HALF THE EARTH

Women's experiences of travel worldwide

-The- rough guides

HALF THE EARTH IS PUBLISHED
JOINTLY BY PANDORA PRESS AND ROUTLEDGE'S
ROUGH GUIDE SERIES

Other available Rough Guides include:
**SPAIN, PORTUGAL, GREECE, YUGOSLAVIA,
FRANCE, AMSTERDAM & HOLLAND,
MOROCCO, TUNISIA, MEXICO** and **PERU**

Forthcoming

CHINA, KENYA, EASTERN EUROPE,

D1166076

Mark Ellingham

First published in 1986
Reprinted in 1987 by
Pandora Press/Routledge & Kegan Paul Ltd
11 New Fetter Lane, London EC4P 4EE

Published in the USA by
Routledge & Kegan Paul Inc.
in association with Methuen Inc.
29 West 35th Street, New York, NY 10001

Set in Linotron, Helvetica and Sabon
by Input Typesetting Ltd, London
and printed in Great Britain
by Cox and Wyman Ltd,
Reading, Berks

Library of Congress Cataloging in Publication Data

Half the Earth.
(The Rough guides)
Bibliography: p.
Includes index.
1. Travel. I. Davies, Miranda. II. Longrigg, Laura.
III. Montefiore, Lucinda. IV. Title: Women's experiences
of travel. V. Series.
G151.H356 1986   910′.88042   86–10223

British Library CIP Data available
ISBN 0 86358 092–0 (pbk)

HALF THE EARTH

Women's experiences of travel worldwide

Edited by
**MIRANDA DAVIES, LAURA
LONGRIGG & LUCINDA MONTEFIORE**
with
NATANIA JANSZ

Maps
**NIKKI GRIFFITHS
AND CHRIS RICKETTS**

Pandora Press/Routledge & Kegan Paul
London and New York

ACKNOWLEDGMENTS

We wish to thank the very many women who responded to requests for accounts and information for this book. At times the undertaking seemed an overwhelming one – we could never have sustained the effort without the continued interest and tolerance of our contributors. Wherever possible we have tried to acknowledge those who helped us collect, modify and expand the information for each chapter within the text itself. There were others, however (some men included), whose contribution to our background research was more general and less easy to categorise. We take this chance to thank: Lucinda Allott, Sarah Anderson of the Travel Bookshop, Margaret Beverley, Carolyn Crane, Christine Davies, Lesley Davis, Jo Hanson, Pamela Holmes, ISIS International, Peggy Jansz, Florica Kyriacopoulos, Clare Longrigg, Daphne Mair, Dorothea McEwan, Brian McSweeney, Clare Sanders, Sisterwrite, Kaye Stearman of MRG, Imogen Taylor, Richard Trillo, Clio Whittaker, Shane Winser and the RGS Expeditionary Advisory Centre, The Woman's Place, Celia Woolfrey and Sue Yates.

For the day-to-day business of upholding morale and helping us to snatch the time and space we needed for editorial work, our thanks to: Simi Bedford, Jill Clarke, Bridget Davies, Jane Ferguson, Ann Goulding, Litza Jansz, Jane Longrigg, Annabell McCluskie, Shaun McVeigh, Michael Reed, Joan Scanlon, Kate Sebag and Judith Watt.

Lastly we'd like to acknowledge a special debt to Mark Ellingham, series editor of the Rough Guides. In making freely available to this project his editorial skills and wide knowledge of independent travel he proved a most generous and valuable resource.

CONTENTS

CONTENTS

◢ NEAR AND MIDDLE EAST

◢ ASIA

◢ AUSTRALIA AND THE PACIFIC

◢ LATIN AMERICA

◤ NORTH AMERICA

HALF THE EARTH

'One of those brilliant ideas which makes you wonder why no one did it before. Practical information, sensible warnings, uplifting tales: it's invaluable for women travellers, inspiring for all women and highly educative for men.' – *City Limits*

'Compact and comprehensive travel guide for women, detailing issues either assumed or ignored by other travel guides, such as safety and harassment and how to get in touch with other women. It covers the continents in a highly accessible mixture of first hand accounts, compiled from contributions of over 300 women, and useful facts and contacts.' – *Venue*

'Contains invaluable information on safety and harassment, the assumptions made about Western women in other countries, and the availability of tampons, toiletries and contraceptives.' – *The Scotsman*

'An inspiring reminder of the endurance, flexibility and independence of the lone female traveller . . . All ranges of experience are here, whether the women are on a bike trip in Holland, a sightseeing holiday in Latin America or (a black woman) visiting England for the first time . . . fascinating reading and an essential index of resources and women's experiences of travel worldwide.' – *Time Out*

'A fascinating collection of women's experiences of worldwide travel . . . just the ticket for armchair travellers wanting to read and relive the atmospheric tales, and for those of us who can't wait to hop on the next plane.' – *Ms London*

'Its immense breadth gives us a rare opportunity to sample countries as vastly different as East Germany and Ecuador, and find that both are recommended for safe travelling.' – *Everywoman*

INTRODUCTION

Our aim in compiling this book was to create a space for women to share their experiences of contemporary travel in ways that would prepare and, we hope, inspire other women to explore different parts of the world.

As a first step we canvassed our friends and advertised in feminist magazines, bookshops, on youth hostel noticeboards, in the *Guardian* newspaper and a wide range of other publications, for women to send in their personal accounts of travel. The shape of the book was still quite vague, although we did stipulate an emphasis on personal experiences and on information of specific relevance and interest to women.

At this stage we expected to cover roughly 50 countries, using one article per country preceded by a brief introduction and ending with a few practical tips, addresses and contacts. However, the response to our search for contributors was quite overwhelming – we must have received around 3,000 letters in the end. Not only was the range of countries wider than we expected, but, more interestingly, women chose to concentrate on a variety of issues from many different viewpoints. For instance, contributions on England ranged from an American account of a visit to Greenham Common that ended in a year-long stay, to the first impressions of a Zambian woman transplanted from Africa to rural Somerset.

For some parts of the world, notably India and the USA, we were inundated by articles and it was hard to choose between them. Other countries, such as Switzerland and Argentina, provoked a very small response. In some areas we accepted the gaps, either in the case of countries little visited for reasons of war, famine or sheer inaccessibility, or else because the particular region as a whole seemed well represented. In others we went out of our way to solicit material, knowing that they were popular with independent women travellers. We tried to include as many countries as we could within the obvious limitations of space, resulting in a final count of 80 countries with often more than one article for each.

From the beginning we had to make certain editorial decisions. The most obvious was to give preference to accounts by women travelling alone, with other women or with children. This was not always possible. For some parts of the world, especially Islamic regions, we received significantly more contributions from women travelling with men. Since this tended to reflect the difficulties of travelling alone – in, Morocco say, or Pakistan – we felt it quite valid to include such experiences; male travellers may provide a cushion of security but you're still treated foremost as a woman with many of the constraints and prejudices that implies.

The second criterion was to focus on independent travel. Package holidays are not only less interesting but, outside Europe and the U.S., they are more often than not restricted to luxury tours. Travel of any kind tends to be a privilege, a fact reflected in the predominance of white middle-class experiences in this book, and to chronicle the more expensive and exploitative aspects of tourism would only have reinforced this point. In order to maintain a traveller's perspective we also decided to request articles from women foreign to the countries concerned.

Certain themes recurred throughout the articles, the most obvious being sexual harassment, an issue almost totally ignored by the supposedly 'comprehensive' travel literature currently flooding the market. We felt it was important to directly address the fears we all have about sexual harassment but without giving a catalogue of disasters or ending up with a definitive list of do's and don'ts which simply further restrict women's rights to travel. We hope that we've managed to provide sufficient information to enable our readers to make their own decisions about where to go, how to dress and how to behave. As far as possible we've avoided making generalisations in any global sense about sexual harassment. Depending on whether you're viewed as a symbol of Western affluence or simply as a more available sex object, there are bound to be subtle variations in what we've come to recognise as the assertion of male dominance. (Less frequent and much harder to ascertain are situations in which you're simply offered sex in what can only be described as a generous spirit, on the understanding that you have the option of saying no.) A more positive recurring theme was the warmth and solidarity described by contributors who'd managed to make contact with communities of women, often within segregated cultures.

We soon realised that it would be necessary to expand the introductions and travel listings to accommodate the diversity of issues covered. Some accounts concentrated on contacts with feminist organisations, for instance in Colombia and Comiso, Italy; some included quite a lot of political information in so far as it affected travel; whilst others were more general intrepid accounts of adventures abroad. The information we've included on feminist activities in the introductions is to provide a context for the contacts we've listed and is meant only as a pointer – the bibliography sections have been specifically compiled for those seeking further information.

Throughout the editorial process we were aware of changing situations – new governments were elected or old governments toppled by military coups, women's groups started and folded – and, as the manuscript finally goes to the printers, we've tried as much as possible to make information up to date.

We see this book as a forum for women to share their experiences of travel and welcome comments and contributions for the next updated volume.

◢ EUROPE

Chapter One

NORTHERN EUROPE

There's an enormous amount of individual and corporate wealth in the countries of **Northern Europe**, and standards of living are generally very high. This makes travel expensive – you have to pay for 'First World' material comforts and for the sanitised efficiency of the road and rail networks, whilst tourism is everywhere well established. Attractions are for the most part well defined. Each country offers a classic range of scenery and historic sites, and the Grand Tour status of the main cultural centres has been little challenged. But despite this circuit, and the Europeans' own holiday resorts, it is also possible to explore, work or live quite apart from the mainstream. **Holland** (above all Amsterdam), **Germany** and the **Scandinavian** countries all have extensive networks of cafés, bookshops and venues – many of them feminist-oriented, some women-only, and often located within a few minutes' walk from the tiny enclaves of conventional tourist interest.

In political terms, recent economic recession and escalating unemployment have meant considerable polarisation – between regions but also within all the large industrial cities. The minority immigrant and migrant communities – Turks, North Africans, Asians, Portuguese – brought in as cheap labour during the 1960s and 1970s have had the worst deal. Reaction and austerity programmes have taken hold even in the traditionally progressive Scandinavian countries, racism is on the increase and 'neo-feminist' groups seeking to 'reaffirm women's unique female nature' (like New Motherhood in West Germany) have carried out major publicity coups. Eurosocialism, wherever it has gained firm ground in power politics also appears to be dissociating itself from more radical agendas, and the proportion of women deputies who retain their seats diminishes at each term.

The **Women's Movement** in Europe is commonly described as being in a latent stage. There is however diverse activism (including increased involvement in ecology and peace groups), with women organising at a local level to expand (and protect) resources – meeting spaces, rape crisis centres, battered women's refuges, transport schemes, self-help and consciousness-raising groups. Women's studies and feminist publications have become well established – in Scandinavia there are women's universities and communes – yet there's a common feeling that these limited gains are tenuous and continued effort is needed if only to retain them.

Unfortunately we've received a poor response to requests for articles on **Norway, Finland, Austria** and **Switzerland**. We would welcome contributions for the second edition.

FRANCE

By far the most visited country of the region, **France** draws pretty much every kind of traveller and tourist – and more French still take their holidays at home than anywhere else. For English-speaking visitors, however, it can be a hard place to get to know in any real way, for all its obvious appeal in terms of food, landscape and city life. There is an image of exclusive chic which attracts people to places like the Côte d'Azur and Dordogne, and to the Alpine ski resorts in winter, and the country as a whole has a reputation for cliquishness. Without educational, business or social connections you may find it hard to slot in – no matter how good your French might be. Regional affiliations are very strong, local communities tend to be tightly knit and local elections get fiercely contested. Travel, though, is usually straightforward and you stand a fairly good chance of paying your way with temporary work – our second two pieces detail the possibilities.

French **politics** are perhaps the most depressing in Europe. The election of the last socialist government under François Mitterand raised hopes until commitments reversed. The nationalism of French foreign policy, and its dedication to all things nuclear, ensures continued nuclear testing in the Pacific, regardless of local rights. And within the country there's been a resurgence of **racism**, paid lip service even within the communist party but made concrete in the growth of Le Pen's *Front National*, the main fascist party. 'Vive Le Pen, France for the French' is a common graffiti in areas with significant immigrant communities, and Spanish, Portuguese and Arab migrant workers are all under threat. Even more than in the UK, if you're black, of whatever racial origin, you may have difficulties getting into the country.

Kate Baillie's article, below, outlines the current state of the **Women's Movement** in France.

▰ **Kate Baillie has spent the last year researching** *The Rough Guide to France*.

You're bound to come across sexual harassment in France. It is generally no worse than in the UK, for instance, but there are problems in judging men without the familiar linguistic and cultural signs. A *bonsoir* or *bonjour* on the street is the standard pick-up opening. If you so much as return the greeting you've let yourself in for a stream of tenacious chat and hard shaking-off work. On the other hand, topless bathing doesn't usually invite bother and it's quite common, if you're on your own, to be offered a drink in a bar, and not to be pestered even if you accept.

On the whole, Paris is by far the most hassling place with constant observation and commentary as you walk down the street.

Very few French women hitchhike except on the Côte d'Azur. If you want to hitch, it's best to use the agencies and go for a mixed ride. Otherwise, take the same precautions as you would at home. Camping rough is not a good idea. You may have trouble at a campsite but at least there'll be people around for support. The *Mairie/Hôtel de Ville* will have addresses of women's organisations (*Femmes Battues, Femmes en Detresse* or *SOS Femmes*). You may be warned against 'les Arabes'. This is predominantly French racism. However, if you are Arab or look as if you might be, your chances of avoiding unpleasantness are very low. Hotels claiming to be booked up, police demanding your papers and abusive treatment from ordinary people is horribly commonplace. In addition, being black of whatever ethnic origin can make entering the country difficult.

According to the media, the Women's Movement died a silent death in 1982. There are no more Women's Day marches, no more major demonstrations, no direct action. Just over a decade since the first feminist meetings during *Mai '68*, bookshops and cafés have started closing, publications reach their last number, girls leaving school deny problems with boys and talk of kids and marriage, and women won't be mobilised. Yet until the socialist defeat this year Yvette Roudy, the minister for women's rights,was doling out money and trotting equal pay and opportunity laws through parliament, and the Elysée palace inviting 400 women for an official celebration of Women's Day. In law, education and work, the sexes are equal; abortion is legal and rape gets long sentences.

The MLF (*Mouvement de Liberation des Femmes*) is not, however, dead, although it is currently in low profile. This has partly to do with the gear switching needed from the Mai '68 decade to 1980s austerity, and partly with the socialists' recent period in power. To enshrine change in laws became for a while easy – the doors to the ministry always open. And 'outside the women's sphere', the socialist government grew steadily more reformist as the economy worsened and cuts in public spending and presidential encouragement sent women back to their homes.

It was as late as 1944 that French women got the vote (and promptly filled more seats in the Assemblée Nationale than they've ever managed since). *Deputés* or not, they were still inferior to their husbands or fathers in the eyes of the law.

In 1949, dismissing all that had been written on feminism in the C19th as 'voluminous nonsense', **Simone de Beauvoir** published *The Second Sex* – the first modern analysis of women's inferior position. But it was not until the 1960s that divorce and marriage laws changed and contraception became legal.

The contemporary liberation movement first achieved public recognition in 1970 at the Arc de Triomphe in Paris when women laid a wreath to the wife of the Unknown Soldier. The following year the group 'Feministes Revolutionaires' organised over 300 public signatures of prominent women who had had abortions. Their campaign had the unified backing of left-wing feminists and mixed groups, and abortion became legal in 1974. The inevitable clashes between communist and socialist women on the one hand and radical feminists on the other was no more of a problem here than in any other country. But the convulsive intellectual culture of Paris spawned another women's group with the title *Psychoanalyse et Politique*, refered to as 'Psyche et Po'. The leader of this elitist and well-funded sect was hailed by initiates as the first coming of a new female being. The messianic Antoinette Fouque owed her vision of anti-capitalist yet capitalist, female yet anti-feminist revolution to the language and practice of her famous ex-psychoanalyst, theoretician Jacques Lacan and, without studying his writings, the talks in Psyche et Po meetings were apparently incomprehensible.

Outside the Paris intellectual milieu Pysche et Po might not have mattered had they been just abstract theorists. But since 1972 they have been out to dominate the Women's Movement. While deriding all feminist practice, they would appear at marches at the last moment with crackshot 'troops' in uniform (red jumpsuits on one March 8) and fight to get their banners to the front. Their limitless funds never went on general campaigns. Instead the money found its way to lawyers for prosecution of non-Psyche et Po bookshops, presses and individuals, and to the media for publicity campaigns propagating the group's exclusive claim to the movement. In 1979 they registered themselves as a limited company entitled 'Mouvement de Liberation des Femmes' thus patenting the name MLF. Thereafter the entire mainstream of the movement from the Feministes Revolutionaires to the marxist *Lutte des Classes* was termed by the media the 'dissident MLF'. Yet they had been responsible for every progressive change in the position of women since 1968 while coping with their own considerable political differences and fighting off Psyche et Po. It is not surprising that exhaustion should have set in, and that the movement needs a breather before rejoining the fray.

In the mid 1980s France still has a long way to go. Women's rights may be institutionalised but *machismo* has hardly been dented. Working-class women organise strikes, factory occupations and other protests, but are still trapped in domestic drudgery even when they work full-time. The educated, middle-class activists may have provided shelters from male violence but men and marriage have never been confronted to the extent they have been in other countries. The appearance of women whether in public or on posters remains male controlled. Without make up, chic clothes and a recent hairdo you cannot be taken seriously. But if you do conform to that image and hold a position of power, male colleagues will say you're too pretty for politics, business, or whatever. The advertising image is whimpering and weak or suspendered and pouting, usually nude and always immaculate. And the manipulators of the trade say this honours feminine beauty. In 1983 Yvette Roudy introduced a bill to outlaw degrading, discriminating and violence-inciting images of women. She foresaw little opposition since a similar anti-racist law had recently been passed. Outrage, hysteria and the amassed fury of male intellectuals, journalists and, of course, advertisers, slaughtered the bill before it could even be debated.

Feminists should not have been surprised by the reaction to the bill. The problem is not complacency. The need for measures – like abolishing the restrictions on abortion – are recognised full well, as is the fact that the Pro-Life forces can outmobilise them with ease in the present climate. Chirac, the new Gaullist Prime Minister, threatened to repeal the legislation altogether before coming to power in March 1986. It seems likely that the Women's Movement will surge back into action, strengthened by the experience of a sympathetic but still sexist government.

◪ **Sally Pitch and Angela Sketcher are working in France, currently in Paris.**

At the time of writing, we have been living together in Paris for a year, and have had wonderful and terrible times, too much to tell in a short space. Neither of us had a job when we arrived – merely £100 each and somewhere to stay (for which we had to pay rent). Subsequently, however, we have both found ourselves in employment which reflects our position as foreign women.

There are a great number of international organisations in Paris so there is a market for English-mother-tongue secretaries. However, despite several years' experience and adequate French, it still took me a month to find a job. The socialist government's protective legislation on temporary work, unfortunately, sometimes works against the interests of those it is sought to protect. An employer taking on secretarial help has to sign a contract for an agreed period, temps are paid 10 per cent on top of their hourly rate (set by the employer not the agency) to make up for not having paid holidays, plus another 10 per cent for instability of work. This means that jobs, although reasonably well paid, tend to be scarce.

Another problem was that I was unfamiliar with the French keyboard. But I found most agencies were very friendly and quite used to this – I was encouraged to go along to their offices as often as I wanted, to practise. To me, French (or French-based) firms seem very formal and strict. In fact the woman who runs the agency with whom I have been most involved confided to me the other day that, when she first saw me, although I did well in the agency tests, she thought I would be unemployable since I had a 'punk' (merely very short) haircut! It was only then that I realised that perhaps I had let my hair grow a bit longer in a subconscious desire to become more acceptable.

Catering is another sector where women can find work, though it is physically demanding and requires a certain resilience to harassment (or 'chatting up') from customers. The competition from the English-speaking population of Paris for jobs in English tea rooms and American restaurants is overwhelming, but twice I have found work relatively easily in fast food restaurants, which have a large intake of immigrant and casual labour. Despite being, in both places, the only English person, I did not have too many difficulties, as the other workers are usually friendly and supportive. Women work the tills, whilst the men are behind in the kitchen; the cleaning is shared. Pay is the minimum wage, with a bonus for nightwork, and whilst it is officially classed as part-time work, you may do anything from 15 to 40 hours a week, often unsocial hours and irregular shifts. To find a job, either walk in, or write to the various companies, or keep an eye on the 'annonces' at the *CIDJ* (Local Youth Information Centre).

As far as grape-picking is concerned women are traditionally regarded as better pickers than men, as it involves fairly nimble finger work. It is also physically arduous, and in some vineyards men are taken on specifically as *porteurs* to carry the full panniers of grapes, usually on their backs. If you have the physical strength, portering is often preferable and sometimes better paid than picking: men usually prefer it. There is, however, enormous unspoken pressure on women not even to suggest that they try portering, and when they are allowed to have a go, it is often treated as a joke.

Rising unemployment is putting added pressure on the demand for such work, and many large farms are now also mechanised or, if not, will probably have a regular supply of local and/or immigrant labour. But casual workers are always needed to supplement the regulars and there are usually far more men than women looking for such work. Many of those we met in the Bordeaux area were unemployed youths from England with only £10 in their pockets. The best way to find work is through contact with a farm, however indirect (newspapers, friends, etc.). It is also a good idea to visit wine town *ANPE* offices (*Agence Nationale Pour l'Emploi* – French equivalent of the Job Centre), as although they are unlikely to be able to offer you any work, you will doubtless meet others in the same situation and jobs are often passed on through word of mouth. Youth hostels too can be good sources of information.

People's attitudes to us varied considerably. On one very small, traditional farm where we were the only foreigners, we were shown great hospitality, although we didn't 'come out' to them. At another where we did, it was the other foreigners who showed us the most support when the nephew of the farm owner and his friend began forms of petty harassment. Ironically, the fact that the boss was a single woman did not ease the tension for us, as we sensed she felt threatened by us.

▨ **Kathleen Griffin adds a note on teaching English.**

It is still easy to find a job teaching English as a foreign language in Paris. If there for a short time you can give private lessons to children and adults. For a long-term job there are two main sources of information – the *International Herald Tribune* and the telephone book. Look up in the yellow pages under 'école de langues', arm yourself with some change and phone around. Always ask for the 'responsable pédagogique'. It may be necessary to work in several schools as one won't be able to fill a timetable. Rates of pay vary enormously from 60 francs an hour upwards. The main books used are the Kernel series and the Strategies series; you're expected to be familiar with them.

TRAVEL NOTES

Languages French. Basque and Breton, as well as regional dialects, are still spoken but losing way. Perhaps more important today are immigrant/migrant languages – Maghrebi Arabic, Portuguese, etc. English is spoken reasonably widely but you'll find it frustrating to depend on.

Transport The French rail network is the best in Europe – efficient and extensive; bus services play a relatively minor role. Cycling is big and you can rent bikes from most train stations and in all towns of any size. Hitching is no more/less safe than Britain, though the French provide an alternative in *Allostop*, an organisation for drivers and hitchers to register for shared journeys.

Accommodation Plentiful, though if your money is tight you'll need to depend on the numerous youth hostels and campsites.

Guide Kate Baillie, Tim Salmon and Andrew Sanger, *The Rough Guide to France* (RKP, 1986). Very up-to-date and good on local, alternative contacts as well as traditional guidebook concerns.

CONTACTS

French **women's centres**, particularly in Paris, are in a state of flux and it's very difficult to give definite addresses – even old-established bookshops have been closing over the last year or two. The following should remain and will be able to provide full and up-to-date contacts for other French cities:

PARIS **Maison des Femmes**, 8 Cité Prost, 11e (Tel. 93.48.24.91). The capital's one secure feminist centre for information, help, food and recreation. They publish a fortnightly bulletin, *Paris Féministes*, run a cinema club and a radio station, *Les Nanas Radioteuses* (101.6Mhz; Wed 6pm-Midnight), and provide a meeting place for most Paris groups (including the 'MIEL', a lesbian organisation who operate the centre's café – *L'Hydromel*).

Feminist bookshops in Paris include *Librairie Anima* (3 rue Ravignan, 18) and *Librairie-Galerie des Femmes* (74 rue de Seine, 6). *Le Potiron* (16 rue du Roule; cl. Sun/Mon) (is the only feminist restaurant in town.

MARSEILLES **Maison des Femmes**, 95 rue Benoit Malon, 5. Again a meeting place for all groups, with people around on Tuesdays and Thursdays 6.30–10.30 pm. *La Douce Amére*, a lesbian campaigning group, can be contacted at the bar *La Boulangerie Gay* (48 rue de Bruys).

NICE **Le Papier Mache**, 3 rue Benoit Bunico. Co-op bookshop, restaurant and arts centre – a friendly leftist haven and meeting place of feminist, ecology and radical groups.

BOOKS

Simone de Beauvoir, 'Feminism – Alive, Well and in Constant Danger' (in *Sisterhood is Global*, Penguin, 1985). *The Second Sex* (1949), *The Woman Destroyed* (1967), both published by Flamingo in translation. One of the founders of French feminism – and existentialism. The *Sisterhood is Global* essay is a good introduction to the present crisis/strengths of the movement in France. Judith Okeley's new revaluation, *Simone de Beauvoir* (Virago, 1986), is also illuminating.

Claire Duchen, *Feminism in France* (RKP

1986) Chronicles the evolution of the women's movement in France from its emergence in 1968 to the present. Highly recommended.

Marguerite Duras, *The Lover* (Flamingo, 1985). Autobiographical novel by influential avant-garde writer.

Marguerite Yourcenar, *Memoirs of Hadrian* (1974, Penguin 1982).

Eveline Mahyère, *I Will Not Serve* (1958, transl. Virago). Powerful lesbian fiction set in Paris in the 1950s.

Roisin Battel, *The Feminist Anti-Text: Recent French Feminist Writings* (1983).

Elaine Marks, *New French Feminisms* (Harvester, 1981). Part of the debate – Beauvoir describes Elaine Marks' book as 'totally distorted'.

Cartoons by Claire Bretecher and Catherine Rihoit.

Thanks to Kathleen Griffin.

BELGIUM

Belgium tends to be a country you visit if you have to: on the way to somewhere else or because you work for the EEC or one of the many European multinationals who have their headquarters in Brussels. Belgians have a reputation of being rather reserved and insular, and although generally polite and accommodating to travellers, they don't tend to be that welcoming. However, the country is easy to get around and presents no particular problems for women, and working in the international community in Brussels is a lucrative experience, highly valued in career terms. Other than that most people stop-over to visit the museums and collections of Flemish art in Brussels, Bruges and Antwerp.

The country is divided into two very distinct communities: the Flemish-speaking majority concentrated in Flanders and the large minority of French-speaking Walloons who dominate the heavily industrialised cities and towns in and around the Ardennes. Brussels has something of both these cultures and is completely bilingual, but the ethnic rivalries at both the national and local level in politics are often extremely acrimonious. At the last National Women's Day, Flemish and French-speaking women celebrated separately and there were no **women's groups** from Wallonia at all. Despite claims of the Council of Belgian Women that improvements have been made in awareness of the conditions of women, everyday life has not really changed. Salary differences between men and women are still up to 30 per cent and reductions in Belgium's textile, banking and retail industries has meant loss of jobs for many women. Meanwhile, abortion remains illegal and harassment continues for doctors who defy the law, although there are now 16 medical centres who have grouped together and will perform abortions.

◤ **Shelley McAlister is a freelance research consultant who recently lived in Belgium for two years; she worked in Brussels and travelled widely in the country.**

Vast, modern motorways speed travellers across Belgium, bypassing most of the interesting sights and cities without so much as a sideways glance.

On the backpacking round-Europe circuit I was urged to miss it out; Brussels seemed famous for nothing more than a statue of a little boy peeing (the Mannekin Pis). Years later, however, I found myself a resident and had time to explore its subtleties.

Travelling about is easy and cheap by train, though in the more remote regions of the Ardennes, you will need a car. On the other hand, a car in Brussels is a positive liability. While courteous and polite in most circumstances, Belgians behind the wheel are extremely intimidating and not always that easy to avoid. 'Mais je suis Belge,' shouted an irate Belgian driver after swerving down the Avenue Louise and crashing into a bewildered American. A more fortunate national characteristic, clichéd but undeniable, is the excellence and incredible variety of food on offer. After eating in Belgium I found even French cooking rather disappointing.

Today the gleaming office blocks and the overwhelming presence of material wealth are evidence that Belgium's capital city is occupied by foreigners: diplomats, corporate executives and coachloads of tourists. The central area is very small and walkable, with its beautifully cobbled streets and gold-trimmed gables of the old Flemish houses. The Museum of Modern Art with its marvellous collection of Flemish paintings, the book and antique stalls of the Sablon and the giant flea market which takes place on Sunday mornings in Marolles should not be missed.

Out of the capital, Bruges is the star attraction, although it features too heavily for its own good on the mainstream 'must see' tourist circuit. Antwerp, a heavily industrialised port, is friendly, relaxed and more interesting – Belgians call it the 'Second Amsterdam' for its tolerance of youth culture. If you want the outdoor life, the Ardennes are pretty and mostly peaceful, although the tourist towns like Spa and Dinant can get crowded in summer.

Belgians tend to keep a safe psychological distance from visitors, while always polite and accommodating in everyday situations. The Belgian family, whether Flemish or Walloon, is close-knit and it is common to see large extended family groups enjoying a camping trip or a bicycle ride together. People generally keep home and work life separate. The ultimate compliment is to be invited to a colleague's house for Sunday dinner when the whole family is there.

Whilst the Catholic religion permeates the society, it does so in an unobtrusive way, unlike in Ireland or Spain. Belgians have a cynical sense of humour and vibrant discussions about religion, politics and economics often take place over long lunches in crowded pavement cafés. They seem to express their individuality by complaining long and loud about everybody and everything. My concierge would constantly hold up the queue at the street market by insisting on careful inspection of every cheese/chicory/guinea fowl and even while counting her change would still be insisting that it could be had fresher, cheaper and of better quality at the stall down the road.

Young women come from the provinces to live and work in the cities, but usually this is a stop-gap until marriage. Their religion and the emphasis on family life mean that domesticity is probably a more common goal for Belgian women than a career. Women do not seem to have benefited from the presence of commercial and diplomatic activity in the capital; behind the gleaming walls of corporate headquarters, they still perform traditional duties as receptionists, secretaries and telex operators. In the commercial world Belgian women do usually win out against their foreign sisters, because of their ability to speak French, Flemish, English and another European language, usually German. But in the large public utilities, although men and women work together, the top jobs are occupied by men and banking is completely dominated by males, except, of course, for the smartly dressed receptionist who greets visitors at the door.

On the other hand, rigid legal systems provide for women in other ways. A couple getting married signs a legal agreement stating what property each of them brings to the marriage. Belgian women retain their own family name legally and few use their husband's name, even socially. Taxes are assessed separately and there is some disadvantage to marrying versus living together. Crèches are readily available, especially in the cities.

The existence of the wealthy, transient foreign community in Brussels has led to an unhappy phenomenon: The Brussels Wife. It is almost impossible for foreign women to find employment in Belgium because of language barriers; even A-level French would not suffice, and generally Flemish and German are also required. The most highly qualified English-speaking woman will suddenly find herself unemployable and with years to kill until her husband's job takes the family back home. For women, the expatriate community in Brussels can be a sad round of collecting the kids from school, shopping and attending cocktail parties.

TRAVEL NOTES

Languages Flemish and French. English and German are quite widely understood.

Transport Like France, best by trains, which are relatively cheap.

Accommodation Generally expensive, though again most towns have youth hostels and campsites.

Special problems If you are planning to live and work in Belgium, you will come up against trivial, unbending bureauc-racy. All residents, whether foreign or Belgian, are obliged to register with the police and carry an identification card at all times. Obtaining one involves days of queuing in government bureaux; fonctionnaires have a reputation for being stern and argumentative.

Guides Martin Dunford and Jack Holland *The Rough Guide to Amsterdam and Holland* (RKP, 1986). Contains a useful section on Brussels, Bruges, Ghent and Antwerp – the Belgian circuit.

CONTACTS

RoSa (*Rol & Samenleving* – 'Role and Society'), Bondenotenstraat 62, 1190 Brussels. Information centre on the Women's Movement in Belgium and elsewhere.

Université des Femmes, 1A Place Quetelet, 1030 Brussels. Provides information on courses and workshops and produces the bi-monthly periodical, *Chronique*.

Vrouwen cafe Chatterbox, Vrijdagmarkt 5, Brussels. Women's café and unofficial information centre.

LUXEMBOURG WOMEN'S CENTRES: **Mouvement de Liberation des Femmes** (MLF), B.P. 174, Luxembourg. **Frauenzentrum** (German speaking branch of MLF) 17 Avenue Monterey Luxembourg.

HOLLAND

There are really two **Hollands**: Amsterdam and the rest. As the centre of West European counter-culture, **Amsterdam** attracts thousands of visitors every year; it has also become a major stopping-off point for independent travellers. The numerous clubs and bars, and the relaxed attitudes to just about everything, have made the city a breeding ground of alternative music and theatre. There are also of course the no-go areas, the notorious 'red light' districts where drug trafficking and prostitution breed their own violence. Much of Amsterdam's counter-culture image and atmosphere derives from the political tension and struggles of the last decades – radical activists (*Provos* and *Kabouteurs*) of the 1960s gave way to the squatters of the 1970s and 1980s, who have staged a long, often successful, often violent battle against the chronic housing shortage in the city.

All of this stands in marked contrast to the entrenched conservatism of the provinces. Outside Amsterdam life can seem parochial and dull, and the countryside, especially in the north, is famously flat. But it is very easy to get around and Dutch women routinely travel alone. Your major problem will probably be the high standard of living which makes existing in Holland very expensive.

The large, diverse **Women's Movement** has its origins in the radical movements of the 1960s. They have fought some impressive and well publicised campaigns – notably, in the 1970s, to legalise abortion. There are now hundreds of local consciousness-raising groups, concerned with specific issues like sexual violence, unequal education, healthcare, and pornography. Most towns have a women's centre, café and bookshop. Many women are active in the peace movement and in various squatting campaigns. Women also keep a high profile in mainstream politics – there are 350 women's groups associated with the Labour Party alone which aim to influence party policy and increase representation in local and national government. The Women's Union, a recognised trade union, was set up to improve the position of housewives and conditions of women doing unpaid work.

▧ **Pat Rush lived and worked in Holland for ten years and still goes there at least once a year. One of her jobs was to produce a radio programme on folk music. In her work she often travelled alone.**

In many respects travelling alone in Holland is no different from travelling alone in Britain. The cities have areas that are best avoided (by women and men), and some of the smaller towns can occasionally seem threatening. But, in the ten years I lived there, the only really unpleasant experiences I had were on late trains out of Amsterdam, where drunken fights were not unusual.

The Dutch are well-used to lone women travellers – at least in the main tourist areas. In Amsterdam, and in other towns with a large population of single young people (university towns, for instance) women do visit bars alone – albeit usually a regular, local haunt. Nevertheless in Utrecht, even with its enormous student population, I was inevitably irritated by constant questions of the 'hasn't he turned up?' variety whenever I ventured into a bar alone at night.

That could, however, have been more on account of my age (early thirties) than my sex in a country where unattached women over 25 seem to be considered somewhat freakish. (Whether an attachment was in the form of marriage or living together, with a woman or with a man, seemed to be of less importance than the fact that an attachment of some kind did exist.) Solo visits to the cinema or to a concert also provoked plenty of stares and the odd unwelcome overture – again perhaps because such places tend to be so youth-orientated. Daylight lounging in pavement cafés, however, seemed to be acceptable virtually anywhere.

In the smaller villages, of course, a lone woman traveller still attracts much more attention. But my own experience was that people were genuinely interested in the visitor, and eager to be of assistance. In fact, it was easy to feel almost suffocated by the hospitality and help offered by people unused to visitors of any kind, let alone a solo woman. It was noticeable, too, that even in towns frequented by tourists, a woman travelling on business is still considered somewhat out of the ordinary. Holland has an exceptionally low rate of employment amongst married women – partly because of the lack of facilities for young children to stay at school during the two-hour midday break or on the free Wednesday afternoon. Certainly there are very few women who would pass a night in a hotel, away from husband and family. At breakfast, I often felt like I was an exhibit in a zoo, and a quiet drink in a hotel bar was rarely a pleasant experience.

My slim executive briefcase also seemed to attract a ludicrous degree of attention. On several occasions I was warned not to carry it with me to an evening appointment, lest I be mugged by someone who thought it was a case full of money. And more than once a passerby – with absolutely no ulterior motive – even insisted on accompanying me and the precious case to our destination! Needless to say, a male colleague with identical case never aroused even a ripple of interest.

As more Dutch women try to combine work and motherhood, or even opt to stay childless in what is still an extremely family-orientated society, attitudes outside the capital will no doubt begin to change.

◢ **Jane Warring spent two weeks in Holland, visiting a friend near Amsterdam and travelling around, mostly by bicycle.**

Cycling around Holland last summer I seemed at times to be the only person on a ten-speed touring bike. This surprised me until I learnt from my friends that many Dutch people have two bikes. They have one, usually the traditional, heavy, sit-up-and-beg type, for commuting to and from work or the shops, and another, a touring or racing cycle, which is taken out for Sunday rides. On my first Sunday in Holland I suddenly felt more 'at home' when many other cyclists on similar bikes came out to join me.

It also seemed at times that I was the only woman who was travelling further than a few kilometres. But, despite this, I met with no problems: even cycling in shorts, I was never hassled or commented at by men. I much appreciated the fact that I seemed to 'blend into' the scenery, although at times I did find this rather disconcerting. In England, as cycling is still an unusual form of transport, I find other cyclists often wave or say hello. Because cycling is so commonplace in Holland it doesn't occur to other cyclists to greet you. In fact the only other cyclists I got chatting to on my trip were Americans.

Cycling in Holland is not as easy as you would think. The terrain is completely flat and the whole country has a network of cycle paths, but the crosswinds are very strong which can make pedalling hard work. (It's also the reason there are so many windmills in Holland.) Another problem I had was trying to work out routes. Unless the map you have is specifically of cycle routes, it is difficult to estimate exactly how long it will take you to get to a certain place because the cycle paths do not always follow the main roads. But, although they may be longer, they are usually scenic, and it is good to be away from the traffic.

I was staying with Dutch friends who live in a small town called Weesp, just outside Amsterdam. I used their home as a base and cycled out every day to places of interest in the surrounding areas, coming back at night to spend the evenings with them. I also travelled south by train and car, and visited Utrecht and Middelburg in the south-west. One of the nicest towns I visited was Leiden, an old university town full of tiny cobbled streets, canals, houseboats, bikes, students, bookshops, cafés and a wonderful market.

Amsterdam itself is incredibly hectic, cosmopolitan, and on the whole tolerant of all kinds of people. There are certain groups at the moment who are hostile towards tourists because they feel the government is putting too much money into the tourist industry and not enough into providing for the needs of Amsterdammers. I saw some graffiti reflecting this attitude but no evidence of it among any of the people I met. I found the Dutch extremely friendly, and everyone I came across could speak at least some English. I wasn't given a chance to practise any of the Dutch I had picked up.

There is much to see and do in Amsterdam, well detailed in some of the guides, but it is interesting to spend time in the places where the Dutch go themselves. The flower market, for instance, which runs alongside one of Amsterdam's many canals, is beautiful, and, if you go at the right time of year, full of tulips. On the wall of one of the buildings overlooking the market I noticed a striking mural. It depicted three women, one controlled like a puppet by strings attached to a large male hand, the other two, painted in vibrant red and yellow, held a pair of scissors, and laughing, had cut themselves free. The painting was gruesome in style but the message was clear.

There are lots of clubs, cafés and restaurants, and I often went to pubs, which are not at all like English ones. They serve coffee and tea as well as alcoholic drinks and are open till about 2 am. People generally go to sit and talk, play cards and other games, and it is quite usual to see small groups of women. The beer is different too – the first time I saw a barman pour out several beers which were almost half froth I was surprised not to hear any complaints, until my Dutch friends explained that there would have been trouble if it hadn't been like that.

One of my favourite places in Amsterdam was the *Melkweg* (Milky Way) at Lijnbaansgracht 243a. It is a centre for plays, films and music. When I was there *Cinemien*, a Dutch feminist film collective, was celebrating its tenth birthday with a festival of films by women directors from countries as diverse as Czechoslovakia, France, Turkey, the USA and Germany. There was also a 'women in rock' week going on. The Melkweg is an old converted warehouse reached by a small bridge over the canal and there are lots of cafés and clubs in the same area. *De Kroeg* (at Lijnbaansgracht 163) is a good one. I saw an excellent reggae band there – black/white and both sexes – which seemed somehow symptomatic of the city. Like many such groups, they originated from different countries but were now based in Amsterdam.

TRAVEL NOTES

Language Dutch. But most Dutch are bilingual in English (and often German and French, too).

Transport Easy in such a compact country: bus and train routes complement each other and stations are usually adjacent. Hitching is good. Bikes can be hired at all main train stations.

Accommodation Hotels are expensive; pensions less so. In Amsterdam and other cities you'll find *Sleep-Ins*, dormitory accommodation heavily subsidised by local councils, and some Youth-Student hotels.

Special problems Bicycle stealing is big business in Holland, especially in Amsterdam (use the bike-pound at the Central Station); pickpockets also work hard on Amsterdam's trams.

Guides Martin Dunford and Jack Holland, *The Rough Guide to Amsterdam and Holland* (RKP, 1986 revision). Comprehensive and reliable. *The Paper*, an alternative English-language magazine, runs interesting articles and details events.

CONTACTS

AMSTERDAM **Vrouwenhuis**, Nieuwe Herengracht 95. Women's Centre – the best overall contact for local groups and campaigns. **Zomeruniversiteit Vrouwenstudies**, Herengracht 508, is a women's studies university. **Xantippe**, Prinsengracht 290 is the main feminist bookshop and there's a women's contemporary art gallery **Amazone** at Keizersgracht 678. Among the **women's cafés** (Vrouwencafes) are *Saarein*, Elandstraat 119, *'t Brune Paard*, Prinsengracht 44, *Orka*, corner of Paleisstraat and NZ Voorburgwal (behind the Royal Palace), *Vivre la Vie*, Amstelstraat 7, and *Françoise*, a coffee shop on Kerkstraat 176.

DEN HAAG **Vrouwenhuis**, Anna Paulownastraat 15 – meeting place and information centre.

Wil Kattenburg, Het Zeiken 186 and *Butterfly*, Laan Van Meedervort 52 – **women's bars**.

UTRECHT **Heksenkelder**, Oudegracht 261 is a feminist bookshop with restaurant and bar.

ROTTERDAM **Emma**, Westersingel 27b is a feminist bookshop and information centre. **Lesbisch Archief Leeuwarden** (lesbian archives) Postbus 4062, 8901 EB Leeuwarden. Large collection of material available for use by individual researchers as well as collectives.

BOOKS

Anja Meulenbelt et al., *A Creative Tension: Exploration in Socialist Feminism* (Pluto, 1985), Writings of Dutch feminists ranging over central areas of debate from internal and international perspective.

Anja Meulenbelt, *The Shame is Over* (The Women's Press, 1980). Introspective account of becoming a feminist.

WEST GERMANY

West Germany – The Democratic Federal Republic (FDR) – is now the richest country in Europe. The rapid industrialisation and rampant consumerism that has characterised its 'miracle' economic recovery since the war (and created the cold, modern cities like Dusseldorf) has not, however, occurred without challenge or dissent. In terms of politics and attitudes, this is probably the most divided European nation. Environmental, civil liberty, left and radical groups – forged over the last two decades – today form a full and organised political stratum, continually at odds with the state.

Support for this grassroots democracy comes from a broad spectrum of housing and workers co-operatives, alternative schools, cafés and bookshops and a flourishing free press. Also from an increasing section of conventional German society, concerned about ecological problems like the acid rain that is destroying the Black Forest. It was from this social fabric that the Green Party emerged and became in 1983 the first ecology party to gain seats in a European national parliament.

Travel poses no particular problems, beyond the obvious expense. To take advantage of conventional attractions – and Germany has some of the best galleries, music festivals and also scenery, around – you'll need to be prepared to spend. But the alternative network, easy enough to make contact with in most large cities, again provides an important resource. And camping is very well established.

The current wave of **feminism** derives from the recent history of alternative politics. Feminist publications (*Courage* and *Emma* are the most widely distributed) proliferated during the 1970s and remain. So too do women's cafés, centres, bookshops and groups – including a large number of lesbian collectives. Current activist campaigns include organising against pornography and violence against women; there are mass 'Reclaim the Night' demonstrations each year in most large towns. Women have retained a high profile in the Green Party, and not only through Petra Kelly, their best known international spokeswoman.

◢ **Hamida Aziz has travelled extensively in West Germany and now lives in the university town of Tübingen.**

The first time I travelled alone in West Germany dates back several years to a long hitchhike from Southern Germany to Marburg, an old town in Hesse. Since then I have travelled a lot, mostly hitching. In terms of safety and the sort of interaction involved, I find hitching alone here differs very little from what I have experienced in England, that is, it is relatively safe and straightforward. The woman traveller does not generally have to suffer the sort of harassment prevalent in the Mediterranean countries and the feeling of confidence with which I could travel was certainly a big bonus and increased my eagerness to explore more of Germany. This was further helped by the fact that many young German people speak some English. However, I would definitely not recommend hitching alone after nightfall (not even short distances in towns). In the summer you can successfully make use of the light morning hours as people start work earlier here and if you have a long journey ahead it is a good idea to get to the motorway between 6 and 7 am.

Most towns (especially those with universities) and certainly the cities, have women's centres, cafés and/or alternative bookshops which you should head for if you are feeling a bit stranded or if you simply seek information not likely to be available at the tourist bureau. In Tübingen, which is a very beautiful university town, the Women's Bookshop runs its own women-only shared lift service. I would recommend enquiring about this sort of service as it can be a good way to meet German women, to establish first contacts here, not to mention being a safer yet cheap means of transport. In towns after 11 pm, public transport is often either infrequent or does not exist at all. In Tübingen, after a long struggle, the Women's Initiative has succeeded in securing funds from the local government for a late night service which will go into operation on a trial basis this summer (1985). Other places may soon offer this important facility, so do check with the local women's centre.

What strikes me most about West Germany is that it is very similar to Britain in its social attitudes. You just have to look at the billboard ads, or flick through one of the glossy women's magazines, to see what position women generally have here. Not quite so apparent (though as significant as in Britain) is the increasing bias against women in the working world, which I feel particularly strongly as the mother of a pre-school child.

In addition to being a foreigner, in my case there is the further factor of my colour. I am frequently mistaken for a Turkish woman (I think Turkish men are the worst off of all the immigrant workers here), or, when they know that I am a British Asian, German men particularly expect me to fit their picture of the exotic oriental woman. For this reason I have sometimes hesitated to wear Indian dress here. But, to be fair, a lot of people are simply curious or admiring – which is much less frustrating than being asked, as I have been in Britain, where I learned such good English!

Another factor, felt by German women equally, that increases the threat of at least verbal harassment in the streets is the presence of soldiers in most sizable towns; they are often the only visible sign that Germany is in fact an occupied country. In this context I should perhaps mention another group, the male refugees, many of whom come from rigidly patriarchal societies. This may mean that they do not regard their advances as sexual harassment when they are directed at German women who, by their standards, appear liberal. Naturally, I would not expect any woman to tolerate sexual harassment. But many refugees live in overcrowded camps, quite isolated from the rest of the community, and over and above the pressure of an uncertain future, they often have to suffer racial prejudice.

The Women's Movement here has its roots in the student activities of the late 1960s. Such groups as the 'Aktionsrat zur Befreiung der Frau' (Berlin) were formed with the aim of freeing women from their traditional chores as a first step in their liberation. The beginning of the 1970s saw a split in the Women's Movement: one part took marxist social analysis as the basis for its strategy, while other women's groups, influenced by the feminists in the USA, put the opposition of the sexes before the class struggle. The #218 (abortion clause) campaign, which drew these two factions together again, brought the Women's Movement much public attention, but the frustration at not having their demands met led to a general withdrawal from this sort of political work. The women's centres of the mid 1970s then took on the character of self-help groups. From this there evolved a feminist subculture with a great variety of long-term projects (i.e. women's publishers, bookshops, cafés, advisory and crisis centres, driving schools, theatre groups, homes, university seminars).

Today the Women's Movement is autonomous, loosely consisting of various independent groups not formally connected but linked by publications, national and international meetings, conferences, etc. It consists predominantly of students (or ex-students), mainly from the social sciences and education sectors, whose education has led them to an awareness of problems and who, in contrast to working women or those with children, have more access to information and time at their disposal to become politically involved. Their basic aim, of course, is to oppose the economic and sexual oppression of women, but opinions differ as to how to achieve this, and particularly with regards to a definition of what is specifically 'female'. Some are concerned with such fields as gynaecology, herbal medicine and magic, and rate 'female' attributes such as intuition and sensitivity positively, while others reject this as the male view of what being female entails. The development of the 'New Motherhood' movement must be seen in this context, although in practical terms it runs the danger of being associated with conservative family politics: a woman's place . . .

Although in West Germany there has never been a women's peace camp comparable to the one at Greenham Common, there are a great number of women's peace groups throughout the country that are actively engaged in anti-military demonstrations, days of action, etc. in their local area, as well as participating in national peace events (for example, the Peace Camp at Mutlangen in Southern Germany). The only all-women's peace camp to have existed here was the Women's Resistance Camp in Reckershausen (Hunsruck) in the summer of 1983.

Because of their policies concerning women and peace, I would finally like to mention the socio-ecologically based groups, now of political party status, of which there is no real equivalent in Britain. These are the *Grunen* (the Green Party), and the *Alternative Liste* (the AL-Party for short), which exists only locally and is represented by the Greens in Parliament. In Tübingen, where they gained 20 per cent of the vote at the last election, it was the ALs who supported the women's taxi service. They also raised funds for the women's home, the youth centre and for improving the bus system. Of course the Greens and AL-Parties are relatively young; yet they may soon be at the stage where coalition with an established party leads to the possibility of gaining regional power. Whether this means the nature of these alternative parties will change (and if so, to what effect), remains to be seen. Personally, I consider the women's and the peace movements essential aspects of life here, and probably the most interesting for those who have the time and inclination to learn about the significant alternative sector of West German society.

◥ **Carol Bayford spent some time in Berlin while researching a dissertation on the Wall.**

However obvious (or morbid) it may seem, the Wall tends to be the first Berlin 'sight' you head towards. If you glimpse it first from the East, as I did, the response can be one of 'is that really it?' – a whitewashed, concrete wall of about 12 feet high. From the West, the sight is more alarming. With the benefit of observation platforms, you see that there is not one wall but two. In the bleak 100 yards of possibly mined no man's land separating the two can be seen the criss-cross of obstruction posts, the searchlights, the Alsatian dogs, the observation towers and the glint of the East German guards' binoculars staring back at you. It's a numbing experience. And although in the West it may have become a 25-mile long canvas for all kinds of graffiti, the Wall dominates the whole nature of Berlin. Some days you can walk for miles, through woods or by lakes, and not see it at all. Others, you meet it at every turn, every attempt you make to move about the city is frustrated, every street a dead end because of it.

It gives West Berlin a 'let's live for today' type of atmosphere with an emphasis on enjoyment, but also a feeling of tenseness, claustrophobia and isolation. West Berlin is awash with colour, neon lights and all forms of entertainment. Luxury goods pack the shops; sex shops abound. East Berlin has little of this colour and appears well-ordered and empty compared with the noise and the bustle on the other side. At night, in sharp contrast to the West, it is virtually deserted.

This is a city where you are aware of the role of government. Travelling by road, there are three routes or corridors through East German territory to Berlin. A time limit is set on your journey and no deviation from the route is allowed. Your passport is checked thoroughly by the West German border guards, the East German border guards, then again by the East German border guards and West German border guards as you enter Berlin. Once in West Berlin, a visit to the East means further border control guards at Checkpoint Charlie, or passing through a corridor at Friedrichstrasse underground station, where you and your passport are scrutinised by a guard seated behind a dark tinted window. Certain underground stations between parts of West Berlin pass under East Berlin and are therefore closed and their entrances bricked up. The train passes through the station slowly but does not stop and in the distant twilight you sometimes catch an eerie glimpse of a patrolling East German soldier.

By accident in East Berlin I found a fairground, and a huge ferris wheel (run by a man wearing a CND badge). It was quite an experience sitting at the top of the 200-foot big wheel with five Soviet soldiers. That's a part of East Berlin: the presence of Soviet soldiers, wandering rather than marching.

The fact that it so clearly is the front line of the Cold War must go some way towards explaining the existence of radical political, ecological, women's and peace groups in West Berlin. The whole German Women's Movement (The Action Council for Women's Liberation) traces its beginnings in 1968 back to this city, and West Berlin has been at the forefront of the movement ever since. It was the first West German city to set up a refuge for battered women (*Frauenhauser*); to organise a German women's film festival; among the first to organise summer courses at its university on women's issues, and is the home of an autonomous Women's Centre for Research, Education and Information. The feminist journal *Courage* is published in West Berlin, and there is a prostitutes-only café.

The Women's Movement in West Berlin, as in the rest of West Germany, covers a wide range of opinion from liberal reform to separatists, and there have at times been quite bitter disputes on certain issues – for example on the existence of a mothering instinct and the failure of the peace and ecological groups to support the movement in some of its campaigns. However the involvement of all these groups in politics is limited by the fact that, under the 1971 Four Power Agreement, West Berliners cannot elect representatives to the Federal Parliament.

There seemed to be little evidence of a separate Women's Movement in East Berlin, and the official attitude is that it is not necessary since the state answers such a need.

Although it was not especially unusual for a woman to be travelling alone in Berlin, I would say that West Berlin feels risky at night, in a way that limits your enjoyment of a city which is alive well into the small hours. Here the Women's Movement has been active in organising 'Reclaim the Night' demonstrations. A girl friend and I were harassed in the street by a man offering us money for sex. My friend shouted at him and he punched her in the mouth, knocking her to the ground. He stood back, looking as shocked as we were, while I helped her up and ran into the road to hail a taxi. The driver told us that one bad experience deserved to be cancelled out, so drove us back to our hotel for free. Generally, men's attitudes to women seemed to me not significantly different here than in any other North European city, though of course that is not necessarily a positive point.

West Berlin is an expensive city, and I found it worth crossing to the East for a cheap meal. I also found that travelling there by coach gave me the chance to gain a couple of addresses of people who lived there. Staying the first couple of nights in the Youth Hostel helped me meet people, and was preferable to moving straight into the isolation of a hotel room. I was advised to avoid the Turkish quarter of the city, but I can't say how valid this was since I took the advice. Finally I think it's worth reading up on the history of the wartime agreements and the events leading up to the building of the Wall, as some understanding of the situation in Berlin today will make your visit more rewarding.

◪ Birgit Griem cycled through Germany, along the Rhine and through the Black Forest. She set out from Breda in Holland.

I had never done any long-distance cycling, hated the idea of carrying heavy gear around with me, and had never really been interested in map reading. However, in spite of initial trepidation, I had a most relaxing and enjoyable holiday doing just that.

Before I left I found really good cycle maps, published in Germany by *Haupeka*. These maps include gradients, the density of traffic on certain roads, cycle lanes, forest paths suitable for cyclists and a whole lot more information which is invaluable if, like me, you are unfit and weary of cars. The disadvantage of the maps is that they are too small for the long-distance cyclist. They only cover an area of 100 square km, which isn't very much if you are, as it were, going straight through them. Towards the end of my trip I needed a new map every other day or so, thereby adding £2.50 (each) to my budget. However, they saved me a lot of frustration, as I found out when I tried to cycle using an ordinary road map.

I managed to keep luggage down to a minimum, didn't carry a tent and always ate in restaurants or when I happened to pass a supermarket or greengrocer. In fact, all my belongings for four weeks were stored in two pannier bags and weighed no more than eight pounds. This obviously made the holiday more expensive, but youth hostel accommodation only costs about £2.50 a night and you can get a great, nourishing three-course meal for around £5.00 at most *Gasthause*. I was a student then and could still afford it.

Next to Holland, Germany is the best country for cycling in Europe. This is largely because the Germans have the right idea about using river banks for recreational purposes. From Cologne all the way to Basle you can cycle beside the river, right away from roads. The only interruption to this occurs in one of the most beautiful sections of the route, between Bad Godesberg and Bingerbrueck. There, the river winds through a fairly narrow wine-growing valley, and there is only room for a motorway type road and a train track on either side of the river. Between Koblenz and Bad Godesberg there aren't even cycle lanes beside the road which makes cycling extremely unpleasant. It is possible to get through this stretch in a day, though, and the superb surroundings (a castle perched on top of a vineyard mountain every mile or so), the picturesque villages and the large number of fellow cyclists more than compensate for the discomforts.

The further south I got the flatter the countryside became. By the time I was cycling through the famous green meadows, bordered by high fragile-looking trees called 'Rheinauen', cycling had become so easy that it was almost second nature. Not having to watch out for cars, which took a lot of the competitive element out of cycling, I had ample time to watch and dream.

When I reached Kehl (about 10 km on the German side of Strasbourg) I felt so fit, competent and confident that I decided to tackle the Black Forest. I avoided the higher parts of it, like the Feldberg and Tittisee, but the cycling was nevertheless quite strenuous. I was there for about a week and a half during which time I probably spent more time cycling downhill than up – my map reading had got quite good by then and I was able to work out routes with short ascents and long descents. That was fun, but I preferred the routine movement of cycling in flat country, where at least I could control the well-being of my legs. Whenever things got too difficult and I could not even remotely appreciate the stunning beauty of the Black Forest, I got on a train.

If like me you enjoy travelling by yourself, cycling is still one of the best ways to do it. The fact that you are a lot faster than people walking provides a definite sense of security, even in the remotest areas. You are likely to get quite a few comments, sexist and otherwise, which is something that you will encounter in Germany anyway, but it is very satisfying to be able to return a comment or sign and then cycle off into the distance before the recipient has had time to get over his astonishment and retaliate.

Amongst cyclists there also exists a sense of solidarity. This means that even if you are setting out by yourself, you are bound to meet people during the day or once you have arrived in a hostel, who you've got something in common with. Most of them will be German or German-speaking though. It seems to be the vogue among Germans to go on long-distance cycling tours, and I met many heroes and heroines who had just come back from Italy across the Alps, swearing that they'd cycled all the way. Don't be put off though. Nobody could convince me that I was not the most heroic of them all, and that I hadn't reached the highest personal goal, regardless of whether I'd just cycled 10 or 80 miles.

TRAVEL DETAILS

Language German. English the first language taught in schools, widely spoken.

Transport Hitching, there are around 50 agencies which arrange lifts. If you are wanting a lift or if you would like to take passengers, call in at the nearest agency. Petrol costs divided between passengers. Headquarters is: *Verband der Deutschen Mitfahrzentralen e.V.*, Dieffenbachstrasse 39, 100 Berlin 61. There are specific agencies for women, *Frauen-Mitfahrzentrale*, in Berlin (Potsdamerstrasse 139), Hamburg. (Rappstrasse 4) and Munich (Baldestrasse 8).

Bicycles can be hired for a small fee from most railway stations. You can transport bicycles on all trains except intercities for around 12DM.

Accommodation Youth hostels in Germany are good but are often booked up months in advance and some can be quite expensive. The headquarters is *Deutsches Jugendherbergswek*, Bulowstrasse 26, 4930 Detmold 1. (Tel. 05231/74010).

Other information *Adresen für die Friedensarbeit* (published in Munich) is a directory for the peace movement. The main contact organisation is *Aktionsgemeinschaft Dienst für den Frieden*, Bluchestr 14, 5300 Bonn (Tel. 0228/229192).

Guides No specific English-language guide seems worth the recommendation. If you're on a tight budget *Let's Go Europe* (St Martin's Press, US) is helpful.

CONTACTS

The **Frauen Adressbuch** (Courage, Berlin) lists all women's centres, cafés, bars, bookshops, etc.; there are also more detailed *Frauenstadtbuchs* for Berlin, Dusseldorf and Munich. Below is a small selection;

BERLIN **Frauenzentrum** (Women's Centre), Stresemannstr 40. Meeting place for a large network of groups – though in danger of closure at its present address. **Zentraleinrichtung zur Forderung von Frauenstudien und Frauenforschung**, Berlin Free University, Postdamerstr 58/11, 1000 Berlin 30. Runs women's courses, seminars and workshops. **Feminist bookshops**: **Labrys**, Yorckstr 22; **Lillith**, Knesebeckstr 86–7; **Miranda**, Nazarethkirchstr 42. **Sozialistischer Frauenbund** (Socialist Women's Federation) Tempelhof 16. Currently planning to set up an institute to analyse the Women's Movement.

FRANKFURT **Feministische Archiv und Dokumentationszentrum** (Feminist Information Centre), Arndstrasse 18. Aims to collect all writings, periodicals, photographs and documents relating to the movement.

Rape crisis centres (*Frauennotrufe*). Berlin Tel. 030–2512828; Frankfurt 069–553559; Heidelberg 06221–13643; Cologne 0221–562035; Munich 089–6519494.

Women-only holidays. *Frauenreisen* (c/o Gabi Bernhard, Kaiserdamm 6, 1000 Berlin 19) run skiing, hiking, historic trips with the intention of promoting contact between European women. *Frauenferienhauser* (Hasenfleet 4, 2171 Oberndorf) operate holiday homes for women.

BOOKS

Petra Kelly, *Fighting for Hope* (Chatto, 1984). Petra Kelly was unhappy about the editing of this, touted as her 'personal manifesto'. Inspiring ideas nonetheless and good background on the Greens.

Gisela Elsner, *Offside* (Virago, 1985). Revealing portrait of women's life in middle-class Germany.

Paul Frolich, *Rosa Luxemburg* (1939, Pluto 1983) Original, revolutionary thinker at forefront of working class struggle and communist party of Germany founder. Definitive biography by revolutionary contemporary.

Look out, too, for novels by Richarda Huch and Gertrud von le Fort – some of which have been translated into English.

Thanks to Marisa Earle for Travel Notes.

DENMARK

With its progressive welfare policies and efficient provision of services, **Denmark** is often considered a bright spot of hope for social reform in Europe. However, unemployment, huge recent economic cut-backs in the public sphere, and a creeping racism directed at 'foreign' or 'guest' workers, are currently contriving to blur that image. The present, somewhat chaotic, parliament is dominated by a four-party right-wing coalition.

Denmark's popular reputation for pornography and sex is outdated – you'll see far more pornography in London or Amsterdam than you will in Copenhagen. Relaxed attitudes to 'alternative lifestyles' do, however, still prevail. Nudity is the famous example – it's not just the young and beautiful who strip off in beaches and parks.

Many travellers make a bee-line for Copenhagen and stay there. But the countryside, while not spectacular, has a gentle beauty and a strange age-old feeling, sometimes at odds with the well-kept roads and clean modernity of even the oldest buildings. There are, too, 5,000 miles of coastline, with some great beaches – and Danish summers are hot and long.

For most **women**, nuclear family units and traditional sex roles are the enduring prototype. Communes and collectives in both agrarian and urban settings have proliferated over the last few decades but they're still viewed as a predominantly middle-class alternative. The recent drastic fall in the birth rate (increasingly referred to as the unofficial birth-strike) has been viewed as a product of dissent – against having to bear the main responsibilities in childrearing and the problems of day-care facilities (though they are in fact more advanced than most other industrialised societies). Since the mid 1970s there has been free abortion on demand and contraception is easily available.

Within fields of adult education, women's studies have made an impact across class and regional boundaries. Courses on aspects of women's lives are now part of most high school curricula and in the south of Jutland the Kvindehøjskolen (Women's School) has been open now for seven years. There are, too, women's galleries and studios in Copenhagen, many formed after the 1975 Women's Exhibition in the city. Among groups, the European trend towards diversification and single-issue groups is evident.

◪ **Lucinda Rathsach travels frequently in Denmark.**

Denmark's social structure is similar to Britain's, but the status of women is more advanced. Danish women gained the vote in 1908, and had elected women to the upper and lower houses of the Folketing, their parliament, by 1918. Nowadays a quarter of the members of the Folketing are women. Most married women and mothers work, and facilities for them are well developed. But, as has been symptomatic in the rest of West Europe, the economic recession has led to women workers suffering most, as jobs in the service industry, teaching and social services get cut or working conditions are left to deteriorate.

Denmark's constitutional monarchy is headed by the popular Margarethe II. Her easy style reflects the general informality and freedom of this country. Dress is casual which makes it much easier to merge in as a traveller. The predominant religion is Lutheran Protestant and there are a number of women priests. Though generally accepted, they are highly vulnerable to the interests and caricatures of the tabloid press. There was a recent major exposé of a woman priest involved in drinking sessions with fishermen among her congregation.

Danish life is dominated by the sea – not surprisingly in a country made up of 500 islands, and with no centres of population more than 35 miles from the ocean. If you travel in by ferry your first port of call will be Esbjerg, on Jutland, and you'll probably find yourself making for Arhus, the country's second largest city. A major attraction, for its life and its vicinity to the island of Funen, Arhus is annual host to a well-established Women's Festival.

Copenhagen is strangely situated, lying in the far eastern reaches of the country on Zealand. Nevertheless, it is home to one and a half million people, an aesthetic town, with houses painted orange, red or yellow, copper-roofed spires, beautiful fountains and statues and a compact historic centre. If you're interested in making contact with feminists in the city visit the Danner House Women's Centre (see Travel Notes for address). You can't miss it, a big red building with the women's sign boldly painted on the main windows. The struggle to acquire the house, and the foundation of the centre, is an inspiring story. It was originally built in 1800 as a shelter for homeless women. Falling into decay, in 1979 it was due to be demolished when local feminists launched a national campaign for funds to buy and restore it.

The whole house has now been decorated and renovated by women, part is closed off and devoted to a refuge for battered women and the rest occupied by some 25 women's groups. The house provides cultural activities (including a festival each January), counselling and courses such as self-defence and assertiveness training, printing and media workshops and, recently, the biggest unemployment scheme for women in the history of Denmark, 'Women Build for Women'. It's also a good place to go for a very cheap cup of coffee and a snack. The café and bookshop selling posters and cards is open downstairs in the afternoons, just ring the bell and someone will let you in. The office is open every day from 9 am to 7 pm. All women are welcome.

Another oasis for the weary and broke traveller is *Use It*, a cheap restaurant, theatre and information centre. Here you will find international newspapers, a noticeboard listing lifts offered both around Denmark and to other countries, maps, and brochures on what is going on in the capital. They publish their own magazine *Playtime* which offers a tongue-in-cheek analysis of what makes Danes great, where to sleep and eat cheaply, sights, tours and events, health shops and alternative Copenhagen. Their leaflets are available in English, and tell you anything from how to see Copenhagen on 6 D Kr a day, to how to order a vegetarian meal. Their office has a book exchange service and a guestbook brimming with weird and wonderful tales and advice from fellow travellers. 'Use It' is also willing to act as a postal address if you are passing through.

◢ Gaye Kynoch lived in Denmark for eight years; she worked 'spare time' with a feminist publishing collective, and adds a note on the Women's School.

It's not really any problem for women to travel in Denmark; you'll probably get less hassle here than most places. There's nothing at all 'unusual' about women going out alone – you may have to fight off a drunk or two – and though lesbian couples may cause comment you're more likely to be left alone. People are generally helpful and friendly, English is widely understood and often fluently spoken, while many people also speak German, especially in Jutland. There's a lot going on for women, and in recent years several places have grown up which perhaps reflect the recent development of the feminist movement: places where women can and do go to be together and study and learn together.

'Kvindehøjskolen' (see Travel Notes) is the Danish Feminist School, a non-profit, government-granted school founded by women in the feminist movement and situated in the countryside in southern Jutland. The school holds courses for Scandinavian women throughout the year, working with a variety of subjects related to the Women's Movement and of varying length, a few weeks or a couple of months. Every summer there is an international course, open to women from everywhere. Kvindehøjskolen has 13 acres of land, with cultivated fields and various buildings, some of them built by women on construction courses.

'Skraekkenborg' (again see Travel Notes), on the little island of Langeland, also runs courses for women. Its site is a beautiful old farmhouse and a couple of barns which have been turned into workshops and a studio, a large patch of land, a few minutes from the sea, and it is much used by women from all over the country. Do remember that neither

Kvindehøjskolen nor Skraekkenborg are holiday resorts. They're busy course centres and homes for many women.

TRAVEL NOTES

Language Danish. English (or German) will get you by.

Transport Efficient public transport network, by train, bus and ferry. 'Nordic passes' can be good investments. Hitching, at least across country, isn't easy, though you can generally pick up lifts out to Sweden or Germany.

Accommodation As in all Scandinavian countries, youth hostels are an invaluable cheap alternative to hotels – but tend to get booked up in summer.

Guides Again, *Let's Go Europe* (St Martins Press, US). *Use It* (see Lucinda Rathsach) publish a useful range of leaflets (Radhusstraede 13, Copenhagen; Tel. 01–15 65 18).

CONTACTS

There are around 50 feminist groups in Denmark, the most prominent being the *Rødstrømper* ('Redstockings').

Danner House, Nansensgade 1, 1366 Copenhagen (Tel. 01–14 16 76). Main Women's Centre for contacts/information on all groups, also counselling and advice.

Kvindehøjskolen, Visby, 6270 Tønder. Danish feminist school (see Gaye Kynoch).

Skraekkenborg, Dageløkkevej 12, 5953 Tranekaer, Langeland Island. Also mentioned by Gaye Kynoch.

KVINFO, Laederstraede 15, 2 sal, 1201 Copenhagen K. Women's Studies research and information centre.

KULU, Køomagergade 67, 1150 Copenhagen K. Umbrella organisation for women's groups concerned with development and Third World contacts.

Kvindemuseumforeningen, Fredensgade 36, 8000 Arhus C. Unique new museum/research centre devoted to Danish women's activities in all fields.

Landsforeningen for bosser og lesbiske, Knabsrostraede 3, Copenhagen (Tel. 01–13 19 48). Lesbian and gay information centre, café and disco.

Women-only holiday camps: Work/holiday activities on various islands. Information from *Ø-lejr-kontoret*, Vendersgade 8, 1363 Copenhagen K (Tel. 01–11 55 81).

BOOKS

Tove Pitlevsen, *Early Spring* (The Women's Press, 1986). Childhood autobiography from one of Denmark's foremost poets.

Inga Dahlsgard, *Women in Denmark – Yesterday and Today* (Det Danske Selskab, Copenhagen).

The **DDS** – The Danish Institute – also have a book on *Danish Women Writers* under production in an English translation. They can be contacted in Copenhagen (Kultorvet 2) and Edinburgh (3 Doune Terrace).

Thanks to Gaye Kynoch who also provided information for the Introduction.

SWEDEN

Sweden's popular image is perhaps the most bland of all the Scandinavian countries. Neutral during the last war, and affluent since, it has high living standards and a virtually institutionalised Social Democratic government. If you visit as a tourist it's likely to be for the countryside – and particularly the wild, unspoilt coastline. Travel is relaxed and very straightforward (although expensive) and harassment as a problem is relatively rare. It can however be quite difficult to actually make contact with Swedes. Outside the capital there are few pubs, and gatherings, such as there are, tend, like most things in Swedish life, to be organised. People go to a meeting with a purpose, like a study group, or to each other's homes where they can drink in private (drinking laws are very strict).

The Social Democrats, who have been in power for most of the last forty years, have poured millions into creating the latest in healthcare and educational facilities. Many Swedes complain of high taxes – but most are eligible for some benefits or grants under the highly developed welfare service. A more serious complaint is the tight bureaucratic control the state exercises over their lives – and the recent election was largely fought on the issue of personal freedom. Most people have a similar, comfortable standard of living and tend to conform to social and professional norms. Unconventionality is rare and not condoned.

The **Women's Movement** in Sweden is both highly developed and well integrated within all mainstream institutions. As in the other Scandinavian countries, there are women's centres and studies programmes in most major towns. Currently the main focus of the movement is on improving childcare facilities and combating sexual discrimination at work. Women have access to most areas of employment but representation at the higher levels is still poor.

After leaving school, Madeleine Bridgman spent five months working as an au pair to a Spanish family in Stockholm.

Arriving at Arlanda, Stockholm's airport, one January afternoon, my first impression was of a small, isolated clearing among fir trees, sinister in the grey, snowy air. There was no suggestion of a major terminal, a capital city, urban life. It was before three and it was dark.

I was going to Stockholm to 'au pair' for a Spanish diplomat's family – a position which, in any country, can be risky, vague and uncomfortable. In my case, there was a strange tension between the legendary Scandinavian efficiency and punctuality and the 'mañana por la mañana' attitude of the Spanish. The British way is probably about halfway between; caught between these two opposites, I found it hard to shake off my national identity.

I was responsible for two small girls. During working hours, I was a substitute mother, travelling around town and suburb with a pushchair. I glimpsed a child's view of Stockholm, and was also impressed by the Swedish attitude to children. In a shop, even on a busy Saturday, the constant undertone of grizzling children and irritated parents, which I was used to from England, was non-existent. A child is warmly received everywhere. The only hostile reaction I personally ever met with came when I dashed into a shop, leaving the baby outside in her pushchair for a minute. The cashier would not take my money until I had gone outside and 'rescued' the baby.

Travel with a child is both enlivening and exhausting but in Sweden it seemed to me less of an ordeal than it might be. On any train or bus, the guard or driver was always willing to help and make sure that child, child's favourite toy, pushchair, shopping bag and me were safely on board. Public and commercial buildings are accessible with pram, pushchair or, indeed, wheelchair. Many museums in Stockholm are designed for child-appeal, with a distinct lack of dusty glass cases, and a profusion of tableaux, audio-visual shows and colourful sculptures to be touched as well as admired. The pleasure is shared between adults and children and you are freed of the effort of making entertainment out of an amenity which is geared to 'adults only'.

During time off, with friends (British, Swedish and Polish), I was free to explore Stockholm. Even at night I generally felt safe. The dark open spaces, the wind in the trees, may have seemed eerie, but I never felt that my right to be out and about and alone was in question. Women are seen publicly in a wide variety of roles, whether patrolling the underground stations in police uniform, or repairing the tracks in overalls. However we were warned about the *Tunnelban*, the underground, at night. You become very aware of the negative side of Swedish life then: swarthy, scruffy men begging cigarettes; a terribly young woman, her face swollen and blotchy, swigging pink fluid from a large plastic container. By and large, though, we encountered no aggression. People had their own problems to worry about.

Wandering the cobbled streets of Gamla Stan (the Old Town) with a camera, I was obviously a visitor, but I was never an object of curiosity and innuendo as I have found myself in British towns. Stockholm is a manageable city. You walk around without feeling overwhelmed. The Kaknastorret, the tallest building in Scandavia, is only 508 feet high, and looking out at dusk, I could see how active and varied, but how small the capital was.

The extreme cold and the short days of the Swedish winter were difficult to get used to. I was told that it was an unusually mild winter but it took a few miserable outings to teach me to wear two pairs of gloves, a long coat rather than a thermal jacket, socks as well as woolly tights. . . . The winter can be depressing. I did not have to go out to work, but the price of staying snuggly indoors with the children was that I did not enjoy fresh air or stretch my limbs for days at a time.

So spring has a very joyous reception. Emerging from the underground one bright, clear morning, I found the square of Ostermalmstorg full of colour. A market had appeared, selling gaudily dyed feathers fixed to twigs, in imitation of the wild flowers soon to transform the woods around Stockholm. By Easter the weather was warm, fresh and cheering. On Easter Saturday, three of us walked along the edge of the city by the sea. A youth whizzed by on roller skates and wished us happy Easter as he passed. I think it was the only unsolicited remark from a strange man any of us had received in Sweden.

It seemed to me that everything was taken very seriously in Sweden. While I was there, a referendum was held on the question of whether or not to build nuclear power stations. Shelves in the local library were devoted to 'atomkraft'. TV documentaries were made by representatives of each side of the debate. They are equally serious in their attitude to leisure. It is difficult to make a bunch of Swedish children build a snowman, or throw snowballs. On the other hand, they can skate and ski almost as soon as they can walk.

One of the greatest pleasures of Sweden is its scenery: green, wild, a density of wild flowers and berries giving a luxurious aspect to a walk. I revelled at being able to stroll home at two in the morning, alone in a fragile pink world, all activity suspended but mine.

TRAVEL NOTES

Language Swedish; English spoken widely.

Transport Regular boat services from mainland to Sweden's many islands, bookable through Norwegian State Railways Travel Bureau. Between towns, trains are frequent and efficient, and tourist special deals available, i.e. *Nordic Railpass* (21–day ticket for unlimited travel in Sweden, Denmark, Norway and Finland).

Accommodation For budget-priced accommodation look for *Rum* (room) signs or ask at local tourist office. Youth hostels are run by Swedish Touring Club, Box 25, S–101 20 Stockholm; cheap rate if you are member of YHA. Budget accommodation also provided by International Youth Centre, Valhalla-vagen 142, S–115 24 Stockholm, and most hotels offer special 'tourist rates'. Many Swedes holiday in hired purpose-built, well-equipped log cabins or chalets in the countryside. Enquire from Tourist Office for information. Lots of cheap camping available.

Special problems It can be difficult to meet people – there aren't really pubs or cafés. You need some kind of purpose.

Guides Again no specific recommendations, though there's a *Rough Guide to Scandinavia* in the pipeline. Meantime *Let's Go Europe* (St Martins Press, U.S.) has a reasonably useful section.

CONTACTS

Fredrika Bremer Forbundet, Biblioteksgatan 12, S–111 46 Stockholm. Organisation dedicated to fighting for equality at home and work, with branches in most cities.

Grupp 8 Snickarbacken 10, S–111 39, Stockholm. Socialist-feminist group which arranges debates, exhibits, etc. Publishes periodical *Kvinnobulletinen*. Lots of local groups.

RIFFI (International Associations of Women Immigrants), Vanadisvagen 7, 3 tr, S–111 46 Stockholm. Set up to help immigrant women deal with isolation and put them in better touch with Swedish society and their rights.

Soroptimisterna, c/o Kerstin Bergstrand, Skapplandsgatan 23, S–414 78 Goteborg. Represents some 40 clubs; emphasis on recruiting women from all walks of life.

BOOKS

Hilda Scott, *Sweden's Right to be Human: Sex-Role Equality – The Goal and the Reality* (Allison & Busby, 1984) Analysis of the Swedish experiment.

Gerd Brantenberg, *The Daughters of Egalia* (Journeyman Press, 1985) Satire of Swedish relationships – actually by a Norwegian novelist.

ICELAND

Half **Iceland**'s population of 250,000 live in the capital, Reykjavik, the rest in the handful of other towns, or in small settlements and isolated farmsteads scattered throughout the habitable, mainly farming regions around the coast. Standards of living are high, even compared to other Scandavian communities, which makes it an expensive place to visit. Anyone interested in geology however, will already be aware of the attractions of Iceland's glaciers and volcanic landscapes. And if you don't mind rain, and like the hardy outdoor life, you will be rewarded by strange, wildly beautiful scenery unlike anything else in this part of the world.

The **Women's Movement** in Iceland first demonstrated its full collective strength in a one-day women's strike ten years ago – an action devised to mark the start of the International Women's Decade. In October 1985 the action was repeated – this time in protest against discrimination in the workplace, and thousands of Icelandic women walked off their jobs, closing down schools, shops, government offices and many businesses. The participation of 160 air stewardesses meant that half the country's aircraft were stranded in foreign airports, while hotels, reputedly, were crowded with men whose wives refused to cook breakfast. This direct action was supported by Iceland's woman President, Vigdis Finnboga-dottir, though little reported outside the country.

One of the other major concerns of the women's organisation, *Kvenna-frambodid*, is to get more women into Parliament. At present nine MPs out of sixty are women, but they have already made a significant impact, refusing to use the obscure language of parliamentary procedure so as to make politics more accessible. Another important issue is the right to abortion, at present legal but under constant threat from the Lutheran church.

◪ **Helen McIlroy spent six weeks in Iceland, hitching and camping with a male friend.**

The Icelanders' own epithet for their country is 'Is ok Eld', meaning Ice and Fire; ice for the long, harsh winters and fire for the constant volcanic activity below the island's surface, visible in some places as sulphur springs and the occasional full-scale volcanic eruption. Much of the landscape bears the scars of these subterranean furnaces – extinct volcanoes, vast heaps of black ash, are dotted around the countryside, and twisted rock formations and lava floes witness past eruptions.

It was the strange, wild scenery that drew me to Iceland, so I spent most of my time in the country away from the main centres of population.

My biggest problem was the high price of virtually everything. To cut costs I hitchhiked and camped most of the time, carrying supplies of food brought out from England and with only the occasional bus ride and stay in a youth hostel for recuperation. The sheer hard work of this kind of travel, and the awful weather, turned my trip from a holiday into a kind of endurance test.

Such rigours aren't necessary, though, if you have money to spare. There are youth hostels, hotels and special tourist offers on the bus network, and on about £15–20 a day you could travel in at least reasonable comfort. The scheduled buses serve all the major settlements, but if you want to visit the interior you'll need either to join a tour or hire a four-wheel drive vehicle, indispensable for the rough tracks and unbridged rivers, swollen during the summer months by the melting glaciers. I did try to cross the interior, from Gullfoss Waterfall in the south to Akureyri in the north, but gave up because of the hopelessness of hitching and the prospect of a 150-mile trudge across the deserted plains.

Icelanders take obvious pride in their country, and they're pleased to meet foreigners who have taken the trouble to go and see it. They are highly aware of their own history, unusual in that it has been written down from the beginning, when a group of Norwegian aristocrats left their country in disgust at political oppression and came with their households and livestock to live on an uninhabited island a thousand miles away. In a hostile land, where they had to rely entirely on their own resources, they survived both the climate and political pressures from abroad to create the first European republic since classical times, predating the French by some nine centuries.

Until the transport revolution of the last hundred years, Iceland was largely isolated from outside influences, and the people subsisted by fishing and farming in traditional communities. The old way of life has today disappeared except in the most remote areas, and more than half the 250,000 inhabitants are town dwellers, enjoying a high standard of living. One feature of their long isolation has, however, survived, and this is their language, little changed from that spoken by the Viking Age settlers of a thousand years ago.

The only Icelander I met who spoke only Icelandic was reputed to be the leader of a revival of worship of the old pagan gods (Thor, Odin, etc.) but our conversation was limited to such items as the depth of snow in winter (deep!). Whatever the truth of his reputation, he certainly looked the part, with a sweeping grey beard, and unusually for an Icelandic man lived alone – in a spartan hut on a windswept mountain, with a tame ram in the garden.

The other Icelandic homes I was invited into, usually for breakfast after camping outside, were very modern, comfortable and well built. They have to be in order to withstand the risk of earth tremors as well as the annual rigours of the Icelandic winter. Full insulation is the norm, and in Reykjavik and other places where there are local hot springs, the hot water is used to run community central heating. Iceland's most northerly point lies just south of the Arctic Circle, and the country has an accordingly dismal climate. For several weeks in midwinter, the sun barely rises above the horizon, and the land is buried under several feet of snow. The Icelanders are used to this, of course, and in the towns life carries on as usual, although in the country households can be cut off for several weeks, so people have to be very well prepared. Because of the difficulty of travel, most children in rural districts go to boarding schools, where they stay almost all winter and then have a very long summer holiday. Social effects of the long winter are hard to gauge. The Icelandic government, like those of the other Scandinavian countries, is very concerned about alcoholism, and the sale of alcohol (obtainable only from government controlled shops) is strictly regulated. I don't know if the problem is real or imagined, and, if real, whether it has more to do with the general affluence than with the months of darkness and twilight.

There are no particular problems for the women traveller in Iceland beyond those faced by anyone travelling on the cheap in harsh conditions. There is a very low rate of violence against women, and I never felt ill at ease because of my sex. Although I was travelling with a man, which can sometimes mask the threat of violence, I never sensed any underlying tension, and I would be happy to return to Iceland alone.

Icelandic women have a high status. Almost all have jobs outside the home and therefore some degree of economic independence, though men still dominate in the more prestigious and lucrative professions. Many women choose to have children outside marriage and this is considered a valid option. In the towns there is state provision of nurseries for children of women who are not married, although there is a shortage of places for children of married women.

Women never change their name on marriage, and titles indicating marital status are used only on very formal occasions, and then only with both the first and second names. A person's real name is their first name, and it is under this that they are listed in telephone and other directories. This traditional naming system has survived, like the Icelandic language itself, because of the smallness of the nation and its isolation from external cultural influences.

TRAVEL NOTES

Language Icelandic, but most Icelanders also speak some English. Icelandic is distantly related to English so there are similar words. It is difficult to pick these out in conversation but simple to learn a few phrases. Anyone who speaks one of the other Scandavian languages has a distinct advantage, especially

Danish, which is spoken by most of the older people (Iceland was under Danish rule until 1944).

Transport Scheduled buses serve all the major settlements. Hitching is pretty safe, probably safer than England, but it can be slow in sparsely populated areas. The Icelanders don't seem to have anything against hitchers, they just don't see many of them.

Accommodation There are plenty of youth hostels and hotels, though they can be expensive. Camping you need only to ask local permission.

Special problems If you plan to go into the interior alone, you must hire a four-wheel drive vehicle, essential for the rough tracks and unbridged rivers. There is very little chance of hitching a lift and if you plan to walk, you should take all you are likely to need as there are no facilities except a few huts dotted along the tracks. It is not safe to leave these tracks as the terrain can be treacherous, and your chances of being found if you have an accident are virtually non-existent. The same goes for glaciers. The maximum summer temperature is about 15° and it is very wet, so if you are planning to camp you will need reliable equipment and efficient waterproof clothing.

Guide David Williams, *Iceland: the Visitor's Guide* (Stacey International, 1985). Large illustrated hardback with useful practical information, though aimed mainly at motorists.

CONTACTS

Kvennaframbodid Gamla Hotel Vik, Adalstraeti, 101 Reykjavik, Iceland. Main office of the Women's Movement, used as a meeting place for various groups and for advice sessions on legal, social and health matters. They also publish a magazine, *Era*, every two months.

Chapter Two

BRITAIN AND IRELAND

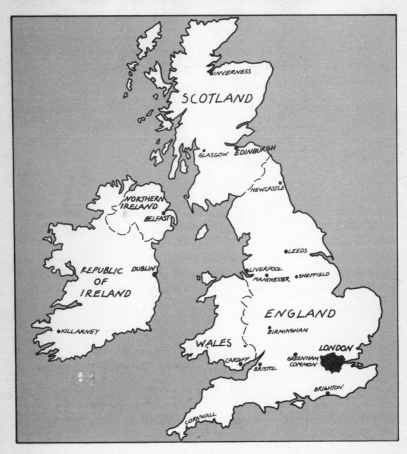

The main problem about travel in **Britain** and **Ireland** is the expense. If your money is limited you'll need to be prepared to camp in all weathers, spend a lot of time hitching and generally avoid eating in restaurants. The cost of living in Ireland is especially exorbitant, though the relative ease of hitching and the hospitality of the people are a big compensation, both in the North and the Republic of Eire.

In terms of safety, you'll probably find harassment far less overt here than, say, in the Latin-dominated countries of Mediterranean Europe, but similar precautions apply: take care if hitching, for instance ask the driver's destination before revealing where you want to go; watch out for your belongings; and try not to walk alone in cities late at night. The latter isn't always easy as public transport tends to shut down by midnight and taxis can be few and far between.

Both Britain and Ireland offer plenty of scope for walking and cycling holidays. In general, Britain is more spoilt, much of its beautiful landscape having to be protected as national parkland, though there are still parts of Wales, Scotland and the north of England where you can walk for miles without seeing a soul. Compared to rural areas, life in the cities is much less friendly and relaxed, but there are other attractions. Despite the handicap of a ruthlessly Conservative government, centres like Edinburgh, Cardiff, Bristol, Liverpool, Leeds and Belfast, as well as London, all have their own women's organisations and radical bookshops and usually some cultural event or other going on.

ENGLAND

For most travellers, **England** begins (quite possible ends) with London, which with its individuality and multi-ethnic mix on the whole lives up to its myths and reputation. But London, like much of southern England, can often seem unwelcoming – and for visitors it is outrageously expensive. Without friends to stay with, the cost of accommodation can be crippling, whilst the city's transport charges are the highest in Europe. They were, for a while, reduced – by the capital's council, the GLC, whose socialist conscience and imagination has helped countless projects over recent years, from arts festivals to feminist publications, anti-racism campaigns to schemes for the disabled. But as from spring 1986 the GLC has gone – abolished by the Conservative central government.

The GLC's abolition is just one indication of the political climate in Britain. The north of England has been especially hard hit by government spending cuts and you may well be shocked by the poverty and unemployment in towns like Liverpool, Bradford and Newcastle, at least in contrast to the more apparently prosperous south. But don't be put off; northern people tend to be very open and friendly with less of the traditional English reserve, accommodation is cheaper and much of the countryside is wild and quite spectacular.

Sexual harassment varies little between England, Wales, Scotland and

Ireland. Apart from the odd wolf-whistle, you're unlikely to be approached by men in rural areas, except in pubs. Big cities, however, pose a definite problem at night, when it's unwise to travel alone. One London borough even has its own safe women's transport service, but without government support the idea's unlikely to catch on to any significant scale. Racism is an additional problem, rooted in Britain's history as a leading imperialist power. You're undoubtedly more prone to abuse if you're black, but even white Australians report patronising, colonial attitudes, especially at work.

The double issue of racism and sexism has become a strong focus of the **Women's Movement** in England, which has many more Asian and Afro-Caribbean communities than neighbouring Wales or Scotland. To understand this commitment you only need turn to one of the two regular feminist publications, *Outwrite* or *Spare Rib*.

Since its inception in the early 1970s, the movement has become incredibly diverse. As well as racism, central issues like health, work, education and violence have been joined by a growing commitment to peace, largely inspired by the women of Greenham Common; the concerns of women's organisations throughout England nowadays range from anti-nuclear protest to consciousness-raising and teaching women practical skills, such as house-building or computer technology; and London alone has three feminist bookshops, plus around six publishers devoted to producing books written by women. All in all, in spite of economic recession and a woman Prime Minister devoted to traditional Conservative values, feminism in England remains very much alive.

▓ **Annie Mubanga comes from Zambia and now is Head of the Housing Team of the British Refugee Council in London.**

I was happy on 6 April 1983, when a female immigration officer at Heathrow Airport told me I was free to enter, especially after the French authorities refused to give me a visa for even 48 hours. My husband is English and so, although I have a Zambian passport, I did not need a visa for Britain.

I have travelled extensively since my arrival. I know Scotland well and the south-west, where I lived in Bath, then in a small Somerset village, for six months. As a foreigner in the south-west I found people extremely polite and obliging, often willing to go out of their way to give me directions. But they tended to be surprised that I'd come to live in Somerset where they felt I'd be isolated from black people. I was also interested to find that everywhere I went there seemed to be somebody who had been to Zambia or had a friend or relative working there. Some had wonderful stories to tell but there was a habit of putting everything in the past, ending with the phrase: 'Oh well, that was ten years ago, but now things are bad.' I just used to keep quiet. What can you say when people run down your country?

We were always being asked when we were going back to Africa. A simple question, but very hard to answer. Also, what was it like over there? The way people referred to Zambia you would have thought it was not on this earth but on some other planet. British people have no idea how big and diverse Africa and Africans are. Their attitudes and questions did not upset me, though, because people did not mean anything bad, the questions were in good faith.

My first Christmas in Somerset was very sad, and I missed my family very much. I was asked what the weather was in 'your country' and when I answered that it was summer the response was – Oh how funny! I was also asked if in Zambia we had 'a proper Christmas'. In my innocence when I asked what a proper Christmas was it turned out to be an English one. Another frequent question was had I seen snow. There is something special and mystical about snow. The Somerset people were very romantic about it. Even when I said that I had seen it in Sweden, this was not considered special. I had to see real snow here.

Having failed to find work in Bath or Bristol, my husband and I were finally offered jobs based in London and so we moved there to live. It's a fascinating city, huge and complex until you discover that it is really made up of many small communities. My job with the Refugee Council involves a lot of travelling, for instance when a client is offered accommodation by the local authorities I go with them to see it, so I've come to know London well, not to mention the problems facing ethnic minorities.

I've learned that black women are doubly discriminated against on grounds of sex and colour. They are concentrated in the worst paid and most dangerous jobs, working in sweat shops or small component factories, as cleaners and domestics, often anti-social hours. I like London, but it's hard to ignore the hostility and racism at times. I've often suffered verbal abuse (skinheads are the worst) and men have felt free to try and pick me up. Bureaucracies tend to be patronising. Women, especially black women, are more often than not assumed to be in the wrong, so it's advisable to be careful about your behaviour. If you travel late (after 10 pm) on public transport, try and go with friends as it can lead to harassment from groups of youths. Don't rely on other late travellers, most bystanders won't come to your help.

Londoners socialise with their close family, work-mates and people they meet in other social contexts, for example sports clubs. My impression is that friendship isn't offered easily. Friendship is seen to result in giving up time and possibly costing money, and people like to be warned of a visit. In other words, you're not expected to drop in on people without pre-arrangements. For temporary visitors this formality means you'll be unlikely to make English friends. One good way of meeting people can be to go to the local library which has information on what is happening in the community. Recently I've met women here for six or eight months who are joining various courses, from language courses to anthropology and development studies, in order to meet other people. The impression that you make friends in pubs is quite misleading. Most people come to pubs in their own groups or to meet old friends, and very rarely mix or join strangers. Besides there's a tradition that people buy each other a round of drinks which can be very expensive, especially in a large group.

London has a lot to offer – you just have to make the effort to find it. There are beautiful parks and some very good street markets where you can buy a huge range of goods from tropical vegetables through to clothes and antiques. Each market has a character of its own and is great fun to wander through. (Prices are usually cheaper during the week so it's well worth buying your fruit and vegetables before the weekend.) There are feminist groups representing many different interests, from lesbians and Third World women to those with disabilities or working in fields such as education or the media. Buying a copy of *Spare Rib*, the national feminist magazine, or *City Limits* or *Time Out* (for weekly information on films, theatre, exhibitions, political events, etc.), you'll always find something interesting going on.

▰ **Fiona Inglis already had the security of a job in London when she came to England. After one-and-a-half years working in a large publishing house, she has just returned home to Australia.**

A fleeting or first visit to London may leave the impression that the women have it OK here: a well-established feminist movement, recognition and acceptance of a large and growing gay population, and a woman Prime Minister. It isn't until one has stayed some time that the enormity of the underlying problems really hits.

My first few weeks in London were spent as a typical pack-lugging under-26-er, taking in all the things we had seen in our primary school geography and history books. It was not until my friends left for further jaunts around Europe that I really began to see London. Aware that living in a cosy Kensington flat with other Australians wasn't the ideal existence in a foreign city, I moved into a flat in a part of London that I hadn't even heard of, let alone seen, with people I didn't know at all.

It was the best thing I could have done and I urge anyone planning to stay in London for a while to escape the security of living with friends from home. After all, what have you left home for? Of course, things aren't all plain sailing. You can't guarantee to hit it off with your flatmates, but advertisements in papers and magazines usually reveal enough to tell you whether or not you'd like to meet them.

There will always be moments of frustration and anger as you try to find your way around the endless maze of London streets, having enquiries met with crusty grunts from newspaper vendors and bus conductors, wondering where you'll end up after half-an-hour on a bumpy bus. Once installed, however, even with only a vague notion of what lies where, it's far easier to see London properly. (You'll find an A-Z your most worthwhile investment.)

During the summer of 1985, a summer which will be remembered as the wettest for many years, the government decided to abolish the Greater London Council. From spring this year, Londoners lost the right for say and active participation in innumerable projects and functions run by the people they have elected to a new, unwanted and chaotic system of government. What has this to do with the visitor to London, you ask? Seemingly the only administrative body that recognised the needs of a large chunk of society (including women, youth, the unemployed and the disabled), the GLC not only attempted to repair some of the damage which government policies did to these groups, it was also responsible for running things like parks, carnivals and sporting events, and providing vital subsidies to the arts; not to mention planning, public transport, housing, education and so on. And the *woman* Prime Minister who has been responsible for its abolition? A value-added-tax (or VAT which you'll get to know only too soon) on Tampax is fairly indicative of how Mrs T feels about the women in this country!

Looking at the Women's Movement in the UK, however, one cannot fail to be encouraged by its lasting strength and achievements, especially in the face of the current government. One need only look at the number of women's presses, publications and bookshops. I'm also impressed by the extent to which the movement seem to be accessible to women at every level of society. My local library – free to all residents, easily located and reached by public transport, with facilities for the disabled and open every day – is full of pamphlets, advertisements and information for anyone to follow up if they choose.

Having said all this, you may well ask how easy it is to meet other women in London. I cannot help but feel that the old English reserve penetrates every Londoner to a certain extent. Walk into a pub or coffee-shop alone and you are likely to remain alone (I have never experienced problems with sexual harassment, though perhaps I have just been lucky). There is no great interest in Australians any more – we are here in such vast numbers that any spark of curiosity perished long ago. This applies to the Women's Movement as well, for the history and policies of Australian women aren't so different from those of our English sisters – we're just a few steps behind, due perhaps to the general lackadaisical and hedonistic attitudes practised in Australia.

If you're a feminist and want to meet other women in your area, buy a copy of *Spare Rib* (available from larger news agencies and women's bookshops) and consult the Classifieds which always list the names and numbers of other women who've either established informal meeting groups or wish to form new ones. The magazine also carries news about conferences, lectures, readings and other events on in London and other parts of the country.

Having recently spent many evenings outside pubs with a wide variety of Londoners, letting our problems melt in the watery sunshine; attended some inspiring and very entertaining fringe theatre shows; and spent days wandering around bookshops, markets and Hampstead Heath (where there's a women's bathing pond), I can only say that London, despite the financial demands, must still be one of the most varied and mentally stimulating cities in the world.

◤ **Ann Arnold, also from Australia, adds a note on work. After some time living in London she, too, has recently returned home.**

As an Australian, I was stunned when I was first referred to as a 'colonial' – a ridiculous reminder of England's outdated imperialism. This notion crops up time and time again in the form of a benevolent, patronising attitude towards 'Aussies', 'Kiwis', etc. Nanny-seeking Hampstead mothers want a 'jolly Australian girl who'll pitch in and doesn't mind working'. Translate: she'll keep smiling when she's told she can't have that promised weekend off, she'll happily prepare a dinner party then politely disappear when the guests arrive, and she'll cheerfully clean the three loos twice a day – on £30 a week.

Nannying, traditionally a popular occupation for young female visitors to England, can of course be enjoyable – I've known many girls very happy with their substitute families. But it is rife with exploitation, as is the catering industry, probably the biggest employment area for temporary workers.

Publicans with rooms to spare offer live-in jobs, mutually convenient for both employer and employee, except that the publican then feels justified in paying low wages for long hours of work. Again there are naturally good and bad amongst the employers.

In a charming fourteenth-century inn just south of London I encountered one of the bad. As breakfast waitress I was part of what the local villagers jokingly called 'the Aussie/Kiwi slave trade'. The staff were housed in practically derelict quarters. I cleaned layers of mouse droppings out of my room when I arrived, and shared one mouldy bath with seven others. The beautiful pub did a roaring trade, while the husband and wife management team ruled with an iron rod, treating their staff with absolute contempt and rudeness.

This type of situation is by no means unique to England, but is able to exist in the extreme here because, amongst other factors, employers know that travellers provide a capable, willing workforce, and are often in desperate need of accommodation and employment. Thus the 'Upstairs Downstairs' environment continues to thrive.

▟ **During a trip to Britain from her home in the States, Sally Marie decided to spend a couple of weeks at Greenham Common. She ended up staying for over a year.**

The Greenham Common Women's Peace Camp was begun in September 1981 by a group of women terrified by the prospect of Cruise missiles being based in England, and has since become a symbol both of world-wide resistance to the war machine and of women's collective strength and spirit. Simply by having a cup of tea at one of the seven camps around the nine-mile fence, the visitor is helping to maintain a constant dissenting presence against the American Air Force base and its miserable arsenal. Any woman travelling in Britain would be doing herself a disservice if she missed out Greenham, whether she plans to stay a few hours or a few months, but be warned: you may find it difficult to tear yourself away.

The Greenham Peace women have become household names in Britain; most people have strong feelings about them, one way or another, though I found that even the most outspoken 'antis' would usually admit to a certain grudging respect. Hitching in England, when I mentioned my intentions to visit Greenham I was often warned against it as a collection of the 'worst kind of lesbians and freaks', living in unutterable filth and squalor much to the disgust and dismay of the 'decent' local population. But I also met many supporters, those who make up a huge resistance network that stretches the length and breadth of the nation. They supply the camp with food, warm clothing, firewood, blankets, sleeping bags, tents and rolls of plastic for shelters, toothpaste, vehicles and cash – vital support, inspired by the many individual women who have been to Greenham or go regularly, and come away empowered and re-energised. Obviously the camp isn't the Ritz, but it's often cosy and comfortable; though the base itself is grotesque and ugly the surrounding Common and countryside is truly lovely; and the company can't be beaten.

There are no leaders at Greenham, no hierarchies, no rules, no fees, no sign-up sheets or duty rotas. There are also no permanent structures, no owned land, no electricity or plumbing. What there *is* is an ever-fluctuating population of women of diverse ages, backgrounds and experi-ence, from all over the world, creating a community that functions on a system of supportive anarchy. During my first weeks I cut my first hole in the fence under the expert tutelage of a 'vicar's wife' from Wales, drank aquavit and danced folk dances long into the night with a cordon of Danish women, participated in a mass action that involved cutting down four-and-a-half miles of fence, and shared many hours of talk by the fire on such topics as vegetarianism, sexuality, our debt to Third World women, and whether or not to dye my hair purple (I didn't in the end dare).

Since it began, the camp has amassed a glorious collection of songs, myths, and herstory, all readily shared with newcomers – women come and go so much you don't feel like an intruder. It's a good idea to visit several, if not all the camps round the base which are situated outside the gates, roughly two miles apart. Each gate has been named and painted from one of the colours of the rainbow; every camp has its own geography and character. Green Gate, for example, is situated deep in a mossy forest; Orange Gate's backyard is a vast stretch of gorse and heather heathland; while the camp at Yellow Gate is perched on an exposed hill overlooking a major road. Women you meet may suggest that you camp at a gate that happens to be low on women, but nobody insists on anything and you'll probably find the one that feels best for you. Greenham having no centre, no headquarters of any kind, means that you must be prepared to take initiative (it took weeks for me to lose the habit of looking for somebody to ask permission of), while keeping the group as a whole in mind.

This includes all the many times of harassment and eviction. The vagaries of British law preclude the forced removal of people from 'common land', but their personal effects may be confiscated. A small brigade of garbage collectors, known as bailiffs, comes round quite often, sometimes even daily, to break up the camps by snatching whatever they can and throwing it into the munching jaws of a garbage truck. This has been going on for so long that women have become adept at whisking essentials – dishes, chairs, food, bedding, firewood, etc. – into camp vehicles, out of the bailiffs' reach, and simply unloading them to set up camp again after the eviction. As far as actual law-breaking goes, many foreign women, myself included, feel a pull towards non-violent civil disobedience at Greenham, but are frightened by the implications of being arrested in someone else's country. As a rule, when I was there foreign women didn't suffer instant deportation and were treated pretty much in the same way as English women, though Irish women, working-class women and women of colour, regardless of nationality, can expect to be treated several degrees worse.

There are precautions you can take against arrest. For example, walking away from a blockade when the police arrive. But before you take part in any action, make sure you talk with several experienced women about the specifics of the legal system. Many have been through the courts again and again and know the procedures backwards. They also have the phone numbers of sympathetic lawyers. On rare occasions women are arrested for no reason at all, so it's a good idea to find out the facts early on if you plan an extended stay.

A NOTE ON MEN Many Greenham supporters are men and they are welcome to visit *during the day* at most gates. Individual men may be asked to leave if women find them dominating the conversation or if they stay too long or women just get weary of male energy. Usually the request will be made politely, but not always. If you're travelling with a man, do yourself a favour: let him explore Oxford for the day while you take the bus to Greenham; or suggest he take a walk around the perimeter fence on his own and chat with the soldiers about disarmament.

TRAVEL NOTES

Language English plus a wide variety of languages spoken by different ethnic groups.

Transport An efficient network of buses and trains covers most of the country, but for long distances coaches are nearly always cheaper. Hitching alone carries the usual risks, although it's fairly easy to get a ride. Bicycling is a good way of getting around cities and seeing the countryside and in London it's not only cheap, but far quicker than relying on public transport.

Accommodation In general expensive, especially in London which is renowned for having some of the most highly priced hotels in the world. Rooms advertised as *Bed and Breakfast* can be reasonable and very comfortable, but fill up quickly in the summer. Most tourist information offices carry a list of rooms available in the area. If you don't mind the regulations, youth hostels are widespread and some of the cheapest places to stay. Camping is safer than in many countries and often free.

For a longer stay in London, try *Spare Rib*, *City Limits* or *Time Out* for Flat Share advertisements or go to the Capital Radio building, Euston Tower, Euston Road, NW1, Tues and Fri afternoons, for their free *Capital Flat Share* leaflet.

Special problems Entrance into England can be a harrowing experience,

especially if you're arriving from a Third World country. Admission is at the discretion of the immigration officer and even marriage to a British citizen won't guarantee you secure entry. Make sure you have all the relevant documents, including entry clearance from the British Embassy in your home country where applicable, and proof of sufficient funds to cover your stay. Black women have been particularly discriminated against by the British Nationality Act. If in trouble, contact the *United Kingdom Immigrant Advisory Service* (Tel. 01–240 5176) which has offices at Heathrow and Gatwick airports; and/or the *Women's Immigration and Nationality Group*, c/o 115 Old Street, London EC1V 9JR (Tel. 01–251 8706).

Unless you're prepared to be ruthlessly exploited (you may have no choice), it's hard to find work without a permit.

Other information Sally Marie has provided the following tips on *going to Greenham Common*:

Greenham Common is about 50 miles west of London on the A4. The main entrance to the base is located on the A339 out of Newbury on the Basingstoke road. Public transport is available from London (train or coach) to Newbury and also to Thatcham which is closer to the camps on the base's north side. From Newbury, you can take a local bus (No.

302) to the Main Gate, USAF Greenham Common (or Yellow Gate). From Thatcham (ask to get off the coach at The Plough) turn right at the Little Chef, and walk the two miles up the hill. After a mile or so you'll pass the train station. At the second intersection, at the top of the hill, turn right: a few hundred yards and you're at Orange Gate. Buses and trains also run to Newbury from Oxford, Reading, and other large towns.

Dress appropriately! Expect rain and cool breezes even in summer. Expect *mud.* Proper footwear is especially important, particularly if you plan to walk the fence. Gifts of books, tampons, loo paper, drink and food, especially fresh fruit, are always welcome – remember that most camp residents are vegetarian and many are vegan (they eat no eggs or milk products). If you're planning to stay overnight or longer, an easily pitched and struck tent is useful, as is a good warm sleeping bag. Don't bring more than you can easily keep track of: bailiffs sometimes arrive early and can be pretty ruthless. Most gates have a vehicle where valuables can be stashed.

You can write to the camp – the women appreciate mail and try hard to respond. The address is: Women's Peace Camp, USAF Greenham Common, Newbury, Berkshire, U.K.

Guides *Let's Go Britain and Ireland* (St Martins Press, U.S., updated annually). Good on practicalities, if sometimes a little crass. Simon Calder, *Hitchhiker's Manual: Britain* (Vacwork, Oxford). Invaluable route information. *Alternative London* (Otherwise Press, 1982). Last edition of a classic hippy guide/directory – still worth hunting out if you plan to stay in the capital some time. Susan Griffith *Summer Jobs in Britain* (Vacwork). Annual work directory.

CONTACTS

We only have space for a small selection of **women's organisations** here, but the **Spare Rib Diary** contains a fairly comprehensive list. It's obtainable from feminist and radical bookshops or by writing to *Spare Rib*, 27 Clerkenwell Close, London EC1 0AT.

The main **women's centre in London** is **A Woman's Place**, Hungerford House, Victoria Embankment, London WC2 (Tel. 01–836 6081), which provides information, books and a meeting place for many different groups. On the first floor is the Feminist Library (Tel. 01–930 0715), open for anyone to look at or borrow from thousands of books. The centre also keeps information on women's studies courses and current feminist research.

These are some more useful London addresses, listed alphabetically:

Asian Women's Resource Centre, 134 Minet Avenue, London NW10 (Tel. 01–961 6559). Provides information on welfare, housing immigration as well as material on the lives and history of Asian women.

Brixton Black Women's Centre, Mary Seacole House, 41a Stockwell Green, London SW9 9HZ (Tel. 01–274 9220/7696). Meeting place and contact for black women's groups in London and around the country.

London Lesbian Line, BM Box 1514, London WC1 3XX (Tel. 01–251 6911). Phone for information and advice, Mon and Fri 2–10pm; Tue, Wed and Thu 7–10pm.

Rape Crisis Centre, Tel. 01–837 1600. 24-hour service.

Release, 183b Prince of Wales Road, London NW5 (Tel. 01–485 4440). Provides legal advice and referral on drugs and the law and abortion.

WISER LINKS *(Women's international information exchange and resource centre)*, 173 Archway Road, London N6 (Tel. 01–341 4403). Mainly geared to linking up and giving solidarity to Third World women.

Women's Advice Centre, c/o Manor Gardens Centre, 6–9 Manor Gardens, London N7 (Tel. 01–281 2205). Free advice and information, Fridays only, 1–3pm.

Women's Health Information Centre, 52 Featherstone Street, London EC1 (Tel. 01–251 6580). National information and resource centre.

London has three **feminist bookshops**: **Silver Moon**, 68 Charing Cross Road, WC2 (Tel. 01–836 7906); **Sisterwrite**, 190 Upper Street, N1 (Tel. 01–226 9782), closed Mondays; and the **Virago Bookshop**, 34 Southampton Street, Covent Garden, WC2 (Tel. 01–240 6638). The first two each have a women-only café and good noticeboards for contacts.

The following **feminist/radical bookshops outside London** are listed alphabetically by town:

BRISTOL **Full Marks**, 110 Cheltenham Road, Bristol (Tel. 0272–40491); and **Greenleaf Bookshop Co-operative**, 82 Colston Street, Bristol 1 (Tel. 0272–211369). The second is also a wholefood café.

CAMBRIDGE: **Grapevine**, Unit 6, Dale's Brewery, Gwydir Street, Cambridge (Tel. 0223–61808).

LANCASTER: **Single Step**, 78a Penny Street, Lancaster (Tel. 0524–63021).

LEEDS: **Corner Bookshop**, 162 Woodhouse Lane (opposite university), Leeds 2 (Tel. 0532–454125).

LEICESTER: **Blackthorn Books** *(Co-op and vegetarian café)*, 70 High Street, Leicester (Tel. 0533–2189).

LIVERPOOL: **Progressive Books**, 12 Berry Street, Liverpool L1 4JF (Tel. 051–709 1905).

MANCHESTER: **Grass Roots**, 1 Newton Street, Manchester (Tel. 061–236 3112).

READING: **Acorn Bookshop**, 17 Chatham Street, Reading (Tel. 0734–584425).

SOUTHAMPTON: **October Books**, 4 Onslow Road, Southampton (Tel. 0703–24489).

YORK: **York Community Books**, 73 Walmgate, York (Tel. 0904–37355).

All these places should be able to provide some information on women's activities in the area. There are far too many women's groups around the country to list here. If you're interested in a particular part of England, contact **WIRES**, PO Box 20, Oxford (Tel. 0865–240991), the internal **newsletter** of the British Women's Liberation Movement.

BOOKS

The 1980s has seen a rapid development of feminist presses and **feminist writing** in England. The titles below represent mainly personal favourites.

Beatrix Campbell, *Wigan Pier Revisited. Poverty and Politics in the 1980s* (Virago, 1984). A devastating record of the extent of poverty and unemployment in the north of England, and a passionate plea for a feminist socialism that responds to real needs.

Jennifer Clarke, *In Our Grandmothers' Footsteps. A Virago Guide to London* (Virago, 1984). The author plus photographer Joanna Parkin have unearthed the memorials to 271 women – famous, infamous and unknown.

Anna Coote and Beatrix Campbell, *Sweet Freedom – The Struggle for Women's Liberation* (Picador, 1982). Two long-term active feminists chronicle the progress of the movement since the late 1960s when it began.

Juliet Mitchell, *Woman's Estate* (Penguin, 1971). Classic socialist/feminist analysis.

Ann Oakley, *Sex, Gender and Society* (MT Smith 1972, rev, Gower 1985). The author draws on biological, anthropological and sociological evidence to examine the real differences between the sexes. Another classic.

Hannah Kantner, Sarah Lefanu, Shaila Shah and Carole Spedding, eds, *Sweeping Statements: Writings from the Women's Liberation Movement 1981–83* (The Women's Press, 1984). Collection of articles and conference papers demonstrating the range of feminist involvement, analysis and action during this period.

Barbara Rogers, *52%: Getting Women's Power into Politics* (The Women's Press, 1983). Compelling argument for the urgent need for more women's involvement in British politics.

Beverley Bryan, Stella Dadzie and Suzanne Scafe, *Heart of the Race* (Virago, 1985). Insights into what it's like growing up as a black woman in Britain.

Amrit Wilson, *Finding a Voice* (Virago, 1978). Experiences of Asian women in Britain recorded in their own words.

Lynne Jones, ed., *Keeping the Peace: Women's Peace Handbook* (The Women's Press, 1983). Personal accounts from women with wide-ranging views. Includes ideas for action.

Barbara Harford and Sarah Hopkins, eds, *Greenham Common: Women at the Wire* (The Women's Press, 1984). Full story of life at the peace camp.

FICTION

Zoe Fairbairns, *Benefits* (Virago, 1979).

Feminist science-fiction set in a not too distant London future where men try to control women's reproduction and the 'victims' fight back.

Pat Barker, *Union Street* (Virago, 1982). About the lives and struggles of seven working-class women and their men in the north of England during the 1973 miners' strike. Also recommended is *Blow Your House Down* (Virago, 1984) which tells the tale of a woman's search for the man responsible for a series of killings of prostitutes in a northern town.

Michele Roberts, *A Piece of the Night* (The Women's Press, 1978). Tells of the contradictions faced by Julie Fanchot, French born, educated in an English convent school, as her life falls apart.

Sara Maitland, *Telling Tales* (Journeyman Press, 1983). Collection of 16 short stories, some set in the present, others featuring women from ancient and biblical history. Very readable.

Jeanette Winterson, *Oranges are not the Only Fruit* (Pandora Press, 1985). Wry, original tales of an evangelical upbringing in the north-west. Quirky and fun.

Buchi Emecheta, *Adah's Story* (Allison & Busby, 1983). Brought from Nigeria to her violent husband, Adah brings up five children, studies, divorces, works in the Civil Service and writes, fulfilling her dreams. Look out also for Emecheta's other novels and children's books.

Sharan-Jeet Shan, *In My Own Name* (The Women's Press, 1985). Autobiographical story of an Indian woman, born in the Punjab and forced into an arranged marriage which brought her to England, where she finally refuses to renounce her right to live her own life. Simply written and very moving.

Angela Carter, *Nothing Sacred* (Virago, 1982). Collection of essays and writings, many of them autobiographical, by one of Britain's leading contemporary novelists.

Betty Vodden, *One Over the Baker's Dozen* (Centerprise, 1985). Autobiography of a woman living all her life in Hackney, London.

WALES

Wales is easily reached from England by road or rail. This accessibility and the unspoiled beauty of the landscape has made tourism one of its biggest growth industries, yet travelling around the country is still like going back in time.

Ever since the annexation of Wales by England in the thirteenth century, the Welsh people have managed to retain a strong sense of their history and national identity, against all odds. Today this sometimes manifests itself in a hostile or at least ambivalent attitude to visitors, but don't be put off. The occasional lapse of courtesy or reversion to the Welsh language amongst locals in shops are only signs of an understandable defence mechanism from a people who have so long felt their culture under threat. Visitors are generally welcome, not least because they represent a vital means of income.

Travelling alone you're unlikely to experience much overt discrimination or harassment, though you'll probably find yourself being stared at. Pubs tend to be the worst pockets of resistance. Several women have reported having to cope with remarks and advances, but they're usually token, almost reflex actions, and easy to manage. Local women are more likely to be found in pubs on Fridays and Saturdays and often enjoy talking with travellers whilst their men get on with the drinking.

▰ **Ceridwen Lloyd-Morgan grew up in north-west Wales. After ten years in England and France she has now returned and teaches women's studies in Aberystwyth. She also writes articles for the Welsh-language press, chiefly in *Pais*, a magazine for women.**

Wales may be part of Britain in terms of government, but it has its own distinct social structures, language and cultures. About 20 per cent of the population is Welsh-speaking; that means roughly a quarter of a million women speak Welsh as well as English. How much you may hear, as a visitor, depends on where you go. Radnorshire, for example, was anglicised a century ago and only a very few people there can speak Welsh. But in the north-west and west the majority do speak Welsh naturally and may feel much less confident in English.

Even in the traditional strongholds of the language, such as Gwynedd and Dyfed, serious erosion has occurred in the last ten years. Tempted by low house prices, clean air and beautiful scenery, many English families, as well as retired people, have been moving in, whilst severe unemployment drives local people away in search of jobs.

When I was growing up in the 1950s and 1960s, such incomers were absorbed quickly and happily. Their children, outnumbered by monoglot Welsh-speakers, were chattering in two languages in a matter of weeks. Nowadays Welsh-speaking children and their mothers suddenly find that they are in the minority. One way they have responded to this situation is by setting up nationwide Welsh-speaking nursery schools (*ysgolion meithrin*), which also take children from English-speaking homes where the parents are keen for them to be bilingual. Parents have to pay, however, and in rural areas expensive and scarce public transport creates further difficulties.

The relatively poor status of women in Wales, and the limited impact of feminism, can be seen in the groups and societies they are involved with outside the home, particularly in the Welsh-speaking context. Perhaps the largest group, *Merched y Wawr* ('daughters of the dawn') was set up in the 1960s as an alternative to the Women's Institute, which was perceived as too English and not political enough. *Merched y Wawr* has a clear commitment to the language and its branches organise Welsh-medium activities of all kinds in the towns and villages. Certain branches are active in the peace movement, for example, organising trips to Greenham and helping to politicise women in the local communities.

For many Welsh-speaking women, the chapel or church is still one of the most important areas of social contact and provides opportunities for organising, public speaking, taking on responsibilities. In many villages it is this dimension rather than a deep commitment to a particular kind of Christianity that makes women regular attenders. (It is worth noting that both the non-conformist denominations and the church in Wales have been far quicker than their English counterparts in bringing in the ordination of women.)

One reason for the slow progress of feminism in Wales is probably its 'Englishness'. People associate it with incomers, bringing new-fangled, foreign ideas with them from outside. Up and down Wales there are women's co-operatives, peace groups, and anti-nuclear groups. There are movements like Welsh Women's Aid, dealing with the specifically female problem of domestic violence. All these groups, which have a basically feminist philosophy, are still perceived by many Welsh women (and men) as alien and irrelevant to their own lives. As the majority of women involved in them are originally from outside Wales and/or non-Welsh-speaking, and meetings are normally conducted in English, a vicious circle of alienation can develop for the Welsh-speaker. It is no exaggeration to say that many Welsh-speaking women feel themselves the victims of a double oppression, by Welsh men and by the English of both sexes.

But one tremendously encouraging development came out of the 1984–5 miners' strike. Women in the coal-mining communities of north-east and south Wales, even those not related to miners, formed women's support groups, and women in other areas helped to collect food and money and distribute leaflets. Going on the picketline, talking to the media, organising and addressing meetings, was a profoundly liberating experience for many. Women who had fought shy of politics became politicised overnight and gained vastly in confidence. It changed personal relationships too, as the men came to admit the crucial importance of the women's contribution to the strike, and to understand that women were more than just sex objects or homemakers.

◪ **Clare Spencer has been living in Wales since 1975.**

The Welsh have a clear stereotype of the tourist. He (and his family) comes from the Midlands, brings his car, and knows what he likes. Among his likes are chicken and chips, caravans, narrow-gauge railways, and heavily signposted scenic walks. Among his dislikes are Dyfed's Sunday pub closing law. Since Wales depends for an increasing percentage of its income on tourism, it can hardly be blamed for conceding to the tastes of this monster. But I'd like to encourage the alternative tourist, the woman who wants to test out her travelling skills by avoiding the main holiday centres and the red roads on the Ordnance Survey maps. Wales is inviting territory, alone or in company, on wheels or on foot. You can even follow a deliberately feminist itinerary, incorporating visits to women's co-operatives (like the Ragged Robin near Lampeter), work-shops, and the Alternative Technology Centre near Machynlleth. A useful point of contact for women in any small Welsh town seems to be the local wholefood shop, which in mid-Wales can provide a strong dose of 1960s nostalgia.

In ten years of occasional residence and frequent travel in mid-, south, and west Wales, I have encountered no face-to-face hostility regarding my status as an English person, and minimal sexual harassment. Obviously, you behave with late-night caution in Cardiff as you would in any major city. And the tradition of the men-only 'smoke-room' bar is unofficially upheld in many town and country pubs. As an unaccompanied woman, you won't get a lot of welcome in the local in, say, a former mining village in one of the valleys. But Wales is one of the few countries in which I have hitchhiked alone, admittedly on minor roads, without qualms; and I have never yet been obliged to refuse a lift through instinctive suspicion of the person who offered it. There is less and less public transport in the rural areas, and more and more demand on people's sense of community.

For the outsider, however, this doesn't mean easy contact. The Welsh language is rarely a barrier, though it can be occasionally disconcerting to find yourself a dumb spectator to a conversation in a village post office. But the economic decline has given women fewer opportunities to break out of traditional patterns of family and home. A female school leaver in an average Welsh town has little local chance of employment except, and even then if they're lucky, shop work. You'll see a lot of bored faces behind the counters of chain stores and ice-cream stalls — and you'll also notice the inflated divide between young and old, many of the generation between having moved away for work in the 1970s. Ironically as a tourist it's probably easier to meet with Welsh women than if you settle. There are quite a few independent craftswomen who sell at local fairs and festivals. And it is possible to plan the kind of travel that will force you to talk to Welsh people, whether by hitchhiking, tracking down women's groups, or exploring some aspect of industrial archaeology. I have been equally absorbed in conversations with an organiser of a south Wales anti-poverty action group, and with a 70-year-old woman who could stand on a ridge above the river Teifi and point out to me the house in which she was born, the manor in which she worked, the smallholding in which she brought up her children, and the cottage which she now maintains, alone.

I've tried not to give an idealised description. Wales is an economically depressed country, with both the progressive, and the conservative, reaction which that condition implies. Chapel morality (not necessarily derogatory of women) still prevails among older rural communities; and rugby club values (always derogatory of women) warp the minds of younger urban men. I've purposely neglected to describe the landscape, which is widely and justly celebrated elsewhere. Try the stretch of coastline covered by the Machynlleth–Pwlleli railway for beaches, castles, isolated villages, and sheep. And I haven't mentioned North Wales and Snowdonia which, if scenically more spectacular, are also more commercially orientated than the inland areas further south.

TRAVEL NOTES

Language Welsh is the national language, spoken by roughly 20 per cent of the population. More or less everyone knows English, but its common usage varies according to area.

Transport Most places are connected by bus, though services are slow and infrequent in the more remote areas. Trains offer wonderful views, but are of limited use as a way of getting around. Hitching is an accepted form of travel for locals and visitors alike, but unless you keep to the main roads likely to be very slow

Accommodation There are hotels, guest houses, bed and breakfast places and youth hostels all over Wales. Prices vary and they get booked up quickly in summer, so it's a good idea to contact the nearest tourist information office. Holiday cottages are advertised in Sunday newspapers and climbing magazines – they're mostly very good value and a lot better than camping when it's very wet.

Special problems Beware of suddenly changing weather conditions. Many of the accidents in the Welsh mountains happen because people start climbing ill-prepared for harsh conditions. Always take warm clothes, waterproofs, a whistle, map and compass, and food and water if you plan any long expedition.

Guides Welsh Tourist Board publications are usually very good. They include *Wales Walking*, a basic guide with maps showing hundreds of walks, and *Where to Stay in Wales*, published yearly. *The Welsh Women's Directory* (published by the Women's Enterprise Bureau, 1984) contains a useful list of addresses, including women's co-operatives, advice centres etc. Available from: WEB, Greenhouse, 1 Trevelyan Terrace, Bangor, Gwynedd – Tel.

0248–351263. It's a good idea to phone first as it may be out of print.

CONTACTS
For information on groups around the country contact either **Cardiff Women's Centre**, 2 Coburn Street, Cathays, Cardiff (Tel. 0222–383024); or **Swansea Women's Centre**, 58 Alexandra Road, Swansea (Tel. 0792–467365). The **Women's Enterprise Bureau** in Bangor, mentioned above under 'Guides', should also have lists of addresses.

Cardiff also has a rape crisis centre – Tel. 0222–373181.

A feminist travel circuit of Wales could include **Oaklands Women's Holiday Centre**, Glasbury-on-Wye, nr Hereford, Powys (Phone first if you want to stay as it gets booked up by groups; Tel. 04974–275. Chaotic and not always very friendly, but worth trying out. Also the **Centre for Alternative Technology** at Llwyngwern Quarry, Machynlleth, Powys (Tel. 0654–2400/2782), which includes a bookshop stocking quite a few women's titles.

For a wider range of feminist books and periodicals visit *One-O-Eight Bookshop*, 108 Salisbury Street, Cardiff (Tel. 0222–28908).

BOOKS
Elizabeth Mavor, *Life with the Ladies of Llangollen* (Viking, 1984). Extracts from the letters and journals of Lady Eleanor Butler and Sarah Ponsonby who scandalised society by eloping in 1783, create a vivid picture of their subsequent life together in the remote Welsh village of Llangollen.

Thanks to Kate Roberts for the general introduction, and Clare Spencer and Georgina Andrewes who provided back-up information for the Travel Notes.

SCOTLAND

Scotland's isolation in the far north of Britain, its untamable landscape and the strong nationalism of its people have allowed it too, even more than Wales, to hold on to an identity all of its own. The lowlands, south of Edinburgh and Glasgow, may be partially anglicised but in the Highlands you enter a quite different world of wild mountain scenery, crumbling castles, and tiny, remote villages and towns.

The Scots are generally friendly and welcoming to visitors which makes hitching relatively easy, especially in isolated areas where the coming of the local bus amounts to a weekly event. Travelling by bus is slow but rewarding, providing you have a comprehensive timetable. Trains can work out cheaper as there are various special deals, but they make travel more limited. Walking and cycling are undoubtedly the best ways of seeing the countryside, but make sure you're well equipped and know where you're going. Like Wales, the weather can be very unpredictable and being stranded in a blizzard is no joke.

As well as the Highlands and Islands (despite the onset of tourism, the Orkneys, Hebrides and Shetland Isles comprise some of the most stunning natural beauty in Britain), Scotland's larger cities are well worth visiting. Aberdeen, thriving centre of the North Sea Oil industry, is prohibitively expensive, but Edinburgh offers plenty of inexpensive accommodation outside the Festival season; Glasgow may be run down, but it's a lively, friendly city with a strong radical tradition; and Inverness is a useful centre for gathering information for a trip around the Highlands.

Most of Scotland's **feminist organisations** are concentrated in these four cities. Edinburgh and Glasgow each have a women's centre and there are three alternative bookshops in Edinburgh, useful for contacts and information on what's going on both here and in the rest of the country.

▟ **Hildegard Dumper recommends travelling alone in Scotland. She did it by bus, concentrating on the north-west coast.**

I chose the area out of curiosity. I wanted to see what life was like up there and how people lived. Travelling by bus I thought would give me a chance to watch people going about their daily lives and, on the way, provide me with a tour of the spectacular scenery I'd heard so much about.

Armed with a book of bus timetables from the Highlands and Islands Development Board I set out, working out each short stage of the journey as I went along. Most towns in that part of Scotland are so small and intimate that most of the time I'd simply get off the bus at my planned destination and stroll down the high street (usually the only one), knocking at houses with accommodation signs in the window. My main contact was with people who ran bed and breakfast places, mostly women, and the bus drivers, mostly men. They were all incredibly kind and helpful. On seeing I was alone, they would often put themselves out to an embarrassing degree, to make sure that I was comfortable and looked after. Women tended to be intrigued and concerned that I was travelling on my own, but they were rarely critical. The drivers I found helpful and courteous. Coming from the city, I wasn't used to such attention and the whole experience was a refreshing reminder of how people can be.

I hadn't been prepared for the amount there was to do in the Highlands. For instance, seal and bird watching are major activities. Every town along the coast provides tours out to sea, either to an island to watch the seals playing among the rocks or along the cliffs to look at the thousands of birds which nest in the crevices. The misty rain somehow makes it all the more bleak and exciting and most accommodation in Scotland provides scalding hot baths to help you recover from the weather.

One of my most memorable journeys was to Thurso. We left on a cold, rainy afternoon, the bus loaded with shoppers returning home. I looked on in awe as the bus gradually deposited each individual in lonely windswept places along the route. I followed the bent figures with my eyes, twisting in my seat to catch a glimpse of their final destinations. Often these were little settlements off the main road, tucked low beneath us in a ravine where the river gushed and spluttered through. Sometimes you could see nothing, just a lone figure painfully climbing home up a sheer mountain track.

The Highland buses seemed to stop anywhere for passengers; sometimes we'd stop for a cup of tea on the way, and once I got picked up outside my door in the morning. Another time the driver shared his sandwiches with me whilst the bus was delayed by a landslide blocking the road. These buses obviously provide a vital communication system for local communities. Drivers seemed never too busy to chat, deliver something or collect a package to deliver further along the route. It might contain a vital piece of equipment needed by a farmer for his machinery or perhaps some jumpers to be sold by a local knitter at the craft shop down the road.

As a woman, I found the main restrictions on my movements occurred in the evening. In the small villages, the pubs were quite friendly, though as a stranger you should expect to be heavily scrutinised. However in larger towns like Ullapool the pubs were filled with holiday makers and loud packs of men and were sometimes unpleasant. At those times I preferred to stay in my room reading or chatting to my host over a cup of tea by the fire.

One of the more exciting aspects of that part of Scotland is the atmosphere of remoteness, which hits you strongly in the towns of Ullapool and Thurso. In Ullapool you can watch the ferry sail out of the harbour to Stornaway on the Isle of Lewis, or the Russian factory ships out at sea sending in a dinghy to collect some provisions. In Thurso the arrival of the ferry from the Faro Isles is an event you get caught up with. Every day, too, there are ships making their way to and from the Shetland Islands.

I have travelled in other countries on my own before and found my experience in Scotland the most relaxed, even when I hitched. Next time I would like to spend longer in the far north and explore some of the islands. For anyone travelling on their own for the first time, Scotland is a perfect place to begin.

TRAVEL NOTES

Language English, but spoken with a strong regional accent and mingled with local words and expressions which sometimes make it difficult even for fluent English speakers to understand.

Transport Similar to England in the lowlands south of Edinburgh and Glasgow. Elsewhere buses, though slow and expensive, are the most usual means of travel. *Getting Around the Highlands and the Islands*, available from the Highlands and Islands Development Board, Bank St, Inverness, provides a map and detailed timetables of even the most obscure bus, ferry and rail services. Hitching is relatively easy, especially in the more remote areas.

Accommodation Many houses offer Bed and Breakfast, sometimes a bit expensive but nearly always comfortable and a good way of meeting local people. Camping is recommended as long as you have the right equipment and a definite liking for the hardy, outdoor life. Otherwise there are over 80 youth hostels around the country.

Guide *Let's Go Britain and Ireland* (St Martins Press US). Useful though it covers only a limited circuit.

CONTACTS

The following addresses of **groups and bookshops** are again taken from the *Spare Rib Diary*. For up-to-date listings of activities watch Spare Rib's classified ads every month.

CUMBERNAULD: **Women's Group**, c/o Liz McLaren, 81 Rose St., Condorrat, Cumbernauld (Tel. 023–6735 138).

EDINBURGH: **Women's Centre**, 61a Broughton St, Edinburgh (Tel. 031–557 3179). Publishes a monthly newsletter. Also worth visiting are three of the city's **bookshops**: Womanzone, 119 Buccleuch St, Edinburgh (Tel. 031–667 0011); **First of May**, 43 Candlemaker Row, Edinburgh 1 (Tel. 031–225 2612); and **Lavender Menace** (Lesbian and Gay Bookshop), 11a Forth St, Edinburgh (Tel 031–556 0079).

GLASGOW: **Women's Centre**, 48 Miller St, Glasgow (Tel. 041–221 1177). Open Mon-Sat, 1–5pm.

INVERNESS: **Women's Group**, c/o 38 Ardconnel St, Inverness (Tel. 0542–40082).

The areas below have **Rape Crisis Centres**, phone numbers only listed.
Aberdeen: 0224–575 560.
Central Scotland: 0324–38433.
Edinburgh: 031–556 9437.
Highlands: 0463–220 922.
Strathclyde: 041–221 8448.

BOOKS

Rosalind K. Marshall, *Virgins and Viragos – a History of Women in Scotland from 1080–1980* (Collins, 1983). A bit academic, but interesting for its exploration of little known ground.

IRELAND

Ireland is divided in two: the 6 northern counties of Ulster, under British rule, and 26 counties making up the independent Republic of Eire. Behind this split lie centuries of conflict, leading up to the present-day 'troubles'. British troops have occupied Northern Ireland since 1969 when the acceleration of hostility between the anti-British Catholic minority and chiefly pro-British Protestants led to an explosion of violence. This has never really abated and many Irish people feel that the British presence only exacerbates the situation in a country tired of being branded a poor relation of Britain.

How far you're affected by the political conflict in **Northern Ireland** depends on your own level of interest in the situation. With soldiers on the streets of Belfast and Derry, security checks and warnings to avoid certain areas, you can't exactly ignore the tension. But there are plenty of lovely beaches and unspoilt stretches of countryside, and the people are amazingly friendly, showing little resentment to British travellers.

The **Irish Republic** is more expensive, but more easily lives up to a reputation for miles of peaceful green and empty landscape, undeveloped coastline and hospitality. Just try and avoid the few more obvious tourist centres. It's good cycling country and hitching is an accepted form of travel, since bus and rail services tend to be limited and/or very slow; like everything else, public transport is also prohibitively expensive. But camping is great if you don't mind getting wet, most youth hostels are open all the year round and there are plenty of Bed and Breakfast places if you can afford them. Eire is based on a traditional rural economy, governed by conservative laws and the Catholic Church. Women being very much bound to traditional roles means that, travelling alone or without a male companion, you may appear rather an oddity, but there's no particular danger of harassment from men.

Irish women have a long history of participation in rebellions against the British. Political protest in Northern Ireland has been strongly entwined with the development of **Irish feminism** since the 1970s and campaigns for battered women's refuges, equal pay at work, an end to discriminatory education, etc. continue alongside efforts to secure the release of, or improve conditions, for political prisoners.

One of the overall most formidable obstacles to the Irish women's movement is the Catholic Church. The rights to contraception and abortion have always been a central issue, the denial of abortion being one of the few areas where Northern Ireland still takes a separate stand from Britain – most women in the Republic still don't have access to contraception.

Today there are quite a few women's groups in both parts of the country, most of which are listed in the *1986 Irish Women's Guidebook and Directory* (see Travel Notes). We regret not including a piece here on Northern Ireland, the only reason being lack of material.

■ **Margaret Greenwood spent a holiday hitching with another woman, from Dublin to the counties of Kerry and Cork.**

We hardly saw any women driving in Ireland and all our lifts came from men. It took us a while to get used to the persistence of traditional values – for instance divorce, a frequent topic of conversation as it was about to be legislated upon, was seen as little more than a joke – but we were mostly treated with great courtesy and kindness by those who picked us up. Archaic attitudes must infuriate Irish women but, being on holiday, we didn't let them worry us.

We had good lifts from Dublin to Limerick and from there set out for Killarney. Not having planned any definite route, we found our decisions being made by the many people who were pleased to give us advice about where to go. In future I'll be more careful who I listen to; people who spend their entire lives in the countryside find it hard to imagine that you might actually *want* rural solitude from a holiday.

This is how we came to Killarney – the most hideous epitome of the tourist town, crammed full of gift shops selling fancy goods, souvenir ashtrays, nodding donkeys and the like. It's right on the package tour circuit and, even in mid-September, English and American tourists were piling out of coaches to spend their money and sample the local customs. However, outside Killarney lies some of the most beautiful, unspoilt countryside I've ever seen – the Ring of Kerry. It's a bit like the English Lake District, but less populated: visions of crags and rugged hillside reflected on mirrors of water, so perfect you can't tell where land and water meet. We hired bikes (about £1 a day), intent on getting as far as possible into the hills, and were lucky enough to meet a man and his son who had given us a lift the evening before. Greeting us like old friends, they offered to drive us into the remoter countryside so we saw much more than we otherwise would have had time to.

It was here that I first understood that if Irish people offer to take you places, or ask you what you'd like to drink, they are not just being polite, they genuinely want your company. Caution is obviously wise at times but, on the whole, stiff, formal English gratitude and reserve is completely inappropriate. From that day on we took offers from people at face value and, apart from a few dodgy moments, this change in our responses proved positive and worthwhile.

From Killarney we hitched through grey drizzle to County Cork. The driver who took us to Bandon said he'd take us the extra 15 miles to

Clonakilty as he'd enjoy the ride and had nothing better to do with his lunch hour. This is one of the many little fishing villages on the coast. In the afternoon we went for a walk over springy brambles and down on to the shore. The sea had a blue-grey calm translucence and the sand was beautifully clean. We followed the coast in and out of the little crooked bays and gullies, keeping to the sand beneath the low cliffs until, so higgledy-piggledy is the shoreline, we couldn't tell which was the direction of land and which way the open sea. Although we were never far from some village, there was a feeling of isolation and quiet which was wonderfully restful.

There are plenty of bars in these coastal villages, open all day, which can be used to punctuate an afternoon walk, and it was here that we had our most interesting contact with women. We spent an entire afternoon in Clonakilty simply talking to the woman serving. We had little money, but there was no obligation to drink in order to stay seated; the place was empty after lunch and she was glad of our company. This was her home. She was training to be a nurse in Cork, but fully intended to return and eventually settle in the place she knew best. Her one idea of freedom was owning a car.

Later on, in Limerick, we witnessed a bar used purely by women. We came upon it by chance, one Sunday. The place was so small it felt like wandering into someone's living room. There were seats for six or seven people at the most, but finding it empty, we decided to risk seeing if we were welcome. The church bells rang outside and we heard the clatter and talk of people spilling out of Mass, getting into cars and disappearing in the windy evening. A group of old women came in, cautiously acknowledged our presence, bought glasses of Stout and settled down to gossip. There was a 'lad' to get crates up from the cellar, but he soon made himself scarce. The atmosphere was marvellous in this female territory, obviously claimed on Sunday nights for its convenient position by the church. Even when the lively banter died down and the unmistakable glow of a television lit up the glazed screen which half divided us, there were soon comments and hoots of laughter as the old women launched into a running commentary on *Dynasty*. Despite being only observers, treated to the odd polite nod or call for approbation on a point, it was a thoroughly enjoyable evening.

These are just a few of my impressions on a short trip hitching round the country. I strongly recommend this style of holiday in south-west Ireland to anyone who appreciates impressive green mountains, lakes and bays; a lazy, meandering itinerary; and incidental company, usually charming, kind, polite, and tinged with a lackadaisical self-confidence.

TRAVEL NOTES

Languages Everyone knows English though it's spoken with occasionally impenetrable accent and quite a few people do speak Gaelic amongst themselves.

Transport Buses and trains are very expensive. A good cheap way of exploring the countryside is to hire a bicycle. Hitching is relatively easy in both parts of Ireland, lack of traffic being more of a problem than reluctant drivers.

Accommodation You can camp more or less anywhere in the countryside, as long as you ask permission of the landowner. Youth hostels get filled up in the summer so it's a good idea to book in advance. Bed and breakfasts are usually relaxed and comfortable, but at least a couple of pounds more expensive in Eire than in Northern Ireland.

Special problems Anglo-Irish conflict, euphemistically referred to as 'the troubles', has led to some hostility towards the British, but it's not usually directed at travellers. Most people are very friendly, often quick to reassure you that you can't be held responsible for the actions of your country. Nevertheless, it's a good idea to familiarise yourself with recent history, out of courtesy if nothing else. Hostility is clearly more common in parts of Northern Ireland and places like Tralee in Kerry which is notorious for Republican sympathy.

Hitching feels generally safe although Margaret Greenwood reports three cases of sexual harassment from single male drivers, all on a Sunday. This is the day when most cars are packed with families. The rest tend to contain single men, pleasure-riding with time on their hands and nothing to do. If a problem arises, it's vital to show your disinterest and disapproval right away. Don't be paranoid, just prepared.

Other information: It's a good idea to check up on the dates of music festivals, fairs and races before you go, whether you wish to visit them or avoid the crowds. The Tourist Information Office in Dublin will give you plenty of general advice, including details of convenient hitching points out of the city.

Guides *Let's Go Britain and Ireland* (St Martins Press, US).

CONTACTS

The *Irish Women's Guidebook and Diary*, co-ordinated by Roisin Conroy and Mary Paul Keane, provides a useful list of addresses. It's available from feminist bookshops in Britain and Ireland or you can send for it from Atticus Press, 48 Fleet St, Dublin 2.

A small selection is included below.

BELFAST: **Women's Centre**, 18 Donegal Street, Belfast BT1 2GP (Tel. 0232–243363); **Rape Crisis Centre**, PO Box 46, Belfast BT2 7AR (Tel. 0232–249696), Mon-Fri 10am–6pm, Tues and Fri 7.30–10pm. Belfast also has a women's paper, *Women's News*, obtainable from c/o Box WN, 7 Winetavern Street, Belfast BT1.

CORK: **The Women's Space** (centre), Quay Co-op, 24 Sullivan's Quay, Cork (Tel. Cork 967660); **Rape Crisis Centre**, open Mon and Fri 9.30–12am, Wed 7.30–10pm, Sun 2.30–4pm, (Tel. 021–504222); **Lesbian Line**, Tue 8–10pm (Tel. Cork 505394).

DERRY: **Women's Centre**, 7–9 Artillery Street, Derry (Tel. 0504–267672).

DUBLIN: **Women's Centre**, 53 Dame Street, Dublin 2 (Tel. Dublin 710088); **Well Woman Centre**, 63 Lower Leeson Street, Dublin 2 and 60 Eccles Street, Dublin 7 (Tel. Dublin 789–366); **Lesbian Line**, Thu 8–10pm (Tel. Dublin 710608); **Rape Crisis Centre**, 2 Lower Pembroke Street, Dublin 2, (Tel. Dublin 601470), open seven days a week, 24hr service.

The following **bookshops** are also good for contacts.

BELFAST: **Just Books/Le Café Hideout**, 7 Winetavern Street (Tel. 0232–225426).

DERRY: **Bookworm Community Bookshop**, 16 Bishop Street (Tel. 0504–225426).

DUBLIN: **Books Upstairs**, 25 Market Arcade (Tel. Dublin 710064).

BOOKS

Eileen Fairweather et al., *Only the Rivers Run Free: Northern Ireland, the Women's War* (Pluto Press, 1984). Through the words of Irish women this book describes their situation and hopes for the future.

Irish Feminist Review, *The Irish Feminist Review* (Women's Community Press,

1985). Collection of articles providing a recent history of the women's movement in Ireland. Includes some useful information.

Minority Rights Group, *The Two Irelands: the double minority* (MRG 2, revised 1984) One of the clearest reports you'll find on Ireland's politics. Essential background.

Eilean Ni Chuilleanain, ed, *Irish Women: Image and Achievement* (Arlen House, 1986). Ten essays by specialist authors trace the position of women in Irish society from ancient to modern times. Recommended.

Nell McCafferty, *A Woman to Blame* (Attic Press, 1986). Brilliant study of the 'Kerry Babies Case', examining the grip on Irish women of the church and patriarch and culture.

FICTION

Frances Molloy, *No Mate for the Magpie* (Virago, 1985). Tragi-comic tale of a Catholic girlhood in Northern Ireland.

Emma Cooke, *Eve's Apple* (Blackstaff, 1985). Set against the 1983 Irish abortion referendum campaign, Cooke's novel describes a woman's isolation and desperation with middle-class provincialism and the hypocrisy of religious values.

Dorothy Nelson, *In Night's City* (Wolfhound Press, 1982). A moving story of sorrow and compassion through the eyes of a mother and daughter on the night of the father's death.

Janet M. Simpson, *Woman's Part: An Anthology of Short Fiction by and about Irish Women* (Arlen House, Dublin, 1984). The stories, some known and some unknown, were written between 1890–1960.

Ruth Hooley, ed., *Northern Irish Women Writers, The Female Line* (Northern Ireland Women's Rights Movement, 1985). Range of stories by known and unknown writers, evoking various aspects of life for women in a country at war.

Chapter Three

MEDITERRANEAN EUROPE

Long hot summers, warm winters, calm blue sea and a relatively cheap, easygoing way of life have long attracted travellers to the **Mediterranean**, but it's only in the past two decades that a full-scale tourist industry has invaded its shores. The Greek islands, large chunks of the Spanish coast and certain parts of Italy and Yugoslavia nowadays receive millions of foreign visitors a year, most of whom simply want a relaxing holiday in the sun. Although not technically a Mediterranean country, Portugal too offers the same attractions.

The incredibly rapid growth of mass tourism has had a dramatic effect both on the environment and on the lives of local people. As more and more tackily built hotels jostle together for space beside the increasingly polluted sea, so thousands of men and women rely ever more on tourism for employment. But, in addition to looking for work, large numbers of men also migrate to the resorts in summer to hunt for 'easy' tourists. Alone or with another woman, you surely won't escape their 'attentions' completely, but confidence, determination and some grasp of the language will go a long way towards ensuring your sanity and survival.

After seaside resorts, big cities tend to be the worst places for sexual harassment. The hissing and passing comments – particularly oppressive in the south of Italy and Spain – can build up to phobic proportions, but use your head, taking special care at night, and you're unlikely to come to any physical harm. Also remember that cities such as Barcelona, Rome, Zagreb, Athens and Lisbon usually house the greatest variety of active women's organisations, often providing support as well as contacts and information about what's happening around the country.

Of the five countries we've included – **Spain, Portugal, Italy, Greece** and **Yugoslavia** – a more reserved national temperament, together with the fact that it's been the least exploited by tourism, makes Portugal the most relaxing to travel in. But in each country, life is notably more hassle-free inland, where extensive bus and rail networks make it easy to get around. Hitching is not generally recommended unless you feel strong and can speak the language. The price of accommodation varies greatly, Italy being the most expensive, followed by Yugoslavia. Wherever you choose to go in the Mediterranean, everything will be cheaper, less crowded and less spoiled off the beaten track, where you'll also find the most genuinely friendly, hospitable people.

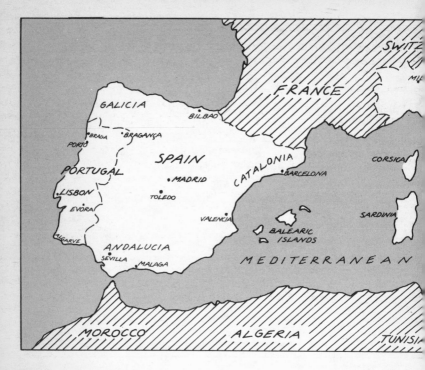

We haven't covered the **Balearic islands, Cyprus, Malta** and the **South of France** in this section, mainly for reasons of space. Nor Stalinist **Albania** – which allows only officially sponsored tour groups. We would welcome accounts on all of these for the next edition.

PORTUGAL

Portugal doesn't border on the Mediterranean sea, but it shares many of the characteristics of its neighbour, Spain, and other Mediterranean countries. The climate is warm, the people hospitable and there's plenty of good, cheap food and wine. In terms of tourism, however, Atlantic Portugal has a definite edge. Even the Algarve, where most of the development is concentrated, incorporates some beautiful stretches of coast, quite untouched by the package holiday industry. And inland there are countless historic sites, picturesque towns and villages, still steeped in tradition, and some magnificent scenery to explore.

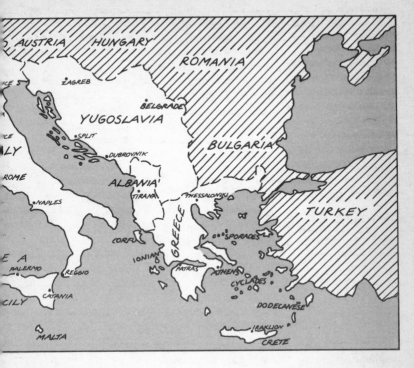

Portugal is a small country and, except in the central and northern mountains, distances are short. A comprehensive bus and rail service connects most of the places you're likely to want to visit. Hitching poses the usual risks, but on the whole *machismo* is less rampant here than in other Latin countries, making it one of the safer places to travel in Europe. Men may hiss and make comments in the streets of Lisbon, the only town of any great size, but elsewhere traditional courtesy is generally accompanied by welcome male restraint.

Given the persistent strength of tradition, it's sometimes hard to believe that Portugal not long ago experienced a dramatic and quite extraordinary revolution. On 25 April 1974 several decades of dictatorship came to an end in an almost bloodless coup, engineered by the army. On top of economic stagnation at home, much of its impetus came from the politicisation of soldiers returning from Africa where their government had sent them, at great expense, to combat the escalating wars of liberation in its colonies. As well as sudden independence for these colonies, the revolution meant massive changes inside the country; amongst them the redistribution of land, the achievement of workers' rights and better social and living conditions, and alterations in the family law.

Throughout this period women campaigned and organised alongside men. Gradually, however, political change seemed to reach a deadlock and with it came the familiar realisation that women's specific needs had actually been submerged in the overall fervour of the revolution. Despite positive legal reforms, the brief emergence of a woman prime minister and the high profile of women in higher education, old attitudes die hard and the Portuguese **Women's Movement** has had difficulties mobilising on any large scale. Compared with, say, Italy or Spain, the movement today is small, but there are at least a couple of central organisations in Lisbon who can put you in touch with what's happening around the country.

◼ Elizabeth Mullet has lived and studied in Lisbon, and has travelled throughout the country.

Lisbon is a breezy, dazzling white city which, having somehow escaped some of the worst symptoms of urban expansion, must be one of the most attractive capitals in the world. I lived there for a while, with a thesis to research, a long list of archives to visit and an irredeemably student income on which to do it. Not quite a resident, nor quite a tourist, I hired a room and traipsed between libraries and the city sights. I explored the frantic covered market on the river front in the early mornings and, from my landlady, learned to cook the sweet rice desserts and the rich stews, brimming with pigs' ears and calves' shinbones.

I also learned to duck the harassment experienced by most young women in the city, finding in museum gardens and monastery cloisters the perfect places to read or write letters undisturbed. Following the example of other students I used to take my books and newspapers to one of the big town cafés in the evenings and sit there with a coffee, half-studying, half-watching the world. Local incomes are low but the habit of an evening out universal; I acquired an ability to stay up until four in the morning to listen to the city's *fado* music (a kind of national blues – worth hearing), to eat breakfast standing up in the busy *pastelerias*, to look people back in the eye and to take lunch seriously.

I was so energetically absorbing a new culture that it took me some time to feel a foreigner's isolation. It wasn't that most Portuguese women my age were locked into family life, married with several children already. More that, despite the relaxing of social attitudes since 1974, women are still essentially seen in the image of their family relationships; somebody's daughter, wife, mother or widow. Acute housing shortages in Lisbon and Oporto and a national minimum wage of less than £100 a month mean that most children leave home only after marriage and often not even then. To be sure, women achieved paper equality within five years of the revolution, but white male socialism has tended to view women's needs and aims as secondary and feminism has had little institutional and popular support. A liberal family background makes more difference than any legislation and if the corridors of the universities are full of women students, access to higher education (around 1.6 per cent of the population) is still largely a privilege of the middle classes. Talking to feminists, I found that the most highly valued opportunity had been to travel, either through work or study, and that way gain a sideways look at their culture and sense of themselves as individuals.

My work took me to Evora, a whitewashed Moorish town in the Alentejo – a region which seemed to me one of the most fascinating. Since Roman times it has been an area of vast rural estates, most of which were seized from the landowners and transformed into collective farms after the revolution. Governments responded first by extending, then restricting, agricultural credits needed by these new farms and now big families are being allowed to return to parts of their estates. The towns are therefore the focus of both the region's poverty and its provincial bourgeoisie. If the narrow, convoluted streets are still lined with sixteenth- and seventeenth-century houses, it's because they've mostly escaped redevelopment; and if the sky on summer nights has more stars than you've ever seen, it's because electricity has not yet reached every house in every town. Evora's main square every Tuesday is full of livestock farmers in dark suits and black hats, negotiating business. At lunchtime they swarm on the local restaurants and fall upon the local goat stews, dishes of pork cooked with shellfish and great steaming plates of salt cod boiled with chickpeas. This is a profoundly masculine society – the characteristic music of the region is that of the male voice miners' choirs – and if you travel from Evora to any of the medieval towns beyond, you'll find cafés the meeting place of men after dinner, and it's rare to see women on the streets after nightfall.

As I moved around the north, to the granite and down-to-earth city of Oporto, and to Vila Real and the castellated hilltowns of the Spanish frontier in Tras-os Montes, I was confronted with a quite different world. This is the area of the great vineyards, but also of small subsistence farming on the terraces of the River Douro and in the handkerchief-sized holdings, with jumbles of cows, cabbages and vines in profusion, infinitely subdivided among families by the inheritance traditions of the Minho district. For the visitor, it's an area which repays a good eye for changing styles of domestic architecture – the granite boulders of the Beiras and the drystone walling of Tras-os Montes; a stomach for the egg-yolk and sugar confections, different in each town; and a taste for the Dão wines and the delicious semi-sparkling *vinhos verdes*, red and white.

To the east the Douro railway line, its extension from Regua through Vila Real to Chaves and the bus journey from Chaves to Bragança, take you through some of the most spectacular scenery in the country, wild and empty. From time to time you pass through villages dessicated by emigration, communities of old people, women and children whose men work in the cities of Central Europe, returning only for visits in the summer months. It's the most conservative area of Portugal, where adherence to the Church and respect for authority have remained strongest and, as 'widows of the living', the wives remain rigidly subject to popular criticism of their social behaviour – as one woman put it, 'what you do *and* what you don't'.

What you do and what you don't, as a visitor, is very much up to you. There are excellent detailed guidebooks and the tourist offices are friendly and helpful about all sorts of unusual requests – where to go to find the country's remarkable wild flowers, for example, or where to nurse a particular ailment or allergy at a spa. Whatever you can learn of this strangest of the romance languages in advance will help immeasurably, but many Portuguese speak some English or French and understand Spanish. And the survival of gentle and courteous social attitudes make it, beyond Lisbon or the busy beaches, one of the easiest Latin countries in which to travel alone.

TRAVEL NOTES

Language Portuguese is a difficult language, especially when it comes to pronunciation but if you know some French and/or Spanish you shouldn't find it too hard to read. English and French are quite widely spoken in cities and most people understand Spanish (albeit reluctantly).

Transport A slow but reasonably cheap and efficient network of buses and trains covers most of the country. Trains are 50–70 per cent cheaper but buses more plentiful – and they'll take you straight to your destination. City buses are expensive whilst taxis are cheap and reliable. Everyone uses them all the time in Lisbon, outside city boundaries negotiate fares in advance. Bicycle hire is a good, if exhausting, way of exploring the countryside. Hitching is the only remotely dangerous way for women to travel and perhaps best not done unless you're experienced and a fast talker in Portuguese.

Accommodation Reasonably cheap hotels and *pensões* are available, even at the height of summer. In smaller towns it's often best to ask the nearest friendly looking woman, who will know who lets rooms; it's quite accepted. Youth hostels are cheaper (there are about a dozen in Portugal, most of them open all year round), but you won't meet Portuguese people that way. There are also about 100 authorised campsites, many of them small and attractive.

Guide Mark Ellingham, John Fisher and Graham Kenyon, *The Rough Guide to Portugal* (Routledge & Kegan Paul, rev. 1986). A mass of information about where to go and how to get there. Reliable and up-to-date.

CONTACTS

There are relatively few **women's organisations** in Portugal. Probably the three best contact addresses for feminist travellers are listed below.

Comisão da Condição Feminina, Avenida de República, 32 – 2 Esq., Lisbon. Researches and maintains a watching brief on all aspects of women's lives in Portugal. They organise meetings and conferences, are very active in areas of social and legal reform, have a good library and are very well connected with feminists throughout the country.

Informação, Documentação Mulheres (IDM), Rua Filipe de Mata, 115A, Lisbon (Tel. 720598). Women's centre incorporating a small library and the one women-only café in Lisbon. Run by a collective of lesbian and heterosexual women, very keen to welcome foreign travellers and publicise the activities of the centre. French, German and English spoken.

Editora das Mulheres, Rua da Conceicao 17 (4th floor), right in the centre of Lisbon. Feminist bookshop, good for contacts.

BOOKS

Maria Velho da Costa, Maria Isabel

Barreno and Maria Teresa Horta, *The Three Marias: Portuguese Letters* (Paladin, 1975). Collage of letters, stories and poems by three feminist writers. Hard to obtain, but worth the effort.

Few Portuguese books, novels or otherwise, have been translated into English but we'd appreciate any recommendations.

Thanks to Elizabeth Mullet for supplying much of the information for these Travel Notes.

SPAIN

Spain is the biggest tourist destination in Europe, pulling in upwards of 3m Britons each year and around 6m other North Europeans. Yet the vast majority of these visitors cling to the package resort areas along the coast – notoriously the Costa del Sol and Costa Brava, almost no part of which has escaped development. Inland, or in the more remote stretches of seaside (in Galicia, say, or around Cadiz), you'll find a different country altogether, and one which lays good claim to being the most rewarding (and least expensive) in Europe for independent travel.

Cliché though it may be, variety is a keynote. The Spanish provinces are each highly individual, quite distinct from one another in everything from climate and landscape to their way of life and attitudes. Galicia – in the north west – is essentially Celtic in culture, and surprisingly matriarchal in its social structures, forged by centuries of work migration. Andalucia, the poorest province, is Spain at its most inflated and stereotyped: stimulating but with a sometimes difficult, rough southern *machismo*. Catalonia, in the north east, has long had a reputation as the most progressive area, the regional pride and activism of its inhabitants intensified by decades of cultural and political repression under Franco. His death, in 1975, heralding democratic change throughout the country, was never more felt than here.

Catalonia's position in the forefront of Spanish radical politics is to some extent reflected in a less rigid attitude towards women. Elsewhere strict morality and conservatism still frequently prevail; girls are expected to remain firmly at home until they marry and go out in the evenings only with an approved *novio* (steady boyfriend). The result is a sometimes suspicious attitude to single women travellers.

Travel in Spain, however, is easy from the point of view of accommodation and transport. There are plenty of good, cheap hotels and an extensive bus and train network. However, sexual harassment is a problem, particularly on the Mediterranean coast where virtually every female tourist is seen as an easy lay. Men tend to stare a lot and make remarks in the street, again more in the highly developed Costa Brava and Costa del Sol where theft, often violent, is becoming an increasing hazard, at least partly due to the desperate level of unemployment. Finally, you may well be disturbed by the proliferation of pornography in Spain, one of the more dramatic aspects of the lifting of censorship when Franco died.

The wave of liberalisation after 1975 was accompanied by the inspired and brilliant explosion of the **Spanish Women's Movement.** Groups sprang up everywhere, eager to gain reform; there were public debates on issues like birth control, abortion and women and work; a national magazine, *Vindicacion Feminista*, was born. Since then, however, the movement has dwindled. Feminists won the right to contraception and divorce, but the battle for abortion continues, leaving many disillusioned.

The Socialist government has not made women's emancipation a priority in its programme for social change and even a plan to legalise abortion on a very restricted basis is threatened because the still powerful right-wing opposition (and many Catholic doctors) are determined to block the bill.

The main activities of the Women's Movement are nowadays undertaken by the Feminist Party, led by Lidia Falcon. The party, one of the few in existence, is a registered political organisation with a club in Barcelona and groups in other big cities. As far as campaigns go, abortion remains *the* major issue. However a recent conference to celebrate ten years of Spanish feminism, attended by 4,000 women, included debates as wide-ranging as disarmament, pornography, education, history, sexuality and work.

▰ **Emma Dexter has travelled around most of Spain, both as a tourist and as a student of Spanish and, later, sculpture.**

A virgin makes her way unsteadily through narrow streets, supported on a huge wooden bier, which in turn is carried invisibly by heaving, sweating men beneath. Weighed down by a gold and silver crown, radiated by frills of lace, half hidden by swelling crowds of white carnations, her face shows resignation to eternities of suffering, infinite degrees of pain. Crystal tears are glued beneath large, false eyelash-trimmed eyes. Her hands jut uselessly in front of her breast. An almost sexual frenzy develops amongst the young men waiting for her arrival, who chant together 'Guapa, Guapa' (meaning 'pretty') in anticipation.

These sculptures undoubtedly inspire pure and devout thoughts in many. However, the emphasis placed on physical perfection coupled with sexual innocence creates powerful stereotypes of ideal womanhood which have been foisted on Spanish women for centuries, by church and state alike. As the influence of religion faded, the purity of the female became enforced by law; until 1978 women could be prosecuted for any sexual activity outside marriage (and they could languish in jail indefinitely until forgiven by their husbands), contraception was illegal, prostitutes were placed in houses of correction – which is still done today. Yet the Virgin is carried down streets lined with kiosks selling pornography.

It is a clash between repressive past and more liberal present that is frequently obvious. A Catalan theatre group staged a firework display in diabolical costumes near the Cathedral in Seville. While pleasing many, it also outraged some, and the following day a demonstration was organised by Catholic students who carried placards reading 'Lord, forgive them for they know not what they do' as an act of reparation. On another occasion, I visited a village that was holding the annual fiesta in honour of its patron saint. An amateur bullfight was about to take place, skinny street stalls were selling music cassettes and sweets, images of the Virgin jostled pornographic playing cards. The local priest invited me to have a drink and meet some of the villagers in a garage that had been specially converted into a party room for the fiesta. As I sipped my sangria I noticed that the walls were covered in pornographic photographs of women, which surprised me as the room was full of women and small children. The woman serving the drinks told us in a tone of weary amusement that the men had been left in charge of decorating the room and this was what they had come up with.

A lot of things have changed in Spain since Franco's death, but not necessarily to the benefit of women. The proliferation of pornography is a 'liberalising' gesture that pleases only a minority of the population and which can always be defended as one of the benefits of democracy. Censorship would be regarded with suspicion because of its long association with Francoism.

When I visited Spain in 1983, shortly after the Socialists' election victory, there was an intoxicating feeling of freedom in the air. The country was breathing a collective sigh of relief at the prospect of change. Inside a year however, the mood had turned to disillusion and pessimism. I found young people particularly cynical, complaining that the Socialist government was compromising, sidestepping or simply botching its most radical election promises. 'Working for Socialism' had lost its idealism and impetus and with it had gone the numerous, diverse and extremely vital campaigns of the opposition years.

Attitudes remain polarised in Spain with religion and conservatism much more entrenched in the countryside than the towns. Villages perhaps only half an hour's drive from a city can be as culturally isolated and as traditionally oriented as if they were several days' journey away. In these places a Spanish city dweller is just as much a foreigner as you are. Rural decline is evident in many areas, with high unemployment and depopulation. Country people will treat you with respect if you show it to them. This means not wearing revealing clothing, covering your shoulders and wearing a skirt, especially on Sundays and religious holidays. There is still a strong tradition of wearing Sunday best everywhere – women wear demure white cotton blouses, knee-length skirts, and high heels. In the little villages, as a traveller, you tend to get stared at and laughed at by little children; but they can also be relaxing and interesting companions, willing to put up with your bad Spanish much more than adults. Adolescent girls seemed particularly curious about me; once a bright, bold girl simply strode up to me and asked what I was doing, where I came from, and whether I was engaged. Most people will probably think you are rather odd not to be married or engaged by the age of 25, but they are polite enough not to mention it.

I would recommend travelling in the Spanish countryside; each inland region has its own characteristics, but they are all equally unspoilt. The people are quick to trust and keen to meet you, and the landscape is wild and beautiful. In a village outside Seville, I asked the Spaniards I was with where I could see genuine flamenco dancing. They laughed and shouted 'Here' and two couples started an impromptu display in the bar.

Travelling on trains and buses is an excellent way to meet people. Spanish people can often be very helpful, and asking directions or information from someone who is also on their own, waiting for a train, can lead to an exchange of addresses and a genuine desire for contact. Share your food and drink with other people in your compartment because the Spaniards do, and it is an excellent way to break down barriers. I shared some water with a girl on a long train journey; when we arrived at our destination, I asked her advice about finding somewhere to stay, which led to her introducing me to all her friends and to many enjoyable evenings. If there is such a thing as a national characteristic, then the Spanish are open and uncomplicated in their expression of liking for you; they don't waste time hiding their feelings.

◪ **Anna Maloney spent two weeks travelling alone around Andalucia last summer.**

With two weeks free in late summer I decided to cut and run on one of those cheap flights to Malaga aiming to do a quick circuit around Andalucia. After a series of dire warnings about Spanish machismo on the Costa del Sol and around, I began to feel that I'd made a bad choice. I think if it hadn't been for the loss of money and, I suppose, the loss of face, I might have considered cancelling.

As it turned out those two weeks were about as near perfect as a holiday can be. I love travelling on my own, making my own decisions, having only myself to look after and always being able to slip in and out of occasional friendships whenever I feel the need to do so. Staying in only one place can get a bit depressing so I tend to move around a lot – planning the logistics of travel can be a good way to keep occupied and it also helps kick off conversations.

Within two hours of hitting Malaga I had found a passable hotel with an amiable owner and was sipping a beer on top of a hill prior to taking in my first bit of Moorish architecture at the Alcazabar. It was also easy that evening to find a cheap restaurant where they seemed quite happy to have a single woman eating, drinking and reading a novel in the corner.

The next day I caught a bus on to Tarifa, passing the embarrassment of Gibraltar on the way. Tarifa, a walled Moorish town, is the most southerly point of Europe and I couldn't get over the excitement of standing in my own continent contemplating a day-trip to Africa. Tarifa is also where the Atlantic bumps into the Mediterranean. There was a tiny Mediterranean beach packed out with tourists, and the usual relaxed Spanish crowd, and a huge deserted windswept Atlantic beach, great for moody walks. After two nights I moved further up the Atlantic coast to Conil, again by bus. (I'd heard mixed stories about hitching in this region and – as the buses were cheap and very efficient – I never really felt any compulsion to put them to the test.) Finding a hotel room in Conil proved difficult but well worth it. It was near another immense windswept beach with sheltered sandy coves only a short walk away. There were quite a few other tourists but it was by no means swamped.

Wandering around, it took me a while to realise that the curious clicking noises from groups of Spanish men hanging out on the streets were aimed at me. I was visually hampered by wearing an old pair of specs which in retrospect might have helped me attain that useful detached 'other worldly' look. The level of harassment I got was never more than an irritation, and as I had already made a resolution not to ruin my holiday by worrying about male nuisances I just ignored it. Two German women I met up with, however, had an entirely different approach. They'd get in first, clicking loudly at any group of men they passed and often hammering home their point with some choice Spanish phrases. It seemed to elicit a sort of stunned, silent disgust. They told me about a bus journey they'd made where the driver, not knowing they were fluent in Spanish, decided to vent his fury against German tourists and particularly 'fat' women (as he described them). They waited till he'd finished, then sauntered up to the front of the coach and let off a tirade against all varieties of chauvinism and a few personal bits and bobs about the physique of Spanish drivers. They were let off the bus. I shared their company for a few days, and found them a great antidote to all the minor hassles you have to put up with, though perhaps not quite in my style.

Cadiz was next. I was impressed by the faded grandeur and the relaxed easy-going pace. Sitting out in the harbour café I was not at all surprised to see an elderly character in linen suit and spats – definitely an ex-Nazi just about to catch a boat to Bolivia. There were also the usual gangs of sailors, this being a large port, but they all seemed fairly well behaved.

Walking down a narrow street in the city two women came up and pressed a leaflet into my hand. Though it was in Spanish, it wasn't hard to make out the 'Greenham Women' message and logo. Inspired, I headed on to the market where I'd noticed two Socialist stalls. Talking was hard, using broken English and sign language, but they managed to get across some sympathy for life under Thatcher and I learnt something about their attitude to NATO. I felt rather ashamed of my ignorance of Spanish and Europolitics.

Apart from this I never really swapped opinions with Spanish people – language and my fear of being misinterpreted as a pushy tourist being the main barriers. But sitting amongst the tables dominated by huge families sharing endless arrays of plates of fish and paella I somehow didn't feel excluded. There were always warm smiles exchanged. The landlady in Cadiz who scowled at me on sight was somewhat of an exception, but then maybe her problem was lack of sleep. At night time the silence around the hotel would get shattered by carousing American sailors, attempting flamenco or singing the blues.

From Cadiz I got a train to Seville, one of the hardest places to find accommodation (apparently during the April Feria it's almost impossible). Street crime is supposed to be much worse in Seville than elsewhere, probably because there are so many tourists ripe for the picking (and a staggering rate of unemployment). I became extra cautious, never flashed my camera and tried to look as if I always knew where I was going – which wasn't at all likely in the winding streets of the Barrio de Santa Cruz area. I found the city so romantic it was almost corny. I especially loved the Alcazar and its Moorish garden in the centre of town. The Moors seemed to have had a good idea of how to create a harmonious peaceful refuge.

On my second day I heard a slight strain of trumpet music wafting up from the Guadalquivir river. I had to follow it. I found a large group of trumpeters playing the traditional scores Miles Davis used in 'Sketches of Spain'.

I never went to any flamenco bars – the authentic ones start up very late and are known only to the afficionados and I wasn't all that interested in the tourist variety. I was amazed though at the way children walk around in groups clicking out flamenco rhythms in perfect timing about as easily as British children sing nursery rhymes. Sometimes you see tiny girls kitted out in full miniature flamenco outfits usually on their way to some club or big occasion. It's a peculiar sight, they play out the almost tarty, super-sexual role with such aplomb.

I loved Spain and I'm going back – that is, after I've finished my course of Spanish evening classes.

TRAVEL NOTES

Languages Spanish; also Catalan, Basque and Gallego (in Galicia). Spanish is an easy language to learn and it always helps if you know some before you set off. If you have time, an alternative to studying it at home is to do a summer course at a Spanish university. It's a good way to meet people, especially if you stay with a family, and the courses are generally good and not too strenuous. For information, contact a Spanish Institute (in London at 102 Eaton Square, SW1).

Transport An extensive bus and train network covers the country. Buses tend to be quicker, especially on shorter or more obscure routes. They're also more hassle-free in terms of harassment. Taxis in cities are incredibly cheap and by far the safest way to travel at night.

Accommodation Cheap and plentiful. Camping rough is not recommended.

Special problems Sexual harassment can undoubtedly be a problem, and there is no simple solution to dealing with it. Unless you're a confident Spanish speaker, it's probably best to ignore remarks. Hitching, generally poor in Spain, is not a good idea unless you're very tough.

Guide Mark Ellingham, John Fisher and Graham Kenyon, *The Rough Guide to Spain* (Routledge & Kegan Paul, 1985). Comprehensive and invaluable – especially on local contacts (and bars).

CONTACTS

All main cities and many of the smaller towns have some kind of **women's centre or organisation**. Below is a selected list taken mainly from the 1984 diary published by Spain's leading feminist publisher, laSal. Address: *ediciones de les dones*, La Riereta, 13, Barcelona 1 (Tel. 329–84 50).

BARCELONA: **Centre d'Informacion i D'Urgència per la Dona**, (women's emergency centre), Tel. 257–81 04; **Club Dona**, Ramblas Catalunya 101 (Tel 215 1533); **Club Vindicación Feminista**, Bailén 18, 3er, la, B–10; **Partit Feminista de España** (address as for Club Vindicacion, Tel. 246–68 88).

BILBAO: **Asamblea de Mujeres de Vizcaya** (Tel. 444–31 93).

BURGOS: **Asamblea de Mujeres de Burgos**, Vitoria 177, 7o.

CÁDIZ: **Asociación Gaditana de la Mujer**, Fernández Ladreda 5, 5o

(contact: Virginia Arizaga); **Centro Asesor de la Mujer**, San Juan de Dios s/n (Tel. 28–56 52).

GERONA: **Casa de la Dona**, information from: Isabel (Tel. 20–70 95), Leo (Tel. 23–24 60), Roser (Tel. 21–29 75).

GRANADA: **Asamblea de Mujeres de Granada**, information from: Mercedes Bellbel Bullejos, Camino de Ronda 71, 7a, puerta 3o.

LA CORUÑA: **Asociación Galega de la Mujer**, San Andrés 139, 3o.

MADRID: **Asamblea de Mujeres de Madrid**, Barquillo 44, 2o, izq.; **Centro de Información de la Mujer**, Menéndez y Pelayo 11, 2o, M 9 (Tel. 276–46 45); **Frente de Liberación de la Mujer**, Fernando VI, 11, 4o (Tel. 429–04 65); **Mujeres por la Paz** (Women for Peace), Almarza 45, M 33 (Tel. 239–42 14 or 266 02 87).

SANTIAGO: **Mujeres de Santiago**, (contact: Marina Santos), República Argentina 43, 1o.

SEVILLA: **Centro de Información de la Mujer** (CIM), Alfonso XII, 5 (Tel. 22–56 20).

TARRAGONA: **Associació de Dones**, St. Salvador 12, esc.21, 4at, 2a.; **Bloc Feminista de Tarragona**, Guirateries 1, 2on, 3a.Apt. Correos 55.

THE ISLANDS: **Asociación de Mujeres Canarias**, Instituto Canario de Estudio Económico, Senador Castillo Olivares 2, Las Palmas; **Centre Feminista, Mallorca** (Tel. 28–51 90 or 23–48 90); **Grup de Dones**, contact: Margarida Bagur, Nou 21, Menorca (Tel. 36–28 52).

Bookshops

Librería Mujer, Centro de Encuentro, Carnicería 1 (Tel. 22–98 82), Granada; **Librería Feminista Fulmen**, Zaragoza 36, Seville (Tel. 22–71 78); **Librería de Mujeres**, San Cristóbal 17, Madrid (Tel. 221–70 43); **Librería Dona**, Gravador Esteve 34, València (Tel. 351–55 36).

BOOKS

John Hooper, *The Spaniards* (Viking, 1986) is excellent for contemporary background.

If you can read Spanish, look out for novels by the Catalan feminist Mercedes Roig.

Thanks to Saundra Satterlee, Debbie Langdon-Davies and Patricia Bannister for additional information.

ITALY

Many Italians regard **Italy** as virtually two separate countries: the north and the south. The first, ending at Rome, enjoys an image of prosperity and innovation; the second, encompassing the notorious Mafia stronghold of Sicily, is considered poor, corrupt, backward and, at least in the minds of most southerners, cruelly neglected. Compared to the thriving industrial centres in and around Turin or Milan, the south is indeed desperately poor. It's also more traditional and conservative and, in this respect, less easy for travellers. But Italy is a country of far more subtle variations.

In a few hours' ride by bus or train you can move from the medieval charm of Venice to the lively, progressive city of Bologna and, further down, Florence and the peaceful mountains and hill towns of Tuscany and Umbria. South of Rome lie beautiful beaches, wild and arid scenery and many more fascinating relics of the past, most famous being the ruined city of Pompei. Italy is steeped in history and every area has its own monuments to an ancient civilisation.

The Italians are very talkative, hospitable people and it takes little to be drawn into long conversations, however poor your grasp of the language. Train journeys provide the perfect setting and, perhaps surprisingly in the light of widespread street harassment, several women report these as among their most enjoyable experiences. Fellow passengers like practising their English and everyone tends to pool their efforts in order to understand your views on the royal family, Mrs Thatcher, the Sicilians or whatever subject comes up. Travelling with a child, you'll be made even more welcome. All over Italy children are doted on and fussed over, providing a wonderful passport for meeting people and gaining their respect. It's quite common in a restaurant for your child to be whisked off to the kitchen and showered with kisses and treats for a couple of hours while you enjoy your meal.

A woman alone or with a female companion is a curiosity and, particularly in the south, may even arouse pity. Italian society (with behind it the weight of the Catholic Church) is so strongly family oriented that it's hard for the older generation, at least, to understand any female desire for independence. Mamma may appear to reign at home, but outside machismo is irritatingly prevalent. Italian men are proud, vain and not easily rejected for, in any situation, they like to at least be *seen* to have the upper hand.

Italian women have a lot to battle against and today every city has at least one **feminist organisation**. In addition several have their own bookshops (also meeting places) and documentation centres. The roots of the movement lie in the generation referred to as the 68ers, political activists who, during that period of social turmoil, gradually saw the need for women to organise separately from men. Many did and still do belong to the huge Italian Communist Party – feminism and communism have always been strongly linked in Italy. *Noi Donne*, the country's first feminist magazine, was started as an organ of the CP in the 1940s – but campaigns for divorce rights and against rape, the successful fight to legalise abortion, and a more recent women's peace movement, all indicate a firm belief in the importance of autonomous organisation.

◪ Caroline Duff lived for three years in Venice where she taught English, first in various schools and then at the university.

Even though thousands of tourists pass through it every year, Venice remains an island cut off from the world and trapped in a watery pocket of time. This is, of course, its attraction and its limitation. Walking in the city you are bound to get lost. Don't worry. It's fun trying to unravel the labyrinthine lay-out, especially as round every corner lies another historic building or picturesque scene. It's best to pursue this aimless wandering for the first few days in order to get used to the lay-out and possibly to escape summer crowds who congregate around six or seven key monuments (in particular, San Marco, the Academia Gallery, Frari and San Rocco).

Despite the hidden alleys and twisting streets, there's relatively little danger of harassment or violence – something of a relief for women travelling from southern Italy. The Venetians themselves seem singularly uninterested in travellers from every point of view except their money. Their city is largely built on foreign trade and Venetians have had foreigners passing through almost since it was founded. But they're not fond of this dependence, nor of the tourist hordes who pass by their doors every day, so don't be surprised by sometimes very off-hand treatment in restaurants and bars, none of which are particularly cheap.

Venetians are also quick to demonstrate the pride they have in their city. Their identification with their roots is even more fierce than the usual 'campanilismo' felt by all Italians. Venice is divided into six *sestieri*, or zones, and these are again divided into parishes. I have spoken to some elderly women who move out of their particular parish perhaps only seven or eight times a year. Small as it is, when you live in Venice, it does begin to close in on you and your mind takes on strange labyrinthine qualities of its own. It becomes somehow difficult to leave the city, though when you do, it is an unforseen relief. Life outside the lagoon often seems very far away and Venetians refer to the mainland as 'terra ferma', giving it a vague, mythological aspect.

But despite these parochial elements, the sophistication of the city contrasts greatly with the simplicity of some of the remote island settlements of the lagoon. Burano, for instance, retains all the bright charm of an isolated fishing village, and the islands of San Erasmus and the Vignole are still farmed by *contadini* (peasant farmers). Pellestrina, beyond the somewhat anomalous Lido with its cars and fashionable beaches, is perhaps the most remote of all.

If you want to see Venice at its best, don't go there in high summer when the crowds and humidity can be stifling. April and May are better months and the October/November period can be warm or misty, producing some very scenic effects. Flooding sometimes occurs towards the end of this period bringing a touch of drama, although for real theatre and burlesque you should visit the city in February during the ten days preceding Shrove Tuesday. It is then that the carnival takes place and San Marco throbs, for once, to sounds produced by the electronic world.

▰ **Angela Morgan spent some time working as an au pair in a small coastal town in Calabria, southern Italy.**

Calabria, right in the toe of Italy, is an impoverished land of forested mountains falling sheer to the sea, with a thin sliver of coastal plain, so dry and hot in summer that it's known as the Italian Africa. Tourists are rare and as an English girl working in a family I was definitely a local curiosity.

The Calabrese are profoundly traditional and women have few of the freedoms which have been gained in the larger cities and in much of the north. Girls are accompanied everywhere, often by an older woman or a male relative and, as I was told, 'good' girls never go out alone. Those that do are considered easy and, though obviously an outsider, the same applied to me. Nearly every time I ventured out I was followed and besieged by young men, on motor scooters and in cars, quite explicitly demanding sex. Saying 'no' seemed astonishingly ineffectual, even when I'd learned to back it up with some much stronger Italian vocabulary. This sort of harassment is much diminished, though never altogether eliminated, if you travel with a man.

As an au pair I was expected to join in completely with the Italian way of life, starting with the evening *passagiata*. In almost every village and town between 7 and 10 pm the entire population put on their Sunday best and congregate in the main square and surrounding streets, literally to walk up and down. On my first evening I was told to wear a pretty dress; my family, being the only one in town with an au pair, wanted to show me off as a sort of status symbol. The passagiata is also an important outlet for marriageable women. Meticulously groomed and often thickly chaperoned, they wander arm-in-arm chatting to their friends but always alert to the sight of an eligible man who, equally vain, might be strolling with his group of cronies the other way.

Calabria is full of beautiful and historical sites: Montralto, the highest peak of the Aspromonte, provides spectacular views across to Sicily and Mount Etna; there are extensive Grecian remains around Locri and Reggio Calabria, not to mention fascinating walled towns, such as Gerace, reached by a road that winds up the mountainside into narrow cobbled streets where black-clad women sit on almost every doorstep chatting. On feast days, especially that of the Assumption of the Virgin Mary in August, families and friends go in large groups to the mountains or the sea. Once arrived, they sit, eat and talk, the children play until everyone returns home. To Italians, at least in the south, family and their small circle of friends is all important; little outside matters.

There's a huge gulf between rich and poor. The children of the family I was working for seemed to regard the inhabitants of a neighbouring block of cottages as forming their own private zoo which they'd watch from the balcony. These neighbours were very poor, with few material possessions, no electric lighting, only an outside sink for all their washing and a charcoal fire. Hens wandered in and out of the cottage.

People in general seemed resigned to their fate and, although posters and Communist Party slogans were splashed on many walls, I came across little enthusiasm for politics and the need for radical social change. Even the Church, probably the most dominant influence on Italian society, appeared to play little part in people's lives – at least not in the family I was living with. They simply seemed to be bound by work, siesta, the beach and the passagiata, an almost monotonous regularity. There was no room for other options – most of the women I met were quite incredulous of my daring in travelling all the way from England on my own; few leave their home town or village for more than a day.

Working as an au pair is a good way of experiencing Italian life, to an extent impossible for the tourist. But the lack of freedom and hazards of travelling and walking alone in the streets can be very stifling. If I returned as a tourist to Calabria, it would probably be with a man.

◤ **Frances Connelly has twice visited the women's peace camp at Comiso, Sicily. Both times she stayed about a week at the camp which is still going at the time of writing (January 1986).**

Sicily is of special strategic importance to the US as missiles can be launched from there to the Middle East. There are 19 American bases in Sicily and cruise missiles were sited at Comiso in March 1984. This increased military activity has strengthened the Mafia who have been involved in land speculation and construction work.

In 1981 a group from Catania went to an international meeting of women for peace in Amsterdam with a statement which pointed out the connections between the nuclear escalation and male violence. On 12 December 1982, women from Catania and Comiso formed a circle in front of the cruise missile base at Comiso, their action inspired by a visit from two women from Greenham Common; they then went on to reclaim the town square.

The following March, about 600 women of different nationalities descended on Comiso for international women's day and to protest against all forms of male violence. Some blockaded the base and despite their non-violence, were very roughly treated by the police. Two women had their arms broken and twelve, one Italian and eleven foreign, were arrested and charged with obstruction, a serious offence punishable by up to twelve years in prison. The foreign women were deported and had to return the following year to stand trial. In the end they were given twenty days' suspended sentence, but it took two long appeals until the original expulsion orders were lifted. It is still very difficult to protest in Italy without incurring these sorts of severe penalties.

From the energy created by that March action a permanent women's peace camp was set up. It's based in a simple house on a small plot of land which, to affirm the international nature of the camp and lessen the risk of expropriation by the military, was paid for by women from all over the world. Each group bought a symbolic square metre. The camp is called *La Ragnatela*, which means the spider's web. It is in a very beautiful and fertile part of Sicily, surrounded by vineyards with orange trees growing nearby. The stone house has been decorated with moons and snakes, and part of the land has been cultivated. There is plenty of room to put up tents and it is usually possible to stay in the house. Groups of women have been living there since 1983. The women are not only concerned about the missiles but also with the wider issues of male violence. The camp is an attempt to create a feminist alternative and to break down barriers between different nationalities. There are Ragnatela groups in several Italian cities – the Florence women have been especially active – but few Italian women can afford to live at the camp as there is no social security in Italy and poverty can be extreme. As a result the majority of women living there are foreign.

If you want to visit the camp, try and talk to someone who has recently been there before you go (see Travel Notes). Bear in mind that Sicilian customs are very different even from mainland Italy and that sometimes the dialect is difficult to understand. It is important to be sensitive to local ways of doing things.

TRAVEL NOTES

Language Italian, with strong regional dialects. If you can't speak Italian, French is useful and quite a few people speak some English, at least in the cities.
Transport Trains and buses are reasonably cheap and run pretty much on time. Hitching is easy enough, but obviously risky, especially in the south.
Accommodation *Pensiones* (and more expensive hotels) are plentiful throughout the country.
Special Problems Machismo rules and harassment can be a problem, especially in the south where some women find it quite unbearable. Railway stations everywhere are particularly hazardous. You should spend the least possible time in them, and never sleep in a station; you run the risk of theft and sexual assault. In general the most obvious strategy is to avoid eye contact. Whatever clothes you wear, you're still likely to be followed, pushed and touched and have your route blocked. Italians are quite amazing at identifying foreigners. Beware of the police, too. According to Diana Pritchard who has lived and travelled extensively in Italy, 'Their conduct is an unpleasant combination of abuse of authority (even the Italian public are cautious of them) and an apparent lack of respect for foreign women. Some of my worst experiences have involved the *Carabinieri* – the armed police – ranging from the indiscreet fondle of my breast as I walked by, to a time when a group of Carabinieri demanded that I open the door of a tiny bedroom in which a female friend and I were staying. Although I eventually managed to get them out of the room, we were followed the next day until we left town.'
Other information *Getting to Comiso:* You can fly to Catania or Palermo and boat trains go from Rome to Catania. From Catania get a bus or shared taxi to Comiso. The camp is about 5 kilometres from the town centre. For more information write to 26 Argyle Street, Cambridge CB1 3LR or, in Italy, phone Florence 665 354. It's very important to contact someone in advance as there are times, mainly in winter, when there are no women at the camp.

You are legally obliged to carry your passport with you at all times in Italy, and in theory you need a *permesso* if you're planning to stay for more than a few days. In practice most tourists don't bother with this document and have no problems but if, in the case of Comiso, the authorities want to deport you, they can use your lack of *permesso* as an excuse. They are available free from police stations and you should be able to get one for three months. You'll need two passport-sized photos and often have to go to the police station early in the morning to fill in forms, returning to collect the *permesso* a few days later.

Non-violent direct action in Italy is very different from England and foreigners should be aware of the risks before doing anything. If you want to make this sort of protest it's a good idea to discuss it thoroughly with some Italians beforehand. If you break the law chances of deportation are very high.

The postal address for the Comiso women's peace camp: *La Ragnatela*, CP 150, Comiso, Sicily.
Guides *Rough Guides* to the main Italian cities and regions, and to the country as a whole are forthcoming. In the meantime make do with *Let's Go Italy* (St Martins Press, US) and, for art and architecture details, the various *Blue Guides* (A & C Black).

CONTACTS

The following is a selected list of **women's centres and bookshops**, as supplied by the Bologna Women's Centre in August 1985. Often bookshops (*librerie*) and centres (*case*) are combined in the same building. A *biblioteca* is a library and suggests a more academic place.

ALESSANDRIA: **Casa delle Donne**, V. Solero 24, 15100

L'AQUILA: **Biblioteca delle Donne**, c/o A.I.E.D., Corso Federico 11 58, 67100

ANCONA: **Biblioteca delle Donne**, V. Cialdini 26, 60122

BOLOGNA: **Librellula, Libreria delle Donne**, Strada Maggiore 23/e.

BOLZANO: **Centro Doc. Infor. Donna**, Piazza Erbe 38, 39100

BRESCIA: **Casa delle Donne**, V. Volturno 36, 25126

CIVITAVECCHIA: **Centro Donna 'Terra-dilet'**, V.G. Abruzzeze, 00053

FANO: **Centro Donna Comune Fano**, C.so Matteoti 68, 61032

FIRENZE: **Libreria delle Donne**, V. Fiesolana 2B, 50122; **Casa delle Donne**, V. Carraia 2, 50127

MILANO: **Libreria delle Donne**, V. Dogana 2, 20123; **Casa delle Donne**, V. Lanzone 32, 20123; **Centro per la Difesa dei Diritti delle Donne**, V. Tadino 23, 20124

MODENA: **Casa delle Donne**, V. Cesana 43, 41100

PARMA: **Biblioteca delle Donne**, V. XX Settembre 31, 43100

PISA: **Centro Documentazione Donne**, V. Puccini 15, 56100

REGGIO EMILIA: **Casa della Donna**, Viale Isonzo 76, 42100

ROMA: **Libreria delle Donne**, Piazza Farnese 103, 00186 (Tel. 05–654 749); **Isis International** (international women's resource centre and information and communication service), V. Santa Maria dell'Anima 30, 00186 (Tel. 06–6565 842).

TORINO: **Casa delle Donne**, V. Fiocchetto 13, 10152

BOOKS

Few books by Italian women have been translated into English. The following two novels are strongly recommended:

Sibilla Alermo, *A Woman* (Virago, 1979). A classic in Italy, first published in 1906, this semi-autobiographical book tells the story of a girl growing up, dominated by her love for her father, but determined to break away and forge her own life.

Dacia Maraini, *Woman at War* (Lighthouse Books, London 1984). By one of Italy's best known contemporary writers, it records, in diary form, a woman's growing self-awareness, beginning on holiday with her husband. The book encompasses weird characters, political argument and a wealth of sensual detail.

Thanks to Diana Pritchard and Joanna Crane for useful insights and Susan Bassnett, a close friend and supporter of Bologna women's centre, who obtained most of the addresses listed above.

GREECE

Literally millions of independent travellers go to **Greece**, attracted by the cheap cost of living, the easy-going Mediterranean culture and ancient sites, so well known as to almost be educational clichés. With the drachma recently devalued, the numbers are likely to increase still further. Athens, a manic overpopulated sprawl of a city, receives an easy two or three million tourists every year. Many, put off by the pollution and anarchic traffic, stay only to traipse round the Acropolis and work out bus and boat timetables. There are numerous cheap hotels and, like most European capitals, women as well as men are on the streets until quite late. You'll find occasional harassment from Greeks picking on 'easy' tourists, but it's nowhere like as oppressive as, say, Rome, and there are plenty of buses and taxis if you ever feel uneasy. There's also a large, if transient community of English teachers and sundry workers and, as Greece phases itself into the EEC, opportunities for work are likely to increase.

Travelling around the main resorts (all the islands on the main ferry routes and a few tourist enclaves scattered around the mainland coast), your main problem will be dealing with the mass of other tourists. According to reputation and the vagaries of package deals, islands tend to be swamped by one or other nationality (Corfu, Rhodes and Spetses are favoured by the British). Greek machismo is strong, but less upfront than the equivalent in Spain or Italy. Most of the hassle you get is from a relatively small population of Greeks who migrate from the mainland with the tourists. As for the main sites, you're as likely to share them with busloads of Greek schoolchildren as regimented crowds of Japanese. Camping nearby or staying in hotels is generally easy and unthreatening.

Attitudes to women remain highly polarised. Legislative reforms, especially the 1983 Family Law which prohibits dowry and stipulates equal status and shared property rights, have had limited impact in the rural areas. In the mountains and inland areas off the tourist circuit you may feel uncomfortable travelling alone. In *kafeneions* (simple cafés, usually packed with old men and often the only place where you can get a drink) your presence will at best be politely tolerated. It's easier travelling with a man – you're more likely to be treated as a *xenos*, meaning both stranger and guest.

The **Women's Movement** has conspicuously emerged over the last few years. By far the largest organisation is the *Women's Union of Greece*, founded in 1976. Whilst it espouses an independent feminist line and has set up numerous consciousness-raising activities across the country, the WUG is very closely linked to the Panhellic Socialist Party (PASOK), currently in power; one of its founder members was Margaret Papandreou, wife of the present prime minister. Along with the Women's Union there are various women's council review committees set up by PASOK to instigate and oversee legislative reforms like the Family Law. There are also several autonomous feminist groups concerned with widening public debate around such issues as sexuality, violence and the representation of women by the media.

▞ **Jo Westbrook spent two weeks island-hopping around the Cyclades.**

We called it the 'island syndrome': the European horde going one way from Athens airport to the bus, to the subway to Piraeus harbour, and up into the huge island ferries, devouring coffee and pastries, escaping the cold, moving ever southwards towards the promised tan. Layers are stripped off over the six-hour voyage to Paros. The pecking order starts here. A full seasoned dark and rosy tan and you're in.

Arriving at Paroikia, Paros' main town and port, we escaped offers of expensive beds and organised camping sites and crammed into a local taxi to the village of Pounda, along with friendly older Greeks amused at our antipathy to tourism. From there a small motorboat took us and four motorbikes over to our hoped-for unspoilt satellite island – Anti-Paros – forty minutes off coast.

Anti-Paros is one street with a tiny port and several seafront tavernas. Small streets leading off the main one hide smaller tavernas overhung with ripe grapes and whitewashed homes. Old women sit crocheting at upper windows and look down at the buzz of activity below provided in the main by boisterous drunk Scandinavians. These are the island regulars; young students who rent double rooms and a bathroom for 400 drachmas a night over the entire summer, living a hedonistic life during the day and showing off their all-over tans during the requisite fashion parade in the evening.

It is impossible to avoid this crowd. Only by walking into the hinterland can you gain peace of mind. Up through the town you can climb up a stony road to one of several tiny white churches commanding a superb view of Paros and of Anti-Paros harbour and beaches. The first night we took the long and dusty road to the campsite, loud music blaring from its restaurant and brown unfriendly bodies emerging from classy bamboo structures. Small bays clothe naked men and women. We moved the second night to a shady room in a house given over to tourists and found a friendlier beach facing Paros where you can walk out for miles without the warm water going above bronzed nipple-height.

This, we decided, was all right, but not all right for us. We took an early morning boat back to Paros harbour. We were heading eventually for Amorgos at the eastern tip of the Cyclades in search of peace and away from these Beautiful People. Naxos was our next overnight stop while waiting for the infrequent sea connection to Amorgos on the good ship *The Marianne*.

Naxos is large and hilly, Apollo's temple welcoming you high up on a hill looking as if it's made out of concrete for the tourists. A small girl on a bike at the harbour offered us a room for 750 drachmas. 'Okay', we said. Her family's house was in a dip a little way out of the town, a courtyard surrounded by small rooms containing an old mahogany bed with hard, lumpy pillows. The family were halfway through their supper, undisturbed by us. In fact we were disturbed by their voices and their television all that night!

Anna Agia beach is a bumpy bus ride away going through the fertile interior. It is one long road with no village, just a few tavernas for the nudists, who have once again built bamboo structures on the sand dunes and live their version of the Garden of Eden. Males here, mainly German and British, strut and preen and glance cursorily at the outstretched females but there's nothing to fear from this lot. We encamped in a goat and mule field and ate sumptuously on roasted half-chickens cooked over a spit at one of the tavernas. The one toilet was an unhealthy hole in the ground. This we decided was not our place in the sun either, so back to the boat.

The Marianne is a small cargo/passenger boat that sails precariously twice a week to Amorgos from Naxos. Bring water, provisions and sunglasses; the trip takes a slow but breathtaking eight hours past Paros, to Iraklia, Kanuffissia, and finally Amorgos. If you want to see Greek island life then this is it, and we had finally found it.

The entire population of each small island comes down to the harbour to meet *The Marianne* and to cart away boxes of toilet rolls, crates of beer and Coca-cola, the odd toilet bowl and boxes of runny baklavas. At Iraklia children were jumping into the sea from a ruin many feet up. A boy of eleven in long trousers and black cap, aping the men, took control of the unloading, a Greek Artful Dodger. A fat woman in a sleeveless dress expertly built a tower from the beer crates. An old man argued hotly with a crew member, waving a list of things that presumably hadn't arrived.

Amorgos is roughly croissant shaped. It appears barren and craggy from the boat, sheer cliffs into the sea. *The Marianne* calls in first to the northern curve, the inlet called Igalia where you should disembark, with the harbour town Ormos, Potomos with its beautiful church above, and the curve of the beach. Two mountain villages, Lagada and Tholaria, stand high up opposite each other, a highly fertile plain stretching miles in between. A tiny monastery is wedged in against one mountain side.

The few tourists who make it here are real travellers, unobtrusive among the fishers and the farmers. The main town Katapoula is far to the south, as yet unconnected by road to Igalia. Accommodation is sparse, the one 'hotel', *Laaki*, is almost hidden by vines. We camped free of charge on the lowest terrace of a disused olive grove out of the main street and washed under the eyes of the people under a fresh water tap where donkeys get precedence over sandy foreigners.

The best of the seven or eight tavernas is *Theos*, near the harbour and overlooking the whole inlet from its rooftop restaurant. The owners are friendly and welcome back Europeans year after year to their fish soup and retsina and their games of backgammon. The best beach is a short but strenuous hike over a cliff, where you can strip off, but not infringe upon local custom.

Sitting watching the sunset one night, the classier cousin to *The Marianne* came in and, as she left, the captain, by way of tradition, sang into the ship's microphone and fireworks were let off, red balls of fire high up in the sky over the harbour, and answered in kind high up from a window of a house in Potomos.

Leaving Amorgos can be tricky. *The Marianne* came in on time en route to Katapoula and thence back to Naxos, but the captain didn't want to go because there was a party on the northern part, so he cancelled the trip. We waited all the next day, hung in suspension, for another boat rumoured to be approaching. Finally it appeared, huge and intruding, an inter-island ferry. We queued up and rejoined the emigrés, waving goodbye to new friends of five days and nights, and munched bread and cheese while the boat heaved from side to side back to Piraeus.

■ **Juliet Martin worked as a chambermaid on the island of Crete.**

Having spent the first week of a vacation working as a waitress in a pub, I took a one-way plane ticket to Crete to search for similar work in the sun. It is not easy to find. I spent the first week unemployed in Heraklion spending what little money I had. You need a work permit to work there – too many tourist police about.

I ended up getting a job in a small resort outside Malia by word of mouth. In return for food and a small room shared with the laundry and cleaning materials I was to work three hours cleaning or occasionally taking the children swimming, etc. The work was tiring in that it took place when the sun was up. Although I was to start at ten it was often later by the time the rooms were vacated. By midday the humidity makes for exhaustion. Weekly, I had to travel up the mountain to clean some villas. For this I was given a moped which often broke down. Pushing it loaded with linen and cleaning materials was more than tiring. The mess left was often unpleasant. A kitchen table covered with brown sticky glue-like stuff proved a minor challenge. It was hot chocolate. On another occasion my employer's husband shouted at me for failing to remove the shit on the outside of a toilet. Somehow it had escaped my attention.

My boss was English. She'd come to Crete as a courier, 'fallen in love with everything' (her words) and stayed to marry. Many of her women friends, also not Greek, had fallen for the apparent dream-like existence on the island, married and become disillusioned. They would sit drinking gin and lemonade discussing their unease. Many husbands were unfaithful, continuing their bachelor existence despite marriage. Nikos took off with a tourist 'for dinner' the evening after his Dutch wife gave birth. This was 'to celebrate'. Such marriages can also cause division in the Greek family who may not accept the foreigner, since she has no dowry. Although it is accepted that men 'play around' with tourists, it is still expected that their wives will be virgin locals.

The foreign chambermaid is caught in the middle; neither part of the family/local scene nor a tourist. Many tourists used me to tell their life stories to. Others included me in their socialising and on their trips over the island. The family frequently entertained relatives and friends for barbecue fish suppers. Although I was welcomed, language was often a barrier to full participation.

From the wings I witnessed the Greek beach-bums (male of course) picking out new tourists fortnightly, declaring unending passion for them, then finding a replacement from the next plane in from Scandinavia. These young men don't work. Their mothers do. They are involved in servicing the hotels often as cleaners. One women stood ironing bed linen all day for a hotel, her calves purple-knotted with veins. Such labour supported her son's endeavours to 'get to know other cultures' – well the female side anyway.

Theoretically I worked only mornings so there was plenty of time to see the island – mainly by hitching. Although the buses are cheap and frequent, hitching is a good option if you're broke. As a woman alone I felt confident hitching by day. Lifts are easy and can be fun if you don't mind the ridiculous conversations in simple English/Greek. Often I'd hitch into Heraklion to walk round the harbour or market or just to sit in the main square with a coffee. It's a big, dusty city relative to the rest of the island, but has its own charm. Men in the towns or those who give you lifts may ask you for a drink or to meet them later. Refusals are quietly accepted. My trickiest situation was being driven to a deserted beach 'to swim'. He stripped off. I looked bored. No, I wasn't joining him. He could go ahead. He didn't. We drove on in silence to Ierapetra. (Worth a visit if you're interested in architecture.)

Mopeds and cars are easily hired for those with a bit more cash. Mopeds have a reputation for breaking down, but some places are only accessible in this way. I got to Lassithi Plateau in a tourist's hire car. It's well worth it, to see the thousands of white-sailed windpumps that serve to irrigate the region. The views are incredible, but take a jumper – it gets blowy.

The most challenging day was spent walking the Samaria Gorge – the longest in Europe. The cheapest way of doing this excursion is to stay in Chania overnight and get the 6 am bus to Omalos where the six-hour descent begins. On the way you'll see 1000-foot drops, beautiful woodland and springs as well as wild goats. Halfway through is the deserted village of Samaria. At the end in Aghia Roumeli is a restaurant (not too pricey considering its position) and a boat which heads along the coast to Khora Sfakion. There a bus takes you back to Chania. It's a long day but well worth the effort.

Anyone wanting to combine work with travel in this way should take enough cash to get home and spend during your stay. You may earn a little but not enough to get home. One-way flights from Crete are very expensive. The cheapest way is to get a deckclass ticket on an overnight boat from Heraklion or Chania to Piraeus, the port of Athens. From Athens you may be lucky to get a cheap plane or failing that, the bus or train.

TRAVEL NOTES

Languages Greek. It's worth learning the alphabet to work out bus destinations and timetables. English (if only tourist essentials) is fairly widely understood. Many Greeks have worked abroad and there's been a recent proliferation of English language schools.

Transport An efficient, reasonably cheap bus service connects main towns and major resorts. Hitching is usually okay (though experiences vary); it's more accepted, but much slower, in the isolated regions where buses do a daily round trip if at all. Be careful of mopeds, hired out on most islands. Maintenance is a joke and accidents common on the dirt tracks. Island ferries get crowded so arrive early and leave time to get back for your flight – bad weather, strikes and out-of-date timetables make them unreliable. There are internal flights to many islands and mainland cities.

Accommodation Plenty of cheap hotels, rooms in private houses and reasonably good campsites. Camping wild is illegal but often tolerated (police attitudes vary). On islands you'll be offered rooms as you get off the ferry – often a good option for the first night at least.

Special problems Kafeneions (cafés) are exclusive male territory. Your presence may be tolerated in the more touristed areas but elsewhere you may be made to feel uncomfortable.

Guide Mark Ellingham, Natania Jansz and John Fisher, *The Rough Guide to Greece* (Routledge & Kegan Paul, 1985). Intelligent, practical and honest guide that doesn't romanticise (or inflate) islands that can sometimes be thoroughly spoilt.

Other information The Greek council for Equality in combination with the Greek National Tourist Organisation and Greek Productivity centre have organised holidays with *Women's Agro-tourist Co-operatives*. They advertise a chance to work alongside Greek women. We'd appreciate any information from someone who's taken this up. Contact addresses are:

Lesvos – Petra, Mytillini Tel. 0253 41238
Hios – c/o The Prefecture of Hios Tel. 0271 25901
Ambelakia (near Larissa, central Greece) Tel. 0495 93296

CONTACTS

Comprehensive **listings** for all feminist groups and centres in Greece appear in the women's *Imerologio* (diary) published in Athens by Eyrotyp (Kolonou 12–24).

Groups listed below are the more accessible contacts, particularly if you don't have good command of Greek.

Multinational Women's Liberation Group Mavromichalis 69, Athens. Produce an English language newsletter, *OUT*, and hold meetings every week at the **Woman's House** (Romanou

Melodou 4 (entrance on a side street off Odos Dafnomili) Lykavitos, Athens; Tel. 281–4823). This is also the meeting place of the **Autonomous Group of Gay Women**.

Greek Women's Liberation Movement, Tsimiski 39, Athens.

Massalias, Sina 38, Athens. The city's feminist bookshop.

Federation of Greek Women (*Omospondia Gynaekon Elladas*). Focuses on discrimination at work and disparities in pay, active in the peace movement. Many branches, including Akademias 52, Athens (Tel. 361–5565)

Movement of Democratic Women (*Kinisi Demokratikon Gynaekon*). Athens branch at Genadiou 5 (Tel. 363–0661)

Union of Greek Women (*Enosis Gynaekon Elladas*) Emphasis on oppression of women in rural areas and Mediterranean women in general.

Responsible for forming the Council of Equality. Branches in all major towns – in Athens at Enianon 8 (Tel. 823–4937) Useful **regional points of contact** are the feminist centres/bookshops in THESSALONIKI (*Spiti Gynaekon*, Yermanou 22) and IOANNINA (*Steki Gynaekon*, M. Kakara 25).

BOOKS

Dido Sotiriou (author of *Endoli* and others) is perhaps the best known and most respected Greek woman novelist but none of her books have as yet been translated into English.

Sheelagh Kanelli, *Nets* (The Women's Press, 1983). A short, lucid novel that reconstructs the events leading up to a disaster in a small Greek coastal village. Though British herself, Kanelli is married to a Greek and has lived there for some years.

YUGOSLAVIA

Yugoslavia may lack some of the hedonistic atmosphere of other Mediterranean countries, but it's well worth exploring. Since becoming one nation in 1918, it has managed to retain a unique mixture of cultures, encompassing three languages and at least three religions, and each of the six republics (Montenegro, Serbia, Croatia, Macedonia, Slovenia, Bosnia and Hercogovina) is almost like a country on its own. Thanks to a wealth of cheap buses it's easy to get around and you can discover an astonishing variety of people and places in a relatively short time.

As usual, tourism is mainly concentrated in a handful of seaside resorts, leaving miles of coastline, many islands and large areas inland virtually untouched by outsiders. Holiday centres attract the familiar brand of southern European men in search of 'available' foreign women. Elsewhere, especially in the poorer and Islamic regions, attitudes are more archaic, and perhaps less obviously threatening. Nevertheless, travelling alone, you will always be the focus of attention and situations like eating in restaurants can be uncomfortable, as offers of free meals flood in and waiters seem to deliberately ignore your wishes. It can be wise to avoid staying out late at night.

The Yugoslav people share great national pride in the state which they feel they have all built together through their own endeavours. It's still a poor country – wages are among the lowest in Europe – but considering the widespread survival of feudalism up to the First World War, there's been great progress towards becoming a relatively industrialised nation. On paper at least, women now have as many opportunities as men. They make up a large portion of the student population and all careers are supposedly open to them. However, away from the cities, many remain dominated by fathers, brothers and husbands into a life of domestic servitude. After World War II, Tito formed an organisation giving all women equal rights as workers and the freedom to explore any chances that came their way. They have long had paid maternity leave, state crèches and nursery schools, all of which help towards economic independence even if they do little to change the extremely chauvinistic attitude of most Yugoslav men. Free from having to fight legal battles, **feminists** concentrate on the need for open debate on issues like rape, health, prostitution and sexism in the media and, above all, the need to acknowledge the existence of a separate 'women's question' outside the framework of party ideology. Resistance is great, but there's a growing movement of autonomous women's groups determined to put feminism, as a vital contribution to socialism, on the map.

▰ **Eve Haslett spent a month travelling round the country, most of the time with two male friends.**

The first place I headed for in Yugoslavia was the Croatian city, Zagreb. I was on a ridiculously overcrowded Italian train from Venice and the only seat I could find was in a compartment packed out with a large Yugoslav family. They were not at all pleased that I had joined them. Just before we reached Trieste about six large bin liners full of new clothes, Levis, etc. were yanked from under seats and off the racks and hastily redistributed amongst the other baggage. Tension mounted in the long wait at the Yugoslav border. Eventually two guards stuck their heads into the compartment, checked everyone's passports, looked around and then left. The furtive glances gave way to huge grins of relief.

Hours later I arrived in Zagreb and went straight to the Youth Hostel. Not only was it incredibly cheap and well equipped, but it was also a great place to meet other women travelling on their own. I had already planned to meet up with two male friends which gave me just a few days on my own to explore this rather grand, green city. It was more than enough time to experience my first taste of Yugoslav machismo – mostly a constant stream of comments and clicking noises (like you use to call a dog to heel) from groups of men hanging around on the streets. Having travelled round Italy and the South of Spain I found this fairly easy to ignore – it never reached the level of my feeling personally threatened. Police and soldiers were around in large numbers but, unlike the machine-gun-wielding Italian guards, they didn't seem interested in deliberate intimidation. Of course, as in any country you could get unlucky and come up against the odd moronic, bored, excessively macho policeman. Most likely he'll hassle you for your passport and ask a few questions. None of them like to be photographed, and anything vaguely militaristic is off limits for holiday snaps.

In many ways I expected Yugoslavs to be hostile towards me as a symbol of the capitalist West. They weren't. But then neither were they falling over themselves to be friendly. In most cases they tend to put their compatriots before tourists, for instance making room for them on a crowded bus before they allow you on, and in my thinking that's fair enough. Waiters and waitresses have a reputation for being extremely curt and abrupt, but then the sort of hours they work and the sheer crassness they have to put up with from hordes of foreign egomaniacs would fray the edges of a saint.

I also had an idea that there'd be food queues and scarcity, a picture reinforced by the farce on the train from Italy. It's true that none of the shops or supermarkets would cause much excitement on a British High Street, but more often than not there was enough choice available to satisfy most Western tastes. Interestingly women do not dominate the menial jobs within supermarkets as they do in Britain, men are often seen at the checkout, stocking shelves or cleaning up. As in any socialist state women are accepted in most areas of work (though there's by no means equal representation at all levels) and sexual equality is enshrined in party doctrine. But this appears to have had little impact on the usual stereotypes of women as passive and submissive and men as active and dominating – at least that was my impression. As I never really managed to learn Serbo-Croat and discuss these issues I don't know how superficial those impressions were. I do know that whenever I was with my two male friends talking to a male Yugoslav (usually a tourist official) I had to struggle and kick my way into the conversation only to have my comments politely disregarded.

The worst was when we got a chance for a free sailing trip. The man who showed us over the boat simply refused to accept the fact that I, rather than one of my male companions, was going to be the skipper. The fact that I was the only one with any experience of sailing was obviously not an adequate explanation. Mooring the boat, especially if it involved anything tricky, attracted little groups of men on the quayside all very evidently willing me to make a total mess of it. There was embarrassment, shame and a smidgeon of disgust when the boat glided smoothly in.

Most of my time in Yugoslavia was spent exploring the very beautiful coastline, using the cheap and efficient bus service and equally good ferry system to reach the Adriatic Islands. I camped virtually everywhere. The campsites were good, you get very little hassle and there's plenty of other tourists if you want to join up with people. The only disadvantage is that they're often a long trek from the town centre. It's not much more expensive to stay in a pension (lists can be obtained from the local tourist offices).

My favourite place was quite definitely Rab Island. Its town is spread along a long peninsula of land, cutting a distinctive silhouette with its three elegant campaniles. Frothing green seems to cap every balcony and terrace and little cobbled streets wind everywhere. But it's not just twee and idyllic, there's also a lively street atmosphere which starts with the evening *corso*, when visitors and townspeople pack the local bars and outdoor restaurants, and continues late into the night. Most Yugoslav women are home by around midnight and staying up later can feel quite risky. It's never a good idea to hang around drinking bars where there are only men. I have heard women describing all-out fights where they've had to cut and run for safety.

Pag town and Island, further to the east, were fascinating. Barren, almost lunar mountains loom around the town, their sole inhabitants being sheep. It's a quirky old place where everything tastes of salt – cheese, milk, even tap water – and where old women in national dress sit out on their doorsteps making lace.

You may be warned, as I was, against going to Kosovo, by far the poorest, least touristed region. There were riots there in 1981 after students demonstrated against high unemployment and what seemed to be cosmetic attempts by central government to boost the regional economy. The majority are of Albanian origin and wish to maintain, in the face of increasingly repressive measures by the police, their separate cultural identity. As I never went, I can't say whether the risks involved in travelling alone in this area are any greater – certainly you'll be more conspicuous and it's more likely that you'll be defined (and limited) by Islamic influenced custom. Explore and stay flexible and you'll get the best overall impression of the country. In general terms the Yugoslavs are very proud of their relatively young nation, there's a strong sense that they helped to build it. Tito is affectionately remembered in the form of monolithic representations of his name scoured out of hillsides or erected on enormous billboards which can be seen for miles. But for the tourist at least this sort of propaganda never feels oppressive.

TRAVEL NOTES

Languages Serbo-Croat is the main language, followed by Slovene and Macedonian. German is widely spoken in the north, but except in tourist resorts few people anywhere speak more than a few words of English.

Transport Buses are plentiful and incredibly cheap, but it's still best to book a seat in advance as they get very crowded. Apart from the north-west, trains are maddeningly slow. Hitching is difficult as few Yugoslavs are prepared to give lifts to foreigners, and it may well pose other problems too.

Accommodation Private rooms are the cheapest option. Some houses have signs, but you can get a list from the local tourist office or just ask around. Make sure you establish the price before settling in. Hotels prices are strictly controlled, but more expensive. Campsites, mainly on the coast, tend to be huge and, again, highly organised, but it's not worth taking the risk of camping rough – it's illegal and quite possibly dangerous.

Special problems Yugoslav men can be very persistent. Be firm from the beginning and you should manage to avoid aggressive situations. If you're travelling alone, avoid bars and walking about late at night. Even in large cities 'nice' women are expected to stay indoors after 11pm.

Guides Martin Dunford and Jack Holland, *The Rough Guide to Yugoslavia*, (Routledge & Kegan Paul, 1985). Specifically geared towards the independent traveller and packed with useful information.

CONTACTS
No information received.

BOOKS
Rebecca West, *Black Lamb and Grey Falcon*, (1938, Papermac 1982). Beautifully written and packed with insights into Yugoslavia before the Second World War.

Thanks to Fiona Lorimer for part of the introduction.

Chapter Four

EASTERN EUROPE AND THE SOVIET UNION

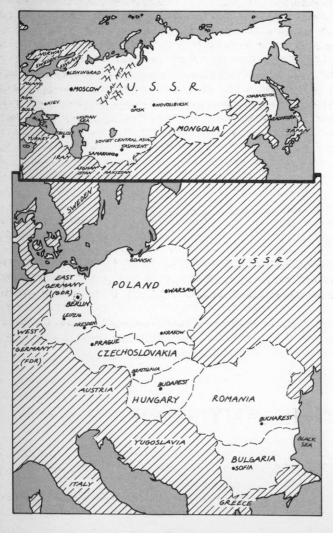

Travel in the **Eastern bloc** countries can be problematic and tedious, reinforcing all the media myths of a controlling state bureaucracy. But it can also be rewarding and – with a few reservations – relatively routine. **Hungary** in particular actively promotes tourism, as much for independent travellers as tour groups; **East Germany**, once you're past the frontier, offers a fairly wide network of hotels and campsites which are normally well run and good value; and in the **USSR**, which you *are* likely to visit in a group, the restrictions imposed by Intourist do nothing to prevent you wandering off within a city on your own. You will be more conspicuous, as a Westerner and as a woman traveller, in **Poland**, **Czechoslovakia**, **Romania** and, outside its Black Sea resorts, **Bulgaria**, and you will sometimes need considerable sensitivity when making personal contacts (and in dealing with food/consumer shortages). Do not, however, allow the cold war images of a homogeneous and drab life 'behind the curtain', with close monitoring of all visitors, to deter you. The communist apparatus has been adapted to every country it is imposed upon – from rigid East German orthodoxy to Hungarian tolerance of a degree of private enterprise – whilst cultural diversity in Eastern Europe (and, obviously, the Soviet republics) is at least as great as in the West.

Paradoxically, the conservatism of many Eastern European and Soviet communities may create most difficulties. The concept of women travelling alone (or together) isn't always understood. Most commonly this just results in courtesy and concern at your well-being but there can be resentment too, at your 'unnaturalness' and freedom to come and go. Travel, though, except in Turkish/Islamic influenced Bulgaria is unlikely to involve any more sexual harassment than you'd experience in Northern Europe and it is very rarely unsafe. What can be hard to contend with is the fairly persistent black market currency harassment, which sometimes carries sexual overtones and can easily verge on intimidation or threat.

We have unfortunately received no substantial account on **Romania**, the poorest country of the bloc. We hope to include coverage in the next edition.

EAST GERMANY (GDR)

East Germany – the **German Democratic Republic** – has an austere reputation in the West. Its government is one of the most effectively pro-Soviet in the Communist bloc; propaganda (against West German/US capitalist imperialism) is all-pervasive; and its frontiers, the Berlin Wall included, are renowned for hostile police and inflexible bureaucracy. Move beyond these factors, though, and you'll find GDR (or DDR as it's written in German) surprising in its interest and in its opportunities for travel, which is cheap and easy. The nation preserves a great deal of 'old German' culture, and several of the grand historic cities, within its boundaries. And, from the feminist viewpoint, it is one of the most radical countries in Europe.

GDR has changed drastically since the war – from a wartorn country, 'liberated' and occupied by Soviet forces, to a successful modern socialist state. Initially its economic recovery lagged behind that of the 'other Germany'. But what was at stake was not just the rebuilding of a country brought to its knees by war but the staging of a socialist revolution, involving the complete reorganisation of society and of the economy. It is now the richest country in Eastern Europe and the ninth industrial nation in the world.

Women have a relatively high status and are represented at more levels of the workplace than in other Eastern bloc countries. Their role in the state's re-formation appears to have been both recognised and valued, and women's rights within socialism have become a subject of much public and private debate. This is most immediately evident from the scope and distribution of East German feminist writing – see Susan Bassnet's piece below – though little of it has yet been translated into English.

◢ Susan Bassnett visited GDR most recently to complete research for her book *Feminist Experiences in Four Cultures*; a writer and poet, she has travelled frequently throughout the country.

Probably the biggest problem about travelling to the GDR is crossing the border. It is often time-consuming, involves standing in queues in squalid surroundings and evokes all sorts of paranoid feelings. Because of the sheer ugliness of most of the arrival procedures, Western journalists have tended to describe the whole country in the same terms. It is worth persevering through the frontier posts if only to prove to oneself that, once you have arrived, the image of the GDR as drab, grey and repressive, is predominantly a media construct with little basis in reality.

Despite being a model socialist country, in many respects GDR is typical of an older Germany. Outside Berlin the pace of life is fairly slow and collective farming has done little to change the face of rural life. There are some fascinating places to visit: the northern Baltic coast, for example, which has good beaches, many of them naturist; and the historic cities of central and southern Germany – Leipzig, Weimar, home of Goethe and Schiller, Jena, Meissen and, of course, Dresden, where the magnificent art gallery stands close to the bombed out remains of a great palace, which has been left as a monument to the fire-bombing that killed tens of thousands of people in 1945.

Travel within the GDR is unproblematic. In all the years that I have been going there I have never encountered any sexual harassment, which makes it unique in my experience. Whether travelling the length of the country by train or walking through the centre of Berlin late at night alone, I have never once had any negative experiences and other women I know can testify to the same. Nevertheless, it would be absurd to assume that sexual harassment and assault is non-existent. I have been told of incidents of both in northern seaports, and a few years ago, when I was researching the position of women in GDR society, the most common complaint of working women in particular was their drunken, violent husbands.

Of all the Eastern European countries I have visited, GDR is the one where the position of women is the most developed. Crèche facilities are good, women have entered the professions in huge numbers, dominating some such as medicine, and the public status of women is high. This is due in part to the fact that after the Second World War, when the GDR was founded, so many men had been killed or gone missing that the country was virtually rebuilt by women – there is a statue in the centre of Berlin that commemorates the women who cleared the rubble of the bombed city. As a result, women have a high public profile and can live, travel and eat in public alone without occasioning any surprise or being automatically treated as sexual prey. Within the family, however, the situation is more complex. Old attitudes die hard, and it is notable that the food queues in supermarkets – Germans seem to queue for everything – are largely made up of women and younger men. Men of the older generation still leave cooking and housework largely to women, and in this respect things are little different from anywhere else in Europe.

The country has no organised feminist movement as such, and many women express some ambiguity about what they will often describe as 'bourgeois feminism'. There are, however, women's trade union associations and community groups – and, talking among these, they appeared to me to be principally concerned with discussing problems of discrimination at work and difficulties within relationships. However, one aspect of Western feminism does cause problems for some GDR women, and that is the question of women's right to define their own sexuality. Lesbianism is still regarded as marginal and suspect, though I did find a striking difference in attitude between women under the age of 25 and those who were older.

Women travelling in the GDR should make a special effort to visit Ravensbruck, the concentration camp exclusively for women and children, north of Berlin on the way to Rostock. This appalling place is preserved as a shrine to humanity and also to sisterhood. In the exhibits in the museum, the toys made of pieces of rag carefully stitched with hair testify to a will not only to survive but to survive as giving, loving individuals. I found Ravensbruck a horrifying but important experience, and going there was a pilgrimage rather than tourism.

One of the striking features of GDR life is the high literacy level. Bookshops tend to sell out of new books immediately because of the rush of customers. In 1983 I was in Weimar when Irmtraud Morgner's new book *Amanda* came out, and managed to get a copy only because a friend rushed out of the hotel as soon as we heard about it, and ran round to the bookshop. Morgner is one of the many excellent GDR women writers, most of whom have not yet been translated into English. Christa Wolf is a notable exception (her latest novel, *Cassandra*, is published by Virago), but Morgner, Helga Konigsdorf, Renate Feyl, Sara Kirsch and many others are still relatively unknown to non-German speakers. The sudden increase in the number of women writing novels has been so striking that critics have begun to talk about the 'phenomenon' of the GDR feminist novel. When Maxie Wander's book *Guten Morgen, du Schone* (Good Morning, Beautiful) came out in 1977, it caused an unprecedented furore. A montage of scripted recordings of women talking about their lives and the problems they encountered in public and private as a woman, the book raised the question of the meaning of feminism *within* socialism and aroused an enormous public response.

Manda Green has lived in Leipzig and visits the GDR for holidays and, whenever possible, for work.

It is difficult as a traveller to get any real understanding of East German society – the similarities, not to mention persistent propaganda and counter-propaganda blur your objectivity. Also, unless you have friends or relatives, you are obliged to stay in the state-owned *Interhotels* which can isolate you, although there is nothing in fact to stop you mixing with Germans. Many are keen to have contact with Westerners, some seeing you as a source of hard currency to spend in the Intershops, others motivated by curiosity and *Fernweh* (the opposite to homesickness – GDR citizens can only travel in a handful of 'brother countries'). Another barrier to understanding GDR is the tendency to think of it as West Germany's poorer cousin. Whilst comparison is inevitable, particularly if you come via Berlin, you need to be especially sensitive to people's strong sense of identity as GDR citizens.

Travelling alone in the GDR I found a similar 'background sexism' to that in Britain – irritating but something you're used to dealing with. Certain places are obviously more fraught than others, the infamous *Mitropa* (railway bars) for instance, and the street lighting of most towns is usually abysmal. But on the whole I felt less constrained and threatened in GDR than in other parts of Europe. The reason for this didn't actually occur to me until I later arrived in Frankfurt and walked the streets, lined with 24-hour sex shows and a parade of prostitutes. There is simply no public, institutionalised sex industry in the GDR – even images of women in advertising are controlled. This gave me a feeling of freedom which I take for granted when I am there but value highly in retrospect.

That apart, my impressions of the country were determined far more by being a 'capitalist' than by being a woman. I became aware that I was making judgments based on all sorts of assumptions and expectations, simply not shared by GDR citizens. For example, I was horrified to learn that students and apprentices are given a planned job years before they qualify; they were shocked that we have to start looking for one ourselves at the end of our training. I suppose it boils down to the fact that they expect security at the expense of some freedom, whilst for us it's vice versa. These are distinctions you need to recognise fast if you're hoping to 'see what it's really like'; as an outsider, the ills – and benefits – of living in the GDR are often invisible and won't directly affect you.

My most clear-cut impression was that although the GDR is a self-professed atheist state, socialism has virtually taken the place of an established religion. Initially I was reluctant to acknowledge this – it seemed too naïvely commie-bashing – but the longer I stayed the more parallels I came to see with a 'church state'. It has its own scripture, prophets, priesthood and even an unwritten bull of party infallibility enshrined in the columns of the national newspaper *Neues Deutschland* – well worth reading to compare the Eastern bloc style of newspeak with ours.

It's hard to escape the state's propaganda – there are agit-prop placards and banners everywhere exhorting the citizen to higher productivity or 'socialist patriotism and proletarian internationalism', lamblasting capitalism, imperialism and revanchism, or expressing adulation of the Soviet Union (another religious parallel: USSR = the Holy Land). The quantity and tenor of the slogans vary according to the international situation. My first visit coincided with the anniversary of Marx's death and the run-up to cruise deployment, so after a couple of months 'the teachings of Karl Marx are all-powerful because they are true' and 'we are the bulwark against the imperialist warlords' were indelibly stamped on my mind.

During my last visit, just before the resumption of arms control talks in Geneva, such aggressive slogans were conspicuous by their absence, which was widely interpreted as a gesture of conciliation. The FDJ (Free German Youth) Whitsun peace rally seemed to me, however, a tired, hackneyed pantomime. All the placards bore variations on the official theme of 'peace despite the NATO arms race' and a friend and I were stopped six times by the *Stasi* (State Security Service) and FDJ organisers for carrying the innocuous banner 'east/west – one world'.

If Christian religion is upstaged by the state religion, it nevertheless plays a vital role in East German society. The churches are one of the few (some would say only) organisations which enjoy some freedom. As a body they are less outspoken and radical than the Roman Catholic Church in Poland, indeed they conscientiously reject the opposition role which the Western press and the Party cast for them, emphasising that they don't want to 'work against or alongside the socialist state but within it'. Their importance lies in the fact that they have become an umbrella organisation which shelters some protest groups, e.g. environmental, peace and women. The scope of action of these groups is obviously limited and they are a fairly recent phenomenon, but their existence is a very significant development.

My visits to GDR have given me not only some insight into 'the other side' but also a greater sense of perspective about 'our side'. It may seem crazy to talk about culture shock, travelling a few kilometres from one industrial country to another (which, in the case of West Germany, shares some common culture and history) but whenever I return to East Germany I am overawed by just how strange – and familiar – it is.

TRAVEL NOTES

Language German; few people speak English.

Transport Reasonably straightforward. Public transport is subsidised and cheap; hitching is no more or less risky than in Britain but can be a slow process as there are less cars on the road.

Accommodation You usually have to stay in state-owned Interhotels and campsites; most, however, are good value.

Special problems Visas are obligatory and the ease of getting one is directly proportional to how much the authorities will earn out of your visit: if you book into one of the state-owned hotels you could get your visa authorisation by return of post; if you are hoping to stay privately with friends, you will have to apply at least 8 weeks in advance and give full details of where and with whom you'll be staying.

You must *register* with the police within 24 hours of arrival and deregister a few days before you leave. They are very rigid about this – any delay can cost you a 25Dm fine and a lot of hassle. Also be aware that GDR citizens are officially supposed to report any contact with 'capitalists'. This is widely ignored, but currency offences are treated very seriously, so you should avoid black market dealings. In any case, you may have more money than you know what to do with after the compulsory exchange of 25Dm per day demanded from all visitors over 16.

Guide *Let's Go Europe* (Columbus Press, US) has a short section on East Germany.

CONTACTS
Autonomous women's organisations are not officially recognised.

BOOKS
Christa Wolf, *A Model Childhood* (1968, Virago 1983), *Cassandra* (1983, Virago 1984): Childhood explores the 'ordinary' experience of life under Nazism.
See Susan Bassnett's piece for novels/feminist writings in German.

POLAND

In the early 1980s, events in **Poland** made world headlines. The rise and subsequent repression of the free trade union Solidarity became the cause célèbre of the Western press, and for a while everything Polish was fashionably radical. But if the outrage which greeted General Jaruzelski's imposition of martial law was genuine it was also ineffective, and media interest since then has slumped once more into indifference. Poland meanwhile has returned to the old 'normality' – its government still intensely resented, its economy floundering, and the black market a mainstay at all levels of society.

Most Western travellers who go to Poland do so to see friends or relatives, or on educational/cultural exchanges. Few places – the beautiful city of Krakow is one – are used to tourists and, travelling around, you'll have to get used to being stared at as a rare Western outsider. On the whole, however, you should find the country safe, incredibly cheap (it is hard to find ways to spend the obligatory £10 a day) and relaxed – Poles have a justly famous reputation for hospitality. The one problem you may come up against is harassment from drunks – alcoholism over the last few years has reached unprecedented levels.

Socially (and politically) Poland remains a profoundly Catholic country, and **women's roles** as mothers and homemakers are deeply engrained. Most women also work outside the home, and have to combine this with running a house and looking after a family – all-consuming tasks, made ever more difficult by the frequent shortages of food and basic consumer goods. Men for the most part consider themselves exempt from domestic labour. And whilst these attitudes persist, the legislative reforms, such as maternity leave (extended to two years by the efforts of Solidarity) and the provision of day nurseries in most workplaces, seem unlikely to bring much relief. There is no feminist movement in the Western sense of the word, although there are official, state-run women's organisations like the *Women's League* – most of them very bureaucratic and limited in scope.

▰ **Laura Longrigg has visited Poland twice, the first time during the heady days of Solidarity in 1981 and then in the summer of 1984.**

I find it hard when I write about Poland to keep my emotion, enthusiasm and very deep concern for the country in check. Most of my impressions are bound up with the highly valued friendships that I made with Polish women and men during my two visits. For me the repression of Solidarity and the continuing economic crisis are linked with images of these friends – resilient and generous, attempting to maintain against all odds some belief in the future and, as women, coping with the increasingly impossible burdens of providing for families while keeping a full-time job.

It's not difficult to make friends in Poland. Poles generally are renowned for their hospitality and it's not just their own that you're pressed to accept but also that of their cousin in Gdansk, friend from student days in Krakow and so on. The immediate practical problem you face is the language. The people you are most likely to come into contact with — waiters, ticket collectors, taxi drivers — won't understand English, another reason for remaining open to any offers of help you might receive.

To begin with I found my appointed role as an honoured guest somewhat disconcerting. I was constantly aware that the speciailties of the house offered to me on the best china had meant hours of extra queuing and the use of valuable ration cards. I also knew that having access to Western currency made me far richer than my hosts and hostesses. In the *Pewex* or international shops, which only accept Western currency, you will not only find 'luxury items' like washing machines and radios but also mundane things like washing powder and toothpaste which often won't have been in normal shops for months. Pewex may seem wonderfully cheap to Western travellers but to a Pole £10 represents several months' hard saving and for that reason I always found shopping in them a very uncomfortable experience. I tried to balance things out a bit by taking a supply of small presents — soap, coffee, nappies, tights and vitamin pills — and stubbornly insisted that people told me (they would never otherwise ask) what I could send them from the West when I returned home. On my first visit to Poland I stayed with a family in Szczecin and gave them some bubble bath. They seemed pleased but a bit mystified. Later I discovered that their bath was only ever used for washing clothes.

Travelling alone on trains and even wandering about the streets of the larger towns I felt relatively safe. The only harassment I experienced was from drunks and in those cases other Poles quickly cut in and chased them off. I did sometimes have the feeling of being an object of curiosity — furtive glances were cast at my, I had thought, none too obvious Western clothing and at my holdall bag, a ludicrous object shaped like a Coca-Cola tin.

A fairly common mistake that people make is in assuming that membership of Solidarity means any particular sympathy or commitment to the political ideologies of the West. This became clear to me when I made the pilgrimage to Gdansk to see the newly erected Solidarity monument. The dreaded Coca-Cola bag stood out like a beacon and provoked open and aggressive hostility from the shift of shipyard workers who filed past me on their way to work. A more difficult affiliation to sort out is that between Solidarity and the Catholic church. They seem to me profoundly linked as signifiers of a powerful subculture, which has developed in a society wholly distrustful of and alienated from its ruling authorities.

Resistance and opposition have gone underground since Solidarity's demise but they're very much alive and show themselves in what, to the Westerner, might seem surprising ways. In the summer of 1984, in the northern town of Slupsk, I was taken to see a wooden cross hanging on the outside wall of an old church. The locals say that on 12 December 1981 – the night Jaruzelski 'declared war on Polish society' – the cross started to bleed. Although it was after midnight and raining, there was half a dozen men and women standing below it, heads bowed in prayer, beside a rack of lit candles. Banked against the wall of the church were about thirty vases of fresh flowers. It seemed both a scene of mourning and of defiance, and made a powerful impression on me.

For Polish women, who have only limited representation in Solidarity, as well as in government and the party, life is very much restricted by the expectations of a deeply religious, conservative society. Women are accepted in the workplace but careerist ambitions tend to be treated with suspicion. Often there's no choice: the sheer logistics of queuing for food and keeping a home tends to preclude taking on the extra work commitments that would lead to promotion. Typically, Polish women are treated with great courtesy by men – much is made of hand-kissing and the giving of flowers – and women are expected to play out their complementary role by keeping to the passive, submissive stereotype.

Staying with Polish friends I found myself initially drawn into male company, taking part in the drinking sessions and rowdy intellectual and political debates. They were attentive, mostly respectful and occasionally flirtatious. The women by contrast seemed quiet, reserved and, I often felt, disapproving. Many are bored, lonely and terribly tired, weighed down by the daily struggle to bring up children in cramped, crowded and deprived conditions. No wonder they distrust these affluent Western women who, having none of their constraints, are able to arrive and monopolise their husbands and menfriends with their Western experiences and curiosity. Tell a Polish woman that she's oppressed and she'd like to throw you down the stairs (that is, if she wasn't so polite). Take time to talk about the day-to-day issues, help out with the children, the shopping and the cooking and you may develop a firm friendship. You'll also be surprised to learn that, once she overcomes her shyness, her English is usually much better than you'd first thought.

Visiting Poland since martial law can be a depressing experience. For many Poles, everything on 12 December 1981 went black – their vision of the future, projected briefly by Solidarity, was smashed. Travellers often return with horror stories of the everyday reality: the queues, ration cards, three generations crowded into a two-room flat, ten-year waiting lists for flats, scarcity of medicines and the frighteningly high rate of alcoholism. Yet both times that I returned from Poland it was on a high.

I came home impressed and inspired by the warmth, courage and patience I was shown, by the sense of humour (often disconcertingly black), and the emotion and the sensitivity I shared.

TRAVEL NOTES

Language Polish. Almost everybody learns Russian at school, although most don't like admitting to it. Some people speak English and older people often speak German.

Transport Mostly by train: always travel *expresobowe* and never *osobowe*, which is the slow train (5 hrs between Katowice and Krakow, for instance, a distance of 60km). Hitching is quite safe, but uncommon. You may often be expected to pay towards (rationed) petrol. Public transport in towns is cheap and frequent and so are taxis.

Accommodation You have to stay in state-run hotels, which can be booked through the official travel agency, *Orbis*. Some may only accept payment in foreign currency.

Special problems Shortages: things you take for granted are unavailable, including: sanitary towels, tampons, paper tissues, toilet paper, shampoo, washing powder, contraceptives, aspirin, coffee, toothpaste, toothbrushes. Western medicines can only be bought from the Pewex shops – most Poles have to rely on herbal remedies.

Every foreign tourist is obliged to change £10 a day into Polish zloty. As the wage of a university professor is about £15 a month, you will probably have more zloty than you can spend. Tourist hotels often ask you to pay in Western currency, and in the Pewex, you always do. You will be constantly approached by people who want to buy your Western currency offering a far better rate than the official one, but it is *very* risky.

Guide *Let's Go Europe* (St Martin's Press, US). Again a small section – but a general reliable one for current travel practicalities.

CONTACTS
No autonomous women's organisations exist, to our knowledge.

BOOKS
Janina Baumann, *Winter in the Morning: A Young Girl's Life in the Warsaw Ghetto and Beyond* (Virago 1986). Account of resilience and courage during the Warsaw siege and Nazi occupation.

Anna Swirszczynska – Poems. Her collections, *I am a Female* (1972) and *Building the Barricade* (1974), have been bestsellers in Poland.

For background on Solidarity and its aftermath: Neil Ascherson, *Polish August* (Penguin, 1982).

Thanks to Barbara Karpowicz.

CZECHOSLOVAKIA

Czechoslovakia is one of the richest and most industrialised countries of the Eastern bloc. It is also ruled by one of the most inflexible, Soviet-orientated governments. As far as many Westerners are concerned, the country lived and died with the events of the 1968 Prague spring – eight months in which Dubček's highly liberal regime was allowed to flourish before being cut off by Russian invasion. Today, with the exception of a fairly large number of West Germans, the country attracts few visitors from the non-communist world.

If you do go — and Prague alone is enough to warrant the effort — you'll probably soon notice the wariness and suspicion that has governed Czech society since 1968 (and, with religious intolerance, and vicious Nazi occupation, through much of the present century). As a Western visitor it is important to be sensitive about making contacts and in playing straight on the bureaucracy which, as in East Germany, involves changing a minimum (currently £12) sum of currency for each day of your stay. It is these factors that are likely to be the most limiting, though sexual harassment, especially from drunks in the cities, can again be a problem. In general, however, Czech men seem to treat women (in public at least) with extreme, almost studied courtesy; if you don't subscribe to the passive, 'feminine' stereotype you may find this in itself a strain.

The double burdens of paid work and domestic duties are as evident for **women** in Czechoslovakia as in any other Eastern bloc country, and financial incentives encourage Czechs to marry young. No feminist organisation exists and if an autonomous group were to emerge it would probably be condemned by the government for undermining 'social solidarity'.

◪ **Susan Bassnett (see East Germany) visited Czechoslovakia on a research scholarship.**

Visiting Czechoslovakia for the first time after several visits to the GDR, I was struck by the enormous difference between these two neighbouring socialist states. It may be due to their very different histories — Czechoslovakia has suffered centuries of religious intolerance, occupation by foreign powers, the suppression of the Czech and Slovak languages until very recently and a particularly brutal Nazi invasion in 1939. All these factors have combined to create an atmosphere of intrigue and wariness, the sort of feelings expressed by Franz Kafka, who was, after all, a native Czech.

This may sound melodramatic, but actually is not. I lost count of how many times, when shown a table in a restaurant with friends, they would deliberately choose to sit as far away from the table recommended by the waiter as they could get. The explanation, always given as a cynical joke, was that the waiter must have some reason for wanting us to sit where he was suggesting. Or, to give another example, it was impossible to ever arrange to meet anyone in Prague inside a café or restaurant because nobody ever knew when anywhere might be open. Time and again I would go to the café in which I had had coffee the day before, only to find it closed, and then call round again later to discover that it had reopened. Everyone I met assured me that this was government policy because it meant that no cliques could form and be certain of a regular place to meet and possibly plan sedition.

In such a climate, the position of women is ambiguous. I met with great courtesy – hand-kissing is still very prevalent, as is the giving of tiny bunches of flowers or even single blooms. All over the place I would see women carrying these little bunches of flowers, and in restaurants, whenever I arrived with my own bunches, waiters would automatically bring little vases. But I did encounter sexual harassment during my visit, and had to devise ways of dealing with it. Travelling home to the hotel in the suburbs of Prague at night, I always wore an old headscarf and avoided eye contact, but still was accosted by drunks on the tram. Alcoholism is very obvious and in the cities there are always drunken men – I never saw any women – staggering round quite early in the day. Moving around Prague or Bratislava, I felt the same wariness I always feel in Italian cities or even in British ones at night alone, a feeling that I have never had in the GDR.

As in other Eastern bloc countries, I was often approached and asked either to change money or sell goods, but I noticed that this only happened when I spoke English with friends. So long as I spoke either German, which was widely understood in Prague and western Czechoslovakia, or halting Czech, I was never hassled. Speaking English, particularly in Prague and particularly at night, caused some very heavy cases of harassment, and it was clear to me that the currency harassment was being linked to sexual harassment unless there was a man with me.

Despite the claims of equality, Czech society is still very much a world in which men see their role as protective and dominant. One incident, shortly after I arrived in Prague, is a case in point. I had gone to one of the many cellar wine bars, with a man who was acting as my academic guide. I had asked to be shown round the bars, he had agreed to take me and I took it for granted that I would foot the bill. However, when I called the waiter over and asked for the bill, total silence fell in the cellar and everyone stared at me. The waiter was embarrassed, my guide was appalled. Afterwards, he explained that it is unacceptable for a woman to pay for a man in public, that everyone must have assumed that he was my fancy man since I was obviously foreign and he was letting me pay the bill. After that, we agreed that I would pass him the money under the table when I wanted to pay my share. It was like stepping backwards in time, and I found it hard to square this kind of behaviour with my expectations of a socialist society.

The Kafkaesque atmosphere of Prague is increased also by the fact that, at least for my generation, the events of 1968 are still a vivid memory. I talked to people about the Russian invasion, and found universal guardedness and cynicism. I met writers who no longer publish and teachers who no longer teach, and the spot in the city centre, where Jan Palach burned himself to death as a gesture of protest was pointed out to me, together with instructions not to linger near it. Nevertheless, I did not meet large numbers of people eager to live in the West. Rather,

I consistently encountered the opposite, with contempt expressed for those who 'sell out' to the myth of free speech and high living standards in Western society. Attitudes to organised women's movements were also discussed and again the general feeling seemed to be that there were other, more pressing matters to be dealt with first before tackling the obviously huge issue of changing the role and status of women in Czech society.

Anglo-Saxon tradition has tended to consider Czechoslovakia as a remote, marginal country, with an undistinguished past. But the Czechs see themselves as continuing a highly developed cultural tradition, and their country well deserves visiting. Despite the slightly paranoid feelings that developed during my stay, I loved the magnificent Tatra mountains, Bratislava and the medieval cities and castles of Bohemia, and especially Prague, which must be one of the most beautiful cities anywhere in the world.

TRAVEL NOTES

Languages Czech and Slovak – similar but distinct languages. German is quite widely spoken (especially among older people); Russian is the second school language.

Transport Buses (slightly faster) and trains are both efficient; for longer journeys book tickets a day in advance. Hitching is accepted and worth trying if you feel confident.

Accommodation Organised by the state through the tourist organisation *Cedok* and student travel bureau, *CKM*; the latter often provides very good value hostels and hotels. Campsites are everywhere and cheap.

Special problems You must change money at the border to cover all of your stay (at the current rate of £12 minimum per day). Exemptions are made only for students on Czech work-camps.

Black market transactions aren't very advisable.

Guides *Let's Go Europe* (St Martin's Press, US) is useful for basics. Ctibor Rybar's *Czechoslovakia Guidebook* and *Prague Guidebook* (Olympia, Prague, 1982/1973) are comprehensive on historic/cultural details.

CONTACTS
No autonomous women's organisations.

BOOKS
Alena Hei Hinger *Women and State Socialism: Sex Inequality in the Soviet Union and Czechoslovakia* (McGill, Ontario, 1980).

Zdena Tomlin, *Stalin's Shoe* (Hutchinson, 1986). First novel by Czech dissident, now living in Britain, which draws from life and events leading up to Prague 1968 (and the subsequent collapse).

Hilda Scott, *Women and Socialism: Experiences from Eastern Europe* (Allison & Busby, 1976). Highly illuminating for Czech attitudes.

For background reading: Milan Kundera, *The Book of Laughter and Forgetting* (Penguin, 1983), other novels, and *Prague: A Disappearing Poem* (in Granta 17, Penguin 1985); Franz Kafka; and Jaroslav Hasek, *The Good Soldier Svejk* (1921, Penguin 1974).

Thanks to Jane Harrison, Sarah Chaplin and Angela Spindler-Brown.

HUNGARY

Hungary successfully promotes tourism. In the summer months there are said to be more tourists in the country than Hungarians. Most of them are from neighbouring Austria and West Germany but there are an increasing number too from Britain and the US. Development, except for a few major resorts around Lake Balaton, is fairly low-key and well integrated. It is possible to rent rooms privately in people's houses; the official currency rate is similar to the unofficial one; and the bureaucracy is fairly easy and routine – including no minimum currency change requirement.

The country's current popularity with Western visitors probably owes as much to its political liberalism as to the attractions of Budapest and the less travelled countryside. Socially there's a notably relaxed atmosphere, with little of the East-West wariness of contact, and in Budapest it's possible to enter into a kind of alternative subculture – centred around the numerous street cafés and fledgling music and fashion scene.

As a byproduct of liberalisation – Hungary's 'market socialism' includes advertising and a degree of private ownership – women are under increasing pressure to subscribe to glamorous, fashionable media images. Representations in advertising and on postcards seem dated in comparison to the West but essentially as exploitative and, unlike in the West, there is little debate concerning the ways in which women are defined and limited by these images. The official *National Alliance of Hungarian Women* supports government measures such as equal pay for equal work but is unable to pursue any separate agenda (such as discrimination within the workplace). No other **women's organisation** is authorised and although there have been occasional independent demonstrations – such as those against the 1973 law to restrict abortion – no autonomous group can survive long.

▰ **Jill Denton has spent much of the last two years travelling in Hungary, Romania and Bulgaria, researching *The Rough Guide to Eastern Europe*.**

Several reasons make Hungary the best place to begin a trip around Eastern Europe. It's close, cheap, easy to enter and has a well-developed tourist industry. German is a common second langauge and English is becoming more popular, particularly with young people.

As I approached the border my usual cynicism gave way to the vague but hopeful expectation that in Hungary at least, sexual equality would be more than party rhetoric. The first thing I noticed were the adverts in Budapest station restaurant. Women's legs and breasts leapt out at me – images which I'd got used to in the West but which seemed to jar in the context of state socialism. The real-life women seemed mainly occupied in waitressing or cleaning jobs or were otherwise looking after children. It's a familiar plot but one which, in the absence of autonomous feminist activity, goes largely unchallenged.

The friends I made – mainly educated working women aged 20–25 years – were horrified when I declared myself a feminist. It had become a bogey-word associated with their mothers' tales of post-war reforms, when all the 'natural order' of the largely agricultural society seemed threatened by state-run nurseries and jobs in industry. My friends had grown up accepting these reforms but remained conservative in their attitudes and uncritical of the expectations they now had to fulfil – like holding a permanent job and doing virtually all housework.

Access to the pill is highly valued – it being the only available form of contraception – though little information is given as to its possible side-effects. Maternity leave of three years on 70 per cent of previous income, with job-back guarantee, is relished both as a break from what is frequently low-paid, boring work; and for the social approval contingent on being a good mother. Many of the women I met studied, though there is considerable under-representation on most teaching staff and in the traditionally 'male' fields of science and technology. Women may now live with their boyfriends but children are usually born within marriage and there are still innumerable obstacles to bringing up a child alone. One woman I knew attempted to do this but received almost no support from her friends or extended family. Another, striking out for more independence from her live-in lover, was warned by female friends about pushing him too far. These two women are still requesting feminist literature. The others mostly agreed that there are more pressing problems than women's liberation and marked me an obsessive eccentric.

As far as travel goes, I found Budapest the least threatening capital I know, even at night. I also felt fine hitching and cycling around the country, despite once being flashed at. From time to time I did have problems dealing with the overly 'gallant' man; 'csokolom' ('I kiss your hand') is the opener, then they insist on paying for everything . . . which lurches easily towards harassment, particularly if you speak no Hungarian or German. A less expected problem was the often over-bearing solicitude of well-meaning families. They'd watch me put up my tent with one eye cast for my escort, then reproach my mother for letting me wander – flatly refusing to believe that I actually enjoyed being alone.

◪ **Dorothy Kidd visited Budapest and Lake Balaton during a month's holiday in Eastern Europe; she travelled with three women friends.**

The queue for the official tourist office at Budapest train station was so long that we decided to take the room offered to us by a tall woman who spoke good English. Eva, as she was called, turned out to be a researcher in her late thirties, and needed the extra cash to buy herself a bicycle for the cottage she had inherited on Lake Balaton. She lived in a tower block on a housing estate in the northern suburbs of Budapest: a twenty-minute bus ride from the city centre and very similar to the estates you see on the outskirts of most European cities.

We were all four to sleep in her lounge-cum-bedroom; there was also a small room permanently let to a local girl whom we never actually saw, I suspect because either she or Eva did not want us to meet. Eva herself slept on her kitchen floor on which she probably found it impossible to stretch right out as she was so tall. It made us wonder how families who are less well paid manage.

We spent the next two days in Budapest, which, with its medieval quarter and beautiful nineteenth-century buildings still has a sense of Europe as it was under the Habsburg Empire. There are plenty of cafés and restaurants in the city centre and we spent long hours just sitting around watching the street life. Coffee in Hungary is excellent, cheap and very strong. On our third day we made an expedition to Lake Balaton. Eva had praised its beauty often and explained that the ambition of many Hungarians was to own a cottage at one of the holiday resorts which pepper its banks. A two-hour train journey took us to Balaton-Fured, a small resort on its northern shore. Eva had not exaggerated: the sides of the lake were covered in tiny cottages. Though not as beautiful as we had been led to expect, Lake Balaton provided a pleasant respite from sightseeing: Hungary in June is very hot and the water was lovely to bathe in. The lake also offers boat excursions and we took one for part of our return journey, in a small craft packed with other, mainly Hungarian, tourists.

Our final day in Budapest was spent trying to spend all our Hungarian money – it is illegal to take currency out of the country. A large sum was in fact spent on 'bribery coffee'. Eva had said it was very unwise for us to be going on, as we planned, to Romania because of the food shortages it was experiencing and the corruption of its officials. Coffee and chocolate, she suggested, would make suitable bribes should we need to force our way into the country.

Eva had told us she was very anxious to come and work in Britain for a year to improve her English which would in turn improve her promotion prospects. We promised to help her in this and I wrote twice after returning, but had no reply. Maybe the letters didn't arrive, though it is difficult not to think that she may have been forbidden to write back as she was, certainly with us, very outspoken. Her criticism of her country, as ever, centred on the influence of the USSR, and she was particularly anxious that we should realise that Russian missiles were already deployed in Hungarian forests.

TRAVEL NOTES

Language Hungarian – which isn't easy. German is very helpful, particularly for travelling outside Budapest, the only place you'll find English at all widely spoken.

Transport Visas are necessary but are issued to road and air passengers on entering the country; train travellers should apply to a Hungarian embassy (in London at 35 Eaton Place, SW1) a few days before setting out. Travel within Hungary is straightforward, by bus and train; the InterRail pass is valid.

Accommodation The few cheap hotels in Budapest are usually full but the tourist organisation, *Ibusz*, arranges private rooms in addition to 'unofficial'

offers. Around the country, *Turistahaza*, dormitory hostels, are useful and campsites plentiful, as well as the conventional hotel network.

Guide Jill Denton and Dan Richardson, *The Rough Guide to Eastern Europe* (Routledge & Kegan Paul, 1986).

CONTACTS
No autonomous women's organisations.

BOOKS
Volgyes, Ivan and Nancy, *The Liberated Female: Life, Work and Sex in Socialist Hungary* (Westview Press, Boulder, Colorado 1977). Very readable, if a little over-journalistic in places.

BULGARIA

Bulgaria has a thriving tourist industry – but one geared almost exclusively towards package holidays, mainly for Austrians and West Germans. Along the Black Sea, and in the mountains, there are large purpose-built resorts. Travelling elsewhere, in the provincial towns and rural areas, you'll arouse a great deal of curiosity; also, if you look in any way unconventional (very short hair, for instance), you're likely to experience harassment, even to the extent of being shouted at in the streets. Until very recently the country outside the capital, Sofia, was made up of exclusively rural, highly conservative communities, influenced in their attitudes towards women by five hundred years of Turkish/Muslim domination.

Unusually, the Soviet influence in Bulgaria is generally accepted. Bulgarian independence from the Ottoman Empire in the last century was gained with the help of Russian armies and everywhere you come upon Soviet-Bulgarian friendship memorials. Russian is widely spoken as a second language and Soviet culture is very dominant, though the Bulgarian Orthodox Church, too, retains wide influence.

There are no autonomous **women's groups** that we know of in Bulgaria. The state, however, gives high priority to education and childcare, women have access to the pill, and maternity leave (even in comparison with other East European nations) is very generous. But as reforms these appear somewhat tenuous in the face of what are still entrenched conservative values.

▰ **Deirdre Rogers has visited Bulgaria frequently over the last five years –
initially with tourist groups, more recently on teacher exchanges, living
in the flats of Bulgarian colleagues.**

The formal constitution of Bulgaria guarantees many things, amongst
them equality between the sexes. Women, when asked about their
position, confirm their importance: 'Without us the country wouldn't
run'. The country has a chronic labour shortage which goes some way
towards explaining why women are valued in the workplace. There are
women running business enterprises, commercial and technical, and
generally holding responsible positions but, as usual, numbers decrease
the higher up the hierarchy you go. At present, however, the number of
young women reaching higher education is equal to the number of men.

During their military service men do work of social value as well as
basic military training, yet most women are still expected to carry the
full burden of career and family. The division of domestic labour has
become an issue increasingly debated by the growing numbers of highly
educated women. It seems unlikely, however, that their arguments will
reach a wider consensus.

State childcare is well developed in Bulgaria. Visit a kindergarten if
you can. They're very well equipped and use a deliberate programme of
work and socialisation, which sounds very formal and doctrinaire, but
in practice is supportive to the staff, to the parents and most importantly
to the children. I asked a friend's son, just about to do his army service,
about his kindergarten days; he suddenly melted and told me 'It was
paradise.'

Due to the housing shortage, young people, single and married, often
live in the parental flat, and it is not unusual to find three generations in
the same house. I was quite surprised to discover how many Bulgarians
try to own their own home. They can get cheap loans from the state
either to build or buy. As well as municipal building there are building
co-operatives connected with enterprises, institutes or trade unions. There
are also some people living in small flats in Sofia or in other big cities,
who are busily building a holiday home-cum-country cottage on a plot
which may be as far as 60 kilometres away from the city.

In the last forty years the population of Sofia, the capital, has grown
to at least one million. It is surrounded by suburbs, nicknamed 'concrete
bedrooms', most of them new and incomplete. In winter, the yet-to-be-
paved public places are muddy and in summer dusty. The spring brings
out the Saturday work groups: local people who tidy up the winter's
rubbish, plant new grass, trees and parks. A lot of voluntary effort goes
into making defined public spaces beautiful. Yet you can go just round
the corner to find a no man's land of neglected waste ground, and there
are amazing contrasts in levels of care and neglect. Some of the neglect

may be attributable to the uprooted feeling of many urban dwellers. Middle-aged Sofia residents will often tell you that they came from this home town or that home town, possibly two or three hundred kilometres away, and they still feel for home. Their children, however, who were born in Sofia, are much more a part of the place and have participated all their lives in local voluntary work. It is a problem to make a concrete suburb for 140,000 into a home. They are working on it.

You can go anywhere in Sofia at any time and not feel threatened. Walking back to my hotel very late at night with a friend, we discussed safety. Sofia is full of open parks and walkways between the blocks of flats. People work all sorts of shift hours and there is almost always someone coming or going. As far as I could make out, mugging, as such, is unknown. Rape is also very rare (though obviously I couldn't say about rape in the home) and you are unlikely as a single woman tourist to feel personally threatened. What you may encounter are would-be, and for the most part male, illegal currency changers. They tend to hang out in the well-known tourist areas. Either ignore them or express blank incomprehension and they will usually get the message and leave you alone.

Easter 1985 found me in maths teacher Maria's kitchen, colouring the traditional eggs. Everyone has eggs, beautifully painted, to crack at midnight, or give to visitors. Easter time also brings crocuses in mauve drifts to the high alpine meadows and the old black-clad women to the churches. In their sharp elbowed determination to be the first for the Holy Light they are dangerous. They, and the great peasant earth mothers of the market, scare me far more than any thoughts of a 'secret policeman to watch every tourist.' 'Just think for a moment,' said Julia, a retired guide. 'In 1955 we opted for a tourist industry. As well as hotels and resorts it involved building the language schools you visited. Nowadays, we have over ten million visitors each year. Even if we wanted to, with our small population, how could we spy on every tourist?'

TRAVEL NOTES

Language Bulgarian. Russian is widely spoken and understood and you'll go some way with German; English speakers are rare.

Transport Visas must be obtained in advance: in London, the embassy (at 186–188 Queen's Gate Gdns, SW7) takes about 10 days to process them. Once in, trains and buses are slow and can be difficult to work out, but they're cheap enough.

Accommodation As from 1985, Western tourists are not allowed to stay overnight with Bulgarians. This leaves *Balkantourist* hotels (relatively pricey) and camping (much less so) the only real options. Your visa has to be stamped daily and details (and cost) of your accommodation recorded on your exchange slip.

Special problems In tourist areas currency harassment is common, and can appear threatening.

Guide Jill Denton and Dan Richardson, *The Rough Guide to Eastern Europe* (Routledge & Kegan Paul, 1986).

CONTACTS
No autonomous women's
organisations.
Thanks to Jill Denton.

THE SOVIET UNION

In a nation of fifteen separate states, stretching across eight and a half million square miles, generalisations can have only limited use. The **Soviet Union** encompasses far more varied cultures than Europe, and, despite popular images in the West, its centralisation often seems little more than a theoretical concept. So too does the official stance of atheism: much of Russia remains Orthodox Catholic, and the republics include large minority communities of Muslims, Jews and Buddhists.

For most people, travel to the USSR is dominated by the experience of being in a group: to go on your own is possible but expensive and, without good Russian, tricky. Whichever way, though, you will have arrangements made through *Intourist*, the official state agency. Most tours take in Moscow and Leningrad, the easiest and most accessible cities, with sites so symbolic as to almost be clichés of Russia's Tsarist and revolutionary pasts. There are also an increasing number of tours on offer to the Muslim regions of subtropical Uzbeckistan and to the Black Sea coast of Georgia; and, if you are making for China or Japan, you can cut across the breadth of the country on the Trans-Siberian Express. On Intourist itineraries, organised activities and visits are never compulsory, and there's nothing to stop you from going off on your own. It is certainly worth doing this, if only to visit a café or ordinary Soviet hotel for a meal, since few Soviet citizens would consider approaching a tour.

Although the USSR has the highest female participation in the labour force of any modern industrial society, **Soviet women** are concentrated in low-pay, low-status jobs. Articles 35 and 53 which instituted sexual equality have had little impact on sexual relations and the division of domestic, unpaid labour. The double burden of domestic and paid work is an entrenched feature of most women's lives and in a society where the logistics of looking after home and family are both complex and time-consuming, it can be crippling. The legislation on maternity-leave (112 days at full pay and partial pay for a year after that) and child care is exemplary but the reality falls far short of the ideal. Day-centres are few and far between, unhygienic and overcrowded. Abortions are easily available (though health-care and follow-up are poor) but birth control methods and education are not. This has led to women resorting to abortion as a form of contraception – the average women in the USSR has six to eight abortions during her lifetime.

These issues are among the concerns raised by a group of Leningrad **feminists** in the *samizdat* (underground) publication, *Almanac – Women and Russia* (see Travel Notes). Four of the founders of this group have since been forced into exile, and the state exerts strong pressure on those feminists still known to be organising, particularly in Moscow and Leningrad.

■ **Catherine Grace travelled alone through the Soviet Union on the Trans-Siberian Express.**

From the time I first heard about it, I had wanted to travel on the Trans-Siberian. I even, hopefully, learned Russian at school. When I was planning nine months' travelling, the Soviet Union was the place to start.

I went on my own, catching the train from Liverpool St. They called out 'Mos-Cow' as though it was a huge joke. I felt scornful and brave. My friends thought I was mad, and would I please send a telegram when I got out safely at Japan.

I started to feel lonely in Holland, solitary in a compartment in the only carriage going to Moscow. Then Olga Petrovna arrived. She was an enormous Russian with an immense amount of luggage. She had been staying with her sister in the West, and the ten vast bundles (including a carpet) were 'presents'. She was crude, she was kind, she was over-whelming. My limited Russian was nearly adequate; we shared food and laughed a lot, mostly through incomprehension.

The Polish-Soviet border was my introduction to Russia's other face. The East German and Polish crossings had been no more than a brief disturbance in the night, a quick passport check. Expecting something similar, I was in my nightdress, a full-length ribboned affair which clearly halved my apparent age. A succession of inspectors looked disbelievingly at me. The food inspector (Olga lost all her fresh food), customs, immigration, tickets all passed me by and pounced on Olga who became more and more flustered. She and ALL her baggage were taken off for examination. I pattered around watching the event of the night – the changing of wheels for the entire train. The Soviet Union retains a different gauge railway system, as a defence precaution, even from its closest allies.

Finally a relieved Olga and I were reunited. I discovered later that I had been very lucky. Several tourists I met had been taken off and been searched, including every single sheet of paper and envelope. My politically dubious lesbian-feminist posters would not have survived.

I learnt a lot from my slow introduction to the Soviet Union. I had had no idea how separate and final the Soviet border was compared to other Eastern bloc countries. I began to realise how real for Soviet people is the fear of invasion. Olga, although flustered, was sure that the officials were right to be thorough, and she didn't question the wheel change. And the number of officials at the border was just a foretaste of bureaucracy to come. I was issued with new tickets at every point along my way, retaining the last one (for the boat to Japan) as long as an hour. Similarly, the sheer quantity of consumer goods and food that Olga brought back gave me an inkling about shortages; I only realised later how generous she had been. Most importantly, I had my first taste of the warmth and generosity of individual Soviet people.

Arriving at the Hotel Metropole in Moscow I assumed that Intourist would be at least a little interested in me and might even tell me what to do. However, once they had my passport I was left severely alone. I overheard someone talking (in English) and asked them what to do about theatre tickets. Thus began my rapid disillusionment as the Intourist staff demanded 'hard' Western currency. They weren't pleased when I produced the exact money – no chance of fiddling the change.

I was lucky to get to the Bolshoi Theatre my first night. Most Muscovites never get the chance. I was sitting next to an engineer who was thrilled to practise her English with me, and insisted on buying me a drink and a sandwich. For the first two intervals she couldn't have been more friendly and we chatted away. During the third she disappeared, and I realised that she had thought better of the contact. It is easy to make one-off contacts, best not to try to pursue them unless you are sure it is acceptable. I only quite enjoyed the opera; it was very heavy, very much a showpiece.

Leningrad lovers don't have a good word to say for Moscow; it's not beautiful, people are dwarfed by the gigantism of streets, squares and monuments. I am not in a position to make the comparison; I loved Moscow. I didn't know what I wanted from this new place and I got a little bit of everything. I suspect it is a very Russian city.

A visit to the Kremlin was an initial shock. It is not a great, grey, grim fortress. It contains some stunningly beautiful buildings; from a distance the white towers and golden domes of the cathedral gleam and glint like a fantasy castle. The Kremlin Wall in Red Square looks as though it came from an Italian Renaissance picture (it was in fact designed by an Italian), and St Basil's, preposterous onion domes and all, is for real.

It's worth branching out, though, from the city's sights and architecture. The centre of Moscow has lots of cinemas and theatres, and you can use the workers' restaurants as well as the hotels. You'll have to queue, of course. But queues and waiting are a basic part of everyday life in the Soviet Union. People on buses and in the street were unfailingly kind and helpful when I asked the way, people in food queues were friendly. (The only thing there were no queues for was bread.)

The longest queue of all, stretching through Red Square and around the Kremlin, was to Lenin's tomb; many of the people were from outside Moscow. As we entered Red Square, we were directed to leave anything we were carrying in a cloakroom, made to tidy up our appearance, and put in an orderly two-by-two line. The guards hushed us when we entered the mausoleum, we descended reverently into the gloom and filed past the body. Early training will out, and I had to restrain an impulse to make the sign of the cross. The evident significance of that visit for the people around me and the 'holy' atmosphere helped me make sense of the huge images of Lenin found in every Soviet city and main street.

Rejoining the Trans-Siberian, the journey took over again. It was I think one of the most sociable times of my life. The landscape across the Soviet Union is not striking, and you inevitably spend much of the time talking. There were many other Western travellers on the train and I discovered for the first time that to travel alone is to be vulnerable to the needs of people travelling in couples who are bored with each other, and not necessarily interested in you. The same people also dish out unwanted sympathy for the (chosen) state of being alone.

I enjoyed myself much more when I struck up a friendship with a Russian family in the next compartment. Galia and Seriozha, a married couple, and Galia's sister, Valia, were travelling the whole way from Moscow to Vladivostock to new jobs. Seriozha had been a chauffeur, Galia a house builder, and Valia had been at school. They did not know what they would be doing in the east and had had to leave most of their belongings, but were remarkably cheerful about it. Conversation was limited, as I didn't want to get them into any kind of trouble; they also quite consistently failed to understand any question if it was clear that an answer might in some way diminish the USSR. They were however very sweet to me, very friendly, became enormously excited at the prospect of having their photographs taken and there were kisses and tears when we said goodbye. I also met Laura, a singing teacher, who was shy but generous. We exchanged little gifts every day, and she attempted the almost hopeless task of trying to teach me a Russian song. I was also in demand as an interpreter, which was difficult, as my Russian wasn't good enough and the conversations seemed stilted.

Intourist had insisted that I travel the next leg of the train journey first class, which was much less fun – the first-class Russians being much more reserved than my previous neighbours.

Life on the train was complicated by the fact that it ran on Moscow times, though we were in fact crossing a time zone every day. This affected the restaurant car, and you could never quite predict when it would be open. Once we were in Siberia, I stopped using it; whenever the train stopped at a station we would all get out and see what was for sale. Middle-aged women were standing behind stalls selling cabbage salads, potatoes and onions – whatever was local. Once it was excellent carrots, once potato pancakes. Another time there were nothing but pine cones, which annoyed me until I made the connection with pine nuts, and joined the Soviet passengers who had rushed to buy them.

It is important to get out at the stations, as it was the only form of exercise available, and it meant fresh air. Our conductress would never allow us to open the windows. All carriages were heated separately by a coal-burning stove, and it was each conductress' responsibility to get the coal. There was hot water available from urns most of the time, and cups of tea were brought round at regular intervals. There was no hot water for washing, though, and the lavatories were grim. I gathered from more seasoned Soviet travellers that we should be grateful they were in working order at all. The Trans-Siberian is a prestige train.

At Khabarovok all Westerners have to leave the train – which in fact goes on to Vladivostock, a military port closed to foreigners – for a connection to the ferry across to Japan. We had one more day and night in the Soviet Union, travelling along the Chinese border. Autumn was nearly over, the trees on the horizon were all quite bare, and we had seen our first snow. Crossing the frontier, and leaving the country, was an anti-climax. I felt sad knowing that if I'd understood more, if I'd been better prepared, I'd have got much more from my stay. I knew that I wanted to return.

◪ **Travelling with a group, Kate Sebag spent ten days in Russia – three days in Moscow and a week in Leningrad – in deepest winter.**

As we waited yet another hour to extract the last member of our group from Soviet customs control in Moscow, my patience was wearing thin. The next day, victims again of the intractable Russian officialdom, we found ourselves waiting once more. This time it was outside a restaurant in Moscow, in which we were meant to be meeting some friends. The tedium was intermittently relieved by having the door slammed in our faces every time we attempted to join the lucky people who, by what seemed a totally arbitrary process, succeeded in finding favour with the porter. Eventually and inexplicably we too were allowed to enter the restaurant which was large and, by most standards, empty. Our friends weren't there.

My holiday in Russia certainly wasn't very relaxed or comfortable, but then I hadn't expected it to be. The food, although not as bad as I had been told it would be, was generally eaten to stem hunger rather than for pleasure. Public refreshment is viewed as thoroughly functional. Cafés are difficult to spot at first as they are not obviously advertised from outside. Explorations of the cities often turned into feats of endurance as temperatures dropped to well below freezing. Leaving the hotel every morning involved serious debate about how many layers of socks and thermal underwear were needed. Further time was then spent negotiating some sort of respectable appearance to appease the censorious eyes of the babushkas (the ubiquitous old matriachs of Russian society) who would cast disparaging looks at our great bulks. Nothing was 'easy' in Russia – I found this particularly so in my first few days there – but I am still glad that I went.

I was lucky to go on a tour organised by people who had lived in Moscow and Leningrad as students, who spoke good Russian and had friends in both cities. So I met individual Russians who were as warm and generous to us as the officialdom was cold. The Russians with whom I discussed the West varied in their attitudes. Some, although critical and cynical about the Soviet system, were in no sense positive about the West, and remained strongly patriotic. To the young, the 'Underground' of Leningrad (this is a sort of subculture, disapproved of by the state, but more or less tolerated), the West represents all things sophisticated and is seen mainly in terms of pop music and clothes.

Less unexpected but more upsetting was a Refusnik family I met. Refusniks are Soviet Jews who have been refused an exit visa to the West. Once people have been refused visas, their jobs are often taken away, making them vulnerable to the charge of parasitism – there is officially no unemployment in the Soviet Union – and thus possible imprisonment. The hostile climate between the Superpowers has meant that in the last five years the number of exit visas granted to Jews has drastically decreased as Soviet propaganda has increased its programme of anti-Zionism.

Although the family I met were not Orthodox Jews, Israel, and even the West as a whole, had become to them the 'Promised Land', symbol of all the freedom and prosperity the Soviet Union denied them. Still smarting from Britain during the miners' strike, we felt duty-bound to point out that our country for one was not such a great place. But halfway through our rant about police violence and biased media-representation it began to seem inappropriate to go on. Here we were talking about censorship to a family for whom, along with the rest of the 270 million people in the Soviet Union, the *only* image of the miners' strike was that of a policeman hitting a picketing miner over the head.

In the flats that we visited living space was, by Western standards, extremely limited. According to Soviet statistics, 20–25 per cent of Soviet people still live in communal flats, in which on average five or six rooms are shared by several families. Kitchen, corridor and bathroom are all communal. One artist whom we met had painted a satirical series of pictures which placed pre-revolutionary figures in some of the sordid, mundane situations of contemporary everyday life. Gogol and Dostoy-evsky could be seen queuing up for the communal toilet, each equipped with the compulsory loo seat.

We met this artist through a black-market dealer, a friend of one of our group. On meeting you his practised eye would scan every piece of clothing and possessions, quite openly calculating your net value as a source of Western goods. Although he was straighter than any of the hustlers likely to approach you on the Nevsky Prospekt (Leningrad's main street) I had the impression that this was mainly because he did not want to lose a valuable trade contact rather than out of any great sense of loyalty to his English friend. The hardened dealers amongst us made some excellent exchanges of 1970s flares and records for wonderful fur hats, but on the whole I would advise against such deals. They tend to be depressing experiences, as you are reduced to $ and Levi signs and find yourself acting in more avaricious and capitalist ways than you could have imagined possible (in fact, perfectly fulfilling Soviet propaganda's image of the West).

I was surprised by the amount of freedom we as tourists were given. The only time I came up against restrictions was when I tried to photo-graph some soldiers clearing away snow from the Tomb of the Unknown Soldier, in Moscow. I was quickly warned away. When you are given your visa you are told not to photograph military installations, bridges, airports and other 'sensitive areas'. This latter phrase, I later found out, can mean queues, drunks, run-down areas, and also soldiers – in fact anything that could be interpreted in an anti-Soviet light.

It is possible and definitely worthwhile to opt out of some of the officially organised and tedious processions of homage to monuments of Soviet achievement and Lenin paraphernalia. However, in Moscow, Lenin's Mausoleum and the Museum of Economic Achievement are musts as, in Leningrad, is the Museum of Atheism, a fascinating place which at times is like entering the world of a fifteenth-century anti-clerical tract. Art enthusiasts should also see the Hermitage, which is all it is made out to be.

No amount of purple prose can describe the beauty of Leningrad in the snow. It's a wonderful city to wander in, not least because the eye is freed from its habitual enslavement of images of Western advertising on posters, billboards and in window displays. Uninterested in, and incapable of reading, the drab Soviet posters, I was free to gaze at the wonderful architecture and at people about their daily business.

▨ **Kate Barker has visited the Soviet Union three times – the first two as a tourist, the last on a three-month student exchange to Leningrad University.**

Arriving in Leningrad as a student was very different from my two previous experiences of the USSR. There was no one to meet us at the airport, no smiling Intourist guide, no room for us to stay in our first night. It had been decided, it seemed, that it was not worth while setting the propaganda machine in motion for a group of Russian-speaking students on a three-month visit.

Our hostel too was not what I had expected. It was well situated, right on the banks of the Neva, and opposite the Hermitage. But it was incredibly run-down. The wallpaper was peeling, the ovens were full of cockroaches and the rooms buzzed with the sound of mosquitoes. In the entrance hall, guarding the main stairs, sat a porter, strict and smiling, or garrulous and charming, depending on whether he had managed to lay his hands on some vodka. All visitors had to leave their identification with him, before they were allowed into the hostel.

Our rooms were on the third floor. They were extremely cramped, with three or four students eating, sleeping and working in each one. I shared a room with one English woman, and one Russian. We did not see our Russian room-mate, Ira, for the first week as she was finishing her compulsory summer vacation job on a collective farm outside Leningrad. She would come back at two o'clock at night, sleep until five, and then she would be up again to work in the fields – harvesting carrots all day by hand.

When we did meet Ira properly, it was difficult to imagine her engaged in such hard manual labour. She was one of the post-war generation of Soviet women who are expected to maintain (always and everywhere) a glamorous image. Every day, she would spend precious hours in front of the mirror, fixing an immaculate make-up mask and practising a smile that she held to be irresistible. Ira and other Soviet women of her generation that we met seemed to us to be caught between a multiplicity of contradictory demands. Whilst accepting passive and coquettish female roles and all the domestic 'duties' of raising a family, she was also trying to pursue, with set determination, the highly competitive career of a political journalist. Her hope was to travel to the West for work.

The male students in the year that we joined considered themselves exempt from the tasks of shopping and cooking and seemed to subsist mainly on a diet of boiled meat and potatoes from the hostel canteen. Everyone, however, including foreign students, had to take part in the hostel cleaning days. On these days the whole place became awash with water and carbolic soap as we scrubbed and polished in a vain attempt to make the hostel look presentable. We soon grew used to this routine of hostel life as we did to standing in queues for the showers, disinfecting our rooms when there was a bedbug scare and washing our clothes by hand in big copper or plastic bowls. This washing, once scrubbed in the brackish Leningrad water, was hung dripping on lines criss-crossing our already cluttered rooms. Because it was such a tedious chore, washing had been turned into quite an event; the washrooms were always full of students singing and gossiping, even playing the guitar. Other popular places for get-togethers were the kitchens and stairwells where groups gathered to sing and talk the night away with a bottle of vodka and a pile of pancakes and sour cream.

Like the hostel, the university itself had become very run-down. Our faculty was reached through a yard full of rusting pieces of machinery and metal cages, in which howling dogs sat waiting to be used in experiments. Our lessons were strictly didactic affairs. We would sit at desks like school children and answer the questions put to us. The Russian education system is geared towards students gaining a detailed knowledge of a specific area, rather than a broad overview, and involves a lot of learning by rote and repetition. Much of the rest of the routine, however, seemed all too familiar, rushing down to the cafeteria between lessons for cabbage pasties and cups of strong black coffee, skipping lessons and working frantically in the library to get an essay in on time.

During my stay in Leningrad, I was a regular visitor to the *Banya* – a particularly Russian hybrid somewhere between a sauna and a public baths. Some of the banyas are an odd reminder of pre-revolutionary opulence, with gilt-framed mirrors, cupids and marble slabs for massage. But the one I visited was fairly modern and functional in design. Nevertheless, it was an odd contrast coming off the street, covered in November snow and entering the clinical looking changing-room where naked women giggled and weighed each other, freed temporarily from work, home and family.

It was fun too joining in some home-grown entertainments; skating in the parks – some of which are frozen over for this purpose in winter – picnicking in the pine forests, and swimming in the rivers. On occasions I'd attend a service at a Russian Orthodox church – a chastening experience but one which is still fundamental to the lives of many Russians. The congregation was almost entirely made up of tiny old women bent double and wizened, yet able to stand through services lasting several hours. The shrill voices of these women, survivors of two world wars, a revolution and Stalin, could be easily heard above the choir.

In adapting to the Leningrad way of life there are, on the whole, few problems. One, which fast becomes obvious, is in gaining an awareness of Russian convention. Anyone wearing even faintly outrageous clothes or make-up is likely to get stared at. A visitor refusing to wear shoes in summer, or a hat in winter, will be subject to constant well-meaning scoldings from matronly 'babushkas' worrying about their health. This can be quite startling if you can't properly follow what they are saying. In other areas of behaviour it is genuinely important to conform. A woman drunk on the streets, quite apart from risking a fine or arrest, is liable to be taken for a prostitute. We were told stories of Western women who had been violently assaulted by local prostitutes on the assumption that they were encroaching on their patch.

TRAVEL NOTES

Languages Russian – though for many only as a second language; minority languages include Slavic, Ukranian, Altaic.

Transport Generally by train (with attendant bureaucracy in booking seats through Intourist); internal flights are cheap and often included in package tours taking in Samarkand, etc.

Accommodation Again, tourists must arrange all accommodation through Intourist – which generally involves little choice but staying in the impersonal, sometimes surprisingly basic, hotels designated for foreigners.

Special problems Bureaucracy – from getting an entrance visa on.

If you use the black market be discreet and don't deal openly on the street; Scandinavian money has the best rate of exchange, US dollars the worst.

Bring tampons and toilet paper, also film (Soviet film has a different processing system). Tights, knickers, postcards and records are appreciated presents but don't assume or patronise.

Guides Collets International Bookshop (129 Charing Cross Road, London WC2) stock a wide range of Soviet guidebooks – to the country as a whole and to all the more visited cities and regions. Let's Go Europe (St Martin's Press, US) is useful on the basics of individual travel.

CONTACTS
All feminist groups remain underground.

BOOKS
Carola Hansson and Karin Liden eds, Moscow Women (Allison & Busby, 1984). Collection of transcripted interviews with thirteen Soviet women, taped clandestinely by two Swedish feminists. Tatvana Mamonova ed., Feminist Writings from the Soviet Union (Blackwell, 1984). These are the articles and essays printed secretly in Russia by the 'Leningrad Feminists' in their Samizdat – compelling reading, they speak out about the position and feelings of Soviet women.

Julia Voznesenskaya, The Woman's Decameron (Quartet, 1986). Written by a Soviet dissident, now resident in West Germany. These are stories about sex, love, men and survival in the USSR – presented through the fictional device of women telling each other their life stories in a Moscow maternity ward.

Andrea Lee, Russian Journal (Faber and Faber 1984). US writer's journal of a year spent on an exchange trip.

Also good on contemporary social background is Colin Thubron's Among the Russians (Penguin 1985).

Thanks to Kate Sebag.

AFRICA

Chapter Five

NORTH AFRICA

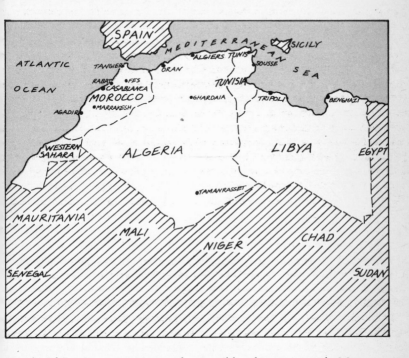

North Africa is an exciting and accessible place to travel. Morocco, Algeria and Tunisia are all within a few hours' ferry ride of southern Europe and to the south the Sahara offers one of the great remaining overland routes. A disadvantage in its being so close is that it can be more difficult to come to terms with the limitations and restrictions of an Islamic, essentially Third World, culture. The familiar feel of recent French colonialism, and the wide usage of the French language, will help you adjust, at least for the practicalities, but they don't go far in terms of attitudes. If you have never travelled in the Islamic world before, the degree and constancy of sexual harassment, in Morocco above all, can be very hard to deal with. In general you will probably feel uncomfortable (if not unsafe) travelling alone or with another woman. Any contacts, any hospitality you receive, and any insights you're likely to gain, will be mediated by men.

The degree of Islamic orthodoxy and of westernisation varies considerably between the North African (or *Maghreb*) nations. **Tunisia**, the Arab world's most liberal nation, is probably the least problematic: recognisably Mediterranean, and sometimes French, in character and with a well-developed tourist industry. **Morocco**, despite its popularity, is the most oppressive – high unemployment and a traditional xenophobia giving all tourists (and women above all) a hard time from 'hustlers' and guides. **Algeria** falls somewhere between the two, having less to do with tourism, but, along with this stance, few facilities outside the cities and established Saharan routes.

We have included a piece on **Libya** in this section although few women (or men, for that matter) would consider it a viable option for travel with its official antagonism towards the West – and in the light of the recent US bombing of Tripoli. However, a small number of women go out there to work, getting high wages on short contracts.

MOROCCO

Until Independence in 1956, **Morocco** was divided into French and Spanish protectorates – and in the north its towns still have a strong European feel. Casablanca, the country's principal port and industrial centre, seems in many ways very much like Marseilles; Agadir, on the southern coast, is a fairly conscious recreation of a Spanish package resort. Yet coming to the country for the first time it is the differences which stand out and initially overwhelm. Morocco is first and foremost an Islamic nation. Women keep a low profile, particularly in urban life, and travelling alone (or with other women) you're likely to be construed as a 'loose' Westerner or, Moroccan's nearest social equivalent, a prostitute. At its best – in the High Atlas mountains, in Marrakesh, and throughout the southern desert routes – it can be a great country to experience. But the level of sexual harassment (and problems with hustlers – getting money from tourists is for many the only viable means of economic survival) can hardly be overstated. Unless you travel with a man it can be virtually impossible to sort out who to trust.

Politically, Morocco's future is highly uncertain. It is at present a monarchy, with Hassan II, the king, appointing all ministers. But Hassan has staked his reputation on a lingering colonial war in the Western Sahara, and at home faces economic crisis and an estimated *sixty* per cent unemployment.

Since Independence women have looked to the state to take over the traditional functions of husbands in providing welfare and educational services for the family, and a small proportion of women have managed to gain access to higher education and (despite intense discrimination) professional employment. For the majority, however, modernisation has brought only the erosion of traditional networks of support, with few alternative resources provided. This has very much increased women's vulnerability to isolation and poverty.

There is one official government **women's organisation** (the *Women's Union*) which has centres running skills training classes in most of the large cities. Since 1983, a feminist group, linked to the left opposition movement has also emerged in Rabat, printing a women's paper *The 8th of March*; distribution is increasing and the group have also organised various conferences, seminars and events in other cities.

◢ Pat Chell lived for two years in Fes, teaching English at the university.

'In Morocco, there are only three kinds of women', I was often told, 'virgins, wives and whores.' It is as useful a proverb as any to keep in mind when you visit – and as a start to understanding the core of the country's culture, Islam and the family.

A woman in Morocco must be a virgin when she marries, and usually she is still expected to prove this on consummation of the marriage by showing evidence of hymenal blood. I have known 'westernised', bourgeois women, no longer virgins but about to marry, who have gone to a doctor in Casablanca to have the hymen restitched. This has not necessarily been done to deceive their prospective husbands, with whom they may have been sleeping in any case, but to 'observe form' and keep the two families happy. I have also known of liberal families who have given their consent for a couple to sleep together, after the marriage contract has been made but before the wedding ceremony, yet have 'satisfied themselves' that the woman was a virgin upon the first occasion.

The only legitimate reason for a woman not being a virgin is if she is a wife. If she is known to be neither, then she will be considered a prostitute. Indeed, once a girl's virginity is lost and her marriage prospects become virtually nil, without family support, she may well have to resort to prostitution as a means of making enough money to live. Prostitution is very common in Morocco. All unmarried Moroccan men whom I spoke to about sex had had their only experiences with prostitutes (apart from those who had been 'lucky' enough to meet tourists who would oblige). On the first occasion this was almost always as an adolescent with a prostitute known for her experience in dealing with 'virgins', though Moroccans would laugh at that expression, as the concept of male virginity does not exist. Indeed, many regard childhood circumcision as equivalent to the taking away of virginity. A bridegroom is tacitly expected to be sexually experienced and one who is not is seen as something of a joke.

Prostitutes (and tourists) aside, Moroccan males turn to masturbation, bestiality or homosexuality. Homosexuality, though it does exist as a sexual preference, is more likely to be thought of as a substitute for the 'real' thing; tourists sometimes misinterpret Moroccan men's show of physical affection for each other as homosexuality, but this is simply a cultural norm. As for women, I'm not so sure that the concept of sexual satisfaction (let alone sexual preference) even exists. Amongst my students at the university, presumably an intellectual elite, the idea of choosing lesbianism, either for physical or political reasons, seemed inconceivable. If anything, it was regarded as another example of Western decadence.

Some of my students did have relationships with men but this was a very risky business indeed. If the relationship was 'known about' and then ended, the woman could be branded as a whore and her life made a misery. I have met female students who have been beaten by fathers or brothers simply for being seen talking to a man. Another, who had been raped, did nothing about the attack even though the assailant was known to her because she was sure that if her family found out she would be taken from the university. Many families are reluctant to allow their daughters to go to university, not because they don't want them educated – they often do as job prospects for women continue to improve – but because they don't want them to be at risk by being in a situation where they can have contact with men.

A number of students, male and female, were obviously dissatisfied with the status quo. A married student I knew attempted to help his working wife with chores until he was forbidden to do so by his mother and his wife was severely reprimanded for failing in her wifely duties. They, like most young Moroccans, were not in a financial position to have a home of their own, even if the family constraints against doing so had not been there. Others of my students wanted to marry Europeans – not so much to have a more equal relationship, nor the financial benefits, but because there was more likelihood of their being able to free themselves from family restraints.

I was only ever aware of one student who did not want to marry. This was Saloua. She was very intelligent and studious, determined to further her studies, which would have meant leaving Morocco, and then returning as a university teacher. She saw this as the best way in which she could help the women of her country. Although she had a very supportive family, she knew that she had to have a strategy to allow her to carry out her plans. She dressed in Western clothes but very demurely – rather middle-aged 'Marks and Spencers'. She was rarely seen alone, thus denying any man an opportunity to talk to her. When with women, she avoided the usual 'gossip' and 'scheming'. In a mixed teaching group she spoke only when invited to do so. If she did become involved in a classroom discussion with males, she would be pleasant but distant, humourless and polite. In other words, she always kept a low profile. She was aware of walking a very tenuous tight-rope to freedom. She was the most courageous Moroccan woman that I met and I wish her well.

Many students, however, equated feminism with danger because they saw it as anti-Islamic. Some of the most politically active women that I came across were involved in Islamic fundamentalism and wanted nothing to do with Western decadence and therefore nothing to do with me.

Moroccans form their ideas of Western women from two main sources, the media and tourists. The cinema is very popular and there is an abundance of trashy European soft-porn films. I have heard great cheers in the cinema when the 'macho' hero has torn off a woman's clothes or physically abused her prior to her becoming a willing sexual partner. One of the biggest culture shocks I had in this respect occurred in a very poor home with no running water, toilet or electricity. There was, however, a television and a wire would be run over the roof to a neighbour's when we wanted an evening's viewing. Every Wednesday, neighbours would gather to watch *Dallas*. It was the only time they had spent time socially with a European and so naturally they were curious. My host had to go to great lengths to explain that I was not a 'Pamela' or a 'Sue-Ellen' and that neither were the majority of Western women. I don't think they were very convinced.

As for tourists, how do Moroccans see them? If a woman is alone or only with women, what kind of woman can she be? No father would put his daughter at risk by letting her travel unless she was already 'worthless'. Her nearest equivalent in Moroccan society is the prostitute. She sits in cafés, drinks alcohol, smokes cigarettes or hashish and will even comb her hair in public. She often dresses 'indecently' – not even a prostitute would do this. Why should a woman want to 'flaunt' her body? She will also often be prepared to have sex if you can charm her into it. These are the kinds of attitudes I heard so frequently.

And, as a traveller, these are the attitudes which you can expect to meet. The forms the inevitable sexual harassment take vary from the relatively innocuous to the absolutely obscene. The most persistent and annoying is a clicking noise made with the tongue every time you walk past a café, for example. Not terribly serious, you might think, but the cumulative effect is very degrading. Then there are more direct, verbal approaches. I would strongly advise against confronting anyone who pesters you, as your remonstrations only provide unexpected entertainment – I've never yet seen a woman come out of one of these confrontations without feeling foolish and humiliated. Your anger will simply not be understood. You are unlikely to receive much sympathy from Moroccan women, either. They will either disapprove of you and think that you must be prepared to accept the consequences of being out in public (i.e. in the man's world) or they will fail to understand your annoyance as there are many young Moroccan women who seek this kind of attention. It is proof of their attractiveness and may be the only kind of contact they have ever known with men.

I don't think as a tourist you can ever avoid sexual harassment completely, but there are certain compromises that reduce its extent. You can dress 'appropriately', in skirts, rather than trousers, and in sleeved, loose-fitting tops. You should avoid making eye contact too, and not start up a 'casual' conversation with a man – there is no such thing in Morocco. Above all, be as polite and even tempered as possible. Moroccans have a highly ritualised, elaborate etiquette, which you will not be able to learn in a short time, but they do respect politeness. Loss of temper equals loss of face, no matter what the provocation.

What I have written are generalisations. There are Moroccan men and women who do not share these attitudes. There are many students who genuinely want to practise their English and can only do so with travellers. Unfortunately on a short stay, the Moroccans you're most likely to encounter are street hustlers only after your money or your body. Sometimes, particularly if you are feeling threatened or insecure, it is difficult to tell whether people are being genuine or 'hustling'. But if you are cautiously optimistic and rely on your instincts, then you might find, as I did, that Moroccans are incredibly hospitable people, many of whom love to have Westerners to stay.

I hope that I haven't put you off travelling to Morocco. Too often, sadly, I met travellers who judged the society with Western values. They saw the men as villains and the women as martyrs.

☑ **Jill Denton spent a summer in Morocco, often looking around on her own but travelling with a male companion.**

Morocco is a completely male world to travel: the streets and cafés are male territory (and harassment our condition of entry), and even contact with women rarely occurs without a male intermediary.

The most publicly assertive women you will see are undoubtedly the Berber peasants, who descend on the towns to trade their produce at the weekly *souk* (market). In consequence they enjoy a measure of economic independence, and their exuberant dress – candy-stripe, sparkling shawls, fluorescent socks and bold jewellery – seems to testify to this greater freedom. Other women, by comparison, are inconspicuous – both in manner and dress. This is most obvious in the small towns and countryside, but in the cities things aren't far different and the moves towards westernisation have often made matters worse. Within the traditional extended family, women and children formed an almost separatist (though male-imposed) community over which older women and the mother with many sons wielded considerable power. But adoption of a 'nuclear family' lifestyle and improved living standards (for example a private bathroom rather than the local *hammam*) are fast eroding the basis of this power. Married women face increasing isolation within the home, whilst at the same time the education and incentives to escape marriage or motherhood are denied them. Small wonder, then, that Moroccans are often suspicious of our values and way of life.

In the steambaths – the hammam – I sat amongst women with henna in their hair and reluctant kids wedged between their knees, and we weighed each other up for a while before beginning to chat in French. I was recommended kids: 'Fun!', and warned off marriage: 'Like another big kid!' Everyone laughed a lot, but then in Morocco single motherhood is still a big joke. The hammam is definitely worth a visit.

Elsewhere, out in the male world, I felt that Moroccan men wanted the best of both worlds – to benefit from Western woman's 'moral laxity' and to retain their strict control over Muslim women. Of the male egos I bumped into, not one could understand that freedom from a husband's watchful eye means also the freedom to say 'no'. I was, however, awarded the status of honorary man. I drank, ate, smoked and slept in one room with three men (one, my travel friend). In the next room our host's 18–year-old sister prepared our meals, washed our dishes. For a month she had not left the house: 'It's the school holidays – where could I go?' Had she merely dined with us, in the presence of her brother's male friends, there would have been dishonour. Predictably, her brother resented the time I spent with her in the kitchen. So too, I think, did her mother. Older women are less likely than their daughters to understand French, but it was really my behaviour which put a barrier between us – male-imposed definitions of dividing women into either 'decent' or 'whore' complicate and restrict any contact.

With the exception of the steambath, in fact, I always met women through men – and I wouldn't have stayed in men's homes had I not been with a man in the first place. It *is* a man's world in Morocco, and even something as apparently simple and casual as a five-minute conversation in a café can be totally misinterpreted. I wouldn't want to put women off visiting Morocco – I had fun there despite the hassles – but don't feel you can act as normal. It doesn't work.

◪ **Lucinda Montefiore also travelled with a male friend. She chose to spend most time in the comparatively relaxed south.**

I felt uneasy about going to Morocco – mainly, I think, because of all the horror stories I had heard about travellers there. The feeling lasted throughout the trip, not because anything terrible happened to me – in fact, rather the reverse, I had a remarkably trouble-free time – but because I was constantly aware of the fact that as a European woman I represented nearly everything that is unacceptable in Islamic terms. However, my sense of unease was not so strong as to prevent me from enjoying my stay.

I took a cheap flight to Morocco and arrived in Agadir, a large package resort on the south-west coast. As an introduction to the country, it's not up to much and I wouldn't recommend staying there. It is a recently built town (the last one was destroyed in an earthquake in 1960) and I found it depressing and characterless, but nonetheless it's a useful base from which to explore the southern desert and the spectacular Atlantic coast.

If you want to be by the sea, I'd advise going to Essaouira – a walled, slightly ramshackle seaside resort with whitewashed houses and blue doors, built overlooking the sea at the end of a great stretch of sandy beach. Of all the places I went to, I found it the most friendly and relaxed. And that's high praise, as Morocco is *not* a relaxing country to travel in. If you're with a man, as I was, the main problem tends not to be sexual harassment but in coping with hustlers. They approach continuously, trying to get money off you, usually by offering their services as guides or pretending to be students or 'friends' eager to practise their English.

There are very few hustlers in Essaouira, partly because it's also a popular place for Moroccan tourists, and they don't make easy victims, and partly because the European tourists who do go there tend to be fairly wealthy (lots of French car drivers stop off in Essaouira) and seem quite happy to spend money unsolicited. There are also other sources of revenue besides tourism – the town is famous for its marquetry and it has a small but active fishing port and industrial base.

I spent a few very self-indulgent days in Essaouira, sitting in open-air cafés, walking along the ramparts, sampling the cakes (there are hundreds of cake shops), and dawdling through the souks and around the marque – try workshops. The one disadvantage was the wind, which blew all the time. I've been told since then that it's windy there nearly all year round – probably the main reason why it hasn't been turned into a package resort.

Heading inland from Essaouira we made for Marrakesh, one of the most exotic and exciting cities I've ever been to. I find it hard to write about this city without resorting to a mass of travel clichés, just because in so many ways it *is* exactly like a tourist fantasy of the Islamic world, with its snake charmers and musicians, its intricate alleyways and lingering smells.

I did a lot of walking in Marrakesh, spending hours getting lost in the souks, enjoying the wonderful smells of cedarwood and leather, spices and herbs. I also had my first introduction to Islamic architecture and found the Koutoubia minaret, the Saadian tombs and the Medrassa so exquisite that I now want to see more.

Wherever I went I always returned to the Djamaa el Fna – the square at the heart of the city – where crowds cluster around the snake charmers, acrobats, fire-eaters and dancers, groups of drummers and pipe musicians, comedians and storytellers. It is for these pleasures, along with the more mundane need to trade, that the southern nomads and the Berbers of the High Atlas have, for centuries, been drawn to Marrakesh – it's not only the tourists who find themselves suspending all judgment.

During my short stay in Morocco I visited only a few places. This was deliberate. It just doesn't make sense to hurtle round the country trying to see everything, and I believe I gained immeasurably by staying in places for a certain length of time. Once you have been somewhere for a few days hustlers no longer bother to approach you. However, without a male companion, the problem of sexual harassment remains the same and I would be very reluctant to return to Morocco on my own or even travelling with another woman.

TRAVEL NOTES

Languages Moroccan Arabic (a considerable variant of 'classical' Egyptian/Gulf Arabic) and three distinct Berber languages. French is widely spoken and is taught in schools.

Transport There's a small but useful rail network. Travel otherwise is by bus (plentiful and cheap) or collective taxi (*grand taxi*) which run between towns according to demand. In the Atlas, and sub-Sahara, you can negotiate lifts on trucks – some of which operate like buses anyway. Hitching is inadvisable and you'll often be asked to pay for lifts, though tourists are often worth approaching at campsites.

Accommodation Very rarely a problem – there are all categories of hotels graded by the state and other (even cheaper) options below them.

Special problems Arrival can be daunting at both Tangier and Tetouan, where you'll find the country's most persistent, aggressive and experienced hustlers. If it's your first visit it makes sense to move straight on – it only takes a couple of days to get used to things.

Many tourists come to Morocco to smoke hashish (*kif*). Although officially illegal, the police tend to turn a blind eye: the main trouble lies with the dealers, who have developed some nasty tricks (like selling you hash then sending friends round to threaten to turn you in to the police unless you pay them off). It's best to avoid the *kif* growing areas of the Rif mountains and the drug centre, Ketama. If you do want to smoke, don't buy anything in the first few days or in Tangier or Tetouan; don't take anything out of the country, and only buy and/or smoke when you feel absolutely safe and confident.

Guide Mark Ellingham and Shaun McVeigh, *The Rough Guide to Morocco* (Routledge & Kegan Paul, 1985). The most recent guidebook published – entertaining, practical and very comprehensive.

CONTACTS

The recently founded *Centre de documentation et d'achion féminin* can be reached at 46 Rue Aboudest–Agdal Rabat. Also try contacting The *8th of March* journal at the Mohammed V University, Rabat.

BOOKS

Fatima Mernissi, *Beyond the Veil: The Sexual Ideology of Women* (1975, Al Saqi, London, rev. 1985). Enlightening study – see the general bibliography – by Morocco's leading sociologist. Very strongly recommended.

Vanessa Maher, *Women and Property in Morocco* (Cambridge UP, 1974). Respected study, though more exclusively academic than Mernissi.

Nancy Phelan, *Morocco is a Lion* (Quartet, 1982). Ordinary, lightweight travelogue – but well observed and includes a variety of inter-views/experiences with Moroccan women, both rural and urban.

Paul Bowles, *The Spider's House* (1955,

Black Sparrow Press, US, 1984). Insightful novel set in Fes during the struggle for independence. Bowles' other Moroccan novels, and especially his translations of Moroccan storytellers, are also worthwhile; most are published by Black Sparrow Press.

ALGERIA

The least known of the three Maghreb nations, **Algeria** has always been considered the most adventurous part of North Africa to travel. The country includes vast stretches of spectacular Saharan desert – from Algiers, the capital, to the south of the country is further than from Algiers to London. But Algeria also has a reputation for danger: exaggerated perhaps, though sexual harassment is common and travelling about with few other tourists, it is easy to feel personally threatened. If you travel with a man, these problems are less noticeable and less oppressive. You will also find it very much easier to accept the frequent offers of hospitality, which, as in any Islamic society, tend to be preferred man to man.

Arriving across the border from Morocco, you will be immediately struck by the absence of hustlers or guides. Tourists are as yet too thinly spread for Algerians to make any sort of regular living from them, and by a combination of socialist reform and Islamic charity most have at least a subsistence income. The government (socialist non-aligned), has actively resisted Western cultural influences. There's a noticeable lack of adverts, pornography and Western films (though *Dallas*, with its extended family, was shown and proved popular). This hasn't coincided with any overt antagonism towards Westerners themselves; any resentments you experience are likely to be a legacy of the French colonial war. It took fourteen years up until 1962 for the French to cede independence.

During that struggle, women fought conspicuously and bravely at the forefront of the resistance movement – and **women's liberation** was a central nationalist issue. Post-Independence betrayal of revolutionary promises has been a key theme, keenly felt, for Algerian feminists. They have had to fight for all advances, and to retain the most circumscribed freedoms. In the 1960s huge numbers of women mobilised against dowry payments, polygyny and disparities in wages, and for better birth control and divorce laws. Twenty years on women organised again, in opposition to a proposed family code, derived from conservative interpretations of

Islamic law and directly at odds with the Independence constitution. The proposal was withdrawn after demonstrations led by women veterans of the revolution, but was passed in secret in spring 1985.

With the exception of occasional reunions of veteran revolutionaries, women are unable to hold public meetings or actively engage others in campaigns. Meetings are sabotaged and members physically threatened by Muslim fundamentalists. Algerian women are looking to the international Muslim Women's community to co-ordinate legal actions against governments who pass unconstitutional legislation and also to a wide range of international groups to help secure the release of women political prisoners.

▨ **Denise Dresner returned to Algeria for a third season's work on an archaeological site in Cherchel, a small town west of Algiers.**

As an archaeologist working a 10-hour day and a 6-day week, my dealings with local people were largely limited to daily exchanges at the bakery where I negotiated in less than rudimentary Arabic for savoury cakes and pizza, and the bar where I did likewise for mint teas and coffees for mid-morning break. In the lively street bustle around our block the townsfolk were treated to the spectacle of an unveiled overalled female balancing a large tray down the slope to the site, across the smooth paving stones of the Roman Forum floor, and delivering it to the 'table top' of a tumbled Corinthian column, whereupon all hands on site downed trowels and shovels and collapsed for a twenty-minute rest.

The fact that we were foreigners, engaged in peculiar activities amongst ruins and trenches twenty feet below street level, was an unprecedented curiosity in itself; the fact that there were three women working on site, *and* directing workmen, ensured the fascination of onlookers and the occasional outburst against such open contravention of Islamic orthodoxy. While my female English colleague and myself were impervious through ignorance to the comments made in Arabic, our Algerian colleague had to tolerate these insults. Being foreigners, and women and infidels to boot, we were not to be held morally accountable, but as an Algerian, Nacera was disregarding tradition and the role of withdrawing, hiding and obeying that it imposes upon women in her country and, in varying degrees of severity, in the Islamic world at large. In a society so resistant to change, where just not wearing the veil can be seen as prostitution, to become an educated/professional/working woman takes as much personal courage as advantages of wealth or status or an enlightened upbringing.

This state of affairs was further illustrated when we visited a family who lived in a flat overlooking the site and who were happy to have us come up to take aerial photographs from their drawing-room window.

The family was represented by five women, ranging in age from about fifteen to fifty, and a young man, a cousin who was there because decorum required the presence of a male (we were a party of two women and a man). Delighted to have us in their home, they plied us with soft drinks and biscuits, which comprise a treat in a place unaccustomed to much variety or luxury in the choice of commodities, and insisted on giving us each a memento upon parting. In the home the women were unveiled, and the younger two spoke, looked and listened avidly, this being the first time they had three foreign persons in their home, two of whom were a similar age to themselves. Two of the older women had been educated abroad, had seen the freedoms and attractions of the Western world, and now they were back here, subject to the old prohibitions, not even allowed to lean out the window for risk of being seen unveiled. They spoke of Algiers as if it were over the border, a place not bound by the strictness of small-town mores, where women did go about unveiled and did go to movies and did enter bars ... At that moment, in that room that was literally a cage, I felt very grateful that my own destiny allowed me to move freely, or at least without that level of religious constraint.

Algeria differs from Morocco and Tunisia in that it has been less open to tourism and fosters a stricter approach to foreigners and to how Algerians behave with foreigners. We encountered none of the hassle or harassment from self-appointed street merchants that is the common experience in Morocco. Both in the towns and more remote areas people were generally friendly and not out to get our money or sell us anything. In fact the most satisfying transaction we conducted was a cash-free one, with a shopkeeper in the marketplace of a frontier town, amidst the full panoply of an African-Arab souk, where we exchanged our cassette recorder for a large woven rug and leather bag.

On another occasion, we found ourselves arriving in the town of Tebessa, near the Algerian-Tunisian border, late in the evening after everything had closed down. The place was a ghost town; we were tired, hungry and road-weary and sat down in the only place open, where all we could get was coffee. When we left and were standing about in the street wondering what to do next, a man came up to us and gave us two loaves of bread and some cheese. I don't know where he materialised from, perhaps he had been at the café or had heard that we were inquiring about where we could get something to eat. In any case this unsolicited gift kept us from hunger that night, as we ended up in the most miserable of accommodations, devoid of plumbing, electricity or victuals. (Tebessa warrants a visit for its Roman amphitheatre and Christian basilica, but an overnight stop should be avoided at all costs.)

With those we lived and worked with in Cherchel and neighbouring Tipasa, there was a further dimension to our relationship which comes about when you return somewhere. On our successive returns over three years we were welcomed as old friends by the workmen, the restaurant people, shopkeepers, café owner, by the elderly caretaker of an ex-French villa in Tipasa who looked after us and our palates with enormous zeal and attention during our stay there, by our Algerian colleagues and assorted personnel and residents. An eclectic crew, somehow bound together by our dedicated if seemingly bizarre mission, day after day beneath the Mediterranean African sun, in pursuit of Cherchel's ancient history, piecing together the pageant of its Phoenician, Roman, Vandal, Byzantine, Arab, Turkish, and French past. Local legend maintained that the statue of a huge golden horse was buried in Cherchel, and the workmen had to reconcile this radiant image with the excitement generated by the finding of little bits of pottery and crumbling green coins.

At the end of my third and last season in Cherchel, the British Archaeological Team in Algeria, all three-strong of us, headed south and east for a driving tour of other towns and sites, a journey through a beautiful country of remarkable contrasts which was to deposit us finally in Tunis, where we made a mad dash through the casbah and ruins of Carthage before boarding the boat to take us back to Europe. It was mid-November and already winter in southern France where we disembarked. Though cold and inappropriately dressed – a few days before, we had been basking in oases on the fringe of the desert – we were giddy with the delights of civilisation – a hot bath, a coffee and cognac and a soft warm bed.

◤ **Jan Wright travelled through the Sahara by Landrover with her husband and three small sons, aged 1, 2½ and 4½ years.**

It was with relief that I crossed into Algeria from Morocco. I was fed up with being hassled and so hoped that Algeria would be different. It was, and as we steadily made our way along the northern coastal strip our mood lightened and we relaxed.

We had come to see the desert, but before we could do that we had to spend several days in Algiers – fighting our way through traffic jams and looking for goods that weren't in the shops. We were soon feeling frustrated again. Even camping was a problem. There was no campsite, and we had great difficulty finding a private spot along the coastal strip, partly because of the heavy military presence and partly because of the spread of the population and cultivation. The seaside resorts offered little consolation. Whilst obviously splendid in French colonial times, they are now decaying and depressed, with rubbish piled high in the streets. Eager to get away from the industrialised and 'civilised' north, we drove south.

We were heading down the trans-Saharan highway, which is extremely broken-up tarmac, to Tamanrasset, the centre of the desert. This once-sleepy desert oasis is now a tourist centre with visitors being flown in on package tours to luxury hotels. By the time we arrived I was in love with the desert. The freedom and solitude of that great expanse was something I had never before experienced. To eat breakfast watching the sunrise, to write by moonlight, and to roll down sand dunes perhaps previously untrodden are things I will not easily forget. To the boys it was one big beach.

Tamanrasset is also accessible by bus (once or twice weekly from Ghardaia – gateway of the Sahara) and from the town there are organised tours into the desert by Toyota landcruiser. In many ways to travel with your own vehicle is to do it the hard way. It's tough driving over long distances, but the obvious advantage is the freedom to explore, and we decided to do just that. We drove through the Hoggar mountains and then up north, stopping at the Touareg village of Ideles. There we were invited into a *zeriba* – a grass house – by a young Touareg girl to drink tea with her family. The Touareg children were crying with hunger and were given sand to eat to put something in their bellies. Our hostess could speak French and asked us for eye ointment to cure blindness. We learnt later that blindness is very common and could be prevented by the use of antibiotics. Peripetetic teachers reach many of the desert villages but not health care. We gave what we could, and left feeling a mixture of anger and sadness for their situation.

Three hundred and fifty kilometres south of Tamanrasset, near the border with Niger, is Gara Ecker, a weird landscape of wind-eroded sandstone rocks. We spent two whole days without seeing another person. It was magic. From here many tourists continue south into Niger. Instead, turning northwards we set off to recross the Sahara, travelling the lesser-used eastern route via Djanet and In Amenas.

This route is much more spectacular than the highway, but it is also much more difficult to drive and there is little traffic. Certain parts have to be driven in convoy for safety. In the hot summer months it can be weeks between one vehicle and the next and a breakdown could mean disaster. We spent the next two weeks in the eastern part of the desert and I enjoyed every minute of it – far more so in fact than the south-bound Saharan journey. I think that was partly because I was so much more relaxed with myself and the people, but also because we were so far off the beaten track that there was an unspoiled air about things.

At Fort Gardel, which is 560 km north-east of Tamanrasset, we spent several days living in a *zeriba* whilst our excellent Touareg guide showed us famous rock engravings in the Tassili mountains. He also drove us right out into the desert to where his brother was camping with the camels. Whilst a Touareg boy caught camels for us to ride, we sat in the sand and ate delicious dried meat, which had been wrapped in dung and buried in the sand. Our guide had two wives, and 12 children all from his first wife. The wives lived in separate *zeribas* and shared their husband. To marry a second wife is a sign of wealth and status and I believe our guide was the only man of his village to do so. We felt very sad when the first wife asked my husband if, in his eyes, the second wife was pretty.

My memories of the drive between Fort Gardel and Djanet are of baking delicious desert bread in the sand under the embers of a fire, of a hummingbird singing on top of our tent at sunrise, and of a sandstorm which kept us huddled in our tent for 24 hours. Temperatures dropped to freezing as the fog of sand completely blocked out the sun.

Driving into Djanet, one is struck by the absence of women on the streets. The men do all the shopping, socializing and business while the women stay at home. Throughout Algeria there are government-run food shops, called national galleries, in an attempt to standardise food prices and it was in one such shop in Djanet that I found myself the only woman amongst a crowd of men pushing and shoving for cheese and eggs after a new consignment had been delivered. These were luxury items.

Further north we visited a really isolated oasis village at the bottom of a canyon. The village chief came out to meet us, or rather my husband Chris, as he totally ignored me. Chris was directed to the chief's house, and I was taken to the women's compound where numerous women and children were congregated feeding and washing babies and small children. I was requested to sit in the centre and breastfeed my youngest son, which I did, much to the delight and amusement of the women. They also insisted on taking off Ed's nappy to discover his sex. Needless to say I was complimented for having three sons and no daughters.

We continued to drive north, over tortuous black rock strewn with corrugations that shook the vehicle nearly to pieces, and past the wrecks of others that failed to make it. Then, passing Illizi, we picked up a newly scraped gravel road that felt like a motorway, and a day later we were on tarmac again, and almost out of 'our' desert. The last 700 or 800 miles to the coast were 'civilised' as a result of the oil industry, and for us the magic of the desert was already a memory.

Whilst we as a family were not hassled at all in Algeria, we did meet five Dutch girls at Tamanrasset who, travelling together in a van, had been followed into the desert by some Algerian border guards and pestered for sex. It might be worth pointing out that they were dressed in shorts which is usually seen as an invitation in Islamic countries. They did manage to retain control over the situation and nothing dire happened. On the other hand, two French girls we spoke to had hitched across the Saharan highway with truck drivers and had no problems whatsoever. I feel pretty sure that had the Dutch girls been travelling the eastern route they would not have encountered the same problem. One is less likely to be hassled the further one is from the main tourist route. By the same token, however, one can also expect to be treated as inferior the further one gets from the beaten track.

TRAVEL NOTES

Languages Arabic and (in the south) Berber dialects. French is very widely spoken.

Transport Plenty of buses on main routes, including the Algiers-Ghardaia-Tamanrasset run. Hitching is possible with trucks and other tourist vehicles. If you're driving, 4–wheel drive isn't necessary for the road to Tamanrasset – many tourists do it in Citroen 2CVs, etc. – but be properly equipped if you leave the track.

Accommodation Most hotels are expensive – cheaper categories don't tend to exist except at a very basic level.

Special problems All tourists (except students) must change $200 US into Algerian dinar on arrival. Needless to say, black market rates are 4–5 times higher, though make use of this with care – the police sometimes crack down. Bureaucracy at Algerian borders is notorious: be prepared to be patient.

Guides Best for general practicalities (hotels, buses, etc.) is the French *Guide Routarde: Afrique du Nord et Sahara* (Hachette, 1985). Simon and Jan Glen, *Sahara Handbook* (Roger Lascelles, 1985) is good for the desert routes.

CONTACTS

The Algerian feminist movement is essentially underground and though meetings take place from time to time they are allowed no permanent office or address.

BOOKS

'Bound and Gagged by the Family Code: An Interview with Algerian Feminist Nadine Claire', in *Trouble and Strife*' magazine (c/o Women's centre,

50 Bethel St, Norwich, UK).

Juliette Minces, *The House of Disobedience* (Al Saqi, 1984) Introduction to the legal status of women in the Arab world and everyday forms of oppression. Case studies on Algeria and Egypt.

Fatma Dussedik, 'Algeria: The Day-to-Day Struggle', in *Sisterhood is Global* (see General Bibliography). Brief statement of the need for a resurgence of the women's movement.

Charlotte H. Bruner, ed., *Unwinding Threads* (see General Bibliography) contains an extract from Fadhma Amrouche's autobiography '*Histoire de ma vie*' written in the lyrical style of Berber (Kabyle) folk music; the book also includes a short folktale *The Story of the Chest* by her daughter Marguerite Amrouche, who continued her mother's tradition, and a short story by Assia Djebar, *Les Impatients*, which deals with the everyday life of Algerian women and her own hopes for emancipation and change.

Ali Ghalem, *A Wife for my Son* (Zed Books, 1985). The painful yet determined struggle of a woman becoming conscious of her own strengths and possibilities.

Paul Henissart, *Wolves in the City: The Death of French Algeria* (1970, Paladin 1973). Grippingly written account of the last months of the war and the resistance.

Pontecorvo, *The Battle of Algiers* (a film – 1965). A classic, clear and powerful on women's involvement in the resistance.

Thanks to Claire Thomas for background information.

TUNISIA

With its Mediterranean beaches and fairly gentle culture, **Tunisia** has developed a highly successful package holiday industry over the last ten years. Most visitors, however, stay in their resorts – mainly around Cap Bon and the 'desert island' of Djerba. In the more remote areas, in the west, for example, you're constantly made aware of the country's traditionally conservative Islamic past. Sexual harassment, in the more developed resorts and in westernised Tunis, is persistent, though basically similar to the sort of pestering you find throughout Mediterranean Europe. In the desert south, where you are defined and limited according to Islamic custom, attitudes are harsher. Here, it is worth considering joining up with a group that includes a man.

The official **status of women** in Tunisia has changed radically over the last thirty years, due mainly to the liberalizing influence of Bourguiba, Tunisia's president-for-life since the country gained independence from the French in 1956. Throughout he has attempted to justify reforms from within original Islamic texts, thus securing the support of Tunisia's religious leaders. Polygamy was outlawed (as Mohammed's stipulation that each wife was to be treated equally was held to be impossible), and women were given equal franchise and statutory equal pay in line with Islamic precepts. Opportunities for work are more promising than in any other Maghreb nation and family planning has been introduced on a wide scale.

Actual social change has, however, been slow to follow these comparatively radical laws – a frequent assertion nowadays being that women have 'too much power'. It's also doubtful whether many of the rural poor are aware of their statutory rights. There remain disparities between the sexes in education and many more women than men are illiterate. In recent years the economic recession coupled with events in Iran have led to an incipient form of reaction. Though many more women work, wages are often paid directly to husbands or used for dowry. Since 1979 increasing numbers of women have taken to wearing the *Chador*, the Iranian headscarf-like veil. As this apparent backlash continues, the overall process of social change is likely to become increasingly complicated. Women are finding themselves caught between, on the one hand, the break-up of the extended family – already causing problems of isolation in the cities – and, on the other, new reactionary pressures.

▧ **Linda Cooley has been working as a teacher in Tunisia for the last six years; she has travelled extensively around the country.**

Tunisian women enjoy a measure of freedom and equality under the law unknown in many other Arab countries. Polygamy was abolished in the mid–1950s when Tunisia became independent. Divorce laws have been altered in women's favour. Most girls attend school. A reasonably large percentage of women are in higher education. Many women work outside the home. There are women in the professions and two women ministers in the government. An established feminist group exists which holds regular meetings, in the Club Tahar Haddad in the capital's Medina, to discuss matters of particular interest to women, although, admittedly, the participants are generally middle-class intellectuals; the mass of working women know little of its activities. There is even a feminist magazine, *Nissa*, introduced in the spring of 1985.

But the presence of so many women in public can be misleading. It may lull you into a false sense of security when you first arrive and lead to false expectations of what you can and cannot do. If you walk around the capital (and remember, this is very unrepresentative of the rest of the country), you will see women in jeans and the latest fashions, sometimes sitting in cafés, even girls walking along holding hands with their boy-friends. But what you cannot see and should know is that these same fashionably dressed girls have fathers who expect them to be home by eight o'clock at the latest, who expect them to be virgins when they marry and who often expect them to marry a relative chosen by the parents. The clothes may have changed in recent years; the amount of women at work may have changed but, deep down, social attitudes have not changed. The Tunisian women you see in the streets are going to work or going home; Tunisia remains a traditional Arab society where the idea of a woman travelling abroad alone is still considered as rather strange. It is changing, but slowly, slowly.

It is important to realise how much the Europeanised image of the capital is superficial. The bar in Tunisia is not like one in France – it's an exclusively male domain and wandering in for a rest and a beer, you are bound to be stared at. Similarly, you can't expect to be able to chat to the man at the next table in the café about the best place to have lunch or the best time to visit the mosque, without your conversation being taken as an invitation. Western movies have done an excellent job in persuading Tunisian men that all Western women spend their lives jumping in and out of bed, with gay abandon, with any willing male.

All this must sound somewhat off-putting. Yet, in six years living in Tunisia, I have often travelled alone; I have travelled with my son; I have travelled with another woman. Perhaps I've been lucky, but apart from the unwanted attentions of a few men, nothing has happened to me. There is no part of the country that it is unsafe to visit. (Though, unless you are enamoured of international hotel architecture – miles and miles and miles of it – you may as well avoid Hammamet and Nabeul, the most developed tourist regions.) You can see the ruins of Carthage, the underground dwellings in tranquil Matmata, the fruitful oases of the south and beautiful Arab architecture all around. You can generally stay in cheap hotels without trouble. (The *Mahalas* in particular are very good value and the ones in Djerba and Kairouan are extremely lovely buildings.) You can see everything. But, travelling alone it's incredibly hard to get to know the people.

You will also find it hard to relax, never being sure about how your behaviour will be interpreted if you do. I learnt to cope by evading direct eye contact with men, and above all never smiling at a stranger – I once found myself being followed home because I inadvertently smiled at a man as we simultaneously reached for the same tin of tomato sauce in the supermarket! Really persistent harassment is not common. It may irk you to keep your silence; not to answer like with like; not to show your disdain; but in the long run it will make your day pleasanter. After a while the ignoring game becomes a reality; you really don't notice that anyone has spoken to you!

If you cannot learn to ignore the hassle from men, you will probably find yourself impatient to leave after a very short time, taking with you an awful image of the country and vowing never to return. It is, in fact, an easy country for a woman on her own to dislike.

Travelling with a man makes it all much simpler. The stereotyped images on both sides (yours of macho Arab men and theirs of loose foreign women) can be dispensed with and everyone can act naturally. Men will talk to you both as you're sitting in a café or waiting for a bus and they're not all hustlers, they often just want someone different to talk to, that's all. You may well get invited home to meet their families, where you will be able to talk to the women in the home too as, unlike in many Arab countries, Tunisian women and men eat together.

You can also go to the *hammam* (public baths) with the women of the house. This is well worth a visit as it is the one place where women can traditionally meet as a group away from all the pressures of what is still a male-dominated society. Unless you speak Arabic it is difficult to talk to the older women there, who rarely speak French, but they are more than willing to show you how to remove the hairs from your body (and I mean your whole body!), to henna your hair, to use *tfal* (a sort of shampoo made from mud) and to give you a thorough scrub with a sort of loofah mitten (and can they scrub thoroughly!). You could, of course, take yourself to the hammam travelling alone, but it's much better to go with a Tunisian woman and, as I've said before, introductions are almost exclusively made through men.

Another possibility is that if you ask around the women you may well find that you can get yourself invited to a wedding (you don't have to know the bride or groom – hundreds of people attend Arab weddings who hardly know the couple), or to any traditional event that is going on in the area at the time. Total strangers can be very hospitable when it comes to sharing their local customs with you. And when it comes to sharing their food. I once had the most beautiful couscous brought out to the field where I was eating my picnic of cheese sandwiches. But then, I was with my son and a man.

Alone or with another woman it is possible, but you will miss a great deal of what is, essentially, Tunisian life. Hopefully through more contact between foreign women and Tunisians a greater understanding will ensue, on both sides, and the lone woman traveller will become more easily accepted.

■ **Yvette Brazier also worked as a teacher in Tunis, the capital.**

Tunis can be hard to cope with – harder, certainly, than elsewhere in the country. For it is halfway Western, the 'city of sin' for provincial Tunisians, and harassment here can often be very upfront. In simple terms, if a Tunisian man does sleep with a woman outside marriage she's most likely to be a tourist. So inevitably they try their luck.

For nine months I lived and worked in Tunis, sharing a house with other English teachers. We enjoyed it, I think, though there was a persistent, and very real, hassle from a group of boys who used to hang around the house at night, making panting noises, jeering and shouting. On one occasion they went further and threw stones. I did something that tourists would rarely consider – I complained to the local police. The next night the boys were back in strength, nearer the house than their usual corner and whooping away. With another woman I left the house by the back entrance and persuaded a policeman to accompany us home.

The boys were still near our house: as they saw us approach, all heads turned to face the opposite direction. 'So you're not going to say anything now we've got a policeman with us, eh?' my friend taunted, and they looked up guiltily. The policeman asked for their identity cards, and told us to come to the police station as soon as possible. Ten minutes later we joined them, now feeling rather sorry for them, though they were no less cocky for having been hauled in, declining to answer questions, trying to pin the blame on absent friends. One received a hefty wack for his insolence from the chief, a big man dressed in a long, brown cloak. My knees started to wobble. Fortunately we were unable to pin any particular offence on any individual, so that no charges could be brought. We talked for a while, the atmosphere clearing, and eventually all apologised to each other. The chief gave us a sheet with the details of the boys' ID cards and said that if we ever received so much as a lustful look, they would either have to pay themselves, or give the names of the offenders. This sounded like virtual bribery to me, but the police were obviously more familiar than I with local habits and morals, and everyone left quite contented.

After that incident trouble was minimal, and if anyone unaware of the agreement did try to bother us, we had only to have a quiet word with 'our lads', and we were left in peace. I couldn't help feeling some sense of triumph in all this.

Although it's become almost a cliché of travel in North Africa, I feel I have to recommend a visit to a hammam – though be warned that the second visit is never quite like the first. On my initiation I felt transported – through darkened rooms and sepia arches – back to at least the last century, only the blue plastic buckets hinting that people do actually have bathrooms in their houses. I sweated in the hot room until a Berber woman with a tattooed face came to find me and rub me down, turning me over, scrubbing my unaccustomed body and pausing only to show her colleagues how filthy I was. Meanwhile there were wedding preparations going on: a procession of women passing through, keening like Red Indians and banging a drum, accompanying a young woman who had come to be cleansed, de-haired (except for her head); the soles of her feet and palms of her hands to be hennaed, made beautiful for her husband-to-be. One moment of glory between the first stage of her life, spent under the eye of her father and eldest brother; and the second, where she is kept by her husband.

Ramadam the month of fasting for Muslims turned Tunisia upside-down. I found people going to bed at 3.00 am, only two hours before their habitual getting-up time. The usually deserted night streets were suddenly light and bustling with men, women and children, walking and drinking tea on terraces of cafés, whose dingy insides were crowded with groups of men intent on games of rummy which might buy them the price of a coffee or 100 Dinars. I had to fast with the Muslims to understand the weary faces on the afternoon train; the silence at sunset, broken only by the clinking of spoons and plates; and the renewed vitality of those emerging from their homes an hour later. Summer, and especially Ramadan, is an exciting time for Tunisian women, since the men are forbidden to 'flirt', and they can go out respectably, even without their husbands.

I was lucky in that I had a Tunisian friend and was able, from time to time, to go and stay with his family on the outskirts of Sfax. I was the first foreigner most of them had ever seen close-to, and the first ever to visit the family. We arrived one night without warning, and they were clearly very mistrustful of me. I had to show my passport and answer a host of questions. But their hospitality could not be faulted as they brought me cushions, food and tea. My friend's father even went to prepare a house for us to stay in – he and his wife opting to sleep in their other son's house during our stay.

Gradually they could see that I liked them, that I was calm and quiet and had not come expressly on a mission to corrupt their youth, their behaviour became more natural. The young people were curious, asking questions in broken French – Do you work? Do many women work in Europe? Can you wear trousers? Why don't you wear a headscarf? Are you going to become a Muslim? Do you not love Allah? I tried not to make my life and freedoms sound too tempting to these young women, brought up to believe that even a trip to Tunis is immoral – and that one is safe there only if surrounded by parents and brothers. They translated what they considered suitable for their elders to hear, though throughout I had the impression that they were indulging in some highly subversive activity with me.

TRAVEL DETAILS

Languages Arabic. Many Tunisians are completely bilingual in French (and often use it among themselves).
Transport Thorough network of trains and buses. *Louages* (collective taxis) are useful; trucks give rides in remote areas, normally for a small charge.
Accommodation *Hotels Tunisiens* are cheap alternatives to the officially graded establishments but some can be on the rough side, occasionally with dormitory accommodation only – unavailable to women. *Pensions familiales* are beginning to appear on the coast, and you are unlikely to leave the country without at least once being offered hospitality for a night.
Special problems If you're dark enough to look Tunisian you may have problems in the south, particularly if you're travelling with a Western male: an idea that's anathema.
Guide Peter Morris and Charles Farr, *The Rough Guide to Tunisia* (Routledge & Kegan Paul, 1985). An excellent guide – practical, informed and culturally sensitive. Includes an interesting section on Women in Tunisia and Bourguiba's reforms.

CONTACTS
Women producing the bi-monthly (Arabic/French) feminist magazine *Nissa*, can be contacted at 8 rue Dar el Jeid, Tunis. Any kind of international support is very much appreciated, especially as Nissa is in danger of folding for lack of funds.
Alliance of Tunisian Women for Research and Information on Women, University of Tunis, Tunis.

BOOKS
Norma Salem, *Habib Bourguiba, Islam and the Creation of Tunisia* (Croom Helm, 1984). Somewhat thesis-like, but a useful study of the man at the heart of the modern nation.
Wilfrid Knapp, *Tunisia* (Thames & Hudson, 1971) The best of several history-cum-background books that came out in the 1970s.
Albert Memmi, *The Pillar of Salt* (1955) Tunisia's most distinguished novelist, and virtually the only one to be translated into English. As a North African Jew, Memmi's work is preoccupied with the problem of identity.

LIBYA

There are virtually no tourists in **Libya**. It's incredibly hard to get a tourist visa (from London it's impossible) and with the prevailing antagonism towards Westerners, fuelled by Gaddafi's powerful rhetoric against 'Capitalist imperialism', there seems little incentive to try. A few women with professional qualifications do however go out on short-term work contracts, joining the large expatriate minority (since the recent *rapprochement* with the Soviet Union many families have moved in from the Eastern bloc). Along with the rest of the country's comparatively small population they live on the Mediterranean coast – the rest of Libya consisting largely of desert.

Since the coup d'etat of 1969, Libya has been ruled by Colonel Gaddafi's revolutionary command council as a Socialist/Islamic state. Oil wealth has bought widespread improvements in living standards (Libya was one of the world's poorest countries in the 1960s) and has been used to underpin major development and education programmes.

Women, mainly urban and middle class, have been active over recent decades in organising attempts to alleviate the two major social problems of illiteracy and seclusion. (In 1951 virtually all Libyan women were illiterate). One of the largest **women's organisations** is the *General Union of Women's Association*, an umbrella organisation formed in 1972 which focuses on 'awareness campaigns', highlighting issues such as dowry. All organisations, including 'revolutionary committees' are under government control – Gaddafi himself espouses a supposedly liberationist stance. Autonomous feminist activities are viewed as subversive, and there are increasing numbers of women political prisoners, especially among the highly educated elite. Others are in exile, many campaigning in groups like the *General Union of the Women of Libya* against the country's current human rights violations and repression.

◪ **Gerda Pickin spent two months in Libya, working as an archaeologist in the eastern city of Benghazi.**

As an archaeologist I have worked in many different countries, rubbing shoulders with their cultures, and awkwardly wrapping my tongue around a variety of languages. But my experiences working in Libya still strike me as the most alien. I was employed to catalogue Greek and Roman pottery from an ancient Hellenistic and Byzantine site in the city of Benghazi. Normally I would have been employed as a supervisor, but Libyan workmen strongly resent a woman boss, no matter how carefully she treads, and this role-reversal barrier which I had successfully overcome in other countries around the world proved insurmountable here.

The workmen laughed when they saw me reading a book; they thought I was pretending to be literate in order to impress them!

Mufta, the university student who was seconded to the site, was more understanding. He was fascinated by me and tried very hard to befriend me, but both of us found the cultural religious differences made real communication almost impossible. Mufta felt he could most easily get on with me by pretending I was a man, giving me the rights and privileges of his male friends. To treat me as he would a sister or a wife would have proved very difficult, since women in Libya are not granted even an iota of the freedom I was allowed. Having a woman as a platonic friend or even as a girlfriend is out of the question, and in Mufta's case even a wife was a far-off dream, as the bride-price he saved up (about £2000) went on a car instead.

Because my time was mainly spent working, I didn't travel extensively, but I did make the journey from Benghazi to Derna or Cyrene several times. I hitchhiked in a group of four, and we easily got lifts from produce lorries, for which we had to pay a modest fee. We hired a car once to go out into the desert a little way, and had planned to cross into Egypt, but were advised that the border was difficult by road, so we didn't attempt it. The other journeys I made in Mufta's bride-price car.

The best thing about travelling in Libya is the almost total lack of tourists. I visited the Greek and Roman ruins at Cyrene and Apollonia along the coast from Benghazi, and was able to explore the well-preserved remains alone. The Mediterranean too was beautiful, the atmosphere created by the columns and statues idyllic. The sharp contrast of lush green coast and sparkling sea to the harsh hot desert always at your back is truly breathtaking. In no other place have I ever felt more off-the-beaten-track.

This feeling of being alone physically was accentuated by the basic hostility I felt when I went out on my own. I was always out of place, with a strong sense of having to be very careful in what I said, did, wore, etc. A typical example was when I tried to go for a swim at the beach in Benghazi. The public beaches are divided up for Males, Females, and Families. The Male section looked like any resort beach, with radios, ice creams, soft drinks, volley ball – all that was missing were the women. The Female beach by comparison was sombre. Most of the women were fully clothed and some veiled. I felt an intruder with my modest, one piece swimming costume, bobbing about with the usual Mediterranean companions of plastic bags and empty bleach bottles.

Libya is an Islamic country first and foremost. All alcohol is illegal, and even a city like Benghazi is not equipped to entertain tourists. Apart from the scenery, the antiquities, and the markets, the visitor to Benghazi must be prepared to entertain herself. Most women are veiled, some 'liberated' women cover their entire faces with a thin black scarf while wearing Western dress. I was constantly aware of the fact that I was in a Muslim country, with the calls to prayer from every minaret a regular feature throughout the day. Every conversation involved religion directly or indirectly, and even on a visit to the doctor I was reminded of the Faith. I had a case of dysentery and visited the local doctor. He was a personable Egyptian who began by apologising that he would not be able to do any physical examination, as it was not allowed. Fortunately for me the diagnosis was simple without one, and medication was provided.

The closest contact I had with Libyan women was through Mufta. I stayed with his family on several occasions, and found his women relatives friendly and curious. Communication was more difficult, as only his sister could speak English, and hers was very halting. Again, they all expressed surprise and admiration at my ability to read! On one visit to Derna, Mufta was to take me to the cinema, which was showing a sub-titled *Sink the Bismark*. Mufta's sister begged to go, but Mufta refused to allow her. She stood up to him, much to everyone's amazement, using my freedom to come and go as an example. But Mufta stood firm, and, as there was no question of her being able to go unescorted by a male member of the family, she was forced to remain behind.

I was fortunate to be invited to the wedding of Mufta's cousin, a shy young girl with no English. Libyan weddings are segregated affairs, and I of course attended the women's festivities. In a large, dimly-lit room, a trio of musicians kept up a constant hypnotic round of Arabic music to which many of the women, young and very old alike, did exotic, gyrating dances. The room became heavy with scent, the odour of rich spicy food, and crowded with women. All sizes and shapes, they wore their most colourful flowing garments, bedecked with tier upon tier of gold jewellery. The bride entered after an hour and sat upon a make-shift throne, laden in even more colourful veils and robes, her gold adornments a dazzling display in the half-light. Every part of the room seemed to be whirling, weaving, and swaying with the never-ending music. Finally, after what seemed many hours, the men's party came to fetch the bride. The groom took her off to his house and all the guests followed. We clustered around the courtyard, for no particular reason that I could fathom. I was about to find Mufta to ask what would happen next, when a cheer rose up from a knot of men under the window. Craning to have a look, I at once saw the cause – a bloody sheet was being waved from the window. The wedding was over, and we each made our separate ways home in the dawn light.

My overall feelings in Libya were of being restricted and nervous. I encountered disapproval whenever I ventured out on the streets alone (being with another woman was more accepted), including having stones thrown at me by small boys. While I did travel alone at times, I always felt uncomfortable, although I never encountered any actual violence or physical unpleasantness. My discomfort stemmed largely from being unable to establish friendly relationships at more than an extremely superficial level. It was difficult to get to know any women, with few opportunities to meet in an informal setting and the lack of language on both sides. Establishing friendships with men was equally prohibitive as I found it hard to interpret the significance of phrases, gestures, etc., and worried lest my own words or actions be misread.

Were I to go again, I would learn more about Islamic customs before going. (I badly offended one man who called to visit at the hostel one evening by putting my feet up on a footstool, exposing the soles of my sandals to him.) I would attempt some basic Arabic, both for use in shops and to be able to talk to more women. At least next time I'll be prepared for salt water coming out of the taps in Benghazi – a shock when you take your first bath or attempt to brush your teeth!

Everywhere I went, people respected and were over-awed by Colonel Gaddafi, and most felt that he had done a lot for Libya. I saw no evidence of trade unions, but the workmen on the excavation were reasonably paid, and told me that there was no unemployment. They were proud of the lack of slums, and there was general agreement that a man who worked hard could do well, with strong family support for the old and infirm.

Despite the headlines which paint an infamous leader and imply vast armies of terrorists, ordinary people were more concerned with the watermelon crop, or whether the wind would blow from the desert or the sea tomorrow.

TRAVEL NOTES

Languages Arabic. English (and Italian, the old colonial language) are generally understood by 'professionals', hotel and shop managers, etc.

Transport There are bus, minibus and taxi services between Benghazi and Tripoli but to travel at all freely you need to hire a car (from Tripoli). Most of the larger cities have a reasonably good local bus service. Hitching is also possible (you pay for lifts), though not recommended alone. Internal flights are quite cheap and you can get ferry rides along the coast.

Accommodation No tourist facilities as such, though most of the larger towns have a few expensive hotels. People working in Libya normally rent or buy flats.

Special problems It is essential to comply with all Islamic codes of behaviour: modest dress, strictly no alcohol, etc.

Guide Nothing recent – old editions of Cook's Handbook to North Africa (which are generally pre-war) include Libya.

CONTACTS
General Union of Women in Libya, Benghazi.

Chapter Six

WEST AFRICA

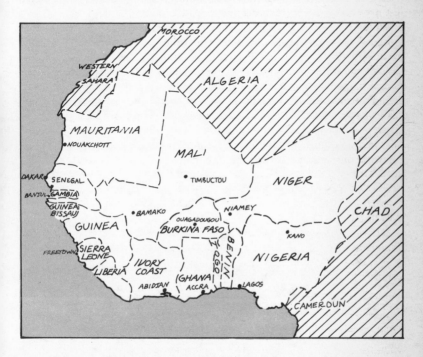

West Africa is a vast, troubled area, on the whole little visited by travellers. The region's history of colonialism – most of it by the French – has left the familiar legacy of dependency and internal tensions, fuelled by the arbitrary boundaries drawn up across tribal and ethnic divides. There are also of course the roads, banks and schools. The French have, for the most part, maintained their various coastal resorts (amongst them resorts in **Senegal** and the **Ivory Coast**) and in the tiny former British colony of **The Gambia** there's now a thriving British package tour industry. Elsewhere, poverty, drought, political upheaval and a high level of crime and corruption have all played their part in putting off foreign visitors.

How far the problems affect you largely depends on how and, of course, where you choose to travel. The **Sahel region**, including **Mali** and **Burkina Faso**, suffers desperately from a lack of fertile land, aggravated by recurring drought. Travel is rough at the best of times and in some areas antagonism is increasing towards the groups of affluent foreigners that cross the desert by truck. As yet though it is surprisingly muted and in most of the rural areas the custom of showing incredible warmth and hospitality to strangers persists.

Islam prevails in most of the West African nations but in comparison with the Arab world its culture poses few particular problems for travellers. West African women are far more visible and much easier to meet than their counterparts in, say, the Middle East. As usual they have to bear the heaviest burdens including the double responsibility of agricultural and domestic work. Travelling around you're likely to find that sexual harassment is much less of a problem than harassment for money. In the larger cities especially you'll be almost continually approached with requests and demands for money – there are no set ways to respond.

We have included pieces on only five out of the seventeen West African countries mainly due to the generally poor response we received for this region. We'd particularly like to include pieces on the Ivory Coast and Sierra Leone in the second edition.

SENEGAL

Senegal, at the westernmost point of Africa, straddles the border of the Sahel region. To the north are large expanses of Sahelian dustland and to the south, richer, tropical lands. The population, predominantly Muslim with large Christian and Animist minorities, has been listed by the UN among those most at risk from famine and drought. Currently the country receives more foreign aid money than *any* other Black African country.

As the first French colony in West Africa, Senegal became the administrative centre for the region and since independence in 1960 has retained close economic and military links with France. French influence is evident in all state institutions as well as the wide road networks and transport system. The country is now ruled as a democratic republic and has maintained a reputation amongst the troubled states of West Africa for 'political stability'. Its capital, Dakar, is a strategic Atlantic port and the region's main transit point for ships heading further south.

In many respects Senegal is an easy place to visit – and not only as part of an expensive package tour. Transport is good, there's a fair amount of accommodation and the Senegalese people are renowned for their hospitality to foreigners (often including invitations to stay in their homes). You do, however, have to get used to being a symbol of affluence.

You'll be constantly approached in the streets and people don't easily understand why you won't give money. How to cope with this (and similarly how to cope with accepting hospitality from Senegalese barely managing to live on a subsistence level) is something you'll need to work out. Bringing and carrying gifts with you helps.

The main **women's organisation,** the *Fédération des Associations Féminines du Sénégal* (FAFS) was founded by the Socialist Party and retains close links with the government. Its chief emphasis is on development and the provision of social welfare and educational services. Although it has a wide membership and has set up a range of local groups, its impact in the rural areas is still small.

A more radical group is the *Association of African Women for Research and Development* (AAWORD), created by a group of African women dedicated to doing feminist research from an African perspective. The group's guidelines and priorities were drawn up at an important meeting in 1977, entitled 'African Women and the Decolonisation of Research', since when it has assisted in numerous schemes emphasising the need for the direct participation of local women in development projects. One of AAWORD's central concerns has also been to counteract Western outrage about genital mutilation by placing it firmly in context as an African problem to be resolved by African people. Sharing these concerns is the International Commission for the Abolition of Sexual Mutilation, who print a quarterly feminist magazine, *Femmes et société*. The magazine, which covers a range of women's rights issues, has recently run into difficulties with funding.

▨ **Kay Sharp has been living for the past two years in Dakar, the capital of Senegal, teaching English as a foreign language to adults.**

Senegal surprised me on first acquaintance by its relaxed public lifestyle, its live-and-let-live attitude to foreigners and the high profile of its women – three things my experience of other Muslim countries had not led me to expect, and which made travelling both easier and more rewarding.

Teranga, an untranslatable Wolof word combining the meaning of hospitality, warmth, kindness and good manners, is probably the most famous Senegalese tradition – and I have met teranga whenever I have travelled, whether alone or accompanied. Add to this the fact that people are used to seeing foreigners come and go in their country, and that Senegalese women, who almost always earn a living outside the home, regularly travel alone from town to town, and you can begin to understand why they are tolerant to foreign women travellers.

Despite the importance of Islam, the women here have never been veiled, so foreign women do not stand out like something that's just walked off a cinema screen. This is not to say that you'll never get hassled, but it's mostly harassment in town from men trying to sell you things. The rest is of the fairly adolescent 'where-are-you-going-can-I-walk-with-you' type. Irritating (sometimes very), but not threatening.

Dakar, the capital, is schizophrenic in the style of most Third World cities, with its rich/poor, high-rise/shanty-town, westernised/ exotic contradictions. I still find it hard to cope with the beggars, often disabled by polio or leprosy, sitting side by side with affluence.

Many tourists divide their time in Dakar between French restaurants and private beaches, with a quick souvenir-buying sortie to a 'colourful' local market. But if you wish to move out of the tourist circuit, then take a stroll through the Medina – one of the oldest and most densely populated quarters. My most vivid images of it are the everyday details: the scraggy chickens and sheep, the glimpses into inner courtyards where women stir pots over charcoal stoves, or sit on doorsteps together weaving cowrie-shells, beads, gold rings and false hair from South Korea into exquisite braided hairstyles.

I remember my initial surprise at children calling *toubab* (white) after me. Mostly they do this out of friendly curiosity and though the term is not in itself an insult – more a recognition that you're white and different – it does inevitably carry all sorts of uncomfortable connotations.

Sunday afternoon is a good time to go to the Medina, as you might see a *sabakh* – a social event when women get together to dance for their own enjoyment. Standing in a circle in the dusty street, they build up rhythm and excitement, clapping with the tam-tams, until someone takes the centre to dance. The dances are mesmerising, and in another context would be easy to classify as pornographic. But with so much female laughter, and with women dancing mainly for each other, the psychology is obviously more complex than that. (It made me think about 'belly-dances' in the harem.) Men do attend, but it's very much a women's event, and well worth seeing.

Outside Dakar you can basically go north into the Sahel, or south to Casamance, where the land is fertile and the influence of Islam is weaker.

I took the 'Casamance Express' from Dakar harbour to the southern capital, Ziguinchor, and it turned out to be the best journey I've made here. You can book a cabin, but I enjoyed sleeping on deck with the tradeswomen who go back and forth dealing in regional produce. They sold me hot coffee when I got up to watch the palm trees go by, and the dolphins following us.

While in Casamance I stayed with village people in their homes and found it a memorable experience. People are very hospitable (teranga again) and will find you accommodation if you arrive in the village and ask. How much you should pay really depends on your means, but it is a good idea to give your hostess something in advance, or each morning so she can buy extra food. Language can be a barrier, as women inevitably get the thin end of education and are much less likely to speak French. Children are often the best translators and notebooks and biros for school are valued 'thank-yous'.

If you don't stay with a family, the best alternative is the *campements*, basic but comfortable hotels in simple buildings. They are often run by villagers and have good local food.

If you have time it's also worth going north to St Louis, if only to see what 'Sahel' means. Apart from the crumbling, picturesque town, I have memory-pictures of endless miles of straight road through flat dustland, with baobab trees, thatched village compounds in the distance, skeleton cows and wild camels.

◤ **Daphne Topouzis spent six months in Senegal researching a PhD; she lived with a Senegalese family on the outskirts of Dakar.**

My original purpose in going to Senegal was to research into the impact of French colonial rule on the development of Black Politics during the 1930s and 1940s. I also wanted to collect material on the Women's Movement in the cities and the role of women in rural development. Yet, it gradually became apparent to me that living with a Senegalese family was easily the most valuable experience of the trip. It enabled me to meet and get close to a large number of women of all ages, from all walks of life, which would have otherwise been impossible.

A friend who had also researched in West Africa helped me make contact with a Muslim family in Dakar. Though we had never met before, the Diops borrowed a couple of relatives' cars and came to meet me at the airport like an old friend. Hospitality is central to Senegalese culture and hosts will go to great lengths to provide their guests with everything they possibly can.

After a short drive we arrived at the 'Keur Diop' (Diop household) in Liberté VI, one of Dakar's suburbs. The hostess, Marianne, had gathered all the family and neighbourhood in the courtyard. After a maternal greeting, she introduced me to everyone and made a little welcome speech. Tea and sugar-coated peanuts were served while the women prepared a number of different dishes from *chicken au yassa* (chicken with onion sauce) to *lakh* (millet porridge with yoghurt). This was clearly a very special occasion.

Curiosity and shyness on both sides made conversation awkward for the first couple of days until the youngest children broke the ice. They taught me my first words of Wolof, reminded me of everybody's names, gave me directions to the bus stop and involved me in family activities. Within a week or so I had settled into a daily routine and had learnt a great deal about my host family and its expectations of me.

Marianne, aged 56, was a secretary in a Dakar hospital, the second of four wives and mother of three daughters and five sons. Just under half of all marriages in Senegal are polygamous (Muslims can have up to four wives) and polygyny is a harsh reality and nightmare for many women like her. It involves economic hardship, neglect of the older wife, favouritism of the younger one, jealousy (wives often share the same bedroom), oversized families and overcrowded households. Yet, the official Women's Movement has not dared question the institution. We spent long periods together talking about most issues, it seemed to me that she enjoyed having someone around who wanted to listen.

Marianne's daughters (aged 16, 22 and 23) were most curious about me and quickly became constant companions. One particular incident a few days after my arrival brought us together After jokingly remarking that my long, straight hair looked quite dull and ugly, they began plaiting it without awaiting my reply: 'Plaits can make anyone look good,' they said. However graceful they looked on them, plaits looked ridiculous on me. Yet the *pagnes* (square patterned fabrics tied around the waist) they offered me did look good and felt comfortable so I began wearing them regularly.

My relationships with the men in the family were friendly and comfortable except for an isolated misunderstanding with the eldest son. But being always a little unsure of my status I tried to maintain a safe distance. I rarely saw Mr Diop (a retired postman) as he spent almost all of his time with his third wife.

On the whole, I greatly appreciated the fact that everyone in the family was discreet, never asking personal questions which might have been difficult to answer (on religion, politics or sex). Part of the explanation might be that I was much more curious about them than they were about me. Yet, despite our differences, they made me feel like a member of their family: they encouraged me to learn Wolof, wear *pagnes*, and allowed me to help with the cooking.

The only two things I found difficult to cope with were the lack of privacy and their unshakeable belief that, being white, I had an inexhaustible supply of money. The lack of privacy meant that I did not have a quiet half-hour to relax, read or write letters. But there was no way around it as the family was large and the house overcrowded. Similarly, I never found a way of resolving the problem of money. Even though I contributed a weekly sum to the family income, regularly bought treats, took the children to the cinema, etc., etc., I was regularly asked for cash. If there was an emergency (medical expenses or school fees) I gave what I could. But often it was for luxuries (new boubous or cosmetics) which seemed essential to them but not to me. I learnt to say I did not have money but that always created some tension.

I also refrained from smoking in front of the elders of the family though

I did smoke with Marianne's children. At home, alcohol was definitely out and I was even reluctant to have a beer in downtown Dakar in their presence.

Except for those relatively minor problems, my life with the family ran smoothly once I established a routine of my own. My day began at 7 am when after a cup of *kénkilibah* (local herb tea) I would take the bus to the 'Building Administratif' where the government archives are held. At 6 pm I would return to Liberté VI, often stopping by on the way amid the tiny dark market stalls, loaded with vegetables and colour.

Marianne's daughters would start to prepare the food in the courtyard while there was still daylight. Evening entertainment consisted in either visiting friends or dancing to the salsa-esque tunes of Dakar's pop bands, Youssou N'Dour and Super Djamono. Social life around the family was so enjoyable that I never went downtown to discos, restaurants or bars. I know they exist, and they are popular amongst the Senegalese, but it never seemed worth the trip. Moreover, Liberté VI was relaxing after a hectic day in Dakar. Everybody knew each other, little French was spoken and no whites lived there. At first I felt uncomfortable being stared at in the streets but gradually people got used to me. As soon as I learnt some Wolof the barrier was broken and I began greeting neighbours regardless of whether I knew them or not.

My first trip outside Dakar was to Fatick, a small town four hours south of the capital. Marianne's son took me to visit his grandmother and her family. The further away we got from Dakar the more we could see the effects of the drought: long stretches of land with dried-up baobabs, cotton trees and abandoned villages. Around Fatick, the dry earth had cracked and dead cattle in different stages of disintegration baked in the sun. We visited the local market to get *gris-gris* and went to a wrestling match. Wrestling is Senegal's national sport and is worth seeing. There is usually an hour of ritual preceding the actual struggle which only lasts a few minutes.

A second trip to Touba was a little disappointing. Touba is the birthplace of the Mouridyyia – Senegal's fast growing Muslim brotherhood. A great mosque and Koranic university dominate the town, which itself is very poor. The contrast between the incredible wealth of the mosque and the poverty surrounding it is quite disturbing. Touba has its own militia who can (and do) arrest people for drinking alcohol or smoking cigarettes within the boundaries.

On another trip, with two women friends, I took the Casamance express boat down to Ziguinchor and visited the US Peace Corps house, which is situated right behind the port. (The Peace Corps is an American voluntary development agency.) Even though I initially had reservations about the organisation and its approach to work in Africa, I found the volunteers friendly, hard-working and eager for company. You will only pay a pound for a night's accommodation and if you shop at the market you can cook in the house. Also, the volunteers are usually delighted to take travellers to their assigned villages. Their knowledge of the local languages and the fact that they are well integrated in the local community are a positive contrast to the Canadian missionaries nearby who seemed totally estranged from their surroundings.

After Ziguinchor I went to Diembering, a small village off Cap Skirring. Villagers were drying fish in the sun, mending fishing nets and repairing pirogues on the beach. I had originally planned to stay for a few days at the government *campement*. But the same evening I began having all the symptoms of malaria: chills and flushes, headaches, hallucinations and diarrhoea. Usually, the first 72 hours of malaria attacks are the worst and after that a large dose of Nivaquine begins to work. I was helped on to the boat back to Dakar and went to the Peace Corps doctor. (They usually only treat volunteers but made an exception in my case.) It took ten days for me to recover and when I returned to the Diop family they treated me as though I had been long lost, showing very real relief and concern.

Soon after that episode I was stopped in the centre of Dakar by a gendarme who wanted to check my passport. As I didn't have one on me I was taken to the station where I encountered at least twenty whites picked up for the same reason. (Every once in a while the police go out on such raids to show foreigners who's boss.) After sitting for hours in the waiting room I began to feel uncomfortable and frightened. The Chief of Police asked me a long series of questions and then calmly assured me that I would be there all day. A few moments later someone offered me a cigarette and I thanked him in Wolof. Suddenly the atmosphere changed, the police became warm and apologetic and I was inundated with invitations and offers of hospitality.

On the whole these problems did not cast a shadow over my stay. They were part of the challenge of trying to lead an integrated life in a very different culture and climate to my own. I've kept contact with the family in Liberté VI whom I consider now part of my extended family and have been invited to return for the marriage of the eldest daughter.

TRAVEL NOTES

Languages French and several African languages – Wolof is the most widely spoken.

Transport The basic transport throughout Senegal is the bush-taxi (*taxi-brousse*). Each passenger pays for a seat, and the taxi leaves only when it is full. Try to travel early in the morning to avoid long waits for other passengers, especially in villages. Prices are government-fixed and fairly low. In Dakar there are taxis and buses.

Accommodation The tourist hotels of Dakar are generally expensive. Outside the capital you can stay in *campements* (cheap but comfortable accommodation in simple buildings). In the rural areas it is likely that you'll be invited to stay in people's homes. You should offer some money or gifts towards your keep.

Special problems You will often be approached for money by 'hasslers', 'beggars' and other people who need it and have none. People have their own ways of dealing with this – most give coins or small gifts.

Guide Mylene Remy, *Senegal Today* (Editions Jeune Afrique) The best general guidebook around.

CONTACTS

Association of African Women in Research and Development (AAWORD), Codesria, BP3304, Dakar. A pan-African women's federation which carries out research, publishes a journal, and campaigns for women's rights throughout Africa.

Femmes et Société, Villa 811, Sicap Baobabs, Dakar. Quarterly magazine published by the *Commission Internationale pour l'abolition des mutilations sexuelle*. Covers a range of issues including genital mutilation, sexual harassment and discrimination at work. The commision, which has offices

across Africa, has a reputation for dynamic and innovative actions.

Council for the Development of Economic and Social Research in Africa (CODESRA):-B.P. 3304, Dakar. One of the 22 priority research themes identified is Women and Development in Africa, though as yet little research has been undertaken by the group.

BOOKS

Mariama Ba, *So Long a Letter* (Virago, 1982) Brilliant portrait by Senegalese feminist of a Muslim woman living in a society of transition. Ba died in 1981. Her second book *The Scarlet Song* (Longman, 1986) focuses on the relationship between an educated French woman and a poor Senegalese man.

Nafissatou Diallo *A Dakar Childhood* (Longman, 1982) Autobiographical account of growing up in Dakar.

Aminata Sow Fell, *Beggars Strike* (Longman, 1981). Fictional tale of a beggars uprising in Dakar by Senegal's leading woman novelist.

BURKINA FASO

Burkina Faso (previously known as Upper Volta) is somewhat of an exception in this region in that only a small percentage of the population is Muslim. The northern part of the country lies in the Sahel (the fringe of the Sahara desert) but, unlike its larger neighbouring countries of Mali and Niger, it does not stretch to the Sahara itself. Nonetheless drought is a recurring feature and it was the disastrous drought of 1973 that first brought this country to the world's attention. Since then the influx of aid and development workers has led to a rapid expansion of the capital, Ouagadougou, which now has a range of Western-style amenities. Recently, with the emergence of cheap French charter flights, the country has been used by independent travellers as a starting point for West Africa.

It is not an easy country to travel around. There's very little transport and the bush taxis which run from town to town are slow and incredibly crowded. Without your own transport it's almost impossible to reach the more isolated villages. Most of the people you'll meet, however, are friendly and welcoming and even travelling alone it's unlikely that you'll encounter any sort of oppressive level of sexual harassment.

In August 1983 a popular Revolution brought the government of Captain Thomas Sankara to power. At the present time Sankara is still in power and the Revolutionary ruling council, the CNR, has begun an ambitious programme of political reform which promises to make far-reaching changes in the social and economic structures of Burkinabe life – educational reform and a primary health care plan are major features. How far Sankara will be successful in this is impossible to tell; after all he still has to contend with the basic features of life in the Sahel – drought, food shortages and extreme poverty exacerbated by world capitalism.

There are also the beginnings of a **Women's Movement,** though predominantly government funded and made up of urban-based, middle-class women. Their main focus, in line with government policy, is on education and welfare reform. In the rural areas increasing numbers of women are involved in self-help community groups – participating in various local development schemes (see Henrietta Moore's piece below for more detail).

■ Henrietta Moore, an anthropoligist, worked for a year in Burkina Faso as a field officer with an all-woman team.

Burkina Faso is a small landlocked country which lies to the north of Ghana. Until recently, the capital, Ouagadougou, was a distant and mysterious town, its name synonymous with the furthest reaches of the European imagination. This Sahelian city was to the French what Timbuctou used to be to the British. Things have changed now, thanks to the Sahel drought and the subsequent influx of foreign aid and ex-patriot workers. Ouagadougou is now an expanding metropolis (it grows at a rate of more than 10 per cent a year), and the air-conditioned supermarkets and aid-organisation Landrovers attest to the changes which the last decade has brought. These changes contrast with the donkeys and bicycles of the urban poor, the lack of water and the flocks of vultures which circle silently over the city.

There are few ways for a traveller to reach Ouaga. The easiest, and perhaps the least exciting, is to fly direct from France, across the great expanse of the Sahara. A gentler and more interesting way to appreciate exactly what the Sahel means is to board the train in Abidjan in the Ivory Coast and watch the subtropical vegetation of coastal West Africa gradually give way to savannah and the arid interior of the north.

Travel inside Burkina Faso is not easy. Roads are improving all the time, but it was only in 1984 that public bus services between Ouaga and Bobo Dioulasso (the second largest city in the country) were instituted. Ouaga itself now has a municipal bus service. Before this came into being the traveller had no way to move about the city except on foot, unless some indulgent resident could be persuaded to lend them a moped. Mopeds and cars fill the streets of the capital (one reason for introducing a bus service was to cut down on their numbers), which has an appallingly high accident rate.

Finding somewhere to stay in Ouaga is little problem. The city has recently become the stepping-off point for young Europeans wanting to explore West Africa and a number of cheap hotels have sprung up to meet the needs of the market. Small bars abound all over town, and provide a limited, but very good, selection of food – mainly, roast meat, salad, and a variety of porridges made from millet, cassava and other staples. Bars in Ouaga are fun and safe. Women travelling together will have no problems and very little hassle. People are friendly, helpful and happy to talk. Many bars have live music. Dancing is a popular pastime, and no traveller should miss the opportunity. West African cities have a lively nightlife, especially in comparison with East Africa or the Middle East.

Leaving Ouaga to go to another main town is not difficult, but to get out into the more remote parts of the country and into the villages can be a problem. There are of course the ubiquitous 'bush taxis' (*taxis brousses*), but these are slow and crammed to capacity by Burkinabe making essential journeys. These taxis ply the main routes, and will take you eastwards over the border to Niger or westwards into Mali if you so desire. However they do not leave the main roads, and it is almost impossible to find your way from roadside settlements into villages, unless you have your own transport. All of which may be frustrating, but it is an inevitable feature of travelling in West Africa and needn't prevent you from meeting people and understanding something of the country.

Burkina Faso is a poor country; only about 10 per cent of the population are literate and only 20 per cent of children attend primary school. After water and food, education and health care are the primary areas of concern. One encouraging development in recent years has been the growth of village-level pre-cooperative groups in many parts of the country. Not all these groups are strong and active, but many are attempting to respond to their community's needs. The present government has set up *Committees for the Defence of the Revolution* (CDR), based on the Cuban model, which are local community groups with social, political, cultural, and quasi-military roles. They act mainly as community self-help groups, and every Sunday groups may be seen building dams or schools, clearing ditches, mending roads and carrying out a host of other activities designed to benefit the community. The spirit of self-help is very strong and the Revolution has produced a new sense of hope which may last the next drought or it may not. Women play an active part in these organisations, and have their own groups to try and raise credits for agricultural or craft equipment.

There is probably the making of a strong Women's Movement in

Burkina Faso, but as is so often the case, the aims of the Revolution must come first. The needs of rural women are not met by the activities of the movement, because it is predominantly an urban, middle-class phenomenon. There is, however, much talk on the radio and in the press of the needs of rural women, sometimes defined as rural mothers. There is also one woman on the ruling CNR, a situation which corresponds well with the situation in the present British cabinet.

TRAVEL NOTES

Languages The official language is French, but it is spoken by a very small section of the population. There are various African languages – the main one is More.

Transport There is a railway route from the Ivory Coast to Ouaga and a public bus service which runs between Ouaga and Bobo Dioulasso in the dry season. Otherwise only bush taxis, which go from town to town, but are crowded, slow and do not leave the main routes.

Accommodation Cheap hotels can be found in the main towns.

Other information Burkina Faso is at present the cheapest country to fly to in West Africa thanks to charter flights offered by the air-charter company Le Point (Point Air-Mulhouse). The flights operate between Lyon, France and Ouaga. The company's headquarters are at Point Air-Mulhouse, 4 Rue des Orphelins, 68200 Mulhouse, France.

Guides Geoff Crowther's *Africa on a Shoestring* (Lonely Planet, rev. 1984) includes Burkina Faso.

BOOKS
See General Bibliography.

THE GAMBIA

A former British colony, **The Gambia** is a classic example of the indiscriminate boundaries drawn up by the colonial powers. It is mainland Africa's smallest state, consisting of a narrow strip of territory which follows the Gambia River inland for approximately 200 miles, but which is rarely more than 15 miles wide. Inland it is surrounded entirely by Senegal, with which it recently formed a confederation (Senegambia). The tourist industry, almost non-existent up until the 1960s, is currently booming. The Gambian beaches are now routine (and cheap) package territory, especially among British and Scandinavians.

Within the tourist complexes, The Gambia is a safe and relaxing place to be and many women holiday there happily on their own. As an independent traveller you'll inevitably see more of the difficulties and poverty common to all West African countries. The dominant culture is Muslim but women, who take on most of the agricultural work, are seen in most public places.

Over half the population live in rural areas, engaged in agriculture, many at a subsistence level, and as a symbol of the affluent West you are likely to be constantly and persistently approached for money. In the capital, Banjul, armed robbery and theft is on the increase. But away from the urban and tourist centres you'll generally be treated as a stranger and welcomed with open friendliness and hospitality.

The country's reputation in the region for political stability was shattered by an attempted coup in 1981. Surface order was, however, quickly restored with the help of Senegalese troops, and has been maintained since then by the establishment of much closer military and economic ties with Senegal – formally recognised in the setting up of the confederation in 1982. Senegalese troops retain an obvious presence, a high priority being to protect the tourist industry.

We have been unable to obtain information regarding women's organisations in The Gambia and would appreciate any information and contacts.

◪ Elizabeth Hart went with her family to The Gambia on a two-week package tour

Injections are your first realisation that The Gambia is going to be different. Yellow fever sounds ominous and I felt twinges of guilt at exposing my son to the pain of these and the possible risk of some unspecified disease. All this faded when we stumbled from our plane into the heat bath of Banjul airport and were bundled on to our coach (not without noticing the ineffectual resentment registering on some white faces as they were given orders by blacks). We were staying in the Kombo St Mary area some 10 miles from the capital, Banjul. It was very dark along the roadside until we came to more populated areas where, despite the fact that it was midnight, groups of people chatted and shops were still open.

The tourist beaches which are vast, sandy and empty are patrolled by guards and we were told that it would not be wise to go beyond the patrol points as there may be armed robbers. Although this provided a sense of security when I went to the beach alone, it also gave me a slightly uneasy feeling of being in a tourist compound. However, though the hotels in this area are grouped together, there is no feeling of oppressive commercialisation despite the strategically placed tourist markets. The people who you have daily dealings with are friendly and helpful; others who hang about the hotels are equally friendly but I soon learned that their greeting 'Welcome, what is your name?' and subsequent speeches usually ended in a request for money.

We were there in April, the end of the tourist and the dry season, the poverty of the dry season was evident. At the enormous Serekunda market the food stalls had but a few fish, black from smoke and flies. These fish stalls were juxtaposed with stalls holding a handful of small tomatoes or two or three cashew nuts. Large gourds full of tomato purée bespoke opulence until we saw that it was sold in a small screw of paper. Other stalls sold half-used bars of soap and partly used tubes of sun tan cream or toothpaste. Such recollections gave me sudden feelings of guilt about bargaining at the local tourist market from our position of privilege.

Our first approach to the capital was along the Bund road, an expanse of mangroves and rubbish tips well patronised by birds and their watchers. Banjul itself has a large sinister market, potholed streets and faded colonial buildings. When we saw it, it was filled with people, some attending a political meeting, others a cricket match. At Banjul the Barra ferry crosses the River Gambia. Having bought our tickets, we waited amidst a patient and quiet crowd. Babies were casually perched on backs and slung under an armpit to be fed. One baby burst into tears on seeing our ghost-like faces; we were in fact the only whites there at the time and felt curiously vulnerable because we were so conspicuous. Vendors wandered round with trays of kola nuts, hard-boiled eggs and vaseline but they did not pressurise you to buy. Some of the women waiting had the most intricate weave of plaits so that their heads looked sculpted and embroidered. The ferry itself was crowded and as the top deck sported armed guards we stayed inside with fish, goats and chickens.

The Gambia is a birdwatcher's paradise – a hundred species a day can easily be seen – and an early morning trip around Oyster Creek enabled us to witness this extraordinary spectacle. The creeks were wide and silent and mangrove swamps were bustling with fiddler crabs, while overhead were pied kingfishers. Other birds included pelicans, darters, several species of tern and heron and cormorants. Only a fish trying to jump into our boat disturbed the voices reverentially hushed so as not to disturb the birds.

One day we followed the motorway to Senegal; a red dust track flanked by typical bush savannah, it led to the customs which it took us an hour to clear. On the way back we travelled through the bush – virtually turn left at the second tree – which must be impassable in the rainy season and arrived back in The Gambia without any customs control.

Elizabeth Everett sailed to The Gambia and spent four weeks travelling up the Gambia River.

I would have taken away far less vivid memories of The Gambia had we just stayed in the capital. Instead we spent four weeks going 170 miles up river to Georgetown and the further we went, the more fascinated we became. Quite soon after leaving Banjul we docked at James Island, a tiny island with an ancient fortress. There was no one else there when we landed. It was totally peaceful, the sounds of the birds and the quaintness of the fort an ironic contrast to its harsh history as the main slave-trading centre for West Africa. We sat on the beach and hunted for trade beads, used as currency two hundred years ago.

The river became narrower, with creeks off to each side. The vegetation along the banks changed as we went inland, from tall mangroves with their strange aerial roots, to flat arid wasteland, to tropical forest. The variety of birds was phenomenal.

The further up-country, the more friendly the people became. Children would run down to the river bank to greet us and lead us inland to their village, which we had already pinpointed by the vultures circling overhead.

There, under the shade of the cotton silk and baobab trees, the men would sit and talk while the women were busy, working the paddy fields, pounding millet, drawing water from the wells, usually with a baby on their back. With us the women were very shy.

Sometimes we were approached by fishermen in their dug-out canoes. They usually wanted something – food, cigarettes, pens or to sell us their fish. They were all very good humoured, and went away chuckling when we told them we had nothing to hand over. In their opinion it was obviously worth a try and they were certainly adept at bargaining.

We passed very few boats. There is one regular passenger steamer, the *Lady Chilel Jawara*, that plies up and down the river once weekly from Banjul to Basse, making frequent stops en route. This for tourists would be the best means of seeing the country in relative comfort. Any trip by road has to be made in a vehicle with 4-wheel drive and these are not easily available. And on the road, you would have to be prepared to rough it, as there is no tourist accommodation available.

TRAVEL NOTES

Languages English (official) and three African languages: Wolof, Mandika and Fula.

Transport Buses serve the area immediately around Banjul. There are also collective taxis that pick up and put down on request. There is a weekly passenger boat that goes up and down the Gambia river; coach and river trips are also laid on for tourists.

Accommodation Cheap accommodation can be found in Banjul. There are also several hotels in and around Banjul geared primarily for package tours. If you want to stay in these it's advisable

to book in advance as they get full up in the tourist season (Nov-May).

Special problems Yellow fever vaccination is compulsory. It is also advisable to take anti-malaria tablets.

Other information There is a thriving black market currency trade and money and travellers' cheques can be exchanged on almost every street corner. Most people obtain their dalasis in this way as it gives a far more favourable exchange rate than the official one. Remember though to exchange all your dalasis before leaving as they are not acceptable in any other country.

Guides Michael Tomkinson, *The Gambia – a Holiday Guide* (Holiday Guides, Hammamet, Tunisia, 1984).

BOOKS
See General Bibliography.
  Also look out for Sarah Hobbs' short film, *The Lost Harvest*, which reports how a major development scheme, designed to increase The Gambia's rice yield, not only ignored the experience of women farmers but took away their land. In the end the women band together, determined to stand up for their rights.

MALI

Mali, half covered by Saharan desert, has been listed as one of the countries most critically affected by the Sahelian drought. Over a million Malians were at risk during the early part of 1985.

Despite this there is a persisting, if small, tourist industry. The country has many historical sites – there's the ancient trading towns of Djenne and Gao and, of course, Timbuctou. American tourists still get jetted in to visit the old mosque and houses of the French explorers and often round off the trip with a tour/safari to take photos of the Dogon tribe in the drought-stricken Bandiagara Escarpment.

By any other approach Mali is not an easy country to visit. Accommodation is expensive and travel, without your own vehicle, slow and incredibly arduous, involving long, hot journeys in overcrowded *taxis brousses*. There are also heavy bureaucratic constraints to contend with and a great deal of your time (and money) will be spent in dealings with SMERT (the national tourist organisation). Outside the tourist areas, however, people will receive you with amazing hospitality and friendliness – it's important to carry gifts with you as some means of reciprocating.

Over the last one and a half decades this predominantly Muslim country has been governed by a succession of Marxist-inspired military regimes. Women are almost entirely engaged in subsistence farming. A **Women's Movement** is developing, though at present it is predominantly urban-based, made up of well-educated, middle-class women. The *UNFM* (*Union Nationale des Femmes du Mali*) is the central organisation and its members campaign for women's rights and participate in meetings abroad. There are also various development centres set up in and around Bamako, mainly co-ordinated by the Centre Djoliba, which provide training skills for girls and women as well as education on nutrition and health, including talks on the health hazards of female circumcision.

▰ **Over several years, Jo Hanson has travelled to many countries in Africa. In the course of one overland trip across the Sahara, she spent a month walking along the Niger River.**

If you look presentable, you might easily fall into the Foreign Aid circuit in Bamako, which consists of men of many nationalities living in styles to which they are probably unaccustomed at home. Exasperated by the two-hour lunches and afternoons beside the swimming pool, I set off to walk up the Niger River towards its source in Guinea.

As soon as I left Bamako and the tarmac road became laterite, good things began to happen. A young man carried my sleeping bag roll and showed me where to buy a cup of condensed-milk coffee, then a half-blind woman took over the bag and led me into a large compound, where I was the centre of attraction for several minutes while I put ointment into her eyes (I always carry a few tubes) and lamented the fact that she was in such a plight only a couple of kilometres from the capital. 'I can't afford to send her to the hospital,' said her husband, but as he was sitting on a good chair surrounded by various sheep and cattle, I wondered where his priorities lay.

Later, in the heat of the day, I was invited to rest by a farmer whose wife was cooking beside the river a delicious-looking fish and groundnut stew. I was looking forward to a taste of this when he pedalled to the village shop and brought back two tins of sardines and four loaves of French bread, obviously thinking that this was what white people must have! When the heat had lessened he led me back to the road (another thing I didn't really want) and proudly showed me the new table-football game a local entrepreneur had set up, penny-a-go. It was the kind where you manipulate handles at high speed to move model players from side to side, and looked a bit bizarre under a baobab tree with a field of maize nearby.

That night I slept on a handy pile of straw at the edge of an Aid project (you can always tell them by the huge size of the fields and the large machinery that is used). Next morning I noticed a Frenchman trying to mend a diesel water-pump, but being an advocate of intermediate technology, I preferred the *shaduf*, an ancient Egyptian device with pole and weight, which was being operated by a market gardener further along the river.

I was invited to fish stew lunch by a family who this time, far from buying French bread for me, eagerly shared the remains of mine. The six sons seemed to be thriving, but at the expense of their mother who looked utterly sapped as well as pregnant. I couldn't speak her language; even if I could, what would I say? I gave her as many iron and vitamin tablets as I could spare, using sign language to tell her 'One a day – not for men,' as I often found that men appropriated the little benefits I gave to their women.

All along the way I was repeatedly asked into huts and given rides on bikes, mobylettes, a donkey cart and even in the car of a gang of hunters who were shooting partridges. I met many strange types: a Jehovah's Witness who tried to convert me in French, a Nigerian seaman who had got stranded and was earning enough to get home by selling face cream made from the boiled root of a tree, and a student of English on a motorbike who stopped me to chat about Dickens. Small-scale trading went on in every village, but there was little enough to buy – maybe a few oranges, bananas or water melons or a bowl of rice and groundnut stew in a 'café' (a mud hut containing a bench).

After five days' walking, I had a rest in a metropolis (well it had a pharmacy and a man who sold matches) called Kangaba. I was taken over by a young unmarried woman called Fatika who was a Community Health Worker. She took me to the Community Centre, a large shed where all kinds of classes presumably went on since the walls were plastered with posters about nutritious food and clean boiled water. I asked Fatika for a drink, thinking this was the right place to be, and she brought me a black cupful from a fetid pot in the corner. As it took so long for my sterilizing tablets to dissolve, I surreptitiously threw it away. This gap between theory and practice is often evident in Africa. I saw it again when Fatika's brother showed me his school books, full of pages and pages of neat writing in French about hygiene – yet they both had dysentery and pleaded with me for a remedy (the pharmacy had run out).

I stayed the night with a couple of Dutch volunteers. They were marvellous people, up at dawn and out to remote villages with a cold box full of children's vaccines strapped to the back of their motor scooters. Consequently for the next couple of days many people I met asked me if I knew 'Nelly-et-Harry'!

I crossed over the river by canoe when I reached the border with Guinea (which was closed to tourists at that time) and started to walk back down the other side. This was a wilder part with less population; in fact I walked all one afternoon in the shallows of the river wearing only bra and pants, with wading birds hopping round and hippos sighing and not a soul in sight. The water was so clear I drank straight from the river. I reached another large village opposite Kangaba and stayed with a nurse-midwife. She was obviously more committed and practical than Fatika, but stymied by an almost complete lack of medicines and supplies. In the evening she had to make two trips to the river to fetch water, carrying on her head a tin tub that I couldn't even lift when it was full. Other women did the same, many of them pregnant, one even saying that her labour pains had started! That night there was a total eclipse of the moon, marked by much drumming and dancing amongst the population, who had been forewarned by news on the radio.

Next day I found myself climbing up a wooded plateau and after several hours' walking through wild dry scrub, I came upon a gold-mining village. Gold is Mali's principal mineral export, but the people who did the labour obviously had no status at all: they were dressed in rags with no school, clinic or facility of any kind in the place. While I was watching the miners lower themselves into deep holes in the ground, a young man on a bike came wobbling through the trees and introduced himself in French as a gold-dealer. He took me on to his father's village, wading over a rushing cold tributary of the Niger, then bike riding *à deux* amongst a wide area of termite hills like a forest of pointed witches' hats. It would certainly have been a tourist attraction if SMERT had known about it!

After that I paid an old man to pole me a dreamy fifteen kilometres down the river in the evening to a rice-processing factory. I expected to find it a hub of activity, but instead it was empty, deserted, thousands of francs (or dollars, or pounds, or deutchmarks) just rusting away. Bats and mosquitoes abounded, and for the first time I had to use my net as I spent the night there.

Although the small town attached to the factory had a road back to Bamako and a once-weekly minibus, it wasn't that day, so I resumed my riverside walk. Gradually it got more and more difficult. I followed lonely cattle tracks over rocks and into small fertile areas, but these petered out and I was faced with a huge area of high elephant grass with no way through. I could walk no further – in any case by now I had given away all my spare clothes and presents. I noticed a man standing on a spit of sand and he told me that a ferry-pirogue might come across some time. I knew I could get a lift or squashed paying ride on the laterite road back on the other side of the river, so decided to wait with him.

He was most solicitous, sharing his food and finding a soft place for me to sit and read, his attitude being typical of all the men I had met. Yet I had never seen one offer a bike ride, carry a heavy load or take the hoe out of the hand of his wife, sister or even mother. It is not difficult to find an explanation for this, but I still regret that the friendly assistance I was lucky enough to receive from men did not touch the visibly arduous lives of the women that I saw on my journey.

TRAVEL NOTES

Languages French and various African languages. The most common is Bambara. Some students speak English.
Transport There is only one railway connecting Bamako (the capital) with Dakar (Senegal). Roads are fairly rough – tarmac up to certain points out of Bamako, the rest sandy tracks. Hitching is difficult as there are few private cars but you can get rides with lorries where you're expected to pay. Shared taxis are also available as well as *taxis brousses*

(crowded minibuses/vans) which go from town to town. When the river is high enough (usually August-December) riverboats run between Mopti, Timbuktu, Gao and sometimes on to Koulikoro, near Bamako.

Accommodation Small hotels are relatively expensive. In Bamako there is a dormitory hostel run by Catholic nuns on Bagaycho Road, and in Gao there are a couple of campsites. Travelling outside the towns and tourist areas you will have to rely on local hospitality – you should offer something (money/gifts) in return for your keep.

Special problems Visas are required by all except nationals of France, and can be quite hard to get hold of. (The nearest Malian embassy to the UK is in Paris.) You cannot get a visa at the border.

You have to register with the police in each town that you stay in overnight. Tourist officials might insist that you use SMERT (The National Tourist Organisation's) official transport at inflated prices. You also have to pay to extend your visa – the initial one is for seven days only; You will need to buy a permit to take photos and you should get an exit visa before leaving the country.

Guide Geoff Crowther's *Africa on a Shoestring* (Lonely Planet rev. 1984) has a few pages on Mali.

CONTACTS
Union Nationale des Femmes du Mali, Bamako (See introduction).
Femmes et Development, Service Quaker, BP 153, Bamako.
Centre Djoliba, BP 298, Bamako. This is the headquarters for seven centres set up around Bamako in order to promote activities such as nutrition and health education, sewing, gardening, etc.

Thanks to Jo Hanson who provided much of the information for the Travel Notes.

NIGERIA

Nigeria has virtually no tourist market. The difficulties of obtaining a visa, vastly inflated prices, political instability and the legendary armed robbers who roam the highways between cities are enough to put off all but the most determined traveller. However, those who do make it often find that the sheer vitality and colour of the country, coupled with the overwhelming hospitality of the people, are enough to make them want to return.

In the 25 years since Independence, Nigeria's progress has been scarred by civil war, assassinations, economic crises and a succession of military coups. Nigerians are a highly divided people, speaking over 200 languages, and there seems little chance of finding a political solution to their tribal and ethnic conflicts. At the time of writing, the sixth coup has overthrown nearly two years of military government under General Buhari. His successor, General Babangida, leader of the Armed Forces Ruling Council, came into power with the well-worn rhetoric of national unity plus a need to rescue the post-oil-boom failing economy. There has been a slight improvement in political freedoms, but the future remains as uncertain as ever.

High prices have long been a focus of discontent and, as consumers and market traders, women have often been at the forefront of protest.

In general, however, Nigerian **women's organisations** are moderate in their demands – the *National Council for Women's Societies*, one of the most established bodies, renamed the 1985 International Women's Day 'Family Day' to reflect their priorities. Although the majority contribute economically to the household and many are financially independent, marriage and producing lots of children are central to almost all their lives. An infertile woman is likely to be rejected by her husband and fall prey to the many private infertility clinics which advertise every few hundred yards along the roadside.

Probably the country's most radical organisation is *Women in Nigeria* which was launched at the Second Annual Women in Nigeria Conference in 1983. Made up of women and men, it sees itself as a political organisation dedicated to overcoming women's problems within the context of the 'exploitative and oppressive character of Nigerian society'. Through a nationwide network of state branches and co-ordinators WIN is currently carrying out a plan of action on issues such as domestic violence, sexism in the media and in education, shared housework and childcare with men, and the need for non-sexist alternatives to government and institutional policies. Although men are incorporated into the organisational structure, this programme indicates a radical departure from the traditional, institutionalised and often church-based women's groups.

◥ **Deborah Birkett has been researching into the life of Mary Kingsley, Victorian traveller and journalist, and went to West Africa to visit the places she had described.**

I had come to Nigeria with the eyes of a Victorian, seeking palm trees, lush undergrowth, and creeks paddled by long slender men in dug-out canoes, chanting. But these images were soon swamped by the practicalities of everyday living. Electricity, running water, telephones, and a reliable postal service were about as rare and valued as a cool evening. The dry heat of *harmattan* – the months before the rainy season breaks – caught in my throat and made simple tasks exhausting. The basic functions of staying alive absorbed the large part of my first few days.

Days started early and abruptly, broke after lunch, then ended as abruptly with the sudden shutting of the sky at 6 o'clock. No dawn and no dusk. The afternoon break was for resting and visiting. With no other communications, calling round is the only way to keep in touch with friends and relatives. Unannounced, a friend will visit with their family and a family with their friends. There is no such person as an uninvited guest. The guests sit in your house as you offer them bottles of soft drinks and ask if they have eaten. There is no pressure to talk, people just sit together through the afternoon.

If people know you have been travelling they will want to hear your tales. Nigeria is a diverse and divided country, an artificial construction – the awkward legacy of colonialism. Civil war has already erupted once in the 1960s, and in the south-east of the country reminders of the famine and violence live in the accounts of those who lived through it and the burnt-out shells of tanks which still sit at the side of the road. Making the two-day rail journey from Lagos in the south to Kano in the north is like passing through a tunnel from one country to another. The Christianity and colour of the south is replaced by the all-encompassing Islam of the north. The southern markets of Ibadan, Calabar, and Lagos are run by women, the infamous market traders whose bright wax-print wrappers and headties and loud haggling dominate the crowded streets. In the north women are rarely seen. Traders and customers are men, and their cloth is a sober embroidered pastel blue, pale grey, and white. The rich green vegetation and humidity of the southern delta is replaced by vast stretches of dry sandy bush. Enormous smooth grey rocks, thrown up from beneath the earth's surface, sit uncomfortably on top of the dusty yellow land. Climbing them, you find ancient iron ore smelting furnaces and grinding holes carved into the hard surface.

Repressive measures introduced by the previous military government included a crack-down on street trading, but even inside a taxi you aren't safe from the hawkers. They thrust their wares through the windows, small newspaper packages of groundnuts and men's underpants stretched over hangers. 'I no go buy 'em', I tried my pidgin.

Statistics say you are 47 times more likely to die in a road accident in Nigeria than Britain. There is no speed limit, huge potholes in the roads, and no new tyres available since the restriction on imports. Even the constant army road-checks don't slow the taxi drivers down. Inter-city taxis have fixed prices; or, like so much else in Nigeria, that is the theory. 'You have to pay one and a half times the fare,' shouted the taxi driver from Calabar to Port Harcourt at a fat Yoruba woman. 'You use up fuel too much.'

Women travelling alone are common, but women without husbands are not. I invented one – giving him a name, job, good prospects, and a residence in the town I was about to arrive in. It avoided long and frustrating questions and the odd proposal.

There are almost no tourists in Nigeria – the exhorbitantly expensive hotels are for businessmen. Tenuous connections with a friend of a friend of a family I knew often provided me with a place to stay, my hosts sometimes moving to the floor to give me their bed. But my embarrassment at arriving on a stranger's doorstep was soon countered by their horror at the thought of a stranger to the country not being received into their home. 'You're welcome,' is repeated over and over again as you cross the threshold, sit in their chair, and are offered your first drink.

Nigerian culture continually questioned the basis of my own life – personal independence – and replaced it with personal responsibility to family and friends. In a society where family and children are central to a woman's life and prestige, and living conditions are generally crowded, aloneness is not considered valuable. There is no public or private space for a woman to be by herself. Sitting in a market or at a roadside someone will always shout 'Sister – how now?', and staying in a Nigerian home means being constantly entertained.

Being alone is even viewed with some horror. Drinking beer by myself in the student bar, I was asked to leave. Eccentricity and deviancy from normal behaviour is frowned upon. Wearing trousers in the north, it was difficult for my friend to get a taxi ride. Other women passengers said she was ungodly.

I often found myself growing angry at this place which seemed to challenge the essence of what I wanted to be and at a climate that made such physical demands on my body – but at the same time I felt that I could not leave. Now, back in London, I am plotting and planning to return to the colour and the noise and the discomfort which from here seem so vital.

TRAVEL NOTES

Languages Quite a few people in cities speak English, the official language. Of the 200 other languages, Hausa is commonly used in the north, Yoruba in the south-west, and Ibo in the south-east. Pidgin is the best language to get you around in the south.

Transport Shared taxis run between all major cities. There is also a limited rail service. Internal flights are reasonably cheap. There are long distance buses run by private companies, no cheaper than taxis but considerably safer.

Accommodation Hotels are very expensive, but missions offer accommodation in some large towns for a reasonable price; ECWA (Evangelical Church of West Africa) are the most common. Also, universities often have guest houses where visitors can stay.

Special problems Visitors must have a visa before entering the country, issued by the Nigerian consulate in your home country. A visa application must be accompanied by a personal invitation from a permanent resident in Nigeria agreeing to be responsible for you during your stay. It is unlikely that you will be given longer than a couple of weeks, but once inside the country visas can usually be renewed at local immigration offices.

Yellow fever vaccination certificates are compulsory. Even with a visa and vaccination certificate, you may have problems entering the country. One person recently was refused entry on the grounds that they had not had a large enough dose of vaccine. All these holdups are ways of asking for money; try to act innocent. If all else fails and you are desperate to get in, you have to pay the price.

The exchange of currency is strictly controlled. You can take in 20 naira (Nigerian currency) and must declare all other currency on a 'yellow form'. When you change this currency the form must be signed and stamped. Make absolutely certain that you get a yellow form and that it is properly completed. Failure to produce it on leaving the country is an offence. Exchanging currency outside the legal market can be considered a capital offence.

Prices in Nigeria are artificially high because of the controlled exchange rate of the naira. Take everything you need – paper, toiletries, books, clothing – with you.

Malaria tablets – double dosage – are well advised, as are innoculations for polio, cholera, typhoid, tetanus and hepatitis. Tampax are £10 a box, so go well prepared. Tap water is not drinkable.

Nigeria is under military rule and there is the constant presence of army and police checks in the street. Never give your passport or any other documents to anyone; it will probably cost you a great deal of money to get them back. Carry photocopies of your travel documents with you everywhere and offer these instead. Expect to be frequently stopped and questioned, and occasionally asked for money. Don't get angry.

The postal service is very unreliable; 30 per cent of letters never arrive. Don't agree to contact friends or relatives as they will only worry when you can't.

Major cities have a NET office where international telephone calls can be made. There is no guarantee, however, that they will be able to connect you, and you may have to queue for a long time. It is very expensive.

Try to avoid travelling between cities or walking around anywhere alone after nightfall. Nigeria's reputation for violent robbery is no myth.

It is advisable to wear clothes which cover the shoulders and knees in Muslim areas, and to avoid trousers. The wearing of shorts anywhere in Nigeria will attract a lot of attention.

Guide There is no travel guide to Nigeria. Geoff Crowther, *Africa on a Shoestring* (Lonely Planet, rev. 1984) contains 15 pages including sample taxi fares and a few recommended places to stay.

CONTACTS

Write to **Women in Nigeria**, PO Box 253, Samaru-Zaria, for details of WIN groups around the country.

The **National Council for Women's Societies**, Tafawa Balewa Square, Lagos. An NGO umbrella group, a focus for all the different women's groups throughout Nigeria. They are not a radical group, though do organise around such issues as marriage law and divorce.

BOOKS

Women in Nigeria, *Women in Nigeria Today* (Zed Books, 1985) A selection of theoretical papers on women's subordination in Nigeria from the Women in Nigeria (WIN) conference.

S. Ardener, ed., *Perceiving Women* (John Wiley and Sons, New York, 1975). Revealing essays on Ibo women.

Molara Ogundipe-Leslie, 'Nigeria: Not Spinning on the Axis of Maleness', in *Sisterhood is Global* (see General Bibliography).

Mary Kingsley, *Travel, in West Africa* (1897, Virago, 1982). A British woman's journals of her independent travels in West Africa in the 1890s.

West Africa magazine, published weekly in London, has up-to-date and in depth news on Nigerian events, as well as many advertisements for cheap flights.

FICTION

Buchi Emecheta, *The Joys of Motherhood* (Heinemann, 1980). Powerful story about the strains of living in a society where women are denied any identity unless they bear children.

Flora Nwapa, *Efuru* (Heinemann, 1966), *Idu* (Heinemann, 1970), *One is Enough* (Tana Press, Eguru, 1981). Nigeria's first published woman novelist, all her work in some way concerns the constraints which marriage has on women. She now runs her own publishing house as an outlet for African writers.

Ifeoman Okoye, *Men Without Ears* (Longman, 1984). The frantic chase for money and the obsession with prestige in urban Nigeria today.

Zaynab Alkali, *Stillborn* (Longman, 1984). Story of a young girl in rural Nigeria torn between village life and the lure of the city.

Thanks to Deborah Birkett who provided much of the information for the introduction and travel notes.

Chapter Seven

EAST AFRICA

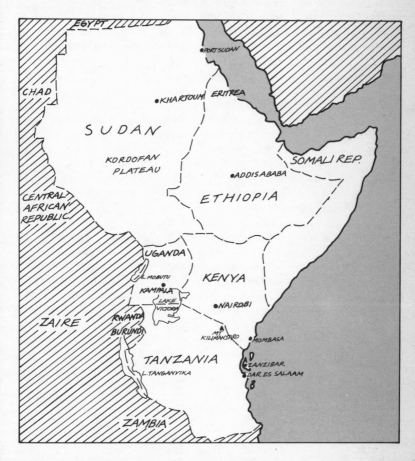

Kenya and **Tanzania** – the two most visited countries of **East Africa** – share a history of Arab domination and British colonial rule. In Kenya the British influences remain strong, with a large expatriate/settler community and a still considerable control of business. Britons too make up a major slice of the country's important tourist industry, attracted by accessible gameparks, beaches and a somewhat overstated image of political stability. Most tend to be on expensive packages – the image is one of organised adventure – though there is a fairly well-established (and growing) independent travel circuit. Tanzania, poorer economically and with its line of Christian Socialism currently looking uncertain, is less well known and less travelled. Its attractions are similar to Kenya's, however, and tourism there looks set to emerge from its recent role as an extension of Kenyan overland/safari trips.

Though many women travel in pairs around both Kenya and Tanzania, few do so alone. Sexual harassment is persistent throughout East Africa and particularly on the Kenyan coast. In the cities – Nairobi above all but to a lesser extent Dar es Salaam – there is also increasing danger of mugging and violent crime. The rural areas, and Tanzania as a whole, are generally easygoing.

We have included the **Sudan** in this section, not entirely arbitrarily, for the black African south of the country shares general characteristics with the region. Again it is not a country you're likely to go to casually. Its recent military coup, which dislodged the Numieri government, has done nothing to halt the secessionist struggle between north and south, and large parts of the country remain critically affected by drought. If you do travel there – teaching jobs or development work are possible sources of entrance/justification – you will find it very much easier with a male companion. Sudanese have a reputation for openness and hospitality, though how you cope with accepting this is at present an uneasy issue.

We have not included in this chapter a 'travel piece' on **Ethiopia**, probably the worst hit of the Sahelian drought nations and also currently torn by civil war. However, we would be interested in hearing from anyone who has recently worked there in aid or development. We would also welcome recent accounts and information on **Uganda**, which under Yower Museveni's National Resistance Army leadership seems to have returned to relative stability after the chaotic last years of Obote and then Tito Okello.

KENYA

Kenya has an image of westernisation and affluence. A former British colony, its capital, Nairobi, is a major commercial centre, crowded with British and multinational firms, many of them trading on the tea and coffee plantation industries. Tourism, along the coast and the upmarket gamepark circuits, is long and well established. But the country's economic advantages, which are rapidly levelling off in the context of world recession, have benefited only a small minority. Stretching north from

Nairobi into the Mathare valley there are vast urban slums, with up to 100,000 people living in cardboard, tin and plastic bag shanty huts. In the north, the edge of the Sahel region, there are areas devastated by drought.

Politically, tribal resentments remain strong, particularly towards economic domination of the Kikuyu tribe, one-fifth of the population. In 1982 the president, Daniel arap Moi, created a one-party state under KANU (Kenya African National Union): a move which strengthened his power base but also led to an (unsuccessful) coup attempt by military and student groups.

Independent travel is relatively straightforward and it is not hard to move away from the tourist enclaves. Many women, however, experience persistent sexual harassment, particularly along the predominantly Muslim coastline. This can be personally threatening and on the beaches it's never a good idea to isolate yourself. Statistics for violent robbery are also high, and carrying any symbol of wealth (in fact anything but the bare necessities) can make you a target.

There are numerous **women's groups** throughout the country, many of them associated with *MAEDELEO ya WANAWAKE* (Progress of Women), a non-governmental organisation. They have been responsible for setting up multi-purpose centres geared towards health education and skills training. There are also literacy groups (according to the 1977 statistics only 10 per cent of women were literate) and also legal literacy programmes. Two years ago the Kenyan Women Finance Trust Ltd, a bank/credit association, was set up to provide credit and security for women-owned business ventures which are usually denied access to mainstream banks. In 1985 Nairobi hosted the conference to end the United Nations Decade for Women.

◪ **Lindsey Hilsum is a journalist and aid worker. Since 1982, she has been working in Nairobi, as an Information Officer for the United Nations Children's Fund and freelance writer.**

December 1982 and my first solo walk through the streets of Nairobi. Having just arrived from Latin America, where I learnt that streetwise means ready to run or ready to fend off catcalls, comments and unwelcome hands, I was on my guard. But in Nairobi no man bothered me. I was profferred the occasional elephant-hair bracelet, the odd batik, but no one tried to touch or waylay me. Some months later, a Norwegian woman friend arrived on her first trip outside Europe. As I showed her around Nairobi that afternoon, men shouted and stared at her. Talking to other women later, I understood the problem. Because I had already learned to walk with confidence and aggression, no one perceived that I was vulnerable. But my friend gave off an aura of uncertainty – she was obviously a newcomer, a tourist and, as such, fair game.

It is possible to travel widely in Kenya using public transport. There are hotels and campsites scattered throughout, and people usually go out of their way to help. A lone woman is something of a curiosity in small towns and rural areas, but people are more likely to be sympathetic than hostile. 'Isn't it sad to be without a husband and children?' I have been asked. My reply that I prefer it that way has started many good conversations! People like to talk – a smattering of Swahili helps, but there are many Kenyans who speak English.

For most visitors to Kenya going to a gamepark is a high priority. The most comfortable way to see the gameparks is to go on an organised tour. I went on one to Masai Mara, and found myself ensconced in a Volkswagen mini-bus with two cowboy-hatted Texans who were 'in oil' in Saudi Arabia, an American couple plus toddler also from Saudi and a lone geriatric British bird-watcher. Other people have found themselves crushed between Germans and Japanese, straining for a glimpse of a lion through the forest of telephoto lenses, and my sister ended up in the Abedares with a busload of Americans wearing name-badges who turned out to have won the trip by being 'workers of the year' at a Coca-Cola factory.

It's more fun to go independently, but only with a reliable, preferably 4-wheel drive vehicle. I spent one hot, frustrating, exhausting week trying to get to Lake Turkana in an ancient Landrover, the remnants of a long-since discarded Ministry of Livestock Development Sheep and Goat project. Accompanied by a friend as mechanically incompetent as myself, I never made it to the lake, but now know all the amateur motor mechanics between Baringo and Baragoi.

Only an hour's drive from Nairobi, you reach the natural rainforest. If you want to explore this region you should go with a guide. It's easy and very dangerous to get lost. Hacking my way through the forest at night, in search of two friends and two small children who had not returned from a walk, I realised how threatening the forest can be. One moment luxuriant and enticing, the next, when every coughing sound could be a leopard and every thud an elephant, it becomes sinister. We found our friends, who had lit a fire and tucked the children snugly into the forked foot of a tree when they realised at dusk that they were lost. We would never have found them without the local Forest Rest House warden, who searched with us as a guide.

One place which has become popular with low-budget tourists is the largely Muslim island of Lamu. With its white-sand beaches and curious melée of backstreets, downmarket restaurants and mosques, it is closer in culture and history to Zanzibar and Ilha de Mozambique than to the rest of Kenya. Sometimes I think I'm just prejudiced against it. The first time I went, my friend Laura and I took the sweltering eight-hour bus-ride from Malindi, and then the boat. The sun blazed down as we left the shore, my period started, and I passed out. Stumbling to the quay at Lamu, I collapsed in the dirt. Laura, pursued by a young man informing her of a nice cheap hotel he was sure she'd like, went in search of liquid. She found a bottle of bright orange Fanta. I took one glance and then vomited. All around me were male voices, saying things like, 'Get her to hospital' and 'Why don't you go back to your own country?' Needless to say, it was two women who helped us find a place to stay.

Personal experience apart, Lamu can be difficult for women. The traditional Muslim culture has been sent reeling by the advent of beer and bikinis; while women tourists bathe topless, Lamu women walk the streets clad in black robes from head to foot. Concerned about the corruption of local youth and the rising numbers of 'beach boys' who hang around tourists, the local authorities are reported to have forbidden young local men from talking to visiting women. The clash in culture has found expression in sexual violence, and there have been several incidents of rape on the beach. I would never bathe topless, and never lose sight of other people on the beach, however solitary and tempting it appears.

Back on the mainland at Malindi the beach is fringed with luxurious hotels, complete with bar service, butler service, air conditioning, chilled wine and four-course meals. Not so far away, the town crumbles into ramshackle mud and wooden dwellings where sewage runs along open drains, and household electricity and water are just promises the municipal council has yet to fulfil.

It's this divide between rich and poor that shocks the first-time visitor to Africa. Personally I avoid staying in tourist hotels, not only because the luxury jars alongside such evident poverty, but because guests are alienated from 'Africa', as alive in a tourist town like Malindi as in any upcountry village where *wazungu* (white people) are rarely seen.

Generally, I stay in a *hoteli*, a small guest-house found in any town. They are cheap, occasionally clean, and almost invariably, the people who run them will be friendly. But single women sometimes have problems with men knocking on their bedroom door (this happens in upmarket hotels too), so I always make sure that my room can be firmly locked from inside.

I think the only way I've come to understand anything about 'ordinary' Kenyan women is by frequenting local bars. In many countries, bars are a male preserve, but in Kenya there are usually women about – barmaids, prostitutes, and in some places women doing their crochet over a bottle of beer. Not many *mzungu* women go into bars, except in tourist hotels, so those that do attract a fair amount of attention. 'People say it is dangerous to come here,' said the proprietor of one bar in Kisumu, 'But you are safe.' I agreed with him, and he bought me a beer simply because I'd dared to be there. As I left, some Asian youths cruised by in their Mercedes. 'Wanna fuck?' they called. That was when I felt nervous, and wished I could find a taxi back to my hotel.

The women tend to assume a protective role. In one bar in downtown Nairobi, a woman kept me by her side all evening. 'No one speaks to my sister without my permission!' she insisted, glaring at anyone, male or female, reckless enough to look at me. As I entered a bar in Kisumu, Jane the barmaid, came to sit with me. A young man slouched towards us from the counter. 'My friend is talking to *me*,' said Jane, and he shrugged and walked away.

Women like Jane have interesting stories, and they usually like to talk. Many come from rural backgrounds, left home to look for a job in the big city, got pregnant, and have been trapped in the circle of barmaiding and prostitution ever since. Options for women are few once you leave the village; with no education and no money, children to support, prostitution is often the only way.

These women may ask you for an address, hoping for a job as a housemaid, or some money to pay school fees, or some clothes. But they're not talking to you because they want something, but because it feels good to talk, and because they're curious, and there is a sympathetic link between women of different cultures, and it is somehow comforting to find common ground with a stranger. 'You can so easily end up in a maternity,' lamented one woman I know, who hangs around the same bar in Nairobi every evening. 'I could be pregnant again. So could you.' Later she took a male friend of mine aside. 'Don't you get my sister pregnant,' she admonished him, 'That would be a very terrible thing to do!' Kenyan men do tend to look upon foreign women as an easy lay, and opening gambits like 'Tell me about free love in your country' are irritatingly common.

If you have any problems, women around will usually help. But beware 'big' men in small towns. If it's the local police chief or councillor who is making advances, it may not be possible for other local people to help out, because of his power and influence. If in doubt, get out, preferably accompanied, preferably in a vehicle. I never walk alone at night in Nairobi, because mugging and raping are quite common, and it's always worth the taxi fare to be safe.

I don't think that Kenyan men are intrinsically any more sexist than men from my own country, England. As a person unfettered by family, educated and employed and travelling unaccompanied, I get treated in some ways as an honorary man. But underneath it all, a woman is a woman is a woman, and most Kenyan men I've met agree with their president who announced in September 1984 that God had made man the head of the family, and challenging that was tantamount to criticising God. And certainly, when I've expressed my doubts, the response is generally that in *my* culture we may have different notions, but *their* women like it that way. I'm not so sure about that.

Throughout Kenya there are large numbers of women's groups which have banded together to earn some money, by making handicrafts, growing crops, keeping bees or goats, or other small-scale businesses. Their success is variable. Some groups have made profits and shared them; in other cases the men have sabotaged the group when they felt threatened by the women's success or have appropriated the money. In others, lack of organisation, inexperience or simply the lack of time among women already overburdened by the day-to-day tasks of survival have built in failure from the beginning.

Women do want better healthcare, contraception, education for themselves and their children, and a higher income. But their needs and wants come a *poor* second to the concept of 'development' which a male-dominated government and which predominantly male-dominated aid agencies promote. The rhetoric of the UN Decade for Women has resounded throughout Kenya, and we all know that small-scale water projects, reforestation, support to women as farmers and access to credit are important. But agricultural extensionists are still men; although it's women who dig the land, women are rarely consulted, and there is a tendency to start 'women's projects' as a sideline to the more serious business of 'nation building'.

Women leaders in Kenya tend to take the attitude that gentle persuasion works better than protest. Many of them are middle-class urban women, whose ideas and problems are often seen as divorced from the reality of ordinary Kenyan women. With their emphasis on educational and welfare and income-generating projects they have been criticised for supporting the status quo and denying the possibilities of radical change.

A Western feminist is often resented. There is good reason for this – many Western women simply do not know about the issues which affect Kenyan women, but nonetheless push their own priorities. On the other hand, the widespread denunciation of feminism (which finds its most outrageous expression in the letters pages of the newspapers) is a way of keeping women down, by telling them that any change is 'unAfrican'. I have come to believe that issues such as accessible clean water and getting more girls into school are more important to most Kenyan women than free abortion on demand or the acceptance of lesbianism and many Kenyan women oppose the latter two. Other issues, such as male violence and access to health care and contraception are as important in Kenya as in any Western country, although the starting point for pushing to achieve these things is different.

Foreign women who have lived in small towns and villages, usually as anthropologists or volunteers, have a deeper understanding of Kenyan women than I do. Many such women leave the country thoroughly depressed, as they see Kenyan women, year after year, accepting violent husbands, a pregnancy a year, children dying, endless work and little reward. Most visitors can't see all that, because it takes time, and nor do they get to see the other side of things, such as the sense of community amongst women and the strength of character that outward acceptance and seeming submissiveness belie.

It's not possible to understand so much on a short visit, but I think that many women coming to Kenya could see and understand a lot more if they dared. It took me a year to dare to travel Kenya alone, on *matatus* (collective taxis) and buses, hitchhiking, going to small towns, being open, talking to people. There's no need for every woman to take a year to pluck up the courage – it's fun, it's interesting and it's worth it. I've been here two years now, and I haven't had nearly enough yet.

TRAVEL NOTES

Languages Swahili is the official language; also Kikuyu, Luo and others. English is widely spoken, routinely so in all tourist fields.

Transport Public transport (buses and a small train network) is reasonable and safe. On well-worn tourist routes there are also collective taxis, usually big Peugeots. *Matatus*, impromptu communal trucks, need more confidence. Hitching isn't advisable.

Accommodation Boardings and Lodgings can be found in any town and are good local value. In gameparks there are very expensive lodges but also *bandas* (small wooden huts with cooking facilities – you bring your own food and sleeping bag) and 'tented camps' (tents provided and set up within lodge compounds).

Guide Richard Trillo, *The Rough Guide to Kenya* (Routledge & Kegan Paul, 1986).

CONTACTS

Maedeleo ya Wanawake. (Progress of Women) Largest and best-known women's organisation with numerous local groups.

National Council of Women of Kenya, PO Box 43741, Nairobi. Produces the publication, *Kenyan Women*.

Pan-African Women Trade Union, PO Box 61068, Nairobi. Continent-wide trade union for women with regular activities and newsletter.

Kenya Association of University Women, PO Box 47010, Nairobi.

Jitegemee Women's Group, PO Box 88, Bumgoma. Resource and information centre for a range of projects (literacy, nutrition, income-generating, etc.).

Viva, PO Box 46319, Nairobi. Monthly magazine combining feminism and fashion in a glossy but appealing package.

BOOKS

Anonymous, *In Dependant Kenya* (Zed Books, 1982). A strident book – which you shouldn't take with you – that pulls no punches in codemning the status quo and Kenya's involvement in the neo-colonial webb.

Patrick Marnharm, *Dispatches from Africa* (1984, Abacus 1985). Sharp, incisive essays on development and politics, concerned in large part with Kenya.

Women's Bureau, *Mid-Decade Report for Women Review Conference* (Ministry of Culture and Social Services, Nairobi, 1980). The position – from an official angle.

FICTION

C. H. Bruner ed., *Unwinding Threads: Writing by Women in Africa* (Heinemann Educational, 1983). Includes stories by the Kenyan writers, Charity Waciuma and Grace Ogot.

Rebeka Njau, *Ripples in the Pool* (Heinemann, 1978). Novel, full of myth and menace, about the building of a village clinic.

Micere Mougo, *Trial of Dedan Kimathi* (Heinemann, 1977). Highly controversial play written with Kenya's most famous – and currently exiled – author, Ngugi was Thiong'o. Many of Ngugi's novels and short stories are also published in Heinemann's African Writers Series; all are recommended.

Muthoni Likimani, *Passbook Number F 47927: Women and Mau Mau in Kenya*

(Macmillan, 1986). Describes, through ten fictionalized episodes, the impact of the 1950s Mau Mau revolt in Kenya on women's daily lives.
Martha Gellhorn, *The Weather in Africa* (Eland, 1985). Three novellas, each set in Kenya and dealing absorbingly with aspects of the European–African relationship.

Karen Blixen, *Out of Africa* (1936, Penguin 1986). A lot better than the film, lyrical, introspective, sometimes intricately (and obnoxiously) racist but never superficial.

Thanks to Sally Fenn, Sarah Oliver and Nicky May.

TANZANIA

Compared with Kenya, tourism in **Tanzania** is fairly low-key. Few travellers venture beyond the 'northern circuit' of Dar es Salaam, the island of Zanzibar, Arusha (Mount Kilimanjaro), the Ngorongoro crater and the Serengeti. It's a huge country and independent travel, without the money to hire a jeep or small plane, can be slow and arduous. The population is made up of a diverse range of tribes and cultures (Muslim, Christian, Animist, Hindu), though none of them dominate; the official language of Kiswahili affords a very tenuous cultural link. Travelling around, most women find the country reasonably relaxed, though the capital, Dar es Salaam, has become more risky, with definite no-go areas. As a general rule you should dress modestly, particularly in predominantly Muslim areas like the island of Zanzibar.

President Nyerere has been in power since the British ceded independence in 1961. In this time he has introduced and determinedly pursued his own brand of Christian Socialism, the most central and ambitious policy of which has been *ujamaa*, villagisation. This has involved compulsory resettlement of populations on a massive scale with the intention of raising agricultural production through local collective farming programmes. At the time of writing Nyerere is preparing to step down amidst claims of local and central government corruption, low-level productivity in the villages and increasing scarcity of basic (imported) commodities. Over the last two years he has introduced draconian steps against 'economic sabotage', involving a clampdown on black marketeers.

The **Union of Women of Tanzania** is a government-aligned organisation which was set up to provide and expand education and welfare projects. Its leaders are predominantly urban, middle-class women who work alongside trainers and teachers provided by VSO and other development agencies. Women attached to the church have traditionally had a high social status and are now often seen working at the forefront of education and medicine. Many women community leaders first learnt their organisational skills in the church. We have been unable to find any additional information regarding autonomous feminist activity.

▨ **Sue Shaw and Lynn Taylor spent several weeks in Tanzania while travelling independently through East Africa.**

Crossing Tanzania to Malawi on a low budget, we discovered that if you don't know what you are doing, travelling as two women is no easier than travelling alone. The path to Ngorongoro Game Reserve is well trodden, but you need time and money to avoid our disappointment of getting within a leap of the crater, and not actually seeing it.

We made our way by local bus from Arusha, which left us stranded at Karatu, where we had to negotiate a lift with the local hotel manager in his open-backed Landrover, along with two goats, eggs, rice and vegetables. Arriving at the gates of the park we were told that the entrance fee and hotel bill had to be paid in foreign currency. A solitary lion, padding past, convinced us that this was not the place to argue about money, so we paid, but without the resources to stay, we reluctantly decided to leave in the morning.

Hitching out proved more difficult that we'd expected. Richer tourists sped past, unwilling to take more than four passengers in their spacious Range Rovers, and it was four hours before we finally got a ride back to the main square of Arusha. With its confusion of rickety buses, fruit vendors and boys selling single cigarettes, Arusha has a small-town friendly feel, but local people warned us not to walk in the mountains alone for fear of armed thieves.

In Dar es Salaam we learned always to look as if we knew what we were doing, even if we didn't. We had only been in the city a couple of days, and on this particular day we were tired, flustered and arguing on the way to catch a bus. We stood, confused and defiantly apart at the bus stop. A man pounced on us and began asking questions so that we had no time to collect our wits as we crowded on to the bus. He continued to distract us, until by sheer luck one of us looked down and saw the razor cut that had appeared, through Lynn's clothes and money belt, leaving her money and plane ticket exposed for the taking.

'You were lucky,' someone told us later, 'if it had been at night, they would have knifed you.' It made us extra cautious walking around Dar es Salaam in the evenings, for the streets were deserted. The liveliest place we found was the hospital, with its babble of visitors. Cafés and bars shut about six, so eat early, because if you leave it till later you might find that there's no food.

The central market, the *Soko*, illustrates this scarcity, for stalls are half empty, and nuts, fruit and vegetables are sold by the handful. The fish market is one place where food seemed abundant. Fried fish, fruit and spices are sold from dozens of stalls, and you can squat under the jacaranda and drink tea brewed in an old oil drum, or eat fresh pineapple.

You only have to sneeze in Dar es Salaam and you are wringing with sweat, so it is advisable to check that your hotel has water. The humidity also means that mosquitoes are rampant, and travellers should be especially careful to take their malaria tablets.

It's worth having a look at a recent map before attempting the crossing from Tanzania to Malawi. The route from Mbela to Kaporo seemed direct to us except for one short stretch that appeared to have no road. This did not deter us, especially when the Tanzanian customs said it was only an hour's walk as they directed us down the track.

Despite the weight of our rucksacks, we set out enthusiastically, through the banana plantation, greeted by little boys herding long-horned cattle, women suckling babies outside mud huts and an old man who gave us oranges wrapped in banana leaves. We walked for two and a half hours before the road split in two. Some women who were walking ahead with bundles on their heads told us to follow them down a small, improbable path. We did, until we came to a muddy, thigh-deep swamp. To our protests that we only wanted to go to immigration, we were told that this was a short cut. So we took off our shoes and waded through, wringing with sweat and trepidation. 'But Malawi, where's Malawi?' we asked. 'Far but not far,' came the cryptic reply.

Through more swamps and a maize field, we were suddenly confronted by the Songwe river, the border between Tanzania and Malawi. It was deep and swirling and the only way across was by dugout canoe. Our plaintive objections were greeted with surprise, for this was routine to our companions. With no alternative, we climbed in.

On the other side, a young man escorted us, slipping and sliding through another swamp, this time a quarter of a mile long, through rice fields and another small village. People laughed when we told them wearily, and now half-heartedly that we were going to immigration. It took a total of six hours solid walking before we reached another road, and hitched a truck which took us the last few kilometres to the long-awaited customs. There is a more conventional way to leave Tanzania – by taking the main road and new bridge over the Songwe.

◢ **Sarah Oliver describes her ascent of Africa's highest mountain, Kilimanjaro.**

Kilimanjaro was given by Queen Victoria to Kaiser Wilhelm as a birthday present, but later reverted to British colonial rule. In the evening sun the magnificent monster looks calm, its white top sparkling out of a shroud of cloud, the foothills dark with forest shadows. An injured young German who had just descended groaned, 'Not for a million dollars! Never again', as he limped by.

The National Park entrance at Marangu has a 'going-up' book and a 'coming down' book. Here we begin. With our guide Anasion Mabando, three porters (who carry warmer clothing and supplies for five days in baskets on their heads), a Dutch volunteer returning from Zambia and myself, we are a party of six.

The porters soon disappear ahead. The well-trodden path leads past eucalyptus trees and Japanese cherry blossom. Singing birds are hidden among dense trees and butterflies fly across the stony track. The walk is pleasant, though warm, and we pause where a deep green shaded stream falls among rocks, refreshing us. After three and a half hours we reach Mandara hut, 9,000 feet above sea level, where we will stay the night.

We sit watching the lights of Moshi town and the mass of stars. Anasion cooks onion soup, goat, cabbage and potatoes – 'food for white people'. He urges us to eat a lot as at higher altitudes we may lose our appetites. He has climbed the mountain over 800 times and has progressed from being a junior porter at 14 to a senior guide. His experience is comforting. We sleep in the wooden huts, well wrapped up against the cold night.

Anasion brings sweet tea at 7 am. The morning is clear and quiet but for birds singing, bees humming and two large white-naped ravens scavenging. We breakfast on paw-paw, porridge and eggs and Anasion suggests we drink a lot of tea. He plans five hours slow walking. We plod up the path into the forest again while the porters leap ahead with their loads.

The rain forest is dense and dark, with drooping creepers hanging from every branch. Loud screeches come from turacos and red-headed parrots which flash in front of us. Suddenly we are out of the forest and on to high savannah. Blinking in the sun, we see Mawenzi peak and further over, the snow of Kilimanjaro.

Here ferns and long grasses replace the wet green of the forest and the sun burns through the dry thin air. We walk slowly, and stop to watch buck and eland. We meet some porters dashing downward with a radio playing. They are followed by some rotund Norwegians who declare that most of their party reached the top.

Then comes the sound of panting and a group of people appears, running. Two rush by carrying a grey-faced boy on a stretcher; his companions pause to explain that he has pulmonary oedela and the only way to save his life is to *run* down to a lower altitude and then take him to hospital. These are fit 18-year-old students – Anasion shakes his head and sighs and warns us to move slowly.

Cloud comes rushing towards us and we are engulfed in cold, damp mist. A piercing whistle from Anasion brings back a porter with the down jackets we hired at Marangu. We don gloves and hoods and plod on through the air which shows our breath. We take frequent rests as the track becomes steeper, and I begin to notice the altitude, as any violent movement results in lightheadedness.

We walk silently in single file, saving our breath. Anasion, last in line, walks at the pace of the slowest, which is me. The mist swirls and we seem to be utterly alone on the way to the top of the world. My sinuses ache and my throat thumps strangely, so I realise I must rest.

At last, through the mist, we see the shapes of the huts of Horombo, where we will stay our second night. It is 2 pm and we have walked for five hours, climbing 3,000 feet. We sleep fully clothed with hats on inside sleeping bags, tossing and turning fitfully. Breakfast is maize porridge again. Then we start walking. We pass the last water source where we fill our bottles. We cross the saddle between Mawenzi and Kilimanjaro, a vast stretch of empty terrain. We walk for five hours and the last part, just before Kibo hut at 15,520 feet, takes a long time; we rest frequently and pant with the effort of moving upwards.

We arrive, tired, and eat goulash which Anasion is delighted we can still manage. We rest, listening to our racing pulses. I sneeze and my nose bleeds. A German woman vomits continuously and another drifts in and out of consciousness, gasping for oxygen.

Anasion rouses us at 1 am, we drink sugary tea and put on our warmest clothing. It has been snowing and the bright moonbeams cast shadows as clear as daylight. Anasion leads, instructing us to tell him if we feel unwell. We shuffle off into the night walking on volcanic scree, using our long sticks to stop us sliding backwards on loose gravel. The moonlight is enchanting, the night clear and quiet; our rasping breath sounds insultingly loud.

At about half past four a cloud covers the moon and an icy wind begins to batter us; between rests we now take eight paces, then six, then four with our lead-like feet. My lungs ache and I feel very tired. Anasion urges us on, chanting 'slowly, slowly, Kilimanjaro,' and we follow. Nothing matters but the next step.

Anasion points to a thin red line in the cloud. 'Alleluya!' he shouts, his voice echoing across the mountain. 'It is morning! Alleluya! Thank you, God!' I am thankful too. The sun's rays warm us and give us courage to continue as we see the beautiful brilliant dawn of Kilimanjaro. In the growing light Anasion points to something white in the rock. It is not snow. It is a flagpole. It is the top.

Painfully and slowly we ascend the rock encouraged by Anasion's chanting, scrambling with our hands over the last little bit. Shaking with the strain but enormously exhilarated I look down on huge glaciers, giant steps of brilliant ice dazzling white in the morning sun. The steaming volcano reminds me of my puniness. A wooden box was wedged between the rocks, inside a book full of triumphant signatures. We had no pen.

We had taken eight hours to climb the peak; coming down took only one hour. At Kibo hut the Chaga mountain rescue men congratulated us. 'Two white women! Really, that is surprising. It's good, very good.' I felt angry, indignant and pleased.

TRAVEL NOTES

Language Kiswahili, English, and numerous tribal languages. It helps to speak even a little Swahili, which is far more necessary than in neighbouring Kenya.

Transport Buses, trains and planes are all stricken by shortages of fuel and spare parts. It is often easier to hitch, or, for a small sum, cadge a spare seat on someone else's safari vehicle. Ask around the Asian travel agents who can be helpful. It is possible to go by ferry from Dar to Zanzibar and from other towns like Bagamoyo and Tanga, but can be difficult to arrange as it is thought to threaten National Security.

Accommodation The YMCAs are cheap, friendly and admit women too; the YWCA in Dar is a good and secure meeting place. Hotels and guesthouses are similar to Kenya, though fewer and less developed.

Special problems Shortages: dispensaries and hospitals often lack vital drug supplies, so take your own (Tanzania is in a high risk malarial zone) plus Tampax, toiletries, any contraceptives, etc.; be prepared too for food and drink shortages, even of Tanzanian products. Official currency rates are abysmal, the black market up to eight times better — but deal at your own risk, penalties are severe on both sides. If you take any photographs ask first and expect to pay.

Guides Nina Casimati, *Guide to East Africa* (Travelaid, 1984). And for hikers — Hilary Bradt, *Backpacker's Africa* (Bradt Publications, 1983).

CONTACTS

No information on specific women's organisations.

Community Development Trust Fund of Tanzania, PO Box 9421, Dar es Salaam. Self-help projects co-ordinating organisation.

Co-operative College: P.O. Box 474, Moshi, Tanzania. Members of the Co-operative college in Moshi have been involved in studying and carrying out development projects with women — useful for anyone interested in women workers' co-operatives.

BOOKS

Ophelia Mascarenhas and Marjorie Mbilinyi, *Women in Tanzania: An analytical bibliography* (Scandinavian Institute of African Studies, 1983).

Goran Hyden, *Beyond Ujamaa in Tanzania: Underdevelopment and an Uncaptured Peasantry* (Heinemann, 1980).

A story by Martha Mvungi is included in *Unwinding Threads* (see Kenya).

Tepilit Ole Saitoti and Carol Beckwith, *Maasai* (Elm Tree Books, 1980). Photo record with interesting text.

Look out too for the work of Tanzanian writers like Hanza Sokko, W. E. Mkufya, Agoro Anduru and Prince Kagwema. Also for the writings of Julius Nyerere — essential insights into the present social structure.

Thanks to Lotte Hughes, Sarah Olney and Jane Longrigg.

SUDAN

Sudan is a divided country, currently in the throes of economic and political crisis. The Sudanese People's Liberation movement, predominantly Black African (Christian and Animist) southerners, are fighting a guerrilla war of secession against Arab Muslim domination by the north. At the time of writing they control much of the south.

On top of this two million people are at risk from drought and famine — a large number of them refugees from neighbouring Ethiopia and Chad.

General Numieri, head of the single-party government, was very recently overthrown by a military coup, his last resort measures of arbitrary price rises and the introduction of Sharia Law (the Islamic legal code) providing the catalyst for protest and dissent. There has been very little information about the policies and affiliations of the new government. Speculation suggests that it's shifting towards a predominantly Libyan position. The borders however are still open from Egypt and Zaire (the Ethiopian border has been closed for some time) and only circumscribed areas in the south are blocked off.

Very few women travel alone around this country, and unless you're with a man you're likely to experience frequent and threatening harassment. You need to dress extremely modestly, particularly in the Muslim areas and wherever you go it's usually best to try and merge in with groups of Sudanese women and their children. Travelling with a man these problems rarely arise – you're much more likely to experience extreme friendliness and hospitality.

There is no real tourist industry, although teaching/development jobs maintain a small number of Westerners. With only one railway line and one major road travel can be very hard. You have to rely almost completely on (paid) lifts on the back of lorries. There are, however, a reasonable amount of rest homes where you can stay. The main **women's organisation**, the 'official' Sudan Women's Union, was closely affiliated with Numieri's Sudanese Socialist Union. It had a very wide membership and was responsible for setting up numerous skills training, social welfare, educational and local income-generating projects. It also published a monthly women's magazine. The *original* Women's Union, an autonomous movement, was forced underground during the Numieri regime but remained active despite constant harassment and intimidation. Its focus was on promoting education (the literacy rate amongst women is around 4 per cent) and women's rights, including campaigns against facial scarification, genital mutilation, male-initiated divorce, polygyny and discrimination in work and pay. Unfortunately we have not been able to obtain information on the status of either group since the coup.

▰ **Rhiannon Lewis spent two years teaching English in Dongola, a small town in northern Sudan.**

The lorry jolted over a sand dune, but the twenty or so people perched on top of the load did not move an inch – except for Mekki, a teacher who'd befriended us at the start of this first desert crossing. His hand once again fell on my knee. I picked it off. Five minutes later his hand was back. Nothing I said or did had any impact, but when Steve my husband exploded: 'Take your hand off my wife's knee!' the reaction was dramatic. With effuse apologies, Mekki shrank away as far as he could in the cramped space between the onion sacks, and remained there. This was Lesson One about life in Sudan: a woman is her man's responsibility. Insults to her honour – which, I was later assured, Mekki's behaviour certainly constituted – reflect more upon her husband/father/brother than upon her.

It was something of a shock and in the following months, as I went about life and work in the small provincial capital of Dongola, I came to learn other things. I should not go out after dark on my own, entertain men on my own, drink alcohol or smoke in public and should dress with a modesty my Baptist forebears would have approved of. Had I been just a bird of passage, a traveller who was passing through, these considerations might have been brushed off as something affecting them, not me, not now. However, being not only a resident but that venerated pillar of small-town life, a teacher, I couldn't afford to be so lighthearted about the religious and social scruples of the society around me. This attitude spilled over into the times when I was a traveller so that, though like all travellers I felt and acted more freely on the road than in my home town street, I was never able to quite forget the preoccupations of the dominant Islamic culture.

I couldn't ignore either the fact that in order to get to know the women of the Sudanese community, I had to gain their trust. Western beliefs in personal freedom, equality of the sexes and accountability to one's own conscience were as strange to them as their segregated society was to me. Accommodating myself to their way of life was therefore a priority. Learning a little Arabic helped greatly in getting to know women, since few of them spoke English. Initial contact was often through their menfolk, or schoolgirls who, having studied English, were more confident of their ability to approach strangers. Once inside the harem, though, there was little holding back and questions about clothes, beauty, family and food were flung at me with increasing speed.

The Sudanese are an open and inquisitive people. Whether itinerant or settled I continually made new friends, and indeed had to struggle at times to preserve a few quiet moments to myself. When settling down to a novel after a hectic morning marshalling classes of sixty at school and battling with the laws of supply and demand in the market, I would be often abruptly interrupted by the clapping of hands as one of my neighbours came in to see me. There were no apologies when I was disturbed in this way; on the contrary, their gregarious culture led them to suppose that a woman on her own must be lonely – so the visits were mercy missions and the breaking of my solitude intended as a gift of friendship. Staying with a Sudanese family was at times an overpowering experience for this reason – wells of warmth and welcome gushing over and flooding me with a tide of smiling faces, glasses of sherbat, sweets and questions.

The questions kept returning to children and marriage, the two main concerns of these women's lives, and a perpetual source of puzzlement to them when they compared their lives with the lives of Western women. They could not understand why I, a married woman, was not keen to prove my fertility by bearing children at the first opportunity, and neither could they understand why those Western women with children had so few. They understood the technical reasons – the pill is well enough known and they often asked whether I took it – but it was the motivation that eluded them. Why should a woman not want to have many children? Children are a gift, a blessing, and give a woman status; why deny the possibility?

Western women who travelled without men also puzzled them, particularly when they got to know and like them. One European friend of mine rapidly won a place in the hearts of the community by her rapid mastering of Arabic, her respect for local customs and her cheerful willingness to spend long hours visiting the harem, whence she would emerge with henna patterns on her hands and kohl around her eyes. She was, though, unmarried, and her single status was an enigma and a challenge to them; they never ceased hoping that she would find herself a good husband. A single woman who chooses to live and travel alone is an unknown phenomenon in respectable Sudanese society, so much so that the Western woman who voyages without a man and fails to win respect through manner and dress can find herself in very deep waters indeed.

During the Eid Kabeer, a major Muslim festival, we were invited to stay in a nearby village by our friends, Ahmed and Amna. We had taken the desert road from Dongola. The first sight of the Nile were a few deserted mudbrick dwellings, and the faint traces of disused irrigation canals; then a thicket of thorned shrubs, grass, and the blue waters of the river. As I stumbled out of the truck, unwinding the scarf which had kept sand out of my hair, nose and mouth during the journey, I became aware of something I had not experienced since leaving Britain: the smell of sweet, green grass. The ferry was an old blue metal landing craft, left by the British when they administered Sudan thirty years ago. The passengers boarded, the women at the back and men at the front, the usual arrangement on these ferries. I stood with Steve somewhere in the middle, wondering whether I should go and stand among the women with Amna or claim the Western woman's prerogative to stand with a man.

From the ferry, the village was a long low ribbon of gleaming white buildings, punctuated by the tall tower of the mosque and many palm trees. A grassy track led us through a field of bersheem (a purple-flowered clover-like plant which is fed to donkeys) to the village. Ahmed and Amna's house would have overlooked the river and fields had there been windows to view the scenery, but like most Sudanese houses, it looked inwards to its courtyard.

The following days were anything but calm. The Sudanese are a gregarious people and a festival is an excuse to be even more sociable than ever. I went visiting with the women while Steve went around with the men. In my best dress and shoes I tagged along after Amna, down sandy lanes overhung with ancient palms where doors in crumbling gateways were pushed open with much clapping of hands. Still clapping, we would walk around the sides of buildings to courtyards where women of all ages sat in the shade on wooden beds, smiling and exclaiming as we appeared.

On one of these visits, I met three little girls dressed like brides. All the children in the neighbourhood had new clothes for the feast, but these three wore dresses of shimmering gold cloth, new red ribbons in their black plaits, henna on their fingers and palms and kohl around their eyes. They clung together, smiling and giggling, and shyly offered their hands to shake. I asked why they were dressed so specially but didn't understand the reply Ahmed's mother gave me; I shook my head and she made a cutting gesture with her finger across her palm, saying as she did so the word 'knife'. At this moment Ahmed appeared and she called him over to explain. He looked embarrassed. 'It is a women's custom,' he said. 'In the Sudan, the women do these things because – ah – they are not educated.' His voice tailed away. 'Circumcision?' I asked. He nodded.

I had read about circumcision before coming to Sudan, and had been appalled. But I was not prepared for this: three giggling, excited girls – they must have been eight or nine years old – dressed like brides, nor for the reactions of Ahmed's mother and Amna, who smiled and laughed as they tried to explain their dresses to me, and were evidently proud.

Visiting the home of one of the girls two days later, I found her lying in bed, wrapped in a green sheet. The women were laughing, and one pinched her affectionately on the cheek. She was one of them now.

Our travels were restricted to areas we could easily visit during limited school holidays. 'Easily' is not a word to be taken lightly when talking of Sudanese travel. It may look a short distance on the map but in reality that road may well be just a set of tyre tracks crossing the desert, or winding up and around boulders and river cliffs. In fact, there is only one major tarmac road in the country, and that runs from Khartoum to Kassala and up along the Red Sea coast to Port Sudan. It is a narrow road and would barely merit a B rating in Britain, but it was a joy to use after the grind and bumps of the sand and gravel tracks I found elsewhere.

We wanted to go south but were discouraged when colleagues were turned back by soldiers. Since then the political situation has worsened. Friends who did manage to travel through the south at that time commented on the lack of food for sale in towns and villages, an observation which must be set against the thought that, to a recent arrival, food stocks in the north would not have appeared particularly plentiful. We also wanted to visit western Sudan, but it was simply too far, given the slow pace of transport, the enormous distances involved and the frequent shortages of buses, trains and planes when the country's fuel stocks ran low.

Health was sometimes a barrier to travelling too; as well as varying degrees of upset stomach, we suffered from malaria and hepatitis which wrecked all wanderlust for a time. Bad health is like the long, uncomfortable rides on buses and trains – worth enduring for the pleasure of coming to the end of it. And, as one fellow traveller said, as we sat on a mudbrick verandah watching the sun sink over the high walls and flat roofs of the town: 'At least you know you're alive here.'

TRAVEL NOTES

Languages Arabic and tribal dialects. English, the old colonial language, is taught in schools and quite widely spoken.

Transport Slow and unreliable – expect long delays. Buses are marginally better than trains; *boxes* (collective taxis) are useful. If you're travelling alone it's always best to sit with Sudanese women – they often use separate compartments to men.

Accommodation Outside Khartoum, the capital, hotels tend to be of the dormitory type; most Sudanese stay with relatives when they travel and hotels are usually a last resort! Catholic resthouses (at Juba, for instance) are good refuges.

Special problems The south-west of the country is at present in a critical position, devastated by drought and guerrilla war. To visit Sudan at all is probably not realistic or useful other than for work. Visas are granted by the Sudanese Embassy in London but not generally in Egypt or any other transit points. If you do visit the north be very sensitive to the strong Islamic culture, both in dress (cover upper arms and knees) and habit (very harsh penalties for use of alcohol).

Guide Kim Naylor, *Africa: The Nile Route* (Lascelles, 1982). Hilary Bradt, *Backpacker's Africa* (Bradt, 1983).

CONTACTS
Sudanese Women's National Assembly (SWNA), PO Box 301, Omdurman. The *original* women's union (see intro), active in development campaigns with rural women.

Ahfad, University College for Women, PO Box 167, Omdurman. Twice-yearly journal on status of women in developing countries.

BOOKS
Marjorie Hall and Bakhita Amin Ismail, *Sisters Under the Sun: the Story of Sudanese Women* (Longman, 1981). Regional study with thorough historical background on the position of women in the Sudan today.

Anne Cloudsley, *Women of Omdurman* . (Ethnographica, 1983).

Eric Hoagland, *African Calliope* (Penguin, 1982). Anecdotal stories of Sudanese life.

Thanks for general help in putting together this chapter to Debbie Garlick and Pat Yale.

Chapter Eight

CENTRAL AND SOUTHERN AFRICA

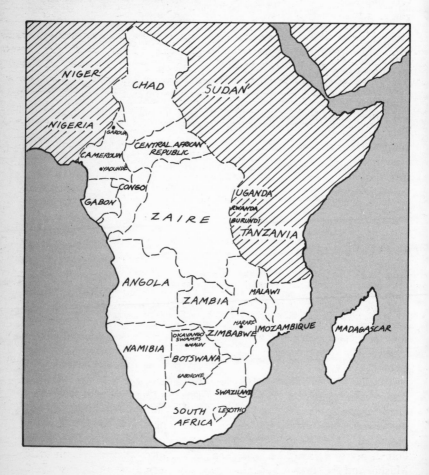

Central Africa, containing some of the smallest and poorest nations in the whole continent, is not a popular destination for travellers, at least not judging from the correspondence we've received. This perhaps applies particularly to English-speaking travellers. **Cameroun, Central African Republic, Congo, Gabon, Equatorial Guinea, São Tome and Principe,** and **Zaire** were colonised by the French, Spanish, Portuguese and Belgians respectively, and very little English is spoken. Few tourist facilities, bad roads, erratic transport, not to mention widespread corruption and some very unpleasant political regimes, all add to the problem. However, if you're adventurous and willing to rough it, there are some beautiful places to see and local peoples are mostly very hospitable.

Southern Africa has long been overshadowed by colonialism, epitomised in the immense political and economic power of white South Africa. But the current unrest in that country, alongside the war in neighbouring Namibia, is likely to reverberate throughout the region. In the meantime **Zimbabwe** and **Botswana** are probably most recommended for travellers. It is still virtually impossible to obtain a visa for **Angola** or **Mozambique**. Of the remaining countries, **Lesotho** and **Swaziland** are too close to **South Africa** for comfort; **Malawi** suffers a ruthless dictatorship under Dr Hastings Banda, and travel in **Zambia** is said to be hampered by widespread police and military harassment.

CAMEROUN

Cameroun stretches from the Gulf of Guinea to Lake Chad, where it narrows into a thin strip of land. Overland access from Europe is a hazardous and difficult journey across the Sahara. Travel inside the country is also not easy, hampered by poor roads, and most visitors tend to stay around the more developed area north-west of the capital, Yaounde.

After being a German protectorate, Cameroun was colonised by the British and the French who divided it between them. Independence was finally granted separately to each section in 1960/61 and despite formal unification, was rapidly followed by a long and bloody rebellion prompted mainly by southern resentment of domination from the north. Politics are also mixed up with religion, the north being predominantly Muslim and the south Christian, with a wide sprinkling of Animist cults. The current president, a southerner, is said to maintain a partial democracy, but in practice Cameroun is an authoritarian state with little, if any, regard for human rights.

Cameroun may be riddled with internal conflict, but people are generally friendly to foreigners, especially in the north. Cheap accommodation is fairly easy to find. Public transport consists mainly of shared taxis or trucks, not much different from hitching which is far slower and still requires payment. We have been unable to obtain any concrete information on the position of women in the Cameroun but, in terms of attitudes to female travellers, it's reportedly more relaxed than most other Central African countries.

◢ **Jan Wright travelled overland to Cameroun during a six-month camping trip around north-west Africa with her husband, and three sons under five. They had only been in the country two days when their Landrover crashed, leaving them bereft of home and transport. Without the accident they would never have experienced life in an African village.**

I came to, lying on the dirt road with the overturned Landrover some 20 yards away. Somehow I managed to climb up and inside the vehicle where I found the boys huddled together and crying, but miraculously unharmed. Fearing an explosion I quickly turned off the engine and got them on to the outside from where I could see Chris, lying unconscious on the road. It took ages for him to respond to my screams and shouts, but he finally managed to stand up and help me get the children down to safety. The relief that we were all alive was indescribable. Nevertheless Chris and I were in a pretty bad way; he had total memory loss and various fractures and I was suffering from a leg injury and bleeding steadily from the head. Eventually a beer truck arrived on the scene and our new adventure began.

The truck driver took us to the hospital at Garoua, the main town in northern Cameroun, while a group of tribesmen from the nearest village, spears in hand, guarded the Landrover with all our belongings. The hospital was a shock. Subconsciously, I was expecting to be looked after but of course there were none of the facilities we take for granted in England. No X-rays or examinations; our cuts were merely washed and we were on our way.

After a miserable night in a hotel with no clothes, shoes, nappies or money, we got in touch with a garage mechanic, recommended by the taxi driver who had taken us to the hotel. Ebode, the mechanic, turned out to be the best friend we could have had. He not only thought he could repair the Landrover, but offered us a mud hut in his village where we could live until it was ready. It was an exciting prospect, especially after a day spent desperately entertaining the children on a hotel bed – I didn't want them running around barefoot for fear of infection – whilst Chris retrieved some of our belongings.

When Ebode delivered us with our bedding and cooking pots to the village we were greeted by men and lots of children, but there wasn't a woman in sight. The men were friendly and helpful and obviously felt very sorry for us. Two of them dug a special loo hole for us since they used the general rubbish heap where goats and dogs scavenged for food. Another man hastily repaired a grass fence around the hut to give us a little privacy. Only when the men had retreated did the women appear, smiling and shy.

We soon fell into a routine. Chris went into Garoua with Ebode every day to oversee repairs to the Landrover and I stayed in the village with the children — a familiar story but with a difference. My day began at dawn when I fed our boys and as many African children as I could manage. Next I lit a fire to burn the previous day's rubbish and swept out the hut. Most of the rest of the day was spent dispensing tea, plasters and aspirin to various adults who wandered by, believing that the white woman could cure all ailments. The villagers had little money and the only doctor they used was the witch doctor. Illness either got better or it didn't. Meanwhile my sons played with the African boys at football with a tin can, drawing in the sand, or just chasing around. The girls were too busy helping their mothers or looking after the younger children. Some of the older boys went to school, but formal education seemed to come second to any work that had to be done.

Washing of clothes was done in the river half a mile away; drinking water came from a nearer swampy hole. We used tablets to sterilise it without ill effects. The African children suffered a lot from coughs and colds and were generally low in energy because of poor diet. They ate only one meal a day in the evenings, usually based on manioch which the women spent a long time pounding. We found that they could not digest milk — it was too rich — and they did not like bread — it was too stodgy.

One eight-year-old girl called Janabu adopted us right from the start. She would arrive at dawn and go home at dusk. Unlike the boys she did not come to play but to help. She wanted to sweep the floor, fetch the water, wash the clothes and above all, care for Eddie our baby. I managed finally to convince her that she needn't work and taught her to crayon and play with Lego. She even began to challenge the boys and join in their games and, by the time we left, had become a force to be reckoned with. I often wonder whether I did her a disservice by sowing the seeds of dissatisfaction since her role in life was so clearly mapped out for her.

Although it must have been very strange to have a white family in their midst, the villagers accepted us with warmth and friendship, as well as natural curiosity. Part of this may have been due to the status of our friend Ebode, who was obviously educated and comparatively rich, but I'm sure that carrying Eddie on my back as I've always done, and breast-feeding, must have helped. Also, having three sons gave me added status. Sometimes I was treated more like an honorary man, not so much for my behaviour as for my knowledge of the world and things I had seen.

In two weeks the Landrover was ready to drive and we prepared to leave, distributing as many of our remaining possessions as we could spare. Any clothes were especially well accepted, although I disappointed the women by not offering bras, considered a real prize. I made up for it with pants! Children's books were another favourite and villagers of all ages would spend ages marvelling at the pictures of white people and their strange possessions.

TRAVEL NOTES

Languages French and English remain the offical languages although a wide variety of African languages are spoken.
Transport Buses are few and far between, especially in the wet season (July/August) when many roads are impassable due to flooding. Hitching is slow and you're expected to pay. Most people travel by shared taxi or truck. Make sure you negotiate a fare in advance – all prices at least double during the wet season – and don't expect to be comfortable, however you go!
Accommodation Cameroun towns generally offer a variety of cheap hotels. It's also possible to stay in a room or dormitory in one of the country's many religious missions, so ask around.
Guides Geoff Crowther, *Africa on a Shoestring* (Lonely Planet, rev. 1984) is the only English language guide to the whole of this region but it does have a reputation for inaccuracy. 10 pages on Cameroun. The French *Guide Routard: Afrique Noir* (Hachette, 1985) is a useful supplement.

CONTACTS
Organisation des Femmes de l'Union Nationale Camerounaise, PO Box 2350, Yaounde.
Association des Femmes Camerounaises, PO Box 1004, Yaounde.
Women's Cameroun National Union (ACWW), PO Box 3, West Cameroun.

These are all likely to be governmental organisations. Unfortunately, we don't have any more details, but it's probably worth writing for information.

BOTSWANA

Almost two-thirds of **Botswana** is covered by the Kalahari desert, yet paradoxically in this drought-prone country, there lies the largest inland delta in the world, the Okavango Basin. Relatively untouched by tourism, the basin is a haven for wildlife and reputedly one of the most beautiful places in Africa. Most of the country's 1m population live around this area, or in the east near the borders with South Africa and Zimbabwe.

Despite scant agricultural resources, Botswana's predominant tribal group, the Batswanas, are mainly cattle herders. Few benefit from their country's rich mineral deposits which are primarily exploited by South African companies. Even before independence from the British in 1966, Botswana's leaders stood up firmly against apartheid, but the economy remains heavily dependent on its imperialist neighbour. However, changing expectations in Botswana – largely a nation of young people – combined with upheavals in South Africa, may herald a dramatic shift in relations, as well as other changes in this usually peaceful country.

Although hitching is easy and a recognised mode of transport among the Batswana, it is hard to reach more remote areas like Okavango. Few people means few roads and very few vehicles, so it's best to try and secure a lift in advance, even if it means going in a group. Unless, of course, you don't mind being stuck in the night in the middle of nowhere. Hotels and lodges are expensive, but there is little alternative apart from camping in the wild. Compared with some African countries, sexual harassment appears to be a minimal problem.

Nearly half of all households in Botswana are headed by **women**, due to male migration to urban centres and to South Africa. The majority work on the land. Hampered by lack of education, women in towns are mainly employed in the service industries as cooks, cleaners, hotel workers, etc. Widows and single mothers often supplement their incomes by brewing beer.

There are few signs of a feminist movement, women's main criterion being a desire to be part of the cash economy.

◪ **Georgina Andrewes spent a month in Botswana on the way home from two-year's teaching in Kenya.**

I loved Botswana; it's a wonderful place for 'wandering' and the one country in East and Southern Africa where I had no problems being a lone woman traveller. But I did have difficulties in finding out how to explore.

I wanted to go out into the desert and through the Okavango swamps, so I went to the tourist office and travel agents in the capital, Gaborone, only to be told there was no option but to fly there and join a safari – in other words that these places were only accessible to a few rich tourists. However, there is an old translation of the Swahili word 'safari'; it means 'to get through some way or another', and I wasn't put off. I bought a map and a volume of Nadine Gordimer's short stories (there's an excellent bookshop in Gaborone, a surprisingly modern city, serviced with luxury goods from South Africa), filled my water bottle, bought some oranges and took the train back to Francistown.

On the train I met some Zimbabwean women who had come down from Bulawayo to 'do their shopping' – dresses, underwear, watches, cups and plates, Tampax and even tea-bags. The train was full of women like themselves, who had saved up to come to Botswana for things which are unobtainable or very expensive in Zimbabwe. Most of them were smuggling back far more than their allowance, at the risk of losing everything to customs officials. There was also a risk of thieves in the night – young men who board the slow-moving train at country stops and break into the compartments with replica keys. Guards patrol the train, but it's still wise to stay awake with the light on.

As we talked through the night I was struck by how much these young women knew about the people and politics of the Western world, compared with how little I knew about their way of life. One of them was a rural development worker. She was optimistic about the future of rural women in Southern Africa: more and more are organising to press for improved healthcare, advice on agriculture and marketing, and for education in basic literacy. Many are now running their own businesses and opening bank accounts, whilst 'the men get left behind, becoming drunk in the bars'. These are important advances in a country where men still retain the 'right' to beat their wives, to have many wives at once, and to demand 'bride price' for their daughters. A lot of fathers demand the latter in cash instead of cattle and can ask for as much as the sum total of their daughter's educational fees; in fact some even keep all the schoolfee receipts to present to the husband-to-be.

My travelling companions not only readily answered my questions, they invited me to stay at their homes in Matabeleland and, of course, insisted on feeding me. I would very much have liked to stay with Batswana people, especially in the bush, but the opportunity never arose. Everyone assumes you want to stay in Gaborone, Francistown or Maun (on the edge of Okavango) and there simply aren't many people or villages around.

In contrast to my train ride I shared the bus from Francistown to Maun with 12 men. I was a bit nervous at first but, as an obvious curiosity, I was treated with great consideration and respect. (This is the only time I've been on a bus in Africa and not in some way been hassled by men.) As we talked I looked out at the dry land, spotting zebra, giraffe and ostriches. I became increasingly aware of the vast flatness of Botswana, miles and miles of nothing but sand and scrub, somehow impressive and yet not at all monotonous.

In the dusty evening light, I saw a solitary Bushman squatting at the roadside, a small wrinkled figure with golden skin. During a month in Botswana I saw only this one 'true' Bushman (there were people of obvious Bushman descent in Maun) so, romantically perhaps, I let him be a symbol for all that I loved about the country. Of all the people there, conservationists, naturalists, agriculturalists, hunters, the Bushmen know most about the intricate balance of land and animals. They are the original inhabitants of Southern Africa, but black and white alike have driven them out of their former hunting grounds into the harshest desert areas. It is a testimony to their intelligence and endurance that the 50,000 or so who remain today continue to live in harmony with their environment.

TRAVEL NOTES

Languages English and Sekalaka.
Transport Hitching is widely accepted, as there are few buses away from the main roads, but you're expected to pay. Entering the country from Zimbabwe, it's best to take the train.
Accommodation Be prepared to pay a lot for hotels. There's little alternative unless you want to risk camping.
Guide Geoff Crowther's *Africa on a Shoestring* (Lonely Planet) has 8 pages on Botswana.

CONTACTS
Botswana Council of Women, PO Box 339, Gaborone; and **Association of Botswana Women**, PO Box 1505, Gaborone. These are the only addresses we've managed to find.

BOOKS
Bessie Head, *A Question of Power* (Heinemann Educational, 1974). Beautifully written exploration of a woman's sanity, as seen through her relationship with two men. By a South African exile writer and set in the village in Botswana where she lived until her death earlier this year. Three other novels/short story collections — by Bessie Head — *Maru* (1972), *The Collector of Treasures* (1977) and *Jerowe, Village of the Rain Wind* — have also been published by Heinemann.

ZIMBABWE

Zimbabwe's organised tourist industry may have suffered since independence, but provided you keep away from certain trouble spots it's a fascinating and relatively easy country to explore. Hitching works well: black Zimbabweans charge a bus-rate or slightly more; whites usually don't charge anything and may well offer to put you up. But, if you're white, beware having to pay in the form of listening to impassioned racist monologues. Given their colonial history, most black people are remarkably friendly.

Most bad publicity about Zimbabwe stems from the complex political situation. As Africa's youngest nation, it gained independence only in 1980 after a long, hard war of liberation from white minority rule. The government was taken over by Robert Mugabe's ZANU party which recently returned to power in the country's first national elections. It was a landslide victory for ZANU, but tension with the main opposition party ZAPU, led by Joshua Nkomo, remains a major source of internal conflict. Political disagreements are mingled with inter-tribal rivalry between the Shona (largely supporters of ZANU) and the minority Ndebele (who mainly support ZAPU), worsened by intense personal animosity between the two leaders. Sporadic violence between rival guerrilla factions is known to flare up in certain areas, notably Matabeleland, and it's important to keep informed of the situation.

In the wake of a war in which **women** fought equally and as bravely as men, the government has always made efforts to elevate their status in society. Several laws have been passed, most significant being the Legal Age of Majority Act whereby a woman, like her male counterpart, stops being a minor at eighteen. However, laws have limitations and women have a hard time battling against centuries of tradition and custom. The Ministry of Community Development and Women's Affairs has made inroads through its focus on literacy and self-help projects in rural areas, apparently met with great enthusiasm by the women concerned, and various other organisations encourage income-generating projects with the aim of strengthening women's economic power. But the tendency is still to concentrate on traditional home-based activities which do little to change fundamental attitudes about women's inferiority. Signs of a growing women's movement, however, and continuing government commitment, indicate the possibility of much deeper, lasting changes in the future.

Kate Kellaway spent three-and-a-half years living as a school-teacher in Zimbabwe.

Independence has meant important legal gains for women. There is a Ministry of Women's Affairs, several women's groups and a slowly growing interest in the Women's Movement. But it is hard to connect these facts to the women I've known and the girls I've taught in Zimbabwe. Only a small educated minority are active in women's affairs or able to protest and it is still the exceptional woman who can define her oppression.

The closest I came to Zimbabwean women was when I was living and teaching in St Mary's, a black township outside Harare. The difference between Harare the town and Harare townships, now euphemistically renamed 'high-density suburbs', is so extreme they shouldn't share the same name. The luxurious 'low-density' suburbs of Zimbabwe's capital are reminiscent of Britain's wealthy stockbroker belt, the style an inheritance of colonialism. The townships, made up of vast complexes of tiny houses, crowded with people deprived of adequate amenities, are a colonial inheritance of another kind.

When I went to live with a family in St Mary's I was congratulating myself on breaking away from the 'British' Zimbabwe to experience the 'real thing'. But it is terrible to make of someone else's hardship an interesting experience for yourself. Besides it wasn't as simple as that. I was there because it was the home of Moses, my boyfriend. Throughout my stay I felt a conflict between accepting hospitality and really looking at what was around me.

St Mary's, without electricity, is the oldest of the Chitungwiza townships, 25 miles from Harare. Imagine row upon row of ramshackle houses, squashed together between miles of dusty streets. You are surrounded by people all day long. There are so many babies that at any given moment one will be crying. Cocks crow dementedly in the middle of the night.

Before I got a job at the local township school my days were spent at home with the women. Moses' sister, Rutendo, has three little girls. She got pregnant at fourteen. Her husband treated her badly and she's glad to be home again. Unlike many women in her position she has managed to get custody of the children, whom she brings up with her mother. Moses' father works far away and, apart from a brother, it's a predominantly female community. Moses' mother is a professional mother. She was my Zimbabwean mother for a while: she accepted me, welcomed and joked with me and tried in every way to make me feel at home.

I didn't speak much Shona, just enough to say a few essential things like 'Ndipeiwo mutsvairo' (give me the broom) or 'Ndine usimbe' (I'm lazy) or 'Ndaguta' (I'm full). I wasn't so much lazy as frightened by the routine of housework that shaped the women's day. Zimbabwean women keep their houses immaculately clean, but in St Mary's it was an unending fight against dust and dirty feet. Rutendo would rise at dawn and sweep the yard with a broom made of twigs, making beautiful patterns in the dust. Moses' second sister, Musafare, applied strong smelling wax polish to the kitchen and dining room floor. The day was punctuated by a trickle of water as children, clothes, floors, pots, selves, everything was washed. Most tasks involved bending – I picture Rutendo and Musafare bending from the hip. Rutendo taught me how to cook *nhopi*, a delicious pumpkin porridge made with peanut butter; she showed me how to scour a pot with sand and how to cook *sadza*. Sadza isn't easy to cook if you're making it for 15 people over a wood fire. It becomes stiff and hard to stir. Zimbabwean women have good strong arms; I felt puny and ridiculous struggling to stir a pot of sadza, my eyes streaming with tears from the smoke. 'Crying for sadza', Rutendo used to call it.

I was the only 'murungu' (white) in the township, but people soon became openly friendly, shouting greetings when I passed. The men were often easier to talk to, partly as they spoke more English. I also think they felt free to talk to me about subjects they wouldn't discuss with their own women. Once Rutendo and I went to see Sissy Elizabeth. She was very pregnant, so pregnant it would have been tactless to ask when the baby was coming. Elizabeth explained that she wanted to be a policewoman after the child was born, but her husband was against it. She asked me to check that her application form was correctly filled. (Later she became a policewoman and her husband beat her up because of it.) I went to talk to Rutendo in the kitchen. She speaks a little English. I chopped the tomatoes small on newspaper.

'Matimati,' I stated.

'Matimati,' Rutendo confirmed.

'Mafuta ekubikisa?' I asked.

'Yes, cooking oil,' said Rutendo, adding it to the pan. In the small black saucepan the sadza began to thicken. Using the *mugoti*, a special stick, I stirred. Rutendo was delighted: 'I'll tell Moses you are a good housewife now.'

Later we sat outside Elizabeth's house, eating sadza and sour milk. The sun burnt my calves. I surveyed my pink espadrilles and the pumpkin leaves swaying in the breeze and was suddenly filled with panic. What was I doing here? What was life like for these women? I watched one idly stitching a border of little green checks onto a loosely woven yellow tablecloth. 'Have a go,' she indicated, thrusting the material into my hands. I didn't, afraid of ruining it or showing myself up as an inept needle-woman. What sort of image was I trying to create with all this knitting, sewing and cooking of sadza? By the time I reached home I felt exhausted from the strain of trying to communicate without enough words. I was so pleased to see Moses' mother, she must have sensed it for she unexpectedly reached for my hand and kissed it.

Women like Rutendo and Moses' mother are authoritative and powerful in the home. How much this has to do with the absence of husbands isn't clear. One of the most popular subjects my students ask to debate is always 'Who is the most powerful, the father or the mother?' There is no foregone conclusion. Other popular subjects include bride price, polygamy and 'a woman's place is in the home'. Students tend to be reactionary, the girls being the most timidly conservative, although seeds of protest often lie beneath the surface. Most of them are prepared to express a distaste for polygamy. Few question the concept of marriage or women's domestic role in the home. I remember a boy named Launcelot saying: 'Women should not go to school. I want a nice fat wife who'll keep me warm in winter and feed me sadza all the year round – that's all she will do.' The day was saved by a boy, aptly named Blessing, who stood up and spoke passionately and eloquently in favour of women's freedom from the slavery of domesticity and cruel husbands. I'm sure that many girls will eventually gain the confidence they need to express their views themselves.

▰ **Georgina Andrewes travelled around Zimbabwe on her way home from teaching on a Voluntary Service Overseas (VSO) programme in Kenya.**

As I headed south from Harare I was struck by the smooth tar road, the miles of wire fencing, the irrigated pastures and neat picnic areas, and by the cleanliness. I had dimly envisaged something of the shambles of East Africa – potholes and broken down buses, cattle hit by cars and policemen doing anything to extract a bribe. In this part of Zimbabwe the only untidiness appeared to be a few discarded beer cartons.

It is quite easy to hitch lifts in Zimbabwe, either paying or free, the latter most likely from white farmers and businessmen who appreciate company on their trips around the country. Every so often the monotony of the fast straight roads is relieved by lacy blankets waving and rippling in the breeze. Women gather at the roadside and string up their crocheted cloths and covers from posts to sell for the much needed cash for clothes and school fees, and for food in times of drought.

In Zimbabwe, as in so many countries, women are closest to the land and so bear the worst burden of hardship when the rains fail. When I was there the country was in the grips of its third year of drought. The day I arrived my attention was drawn to a short newspaper article announcing that groups of women were to be taken to see how low the water level of Lake McIlwaine had fallen, so that they would realise the need for rationing. Two months later, after very heavy rainfall, the lakes and dams were full again. It was then that a group of 'important' men set off for the banks of the same lake to celebrate the rainfall by drinking champagne!

Nevertheless, I got the impression that women do have a powerful voice in Zimbabwe. Improvements such as free healthcare and primary education, land resettlement, the removal of tax on basic foodstuffs, and higher minimum wages have directly benefited rural women; and there are quite a few women's groups. Of greater concern appeared to be the continuing inter-tribal tension. Travellers are by no means immune from the conflict and it's wise to keep well-informed of the current situation.

Probably my happiest days were spent hitching and walking out in the Eastern Highlands near the border with Mozambique. Together with another traveller whom I met in the youth hostel in Harare – a cheap and pleasant place to stay and a useful meeting place – I hitched most of the way in one long ride on the back of a lorry. Huge granite boulders lie scattered and balanced all over Zimbabwe, but I had seen nothing like these before: vast rocks, three thousand million years old, toppling yet frozen still against the sky.

After a night at Nyanga we decided to walk across the Inyanga mountain range to Troutbeck in the east, a tourist spot and beautiful. It was one of those walks that tests endurance: wonderful to begin with, climbing up and up through the pink-leaved Msasa trees, with always another peek to go; then slithering down rocks and dry earth into dense vegetation, through bamboo and savannah grass the height of man, over boulders, under trees, through bush, sweating, thirsty and scratched.

Troutbeck is a kind of African Scotland where the sun is hot, the lake waters cool and the pine trees are dark and sweet-smelling. It's the sort of place to go for complete calm. But hotels are expensive. We swam and rowed on the lake, ate tomato sandwiches with tea, and then moved on. After what seemed like hours shivering by the roadside, a Landrover picked us up and took us to Rhodes Dam where we stayed in one of the excellent lodges which can be found in all the country's national parks. These are self-catering and usually need to be booked in advance – we were lucky this time.

TRAVEL NOTES

Languages English is the official language. Shona is most widely spoken, followed by Sindebele.

Transport A good railway network connects all major cities. Buses are slow and usually very crowded, but they're cheap and travel almost everywhere. Hitching is easy and seems to be quite safe.

Accommodation All hotels tend to be expensive. Lodges, to be found in all the national parks, are cheaper but nearly always self-catering. Book in advance by writing to the Travel Centre, Stanley Avenue, PO Box 8151, Harare. Also check that lodges are open all the year round.

Special problems Take care when travelling between Bulawayo and Victoria Falls. ZAPU guerrilla activity can make it dangerous, especially at night. Don't hitch and make sure you keep informed of the situation in this area.

Guide Geoff Crowther, *Africa on a Shoestring* (Lonely Planet). Contains an update on Zimbabwe in the 1984 edition. Hilary Bradt, *Backpackers Africa* (Bradt, 1983).

CONTACTS

Women's Action Group, Box 5, Harare. At present the group holds meetings on Tuesdays at 6pm in the Catholic hall, on the corner of Fourth Street and Rhodes Avenue. It was initially formed in response to a massive and widespread police round-up of women, apparently suspected of being prostitutes, in 1983.

Zimbabwe Women's Bureau, Munndix House, Cameron Street, Harare. The Bureau's main aim is to promote the economic self-sufficiency of women outside the formal waged sectors of urban and rural areas. Helpful if you're interested in visiting various projects. Try asking for Mrs Khumalo.

Voice, 16 Samora Machel Avenue, Harare. Co-ordinating body of non-governmental or volunteer organisations. Not a women's organisation but very useful for gathering information.

BOOKS

Zimbabwe Publishing House has a fast-expanding women's list, fiction and non-fiction. For details write to ZPH, PO Box BW–250, Harare.

Sekai Nzenza, *The Autobiography of a Zimbabwean Woman* (Karia Press, 1986). Sekai is Zimbabwean–the book is about her life and shows the issues facing black people, from a Black Woman's perspective, and the contradictions resulting from the long oppression of white minority rule.

Ellen Kuzwayo, *Call Me a Woman* (The Women's Press, 1985). This remarkable autobiography, drawing on the experience of 70 years, movingly reveals what it's like to be a Black woman in South Africa. Much of the book, notably life in the townships, can be related to Zimbabwe.

Also look out for short stories and/or novels by Nadine Gordimer and Doris Lessing.

Thanks to Claire Sanders for helping to edit this chapter.

NEAR AND MIDDLE EAST

Chapter Nine

TURKEY AND THE OVERLAND TO ASIA

In the late 1960s, and the first years of the 1970s, thousands of independent travellers passed through Turkey, Iran and Afghanistan en route to India and Nepal. With recent political events, however, the overland trail has all but petered out. Afghanistan, under Soviet military occupation, is closed to tourists; Iran, at war with neighbouring Iraq and under strict Islamic rule, is not welcoming.

Turkey itself, though, is at present in the midst of a tourist boom. Tour companies, finding Greece increasingly overexploited, have been quick to invest in the country since its 'political stabilisation' under the military. And, for Europeans, it is one of the most exciting and accessible travel destinations, combining Mediterranean and Black Sea coastline with classical and Islamic sites and, in the east, spectacular mountainous isolation. Its traditional Muslim culture is tempered by a long-established secular state. Travel can be as adventurous as you want, though main routes are well covered by buses and accommodation plentiful and cheap.

It is still possible to travel through **Iran**, and a handful of tour operators continue to run overland trips, entering at the Turkish border and exiting into Pakistan. Doing it by yourself is considerably more daunting, although the Iranians are generally prepared to grant two-week transit visas and there are buses and cheap accommodation along the way. Iran, however, has never been an easy place for a woman traveller and at present is particularly oppressive. If the modesty of your clothes (or behaviour) is deemed 'incorrect' you can expect public hostility and rough treatment from the Revolutionary Guards. If you do decide to travel through the country, consider going in a group.

To an extent, similar factors apply to **Iraq**, never greatly visited due to a refusal in the 1960s/1970s to grant tourist visas. This position has now changed, and official government policy is to encourage foreign tourists. Attempts to do so, however, have largely been disrupted by the war with Iran, which in the south-west is currently a full scale military conflict.

If or when **Afghanistan** opens to travellers, we would welcome any contributions.

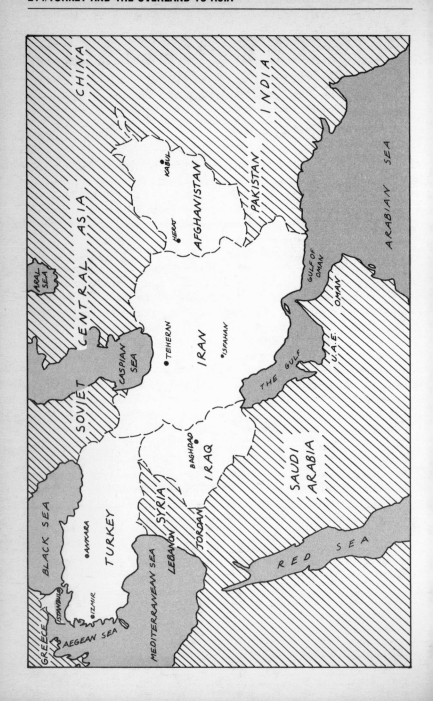

TURKEY

As **Turkey** emerges as a major European holiday resort, so it is becoming more Westernised and tourist-orientated. But this applies only to the most accessible and obvious attractions: the Aegean/Mediterranean coast, the circuit of classical sites, and Istanbul. Head east and you will find the country rural, undeveloped and highly traditional in attitudes. Obviously, the difficulties of travel depend on how far you move away from the established circuits and major centres. In terms of sexual harassment, however, you may find the more popular areas, and especially Istanbul, the most uncomfortable. Turks in general have a reputation for friendliness and hospitality, though, as might be expected of a Muslim nation, you will find this is most generally proferred man to man. Travelling alone, it can be hard to work out who to trust.

Political instability in Turkey reached chaotic and violent proportions in the late 1970s, and the military coup, in 1980, was, initially, widely accepted. It very quickly developed, however, into a right-wing and highly repressive military regime: in 1982 a reported 23,983 people were jailed for political and ideological crimes. Today, there has been a limited return to democracy, with military-regulated elections in November 1983. But the military establishment, with the president, General Evren, continue to exert a controlling influence; political dissent is barely tolerated; and thousands of Turks (including the president of the Istanbul Law Association and the entire Peace Committee) remain imprisoned.

The position of Turkish women is covered in some detail by Mary Harris (see below). A **Women's Movement** is just beginning to emerge, most notably with the 1984 foundation of the *Kadin Çevresi* (Women's Circle) – a feminist publishing firm which is producing translations of feminist classics as well as original works in Turkish. They have already set up a 'Readers Club', where women can meet weekly and also attend seminars and conferences, and a legal advice office, and have plans to set up a medical centre, coffee house, video-cinema and theatre, and a regular feminist review. However in an environment where political activity is not well received (and can be dangerous), they intend to restrict their activities, for a while, to the media.

▰ **Mary Harris has travelled around most parts of Turkey, over several years; she most often travels alone.**

It sounds like a cliché but Turkey really is a country of natural beauty, long and ancient history, and cultural and artistic diversity. I first went there because I have a long-standing interest in the history of the Middle East which I could not indulge until my children were grown, but on my first visit I fell for the people, the country, the food, the architecture and the arts. Since then I have returned again and again as my interests have broadened and deepened. I still normally travel on my own and, though very nervous at first, I am convinced that for me it is by far the best way to go.

Anyone who wants to understand the country today, the position of Turkish women within it, and the reaction of the Turks to foreign women, needs to try to understand at least some of the apparent paradoxes that have been thrown up by Turkey's incredibly complex recent history. Most of these stem from the fact that Turkey has chosen to be a secular state, yet 99 per cent of its people are Muslim, and for Muslims Islam *is* the state. It is the philosophical resolution of this paradox which has been behind many political developments in Turkey – the climax of which came with the person of Mustafa Kemal, the Ataturk. Ataturk led the resistance against threatened domination by the Allied armies of Britain, France and America at the end of the 1914–18 war and against the subsequent Greek invasion of Anatolia. In the course of these struggles throughout which women played a conspicuous part, he made the first definition of modern Turkey. As a part of a bourgeois revolution 'from above', and in setting the norms for a modern secular state, Turkish women were given legal and political status unheard of in Islam and not exactly common in the West. (Even before Ataturk, during the Young Turks revolution of 1908, the Union and Progress Party defended feminist principles, but in this case it was from a highly intellectual and abstract point of view.)

Between 1934 and 1946 increasing numbers of women gained access to education, were admitted as representatives in Parliament (all were back benchers and most lost their seats with the demise of the one party state) and, as far as legislation could proscribe, the 'Harem' value on women was removed. As usual, however, these formal changes had little impact on sexual relations and women continued to be dominated by men at the head of the family. As far as most people were concerned Ataturk was instituting a form of 'state feminism' which was enacted without consultation or popular consensus. Much of it did not last.

In the more open political climate of the 1960s feminism was excluded from debate on the grounds that women and men were already equal. Later, socialist movements had women's groups but they were political rather than feminist. After the coup of 1980, when there was a political clampdown, women paradoxically were allowed to meet again as feminists, even having their own page in a weekly paper. Against feminism today is the Ottoman legacy that women's emancipation is 'unnatural' and the Ataturk legacy, maintained by the present regime, that all that can be done has been done by legal reform.

Meanwhile, though many and increasing numbers of women work in the professions, the traditional divisions of labour remain. The vast majority of Turkish women work in the home and in the fields. Change is coming, but slowly. A friend recently took me to visit her parents in southern Turkey. She, her brothers and sister are all professional people. Her parents worked the land on a small farm and her mother, small and bent, started life working horribly long hours in cotton fields between the remains of Roman aqueducts. Now there are modern aqueducts, though they didn't come in time for her, and a great new co-operative cotton factory. Her daughter also works horribly long hours but in a university. She can have tertiary education and the right to vote and to be a Muslim, but she is not allowed to wear her Muslim head scarf; she will be prosecuted if she does.

Thus in spite of the fact that, by Western-Christian standards, and that means increasingly Turkish-secular standards, Turkish women, particularly Turkish working-class women, are oppressed, the articulate voices of the educationally privileged don't really see Western-Christian feminism as the answer. They are working out their own solution at a time in history when grass-roots movements are banned and where on the whole they still work from the security and social service of their families. Already they are ahead of their sisters in Islam and I for one have no doubt that their solution will come, and that it will be a practical and uniquely Turkish one.

A woman travelling alone in Turkey presents an enigma; she could be a professional Turkish woman travelling alone (and Turkish men don't publicly molest Turkish women – under the concept of family honour all hell would be let loose if they did); she could be an unchaste loner and worth a go; or she could be what many of the Muslim countries now have and that is virtually a third sex for emancipated Western women, independent and 'unavailable' for sex. That is what I now aim for, but it has taken a while to work out the formula and it takes stamina to maintain it.

Before I could speak some Turkish I found that the quickest way of dealing with a persistent pesterer or follower was to go and stand next to any middle-aged Turkish person and make a fuss in English clearly indicating both the culprit and my distress. The effect is immediate but can be very aggressive so that you almost feel sorry for the man. I have not tried asking the Turkish police to help, partly because among the plethora of police uniforms I forget which are the Tourist Police, partly because I suspect that under his uniform a policeman is still a red-blooded Turk, and partly because I have seen Tourist Police being very, very tough on someone who cheated a tourist.

The best defences of all are to show obvious respect in dress and behaviour for the dominant Muslim culture, to learn the language and to get to know the women. Turkish women are wonderfully warm and affectionate in their hospitality. One incident sums it up, though I could quote very many. I was on a crowded Bosphorus ferry in the heat of the day, just me and a ferry full of working men. I was hiding behind my sunglasses and watching the view when there was a tug at my skirt and a small boy grabbed my hand, leading me to the wheelhouse. Three women and some small children were sitting there out of the sun, they had moved over to make room for me and sent a child to fetch me to join them. We had few words in common but one of the babies was planted on my knee and I was absorbed into warm, protective woman-hood that, to me, seems to happen in this way only in Turkey.

▨ Rosie Walford spent two weeks travelling around the east and north-east of Turkey, with a male friend.

I left for Turkey with certain reservations, some associated with the country's atrocious human rights record and some with nightmarish scenes that I remembered from *Midnight Express*. I returned with a very much less sombre impression.

To begin with I was wary of the people. Having never travelled before in an Islamic society, I had to adjust to being always and only approached by men. But my wariness on the whole was unfounded. We were shown great kindness and friendliness – men who we approached for directions went miles out of their way to lead us to our destination; street vendors often gave instead of sold me the fruit that I wanted to buy, and quite often we were simply adopted as a 'brother' and 'sister' and offered hospitality for as long as we remained in the town. This rarely seemed to conceal any ulterior motive though at times it did get claustrophobic, making us value rather more highly our privacy and freedom.

I can't tell how many of my positive experiences were related to the fact that I was travelling with a man and that we kept largely to the rural areas. I very much doubt if I would have been offered (or would have felt able to accept) so much hospitality had I been on my own. Other travellers I met described various experiences of both hospitality and harassment. Sexual harassment on the whole is surprisingly rare, you don't get the sort of petty interference that, travelling around the Mediter-ranean, builds up to almost phobic proportions. But when it does occur it feels more threatening and dangerous than in many countries. Wearing concealing clothing and acting inconspicuously really does seem to make you less vulnerable.

As foreign travellers we saw nothing of the ugly political side of life. It was easy to forget about this aspect of the country and to leave with an unrealistic view of stability. We did, however, notice the heavy military presence wherever we went – the menacingly armed officers who stood outside every post-office, bank or bridge. The government's intolerance of dissident opinion is clearly rigorously enforced: we found that people would refuse to discuss anything vaguely political, even in a moving car, for fear of being overheard.

Our only encounter with the police was when we had overslept our early-morning coach stop and jumped out at a petrol station to hitchhike back. As always there was a police car watching over. The uniformed officer inside beckoned to us with his pistol and we walked towards him somewhat apprehensively. However, as soon as he had ascertained where we were going he hailed down a worried looking lorry-driver and ordered him to drive us there. For us, this was easy hitchhiking, but also a demonstration of how the police command their absolute authority through fear.

Moving from place to place was generally easy and fast. Private coach companies compete for passengers, giving out cool palmfuls of cologne and free iced water on every route. Like most transport in Turkey, the seating is segregated with women placed at the front, which means that you always get a seat no matter how crowded the coach gets. Sitting for hours on some of the longer journeys, surrounded by Turkish women, I would become disheartened by their very obvious reluctance to enter into any sort of interchange. There seemed little that I could do to break down the barriers of communication. I was never quite sure how much of this was to do with shyness or language problems. They may have simply preferred to dissociate from me as a symbol of the immoral, ungodly West.

In the north-eastern corner of Turkey, where there are no major roads and the coaches do not run, we hitchhiked to a small farming village in the beautiful alpine mountains. Staying in this remote and primitive place I felt I could have been in a different country altogether. High in the summer pastures which were always enshrouded by clouds, the houses were built of rough stone and wood, heated only by a tin stove and the cows beneath the floor and with only the barest essentials of living inside. The women here seemed to be treated as unwaged labour, leading a life far removed from their veiled and housebound counterparts in the towns. Brightly dressed, with their arms and legs left free for working and their heads only covered from the rain, they worked all day cutting, gathering and baling hay by hand. At the end of her long day the woman we were staying with first made food for the men in the house and then disappeared to milk cows, churn cheese and bake bread for the next day before she herself stopped to eat. Although the women here clearly participated more in community life and were active outside the home, they still appeared to have very low status.

TRAVEL NOTES

Languages Turkish. Some English is spoken but German is more common.
Transport Most people travel by bus. The service is extensive and efficient and the buses are cheap, fast and comfortable. Trains are even cheaper but they're slower and the network is far more limited. Shared minibuses (*dolmuses*) are also available – they cost little more than buses and go to even very remote villages. Another affordable option is to travel by boat (along the Mediterranean and Black Sea coasts) on the *Turkish Maritime Lines*.
Accommodation In all main resorts and cities there's plenty of cheap accommodation. In the east, you'll be able to find places to stay but the choice is far more limited.
Special problems If you're travelling alone or with another woman, you're liable to be harassed a fair bit. It does help to dress reasonably modestly, i.e. cover your shoulders and don't wear shorts.
Avoid drugs – penalties are very severe even for possession of a small amount of cannabis.
Guides Diana Darke, *Turkey's Aegean Coast* (Michael Haag, 1986). Perhaps the most reliable. Tom Brosnahan, *Turkey – A Travel Survival Kit* (Lonely Planet, 1985). Useful on practicalities though not up to usual Lonely Planet standards. For cultural/historical details, George Bean, *Turkey's Aegean Coast* (John Murray, rev. 1984) and John Freely, *Companion Guide to Turkey* (Collins, rev 1984).

CONTACTS

Kadin Çevresi Yayinlari, Yani Hamam Sok. Öztel Işhani, 13/7 Beşiktas-Istanbul, Turkey (see introduction for details).

BOOKS

Pembenaz Yorgun, 'The Women's Question and Difficulties of Feminism in Turkey', in *Modern Turkey – Development and Crisis* (Ithaca Press, US, 1984).
Freya Stark, *Alexander's Path* (1956, Century 1984). Classic travels in Asia Minor.
Rose Macaulay, *The Towers of Trebizond* (1956, Futura 1981). Beautiful and quirky novel of intrepid camel-travelling and High Anglican angst. Greatly recommended.

IRAN

Though it is now possible to get into **Iran** again on the standard two-week transit visa it is difficult to contemplate travelling through this country with any degree of sanguinity or pleasure. The repressiveness of the regime is felt daily in the high level of propaganda, in the constant searchings of the Revolutionary Guards, in the omnipresent face of Khomeini and more particularly in the restrictions imposed upon you as a woman. The most obvious one is that of dress – you must cover up completely, and that includes wearing a veil that covers every inch of your hair. Nonetheless, there are positive aspects to travel in Iran. Roads and buses are good and budget hotels are plentiful. And, more importantly, the current regime's anti-Western stance does not seem to have affected the Iranians themselves, who remain for the most part, both men and women, extremely friendly and welcoming. This, and the undeniable attractions of seeing 'Persia' and travelling to India overland have meant that a small but growing number of women do visit the country.

Before the 1979 revolution the Iranian **Women's Movement** was strong, widespread and very active. Despite continual opposition from fundamentalist religious groups, it managed to achieve widespread gains for women in education, in the workplace and in legal reform. After the revolution, and Khomeini's seizure of power, the picture was reversed: virtually all legislation favouring women's rights was abolished; women who went unveiled were called prostitutes and many lost their jobs for refusing to conform to strict Muslim dress. Large numbers of Iranian women, many of whom had played their part in the revolutionary over-throw of the Shah, took to the streets in protest in the first weeks of Khomeini's 'Islamicisation' of the state; they were beaten and imprisoned. Thousands subsequently fled into exile, yet it is still estimated that by 1983 over 20,000 women had been executed for 'counter-revolutionary' or 'anti-Islamic' activity. All feminist groups in Iran have been forced underground, but women and women's groups are active in anti-Khomeini organisations both inside and outside the country.

◪ **Jennifer Luesby travelled through Iran, en route to Nepal, as part of an organised overland tour.**

Rural life in Iran is typical of underdeveloped Asia – centering on survival. The people remain largely uneducated and unwaged. The villages vary from scruffy concrete complexes in the west, to traditional straw-roofed huts in the far east. In contrast, the towns and cities with their wide tree-lined streets, Moghul remains and Western layouts present a veneer of sophistication. The infrastructure is impressive, reflecting significant past investment. The impression of order and stability fostered by the kerbed pavements, fenced-off parks and laid-out flowerbeds belies the current state of political and social turmoil.

The revolution of February 1979 established a fundamentalist Islamic dictatorship, under Ayatollah Khomeini, which has led to a total trans-formation of Iranian society. The propaganda is all-pervasive and shocking. The central theme is one of world domination, with 'The World Equals An Islamic World' a commonly expressed sentiment. There is a great deal of anti-everyone graffiti. The majority of hatred is directed at the Iraqis, Americans and Israelis, with the Russians, French, Canadian and British following closely. The type of imagery used is violent, with posters of spears raining down on a sea of Caucasian faces, bayonets crossed at an Israeli soldier's throat, and bloody scenes of the ongoing war with Iraq. Pictures and slogans are liberally plastered over every available wall and there are even purpose-built placards around many of the parks and monuments. The most sinister aspect is the saturation coverage of the Ayatollah. This Islamic 'Holy Man' peers at you from every street corner, highway and byway, resulting in a distinct 'big brother is watching you' reaction.

Women are the most deeply affected by the Islamicisation programme. Even as a woman traveller, you are obliged to keep your body covered, with the exception of your face and hands, at all times – which involves the compulsory wearing of a headscarf. Your treatment differs from that of an Iranian woman in that these restrictions do not extend to the obligatory wearing of a *ropush*, or kneelength coat, and trousers are acceptable. However, a note of warning, one of my fellow travellers had a particularly unpleasant encounter with the Iranian authorities following a brief public appearance in a track suit. 'Trousers' do not include ski-pants, tracksuit-pants or anything similar – take loose, baggy clothes.

That women are second-class citizens in Iran is a fact you are rarely allowed to forget. Your different colouring, clothing, and behaviour make you a particular focus of attention, much of which takes the form of sexual harassment: being jostled in the streets, being stared at continuously, sometimes too being followed. The black spots for this kind of treatment are the urban bazaars or market areas. The key to deterring abuse is to avoid eye contact. It is a dictate of the Muslim religion that men and women should avert their gaze from one another. For the men this transgression is circumvented in the case of Iranian women by their enforced shrouding, and seemingly condoned when directed at Western women. However, for women it is a code which must be observed; to break it is seen as a declaration of wantonness and is responded to as such.

The duality of the Iranian woman's role is quite strange. This Islamic dictatorship cannot afford to dispense with the Shah's legacy of a generation of skilled and educated women. Thus, whilst subject to Islamic strictures, women contribute actively to the economy. From customs officer to television news announcer they retain an unusually high profile. This obviously opens up a minefield of contradictions, by creating a class of economically independent women within a male-orientated society. The inconsistency remains unresolved. In the meantime it is relatively easy for the woman traveller to interact with Iranian women.

The climate of terror, induced by the propaganda, has certainly not destroyed the friendliness of the Iranian people. Whilst my fellow travellers and I were subject to open hostility on occasions, the chief source was officialdom, and a tiny minority of the men. Significant was the number of Iranians, both men and women, who actively sought us out and made friendly overtures. However very few were willing to discuss the values or laws of their new religious state – their amiability was tempered with well-founded fear.

It may be difficult at this point to understand why any woman should want to travel to Iran. The attractions are numerous. The buildings of Isfahan, lavishly adorned with blue mosaics, are just one example of this land's unique history and culture. In the towns one can find elegant marble-floored cake shops, highly worked silver and beautiful silks. Only minutes away, weights and measures are cast in open kilns using sand moulds, ornate brass and pewter plates are beaten by hand and, of course, Iran is the home of the famed Persian carpet.

I am, on the whole, glad that I visited Iran. But I didn't love the country – I was essentially shocked by it. The new rules must be kept and a clear head and ability to cope with potentially difficult situations is essential. Don't go alone if you can do otherwise. But if you can't and you still wish to go, stick to the towns, where you're safest. Avoid the rural areas and Teheran.

An **additional contribution** on Iran can be found in the following section on Iraq where Emma Duncan compares her experiences of the two countries.

TRAVEL NOTES

Languages Farsi, Turkish, Kurdish, Arabic. In the main towns and cities, quite a number of people speak some English.

Travel There is a railway network and coach service both of which are relatively cheap. In the former there are women's compartments which makes one feel fairly safe, but it is not an extensive service. Probably the best option for independent travel is the inter-town coach system which is generally quite comfortable and efficient. In some cities segregation rules in buses have been enforced.

Accommodation Plenty of reasonably priced hotels remain in the medium-sized towns.

Special problems You must dress appropriately otherwise you'll find yourself in serious trouble. You need to cover yourself completely, preferably in sombre clothing and that includes wearing a scarf that covers all your hair.

Security is stringent and revolutionary guards will stop and search coaches fairly frequently. You might also be body searched when you cross over the border into Iran.

Travel is restricted in the south-west as long as the Iran/Iraq war continues, but otherwise is unhindered.

Guide There are no specific guide books available on Iran. Susan Griffith's *Travellers Survival Kit to the East* (Vacation Work, 1986) provides some information on travel restrictions, transport, accommodation, etc; Geoff Crowther, *West Asia on a Shoestring* (Lonely Planet, 1984) also includes a section on the country.

CONTACTS
Women's Section of the **Iranian Community Centre**, 465a Green Lanes, London N4 (Tel. 01–341 5005) Resource centre, newsletter in Farsi.

Women & Struggle In Iran A quarterly publication produced by the Women's Commission of the Iranian Students Association in the USA. Copies available from ISA, (WC-ISA), P.O. Box 5642, Chicago, Illinois 60680.

BOOKS
Tabari Azar, et al., eds, *In the Shadow of Islam: The Women's Movement in Iran* (Zed Books, London 1982). Written by three Iranian women, this book covers the Women's Movement in Iran since the Revolution of 1979, focusing on the relation between Islam and the struggle for women's emancipation.

Farah Asari, ed., *Women of Iran* (Ithaca Press, 1983). A collection of papers by socialist-feminist Iranian women which bring a fresh approach to the political debates surrounding the revolution in Iran.

Manny Sharazi, *Javady Alley* (The Women's Press, 1984). An outstanding novel set in Iran in 1953, and seen through the eyes of a seven-year-old girl whose childhood certainties are coming under threat.

Freya Stark, *The Valleys of the*

Assassins. (1934 Century 1984). Another world – and another classic piece of travel.

In *Third World Second Sex* (see General Bibliography) an extract is included from a booklet entitled 'Iranian Women: The Struggle Since the Revolution', produced by the London Iranian Women's Liberation Group.

IRAQ

Westerners used not to be welcome in **Iraq**. This has changed in recent years but the government's attempts to encourage tourism have largely been disrupted by the war with Iran and by reports of the all-pervasive state repression – particularly against the minority Kurds. Few people would at present consider visiting Iraq for a holiday.

The current dictatorial regime – Saadaq Hussein's Ba'ath Socialist Party – has been in power since 1968. Using revenue from the country's oil-fields, it has implemented a rapid programme of modernisation, now foundering under the economic pressures of maintaining its war with Iran. Inflation has been rapid, and Iraq is at present an expensive country to visit.

Iraq is a secular state, something it emphasises in response to the Iranian Islamic government, and **Iraqi women** are noticeably more emancipated than women in most Arab countries. However, amongst a population which is almost entirely Muslim, social attitudes towards women's sexuality have hardly altered at all. Exceptional importance is still attached to women's pre-marital virginity and it's generally unacceptable for an Iraqi woman to live on her own. Despite the high profile and Western-style clothing of Iraqi women, a Western woman travelling around alone will still be considered 'loose' and is likely to be subjected to fairly persistent harassment.

The Ba'ath Party actively promotes the interests of women, encouraging education for girls at all levels, non-segregated schools and women's employment in a wide range of fields. Affiliated to the government is the **General Federation of Iraqi Women**, a large state organisation with headquarters in Baghdad and eighteen main branches throughout the country. The Federation participates in international women's activities and acts as an apparently effective pressure group to bring about the integration of women into the economy. Though the position of women has noticeably improved in the cities, change has yet to come to most of the rural areas.

▰ **Emma Duncan is a journalist who paid two short visits to Iran and Iraq to report on the war.**

Women in Iraq have a whole range of freedoms which are unavailable in Iran and for that matter, most of the countries around the Gulf. The attention paid to improving the position of women is one of the few tangible gains for which the Iraqi regime is responsible. Women's access to education is well established, they are encouraged to compete for high-powered jobs (the proportion of surgeons who are women is higher than in Western Europe) and there are women in both the ruling Ba'ath party and in the rubber stamp Parliament. In Baghdad, women generally wear Western-style clothes, drink, and go to restaurants and night-clubs. Understandably they react with horror at the idea of an Iranian invasion that would impose strict Islamic codes of behaviour on them.

But if the 'liberal' attitude of the government has had some effect on the way Iraqi men regard Iraqi women, it has not much changed their view of Western women. This, I think, is partly to do with their general attitude towards foreigners.

Iraq has for a long time been a much more closed society than Iran. Until the economic strains imposed by the war forced the government to look for any help it could get, it positively discouraged Westerners from entering the country. It was friendly with Russia, but nobody else. Even now, although the government encourages foreign business and invest-ment, the Iraqi people try to avoid contact with foreigners.

Iraq is also a well-established police state. There is a huge political party network which the government can and does abuse for information on potentially subversive citizens; there's a large and effective secret police, and a plethora of other security services. The effect of all this is that most Iraqis feel that they are being watched all the time. Anybody may be an informer: if it's not one of your next-door neighbours then it must be the other.

The government similarly appears to be paranoid about foreigners and Westerners in particular. It seems most likely that this is a hang-over from the days of active hostility to the West, combined with general paranoia created by war, successionist struggles and internal dissent. Whatever the cause, it is extraordinarily difficult to meet Iraqis socially. Obviously, you meet them if you are doing business – I was there as a journalist covering the war, so had a lot of dealings with government bureaucrats – but you can rarely go to their homes or invite them to visit you. One diplomat I talked to who had been there nearly two years showed great excitement over the fact that he had just been into an Iraqi's house for the first time: his driver had invited him in for tea. People's nervousness seemed to me entirely justified. There are too many stories of people being dragged in by the security services and 'questioned' for twelve hours for talking to a foreigner.

One obvious result is that Iraqis have not had much contact with the reality, as opposed to the fantasy, of Western women, who remain foisted with the myth that they are loose adventuresses, willing to sleep with anyone. This seems to evoke a mixture of desire and hostility with men, who follow you in cars as you walk along the pavement and finger you in the street. It didn't seem to matter that I was dressed much more modestly than most Iraqi women, in baggy clothes covering every conceivably interesting part of my body. I was quite obviously a foreign woman, and that in itself was enough of a turn-on. I was never actually threatened, yet the feeling was sufficiently intimidating for me to want to spend as little time out of my hotel, alone, as possible. The looks and stares persisted when I was with men, but having friends around, it didn't bother me so much.

Professionally, I was treated no worse than the other male journalists – that is, we were at the mercy of a Kafkaesque bureaucracy, restricted in our movements, watched, and not allowed to talk to anybody who was likely to tell us an alternative version about what was going on. The bureaucracy in a police state that runs on fear is particularly difficult to deal with, because everybody is reluctant to take decisions. The penalties for making mistakes are tough – sometimes death – so nobody wants to put themselves in a vulnerable position. You are, therefore, endlessly shunted from office to office, with everybody claiming that whatever you are asking is somebody else's responsibility. I attributed the fact that I was not treated any differently to men largely to the fact that sexual equality is party ideology, and government officials have to conform to it.

Most of this stands in marked contrast to life in Iran. In Iran, discrimination is part of the state ideology. When you are there, you have to behave as the government expects its women to behave. Don't be fooled by the embassy in London, which told me that it would be sensible for me to wear some sort of *chador* (veil) because I would feel more comfortable. You have to, or you are liable to get roughed up by Revolutionary Guards. Ideally, you should have a large, preferably dark, scarf, a long dark raincoat, trousers, dark socks and flat shoes. The scarf must cover all your hair: even bits of fringe sticking out are unacceptably risqué.

Women's dress is an important political issue, and one to which the government and its opponents pay a lot of attention. Immodesty is a sign of being morally lax and un-Islamic. The government is criticised by its right-wing opponents for not being sufficiently strictly Islamic, and one way of deflecting that sort of criticism is to try to prove your Islamic credentials by insisting on rigorous adherence to the superficials, like proper dress. There have been signs, recently, that women may be forced to wear the full chador – a black sheet draped over the whole body and held from the inside so as only to reveal the eyes – because the government wants to be seen to be even more Islamic than its opponents.

This sort of fetishism is strange stuff to a Westerner. To me, it seemed to imply an obsession with sex – that unless every inch of flesh or strand of hair which might turn a man's head is covered up, nobody will be able to think about God, the war or the balance of payments. Of course, covering things up doesn't stop men thinking about sex – rather the opposite. A journalist who had been in Teheran for three months told me with horror that he had already started eyeing women's ankles.

The Iranians I dealt with – mostly in the felicitously named Ministry of Islamic Guidance – were aware how bizarre, not to say distasteful, I found all this. They were pleasant, helpful, and rather apologetic. They pointed out with some embarrassment that the scarf I had arrived with was too small: bits of my neck showed, and I could not go and interview anybody looking like that. They were certainly revolutionaries, convinced that the Islamic revolution was good for Iran; yet they were much subtler, much more aware of my point of view, than were the Iraqis.

Five years of revolution cannot wipe out decades of friendly contact with the West. Strangely, given the regime's anti-Western rhetoric, I felt I was viewed with less hostility than I was in Iraq. People in the streets either ignored me or, if I looked lost, showed me where to go. Men in shops and hotels flirted in a rather Mediterranean way. I was not made to feel abnormal. People talked to me, and invited me to their houses, which was a revelation. Middle-class life in Teheran continues behind people's front doors: the chador comes off, drink flows (mostly vodka, made with medical alcohol and distilled water: it tastes of nothing and doesn't make you blind), people talk politics, criticise the regime, complain about getting poorer, grumble about the price of food and the pointlessness of the war – the kind of talk that would have been unimaginable in Iraq. These things can happen because Iran is not yet an efficient police state in the way that Iraq is; the government doesn't have the sort of network of informants required.

Even so, I do not suggest that Iran is fun for a woman to be in. I was all right: I was on a short trip, and amazed, given all I had heard about the place, that so much un-Islamic activity went on. But the foreign women I came across who had been there for a while were unenthusiastic. There is nothing to do in Teheran: restaurants are barely worth going to, plays and films are Islamic, even to go out shopping or for a walk you have to conceal yourself completely. They felt caged by Islamic regulations, and very bored.

TRAVEL NOTES

Languages Arabic is Iraq's official language; Kurdish is spoken in the north. You'll find English is widely spoken in Baghdad.

Transport Railways and buses connect the larger towns and cities and domestic flights also connect Baghdad with Basra and Mosul. Within the cities taxis are easily available, but they're very expensive (you should agree a price at the start of a journey).

Accommodation There are many hotels in Baghdad. There's also a network of government rest houses and hotels (all owned by the state tourism organisation) along main roads and railway routes and at tourist sites. Prices, though, are generally high. Hotel bills have to be paid in foreign currency, not in Iraqi dinars, unless you have a work permit.

Special problems Inflation has been high in Iraq, largely as a result of the war and most things are expensive.

Security is very tight especially in the airport. Certain areas too are out of bounds because of the war with Iran.

Guides There are no specific guide books available, though Susan Griffith's

Travellers Survival Kit to the East (Vacation Work, 1986) provides some information on transport, sites, accommodation, etc. The State Organisation for Tourism also issues a Tourist Guide. You can obtain a copy if you write to: PO Box 10028, Karradh, Baghdad.

CONTACTS

The General Federation of Iraqi Women, Abi Talib Street, Alwaziriya, Baghdad, Iraq.

International Committee for the Release of Detained and 'Disappeared' Women in Iraq, PO Box 9308, London WC1. Write for campaigning information and details.

BOOKS

Doreen Ingrams, *The Awakened Women in Iraq* (Third World Centre for Research and Publishing, London, 1984) Survey of position of women in Iraq including chapters on minorities; women pioneers; the General Federation of Iraqi women; women and the professions etc. – informative but mostly uncritical.

Chapter Ten
THE MIDDLE EAST

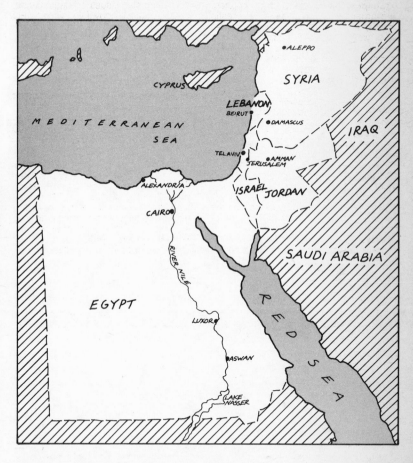

The historical/tourist interest of the **Middle East** is matched only by its political instability. In shaping this chapter we have had to make decisions both about naming territory (we settled on an all-encompassing Israel-Palestine section) and about including pieces on countries recently changed beyond recognition (we dropped Lebanon for this edition).

Egypt, by far the most travelled country of the region, provoked one of the larger responses in our appeal for contributions. Many, however, were surprisingly negative. The scale of Egyptian tourism, and the network of guides and hustlers around the major sites, can feel both oppressive and at times personally threatening. **Syria,** by contrast, is at present almost unvisited. Its sites, both Islamic and Roman, are perhaps the most exciting and beautiful in the Mediterranean or Middle East; its level of harassment, on the whole, low.

Travel in **Israel-Palestine** demands an individual reaction, based on your own personal politics. The one aspect that is undeniable is the reality of militarisation as the state of Israel continues, supported by the West and unrecognised, outside Egypt, by the Arab World. We have included two experiences – one of working on a kibbutz, the other teaching in the West Bank – and hope to broaden this range in a future edition. We would also be interested in contributions on travelling in **Jordan**.

EGYPT

Egypt is well used to tourism. It has a long-established and very well-organised holiday industry, geared for the most part towards shunting visitors along the Nile to Cairo, around the Pyramids and on to Luxor and Aswan. If you want to travel independently, and you can take the heat, it's best to go in the middle of June, the only time when the crowds really thin out.

The country, and in particular the capital, Cairo, can be initially confusing and intimidating. In all the main tourist areas you'll need to cope with hustlers and guides – and come to terms with genuine poverty. Harassment too is a problem and you'll need to dress very modestly to command respect. As ever, though, these are factors that become less intense as you grow more used to travel, or live for a while in one place, or if you're touring with a man.

Politically, Egypt's 'open door' economic policy has attracted an enormous proliferation of multinational enterprises – their effect has been to widen the already extreme poverty gap. Unemployment and homelessness are approaching ever more critical proportions. Over the last decade, as part of the reaction to these rising encroachments of Western capitalism, there has been a powerful swing towards Islamic fundamentalism. The government, whilst attempting to subdue fundamentalism as a political movement, has, socially, made concessions. **Women** are returning, sometimes voluntarily but also under considerable social pressure, to traditional roles. The familiar scapegoating of women who attempt to retain their positions in the workplace during a climate of economic recession and high unemployment is particularly strong in Egypt. In rural areas women continue to labour for long hours under arduous conditions to maintain a subsistence living.

For information on the **Egyptian Women's Movement** see Kate Baillie's piece, below.

▰ **Kate Baillie lived in Cairo for two and a half months, teaching English and learning Arabic.**

Egypt is the West's pet Arab country, 'moderate' being the favourite adjective. It's important to know that this reflects nothing of the internal situation, simply Egypt's pro-Western economic and diplomatic policy. The fact is, it is not unknown for Egyptians to be imprisoned for criticising the government, censorship of the arts and media is commonplace, political parties are suppressed, and the capital is infested with armed soldiers. In the press and television centre, levelled rifles greet employees from a sandbag emplacement inside the foyer. The oppression is not quite as bad now as it was under President Sadat, but while a few political prisoners are released and the odd paper is allowed to publish again, American enterprise continues to prise apart Egyptian culture, values and, of course, the economy.

A new polarisation has appeared above the basic division of peasant and bourgeois, villager and Cairean. Those in the pay of the multi-nationals form their own super class. Speaking only English, adopting Cindy Doll and grey-suited dress, their living standards leap while their lives become subservient to work patterns evolved for a very alien climate and culture. Speed, greed, glamour and competitiveness are the requisite values. Meanwhile, the majority, who don't or can't choose that rat race, remain in their desert robes and poverty, upholding values and a vision of society derived from a history much older than the West now knows.

The re-emerging strength of Islamic fundamentalism has to be appreciated in this context. An apparently fanatical religious social movement is hard for us to comprehend. What has to be grasped is that Islamic fundamentalism is both political and religious and there is no distinction because of the nature of Islam. The Muslim faith is a set of rules for a state, not just for individuals and it is in this that it differs so much from Christianity. Inevitably, the religious text, the Koran, is open to all manner of conflicting interpretations. It can be argued contrary to actual practice in Egypt that the Koran stipulates the right of women to choose their husbands and to leave them. The financial rights it lays down for women were not achieved by European women until the 19th and 20th centuries. Its banking policy would make you open an account tomorrow. Its precepts on virginity and menstruation would make you run a mile. During the prophet's lifetime, some women complained that only men were being addressed. From then on, the two words for male believers and female believers appear. There is nothing in the Koran about female circumcision.

Leaving behind the 5th and 6th centuries, the struggle for emancipation was started by Egyptian women at the start of this century. In 1962, under Nasser, they obtained the vote, access to free education at all levels, and a woman minister for social affairs was appointed. In the last twenty years, women have entered the professions, factories, the civil service and business, though they are not allowed to be judges. In the public sector, equal pay is legally enforcable. Woman now comprise almost 50 per cent of the workforce though nearly half of those are peasant women working in the fields with their men as they have done for centuries. Abortion remains illegal and clitoridectomy, proving virginity on the wedding night and the punishment of adultery are still practised.

Sadat created an official Women's Movement with his Madison Avenue-bedecked wife Jhan as president. It was little more than a tea party circle of her friends enjoying the freedoms of power and riches. She is reputed to have approved a World Health Organisation scheme to put a sterilising agent in a village's water supply without informing, let alone consulting, the inhabitants. The real Women's Movement, though inevitably made up of educated urban women, is pan-Arab and takes its position from Arab history and experience, not American or European feminist texts. In the villages and amongst the urban poor, where feminism is unheard of, there is a communion between women who share work in and outside the home, in ways that our Western conception of sisterhood could never emulate.

In Cairo, I experienced from women this almost instinctive kind of care and protectiveness. On several occasions women who were strangers to me and spoke no English, rescued me from situations in which I was unwittingly at risk. Wandering, heat-dazed and lost, in a slum behind the Citadelle, a woman took my arm, smiled at me and led me out of the maze, shooing away the men and little boys who approached us. A few days later I tried sleeping in Al Azhar mosque, unaware that this is forbidden to women, let alone infidels. A soldier appeared with the intention of arresting me, but I was saved by a woman who sat me behind her and talked at length to what were by now five soldiers and seven other men grouped round. Presumably she explained my ignorance: the only words I could catch from the men were 'Police' and 'Koran'. But she succeeded, the men left and the woman smiled at me and patted the ground to show I could stay.

Aside from the pyramids, the mosques are the sights to see in Cairo, both from the gaping at beautiful buildings point of view and to experience the use Muslims make of their places of worship. A note on dress – you always have to take your shoes off and in the more tourist-frequented mosques you may have to pay to get them back. Though not usually enforced, I'd advise wearing a scarf, out of courtesy if nothing else. As for shorts, short skirts, punk hair styles and bralessness with clinging clothes, forget it, whether in mosques or on the street.

Mosques can also be the best places to meet Egyptian women – especially where a women's area is curtained off. Not long after the incident in Al Azhar, I was very comforted to be separated off from the men. But I still wasn't sure about the sleeping rules, so I gestured an enquiry to a woman, in her fifties I supposed, veiled and gowned to the floor in black. She immediately bounced up to me, talking nineteen to the dozen and then went off to fetch two friends who spoke some English. With their fifty odd words and my fifteen of Arabic, gestures, pictures and a dictionary, and joined by two more women, we passed several hours together in enthusiastic discussion. They asked me the two standard questions that had opened every conversation I had had in Cairo with men or women: 'What's your religion?' and 'Are you married?' The latter, once answered negatively, would be replaced by 'Where's your friend?'. The first question had involved me in metaphysical arguments I had long forgotten, and I learned to avoid any words the dictionary gave for 'atheist' which carry the same moral connotations as saying you eat babies. I don't know what these women understood about my religion or lack of it, but they burst into delighted laughter at the fact of my having not one 'friend' but lots. They removed my scarf, combed my hair, called me *halwe* (sweet, pretty) and invited me to eat with them later.

Egyptians are renowned for their kindness, humour and generosity. It was these qualities that I appreciated in the Egyptian men I became friends with. I was treated with great respect and my views were listened to without having to force a space to speak. But when it came to anything to do with sex, they were pathological. One group of colleagues assumed, on zero evidence, that I was having an affair with one of them. They persuaded his wife that I was, expected their turn to be next, and were baffled by my astounded refusals. Their image of Western women and their idea of American companies are similar illusions: free sex and fast money. What I found again and again after similar and worse experiences, was a childlike shame, profuse apologies and misconception of my attitude when I taxed them with their behaviour. These men were all liberals or socialists and well educated.

However, don't let this put you off getting into conversation with Egyptian men. Though I don't know the statistics for rape and assault, I'd stake a lot on Cairo being a safer place than London for a woman on her own. But even if you encounter no unmanageable difficulties, Cairo is an exhausting experience. Oxford Street during the sales has nothing on every street in the centre of the city all day and most of the night. Crossing roads is like trying to fly a kite in Heathrow. The fumes, heat and dust, the noise of car horns and shouting, and the spilling, squashing buses are a nightmare. And manoeuvering through this you have to contend with constant pestering, mostly verbal, from the passing male masses. There are times when you feel very exposed and wish you were robed and veiled.

TRAVEL NOTES

Language Arabic. English is spoken in the tourist areas but it's useful at least to be able to read Arabic numerals.

Transport Buses and trains are cheap, but buses particularly are very crowded. Trains going south to Luxor/Aswan often get full up so book tickets well in advance. Taxis are readily available in the cities and main towns.

Accommodation There are hotels at all prices. In the high season (Oct-March) the expensive places tend to be fully booked, but finding a cheap room is not a problem. If you end up late at night booking into a hotel that makes you feel uneasy or unsafe, move on the next day – there are always plenty of alternatives.

Special problems Harassment – particularly if you're on your own. In crowded buses, women often get groped in the crush.

Though many tourists do travel around in shorts and sleeveless T-shirts, it's advisable to dress modestly – you're less likely to get harassed or cause offence.

Changing money on the black market is common, though it can lead to problems with out-of-date currency slips at the end of your stay.

Other information Along the Mediterranean coastline there are both private and public beaches. On public beaches there are few foreign tourists and almost all Egyptian women swim in their clothes. Private beaches do not cost much and you'll feel far less self-conscious as you'll be amongst other women (both tourists and Egyptians) who will be wearing swimming gear.

Guide Michael Haag, *Guide to Egypt* (Travelaid, rev. 1985). By far the best guide to the country – well informed and practical (if not always too helpful for the cheaper hotels).

CONTACTS
No information received.

BOOKS
Nawal El Saadawi, *The Hidden Face of Eve* (Zed Books, 1980) Covering a wide range of topics – sexual aggression, female circumcision, prostitution, marriage, divorce and sexual relationships – Saadawi provides a personal and often disturbing account of what it's like to grow up as a woman in the Islamic world of the Middle East. Also highly recommended are Saadawi's novels, *Woman at Point Zero* (Zed Press, 1983), a powerful and moving story of a young Egyptian woman condemned to death for killing a pimp, and *God Dies by the Nile* (Zed Press, 1985), the story of the tyranny and corruption of a small town mayor in Egypt and the illiterate peasant woman who kills him.

Alifa Rifaat, *Distant View of a Minaret* (Heinemann, 1985) Well-known Egyptian writer in her fifties. She expresses her revolt against male hegemony and suggests solutions within the orthodox Koranic framework.

Nayra Atiya, *Khul-Khaal Five Egyptian Women Tell Their Stories* (American University in Cairo Press, 1984) A collection of oral histories of Egyptian women from peasant backgrounds.

Huda Sha'rawi, *Harem Years: The Memoirs of an Egyptian Feminist* (Virago, 1986) A unique document from the last generation of upper-class Egyptian women who spent their childhood and married life in the segregated world of the harem.

An excellent article on Egypt by Angela Davis can be found in *Women a World Report* (see General Bibliography).

For background on the rise of Islamic fundamentalism: Gilles Kepel, *The Prophet and Pharoah: Muslim Extremism in Egypt* (Al Saqi, 1985).

Thanks to Kate Figes.

ISRAEL-PALESTINE

Most visitors to **Israel-Palestine** go either to see the biblical/historical sites or to experience work on a kibbutz. Once in the territory, however, you will probably find yourself facing additional choices of travel – most obviously whether to visit the 'Occupied Territories', the Arab Palestinian homelands of the West Bank and Gaza strip, colonised by the Israelis after the 1967 war. If you choose to do so, as a tourist, it is important to be aware of the implications of the political situation and of travelling in areas which remain under direct military occupation.

Within Israel itself, established as an independent Jewish state in 1948, the presence of the military will again be an enduring image. Travel, however, is fairly straightforward: distances are small, transport plentiful, and there's a well-established network of hotels and hostels. And the sites and landscape, and the city of Jerusalem, are certainly compelling.

The Israeli political spectrum is wide, reflecting both political ideologies and ethnic origin – from European Ashkenazy beginnings the population is now dominated by Sephardic Jews who have emigrated from North Africa and the Arab world. The current government coalition is an uneasy compromise between the moderate Zionist Labour party's desire for peace (with the possible exchange of territory in settlement) and the Likud's Old Testament designs for a Greater Israel. At its fringes is the increasingly alarming spectre of a rabidly anti-Arab far right. Palestinian Arab politics are also splintered, though within the Occupied Territories there is general widespread support for the Palestinian Liberation Organisation (PLO).

Palestinian women have always been involved in the resistance movement – against British occupation before that of the Israelis – and have developed a grass-roots movement with centres, committees and unions in most of the towns villages and refugee camps. There are four main women's committees aligned to different political groups, the most active of which are the Women's Work and the Worker Women's committees, which have set up over a hundred centres throughout the West Bank and Gaza strip. Besides co-ordinating (on a self-help basis) social service, welfare and educational provisions, they have also set up numerous income-generating projects for women and organise various campaigns and demonstrations around issues of women's rights as well as women's cultural events. Participation in this movement has enabled many women to extend their traditional roles within the Islamic culture towards greater independence and to an active awareness of the double struggle they face – for national and sexual liberation.

The **Israeli feminist movement** emerged as a separate political force during the early 1970s and in 1978 the first national feminist conference was held in Haifa. Sexual equality has, however, long been an issue of public debate. Many educated European women were attracted to the fledgling state during the first waves of migration on the promise of sexual egalitarianism. Women have retained a role within the labour force and also in the army (military service is compulsory for women aged 18–36, though they are barred from combat roles). The spectrum of feminist activity is similar to that of Europe and the USA with women organising around issues such as violence against women, discrimination and media representations of women. Women also have a strong voice within the peace movement and are using it to widely publicise the contradictions between feminist values and increased militarisation. Working together with Palestinian women, some groups of Israeli feminists are also demanding the withdrawal of troops from the occupied territories.

◢ **Emma Paterson spent four months working on a kibbutz and travelling around Israel.**

I went to a kibbutz, the Neve Yam, just after I left school. For me it seemed an exciting proposition – it was my first chance to travel any distance from home and to an intriguing, hot and exotic place, with 'a place to belong' and a chance to become part of a society which I envisaged as being both open and egalitarian. I suppose I also fell for the 'holiday camp' type of image, easy-made friends, plenty of fun and none of the usual problems about what to do in an evening.

On arriving it was easy to see why the representatives in London had depicted Neve Yam as one of the most picturesque settlements in Israel. There were four main communal buildings and a hundred or so smaller whitewashed bungalows set out on a large expanse of well-kept lawns, dotted by hydrangea bushes and bordered by a continuous bank of golden sand dunes. The first day was set aside for general induction and meeting the other volunteers. The work supervisor assigned me a job and advised me to get a good night's sleep.

The next day came as a shock. I and some other volunteers were picked up by tractor at 5 am and taken to a set of fields just outside the main kibbutz complex. We were handed weighty pickaxes and advised on how to weed the fields: 'stand with your feet well apart, raise the pick behind your head and then bring it down with your full weight behind it'. It made the work sound easy and for the first two minutes or so it was. But after six hours of hacking away frantically, then wearily, then not at all, my condition began to verge on the comatose. Those with enough energy to talk shared their sense of outrage – surely this was slave labour? How could anyone possibly survive four months of it?

Of course our bodies began grudgingly to adjust and we became more aware and more open to what was happening around us. The resentment was still there but its basis began to shift. I realised that the volunteers (of either sex, there was no discrimination, though in this respect you hear different stories on other kibbutzim) were allocated the more mundane or physically demanding jobs, creating a divide between us and the members. It was my first point of disillusion with kibbutz life.

Throughout I wished I could have had more contact with the kibbutzniks themselves. I know that in some kibbutzim members are appointed as a key friend/mentor to each volunteer. That wasn't the case with ours – the members led completely separate lives. As far as most of the older members were concerned we were just another transient group. The younger ones also seemed largely indifferent, though there were a few who bounced from volunteer to volunteer forming immediate but very superficial friendships (one way of coping with the constant turnover, I suppose). One or two developed quite intense relationships and there were many promises of visits and letters when their partners left. I felt that in identifying themselves with us they were in some way rebelling.

The lack of communication meant that I could never talk out my discontents. I could never seek an explanation as to why my understanding of kibbutz ideology seemed so obviously divorced from the reality. For instance it quickly became clear that in this supposedly egalitarian society some had more prestige, status and an easier life than others, but I couldn't be sure why or what the currency was. Also, women seemed to be confined to the classically feminine roles of looking after the kindergarten, dining room and launderette and yet sex-role stereotyping was supposed to have been abolished with the ethos of the nuclear family. I know that at the time I was very naive about such things and prone to see reform in black and white terms but I had no other resources to reanalyse what I saw. The fact that no one cared if we approved or disapproved, dissented or complied, with the system added to the feeling I had of being used.

There was very little either of the jolly and active nightlife I'd anticipated. Almost no attempt was made to provide entertainment for the volunteers and any activities were sorted out on an impromptu basis amongst ourselves. Boredom was perhaps the worst problem to contend with after I'd overcome physical exhaustion.

This was common also, though much more ingrained amongst the younger members. Many looked to their forthcoming military service as an escape. It seemed paradoxical to me that the security and seclusion which had played some part in motivating the older people to join were precisely the factors that prompted the young to leave. For the volunteers boredom came and went in waves – people coped unpredictably. The most usual was the drunken orgy or the creation of all sorts of unnecessary complications in terms of sexual partners.

Knowing exactly what you're going to do the next day or the next week or the next month does, however, have its advantages. It releases you from the usual preoccupations of travel and the space for introspection can be valuable. It also forced me to make the most out of my three days per month leave – never enough though to really get used to being on your own again. The day I said goodbye, carried my bags to the side of the road and stuck out my thumb, I felt an almost overwhelming sense of freedom and autonomy.

Getting lifts in Israel was to prove incredibly easy and, consequently, it wasn't long before I was offered my first ride, up to Nazareth. I had decided to visit Nazareth because of its biblical connections, but on arriving I realised that I had failed to take into account the fact that this was an Arab town. Easily identified as a kibbutz volunteer, and in their view, immodestly dressed in shorts and T-shirt, I was both sexually intimidated and treated to a host of verbal abuse. I felt extremely uncomfortable being there, and had to leave almost as quickly as I arrived.

The next week I spent touring around the north of Israel and then moved further south. I enjoyed my travels in the south far more, mainly because of the dramatic, desert scenery which I found so much more exciting than the green rolling hills of the north. Mixed with my feelings of delight, however, were ones of anxiety about hitching alone in such isolated parts, and vulnerability. There were several occasions on which drivers had made subtle and not so subtle passes at me, and because of this sexual harassment, the mistrust which I had formerly relinquished in the kibbutz re-emerged. The fact that most people spoke English, however, did somewhat ease my sense of insecurity and enabled me to continue my travels through Israel. Many Israelis who gave me lifts seemed disappointed that I wasn't Jewish, something that had never arisen whilst at the kibbutz.

What I now regret most about my travels in Israel was that after my first unfortunate experience with an Arab township, I purposefully confined myself to Jewish territory, something I could have avoided if I'd been more aware of the kinds of behaviour acceptable to an Arabic community. I feel it's also important to add that my not entirely positive account of kibbutz life was perhaps atypical – referring only to my own personal expectations and disillusions in one particular kibbutz. Some women certainly have felt invigorated and inspired by their stay on a kibbutz and return time and time again.

▰ **Working in conjuction with *UNIPAL* (Universities Educational Fund for Palestinian Refugees), Salli Ramsden taught English for two months in the West Bank.**

On reading my diary a few months after returning to England, I was shocked to realise how quickly the impact of the Palestinians' day-to-day oppression in the Occupied Territories had become subsumed into my own worries about essays and exams at university. The curfews, street patrols, road blocks; the deportations, prison sentences, house and town arrests; the press censorship, the bulldozing of houses, the appropriation of land, the closure of universities; the unattainable licenses required from the Israeli administration for exports, travel, municipal services, development projects. . . . All this now hardly seemed real viewed from the comfortable distance of my life in England.

For two months, I lived with a group of volunteers in Nablus, the largest town in the West Bank, and taught English to 13–year-old girls in Fara Refugee Camp. The difference between women's situations in the towns and camps, only an hour's journey apart, seemed very great. In the towns women tend to be more westernised in their dress and lifestyles than those women from the outlying camps and villages who often wear traditional costume and adhere to more traditional codes of behaviour.

Enthusiasm for my English lessons never waned, since they provided most girls with their one opportunity during the long summer vacation to leave the house, and their domestic duties. Whereas in the towns almost all girls now complete secondary education, those in the camps are more likely to leave school early so as to marry, or to look after younger brothers and sisters. Two of my pupils were already engaged and only one did not intend to marry before the age of twenty. Those that did want to go on to university felt that marriage was the only 'career' open to them.

The emphasis placed on the roles of mother and housewife seems to afford Palestinian women relatively little status even within the home. In some households I would find myself sitting down to a meal which had taken the women several days to prepare. Yet once the food was served the women would disappear, leaving the men to talk politics with me. On one occasion, I was not even allowed to see the women in order to thank them for the meal.

However, by no means did all the women I met share my frustrations at what I felt to be an incredibly limiting definition of gender roles. Some in fact condemned me for my independence in leaving my family, remaining unmarried and travelling abroad in a mixed group of volunteers. Due to the strict segregation of the sexes operating in some Muslim families we were sometimes forced to say that all ten of us were brothers and sisters! On the other hand, some women envied my greater freedom and the opportunities available to me in Western society. The women who lived next door to us in Nablus wore jeans and watched American soap operas on TV but rarely left the flat. When I went to say my goodbyes one of them confessed to a boredom which had verged on suicidal depression until her children had filled up her life. For the Palestinian teacher helping me in the camp, our friendship resulted in a temporary lifting of the restrictions which she found oppressive in her life. She visited Nablus more frequently, took part in all kinds of discussions and social events that were new to her, and even stayed the night in Jerusalem with us. Then I walked out of her life just as I had walked into it two months earlier, leaving her to cope with her now increased dissatisfactions.

Some women have gained greater rights for themselves through their participation in the national struggle. In 1969 the General Union of Palestinian Women was formally integrated into the PLO and various women's committees now play a key role in providing essential municipal services, education schemes, cultural programmes etc. I met several women who had been imprisoned for their political activities. One told me how she had taught herself English during a ten-year prison sentence. She now teaches adult literacy classes, despite suffering from physical disabilities sustained under torture.

Almost every woman that I met held strong and well-informed opinions on the political situation in the West Bank and it was my 13–year-old pupils more than anyone else who kept me abreast of the latest developments under the Occupation. Given the oppressive military regime under which they live, many of the women that I spoke to regarded the struggle for women's rights as very much secondary to the need for national self-determination. Others felt that their commitment to the national cause would be all the more effective once their position as women had improved. The complicated political situation with which Palestinian women are confronted, not to mention their different culture and religion, brought home to me how much their experience differs from that of most feminists in the West. It forced me to re-examine my Western feminist assumptions and their relevance (or otherwise) to women in different situations. Yet despite the differences between us, I ultimately came away more than ever convinced of the solidarity which arises out of our shared oppression as women – and of the possibility and importance of working together on an international scale to overcome that oppression.

On a practical note I would advise anyone wishing to visit the Occupied Territories for the first time to arrange it through an organisation, as without contacts it can be difficult to meet people. I found the basic Arabic greetings and visible signs of friendships (a pendant with my name inscribed in Arabic, Palestinian earrings) the best way to overcome suspicions about my foreignness. The right clothes – loose dresses, long sleeves and baggy trousers – provide a double protection, against the heat and against sexual harassment.

TRAVEL NOTES

Languages Arabic, Hebrew, Yiddish; English is quite widely spoken. When talking to Palestinians remember always to use Arabic rather than Hebrew names – for Jerusalem, for example, *El Khudz* rather than *Yerushalayim*.

Transport Trains run between a few major cities but buses are the usual form of transport – they're generally efficient. Travelling to/around the Occupied Territories, use Arab buses rather than the Israeli *Egged* lines, or *servis* (collective taxis). Hitching is widespread among Israelis, though not especially safe.

Accommodation Israeli hotels tend to be expensive but there's a good network of hostels and youth hostels; there are few hotels in the Occupied Territories and it's best to have contacts if you want to stay.

Special problems Harassment is fairly common, especially of single women; Jerusalem Old City is not considered safe at night.

Visiting Arab or Orthodox Jewish areas you should dress modestly (covering arms as well as legs).

Guides *Let's Go: Israel and Egypt* (St Martin's Press, US) is useful for budget information; Kay Showker, *Jordan and the Holy Land* (Fodor, 1984) has the best detail on the Occupied Territories.

CONTACTS

Palestinian groups

It is not difficult to contact **Palestinian women's organisations** but most request that details are not printed. For initial information you may find it useful to talk to **ZATAR** (Middle East Community Development) 21 Collingham Road, London SW5 0NV – a British-based organisation which provides a link between the West Bank and Gaza Strip Women's Committees (and other projects), and individuals and organisations abroad.

Israeli groups

Israel Feminist Movement, Tel Aviv, PO Box 3304 (Tel. 03–234314/917) Established in 1972. Its main current project is Tel Aviv rape crisis centre (see below). It also offers consciousness-raising groups and has recently opened the Tel Aviv Feminist Centre at 82 Ben Yehuda Street.

International Feminist Network – Israel Representative, c/o Yarron, 1 Stand Street, Tel Aviv (Tel. 03–234144) Geared to circulating information on feminist issues to women all over the world.

Herzlia Women's Aid Centre – 58 Sokolov Street, Herzlia, Tel Aviv area. Tel. 052–83856. Established in 1978 to co-ordinate campaigns against violence against women.

Tzena V Rena, 14 Mazeh Street, Tel Aviv. Feminist-run bookshop and cultural centre.

Kol Haisha Feminist Centre and Book Store, 4 Histadrut Street, Jerusalem (Tel. 02–245971).

Second Sex Publishing House, 55 Sheinkin Street, Givataim (Tel. 03–312349) Translates feminist works into Hebrew.

Rape Crisis Centres Tel Aviv, PO Box 33041 (Tel. 03–234314/917). Haifa, PO Box 9308 (Tel. 04–88791). Jerusalem PO Box 18024 (Tel. 02–810110)

BOOKS

Palestinian experiences

Raymonda Tawil, *My Home, My Prison* (Zed Books, 1983). Powerful autobiography, written whilst under house arrest, by a Palestinian woman living in the West Bank.

Ingela Bendt and James Downing, *We Shall Return – Women of Palestine* (Zed Books, 1982). Based on extensive interviews with Palestinian women living in refugee camps in the Lebanon.

Sahar Khalifa, *Wild Thorns* (1976, Al Saqi, 1985). Superb novel by a Palestinian woman writer, of everyday life and personal relations under the occupation. Very highly recommended.

An absorbing collection of interviews with Palestinian women, selected from transcripts first published in the Journal of Palestine Studies, can be found in Miranda Davies ed. *Third World Second Sex* (see General Bibliography).

For general political background: *The Palestinians* (Minority Rights Group Report, no 24, [rev.] 1984).

Israeli experiences

Khamsin Journal, *Forbidden Agendas* (Al Saqi, 1985). Wide-reaching collection of essays on Israel and the Middle East from the Israeli journal *Khamsin*. Particularly useful in understanding the tensions between European and Oriental Jews.

Susanna Heschel, ed., *On Being a Jewish Feminist* (Schocken Books, US, 1983). The experience is mainly Jewish-American but includes an essay on Israeli women and is enlightening in its general exploration of the conflicts/possibilities of Judaism and feminism.

Nira Yuval-Davis, *Israeli Women and Men: Divisions Behind the Unity* (Change, 1983). Pamphlet on the position of Israeli women.

For background: Amos Oz, *In the Land of Israel* (Flamingo, 1984) is an insightful book of very diverse interviews. Amos Kenan's recent novel, *The Road to Ein Harod* (Al Saqi, 1985), taking the form of a political thriller, confronts the conflicting utopias of Jew and Arab in Israel today.

Thanks to Sarah Gowen for information on Palestinian women's organisations.

SYRIA

Syria possesses considerable tourist attractions: an abundance of ancient and historical sites, and a beautiful Mediterranean coastline. Yet, from the West at least, there are virtually no tourists. What keeps them away, is the country's political image: a succession of wars with Israel, anti-Western rhetoric from Damascus, and the fact that Syria is now in the Soviet sphere of influence. In practice, these issues are unlikely to affect you: if you're white, you may find yourself mistaken for a Russian or Czech – no more than that. Syria's predominantly Muslim society seems to pose few problems for women travellers. You will certainly provoke curiosity, but the attention you receive usually takes the form of a barrage of questions and invitations of hospitality and is rarely threatening.

The present Syrian government, under President Hafiz el Assad's Ba'ath Party, rules by a combination of Arab socialism and military muscle. Assad has considerable personal popularity, through his strong international image and the uniting threat of Israel (and its US ally). There is, however, a growing fundamentalist influence in the country that opposes the carefully secular nature of his government.

Ba'ath commitments to improve the **position of women** – perhaps the most contentious instance of secular socialism in action – has led to some advances. The number of girls in schools and continuing at university has risen steeply, and there are small numbers of women now entering the professions – even a few women deputies in parliament. Traditional social constraints still, however, control the lives of most Syrian women.

▨ **Heather Claridge lived in Damascus for four months, studying Arabic; during this time she travelled widely in Syria.**

•

The rarity of Western visitors in Syria does have its advantages for those who make it there. One is conspicuous but welcome, and the lack of a tourist infrastructure for all but the major attractions can often make you feel like an explorer, in the tradition and footsteps of the Victorians and Orientalists who came before.

From the moment I stepped off the Greek cargo boat in Tartus I felt I'd been somehow raised in status. I was rushed through customs, men carrying my bags for me throughout, and before I could even think of investigating the rather decayed seaside town, I was placed in a taxi, money was changed for me, the driver paid. It felt like I was being smuggled into or out of a war zone. The other passengers in the taxi were men and in uniform; neither they nor the driver spoke a word to me during the three-hour journey to Damascus.

My stay in Syria was free from sexual hassles – the only pestering was from men who wanted to know about language schools in England. In fact as I got more confident I found myself striking up conversations with men as well as women on buses and elsewhere, something I hadn't expected would be possible. Time and again I was told. 'You honour us'; and it seemed that the greatest honour I could do to people was to accept their invitation and visit their homes. Being an honoured guest has its obligations, however – you have to be entertaining and appear to be entertained. I was cajoled into attempting to belly dance in front of a group of women in Damascus, and sat for hours watching Arabic soap operas on television, drinking endless cups of tea. It's best to be selective about the invitations you accept; otherwise you can get the feeling of being over-protected and overwhelmed, especially if you're a woman on your own.

Even with Ba'athist centralisation, the different regions of Syria seem quite separate: Bedouin tribes in the desert, secluded religious minorities in the mountain districts and between the two extremes, the fertile strip, dotted with towns and cities which are the traditional strongholds of Sunni Islam. In the past twenty years or so 'the great socialist march forward' has affected the towns and cities in the plain more than other parts, and in each of them there still seem to be two cultures: that of the old city with its walls, mosques and souks, and, outside it, the new city with its Ba'ath party headquarters, army barracks and rows of Soviet-style apartment blocks.

Syria is littered with ruins from a score of civilisations. It's worth having a good guidebook, since a lot of them go unmentioned in the official tourist literature. One very exciting day was spent searching for a castle of the Assassins high in the Nosairi mountains. The Assassins were a secret order of medieval Islamic anarchists who set out to undermine existing authority by murdering selected individuals. They would get high on hashish before undertaking what were often suicide attacks, hence their Arabic name Hashishiyeen, and from that the English word 'assassin'. Their bases were notoriously well-hidden and, inaccessible, and although we did find the castle after several hours' searching, the Assassins kept the edge on us with their concealed entrance; we never found the way in.

At present Damascus itself looks more Islamic than it has for years. This is one result of the rather unlikely alliance between the socialist government of Syria and Khomeini's Iran. Each week several thousand Iranian tourists (reputedly families of 'martyrs' in the Iran-Iraq war) arrive in Damascus for a holiday at the Iranian government's expense. Like all tourists, their territory is the streets, and the narrow lanes of the Old City are congested with women in *chadors*. Syrian women are less in evidence in the cities, and the ones I did get to know through being invited home by their menfolk could see little point in going out in the streets. Their homes were their only focus of interest, families their greatest source of happiness in life, and they pitied me dashing around and thought I must be missing my family. I found it helped having photographs from home – it made me seem more human.

I left Syria with contradictory images. On the one hand the groups of women in their homes, dancing, telling jokes, drinking tea. On the other, the streets full of soldiers, posters of the President everywhere, tanks returning in the evening from what seemed like a commuter war in Lebanon. On a Muslim feast day I went with some Syrian Christians to a popular restaurant in the mountains above Damascus, a few miles from the Lebanese border. The place was packed with families eating stuffed pigeon and drinking arak among fountains and cherry trees. In the background every few minutes there was the sound of a great thud, slightly muffled. No one seemed to react at all. It was only on returning to Damascus that I learnt there'd been an Israeli bombardment of Syrian positions in Lebanon, a few miles from where we'd been.

TRAVEL NOTES

Languages Arabic, with Kurdish, Turkish, Greek, Armenian, Circasian and Aramaic minorities. In the cities many Syrians speak English, some of the older generation French and a few Russian; outside, you'll need to master some rudimentary Arabic.

Transport Generally by bus. There are two kinds of services: *Karnak* coaches, comfortable and quick but only between main cities, and *microbuses*, which leave (like collective 'service taxis') when they're full. Hitching is fairly common amongst Syrians, and where there are no buses you're likely to get offered a lift.

Accommodation Hotels can be scarce

– even in the main cities. If you're happy to take what's available, though, you should have few problems.

Special problems If you visit the coast, you'll find Syrian women swim in full attire – from headscarves down. Swimming costumes attract a lot of attention.

All foreigners are required to change the equivalent of $100 into Syrian pounds on entering the country and to register with the immigration authorities within seven days (bring four passport photos for this).

Guide *Syria Today* (Jeunes Afriques, Paris, 1978). More or less unavailable but there's nothing else.

CONTACTS
No information received.

BOOKS
Tabitha Petran, *Syria* (Benn, 1982). Readable history with 20th-century slant. Comments by Petran on the position of Syrian women can be found in the Minority Rights Group report, *Arab Women* (see General Bibliography).

Thanks to Heather Claridge for the introduction.

Chapter Eleven

THE GULF STATES AND YEMEN

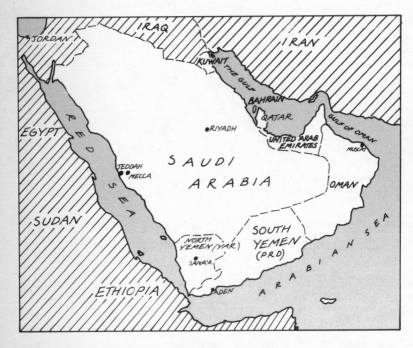

Among the six **Gulf States,** only Bahrain and the United Arab Emirates issue visas for individual Western tourist visits – and even then with restrictions. For the rest, work, or a member of your family (occasionally, with persistence, a friend) who is working in the country, is the only real condition of entry. There has recently been some experiment with organised tours but these remain of an isolated, luxury nature – and very expensive.

Once in, ease of travel varies considerably, in line with the States' differing degrees of Islamic orthodoxy. **Saudi Arabia** is the most stringent, with its notorious ban on women driving, and an antagonism towards Western influences that places severe constraints on all foreign women. Others, perhaps most notably the UAE, are more relaxed, with well-established expatriate communities and (internal) tourist facilities. **Oman**, which with Saudi is featured in this chapter, falls somewhere in between, its swift modernisation reasonably accepting of cultural differences with the West. It is too, less likely to pose the problem of sexual harassment, which in Saudi can be particularly intense if you are working as a single woman.

The two **Yemens** – set apart from their peninsular neighbours by lack of oil fields – are the least-known countries of the Arabian peninsula, also the most spectacular, with high altitude and extraordinary traditional architecture. In (capitalist) North Yemen, tourism is just beginning to emerge, and visas quite easily obtained. The immediate future in **South Yemen**, however, after its week-long civil war in early 1986, its at present hard to predict.

We have included pieces in this section only on Saudi Arabia, Oman and North Yemen; we are interested in expanding coverage of the region for the next edition and would particularly welcome contributions on **Bahrain** and the **UAE**.

SAUDI ARABIA

Islam of the stern Wahabite tradition dominates all aspects of life in **Saudi Arabia**. Although Western technology is welcome, its culture most clearly is not. The country permits no tourism. With the exception of Muslims who can obtain pilgrimage visas to visit the holy sites of Mecca (Makkah) and Medina, foreigners can only enter the country on work or family visas.

Due to Saudi Arabia's oil industry – it is the world's leading exporter – foreign workers make up a significant part of its population. Amongst this large community, the vast majority migrant workers from the Arab world, are several thousand Westerners. Most women among them are on family visas, accompanying their husbands, but a significant number come independently as teachers, doctors, nannies and nurses.

Western women living in Saudi Arabia are faced with numerous restrictions. It is illegal for a woman to drive; it is essential to dress extremely modestly and to keep to the areas marked out for women, i.e. the rear of buses, the 'family section' of a restaurant. Failure to observe these and other practices (see travel notes) can lead to severe trouble with the authorities. At the same time, Western women, particularly single workers, are very vulnerable to harassment – both from Saudi men for failing to conform to the role expected of women, and from the large numbers of foreign men with bachelor status. It's not easy to explore the cities, let alone travel around the kingdom on your own, and most women join up with other expatriates for trips around the country.

Traditionally **Saudi women** are expected to lead secluded lives with roles strictly confined to that of wife and mother. On the rare occasions when they go out, they are heavily veiled and accompanied by their husbands, fathers or brothers. Their participation in the open labour force is one of the lowest in the world. In recent years though, with the widespread introduction of female education in the 1960s, changes have started to take place. Women are now encouraged to work in segregated female sectors (as teachers, doctors, social workers, nurses, etc.) and the government has also begun to consider the economic advantages of employing women outside teaching and social services instead of relying on a large foreign workforce. Moves in this direction provoke much opposition from the conservative Muslims in the country, but at the same time there is a growing movement amongst Saudi women, backed by liberal men, advocating for women's greater participation in the economic and social life of the country.

◢ **Alice Arndt first went to Saudi Arabia in 1975, on a two-year teaching contract; in 1983 she returned to live, with her husband.**

Ten years ago, when I arrived in the Kingdom washed in on the wave of modern technology, foreign workers and petrodollars that were flooding the country, I assumed without question that the East-West gap would gradually close up. I took it for granted that exposure to Western customs and values would inevitably lead to their adoption in Arabia. Saudi society was bound to liberalise. If you had asked me then, I would have told you that, of course, in a few years Saudi women would be driving cars, veils would gradually disappear, the shops which closed their doors at prayer times would constitute an ever smaller minority. I noted the increasing educational opportunities for women, and felt certain that they would soon lead to demands from the women for further opportunities and ultimately for emancipation in their society. And the large number of young Saudi men who were being sent to other countries for advanced degrees would surely be infected with more liberal attitudes toward their women at home.

Today, a decade later . . . well, it hasn't turned out that way at all. It is *still* illegal for a woman to drive, or own, an automobile or to ride a bicycle. Today, virtually every shop closes up tight during the several daily prayers; and any shopkeeper who's slow to lock his door or pull down the shutters is likely to find the *mutawa*, the religious police, brandishing a long stick in his direction. Even television programmes are interrupted by a 'Prayer Intermission'.

Women in the Kingdom must dress more conservatively than ten years ago, and that includes foreigners as well as Saudis. My husband's company issues regular bulletins about the 'Dress Code' for employees and their families. The long skirts which I used to wear are now considered to be too form-revealing because they have a waistband; a long, loose dress is preferred. For the same reason, trousers must be covered by a long tunic top. Did I really wear sleeveless blouses in the summer heat a decade ago? Not today.

Recently with my family and friends I ventured into a very old market area of a conservative town in the centre of the peninsula. Although I wore a black silk *abaya*, a long cloak that extends from the top of my head to my feet, covering all but face and hands, the local residents – both men and women – were not satisfied until I was peering out at them in astonishment through three layers of black gauze which hung before my face.

When I first arrived in Saudi Arabia, I got a job teaching English and mathematics to young Saudi men in an industrial training school. Although it was somewhat remarkable for them to have a woman teacher, my skills were needed at that time and most of my students accepted me with friendly good grace. Today, women are not permitted to teach in that school. In some of the women's colleges, there is a shortage of qualified instructors similar to the situation at my training centre years ago; when it is necessary for a man to teach a class of women, he lectures to them from behind a one-way glass which functions just like a veil: they can see him but he cannot see them.

This is how the Saudis always said it would be. They insisted from the very beginning that they would take Western technology without taking Western culture. They warned that they would hire foreign workers when they needed them and send them home the minute they had trained Saudis to do their jobs. Today, with oil production at a twenty-year low, thousands of foreigners are leaving the Kingdom every month, returning to homes all over the world.

In addition to preserving their traditions and customs in the face of modernisation, the Saudis are participating in that broad political and religious conservatism which has swept across both East and West. Fundamentalist Muslims, within and without the Kingdom, are urging the Saudi government, as Guardian of the Holy Cities of Mecca and Medina, to be ever stricter in adhering to and enforcing Islamic principles.

Most of the Saudi women I met were disapproving of their sisters in the West. They see Western women as unprotected, living in dangerous cities and unable to rely on the men of their family to escort them on the streets. A strong sense of sisterhood has always been a part of Arab culture, and constant familial support buoys Saudi women throughout their lives; in contrast Western women's lifestyles appear to risk loneliness, promiscuity, and abandonment by their children in their old age.

In public, men and women are separated. Schools are segregated by sex. All museums and public exhibits have 'men's days' and 'women's days' during the week. The few women who venture to worship in a mosque are confined to a special section. Even weddings are celebrated with a men's party and a women's party.

Education for females outside the home is a new phenomenon, beginning only 30 years ago. Today there are girls' schools at every level, including women's programmes at several universities scattered around Saudi Arabia. Older women are included in a national literacy campaign. Opportunities exist for women to study abroad (usually with their husbands). A woman may become a teacher (with female students) or a doctor (with female patients) or a businesswoman (whose brothers provide the interface with the male world). Several banks have established branches just for women. The Government has recently begun to consider whether putting their own women to work would be less disruptive to their society than bringing in masses of foreign workers, and is looking for ways to create more 'women's jobs'.

I am acquainted with a few Saudi women who refuse to wear the veil (they are fortunate in that their families support them in this move) and a couple who rankle at government censorship and what they see as religious coercion. I know of several who feel depressed by the numerous restrictions placed on them. But they all consider themselves to be good Saudis nonetheless, and are devoted to their families, culture, religion and country. There is no political action group in Saudi Arabia, male or female. Women are not agitating for 'liberation' or 'equality'. Change in Saudi society will come from the inside, from within individual lives, homes and families, and at a pace consistent with the Middle Eastern concept of time, one profoundly different from the Western concept.

Thanks to the Oil Boom of the 1970s, the Saudis' material needs are basically met. The country is now self-sufficient in food production; electricity has reached a large number of towns and villages; education is free and available to everyone who wants it; hospitals are well-equipped and their number is growing as fast as the staff can be found; even the nomadic Bedouin have access to new water wells drilled here and there in the desert. These material advances can free the people to turn their thoughts and energies to the larger questions of life, to contemplate, perhaps, among other things, the role of women in this modern manifestation of their ancient culture. And that has to be good for Saudi women, for their men, and for both halves of the earth.

TRAVEL NOTES

Languages Arabic. English is widely spoken and understood.
Transport There are frequent and reasonably priced plane services between all the main cities in the country. There is also a network of good

roads, and rental cars are available in all areas. However, as a single woman you will have to obtain a driver, since it is illegal for a woman to drive, and it is advisable only to go with a driver who has been highly recommended by someone you know well.

Outside all airports are the white cars of the Saudi Limousine Service. They are metred and will ferry you about safely. A single woman should not hire any of the yellow cabs as they are not regulated. The larger cities have a public bus service. Each bus has a special compartment for women, which is closed off from the rest of the vehicle and is entered by a separate door.

Accommodation The government has recently decreed that a woman may check into a hotel alone without a letter of permission from her husband or father – some hotels though are still reluctant to register single women. Bearing this limitation in mind, there are many hotels in Saudi Arabia – some are incredibly luxurious, others designed to provide simple lodgings for pilgrims. During the *Hajj* (pilgrimage season) hotels become very full and you'll need to reserve a room well in advance.

Special problems You cannot enter the Kingdom without the appropriate visitor's visa stamped in your passport. Generally, visas are issued to Muslims wishing to make the Pilgrimage, to workers travelling to a job already obtained in the Kingdom, to women and children on family visas, and to visitors attending a conference or invited by an academic or commercial institution. Tourist visas are not available and it has become more difficult recently for single women to obtain a work permit.

Customs officials search luggage thoroughly for alcohol, drugs, medicines and pornography. Penalties for attempting to bring any of these items into the country can be severe. (If you absolutely must carry a medication in with you, bring an official letter from your physician explaining the necessity.)

Western women, in particular single ones, are subjected to both verbal and physical abuse for failing to observe Saudi cultural practices regarding women (i.e. going out on the streets unaccompanied by a male family member; not wearing the veil; working in non-segregated jobs, etc.) Harassment also comes from the large number of foreign men working in the country.

Modest dress is essential. Short skirts, sleeveless tops and tight and low-cut clothes on women are considered offensive. Trousers should be covered by a long tunic. A long dress is the preferred clothing for Western women and in many areas a woman should cover her hair.

Guides Madge Pendleton ed, *The Green Book: Guide for Living in Saudi Arabia* (Middle East Editorial Associates, Washington, 1984). Trevor Mostyn ed. *Saudi Arabia: A MEED Practical Guide* (Middle East Economic Digest, London, rev. 1983).

CONTACTS
We were unable to obtain any addresses, but there are many **women's groups** in the country, organised for social and charitable purposes. In addition, there are **women's centres** in Jiddah (Hijaz) and Al Khobar (Eastern Province) which offer classes in such subjects as child care, nutrition, languages and sewing.

BOOKS
Marianne Alireza, *At the Drop of a Veil* (Houghton Mifflin, Boston 1971).
Eleanor Nicholson, *In the Footsteps of the Camel: A Portrait of the Bedouins of Eastern Saudi Arabia in Mid-Century* (Stacy International, London 1983).

Useful information on Saudi women can be found in *Sisterhood is Global* and in the Minority Rights Group report *Arab Women* (see General Bibliography).

Thanks to Jean Grant Fraga for contributing to the introduction.

OMAN

Oman's development into a modern, oil economy state has been the most recent, and in some ways the most dramatic, in the Gulf. It was until 1970 an impoverished, essentially feudal society, governed by a reclusive sultan who banned all aspects of Western, non-Islamic influence – including drilling for oil. Then, in a bloodless coup, the sultan's British-educated son, Qaboos bin Said, seized power. All restrictions on Oman's economic development were lifted and a centralised bureaucracy installed to control the traditional power of local sheikhs and walis. Qaboos' autocratic rule, and kingdom-forming, however has not been without conflict. The southern Dhofar region, populated by an ethnically distinct tribe whose affinities seem closer to neighbouring (socialist) South Yemen, took part in armed rebellion in 1972–6, and were defeated only with US and (pre-revolutionary) Iranian aid and direct British military involvement.

Omani society, despite Qaboos's slant towards Britain and the US, remains orthodox Islamic with little privelege and a low profile given to Western culture. With the recent oil prosperity there have of course been prestige projects – road links, ministries and the university touted for by the Thatchers (mother and son). But foreign visitors are carefully limited and, apart from a few organised tours, admitted only with a work link. Most women visit Oman on family visas – only a few work in the Sultanate as teachers and nurses. Travel within the country is reasonably easy and unproblematic, though Islamic custom, particularly with regard to (very modest) dress must be respected.

The last decade's development has included a rapid expansion of educational facilities, open to both sexes, and an increasing number of **women** in the towns go unveiled and work in unsegregated jobs. In the mountainous, rural interior, however, women are for the most part illiterate and lead traditionally secluded lives. The *PFLO*, the Dhofar revolutionary group still active (though not militarily) along the Yemen-Oman border, includes a women's organisation with the objectives of emancipation; within their 'refugee territory' they have established training programmes in literacy, political and cultural education, with childcare facilities to allow women's participation.

◤ **Carolyn Milner, whose family is based in Oman, has visited the Sultanate several times over the last few years.**

As you drive along the gleaming new freeways around Muscat, the Omani capital, a common sight among the tankers and Mercedes are battered Toyota pick-ups laden with sacks of dates, grain, sheep and strange black figures with faces like grotesque birds. It comes as something of a shock to realise that these creatures are not the victims of some terrible deformity, but women. These women, who generally come from the interior, wear the traditional *birqa*, a stiff, black mask with a huge flap running down the centre of their face. In the incongruous setting of a Westernised modern city, they symbolise the general position of women in Omani society: surrounded by apparently archaic custom and repressive taboos, and caught amid the contradictions of a rapidly developing oil-rich state.

The Omani government's modernisation programmes have strongly emphasised housing and welfare, and on the nightly TV news you are forever seeing new roads being opened, a roof put on the university building, or the opening of a new oil field. On the streets of Muscat, too, you see few signs of underdevelopment or poverty. It is not that they don't exist – there are areas of wasteland and dilapidated hovels along the city outskirts; but the authorities, embarrassed by their presence, erect miles of white boards along the roadside to keep them from outsiders' sight.

Most foreigners who work in Oman live in Muscat, and if you visit it is likely to be the first place on your itinerary. It's an odd city to get to grips with, its quarters strung out over a large area. The actual city of Muscat is essentially a setting for the Sultan's new palace, a garish but imposing collage of stained glass and gold tiles. The commercial centre of the capital is a few miles away in Ruwi. Here the contradictions of the new nation are most strikingly apparent. Shabby huts, selling brass-ware and spices, stand side by side with chic French perfumeries, and goats jump nonchalantly on to the roofs of spotless Cadillacs.

Muscat and the two other cities of Nizwah and Salalah are fascinating in themselves but to get a real sense of Oman you should take an excursion into the interior. For this, a four-wheel drive vehicle is essential because, despite the continuing road-building programme, only the major towns are as yet connected by tarmac roads. But even within a few hours' drive of Muscat there are villages set in stunning mountain landscapes which appear unaffected by the 20th century. In Misfah, a village built high on a hillside, the streets are so narrow and steep that you must leave your vehicle on the plain and enter the village on foot. Along the coast, tiny fishing villages have makeshift souks right on the beach where the fishermen unload their catch.

If you want to turn an excursion into an expedition, there are areas of really stunning natural beauty further into the interior. About five hours' drive to the south of Muscat are a series of beaches which at certain times of the year are filled with huge turtles from the Indian Ocean which come ashore to lay their eggs. If you pitch a tent here, it will soon be surrounded by these enormous reptiles, apparently oblivious to your presence. Even further south is the fertile plain around Salalah, where the landscape suddenly becomes damp and overgrown and where flocks of flamingos crowd the tropical marshes near the coast. And from there, inland, lie the green mountains and river valleys of the Dhofar province, which must be one of the most spectacular areas in the Middle East.

The hospitality of the Omanis is proverbial. You only have to stand still by the side of the road, even if it is a busy dual carriageway, for cars to screech dangerously to a halt in order to let you cross. I know from experience that this must be one of the most relaxed Arab countries for a woman to travel in. As in other Middle-Eastern states the Omani government is reluctant to grant tourist visas to unaccompanied women unless they know an expatriate in the country or are part of an organised guided-tour. Once in Oman, however, women tourists are free to travel anywhere and the type of harassment that would be taken for granted in a North African country, for instance, is unknown in Oman.

One must of course, respect Omani customs. It is both polite and prudent for women (and men) to dress in an unprovocative way. I know of one English woman living in Oman, who went into a local supermarket wearing a tennis skirt. A policeman saw her and within half an hour, she was at the airport and deported on the next flight to England. If you are respectful and courteous, however, your welcome in Muscat as well as the remotest parts of the interior, is likely to be often overwhelmingly warm.

TRAVEL NOTES

Languages Arabic. Many people speak a little English.

Travel There is a good bus service around the capital area and regular (but expensive) flights between the main cities. To travel further afield you need to hire a four-wheel drive vehicle. There is no ban on hitching, but it is rarely done.

Accommodation There are a number of hotels around Muscat and some in Salalah, but few (as yet) in provincial areas. Camping is generally possible.

Special problems Visas are almost certain to be refused unless you have family or friends working in the Oman, or can afford to join a tour group.

Bathing is possible at hotels – many have swimming pools or private beaches; elsewhere you risk running into trouble with the police.

Other information No tour operator as yet has a regular trip to Oman, though occasional tours are becoming more frequent.

Guide John Whelan, ed., *Oman A MEED Practical Guide* (Middle East Economic Digest, London 1981).

CONTACTS
No information received.

BOOKS
F. A. Clements, *Oman – The Reborn Land* (Longman, 1980) A recent general survey of the country, which is useful although rather over enthusiastically pro-Qaboos.

An extract from the PLFO women's organisation manifesto, 'Women and Revolution in Oman', appears in Miranda Davies ed. *Third World Second Sex*, A brief introduction to the role of Omani women is included in the Minority Rights Group report, *Arab Women*. See General Bibliography.

NORTH YEMEN

Mountainous and isolated, **North Yemen** (Yemen Arab Republic – YAR) is a society and economy in considerable flux. It is one of the world's least-developed nations, with little industry and no oil of its own. Yet due to the mass migration of (male) Yemeni workers to Saudi Arabia, it has acquired a recent veneer of booming capitalism – at least in the cities.

It is a Muslim country and, in contrast to neighbouring socialist South Yemen (the PRD – People's Democratic Republic) the traditional code continues to dominate all aspects of life. Foreigners are a rare sight, though various development agencies are active in the rural areas, and the startling Arabian architecture of the towns and villages is attracting a small but growing number of tourists. Visas are obtained without difficulty. Travel within the country can be arduous but, outside the capital Sana'a, sexual harassment is relatively rare.

North Yemeni **women** are for the most part bound tightly by traditional social constraints: the vast majority are veiled and remain secluded from male/public spheres. Yet the widespread migration of men to work in Saudi has made this position increasingly problematic for some women. Left behind, sometimes in villages with no adult male workers at all, they have had to expand their work role without the social sanction to do so.

Development agencies have begun to initiate a series of 'home economics' projects, involving agricultural training as well as healthcare, literacy and handicrafts education, for rural women. They have been lent support by the **Yemeni Women's Association** and in some villages have met with considerable success; in others, the opposition of men to what they perceive as 'politicisation' of women remains a seemingly impenetrable barrier.

◪ **Whilst working in Egypt, Gill Hoggard took a holiday in North Yemen; she travelled with a woman friend.**

You cannot go to North Yemen without romantic baggage: travelling in the footsteps of Freya Stark, veiled women, austere mountains, clifftop fortresses and swirling cloud. But tempering romanticism with practicality, I stocked up in Cairo with insect repellent, malaria pills and appropriate clothing (baggy trousers and loose kaftans). Bleary eyed from the flight, I watched as our plane circled the mountains and flew low into Sana'a as the rising sun caught a jumble of mud-brick houses, spectacular free-standing minarets, and occasional familiar concrete apartment blocks.

Sana'a airport was in the process of being modernised, and on emerging from the concourse into the brilliant morning sun I was met by a cacophony of bulldozers, pneumatic drills and dumper trucks. I was somewhat unsettled by the people – a crowd of fierce-looking men, each of whom displayed a large dagger on his belt. Unsure how to interpret this, I fled back to the safety of a group of American missionaries I had chatted to on the plane. It was thus, crowded Yemeni style into a Peugeot taxi, and with the gossip of someone's high school graduation in Milwaukee flowing comfortably around me, that I caught a first glimpse of Sana'a's extraordinary and beautiful architecture. Everywhere was fretwork and tracery, picked out in white against the brown mudbrick. Gutters, drainpipes, latticework balconies and zig-zag ramparts rioted over the house-fronts, and on the flat roofs washing flapped in the wind.

In the course of my stay I saw few women. Like all Arabs, Yeminis regard the modesty and chastity of their women as paramount. They are required to wear not just one veil but two: the inner, covering most of the face except the eyes, and the outer, a kind of thin scarf which may be raised only for close relatives. I found it quite unsettling to attempt a conversation with, literally, an unseen person. Those women seen on the streets, shopping or (rarely) selling food, belong to the poorer classes; it is considered shameful for those of any wealth or position to venture out. Instead one sees men doing the shopping and all external business.

Once, manoeuvring my way through the souk, I came upon a whole row of women, side by side, giggling and chattering and selling bread. Unusually they were only half veiled. I surreptitiously took a picture, but was angrily bumped and jostled by the men: they do not want anyone, even another woman, to take pictures of their own women. I had ventured out into the qat souk – the market for the narcotic leaves which Yeminis chew for relaxation. Serious buying begins around 11 am in time for the afternoon, and everywhere earnest groups of men can be seen bargaining over large plastic-wrapped bundles of what look like a small privet hedge. Alcohol is strictly forbidden and tobacco rarely smoked but chewing qat is a national pastime. Everywhere in Yemen, as the afternoon draws on, can be seen the unfocussed eyes and vacant grin of those under the influence. Qat is easily grown, fetches a respectable sum in the market-place and whole mountainsides, which used to grow coffee, have been turned over to its production.

Yemini women as well as men chew qat and throughout one bus journey we made into the mountains, two heavily-wrapped ladies besides us plucked demurely at their bundles of leaves and slowly subsided, like the rest of the passengers, into a quiet and dreamy trance. On that occasion, as on several others, my friend and I had been ushered to the 'best' seats – the front – from which we had all too clear a view of the spectacular gorges and canyons which fell away below the road. Apart from some nerve-racking mountain roads, we didn't find it too difficult travelling around the country. Between all the major centres of population there are good tarmac roads and also a regular and punctual bus service. Although we were often the only women on the buses and always the only Westerners, we were met by unfailing courtesy and friendliness.

The place which left the strongest impression on me was the village of Al-Manakah, high up in the mountains south of Sana'a, and the objective of our qat-powered bus trip. Its 'hotel for travellers' proved to be of ancient Yemeni design, a warren of tiny rooms, passageways and mysterious inhabitants, laughing and chattering in the unseen lower quarters. We had met, briefly, the woman who appeared to be in charge of the hotel in order to settle the business details. From then on our food was served by a heavily veiled and very timid girl of about 12, probably her daughter, and thereafter, except for the muffled thumps, giggles and bangs emanating from downstairs, we saw no sign of anyone else. The unusual thing about this was that we had seen the woman and the girl at all: normally all strangers would deal only with the men of the house. But Al-Manakah, like so many other villages in the High Yemen, had sent its men to work in the Gulf, leaving the women in charge.

While we were there we followed the track out beyond the village and frequently encountered groups of men, either desultorily keeping an eye on their goats or more usually, squatting in the road to brew coffee over a small fire. We called out the Arabic greeting 'Peace be on you' – both to let it be known that we spoke the language, and to lessen the likelihood of any unpleasantness. Traditionally if one has replied 'And on you be peace' it is morally unthinkable to insult or injure one's interlocutor. There was, however, not the slightest reason for unease: we were frequently invited to share in the coffee-drinking, or simply encouraged as to what we could find further on.

In Sana'a, however, we met Women Peace Corps members who told us of increasing incidents of sexual harassment on the city's streets after dark. They attributed this to the recent importation of pornographic videos from the West, one amongst a whole number of 'luxury' goods that have started to enter the city. American chains such as the Hiltons and MacDonalds have also been established and the city as a whole is becoming increasingly open to Western influence. Yet it is still expected that these new and gleaming Western establishments will be exclusively staffed and patronised by men.

TRAVEL NOTES

Languages Arabic. It is definitely worth learning the basics before you go (numbers, simple questions) as very few people speak English.

Transport Within Sana'a there are shared taxis which are expensive (as is everything in Yemen) but the only means of getting around. A reasonably good bus service runs between main towns – most buses leaving early in the morning to complete the journey within daylight hours. Once a bus is full the driver will leave, no matter what the clock says, so it's worth arriving in good time. Internal air flights are also available, but besides being vastly expensive mean that you miss out on the spectacular mountain scenery. Amongst foreigners, hitching is rare if not unknown, and given the precipitous mountain roads, erratic driving, widespread chewing of narcotic leaves, and the fact that Yemen is a Muslim country, probably inadvisable.

Accommodation In Sana'a there are several grades of hotels but prices are high even for quite basic accommodation. In the mountain villages you find *funduks*, ancient hostelries which now take in foreign travellers; they are reasonable but very basic – you sleep on floor cushions and squat over a hole.

Always ask people for a funduk and not a hotel if you want the cheaper, more basic accommodation.

Special problems Yeminis are strict Muslims and find bare flesh offensive – they particularly object to women's upper arms being uncovered. Clothing therefore should be loose and voluminous and cover the arms at least to the elbow.

Standards of hygiene are low – drink bottled water and come equipped with diarrhoea pills, and, for staying in funduks, insect repellent and a sheet sleeping bag. Temperatures vary greatly – take warm jumpers and a sunhat.

Guide None as yet.

CONTACTS

If you are interested in women's development programmes, make contact in Sana'a with either the **Yemini Women's Association** or the Unesco-backed **Tihama Development Authority** or **Southern Uplands Rural Development Project** (**SURDU**).

BOOKS

Carla Makhlouf, *Changing Veils: Women and Modernisation in North Yemen* (Croom Helm, 1979).

ASIA

Chapter twelve
INDIA AND THE SUBCONTINENT

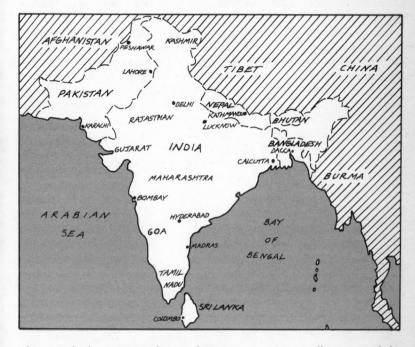

There's a fairly strong tradition of Western women travelling around the **Indian subcontinent**, connected in turn with the years of the Raj and with the relatively brief, but significant, hippy era.

Whilst the lingering hippy stereotype can be burdensome, connoting scruffiness, licentiousness and drug abuse, it also has a positive side in a legacy of cheap accommodation. Transport too is in plentiful supply and, with the exception of the strong Muslim areas, sexual harassment rarely becomes restrictive or oppressive. Much harder to contend with is the sheer pressure of people, the unremitting poverty and the numbers of hustlers and beggars. How you cope with the outrageous disparities of wealth is up to your own personal politics. But whatever you do, or don't do, you'll need to come to terms with your comparative wealth and outsider-status – and the attention this inevitably attracts.

India, with its spiritual heritage (and sights), holds the most obvious and enduring fascination. It remains idealised, sometimes poverty and all, but the terms of reference have shifted since the 1960s. Though you still come across occasional pockets of hippies, those who travel nowadays are generally self-supporting and more respectful of the diverse cultures they meet.

Nepal is currently in the midst of a tourist boom, and with the opening of its border with Tibetan China numbers are likely to increase still further. **Sri Lanka**, recently extremely popular, is now struggling to retain a tourist industry amidst an escalation of inter-ethnic violence. Far fewer women would consider going to **Pakistan** or **Bangladesh**. In Pakistan there are the pervasive restrictions of a neo-fundamentalist Islamic state, whilst in Bangladesh, still a desperately poor country, tourism has little place – most women who go there are involved in aid or development work.

INDIA

India, one of the most travelled countries in the world, is perhaps also the most overwhelming. People find themselves reacting intensely, as much to the difference and richness of the culture as to the unbelievable poverty and the constant pressure of people.

In many ways it is misleading to talk about India as one country. With its six major religious groups, its differing stages of development, its widely varying landscape and its proliferation of local cultures and languages, India is easily as diverse as Europe. For a traveller on a short trip one or two areas are more than enough to take in.

Countless women travel the country alone and sexual harassment is not a great problem. This is not to say it doesn't occur. Muslim areas are especially difficult and you might also be harassed in cities and on crowded buses and trains. But it is rarely very aggressive and dangerous situations can mostly be avoided by making a public statement or outcry – passers-by or fellow passengers are bound to help you. There are however many different pressures: persistent street hustlers, infuriating bureaucracy, long and exhausting journeys, and beggars, often with appalling deformities. Some women find it all too much and return home mentally and physically frayed. Yet for the vast majority, India, in spite of its many problems, is entrancing.

The **feminist movement** in India has become increasingly strong in recent years, though it remains concentrated in the cities and the women involved predominantly highly educated and middle class. But many women's centres and action groups have been set up and with women's magazines such as *Manushi* and the feminist publishing company *Kali for Women*, the feminist network is widening daily. Local actions like the organisation of lower caste street workers in Ahmedabad into collectives as a means of protecting themselves from police harassment and the exploitation of money lenders (see Una Flett's piece) have been both creative and diverse. One of the chief concerns of the feminist movement is to involve more rural and urban-poor women in various broad-based campaigns – against dowry (the number of dowry deaths remains alarmingly high), discrimination in the work place and disparities in pay and education.

◢ **Una Flett was born in India but left at the age of five. She returned for the first time five years ago for a trip of two months and followed this up recently with a four-month visit.**

Somehow, oscillating between resilience and fatalism, India keeps going – keeps going in spite of her 714 million, nearly half of whom are unemployed. This is the enduring image of India, the crowds upon crowds of people everywhere. Most of the population live in rural villages but increasingly they migrate to cities to live in the great sprawls of shanty towns (*bhastis*). The sight of pavement sleepers, beggars and hustlers, tearful young graduates telling you of their destitution, not enough space on buses, queues like insurrecting armies; these are all part of the day-to-day experience. Everything, from buying a stamp to boarding a train, will be done against the pressure of competing hundreds.

As a foreigner, particularly a woman travelling alone, the first thing you encounter is the stare, the open curious gaze, followed usually by the open curious question. Indians are avid 'collectors' of foreigners, not by any means always in a predatory spirit. To the crowds of unemployed young men who hang around every public place, the foreigner is entertainment, also – my personal theory – a kind of token substitute for travel. Most of them will never 'go foreign' but, because the West still represents much that is desirable and prestigious, any kind of contact is prized.

There is a difficult ambiguity in these encounters. Are you being chatted up by a hustler or not? I have been made miserable by my own suspicions of some innocuous men who simply wanted to talk and alleviate the long day's boredom, as I have been enraged by an attempted rip-off – though the first thing to learn is to economise in anger. It gets you nowhere and is exhausting. But there is a long and pushy list of people trying to engage your attention for money, offering to be your guide, find accommodation, rent you a houseboat in Kashmir, show you the local handicrafts, besides the shoal of aggressive sellers of all kinds of pitiful junk.

In big cities the likelihood of outright harassment is much higher than on trains or in smaller places. 'Eve-teasing', the term coined by the Indian press for feeling up, provokes long scandalised articles in the dailies and is for Indian women as much as foreigners a hazard of city life, particularly on buses (so is pick-pocketing and jewellery snatching). Sikh and Muslim men are on the whole much more sexually aggressive than Hindus. A memorably unpleasant experience was being pulled round Lucknow (a predominantly Muslim city) in an open rickshaw, a sight that triggered off shouts, solicitations, jeers and cheers from every man I passed. It was the one place where I chose to go hungry rather than venture out and look for somewhere to eat on my own.

I travelled clockwise round India by train, a slow and tiring kind of journeying but a certain way of getting the flavour of the country and above all the people. For all life takes place in stations. Travelling is endemic among Indians – to visit relatives, to take produce to markets, to make pilgrimages, to look for work. Besides travellers, stations have their quota (sometimes enormous as in Howrah station in Calcutta) of permanent residents, homeless families who have settled in with their cooking pots and babies and cloth bundles. There is an amazing sense of private family life being lived in the open, among travellers and others. It is, after a little practice, curiously relaxing. You lose the sense of a rigid self-conscious boundary between 'public' and 'private', as it exists in a Western society. The small space occupied by your bags in the middle of the waiting crowd becomes a sort of privacy. I ended up quite naturally unpacking and repacking my possessions on platforms, settling in to write up notes and generally behaving in a 'domestic' manner.

I grew to love stations as much as I dreaded them in the early stages. They are bewildering ant-heaps until one knows one's way around, but there are plentiful supplies of coolies (wearing red waistcoats for identification) and they know platforms and departure times rather better than the station staff. There are also plentiful supplies of friendly people. Indians are well aware of the impenetrability of their booking system for foreigners and love to help you out. Above all, there is the fun of eating in stations where there are all sorts of oily cooked food snacks, fruit and hot sweet tea served in little clay cups which give the tea a slightly earthy taste and which one smashes to shards on the railway lines after drinking.

Both sexes found the fact that I travelled alone quite extraordinary. 'Lonely you come?' they would ask, incredulous. Although it was by their standards bizarre, it was entirely tolerated. I was asked about our marital system, or lack of it, and asked in turn about theirs. Although love matches do occur across caste and religion (disasters in the eyes of most families), the system of arranged marriages has not been seriously questioned. Freedom of contact between the sexes is rigorously prescribed. College students lead segregated lives. There is no mixing among the young in public. In some states I found separate compartments on trains for women – good places to talk – and special seats on buses.

Women are still seriously hampered at all levels except at the very top by their subordinate and dependent status. Apart from the small group of highly educated and very able women in academic, professional and commercial jobs – a Westernised elite – the rest of the country's women are restrained either by tradition or poverty or both. The dowry system, though made officially illegal some years ago, persists with all its iniquities. Higher education for girls is more a 'selling point' in the marriage market (see the personal ads column in any English language newspaper) than a means of entering employment. The large bulk of Indian women do not work after marriage, for that reflects poorly on the husband. Only those at the top and those at the very bottom do so.

Women of course do much of the agricultural work in the villages. In towns they do some of the hardest and worst-paid heavy labouring jobs. They face two kinds of sexual discrimination in earnings. Either they are confined to certain tasks within an industry – in brick-making they may only carry loads, not mould the bricks – or, in an industry where there is some overlap of men's and women's work, they are simply paid at a lower rate.

However, among women at the desperate bottom of the heap an amazing potential for self-help can be tapped. In Ahmedabad, a union for self-employed women – rag and scrap sellers, quilt-makers, joss-stick rollers, and market women of all kinds – was started in the early 1970s. By setting up banking and credit facilities, training schemes and protest groups *SEWA* (Self-Employed Women's Association) has managed to rescue its members from the hold of money-lenders, make an effective case against constant harassment by police, and to develop – from a baseline of total ignorance – a remarkable degree of financial competence. Women have also asserted themselves in ecological issues, most notably in the Chipko movement to save the deforestation of the Himalayan slopes. However, the power of tradition is vast, a force that locks people into a sense of pre-ordained order. To do exactly as it was done before is an axiom of life in India.

If you go, don't try to do too much. Your senses will be at full stretch all the time because there is so much to take in. The stimulation is tremendous. So is the exhaustion.

◪ **Susanna Hancox has visited India twice. On both occasions she spent nearly three months, combining travel with research on Hindu religions.**

It can be a shock for a conscientious traveller in the 1980s to find her experiences affected by stereotypical views of the 'hippy' era. Understanding cultural difference and the causes for misunderstandings can go a long way in alleviating anxieties. For instance, the idea that wealthy Westerners should actually want to look like peasants by adopting 'ethnic' embroidered skirts, hand-made sandals and heavy jewellery, however intricate, is considered strange in a society intent on becoming more, not less industrial and urbanised. Cosmopolitan Indians are increasingly adopting Western clothes, but it's the pristine jeans, natty handbags, neat dresses and the high-heeled look of the Bombay and Delhi fashion pages. If you don't look like one of these models, or indeed like Margaret Thatcher (who's very popular in India), you'll be called a hippy and teased on occasion. This is most likely to happen in Delhi, which seems a coldly conservative city, and in the provincial towns and rural areas. Calcutta and Bombay are tolerant by contrast and far more accepting of differences. Drug-taking and promiscuity, however, the most offensive aspect of this stereotype for most Indians, are still a source of tension, especially in the Kulu valley in the Himalayas and in Goa on the west coast where children still chase after you shouting 'Hippy, Hippy, Hippy' and adults appear wary of making contact.

To be considered personally unclean is about the worst possible Indian condemnation and it's therefore wise to know something of normal standards of hygiene. Every morning, wherever they find themselves, Indians perform elaborate ablutions with much loud clearing of the throat, gurgling and spitting. After washing all over, clean clothes are put on for the day. By contrast Europeans tend to be far more flexible about when they bathe, yet it's important to keep as clean as possible when travelling and discard any torn or tatty clothing. Washing hands before eating is also imperative. Although you'll sometimes be given cutlery, food is generally eaten using the right hand – if possible using only the finger tips up to the first joint. Never use your left hand as this is for washing your backside. Also anything that has been touched by the mouth of another is considered filthy, a feeling contained in the word 'Jūthā'. On buses and trains people are often generous and share food. To take a bite out of a banana or chapati and then pass it on would be anathema, as would drinking from somebody else's bottle of Campa Cola.

As far as clothes were concerned, I found that the *salwar/kameez*, pyjamas and long shirt, worn by many north Indian women the easiest and coolest for moving around. It also seemed to engender a certain amount of warmth and acceptance. I've never been convinced of the value of wearing a sari. As an article of clothing it has a special status and is meant to be worn in an elegant way which tends to elude the uninitiated. I've heard harsh criticism of Westerners who wear it badly – in any case it restricts movement.

But whatever cultural form you adopt, you can't hide the fact that you are European and therefore, in relative terms, extremely wealthy. Wherever you go you will be approached by multitudes of beggars many of whom display the most horrendous deformities. Response to this is personal and I don't think can be anticipated. I would always try to give food rather than money but it can only be a drop in the ocean. Biros, plastic combs and hairslides go down well everywhere as gifts.

Relations between Indian men and women remain rather distant and formal in public with little touching or incidental contact. The relative freedom of Western women to associate with men of their own choosing is often interpreted as licentiousness and for these reasons, unless you're married, travelling with a man would not necessarily afford extra protection. I once made the mistake in Delhi of sharing a room with two male friends to economise while waiting for a return flight. One night we all three went to the pictures but, feeling tired, I decided to go back half-way through the film. The men at the reception desk leered ominously when I primly explained that my friends would be following me shortly and bade them good-night. I then spent an anxious couple of hours sitting in my room listening to creaks and muffled voices outside my door. Later on, an Indian woman told me that I must have seemed looser than loose to be sleeping in the same room as *two* men and that the hotel staff were simply seizing the chance to try their luck.

The extent to which a European traveller adapts her behaviour to fit the values of local inhabitants, is also a matter of individual choice. Goa provides a final and vivid illustration of an instance where varying cultural outlooks regarding women, meet. For a Westerner, the miles of white sands, rolling warm waves and coconut palms, create a desert-island type paradise. Save for the odd village or hut and the occasional cluster of fishing boats, the coastline seems unpeopled to an extent far greater than anywhere in the occident. The temptation to revert to the 'primitive' is great, and many young Europeans spend days on the beach nude, wrapping only a flimsy cotton lungi around them before drifting back to lodgings or to cafés where Dire Straits and Bob Marley are played at top volume. Goa is seen by Indians as the place, *par excellence*, where hippies congregate with their sex and drugs and rock' n' roll. Until the 1960s, it was a Portuguese colony, and there remains a pious, respectable, Roman Catholic element in the culture as a result. Many Goans are deeply offended and disturbed by the behaviour of Europeans. However, Indian tourists also go to the beaches in cars and coachloads. The women paddle coyly at the water's edge and occasionally submerge themselves, fully clothed in saris. Often groups of men hike up the beaches in the hope of finding a notorious nude, though a bikini-clad woman is sufficient to draw a large crowd who will encircle her, quite blatantly ogling. Little is to be gained by getting angry since the reasons for the fascination are obvious. The beaches are vast enough to find a secluded spot and I would urge discretion.

All these comments on cultural differences as they affect women in

India, though, are meant as a guide and not as a deterrent. Nowhere in India will being Western and female automatically endanger you.

Peggy Gregory spent nearly two years travelling around India. She stayed for three months in an *ashram* and spent six months living alone in a rented house in Bengal.

Before I left for India I talked to people who had already been, attempting to grasp what it would be like, and to gain more confidence about going. Talking helped, but I still had doubts – maybe these other people were simply better travellers, stronger, more open and more resilient than I was.

I had managed through a connection in England to arrange a room with a family in Delhi to cover my first few days. That way the initial shock was softened, as I could make forays out into the hustle for short periods and then retreat into the warmth of a family atmosphere. It was colder than I'd anticipated (in December) and the city seemed surprisingly pleasant, almost sedate. The old part of the city however is less congenial, crowded with people and vehicles, very dusty and chaotic; it was enticing, but I felt too raw – too intimidated by the constant staring, comments and questions that assailed me as I walked around or sat resting for a while. I wanted to merge in with the crowds and observe everything unnoticed.

When I started travelling I compensated for my lack of experience by finding other single women to travel with – either another recent arrival with whom I could share my uncertainties, or people who had been in India for a longer time from whom I could gain confidence. From one woman I learnt to speak some Hindi and to read the alphabet, particularly useful for reading timetables at bus stations. Generally just talking to other travellers was helpful, to find out which places were interesting to visit, how they approached travelling and what they had learnt from their experiences.

There are a lot of foreign travellers all over India, especially in main towns and cities or any place mentioned in the guide books as being interesting because of temples, art treasures or atmosphere. I set out with a guide book, which was useful for general hints and finding hotels but soon became redundant. I usually stayed in dormitories in cheap hotels – they are less expensive than rooms, and it's easy to find companions, although you don't have any privacy. I spent the first month travelling around Rajasthan, an increasingly popular state with tourists.

My confidence grew quickly. With it came the realisation that I wouldn't learn much by confining myself to the tourist route or by hanging around with other Westerners simply for the sake of emotional security. The most important thing I learnt during that time was to judge a situation by its atmosphere and to promote an atmosphere myself of being open to unexpected events or meetings – not to jump feet first into any situation I was unsure of.

For the next four or five months I stayed in cheap hotels, occasionally with families and once in an ashram – sleeping on station platforms or trains when in transit; a passive observer to the life and activity around me. I was gradually changing, relating to things with regard to where I was the month before rather than in contrast to England, which began to feel a long way away. The persona I developed was of a 'nice girl', strong but 'odd' as a buffer between me and the world outside: one which both allowed me to communicate and also protected me.

I felt safe, even when walking around at night, travelling in trains or staying in hotels. At night, for instance, in cities many people are still shopping until quite late, and there are women and children on the streets. However I tried to stay clear of the predominantly Muslim areas at night as the total absence of women made me uneasy. In the countryside it's also not so safe, but when staying in these areas I was often with someone or could use a bicycle. Anyhow, whenever in doubt you can always catch a rickshaw.

I was very rarely sexually harassed and never in any sort of aggressive or threatening way, but I did get my share of the street hustlers. Stallholders in the market often pick on foreigners, and leaving a train or bus station with luggage almost invariably brings a rush of rickshaw cyclists and touts insisting on taking you to the 'cheapest' hotel in town. If I felt slightly battered after a journey I'd deal with that by dumping my luggage in the left luggage. I'd then hang around for a while and leave the station to look for somewhere to stay, collecting my luggage later. Most situations, however, depend on your reaction and state of mind; if you're feeling bad any hitches or hassles are irritating, but if you're feeling good it is fun. Generally I felt I was hassled less as time went on, partly I think because I had learnt to dress and move around in a less conspicuous manner.

I worked my way southwards over a period of six months. By the time I arrived in Tamil Nadu I began to feel ill. So much so that I had to retreat to a hotel room where I spent a lonely and painful week unable to sleep, eat or do more than shuffle to the toilet twice a day. I had hepatitis. I knew it as soon as I caught sight of my yellow eyes and skin. Gathering the little strength I had, I moved to a local Christian ashram at Shantivanam where I spent a week until they sent me back to Tiruchi to a hospital. Ashrams don't usually like people visiting if they are ill but when my symptoms disappeared (after a week) I was welcomed back. I was lucky to have gone to that particular ashram as they did genuinely seem to care. They even sent someone to visit me every day while I was in hospital.

Illness of some sort is almost inevitable if you spend any time in

India. I was, however, unlucky to catch both hepatitis and later amoebic dysentery, both through contaminated water. I took the usual precautions for the first three months but drinking only sweet tea and soft drinks is expensive and anyway is extremely difficult if you're staying in rural areas – I lapsed, accepting the possibility that I might get ill.

With a fairly poor diet it took a long time to regain strength so I was at the ashram for about three months. Looking back, I realise it was the best place to have convalesced. There was a ready-made structure to the day which I appreciated after so long on the road; and a gentle and open approach to life and 'spirituality'. I had gone there rather uncertain as to how a casual and unconvinced visitor might be welcomed. The only other ashram I'd been to was a Buddhist one in the north (Igatpur) where I'd gone specifically to do a meditation course. I discovered later that ashrams are usually open to anyone as long as they approach with a genuinely sympathetic attitude. Some have become wary as they've been abused in the past for free accommodation – it is often best to write in advance to say you are arriving.

Most people I met had been disappointed by the lack of harmony they encountered in some ashrams. It's something I felt myself when I stayed in Igatpur. Everything had been fine during the meditation course, perhaps because we were under a vow of silence and concentrating solely on meditation. Staying on to do some voluntary work around the ashram (which everyone was asked to do, although this is not so in all ashrams, rules vary), I became disheartened by obvious rivalries that emerged between people. Their frustrations and antagonisms weren't particularly new but they seemed out of place. This was true also to a lesser extent in Shantivanam, but by then I was less naive – you can't expect people to become suddenly calm and open the minute they walk through an ashram gate. Often the process of introversion and speculation that people enter into can have paradoxical effects – breeding a sort of paranoia.

Moving on, I began to feel more and more the need for some sort of structure – I wanted to become more involved in learning about Indian culture. In Pondicherry I started to learn tabla, the percussion accompaniment to classical Indian music and for the following nine months was completely involved in learning the technique. I eventually settled down in Bengal in a small town called Shantiniketan, which has built up around an ashram, school and university set up by the renowned poet Rabindranath Tagore. It's an extraordinary, peaceful place. I felt at ease immediately, found a music teacher and rented a room. I also started to learn Bengali and taught English privately. I was extremely happy there, and even when the time came when I wanted to return to England I found it hard to wrench myself away from what had become my home in India.

I could have remained in India, and if I had done so it would probably have been for a long time. Yet I was tired of making the compromises necessary to live in a country as a foreigner; and it was that which eventually made me decide to return.

Returning to England and having to adjust to a more complex lifestyle, having lived so simply for such a long time, was very difficult. I felt disorientated for several months, not sure that I had made the right decision. Looking back, it was a good decision, for what I had learnt there had to be put to the test in another environment; much of it has fallen down and much remained.

TRAVEL NOTES

Languages Hindi is the official national language but it is by no means universally spoken and there are hundreds of other regional languages and dialects. You will find that English (an associate official language) is widely spoken, particularly amongst educated Indians.

Transport There is an extensive railway service in India. Most tourists use 2nd class reserved seats (2nd class unreserved gets ludicrously crowded and is best avoided). Some trains also have compartments reserved exclusively for women. Buying and reserving your tickets can take hours; it's best to do it a few days in advance as seats often get fully 'booked'. Sometimes there are separate queues for women – worth taking advantage of since they massively cut down time. Tourists can also buy *Indrail* cards which give unlimited travel for a specified period and will nearly always get you a reservation but they are economic only for long stays.

If you've got money you can fly between major cities but with frequent delays and booking difficulties it's not as quick as you'd think.

Accommodation A whole range of hotels from expensive luxury palace style accommodation to smelly bug-ridden cells. There is no shortage of cheap, clean and perfectly safe accommodation. A Government Tourist Bungalow (middling price range) is usually a safe bet. With so much choice there's never any need to stay in a hotel if you feel uneasy there.

Special problems You're quite likely to get ill in India. Various kinds of dysentery and infective hepatitis are real hazards, though you might get away with just a dose of 'Delhi belly'. If you're there for

just a short time it makes sense not to drink unboiled water or buy peeled fruit, but for any longer, or travelling in rural areas, you will find these precautions difficult to observe.

Theft is common and you should always keep your money and valuables securely on your person, preferably in a money belt. Beggars are very, very common – reactions to them vary. It's a good idea though to carry small change – a few paise is all that is expected, or a little food to share with children. You will also find hundreds of hustlers fighting for your attention. Try not to let yourself be pressurised into acting hastily.

Guides Tony Wheeler et al, *India – A Travel Survival Kit* (Lonely Planet, 1981, rev. 1985). Invaluable, at least to begin with; later you may feel you need to break out of 'the circuit'. Lonely Planet also publish a regional guide to *Kashmir, Ladakh and Zanskar*, and a *Trekking Guide to the Indian Himalaya*. For cultural detail the *Murray's Handbook to India* (John Murray, London), though originally published half a century ago, remains in a class of its own.

CONTACTS
Saheli Women's Resource Centre Under Defence Colony flyover, New Delhi 110024.

Institute of Social studies (ISS) 5 Deen Dayal Upadhyaya Marg, New Delhi 2, voluntary, non-profit research organisation – concentrates on women's access to employment and role in development, also on strengthening women's organisations. The group publishes a newsletter.

Centre for Women's Development Studies: B–43, Panchsheel Enclave, New Delhi 110017 – undertakes research on women and development, and is currently developing a clearing house of information and ideas.

Indian Social Institute (ISI) Programme for Women's Development, Lodi Road, New Delhi 110003, aims to increase the participation of women at different levels in the development process through training courses for community organisers.

Indian Council of Social Science Research (ICSSR) 11PA Hostel, Indraprastha Estate, Ring Road, New Delhi, 110002 – has a women's studies programme and carries out wide-ranging research. They also organise numerous workshops and symposia on feminist themes.

Manushi; c/202 Lajpat Nagar, New Delhi 110024, publishes the monthly journal *Manushi* – an excellent source of information on news and analysis of women's situation and struggle in India. Written in English and Hindi.

Kali for Women (feminist publishers), N 84 Panchshila Park, ND 110017.

Feminist Resource Centre (FRD) 13 Carol Mansion, 35 Sitladevi Temple Road, Mahim, Bombay 400016 – carries out action-oriented research from a feminist perspective on range of issues (health, sexuality, violence against women, discrimination at work).

Women's Centre, 307 Yasmeen Apartments, Yashwant Nagar, Vakola, Santa Crz East, Bombay.

Research Unit on Women's Studies SNDT Women's University; 1 Nathibai Thackersey Road, Bombay 400 020, publishes a quarterly newsletter of the Research Unit on Women's Studies – useful resource about organisations and institutions in India involved in research and projects on women and development.

Forum Against the Oppression of Women, c/o Vibhuti Patel, K 8 Nensey Colony, Express Highway, Borivili East 400066.

SEWA (Self Employed Women's Association), Textile Worker's Union Building, Ahmedabad (see introduction).

The journal, **Manushi**, can be obtained in the UK from *Manushi* c/o 17 Colworth Road, London E11; in the US from *Manushi*, c/o 5008 Erringer Place, Philadelphia, PA 19144.

BOOKS

Madhu Kishwar and Ruth Vanita, eds, *In Search of Answers: Indian Women's Voices* (Zed Books, 1984). Collection of articles from *Manushi* which provides a comprehensive, powerful and lucid account of women in Indian society.

Jeneffer Sebstad, *Women and Self-Reliance in India: the SEWA story* (Zed Books, 1985). Account of the formation – and achievements – of SEWA (see introduction).

Joanna Liddle and Rama Joshi, *Daughters of Independence – Gender, Caste and Class in India* (Zed Books, 1985).

Gail Omvedt, *We Will Smash This Prison! Indian Women in Struggle* (Zed Books 1980). A compelling account of women's struggles in western India in the 1970s.

Patricia Jeffrey, *Frogs in a Well: Indian Women in Purdah* (Zed Books, 1979). A comprehensive study of a community of Muslim women in the heart of New Delhi.

Ved Mehta, *The New India* (Penguin, 1978). Deals mainly with the ten-year period of Emergency Rule, and Mrs Ghandi's style as a political leader, but also carries a strong sense of the precariousness and anarchic threat of life in India.

Gita Mehta, *Karma Cola* (1979, Fontana 1981). Subtitled 'Marketing the Mystic East', this is a sharp and cynical look at hippies (and their successors) in India – and how Indians see them.

Dervla Murphy, *On a Shoestring to Coorg: An experience of Southern India* (1976, Century 1985). An intrepid journey – by the well-known contemporary traveller and her 5-year-old daughter.

Neera Desai and Ibhuti Patel, *Indian Women* (Sangam, 1985), An examination of the impact of International Women's Decade on the lives, status and struggles of women in India.

There are interesting contributions on India by Marilyn French in *Women: A World Report* (Methuen), by Devaki Jain in *Sisterhood is Global* (Penguin) and by the Manushi collective and an Indian Women's Anti-Rape Group in *Third World: Second Sex*. See the general bibliography for details/dates.

Minority Rights Group, *India the Nagus and the north-east* (MRG No. 17 1980). Also, *The Untouchables of India* (MRG No. 26, 1982). and *The Sikhs* (MRG No. 65).

FICTION

Sharan-Jat Shar, *In My Own Name* (The Women's Press, 1985). Autobiographical account of growing up in the Punjab, a life that includes forced marriage and emigration.

Padma Perera, *Birthday, Deathday* (The Women's Press, 1985). Short stories, mainly exploring the contradictions for an Indian woman educated in the West on returning to her homeland.

Truth-tales: Contemporary Writing by Indian Women (Kali for Women, 1986). A collection of stories many of them translated into English for the first time, by contemporary Indian women writers.

Anita Desai, *Fire on the Mountain* (Penguin 1981). Aged Indian woman is visited in her mountain retreat by her great grandchild.

Ruth Prawer Jhabvala, *Heat and Dust* (Futura, 1976), *A Backward Place* (Penguin, 1979), and others.

Thanks to Mary Lightfoot.

NEPAL

Up until the 1960s **Nepal** was virtually untouched by the outside world, an isolated mountain kingdom and highly traditional Hindu society. It is today in the midst of a tourist boom, with travellers pouring into the capital, Kathmandu, and, accompanied by local guides, out along its spectacular Himalayan trekking routes. As from 1985 there is an added lure in the possibility of crossing the Chinese border to Tibet (see. p.328).

As a primarily rural and Hindu society, Nepal is a relatively safe place to travel; you are treated first and foremost as a foreigner, rather than a woman, and harassment is uncommon. What is disturbing is the pattern that you and your fellow tourists are creating. Kathmandu has changed suddenly and sadly under tourist developments, and the trekking industry, for all its supposed 'contact with local people', is as prepared as any other to exploit workers with low wages and poor conditions. If you want to feel good about trekking here choose your tour with care – or go it alone.

Under the partyless 'Democratic Panchayat' system of King Birenda, autonomous **women's groups** are considered divisive. (It is illegal for any political group to function without prior government consent.) There are a few officially sanctioned bodies – notably the Nepal Women's Organisation – which are oriented mainly towards providing educational and social welfare services. The NWO has initiated campaigns on issues of property rights, polygamy and child and forced marriages, but these have been criticised by Nepalese feminists as being largely tokenistic.

◪ **Bronwen Lewis spent two months in Nepal, trekking and touring alone.**

In the trekking centre of Pokhara in western Nepal, I was variously told that solo trekking was too dangerous for women, that a porter was needed to carry kit on such hard trails, and that a guide was necessary to find one's way in the mountains. This was all disheartening advice, as I'd wandered alone through Asia so far, and had neither the money nor the stomach for guides and porters. The guide books available tended to be of little help as they were almost all written by men in charge of trekking companies. However, one day, I happened to see a guidebook photograph of a woman alone in the mountains, rucksack on her back. The next day I got a trekking permit and set off.

The route I chose was the popular Dumre to Pokhara trek, via Manang and the 5330 metre Thorong La pass. This seemed ideal, because it was a circular route with a wide variety of scenery, actually crossed the Himalayas, and was the only longish (three week) trek where food and overnight accommodation would be available daily.

The gloomy advice proved unfounded. I met a lot of solo walkers though sadly, virtually no women – Nepal seemed the safest country for solo travel I've ever visited. On the trek, even tales of theft were very rare, and I left my open rucksack unattended on footpaths while bathing. The men I met were often shy, even the young men, who shared the delusions of many Asian men about Western women, were friendly rather than threatening and the only harassment I suffered was from children, who pester all foreigners for sweets, money and schoolpens. From a safety point of view, my well-travelled route was a blessing, but it wouldn't suit real wilderness lovers.

As for guides, advice en route was plentiful and free. I did get slightly lost almost every day, owing to a fondness for crossing every rickety suspension bridge I saw, and meandering off the path in the forests, but inevitably a porter or woman farmer would appear and point me in the right direction. With a good (locally available) map and local people's directions, it wasn't possible to get lost in the mountains.

On the trek I chose, no tent or food had to be carried, so I had no difficulty carrying a seven kilo pack of essential clothes, sleeping bag, medicine etc. The walking was fine, once my muscles had got used to the idea, and an unpractised walker could always get a four-week permit, and do the trek in smaller daily stages. The only really hard part was crossing the high Thorong La pass, due mainly to the high altitude (which made the going painfully slow), ice on the narrow trail, and the fact that it had to be crossed in only one day. When the pass is open, there are always small groups of trekkers staying at the huts below so it's possible to meet people at night and arrange to climb with them the next day. If you prefer to go it alone it is at least advisable to climb in sight of other people in case of altitude problems. But the pass involves no hard climbing, so if walkers acclimatise slowly, it shouldn't be a problem for anyone who is reasonably fit.

There were minor problems. My kit wasn't ideal; I had no walking boots, and my other mountain equipment was hired in Pokhara. (A far better selection is available in Kathmandu.) At these altitudes, equipment must be both warm and light, which means expensive. I was sometimes very cold in my cheap and nasty gear. Lack of clean drinking water also means health problems; about half the trekkers I met had been mildly ill. Often a day's rest is enough – pity the poor trekkers in large groups who are forced to stagger on regardless – but many carried treatment for diarrhoea, worms, and giardiasis (stomach parasites), as well as something to purify water if they drank it unboiled.

I soon saw why the guide books called this the best trek in Nepal. The scenery is fantastically varied – rice fields, forested gorges, snowy peaks, glaciers and moonscapes with Buddhist monasteries and fluttering prayer flags. The villages are often architecturally interesting, and I found the food plain and good. In the small tea-shops-cum-hotels, people are friendly, and guests often sit and sleep near the central fire, where the women are churning yak butter and stirring porridge. Some of the tea shops are run by women, who speak some English, and appear to have a fair amount of status and independence. They may, in honour of a British guest, tune in to the BBC World Service, so that the rattle of grandmother's prayer wheel mingles with *Baker's Dozen*.

▨ **Kathleen Muldoon lived for a year and a half in Nepal, completing fieldwork for an anthropology PhD.**

For virtually my whole stay in Nepal I lived in a village in the Himalayan foothills, in the far north-west. The people were Hindu and their livelihood was subsistence farming – typical in both respects of the country's population outside Kathmandu.

To say that this village was Hindu does not mean its gods were the conventional Shiva, Vishnu and their various incarnations. In most Nepalese villages, the people know little or nothing about the formal Hindu pantheon; they have their own gods and goddesses and communicate with them through the medium of possessed oracles during seances. But worshipping the gods is only one part of Hinduism. As a religion it is infinitely broader in its scope – encompassing a world-view and way of life, decreeing or rationalising (or both) a whole social order that designates men above women, and one caste above another. There is an ancient Hindu saying: 'A woman is never fit for independence. As a child she belongs to her father, in womanhood to her husband, and then, when her lord is dead, to her sons.' And, for many women in rural Nepal, this is still the reality.

In the village where I lived, a girl is usually betrothed to a boy of her father's choosing when she is very young, maybe only two or three. When she reaches puberty she is sent to live with him and his family, often to a village some distance from the one where she grew up. Here, she finds herself an outsider in a closely knit extended family, sometimes of three generations of related men and their wives and children. A stranger, even to her husband, she feels isolated and lonely, is expected to work harder than anyone else in the family, and makes an easy scapegoat when things go wrong.

The young wife of one of the sons in the household where I lived often went to work in the fields before anyone else was up. Generally, she came back as it was getting dark and ate her meal in silence, her face and head shrouded by her shawl. As is usually the case, her status improved with the birth of her first son. Only then was she regarded as a member of the family, rather than a barely welcome burden on its scant resources.

But motherhood has problems of its own. Large families are considered a source of pride and happiness and, as long as there is sufficient land, of wealth. So women bear child after child, from puberty, when they marry, until old-age declares them infertile. In addition to bearing and rearing children, women in Nepal do about 50 per cent of the agricultural work and most of the domestic work, fetching water, grinding grain, husking rice, cooking, etc. These conditions – incessant childbearing, poverty and over-hard work – combine with poor health care to make Nepal's infant and maternal mortality rate one of the highest in the world.

It is a strange irony that although a Hindu woman's status is enhanced by motherhood, all manifestations of her fertility are polluting to men. Another young woman in the household where I lived had a miscarriage one night and was rushed to the stable by her mother-in-law because she was polluting the house. She stayed in the stable for ten days and then, on the morning of the eleventh, she went to the stream and washed and drank a few drops of cow's urine (all the products of the cow are purifying to Hindus) and her pollution ended.

The same rules apply for childbirth and for every monthly period, when a woman spends the first four days of bleeding in the stable or in a special hut behind the house. Most women, polluted in this way, continue to work in the fields, but they must not fetch water, cook or touch any man. (Untouchable castes are polluting to higher castes in a similar way, except for them it is a permanent state.)

Some of the most moving memories I have of that village are of the times I spent with groups of women who had come back from their husbands' villages to their parents for a few days during festivals. These are their holidays, rare times when they are indulged and don't work in the fields. We would spend hours together, washing at the stream, sitting in the sun, combing, oiling and plaiting each other's hair, talking about children, food, clothes and jewellery, and laughing about their impossibly difficult husbands and parents-in-law. There seemed to be a familiarity between us that overrode the enormous differences of our worlds and life-experiences.

But when I was travelling in Nepal, in all but the very remote parts, I was not treated as a local woman (no one seemed to be concerned, for example, whether I was menstruating), nor, particularly was I treated as a woman at all (there was almost no sexual harrassment and few jibes). I was type-caste as a foreigner, a role on which gender has little bearing.

Being foreign implies, above all, two things: wealth and leisure. However poor you may feel and however frugally you think you are living, there are glaring inequalities that can't be disguised and often don't pass without comment – such as the fact that you have the leisure to wander round the countryside when local people are working in the fields, that when it's snowing you have your down jacket and walking boots, when many are barefoot. People will ask how much your fare to Nepal was, how much your camera cost, what your salary is. And if you tell the truth – which I can't say I always did – you will be regarded with wide-eyed incredulity.

It's difficult to tell how much resentment rural people actually felt and how much I projected on to them through my own sense of guilt. It may be surprising, given the predominant poverty, that outside the urban areas, there is little theft. Things are usually only stolen as a result of your own carelessness or insensitive flaunting. But what has happened is that the attitude that foreigners are an 'easy touch' is spreading, partly, of course, through our own fault.

One thing I was never able to desensitise myself to was the endless requests for medicine. People would come up to me, sometimes faking, it's true, but often distraut, with infected wounds, stomach aches, tubercular coughs, malnourished babies – pleading for medicine. Usually, I had no choice but to send them away, suggesting that they try the nearest health-post (which, we both knew, was probably at least a day's walk away, and possibly unstaffed in any case). What hurt me most on these occasions was the conviction in the sick person's eyes, that I did have the medicine, but was too mean to give it to them.

Most of what I have written presupposes that you will go trekking. But it is easy to enjoy yourself for at least a couple of weeks, when you first arrive in Nepal, doing all the things that are more readily accessible to tourists. Just wandering through the streets of Kathmandu, going into temples, looking at the stone- and wood-carved statues of gods and goddesses, can be spellbinding. And when you tire of city life there are buses that go south to the Terai, and the National Game Reserve in Chitwan. It's also possible to take a bus north to the Chinese border (and, since 1985, into China itself), and west to Pokhara, a lakeside tourist resort.

But, sooner or later, you will see a chain of mountains on the horizon turning from grey, to pink, to orange, to white, as the the sun rises, and the temptation to leave the motorable roads and head for the Himalayas will be hard to resist.

As you walk northwards, beyond the lower foothills and the Hindu villages, the landscape becomes progressively more inhospitable. Gradually, the rich colours of fertile agricultural land fade. Eventually, they merge into varying shades of grey – grey rocky earth, banks of scree, stone houses nestled into bare cliff-sides as shelter from the relentless dust-blowing wind, that sweeps its way down from Tibet.

The people who live at this altitude are mainly Tibetan Buddhists whose livelihood is based, primarily, on animal husbandry and trade. Often you pass their caravans – heavily laden mules and yaks, with red plumes and jangling bells – laboriously making their way down the steep and winding tracks between north and south, Tibet and India.

One of the most tragic, and yet (for us as foreigners and adventure-seekers) most precious things about Nepal, is the virtual impossibility of constructing roads in the Himalayas. It makes the logistics of development programmes daunting; but it also means that if you do make the effort to walk, you will be rewarded by finding yourself in a still relatively unchanged, traditional culture.

TRAVEL NOTES

Languages Nepali and regional dialects: some English spoken on tourist circuits.

Transport Within the Kathmandu Valley there are buses; further north trekking is the only option, other than a small network of flights (expensive and unreliable – though if time is tight you can fly out into the Himalayas and trek back).

Accommodation Plenty of cheap places to stay in Kathmandu and surrounding areas; also small hotels on regular trekking routes. On more remote routes, there are virtually no tourist facilities and you'll have to carry your own tent or join a trekking party with porters. An alternative is to stay in people's homes – there is nowhere in Nepal that you would not be taken in – though if you do this be aware of the acuteness of food shortages in much of the country.

Special problems In the more orthodox Hindu far west you may be asked – as a foreigner (and therefore untouchable) – to sleep outside the main living room. Everywhere you should try to avoid touching cooking utensils or food that is being prepared, and if you're given water to drink from a communal vessel avoid any contact with your lips. Trekking demands proper clothing and equipment. Altitude sickness is a common problem.

Guides Prakash A. Raj, *Kathmandu and the Kingdom of Nepal – A Travel Survival Kit* (Lonely Planet, rev. 1985). The most useful basic guide. Best of the specific trekking guides is reckoned to be Stephen Bezruchka's *Trekking in Nepal* (Mountaineers, US, rev. 1985).

CONTACTS
Nepal Women's Organisation, 16/33 Rama Saha Path, Kathmandu.

BOOKS
Lynn Bennett, *Dangerous Wives and Sacred Sisters* (Columbia University Press, New York, 1983) Good insight into life and position of Hindu women in Nepal.

Lynn Bennett, ed. *The Status of Women in Nepal* (CEDA, Tribhuvan University, Nepal). Lengthier, more academic study.

SRI LANKA

Up until the last two to three years, travellers tended to use **Sri Lanka** as a gentle introduction to Asia and the Indian subcontinent. Though pervasively poor, and with persisting problems of unemployment (especially among the large numbers of graduates), it has never had the desperate, all-permeating sense of poverty of, say, parts of India. The mild climate and fertile soil somehow allow most people to feed themselves. To tourists it is promoted as an 'island paradise', combining an easy, expansive approach with a range of facilities, lush scenery and all the exotic pleasures of a tropical coastline.

This remains – though the paradise image has been all but lost amongst the recent inter-ethnic conflicts. In 1983 there was an eruption of violence between the Tamils (the mainly Hindu minority) and the majority (largely Buddhist) Sinhalese. Radical Tamil groups, increasingly using guerrilla tactics, agitated for a separate state of Tamil-Eelam in the north. Since, the situation has developed into one of sporadic violence and unrest, with the use of curfews and military manoeuvres along the north and east coasts becoming routine.

The government is at present attempting to revive the holiday industry, but the situation, together with televised scenes of anti-Tamil riots in the capital, Colombo, and the news of many Tamils attempting to leave the country, continue to keep the numbers of visitors low. Whilst there is in fact little direct danger to tourists – who have never been ostensible targets of political activism – Jaffna in the north and now parts of the east coast are off-limits. Travelling in tourist areas your main problem lies in being hassled as one of few potential customers. Sexual harassment is a less direct concern: men honk car horns or shout comments but this rarely feels personally threatening.

Voluntary **women's groups** working alongside government-sponsored organisations have played an increasingly important role in the provision and delivery of social welfare services throughout the country. Mostly they have been concerned with setting up educational and income-generating projects (handicraft co-ops, etc.) amongst rural and urban-poor women, and with running social service institutions such as kindergartens, orphanages and hostels. There is also a small number of groups such as the *Kantha Handa* (Voice of Women), the *Katha Shakthi* (Women's Liberation Movement) and *Vavuniya* (Tamil women's liberation Movement) which take a more structural approach to the issues of women's oppression, emphasising the importance of consciousness-raising. Of particular current concern is the exploitation of women's labour in the Free Trade Zone and in the tea, rubber, coconut and allied trades linked with the export economy.

(The events in Sri Lanka have overtaken us. The following two articles were written before the most recent escalation of violence.)

◪ **Ruth Crosskey spent two months in Sri Lanka. She travelled mainly alone, and spent some time working on an archaeological project.**

In the more touristed areas of Sri Lanka a single woman attracts a great deal of attention – mainly from hustlers and traders attempting to sell their wares, postcards, gemstones and 'antiques'. This needs a certain firmness to shake off, but there's little aggression in it and, if I had to generalise, I'd say the country is not a difficult one for women travellers. It can be frustrating, however. When making my way around the island I found I had very little contact with any Sri Lankan women. It is the men whom you meet – the traders, hoteliers and hustlers. Women, generally less familiar with English, tend to be preoccupied with children and purchases when outside the home.

I had friends working on the Cultural Triangle archaeological project, and an archaeology degree myself, so for a time I worked as a volunteer at the site of Sigiriya. This proved a rewarding task, and a good source of contact. I found myself with two young Sri Lankan assistants, both women. Both were Buddhist Sinhalese and seemed to me very innocent. They followed the principles of abstinence almost automatically: a vegetarian diet, no smoking or drinking, and certainly no sex before marriage. In fact they were supposed to be completely ignorant of sexual matters and, as this didn't seem merely assumed, questions about boyfriends in England proved sometimes quite difficult to answer.

They would dissolve into delighted giggles if you asked them about their own boyfriends, and would let you peep at their photographs. But it seemed that they did not know them very well, the love-match, their parents' interests and the future prospects for the potential bridegroom seemed to weigh equally in their choice. Once a girl marries she is looked up to by the rest and acquires an aura of knowledge – real or assumed.

The men working at Sigiriya tended to lapse more from their roles as good Buddhists, and made more of a virtue of following the religious rules. Although they would not admit to drinking arrack, they would sneak off in groups in the evening sometimes. Arrack drinking is especially frowned upon, as the sole purpose is to get blind drunk, with no half measures. The men suspected that we drank arrack too but, being Western, we escaped the condemnation a Sri Lankan girl would experience. The men's attitude to girls who did break the unwritten rules was as important in making them toe the line as their own feelings. Most of the men were unmarried, but did not have any close relationships with the girl graduates. When they had some prospects they would expect to start courting a girl, usually from their village, and usually for some years until they had saved enough to marry. Even then, if they had jobs in different places, they would live apart for some time until they wished to have children.

The graduates tended to look down upon the labourers. A village woman who worked in one of the laboratories was by far the most apt and conscientious worker, making the graduates by comparison seem lazy. Not only was her contribution undervalued but she was consistently given unpleasant jobs, and sometimes much of the graduates' own work as well. As Westerners we had to be careful not to offend. We tried only to drink, smoke and swear in private. Our positions of authority and more assertive approach to life could have given rise to envy and confusion. We had to be extremely tactful, especially about trying to step up the rate of work. As part of a co-operative, the Sri Lankans seemed to adopt a protective attitude towards us and in turn we developed an enduring affection for them. The labourer who carried the survey equipment became a good friend, and we spent a happy day cycling over to his village to meet his friends and his mother (ancient but much-adored). I found myself much embarrassed, trying to fend off presents from really very poor people, with very little success. It was strange that in the village I experienced the exact opposite of the treatment I had as a single woman in touristed areas. Here I was an object of great curiosity, but as such I was shown great respect.

▉ **Sue Eckstein spent two years in Sri Lanka, working in Colombo as a teacher.**

In many Colombo houses there are two kitchens. One is a bright plastic-tiled room, equipped with the latest cookers, stainless steel sinks and microwave ovens. The other is a dark, stone floored pantry with an open hearth with soot-blackened pots resting on a wood fire. Visitors will be assured that food cooked this second way tastes much better. You get the real 'Sri Lankan curry taste' which you cannot possibly get from the hot-plate of a modern cooker.

This love-hate relationship with all that is imported can be applied to more than kitchen equipment. As a white woman living and travelling alone in the urban and tourist areas of Sri Lanka I was regarded simul-taneously as desired object and unwelcome intrusion, status symbol and sex symbol, a personification of a coveted import from the West which was also vastly inferior to the local product.

This gave rise to a curious kind of sexual harassment, which though rarely intimidating was nevertheless an irritating part of my life and travels in Sri Lanka.

I first began to appreciate what concepts of Western women prevailed here when, shortly after my arrival, I went to look at a room that was to let. 'You can't have any male visitors in the room after 6 pm,' the landlady informed me. 'I know what you foreign girls are like. I've got my three daughters to think about.'

One of my students, a fifteen-year-old Sri Lankan girl, confirmed this opinion in a grammar exercise practising the comparative form: 'An Eastern girl is more innocent and modest than a Western girl.'

I found it almost impossible to walk around alone in the evenings. It seemed that few drivers including the Police, could resist a quick shout out of the window or a blast of the horn. Cars frequently crawled along the curb while the drivers peered out to see if I was worth stopping for. I had offers of lifts in cars, on the back of motorcycles, and even in the odd bullock cart. I lost count of the number of cab drivers who felt it part of the service to enquire after my marital status.

Once I went to a beach resort on the west coast with a Sri Lankan friend, on the back of his motorbike. We saw a small guest house and decided to stop for lunch. The manager looked me up and down, grinned knowingly at my friend, and asked in Sinhala. 'Did you pick her up at the bus-stand?'

I found too that the 'go-between' still has a function on the Sri Lanka social scene. I was sitting reading at a swimming pool in Colombo once when a young waiter came up to me. He needed my name and phone number, he said to report the fact that a fly had chosen my bottle of Fanta in which to drown itself. I expressed surprise at his rather uncharacteristic concern for hygiene and told him I had no phone. The fly turned out to be incidental, as I saw the waiter go and report the information, or lack of it, back to a man who had been staring at me for the past hour.

I never encountered any kind of sexual harassment when I travelled alone in the more rural areas of Sri Lanka. One of my most enjoyable and memorable days was spent on a journey to an isolated village in the Dry Zone, north of Hambantota, a village not unlike the one Leonard Woolf described in *A Village in the Jungle*.

I changed buses in a tiny town built around a crossroads and sat down on a bench outside a mud-walled house to wait the hour for the connection. I watched the cows that wandered past snuffling in the gutters, the villagers riding past me, two or three to a bicycle, the women buying rice and chillies in the store opposite, listened to the sounds of the mynah birds and crickets and smelt the smell of cooking rice and decaying refuse. A small child came and sat by me and watched with me. Another child ran out of the house, over to the store, bought a small bag of sugar and disappeared back into the house. A few minutes later, a woman emerged followed by five or six children, carrying a glass of sweet tea which she gave me, telling me in Sinhala to drink. When I left a crowd of children ran behind the bus waving and shouting 'Goodbye! Goodbye!'

Rural Sri Lankans who have not had much exposure to the celluloid images of Western women, and who have not encountered such alien phenomena as topless bathers or tourism as a source of income, are likely to view Western people travelling alone as a source of interest, regardless of their sex. And there are still areas where very few Westerners have ever been. Women will undoubtedly arouse curiosity when travelling in remote parts of Sri Lanka, but it is a gentle curiosity and inquisitiveness compared to the frenetic attention of the cities and resorts.

TRAVEL NOTES

Languages Sinhala and Tamil. You'll find English is widely spoken and understood.

Transport There is an extensive bus service and a rather more limited train service. They are both very cheap but buses are often old and uncomfortable. If you are travelling at night by train it is advisable to carry a timetable which counts out the stops, as Sri Lankan train stations are very badly lit. Hitching is uncommon and not worthwhile as public transport is generally cheap.

Accommodation Plentiful. Small guest houses run by families are often a good bet.

Special problems Because of political instability in the Tamil-dominated north of Sri Lanka, the ferry between Talaimannar and Rameswaram in south India is no longer operating. The only approach is by air to Colombo International Airport.

As throughout Asia, it is best if you can avoid tap water and you should also take malaria precautions. Mosquitoes are legion, but even the most modest guest houses supply mosquito nets.

Guides Tony Wheeler, *Sri Lanka, A Travel Survival Kit* (Lonely Planet, 1984). *Insight Guide to Sri Lanka* (APA, 1984). *A Traveller's Survival Guide to the East* (VacWork, 1985). No particular recommendation.

CONTACTS
Kantha Handa (Voice of Women), 529 Baudhaloka Mawatha, Colombo 8. Feminist journal that comes out sporadically in Sinhala, Tamil and English.

BOOKS
An article from Kantha Handa appears in *Third World: Second Sex* (see general bibliography).
Else Skjonsberg, *A Special Caste: Tamil Women of Sri Lanka* (Zed Books, 1982). Anthropological study of sex, class and caste relationships in a fishing village.

Thanks to Susan Griffith.

PAKISTAN

The number of women travelling in **Pakistan** has much diminished over the last decade. This is due partly to the closure of the overland route to India via Afghanistan (few women would consider the option of driving through Iran) but it is mainly because of the increasing limitations and restrictions imposed by General Zia's neo-fundamentalist Islamic state. Away from the 5-star hotels, it takes a fair amount of resilience to cope with the harassment and muted antagonism shown towards you as a symbol of the decadent, licentious West. If you travel with a man this is less noticeable, and attitudes generally tend to become more relaxed towards the border areas. For some the spectacular scenery of Pakistan's mountains and ravines are sufficient compensation.

Since General Zia introduced his Islamicisation programme, women in Pakistan have had to concentrate on retaining even the most circumscribed and basic freedoms against wave upon wave of retrogressive legislation – and in a country where dissent is punished swiftly and harshly. Women today cannot testify in a murder case, cannot secure a rape conviction without four witnesses (their own evidence being inadmissible) and in the case of compensation, a woman's life is valued at half that of a man. Under discussion are bills to lift dowry restrictions, lower the minimum age of marriage to puberty and ban women under 50 from public office.

Opposition to Zia within Pakistan, however, is centred on one woman – **Benazir Bhutto**, daughter of the executed former prime minister. Her nine-year campaign to reinstate democracy, fuelled by an unabashed if eloquent re-write of her father's years in office, has recently culminated in mass demonstrations of support in Karachi and throughout the country. Zia remains (at the time of writing) very much in control, supported a little uneasily by the US, aware of the possibilities of a 'second Corrie Aquino' in what is for them a vital front-line state in the covert war against Afghanistan. But how long this position will remain is highly unpredictable. Uniquely, there is a real and increasing chance of a woman obtaining power as premier of an Islamic nation.

The **Pakistan Women's Action Forum**, the main feminist force, was founded in 1981 to campaign against a law which removed legal protection for women whose husbands took a second wife. Within months WAF groups, with an increasingly wider brief, had been established in all major towns. Simultaneously groups such as the All Pakistan Women's Association, Punjab Women Lawyers, Young Women's Christian Association and many others were becoming increasingly politicised in opposition to the government's programme. The movement focused on one particular bill, the Law of Evidence, which proposed the equating of the legal testimony of one man to that of two women. This was seen as totally at odds with the Muslim precept of equality. Two hundred women staged a sitdown protest outside the Lahore High Court where they had been thwarted in an attempt to present a petition. They were charged by police wielding metal tipped clubs, forty were injured of whom at least six needed hospital treatment. In the ensuing outcry the banned opposition parties, the media and many women's organisations united to openly condem police brutality. The Women's Movement entered a new phase.

◢ **Sarah Lyne spent six weeks travelling in Pakistan, enroute to the north of India.**

To cope with Pakistan you must swallow your pride and silently accept the assumptions and restrictions implicit in their idea of a woman: your own must be kept more or less in *purdah* In practical terms this entails dressing with extreme modesty (I wore the *shilwar*, flared trousers that come down over the ankles and a *qumiz* or long-sleeved shirt) and, wherever possible, teaming up with a Western man. As in many Muslim countries, a white women travelling alone is regarded as a whore, her excessive personal liberty and inordinate concern for her individuality being incomprehensible to most of the people. Once with a man, your presence becomes less offensive, smiles become kind (if patronising) rather than mistrustful and life generally seems a lot easier. This won't necessarily however, affect the amount of sexual harassment you'll get. Being whistled after or leered at is something you have to quickly come to terms with. But it rarely takes any physical form or gets more extreme than this and if you stay in any one place for more than a few days, it noticeably diminishes.

When using public transport of any kind it is important to be aware of your 'place'. This is with the women and children, at the back of the bus, or in a separate compartment in a train. It is a segregation that can be a life-saver when everything, just for the moment, gets too much. Babies are put in your lap, your hair is plaited by your neighbour, and although no one understands a word you say, fun is had by all. If you are travelling with a man you sit with him, making sure that you are by the window, he on the outside of you. Travelling down from the Swat Valley to Peshawar, I could not understand why the seat we were on was empty but for us, and the rest of the bus bursting: everyone on everyone else's lap, several on the driver's, chicken and various livestock piled to the roof. Someone with a bit of English and fluent sign-language finally made us realise that I was the reason for the jam; I moved next to the window and a dozen people and chickens descended.

The religious intransigence which fosters this way of relating to people has very much intensified under the regime of General Zia-al-Haq. This has not, however, been without internal dissent – a major contention being that the practical compassion of the Muslim faith has become cynically subverted by Zia and his military supporters for political ends. Spreading out from the centre towards the frontiers of the country the laws of the 'Pure Islamic State of Pakistan' appear to be less and less rigidly enforced. People in the border areas seem generally more tolerant of, and responsive to, outside influences.

Peshawar, the nearest large town to the border with Afghanistan, is filled with Afghani refugees who have smuggled themselves over the border. I was told that the easiest way was to dress in purdah; no woman would be searched. Children turn up with Russian skin and faces. The market is run largely by refugees, who will give you tea, make trousers and talk of the life they have left, no matter who you are.

Further north where the border moves in an arc, the people seem far removed from conflicts of national politics, concerned instead with more local tribal differences. The Swat Valley, for instance, seems to be a separate nation as until recently it was. It was in this area that I felt least encumbered by being a woman, because most people there are rebelling against something. The prospect of a woman is more easily accepted as just another rebel. Pathan tribesmen would talk to me, even about the intricacies of the new guns laid on the table in front of them. This is by no means to say that you should search out trouble, but be aware of the places, like Peshawar and the valleys north of it, in which boundaries are dotted lines, moved backward and forward from day to day. It is here that you will find other boundaries, if not disregarded, at least flexible.

◪ **Carmel Pavageau spent two weeks in the Northern Territory, travelling with her husband.**

We travelled the spectacular Karakoram Highway from Rawalpindi to Hunza. The road surface is mostly excellent, but the trip can last easily 22 hours, even with the driver going like a bat out of the Muslim equivalent of hell. Occasionally we spotted the sobering results of just too much speed – burnt-out skeletons of coaches lying at the bottom of ravines. And there was always the danger, we knew, that the mountain-side might at any time just fall away. Five hundred men lost their lives building the highway and the whole Karakoram range is notorious for its instability.

We travelled up on a bus booked by a bunch of university students (male of course) for a week's holiday. Their consistently childish behaviour, giggling and chucking cushions at one another, came as a bit of a surprise. So too did the gentleness they showed one another, tucking cushions under sleeping heads and passing round food. A couple attached themselves to us at the various stops and showed us where we could eat. They also got the stereo turned down when it nearly blasted us out of our seats and asked the driver to slow down when I turned a shade of green. I don't know if they would have approached me in this way if I had been on my own – so often a male companion can act as a point of contact (as well as a buffer).

Fundamental Islamic practices are not too obvious in this Northern Territory, especially in the Hunza Valley where the people still cling to their own particular brand of Islam. They are Ismailis, followers of the Aga Khan. The women are unveiled, working in the fields and always ready with a smile as you pass. Some (very unusually) even allowed me to take a picture of them. And the *muezzin* keeps a low profile here, the locals obviously calling themselves to prayer when it suits them.

The Valley bursts into view like a bright green chessboard of fields as the bus swerves out of a narrow defile of grey shale and rock that lines the Karakoram Highway. The journey up is spectacular. The Highway climbs high above the Indus so that rope bridges far below look no more than threads; across the other side of the valley are old pre-Highway paths that are mere goat tracks. All seem to end in a heaped landslide. Now and then we passed whole troupes of nomads, trailing sheep and goats and camels. Hunza's tiny fields are skirted by glacial streams and shaded by willow, mulberry and apricot trees; and low stone walls blend almost imperceptibly into the small houses.

Further up the valley, at Pasu, it's a different scene. The valley is desolate, wide and flat; full of stones and scarcely a plant to be seen. Virtually the only sign of habitation is a soldiers' barracks and an inn. But around that is the most staggering arena of mountains I've ever seen. Razor-peaked Mt Tupopdan across the river lightens and darkens as clouds cast shadows across its ridges. Sheer walls of rock flank its spires and the occasional thunder of a landslide is heard as shale slides heavily into hidden crevasses. It's all quite unnerving. Pasu is the point of return for foreigners. Eighty miles further on is China's back door. Only Pakistanis or Chinese are allowed passage at the moment, but there are plans to open up the border to tourists perhaps in 1986.

TRAVEL NOTES

Languages Urdu, Pushtu and many others. You will find English speakers fairly easily in the main centres.

Transport In town there are buses, mini-buses, three-wheeled motor scooters (auto-rickshaws), horse carriages (tongas) and taxis; all are reasonably priced. People tend to be very helpful in directing you to the bus you want, or even taking you there.

Outside of town, the buses are fairly cheap and very fast, often frighteningly so. There is also a small railway network. see Sarah Lynals piece for details on train/bus conventions.

Accommodation Wide range, from top-class international-style hotels to small very basic inns.

Special problems Harassment can become restrictive and oppressive. It's worth taking care over your dress. Trousers are better than skirts since ankles are strictly taboo; loose T-shirts are OK but large long-sleeved shirts are better. The Pakistanis' own clothing (the *shil-war-quimiz*) is perfect and you can get a tailor, found in all market areas, to make one up for you in a day.

Guides Jose Roleo Santiago, *Pakistan – A Travel Survival Kit* (Lonely Planet,

1981). Christine Osborne, *Pakistan* (Longman, 1983).

CONTACTS

Women's Action Forum (WAF), PO Box 3287, Gulberg, Lahore. Holds monthly public meetings, and workshops, seminars and discussion groups in both Urdu and English.

Asian Women's Institute International Office, c/o Association of Kinnaird College for Women, Lahore–3, Active in the field of education and women's studies, also in rural development projects for women which emphasise consciousness-raising as well as economic growth.

BOOKS

Dervla Murphy *Where the Indus is Young* (1976, Century 1985). Lively account of a journey through the more remote parts of northern Pakistan which the author made with her seven-year-old daughter. Geoffrey Moorhouse, *To the Frontier* (Hodder & Stoughton). Wide-ranging travelogue of modern-day Pakistan.

Thanks to Jennifer Luesby who supplied information on the Women's Movement.

BANGLADESH

In the minds of most Westerners, **Bangladesh** remains synonymous with the worst ravages of war, famine, poverty and disaster. Since the very bloody war of independence from Pakistan (1971–2) the country has remained in a near constant state of political instability, with nine successive presidents, and of devastating economic crisis. At the time of writing the military, under General Ershad, are enforcing martial rule.

It is not a place you visit casually. The degree of poverty comes as a shock even if you've travelled extensively in India, and, although not formally an Islamic state, rigorous constraints (including the veil) are imposed on women. A number of Western women, however, work in Bangladesh as part of development and relief organisations, and reports are that it is easier to travel alone than in Pakistan.

Aid and development agencies within the country are increasingly recognising that the long-term survival of impoverished rural communities will depend on how much **women** can be supported in their role as caregivers and providers. Operating at a very local level – and within the confines of Muslim custom – projects have been set up to educate women in health care, nutrition and literacy. Christine Morton's piece, which follows, details this more fully.

▨ **Christina Morton went to Bangladesh to take part as a volunteer in development work.**

During a three and a half month stay in Bangladesh I experienced complete and profound culture shock – I doubt even now I can write objectively about what it's like to visit the country. I did not go as a tourist – few people do. My purpose was to observe, and as far as possible to participate in, some of the innumerable development projects which have sprung up since the war of independence with Pakistan.

In Bangladesh poverty permeates every facet of human existence, and emotional, cultural, social and political interactions are all to some extent determined by this. I would not though discourage anyone from visiting the country provided they were really prepared to open their eyes, their ears, their hearts and their minds to the society around them. This of course takes time and commitment, and it's debatable whether a very short stay would afford great insights.

I was lucky in that for most of the time I wasn't forced to stay in hotels but was able to live with Bengali families, urban and rural, poor and not so poor. Also, though my status of single woman closed a few doors (inevitably of mosques and shrines), it brought me the huge advantage of contact with Bangladeshi women. Having been given initial introductions – most often, from men – I was allowed behind the veil of purdah to see the hardness of women's lives and feel their warmth, their gentleness and generosity. This process was never easy and I would be emotionally exhausted at the end of a day. Bangladeshi women lack any comprehension of Westerners wanting privacy, and in addition I sometimes felt that I was not appearing as a person with depth, humanity and personality but as a symbol (of promiscuity perhaps, of beauty – they have a high regard for white skin – but above all of affluence). Yet it was an unfailingly rewarding process to strip away layers of cultural differentiation, to build a bridge across the gulf that separated us in terms of economic circumstance, and to achieve on occasions, that truly human contact which is the reward of all travellers.

Language was sometimes a problem. I never picked up as much Bengali as I could have wished, but there are sometimes better ways of communicating – signs, touch, laughter. Indeed there were times when I was positively glad to be unable to understand Bengali. Bangladesh is an Islamic country (not, like Pakistan, an Islamic State but under the influence of aid-giving Middle Eastern countries such as Saudi Arabia it becomes more dogmatically religious every day) and women are simply not seen in public places without the veil, or at least a male escort. Women who do venture out, women who like me walk about alone in the streets, are considered whores and are called after as such. Sometimes my short hair and my unconventional clothing (I usually wore for modesty's sake – and I would advise any woman to do the same – a long-sleeved hip-length shirt over trousers or a longish skirt) invited men to speculate about my sex and one of the names which was called after me was the Bengali word for eunuch. This did not really upset me, because on the whole I had anticipated far worse sexual harassment than I ever actually experienced and indeed I often felt safer travelling alone in Bangladesh than I do crossing my home town in England. My hosts, my fellow travellers and the friends I made were often beside themselves with anxiety on my behalf. 'Where are your brothers?' they would ask, 'Don't you need your father to protect you?', 'Don't you miss your mother?' An independent and self-sufficient woman is indeed an enigma to them.

People are what a visit to Bangladesh is all about. There is little point in going if you are more interested in monuments (there are none) or a fun time (forget it). The only places that could be described as being of 'tourist interest' are Sundarbans in the south (last remnants of genuine jungle, where people motorlauch into the forest waterways in search of wildlife) and the 70-mile beach at Cox's Bazaar. But even if the will is there, the near total dearth of tourist facilities makes the usual indulgent 'holiday resort' lifestyle impossible.

People, however, are everywhere, 100 million of them squashed into a country which is no bigger than England and Wales. The vast majority live in the villages but even the ten million or so who form the urban population are sufficient to throng the streets and cram the public transport to bursting. Every bus and railway carriage has almost as many bodies hanging from the outside as are squashed into the interior. On a few occasions I visited villages where a white face had never been seen and where England (*Bilat*) was the stuff of legends and faded memories. In any such place I would be surrounded by crowds – sometimes scornful, suspicious or even hostile, sometimes merely curious, but mostly, or so it seemed to me, gentle and welcoming and always ready with hospitality – water, rice, the juice of the date palm, precious eggs.

Women in Bangladesh carry simultaneously the burdens imposed by economic exploitation, from both national and international sources, and a society which in both its religious and secular aspects is stubbornly patriarchal. Uncharacteristically however, the government has legislated for a quota of 10 to 15 per cent of women in employment in all areas of administration and industry, and several of the leading figures in the opposition political parties are women. But far more significant I felt was the relative effectiveness of development schemes which have grasped that the recovery and advancement of the entire country would stand or fall on the improvement of the position of women – their health, their education, their nutrition and their participation in the political and economic organisation of their society.

Bangladesh is, in the villages at least, and particularly where endemic landlessness has rotted the social fabric from within, an embryonic society. To visit it is to time travel, to observe at the micro level the gathering together of the fragments of a ravaged social structure into what is as yet the flimsiest of edifices – so fragile in the face of the odds stacked against it that you tremble for it. What hope have 100 million souls, half of which hover at or below the poverty line, chronically malnourished, in the face of increasing landlessness among the peasants, a rocketing population (which is predicted to reach 150 million by the end of the century), an escalating national debt, a dearth of commodity resources and a heritage of feudalism and imperialism? All the problems which we now so glibly label 'Third World' are concentrated in Bangladesh to a degree which will inevitably shock.

But projects such as *Gonoshastraya Kendra* (the People's Health Centre) just north of the capital, Dacca, and those working under the auspices of the Bangladesh Rural Advancement Committee (both entirely indigenous organisations incidentally) have recognised the enormous potential for radical change and development which lies in the hands of women. Women who are healthy, properly fed, basically literate and skilled, who have, in other words, access to the opportunities available in their society now and to the chance to create further opportunities for the future – in their hands lies not merely *a* hope, but *the* hope of Bangladesh's future generations. I could not avoid reflecting that this is a concept of social development with which the most advanced Western nations have in large measure yet to grapple.

TRAVEL NOTES

Languages Bengali. English is widely spoken.

Transport Flights between towns are incredibly cheap. There's a limited rail network and a few buses but they can be desperate – literally falling apart in transit. In the south boats, paddle steamers and motor launches are more usual forms of transport.

Accommodation Outside Dacca tourists (and tourist facilities) are sparse; there's the range, but nothing like the number of hotels you find in India or Pakistan.

Special problems As a Muslim country you're expected to dress extremely modestly. Health problems (and malaria) are common: take all precautions and inoculations.

Guides Jose Roleo Santiago, *Bangladesh – A Travel Survival Kit* (Lonely Planet, 1986), and Don Yeo, *Bangladesh – A Traveller's Guide* (Roger Lascelles, 1984).

CONTACTS
Bangladesh Rural Advancement Committee (BRAC), 66, Mohakhali Commercial Area, Dacca 12. Private, non-profit making organisation of Bengalis engaged in development work. BRAC initiated the Jamalpur Women's Program in 1976, which focuses on skills training, health education and literacy. It has also set up many women's work co-operatives, and produces a regular mimeographed newsletter.

Gonashasthaya Kendra (People's Health Centre), PO Nayarhat via Dhamrai, Dacca Development organisation.

BOOKS
Betsy Hartmann and James Boyce, *A Quiet Violence – View from a Bangladeshi village* (Zed Books, 1983). Ethnographic account of women in a rural society.

Chapter Thirteen

SOUTH-EAST ASIA

Like India, **South-East Asia** saw an explosion of independent travel in the 1970s. Australians, particularly, began to take advantage of the tropical island beaches and varied ethnic cultures, creating a network of cheap dormitories and hostels. Today these are increasingly juxtaposed by luxury and package-holiday tour developments – just part of the vast multinational interests in the region.

The six countries – **Singapore, Malaysia, Thailand, Burma, Indonesia** and the **Philippines** – share only casual similarities, as do many regions within the countries themselves. There are religious divides, predominantly Buddhist/Muslim; outrageous economic divides, with Thailand and the Philippines offering some of the ugliest examples of capitalism anywhere in the world; and bizarre social shifts, from Westernised cities like Singapore or Manila to areas of dense jungle where traditional tribal cultures remain relatively intact. The one unifying factor, for all except isolated socialist Burma, are the agribusiness conglomerates. These have dispossessed large populations of rural workers, leaving them the option of selling their labour back to the various enterprises or migrating to the city 'sweat shops'. In Thailand, developed as a 'rest and recreation' centre during the Vietnam war, a third, prevalent option for rural women is prostitution. The sex business in Bangkok is a major growth industry, as too is sex tourism – foreign businessmen fly in in groups for package deals. You may at times find it hard to come to terms with your own privileged presence.

Travel, however, is relatively easy, at least on the established circuits. Malaysia, the most rigidly Muslim country in the region, is probably the only place where sexual harassment will hinder your freedom of movement. Burma, which you can visit for a maximum of seven days, has a reputation for being one of the safest Asian countries. Everywhere, away from tourist centres and main cities, you are likely to find yourself an object of continual, unabashed curiosity.

MALAYSIA

Malaysia – former British colony and today one of the richest Asian nations – is patently unpopular with independent travellers. It is a predominantly Muslim country and travelling alone outside the cosmopolitan business centres of Kuala Lumpur or the highly developed and very expensive west coast you're likely to feel uncomfortable. Sexual harassment is common, especially along the isolated east coast where there's been a recent resurgence of Muslim Nationalism. By far the majority of tourists however are on stop-over package deals to KL, en route from Bangkok to Singapore or vice versa. Very few explore the country at all, and even fewer make the four-hundred-mile journey across the South China Sea to tribal East Malaysia (Borneo). Around this area, adherence to Islamic principles is less rigid and attitudes towards foreign women tend to be more relaxed. The main problems are the unpredictable monsoons that sweep the coast.

Over recent years the racial tensions between the Malay majority and the very large Chinese and Indian minorities have erupted in violent race riots. Since independence, these minorities have seen themselves increasingly disadvantaged by pro-Malay legislation. Under British colonial rule they had established a fairly clear monopoly over much of the business and cultural life of the main cities. Hopes of achieving some sort of long-term harmony at present appear slight.

Women's lives are dominated by the restraints of Islam and oriental traditions. Although all children get free primary school education, only a few girls go on to the secondary level. Marriage and child-rearing are at the focus of most women's lives – very few continue working after marriage. The government has a fairly progressive attitude towards birth control – contraception is available to all – though in matters like divorce and abortion, Islamic laws apply. In the tribal villages of East Malaysia women lead segregated lives, but their control over domestic affairs is well established.

◢ **Coral Beadle visited Port Dicon and Kuala Lumpur during a three-month tour of South-East Asia.**

We arrived in January, confident that as two women together we would be able to cope with this Muslim country. But I for one was unprepared for my first taste of Islam. Next time I will wear loose trousers, long-sleeved shirts and – without doubt – a bra. If I ever again venture onto a Malaysian beach, it will be in more than a bikini, and my gaze will remain permanently fixed to the sand. Another error – before leaving home a Malaysian friend had said we had picked entirely the wrong time of year to go there. We thought we had planned well: to be travelling up the west coast just after the east-moving monsoons had finished, coming back down the east coast when the rains had passed, and finally crossing over to Eastern Malaysia, where there was no hope of avoiding the storms. In fact it was so hot and humid on the west coast after the monsoon that the business of acclimatising was doubly hard.

But we were right in one assumption. The affluent, still 'English-colonial' country is an ideal place from which to ease into eastern culture. We took the bus from Singapore up to Melacca, a beautiful little port if you can look beyond the heat, the dirt, the traffic and the smells. We allowed Ah Tee – 'the Rickshaw Diplomat' according to the newspaper cutting mounted on his bike – to lead us to a dirty hotel above a 24–hour market. It turned out to be a brothel – he turned out to be genuinely nice, buying us breakfast though he knew we had no money to spend on a further rickshaw tour. But a couple of days was enough time to see the pink buildings left by the Dutch and we then moved on to Port Dickson, army garrison town and weekend beach resort for Malaysians escaping the capital, Kuala Lumpur.

Consulting *South East Asia on a Shoestring* for somewhere to stay, we plumped for the out-of-town youth hostel, billed as beautifully quiet, cheap and only a few minutes from the sea. So isolated in fact that it was easy for a boy to follow us back from the beach and, armed with a knife, threaten to rape us. We were fortunate. He could speak English and we talked our way out of it, got him into a public place and were finally rescued by another Malay.

Our good samaritan took us home to his family, and we ended up spending several days staying with them. They lived in a compound of former colonial houses occupied by young families, with a clear, sandy sea just over the end of the garden wall. The lack of privacy was a shock. The family lived largely out of doors under the constant gaze of neighbours on adjoining patios, with competing stereos blaring from nearby homes. Equally surprising was our celebrity value. Weekenders from the capital and grandparents were among the many who came to meet us. But, with the easy pace of life, partially attributable to the heat, we couldn't help but relax. Yet what was really crucial to the experience was our relationship with his wife. She had a young child to bring up, a full-time teaching job, and was studying in the hope of going to university but she also found time for us and was as keen to learn about our lives as we to understand hers.

It was with these Malaysian friends that I first learned the extent of Asian hospitality. Guests never pay. We often ate away from home at sit-down street stalls but weren't allowed to meet the bill. We did find one method of saying 'thank you' – we cooked a roast dinner complete with specially requested mashed potato. Virtually the only other item we bought was beer which, of course, we drank alone because we were guests in a non-drinking Muslim household.

We were lucky to make friends in Kuala Lumpur and the Cameron Highlands as well. In KL they taught us to appreciate the new capital emerging out of the shanty sprawl, taking us to the muddy river mouth from which the city takes its name, and up to the Hindu Batu Caves, ranked as one of the natural wonders of the world. And, with an Indian woman, we ventured one lunchtime into the National Mosque, dressed, like three witches, in black robes. Whilst we sweltered in dark shrouds designed to cover our dirty flesh, male worshippers changed from their business trousers into sarongs in open view.

Up in the Highlands, we were privileged to be invited to a party, an 'open house', which ended abruptly at 8 pm, as is the Malaysian norm, and were taken in the cool air on jungle walks. We ended our Malaysian travels in Penang, surrounded by fellow travellers in one of the clean

Chinese hotels which are always full and can't be booked in advance. The local beaches were dirty and lined with ogling groups of men. I had planned to continue to the east coast, but splitting up with my companion, felt this would be too much of a risk. But I do certainly plan to return, despite the drawbacks.

▨ **Judy Tice visited Borneo (Eastern Malaysia) on her way back from Australia to the UK. She was travelling alone and spent seven weeks on the island.**

Two young German men who arrived with me at Kuching airport were the only Western travellers I met in Borneo. I was given a month's visa, they, two weeks. It was February, towards the end of the rainy season, so travel was slightly restricted. The rivers were high and muddy, but the rapids were fast and exciting. Few roads are tarmacked so they were impassable to public transport. The leeches were also in abundance, but they are only a problem if you intend to trek in the forests. I was advised to visit in June, the dry season and the time of the many festivals celebrating the end of the rice harvests.

Kuching is a small city, full of contrasts. The old palaces of the colonial rulers, James Brooke and his family, called the Astana, are beautiful white colonial buildings. Nearby is the famous Sarawak museum, housing the best collection of tribal artifacts in all Asia. At the wharf houseboats, Japanese and Filipino trading boats pull up beside the market, where everything from fabrics, chickens, snakes, cakes and water buffalo are sold. Yet most of Kuching is post-war housing blocks and with the recent wealth created by the lumber industries new buildings are shooting up and people encouraged to leave their *kampongs* (villages) for the city. I stayed in a part of the Anglican cathedral, surrounded by a beautiful tropical garden. The Chinese chaplain befriended me, took me to his sister's birthday party and gave me useful addresses and information for the interior.

One day I went out without my umbrella, got soaked and hitched a lift in seconds. A young man drove me all around the surrounding area, which I would never have visited otherwise, as buses tend to go one day and return the next, which makes it tricky if you don't have a lot of time. He drove a BMW yet his apartment, where our trip ended, was tiny and stark. He obviously wanted sex but like every other man I met in Borneo he was never aggressive. 'No' said a couple of times sufficed. I often think that as a woman travelling alone you cause more enquiry, more people will help you, and if you judge characters wisely, you can get to places a man would be unlikely to be invited to. If I sat down at a stall to eat, nearly always some man or men would join me and then insist on paying for the whole meal. They usually had their motives but I learnt a lot from talking to them and I would not have wanted to isolate myself.

The men were very physical towards each other, going about arm in arm and embracing, though I never saw such outward affection between a man and a woman. I would often ask 'where is your wife?' to be told that she was at home, she was very understanding, she has many children. My main contact with women was in shops or in the market place. They tended to appraise me, even stare. I think my size, though not particularly large by Western standards, amazed them. I never saw any women in the bars at night.

Along the Rejang River, there are tribal longhouses, some of which have now become little more than tourist ghettoes. I stayed in one belonging to the Kayan tribe, where about fifty families shared communal chores and facilities. Having the bare minimum with me, I had a problem when my period arrived unexpectedly. The women were great, laughing with me, lending me sarongs and pointing me in the direction of the river to wash. The younger men were away for a few months working the paddy-fields. The women worked the rice on bamboo mats in bare feet to separate it from the husk. They also made wonderful handicrafts, embroidered bamboo hats, baskets decorated with a pattern of beads in which they carried their babies. It is customary to take people some gifts, but packet cigarettes are not appreciated because they prefer their home-grown mix, wrapped in a fine piece of bamboo. They make rice wine and all visitors are generously treated.

I had a very amusing time, staying in the headman's room, drinking, smoking and communicating by hand actions, as no one spoke English. I discovered that some children, usually the eldest boys, were now getting formal education in the interior but that this was rather dependent upon the need to include children in the agricultural workforce. I was proudly told of one English teacher, Miss Leslie, who was known and loved by all around Kapit – about four hours up the Rejang River by express boat – and whose fame had obviously spread far and wide.

I did not find religion very dominant, although I was always aware of its presence. Some Malays joked with me that they were Chrislam (Christian/Islam) because they drank beer and smoked, yet would never touch meat. They would go to the mosque occasionally, as suited, or pay their respects when somebody died. I often saw women in the mosques, at all times of the day, sometimes veiled for prayer. There are some interesting Chinese Buddhist temples too, but I rarely saw anyone praying in them. There are still a lot of practising Christians, evidence of British missionary education. The old missionary churches, mainly Methodist or Anglican, remain, but most of them now only provide cheap and relatively clean accommodation.

I highly recommend a visit to the Niah caves, to the Orang-utan sanctuary and climbing Mount Kinabalu, the highest mountain in South-East Asia. If you like adventure and being outdoors, don't let the expense of Borneo put you off. It is becoming more accessible though when I was there, I still felt like an explorer.

TRAVEL NOTES

Language Bahasa Malay is the national language, with minority Chinese and Tamil: English is widely spoken in West Malaysia.

Guides Geoff Crowther and Tony Wheeler, *Malaysia, Singapore and Brunei – A Travel Survival Kit* (1982). Again most travellers' first investment.

Travel Excellent railway from Singapore to Kuala Lumpur and on to Thailand; 30-day rail pass available for tourists. Good taxi and bus services. Hitching possible but *not* recommended. The cheapest flight to Sarawak and Sabah from Peninsular Malaysia is from Johore Bahru. Travel in Eastern Malaysia is mostly by boat and irregular buses – but watch out for air-conditioned buses, you'll freeze.

Accommodation Youth hostels mostly provide good clean, cheap accommodation and so do Chinese hotels; YWCA in Georgetown is reasonable though inconveniently situated out of the city. Hotel prices tend to fluctuate, so check with railway stations and tourists offices who usually have up-to-date lists. On Sarawak and Sabah good places to stay are the tribal longhouses though some are now becoming packaged exclusively to tourism; otherwise accommodation (and everything else) in this area is very expensive.

Special problems Monsoons – plan the time of your visit carefully, especially to Eastern Malaysia. Drug penalties are extremely severe.

CONTACTS

There is a Malay Women's Movement but we haven't received any information on its activities – or a contact address. You may be interested in talking to **The Consumers' Association of Penang**, an independent organisation involved in the protection of consumers' interests, which does a lot of research into the specific problems of women. Areas of study and campaigning include nutrition, housing, environmental balance and the exploitation of women in the media.

Sahabat Alam Malaysia, 37 Lorong Birch, Penang (04 376 930) are a Third World development and ecology group affiliated with Friends of the Earth.

BOOKS

Mum Simgrafik, *Where Monsoons Meet: A History of Malaya* (Marram/Zed Books, 1979). Radical cartoon history.

Redmond O'Hanlon, *Into Borneo* (Penguin, 1984). A good read if you plan to visit East Malaysia, or if you're interested in the region's natural history.

Thanks to Jane Linn for compiling the Travel Notes and to Coral Beadle for introductory information.

THAILAND

Thailand's capital, Bangkok, and resorts like Pattaya and Phuket, are amongst the most touristed spots anywhere in Asia. Over two million people visit Thailand every year, and the last two decades have seen its tourist industry explode. Bangkok's popularity with American soldiers during the Vietnam War initially determined the nature of that industry, and sex tourism is now big business – there are over 300,000 prostitutes in Bangkok alone. All the big resorts too have been extensively westernised, with plenty of expensive shops and luxury hotels, although away from the tourist enclaves, especially in the north, much of Thailand remains rural and undeveloped. For women travellers, it is relatively safe and easy to get around, though you should beware the many thieves and pickpockets in Bangkok. There is sporadic guerrilla fighting in the border areas, but travellers are unlikely to be affected – or allowed into sensitive regions.

Eighty per cent of the Thai population are Buddhist practising Thais, but there are also hill tribes in the north, and a large Malay Muslim minority in the southern provinces. Corruption, military dictatorship, armed coups, student revolts have littered Thailand's recent history. The present government, with the help of US aid and advisers, takes a strict anti-communist line, its main concern being to stifle guerrilla activity along the borders with Laos, Kampuchea and Burma.

The country's huge moves towards Western capitalism have given some women, especially professional middle-class ones, the opportunity of Western-style freedom. But for poorer, rural women the changed economic condition has proved disastrous. The growth of big agribusiness means fewer Thais own and work their own land and to make a subsistence wage many have to sell their labour back to agribusiness and increasingly to the tourist service industries and prostitution. Hundreds of women arrive every month in Bangkok looking for work to help support their families, and often very young, far from home, and desperate for money, they are easy targets for exploitation. Various women's organisations, such as the associations of women doctors and women lawyers, and the National Council of Women, have been campaigning against such exploitation, but it is hard to see the authorities doing anything except continue to turn a blind eye and collect the revenue.

◪ **Katie Cohoon spent four months in Bangkok, whilst working.**

Brash and commercial with a population of around 5 million, Bangkok is Thailand's chief port and cultural and commercial centre. It is also the main centre for prostitution in South East Asia – ironically, the local name, *Krung Thep*, means 'city of angels'.

The city owes this position to the American war in Vietnam when it became the region's principal 'rest and recreation' centre for off-duty GIs. The bars and massage parlours remain and sex is big business in the city. Hub of the infamous red light area is Patpong Road – a street lined with discos, go-go bars, live shows and home for the pimps, con-men and hustlers. It is an area you will probably find disturbing – the exploitation is not concealed – but one I personally didn't try to avoid.

The girls that I met in the bars seemed to have their own sisterhood and a kind of independence because they have broken away from the restraints that society imposes on the more 'respectable' Thai women. In many cases, however, their lifestyle has to be kept secret from the families whom they support. A few of them get a glimpse of another way of life and the chance to escape the trap by moving abroad. Towards me they were very protective, warm, friendly and funny and the brief friendships I shared with them are among my fondest memories of the city.

Away from the more luridly publicised attractions of Bangkok, the city has a lot more to offer. Eating out is one of the best features and an important part of Thai social life. Pick any cuisine from around the world and you will find it here, from fast food burgers to English steak houses to Japanese sushi bars.

The maze of streets in the market areas were perhaps my favourite parts of the city. Dirty and usually extremely smelly, they were also lively, and full of atmosphere. And when the hubbub of the streets got too much, I could always escape to the river. The Chao Phraya river and the network of klongs or canals are important thoroughfares in the city, although the famous floating markets are now little more than shows staged for the tourists. Travelling past the lush vegetation and the shanty-style villages, it is difficult to remember you are in the middle of a vast city. Bangkok lacks open green spaces but about an hour's drive away is the Ancient City – a huge outdoor museum with replicas of many of Thailand's most historic temples, palaces and monuments. A peaceful break from the metropolis, the parkland is stunning and the atmosphere calm and tranquil.

The old cliché East meets West comes true in Bangkok. As hundreds join the traffic queues before they start work in their air-conditioned offices, saffron-robed Buddhist monks can be seen begging for their early morning alms as they have done for centuries. Amongst the glass and concrete of the tower blocks, crowds still gather before the ancient shrines to offer gifts and prayers before their gods. Time is still spent teaching the traditional steps and stories in the graceful art of classical Thai ballet. Behind the hectic pace of modern life and the trappings of Western society, you can still find the elegance and splendour of another culture, the shadow of another age.

◩ **Sarah Coxon spent three weeks with a male friend trekking in Northern Thailand and visiting the villages of the hill tribes.**

To the north and west of Chiang Mai, once Siam's capital, are rolling forested hills occupied by tribes who for centuries have wandered through the area regardless of national boundaries. There are many tribes, of whom the most prominent are the Lisu, Akha, Karen and the Meo. Each preserves its highly individual customs and identity. The main cash crop for many is opium, but this is now being rivalled by tourism as a source of income. As a result, the politics of the region are complex. For a long time little attention was paid to the tribes' activities, but increasing pressure from the American government to stem the flow of heroin has brought the communities into the public eye. Programmes were started to encourage them to grow new cash crops which they could sell themselves, rather than opium whose profits and production are mostly controlled by the powerful Kung Sa and his local Shan private army. These changes have been widely resisted and although Thai troops have been used to try and combat the trading their main effect has probably been to corrupt the region still further.

There are frequent stories of parties of tourists being mugged by armed bandits, but from my own experiences I would say that though there is a certain element of danger, if sufficient care is taken you are unlikely to encounter any serious trouble. Organised tours tend to steer clear of the problem areas and if you're travelling alone, the local people are happy to advise you of any particularly sensitive places to avoid. Increasingly a visit to the hill tribes is on everyone's itinerary during their stay in Thailand and the main centre for such a trip is Chiang Mai, about twelve hours' north of Bangkok by train. Here guides and organised tours abound, almost at every guest house. Tours usually last five days and follow the format of daytime trekking and nights spent in a selection of villages. However, such tours can be very sterile affairs as they tend to visit the same villages over and over again. These are now little more than human zoos, putting on traditional clothes and doing dances when the tourists come.

We decided to avoid such a group tour and to go it alone. We headed north by bus to Fang where we met a guide who talked us into taking a trip to visit a Black Lahu tribe in the hills nearby. After an easy day's walk we reached the village, which was made up of ten or so bamboo huts built on stilts.

The people of the tribe were very welcoming, especially the children, who were far from overawed by our presence. From an early age they take on many of the responsibilities of their elders, and even the youngest ones spoke freely to adults and were afforded the respect of equals in conversation. We never saw a child being chastised or forced to do anything against its will. However, older girls were expected to look after the babies of the village whilst their parents worked in the fields. It was not uncommon to see a girl of under 10 walking around smoking a cigarette and carrying a baby on her back. The women tended to perform more traditional roles of child-rearing, cooking and the manufacture of clothes. However, they also seemed to have a say in community decisions and in one or two villages a form of matriarchy appeared to be in operation.

In the evening a communal meal was prepared by our guide with food he had brought from the town. This seemed to be the village's reward for putting up with us. Afterwards our guide interpreted their questions – where we were from, were we married, how many children we had. The fact that we had none caused some bemusement and even suspicion, but that quickly turned to pity.

There seems no reason why lone women should not travel in this area although I think it would be safer for two women to travel together. The travellers I talked to had encountered practically no sexual harassment but were very wary of soldiers who seem to be able to do what they like. On one occasion whilst we were in a Meo village, three soldiers arrived and accused us of smoking opium, obviously hoping for a bribe. We pretended not to know what they were saying and asked about their guns and they let the matter drop. Later we found them vomiting outside our hut, a sign that they themselves had been smoking opium.

On the whole I thoroughly enjoyed my stay in Northern Thailand, although there are places there now which led me to wonder at times if it was morally defensible to be there as a tourist at all. I would hope that those who do explore this area do so with a conscience, and try not to pollute it further.

◤ **Catherine Black spent three weeks in Thailand, travelling alone.**

There are two very different kinds of tourism in Thailand. The independent travellers, the more affluent (and generally more sensitive) descendants of the hippies, create resorts in their own image, staying 'native style' in local, often pretty basic, beach bungalows. Come on a package deal, though, and you'll probably have a stay in the capital combined with a developed resort, usually Pattaya or Phuket. If it's Phuket you're lucky – though increasingly popular it remains generally relaxed. Pattaya is something else. Having spent most of my time in the country 'roughing it' I went there for a change, to be pampered in a hotel and relax on a beach getting a suntan. I would be reluctant to go again.

The problem is not so much the town – which with its plush hotels and upmarket shops, restaurants and nightclubs could be any westernised beach resort – as the tourists. Most of them tend to be middle-aged, European men, and you see them walking arm-in-arm with their latest under-18 Thai girl. It would be hard not to find the pattern of exploitation offensive and there is quite obvious resentment shown by locals to the Westerners who have turned their town into a brothel.

I spent one long evening discussing the problem with some of the hotel staff. The men seemed very concerned about the numbers of Thai girls who had taken to prostitution, as they saw it, as the easiest (only) way towards independence. The women were equally concerned, sensing that prostitution as a way of life for so many is bound to make it harder for women to get any other sort of employment.

To my own way of travelling, as a single woman, the staff (like so many Thais), expressed incomprehension. Not with my right or ability to do so but at my wanting to, alone. They expressed concern, too, that I might be mugged or attacked, above all in Bangkok. But I found that dressing inconspicuously and never carrying any more cash (or apparent wealth) than necessary made me an unlikely target for such attacks.

I never came across any deliberate or aggressive sexual harassment, either. Western women, especially with blonde hair and blue eyes, can however expect to be stared at, pointed at, and sometimes touched – by women as well as men. Thai people seem to have a childlike fascination with *farangs* (foreigners), which provides an initial boost to the ego and then quickly becomes irritating. But it *is* just simple curiosity, not intended to be rude or sexually intimidating, and has to be accepted. To lose your temper, the height of bad manners in Thai society, would be unreasonable and would achieve nothing.

TRAVEL NOTES

Language Thai and tribal languages; English is the language of tourism.

Transport It's easy to get about. There's a good bus and rail service, both with air-conditioned coaches. Cities have local bus services and plenty of taxis. The one real problem (other than expense) is theft: try to avoid night travel and wear a moneybelt for valuables. Be wise too to the practise of drugging food served on long night trips to ease theft.

Accommodation Wide network of cheap hotels and dormitories, and camping, in most towns, resorts and in the National Parks. Real luxury, too, if you want, or can afford it.

Special problems Smoking opium in Thailand is cheap but illegal: if caught the best you can hope for is a hefty bribe (as much as $2,000 for heroin possession). Thai jails are to be taken seriously.

Guides Joe Cummings, *Thailand – A Travel Survival Kit* (Lonely Planet, 1984). Practical and useful, though like all Lonely Planet guides, its success is in some ways a drawback – the guide *is* the independent travel circuit. *The*

Insight Guide to Thailand (APA Publications) is good on cultural/historical background.

CONTACTS
Friends of Women, 2/3 Soi Wang-Lang Arunamarin Road, Bangkok 10700. Independent group made up of both men and women which seeks to understand the condition of women in Thai society. Activities include counselling on women's rights, setting up women's groups, running an information service and publishing a quarterly magazine.

BOOKS
David Elliott, *Thailand: Origins of Military Rule* (Zed Books, 1979). The political background to Thailand's present form of government.

BURMA

Burma is very different to the rest of South-East Asia – long isolated from the rest of the world and suffused in Buddhist tradition. It is well worth visiting even though you can only stay there on a seven-day visa – a system strictly enforced by the authorities and which (with Burmese public transport) ensures that foreign visitors get to see only a small part of the country. Travel in fact can seem like playing a very complicated boardgame, with the time limit, and with the bureaucracy of the government agency, *Tourist Burma*. But sexual harassment is almost unheard of and it is probably one of the safest, easiest countries in South-East Asia for women travellers.

By its policy of isolation, Burma has distanced itself not only from the effects of mass tourism and Western-style consumerism but also from the damaging power struggles of the region. It does however have serious internal troubles – various tribal groups, notably the Shan and Kachin, have been in open conflict with the government for many years, fighting for secession from the Burmese Union. Despite massive armed spending and regular military offensives against them, the guerrilla forces now control considerable areas in the north and west of the country, successfully supporting their activities with banditry and opium smuggling. The national economy meanwhile is in a state of ongoing crisis. A massive, unwieldy bureaucracy, dominates all aspects of Burmese life, and there's a booming black market.

Under the socialist regime, **Burmese women** have equal status with men and, in law, equal rights. Women certainly seem free in their public lives: they don't change their name on marriage and can be seen in all types of work, including in building sites and road gangs. Against this, there's the fundamental Buddhist belief in the concept of hoon, the male religious essence which places men on a higher plane to women. Safeguarding the hoon of her husband/father/son is part of a woman's duty and as spiritual ritual is central to Burmese life, it inevitably dominates all her social relationships. In the home her inferior status to men is reinforced by the image of 'little woman' she is supposed to act out: at a dinner party, for instance, she and her daughters do not participate in the meal but wait on husband and guests. So far we've been unable to find any information regarding women's organisations in Burma.

◤ **Delia Pemberton helped escort a two-week Christmas holiday tour to Burma and Thailand.**

Specialist travel companies like the one I worked for run group holidays in South-East Asia which incorporate tours of Burma. These tend to be very expensive, but it's not a bad idea to consider a prebooked tour for the Burma portion of a longer trip, even if you're not normally a 'package tour' person. This is because Burmese bureaucracy is geared to the concept of group travel, and hotel/transport booking is allocated accordingly. The independent traveller can run into difficulties, particularly during the November to February 'high season'.

Arrangements for a tour of Burma can be made through a number of British/Australian/American 'Adventure travel' agencies, and also in Bangkok and Singapore. Groups are normally small, ours (of 16) was the largest we encountered, so it's hardly mass tourism. A typical tour takes in the Burma 'loop', starting and ending in Rangoon, with a succession of internal flights to Pagan, Mandalay and Heho (for Inle Lake and Taunggyi). Independent travellers also loop from Rangoon (you're legally obliged to spend your last night there to make sure you don't overstay your visa) but would probably find it difficult to visit all these sites. In theory it's possible to 'do-it-yourself' in a week, but the time spent arranging transport/accommodation might not leave much over for having fun. I'd love to go back on my own, but would definitely only attempt to visit one or two places – that way, I feel, the laid-back Burmese attitude could be a source of enjoyment rather than frustration.

What makes Burma really special is almost indefinable – a sense of peace and tranquillity which seems to permeate every aspect of life, springing from the nation's deep devotion to Buddhism. Over 90 per cent of its 30 million population are adherents of the faith, and its precepts govern every aspect of their lives. It's impossible to overstress this influence. One example of it was the national argument which took place prior to the introduction of insecticides, when a powerful Buddhist lobby opposed the innovation on the grounds that the taking of any life, however small, was against the teaching of the Law.

Pagodas, which house Buddha relics, are the focus of Burmese religious life and to some extent a symbol of national identity – in Mandalay alone there is said to be one to every dozen of the city's population. Sometimes the pagoda complexes contain shrines, not only to Buddha but also to *nats*, the native Burmese spirits. The little house-like structures attached to trees or standing at the side of the road are also nat shrines – evidence of the survival of ancient beliefs in the heart of Buddhist Burma. Most Burmese people say that they 'don't believe' in the nats, but nearly every house will have a coconut hanging from its south-eastern corner pillar for Min Mahagiri, the house nat, and even the devout Buddhist undertaking an important step like a journey or examination is likely to make an offering to the appropriate spirit.

All Burmese people, men and women alike, are expected to enter a monastery at least once in their lives in order to study the Buddha's teachings. As Buddhism regards women as being inferior to men, however, nuns are not allowed to preach, but otherwise live exactly as the monks do, owning the same minimal possessions, shaving their heads and eyebrows, begging for their food, and living a life of prayer and meditation. Monasteries, although principally religious institutions, also fulfil important social functions, providing educational facilities, healing and shelter for the old. Today, there are around 13,000 monasteries in Burma, and a quarter of a million people living the monastic life.

The Burmese are the nicest people you are ever likely to meet – kind, gentle and considerate – and there is a calm and delicacy about everything they do that I often found very moving. (At other times, it made me painfully aware of my own clumsiness!) After years of being molested to distraction around Egypt and North Africa, I had come to regard harassment, like tummy upsets, as a normal hazard of overseas travel. In Burma, it just doesn't happen – during my stay I wasn't bothered once. It was quite a heady experience to be able to wander alone and at leisure through the streets, markets and monuments. Not that I wasn't approached – like all tourists (who are still quite a rare sight in Burma) I attracted great interest, but soon realised that people who stop you in the street really aren't after anything more than a chat that gives them a chance to practise their English.

Of all the countries I have travelled in, including mainland Europe, Burma is the one place I'd have no qualms about returning to alone. Since my return, I've spoken to other women who've been there, and they were of the same opinion. Obviously it makes sense to take normal safety precautions, like not going out alone late at night (there isn't anywhere to go, anyway), but with common sense and good manners (politeness is extremely important in Burma) you should have no problems at all. Except for the problem every traveller to Burma shares – you can only stay for a week.

TRAVEL NOTES

Language *Birman* (Burmese) and over 100 different languages and dialects; many Burmese also speak some English.

Transport There is no legal overland route into Burma, so entry has to be either by air or sea. Transport in Burma is dependent on weather and political conditions, but basically you can travel by air (Rangoon to major centres – don't be put off if you see ground crew pushing the plane), rail (Rangoon to Mandalay, Thazi, Prome and others) and river steamer (Rangoon to Pagan, Mandalay, Minghla, etc). Road transport, trucks or buses can be erratic.

Accommodation Varies greatly in standard; *Tourist Burma* in Rangoon can help with bookings. YWCA in Rangoon is good.

Guide Once again Tony Wheeler – *Burma – A Travel Survival Kit* (Lonely Planet, 1984). Invaluable for the possibilities of 7-day circuits and packed with off-beat information.

Special problems Bureaucracy – both entering the country (make sure your visa dates are exact) and travelling around it (all financial transactions must be recorded on a declaration form). Changing money on the black market isn't recommended though a lot of travellers exchange or sell goods. Malaria precautions are essential. So is health insurance.

CONTACTS
No information received.

BOOKS
Mi Mi Khaing, *The World of Burmese Women* (Zed Books, 1984). Sensitive portrait of women in Burma today.
For colonial background, George Orwell's *Burmese Days* (1949, Penguin, 1967).

Thanks to Carmel Pavageau.

INDONESIA

Indonesia extends over a vast chain of some 3,000 islands, of which the most commonly visited are Bali and Java. Although remote and exotic as far as Europeans and Americans are concerned, it is the nearest form of abroad to millions of Australians and New Zealanders. This means that there's an established package-tour industry (with developments particularly along the beaches of Bali), while all the better-known islands also have extensive networks of basic cheap accommodation and are well used to independent travellers. Indonesians are predominantly Muslim but their style of Islam is quite liberal and tolerant and you are unlikely to encounter the sort of aggressive sexual harassment that is directed at women travellers in some parts of Malaysia.

Indonesia is a country rich in resources but generally the standard of living is very low, exacerbated by an ever-growing population – particularly on the island of Java, whose capital, Jakarta, is the nation's administrative centre. Java's influence – the 'sistem Jakarta' – is resented, and often disparaged as the successor to Dutch colonial rule. The islands have an image of relative political stability, and the various cultures and religious groups appear to peacefully co-exist. But the underside of this is the harsh, swift and often brutal suppression of any opposition to General Suharto's regime. Resistance to the forced military colonisation of East Timor and West Irian has been crushed by systematic mass murder.

Indonesian women seem more independent and visible than in most Islamic countries. The islands' interpretation of Islam does not demand that women are veiled; government schools are co-educational and there is relatively little discrimination between the sexes with respect to subjects studied and the number of years spent studying. Whether this will endure is uncertain. Despite government curbs, Islamic fundamentalism has recently gained ground, attempting to re-affirm Malay culture in opposition to Western influence.

There is a long tradition of organisation among Indonesian women. Voluntary women's groups have played an increasingly important role in the provision and delivery of social welfare services throughout the country. The Indonesian Women's Congress, a federation of the main **women's organisations** originally set up in 1928 and known as *KOWANI*, runs a 'legal literacy' programme and helps rural women to understand legal rights (such as the legal stipulations surrounding polygyny and forced marriages included in the 1974 Marriage act). Besides campaigning for a more uniform marriage law that will not only limit but prohibit polygyny, child marriage and arbitrary male-initiated divorce, KOWANI is also lobbying for equal inheritance laws and has autonomous groups focusing on a range of issues including reform of the abortion laws. In some areas these groups have to operate amidst considerable (and escalating) harassment from the emerging Islamic Fundamentalist Movement.

▨ **Maria Maw has visited Indonesia twice recently, for a total of six months. She travelled alone, mostly in Java.**

Arriving in Indonesia, and particularly Java, because it is Muslim, densely populated and less popular with tourists than Bali, can be something of a culture shock. Most visitors will be bombarded by a hassling mob of taxi *becak* (a tricycle with covered passenger seat) and bus-drivers. Here the first and hardest lesson begins: loss of privacy. Indonesian people have little concept of personal space and they are curious about other people, especially Westerners, whom they have definite ideas about from the media. They (usually men) will ask numerous questions about you and your reasons for travelling, and for a person alone these are always preceded by, 'Where are your friends?' A single Western women is generally regarded on the one hand with pity for her loneliness and on the other with admiration for her bravery. A traveller who can temporarily sacrifice her privacy and welcome what is basically friendly interest will be rewarded with unconditional acceptance and hospitality.

As I learnt to relax with people in mutual acceptance and trust, I became increasingly aware of the beauty that surrounded me. Java is lush and extremely fertile due to the lava-rich soil washed down by heavy rains from its blue-tinged volcanoes. Most of the land is cultivated; the low-lying country is terraced to form paddy-fields, intricate patterns of watery mirrors which later become emerald seas of rice shoots; the mountain slopes are planted in neat rows of cassava, rubber, coffee, tea and hardier fruits and vegetables, all interspersed with pockets of bamboo and canopied, tropical forests.

The majority of people work on the land as there is little industry or even mechanisation. Local government and tourism are the other major employers. For an over-populated island there is surprisingly little unemployment and few beggars. The Javanese are incredibly enterprising, creating their own employment and sharing what they earn within the family. Those who can afford to feed someone else will often take in a poorer person (usually a young woman from a large family in a nearby village) as a home-help. There is very little job discrimination between the sexes, men and women work together, with the exception of housework and the uniformed forces. I was struck by the sense of family and community, and the love, friendship and respect which is communicated within these. The magic ingredient seemed to be the unique (to me) way of socialising children. They are considered small people, their needs and opinions are respected and they are seldom excluded from adult company. Babies are carried almost continually, and children are cared for not only by their family but by all their relatives and friends. A baby's cry is a rare sound and I have only seen one child physically punished.

The government plays a significant role in the lives of all Indonesian people, although many are unaware of its subtle influences and intimidations. It uses advertising campaigns and sporadic educational schemes to promote health, smaller families, agriculture, and the transmigration of people from overpopulated Java to other islands. The national flag, emblem and a list of the five basic principles of the *Panca Sila* (the country's philosophy which is based on one God, one nation, one people, democracy and equality) are displayed everywhere.

In order to exert its influence and to monitor any subversive activities even in the remotest islands, the government uses a system based on the communal nature of people's lives. Each household is part of a *kampung* a small community similar to a village, and kampung leaders meet regularly to discuss community issues. Information is passed up and down through these meetings, usually down. Other political gathering is prohibited for fear of communism, and, for fear of being labelled a communist, people will refuse to talk about politics except with close, trusted friends. An economics student at the university explained to me her frustration at not being able to discuss honest political opinions, even in tutorials. The majority of the people live in ignorance and fear of the corrupt bureaucratic system and the armed forces.

There are exceptions to the government's prohibition of political groups, and one of them is an organisation called *Dharma Wanita*.

Membership to it is automatic if a woman works for the government or marries a man who does. It reminded me rather of the Women's Institute, and is primarily involved in social programmes to promote health, education, community spirit and co-operation; like the 'Panca Sila', its ten-point programme is displayed in conspicuous places, although there is no reference to women in it. The Dharma Wanita presides over similar women's organisations which are open to all women, but I personally saw little evidence of their activities except for a ceremony on Kartini Day.

Every year, local groups sing and perform traditional dances on Kartini Day, in remembrance of Indonesia's leading heroine, Raden Adjeng Kartini. The educated daughter of a Javanese major, she wrote letters to her Dutch friends about the social status and lives of Indonesian women, the need for education for girls, and the evils of polygamy and the paternalistic Dutch colonialism. She died, aged 24, in childbirth. In recent years her writing has been revived with the publication of a serious women's magazine called, appropriately, *Kartini*.

The sisterhood of Indonesian women is very evident – women spend a lot of time together, sharing work, childcare, entertainment, confidences, and times of idle leisure. But most tourists have little contact with women other than to be served by them, and it is usually the men who will seek out Westerners and approach them. Other than on buses and trains the most convenient way to meet local people is at a *warung* (a small eating stall with benches) which can be found anywhere, day or night. Women travellers have an advantage over men in that it is acceptable for them to be in women's space as well as men's. But it is up to the woman traveller to make the effort to approach a woman or group of women. Lone women travellers are considered rather odd by both men and women, especially as they are usually older than the average age at which Indonesian women get married. Many women remain baffled by you, but many men seize the opportunity to try their luck, if usually in a fairly good-natured, easily rejected, way.

Unlike most tourists I did not rush through Java, staying a few days here and there and trying to see as many sights as possible between long journeys on stickily-crowded public transport. I stayed in three places, Surabaya, Yogyakarta and Pangandaran and made a few short trips from these. Surabaya is Java's second city, a dirty, decaying, sprawling place vibrating with life, a more typical urban community than Westernised Jakarta. I stayed in a kampung, taught English part-time and mixed mostly with university students, some wealthier than I could imagine, and some barely subsisting whilst maintaining a social image befitting their education. I spent a couple of weeks in Yogyakarta studying the basics of batik painting. In the peaceful, relaxed fishing town of Pangandaran, where the sun rises and sets spectacularly over the ocean, I practised batik with a local friend and took long walks in the nearby jungle and along the miles of deserted palm-fringed beaches. In the evenings locals and tourists would gather in a warung or on the beach beneath the stars, for impromptu parties and music sessions.

I have a few unpleasant memories: occasional longings to meet an English-speaking woman and a couple of nervous nights as the only westerner in a *losmen* (guesthouse) with men prowling around outside my room. But these were exceptions, now half-forgotten in the myriad of memories of times spent alone with Indonesian people, feeling a part of the harmonious flow and cycle of life.

TRAVEL NOTES

Languages Bahasa Indonesia is the national language and its pidgin, pragmatic structure easy to learn; over 200 other languages and dialects among ethnic groups. Younger people and the tourist industry generally speak some English.

Transport Boats and *bemos* (buses) are plentiful and cheap; hitching is uncommon but possible and relatively safe.

Accommodation Wide range – from luxury hotels to beach-huts.

Guide Bill Dalton, *Indonesia Handbook* (Moon Publications, US, 1984 update). A classic guide – so fascinating that it has been banned for sale in Indonesia (though you can carry it in).

CONTACTS
Organisan Wanita Jakarta Raya, (**KOWANI**) Jalan Diponegoro 26, Jakarta, Pusat. See introduction.

BOOKS
Raden Adjeng Kartini, *Letters of a Javanese Princess* (Heinemann Asia). Letters of an early Indonesian feminist and national heroine.

Nina Epton, *Magic and Mystics of Java* (1974). Interesting travelogue with anthropological slant.

Vicki Baum, *A Tale from Bali* (Oxford University Press).

Hamish McDonald, *Suharto's Indonesia* (Fontana, 1980). Thorough political account of events since 1965.

Minority Rights Group, *Women in Asia* (MRG, 1982). Contains an interesting section on Indonesian women.

New Internationalist magazine, no 116. Useful on background, with a range of Indonesian interviews.

Thanks to Gwyneth Jones.

THE PHILIPPINES

The Philippines, with its beautiful beaches and spectacular mountain scenery, is commonly packaged and promoted as a tropical island paradise. But beyond the luxury hotels of Manila and the fashionable resorts of Luzon and Cebu, are the pervasive signs of gross exploitation and unmitigated poverty. Most cities are bordered by sprawling, poverty-stricken ghettoes where unemployment has reached an unprecedented level. And on many of the islands where huge agribusiness conglomerates have dispossessed rural Filipinos, poverty and deprivation are even more intense.

How much of this will change – and how quickly – with the revolutionary ousting of Ferdinand Marcos is hard to predict. At the time of writing, Corrie Aquino, the new president voted in and then installed by 'peoples' power', has made important gestures towards the urban poor and in favour of rural land reform. But however genuine – and impressive – her personal credibility, the will to change has to overcome a political infrastructure that remains (even in Manila) relatively little changed. Twenty years of dictatorship don't disintegrate overnight, at least with the chosen 'democratic' path. And Philippine government authority in any case doesn't stretch throughout the islands: large tracts of the nation were 'liberated', well before Aquino, by the communist New People's Army – and *their* status is equally unsure.

As far as the visitor goes, if you travel outside the tourist enclaves you're likely to find yourself an object of curiosity, but treated with courtesy and generosity by Filipinos, especially by the women. The population is largely Roman Catholic, the indigenous Malay culture having been subsumed by first Spanish and then American influences. Transport can be inefficient and uncomfortable but it is generally safe. Travelling around, though, you shouldn't underestimate the problems of dealing with extreme heat and the general lack of food. You will automatically be warned away from the no-go areas where armed insurrection is making gains. At the moment these are limited mainly to the islands in the south but the war is spreading.

The growth of agribusiness and of labour-intensive industries like textiles and electronics was engineered by the Marcos government to tap the country's resources of cheap labour. One of the worst results of their policy are the 'free trade zones', where workers, often housed behind high wire fences, live in dormitories, sometimes even sharing a bed as one or other is always working. Most of the workers in these zones are women – preferred for their docility and nimble fingers. Some have recently unionised and there have been sporadic strikes and other forms of resistance. But these have been swiftly and brutally suppressed by employers. Wages remain unbelievably low and basic labour rights (sick leave, holidays, maternity leave) consistently denied. In addition, Filipino women's participation in public life and politics is almost non-existent. In law their rights are restricted, in relation to property, legal separation and widow's rights.

There is a national Philippines **Women's Movement** called *Gabriela* which is achieving a high profile across the islands. They are confronting major structural issues like liberation from dictatorship and American imperialism, and aim to mobilise women for development and peace in the face of economic crisis and increasing militarisation.

Karen Crane spent eight months in the Philippines, living with a village family in the northern province of Illocos Sur, and travelling alone around the islands.

I had only planned to spend two days in the Philippines en route for Australia and ended up staying eight months. On a cold, snowy Saturday in early February, I arrived at Gatwick Airport with my rucksack, a ticket to Manila and the address of a dormitory there. During the flight, I began to get very nervous about arriving in a country I knew nothing about, but when the plane landed and I realised there was no turning back, I suddenly felt strong and confident – ready to take on the world if necessary. This was lucky, as the customs official said to me as I walked through 'You must be very careful. The people here are not good.' I found out later that this was a common attitude held by those in positions of power towards the poor.

Coming out of the terminal building, I was mobbed by people clamouring for my baggage and custom. The culture shock was immense, I felt totally disorientated and only managed with great difficulty to select one of them. The drive from the airport was a moving experience for two reasons, the first being the setting of a very large sun of flaming red which appeared to take up the whole sky. I felt as though it was shining for me and took great comfort in this. The second was that we drove through the tourist belt and then in stark contrast the shanty towns with massive potholes in the road, with people lying in the street either resting or too weak to move, and every few yards a stall selling anything from fishballs to green mangoes and salt. Common to both areas were the *jeepneys*, brightly coloured jeeps holding up to twelve people with ornate models and tassles adorning their bonnets, and the pollution from their exhaust fumes.

My arrival at the dormitory, in Sampaloc, created a sensation. It was a women's dormitory and the residents were very curious about me and seemed to find my presence a great honour. They wanted to do my washing and cooking and generally look after me and I began to feel trapped. I tried to explain that I had little money and did not expect this sort of treatment. But I soon realised that they were just happy and proud to take care of me and in return to introduce me to all their friends and family. The living conditions also took some getting used to: I found myself washing in cold water, squatting over the toilet and sleeping on a bed which seemed like a table. At first I just wanted to go home; but one morning, squatting on the loo, I decided to stop being negative and make the most of every minute of my stay in the Philippines.

It worked, for the next day I found myself on a bus, accompanying an old woman called Nana Conching, who had been staying at the dormitory with her daughter, to her home in the northern province of Illocos Sur. It was an eight-hour journey and the bus was loaded with sackfuls of goods bought in the capital, which were tossed off at stops along the way. Buses coming into Manila from the provinces are similarly loaded, with sacks of garlic, tobacco, peanuts, sugar cane and also goats, piglets and chickens besides the passengers. These bus journeys are definitely not for anyone with a weak stomach. On another eight-hour journey, I sat on a sack of garlic the whole way, its smell mingling with the sweat of the passengers. There are a few air-conditioned buses, but they are too expensive for most local people. In this as in most things, the poor in the Philippines are very definitely at the bottom of the heap.

My first journey ended at Sinait, a beautiful *barrio* (village) by the sea, set among palm trees and banana plantations and with houses built of bamboo. My appearance again caused great excitement – especially among the women and children, who called me 'Americana'. As in the dormitory, few could speak English, but I felt immediately at ease among them as they gathered round me. The children were apprehensive at first but soon came to say 'hello', which many of them knew. I spent that first evening in Sinait on the beach, watching the sun set.

On the surface it seemed like paradise, but the reality was very different. The quaint-looking houses were practical but not comfortable and contained only the bare necessities. Cooking was done outside on a fire in all weathers, even in monsoon rain or when a typhoon was blowing. The women were expert at keeping the fire going, even with wet wood. There was no proper water supply, sanitation was poor and the electricity supply erratic. Apart from farming and fishing, there were no jobs except for a few teachers in local primary schools. Most people owned a patch of land and a carabao, a very powerful animal which was used to pull the plough.

During the time I spent travelling among the islands of the Philippines, I learned the art of survival in an under-developed country, where the hardship caused by absolute poverty is almost unimaginable to the average person from the West. Yet the people, particularly women, seem incredibly positive in spite of everything, and they welcomed me into their families once they discovered I was no kind of a threat to them. I have an unqualified admiration for Filipino women who seem to spend their whole lives in a completely circumscribed manner. Little girls cannot do many things boys are allowed to do; their education is seldom taken seriously and when they marry, as almost all do, their husbands will very likely take their labour and support for granted. Most women have about six children, whom they must bring up with very little money or food, spending their days in domestic chores and agricultural labour. Meanwhile the men can while away time drinking rice or sugar cane wine, gambling and smoking. Marijuana is illegal, but widely smoked. Some men do work very hard on the land, but unemployment has drawn many, sometimes taking their whole families with them, to the city shanty towns.

I stayed in Sinait for nearly two weeks, as the guest of Nana and her daughter. After returning to Manila to extend my visa, I then spent nearly two months travelling to other islands, but all the time thought of Sinait and finally went back there for the remainder of my stay in the Philippines. Nana was 68, a widow for the past ten years. She had eight children, most of whom lived in Sinait. With her lived two daughters, a granddaughter and great-grandson. One daughter, Puring, was a schoolteacher and her small income kept the household going. The house was one big room, the sleeping area partitioned off. I learned to cook rice and vegetables on the outside fire and was soon taking turns to cook. Food was scarce and in bad weather, such as a typhoon when fish could not be caught, rice (and leaves cooked in monosodium glutamate) would be the sole diet.

All water was carried from the well behind the house, and an important part of every day for the women was the washing of clothes. They would collect round the well with very large galvanised iron bowls and wash their faded garments with great care, though the bars of soap would leave craters in their hands. This was where the local news was passed around. Ironing was done on a table, with a heavy iron filled with charcoal – a very difficult operation and whenever I tried ironing my clothes, they became black.

Nana Conching washed, ironed, fetched water, fed the pigs on ground-up trunks of banana palm, and also fed the chickens, guinea pigs and dogs, talking to them as she did so. She planted rice in season, chopped wood, collected crabs on the seashore and pulled in the fishing nets. I came to have the greatest admiration for her. She never complained, was very religious, giving out an aura of calm and strength, and totally devoted to her children. Her English was pretty good, so I came to learn a lot about her life, and during that second stay I tried to show some of my gratitude for her hospitality in helping out with all the chores.

By the time I left Sinait I was suffering physically from malnutrition –

a solid expression of the poverty everywhere behind the Philippines' paradise image. But the experience of living in the barrio will stay with me, and it is the generosity, kindness and openness that I most remember. Just before leaving, Lina, Nana's granddaughter, gave birth and gave her daughter my name.

TRAVEL NOTES

Language Filipino (Tagalog) and numerous local dialects. English and Spanish spoken quite widely in cities and tourist areas.

Transport Boats between islands, and buses around them, are very cheap – though heavygoing. *Jeepneys* (taxis) in towns are also inexpensive.

Accommodation Few if any cheap hotels. In Manila and other cities you can usually find dormitories in the university area. Elsewhere negotiate locally for rooms.

Guide Jens Peters *The Philippines – A Travel Survival Kit* (Lonely Planet, 1983).

Special problems Due to the continuing guerilla action, or NPA occupation, many of the southern islands are now impossible (and perhaps unsafe) to visit. Check bulletins and get up-to-date advice.

CONTACTS

Gabriela (Women's Movement), Room 221, PCIB Building, Greenhills Commercial Center, San Juan, Manila.

TO-MAE-W (Third World Movement Against the Exploitation of Women), PO Box SM–366, Manila. Very dynamic organisation, established in 1961 to co-ordinate research and action on issues such as tourism/prostitution, sexism in the media and the plight of women workers throughout the region and the Third World.

Commission for Filipino Migrant Workers and London Philippines Support Group, c/o St Francis of Assisi Community Centre, Pottery Lane, London W11 (Tel. 01-221 0356).

BOOKS

Linda Ty-Casper, *Awaiting Trespass (A Pasión)* (Readers International, 1986). The first of Ty-Casper's novels to be published in the West (and a book which could not be published in Marcos's time). Set in the days before the Pope is due to visit Manila, it combines a personal awakening with powerful social satire.

James Fenton, *The Snap Revolution* in *Granta 18* (Penguin, 1986). A brilliant and extraordinary piece of journalism. Fenton arrived in Manila to cover the phoney election called by Marcos and found himself caught up in events, joining in the looting of the Presidential Palace after the Americans had flown Marcos out. Essential reading if you plan to visit.

Chapter Fourteen

CHINA AND NORTH-EAST ASIA

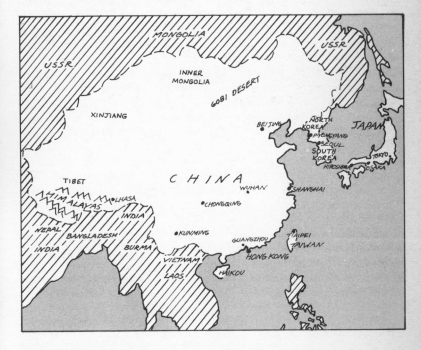

China inevitably forms the largest part of this chapter. Closed to the West for almost thirty years after the 1949 revolution, it has, in the last five, radically changed its stance towards tourism – first admitting 'cultural exchange' tour groups, then, in 1981, beginning to issue visas for independent travel. Today Western currency is a major priority, tourism a growth industry and getting in (through Hong Kong) routine. This is not to say that Chinese travel is straightforward or easy: bureaucracy restricts all spheres of life, public transport can be a struggle and information, even about which cities you can visit, is hard to come by. You will need endurance.

Of the other countries in the region, **Japan** and **South Korea**, as well as **Hong Kong** and **Taiwan**, are all considerably Westernised, with well-established tourist industries. Facilities, however, tend to be geared towards visiting businessmen. Independent travellers will find these places easy to get around but pricey. You may decide to combine travel with work – both Hong Kong and Japan offer secretarial and other possibilities.

Coming from Europe, America, or Australia, probably the biggest problem you will have is in adjusting to the very different social and philosophical attitudes. The cohesion of the extended family unit, which inevitably excludes strangers, takes some getting used to, as do the ever-present crowds and people's blatant curiosity about foreigners. Sexual harassment, however, is not generally a concern, and in China and South Korea it is virtually unheard of.

Throughout the region traditional Confucian beliefs in women's subordinate status and special role as family and home-makers persevere, despite the craze with Western values in Japan and the professed sexual equality in Communist China. In South Korea and Japan the sex industry is big business, and there is equally vicious exploitation in the textile, food processing and computer industries, which rely on cheap, female labour. Developing such industries is an important part of China's modernisation programme, which is a cause of great concern to the All China Women's Federation, an organisation which was set up to protect China's women.

We have been unable to commission pieces on **Taiwan**, which can be visited routinely, nor on **North Korea**, which was virtually inaccessible to Western tourists until 1985. North Korea is now experimenting with tourist groups. We would welcome accounts on both for the next edition of this book.

CHINA

The possibilities of travel in **China** – with its regions as vastly different as Canton and Tibet – can hardly be overestimated. Nor, however, can its difficulties. The road and rail systems are inadequate, food and hotels generally rough, and bureaucratic restrictions (literally) unbelievable: it's hard work. But take confidence from the fact that you won't be alone. For Australians a trip to China, or at least into Canton is now an established part of the long-haul route to Europe, and increasingly popular as an individual destination. And harassment is unlikely to be a problem; 'hooliganism', which includes sexual harassment, carries a 7-year prison sentence and rape can be punishable by death.

You can get into the country most easily through Hong Kong, where a number of operators issue visas along with a flight to Peking (Beijing) or train ticket to Canton (Guangzhou). Canton, if time is limited, is the easiest part of China to travel: traditionally sophisticated and currently very much the leader in 'Westernising' influences. A more adventurous, and at present highly uncertain, approach is through Nepal into Tibet – itself only recently opened by the Chinese authorities. Once in China most independent visitors want to travel as widely as possible: like India this is a nation of distance and peoples. But bear in mind that itineraries need to be flexible and that the majority of casual Western visitors end up spending less time in China than they had planned. China is not on the whole a country of great monuments (the Communists, like all dynasties before them, have destroyed earlier showpieces) and its cities can seem depressingly drab and uniform.

As far as the **position of women** is concerned, the Confucianist revival and recent development of traditional female labour industries like textiles, food processing and tourism are bound to have a detrimental effect. The Communist era heralded enormous changes for women, but it also institutionalised the problem of dual labour. According to Mao's two zeals, women were expected both to help build the socialist future and fulfil their traditional role of taking care of their families. Many women now have full access to education and employment; contraception is free, abortion legal and divorce instigated by wives common. But the traditional view that women are specially suited to certain jobs (childcare and housework) and incapable of others (anything too mentally and physically taxing), as well as the Confucian ideal of the three obediences (to father, husband, son) are as strong as ever. The clearest and most frightening demonstration of women's subordinate status has been the increase in female infanticide, associated with the introduction of the one-child-per-family policy.

The *All China Women's Federation* was set up in 1949 under the umbrella of the Communist Party and is charged with representing 'the deepest needs and rights of women'. It has been criticised for assuming that the Party line provides all the answers, but many of its local branches are now a crucial source of help and protection for women. Recently, the ACWF has launched a nationwide campaign to inform women of their legal rights, convince them of their own worth (the so-called '4 loves' – self-love, self-respect, self-confidence, self-determination) and prepare them for leadership and financial independence. But it will need positive action by the government if this is to have any impact on the lives of most rural women.

▰ **Alisa Joyce taught English for a year in Beijing and then travelled extensively in the country.**

A Westerner in China is never allowed to forget or ignore her status as a foreigner and outsider. The Chinese language itself reinforces this idea by calling the nation the 'National Family', the people 'the old hundred names' (the 100 common Chinese surnames), and everybody else *wai guoren*, literally 'outside country persons', a generic label for any non-Chinese. As individuals, Chinese men and women turn to the family for support and for the luxury of personal expression; the family turns to the larger work unit wherein they live, learn and work; and these work units turn to the state, the National Family, as the largest common denominator.

As a Westerner, participating in life only to the extent allowed, you stand outside the values and mores of Chinese society. Despite your proximity to the society, and the occasional intimacy with Chinese friends, you cannot share in the family-like security of Chineseness.

'Wai guoren!' the children of my work unit's primary school scream and run away as I approach. It is a game we have played, half-seriously, every morning for two years.

'Because you are not Chinese,' a good friend will say, 'you will never understand China.' Because you are an oddity, you have the freedom to be audacious and carefully iconoclastic. Because some will see you as a role model, however, you must be conservative and culturally sensitive.

A Western woman in China is a prominent and striking example of the differences between West and East. The very fact that she has travelled across the world, away from her mother and 'motherland', without husband or children to cement her in the family structure, makes her an incomprehensible entity to most Chinese. Many will shake their heads in disbelief at the audacity of such liberality. Others, mostly young women straining to come to terms with the world beyond Chinese borders, admire the boldness and regret the social necessity of their own timidity. The confidence and independence that a Western woman may take for granted are sometimes seen in terms of an awesome power and freedom. It is humbling and almost frightening when a young woman student suddenly declares: 'I hope someday I will have the strength to be like you.'

There is an attitude of rueful conservatism among many young Chinese. They acknowledge the disadvantage of the restrictions that both two thousand years of feudal Confucianism and thirty years of Maoist/Marxist morality have placed on them, yet they generally accept the unavoidable: 'It is our habit; we are accustomed to these ways.' Women in China today must still seek fulfilment and social sanction through marriage. The intelligent university student must stifle her superiority for fear it will discourage suitors and she will most frequently choose a man for his social position and earning potential. 'A boyfriend,' in the vernacular of young Chinese, means the man you will marry and therefore relationships between the sexes are taken extremely seriously, even tragically. Two suicide attempts – one successful – by women in my department in 1983 were caused by relationships that were broken off.

The contradictions between theory and practice – in this case between the belief that the advent of Chinese socialism liberated Chinese women from oppression and the reality of an extremely conservative society where women are locked into restrictive roles – create much confusion and frustration. But, like most conflict in China, it is largely a silent and brooding frustration. In teaching a class on American literature, the topic of women's liberation arose and I asked my class their opinion of this problem. A young man spoke immediately. 'In China women are completely liberated and equal to men.' This is the accepted line. I said, 'Okay,' and watched as the women in the classroom silently grimaced and looked at their desks.

Although what we called the 'little cat' syndrome (women who simpered and were coy, living up to archaic conventions of the demure Chinese female, an obedient and sweet *yin* to the masculine *yang*) was prevalent in many Chinese women I met, there was also a courage, perceptiveness and inner strenth. As far as I am aware there is no distinct 'Women's Movement' in China – Chinese have had enough of movements. There are feminists, however, in the sense that many Chinese women are aware of the problems they face. The changes that have transformed the social and economic structure of China during the last thirty years have had a great impact on the role of Chinese women and on their perceptions of that role. But in the past, the priorities of nationalism and modernisation have overridden those of women as an independent social force. Today, with the increasing Western influence on China, new population policies which limit couples to one child, and the acceleration of change in the society and economy, women are slowly beginning to recalculate the ancient yin and yang balance of their society.

As you travel across China you will meet women at all the different levels of this transformation: a young intellectual, knowledgeable of the West and of Western women, curious about our freedom and independence; a factory worker, tough and self-possessed, and proud of her own degree of independence; a peasant whose innate conservatism and ignorance of the world outside her county or village will inhibit change for several generations more.

These women will certainly be curious about you – not as a woman, but just because you are that rarely seen animal, the foreigner. They will stare, some friendly and some hostile and defensive. If you can communicate with them, they will ask endless questions about how much your clothes or Walkman cost, and how much you earn, and why you aren't married. Most will be courteous, but few will understand your desire to leave your family and country and come to China. In seeking out these encounters – with the help of someone who speaks both Chinese and English – you will discover both the graciousness and reticence of Chinese women. As they learn more about you, their concepts of a woman's role will be at least mentally altered; and as you learn about them, your own preconceptions of women's strength and independence may change.

For women travellers, China must be one of the safest countries in the world. Because of your status as a foreigner you are a guest and generally treated with kid gloves. It is only in north-western China, where the population is largely Muslim, that recognisable and troublesome harassment may occur. In these areas it is advisable to wear a scarf on your head, as all Muslim women do, and not to wear clothing which is any way revealing. This advice holds for most of China, actually, as women are modest to an extreme and what may pass as attractive and comfortable in London will be seen as shocking and provocative in China.

Although travelling alone in China would not be dangerous, it is unadvisable. Many areas have been open to foreigners only very recently and the Chinese are excessively curious about their strange, new guests. Wherever you go outside Beijing, Shanghai or Canton, you will be stared at continuously, often surrounded by groups of curious people, followed by crowds and even poked at and prodded. Some travellers don't mind this interest but I found it extremely trying when travelling by myself not to have another Westerner with whom to share the attention.

Travelling in China can be a disappointing, extremely uncomfortable and disillusioning experience if you are not prepared. Most of the cities you will visit are not beautiful, most of the hotels are not comfortable and most of the food is less than appealing. Yet, for me, and for most people I met, the opportunity to travel through this enormous and varied land made the little inconveniences worthwhile. China has not been opened to the curious eyes of the West since the days of the missionaries when Westerners overran the country with their religions and their trade.

In our willingness to endure the discomforts and frustrations of travelling in a country totally unfamiliar with our demands and needs, we are given the chance to penetrate deeper into the heart of the world's oldest civilisation than ever before. Moreover, China in the 1980s is changing rapidly – so quickly that it astonishes even the most radical proponents of change. To observe the evolution of socialism in China, and the coming alive of her population – both men and women – is a very exciting experience. Just approach it with the right attitude: your expectations have to change. You can't expect anything to happen the way you hope or want it to. You have to slow down and not expect efficiency or speed in service, and not hope to keep a tight travelling schedule. You must be flexible in everything.

▨ **Kaye Stearman first visited China in 1982 when she journeyed around central and southern China. She returned recently for a long trip from Hong Kong to Beijing.**

China, like India, does not have landscapes but peoplescapes. Even in the most isolated or desolated regions there are people. In the fertile plains the density of the population is immense, with villages only a mile or two apart. The cities are sprawling, congested areas, with the majority of their inhabitants living in cramped, wooden or brick shacks, or in depressingly uniform and often jerry-built concrete dormitory blocks. Yet although there are people everywhere there is little sense of that confusion and chaos which, to me, characterises India. The numbers of people may be bewildering but their sense of purpose and direction are not. In China there is a system of living and working which may be slow, frustrating and difficult for the Westerner to understand and appreciate, but which nevertheless does work, and most of the time works fairly well. It is a system which ensures that most Chinese are well-fed, adequately clothed, reasonably healthy and fairly productive. By and large it is not a system which is intended to encourage creativity or individuality, except recently in the materialistic sphere.

Yet it is wrong to imagine, as I had done, that the Chinese were merely variations on one pattern. Contrary to the general myth, not all Chinese look, dress and act alike. There are many regional variations both in the physical type, appearance and language. A substantial minority of people are not 'Chinese' at all, like the hill-tribe people in the south or the Turkish people of the west. The drab blue and olive of everyday dress is often relieved by splashes of violent colour – magenta and saffron vests, orange and pink quilted jackets. Babies and young children are bundles of colour and pattern. Nor are the Chinese the commonly depicted mindless, fanatically collective automatons. They can be friendly or cool, curious to the point of infuriation or totally indifferent, ready for a joke or (very occasionally) hostile. I found little of the 'inscrutable oriental' and a far greater degree of spontaneity than I had expected.

Since most Chinese, even in the big cities, rarely if ever have the opportunity to meet or talk with a foreigner, they are still objects of intense curiosity. And curiosity in China can be open, even brazen, and continuous. This is something which most travellers find hard to accept. Being thin and dark probably made it slightly easier for myself, but every foreigner in China must accept that they can never be anonymous, can never blend in with the crowd, and will always be different (this also applies to overseas Chinese). It is this, as much as the restrictions placed by the Chinese government, which is a limiting factor in deciding where to go, but once you accept your own strangeness you can begin to take the constant surveillance in your stride. Staring is not considered especially rude in China, there is little open hostility and most staring is either friendly or merely curious. Generally a smile or greeting to the starer will break the ice, and, refreshingly, the staring is non-sexual, even by young men. I found it irritating, but never offensive or threatening although I met many travellers who couldn't cope with it. The best tactic is to accept it as inevitable and turn it to good account. If people can stare at you, you can also stare at them.

The men I met travelling in China said that they had not met or spoken to any Chinese women apart from those in hotels and shops or introduced through the medium of a man, usually a husband or brother. But I found it very easy to meet men and women and could approach and be approached by both in a spirit of friendly curiosity. Communication was limited as my Chinese was very basic and most women, apart from intellectuals and students, spoke no English. But there was always great curiosity and questioning – about my name, age, nationality, whether I was married and had children, where I was going, what I liked and disliked about China – could go on for hours. A lot of these encounters took place in the long-distance trains, especially in the hard sleeper class which was far less crowded than the hard seat class, and where there was more chance of meeting educated Chinese who were interested to learn all they could of the outside world and/or practise their English. Sometimes this would prove frustrating if I wanted to practise my Chinese. But with a smattering of both languages I usually managed to get the basic facts across. Hotels and cafés also proved a good meeting place, especially the shabby provincial hotels where foreigners were few and dormitory rooms common.

On the outward level I encountered only friendliness and only one case of outright hostility. But I may have been lucky. A travelling companion on my first trip who returned during the 'spiritual pollution' campaign in mid-1983 when foreign influences were discouraged and there was a general crackdown on crime (which resulted in about 10,000 people being executed) found that most people were afraid to associate with foreigners. Chinese people who are friendly with foreigners can later be picked up by the security police and questioned. This is one reason why they tend to be interested mainly in superficial aspects of foreigners' lives and why they are reluctant to talk about the negative aspects of their own. It is my impression that people are freer to communicate in the south of China than in the north where bureaucracy is more pervasive and control tighter. It is always important to remember when speaking to Chinese people that they may be watched by their neighbourhood committees and can be called for questioning by the police. As a foreigner you are unlikely to be affected; they may be.

The people I most easily identified with were the educated ones in their late twenties or thirties. These are the generation who were sent from the cities to the countryside as Red Guards. Most had to leave school early or abandon college and university courses and to accept life in a remote village, often in an area of the country far from their home and with a people whose dialect they found incomprehensible. For most the process was simultaneously exhilarating, bewildering, depressing, disrupting and – ultimately – disillusioning. Some remember the excitement of travelling around China with a group of Red Guards (few Chinese have opportunities to travel), some their shock at primitive village conditions. Others recollect their horror at seeing friends and relatives denounced as counter-revolutionaries. Today the Cultural Revolution is generally regarded as a dreadful mistake which disrupted Chinese society and retarded economic growth. Many former Red Guards have returned to the cities, some are on training courses or have returned to higher education. They were some of the most interesting and critical people I met and although it is worth being circumspect (because of the police as I noted above), you can learn a great deal from the 'wounded'. The new generation of students appears blander, encouraged both to conform and compete.

Some aspects of Chinese life I found immensely annoying. The constant smoking, mainly by men, was one. The dry cold winter and the colds I could never shake off were another. The problems of bureaucracy, especially in Beijing, could be trying beyond patience. The evidence of political repression – in the ubiquitous street photos of trials and executions – is depressing. So too is the pollution-laden air of most cities and the depressing uniformity of most modern architecture. China is a Third-World country and poverty is often visible, although not to the extent or depth of many other countries.

But for me the highlight was the discovery of the Chinese as ordinary human beings, neither to be feared nor idealised. Within the limits of fragmented and sporadic personal communication they are a friendly, spontaneous and lively people who deserve better conditions from their government and a better understanding from the outside world. Over the past few years China has slowly opened up to the West. It is up to the traveller to make the best of this small opening and not to abuse or reject it because of the social and political differences. China is not and cannot be a replica of the West, but nor is it a people beyond understanding. I have met many travellers who disliked the Chinese and their way of life and saw their time there as an endurance test. But for me it was only the beginning of a journey into another world, both less foreign and yet more strange than I had imagined.

▉ **Sue Daish spent a month in China, travelling around and also staying with friends in Shanghai where she met Chinese teachers, students and members of the Shanghai Women's Federation.**

I arrived in March, at the tail end of winter, to spend a month visiting Australian friends in Shanghai and exploring as much as time and money would allow. I never once felt threatened in any way, nor did I personally encounter sexual discrimination. I spent about two weeks in Shanghai, probably the most cosmopolitan of Chinese cities, and divided the rest of my time between Beijing, where the Great Wall and the imperial splendour of the Forbidden City are not to be missed, Hangzhou, recommended by many including Marco Polo for the beauty of its lakes and surrounding scenery, and Shaoxing, a canal town famed for its wine and porcelain, and birthplace of the writer, Lu Hsun. I would like to have travelled further afield to see, for example, the spectacularly beautiful karst limestone scenery at Guilin and the renowned terracotta warriors at Xi'an. However, apart from time being short, fellow travellers reported that an outbreak of cholera at Xi'an had resulted in the temporary closure of hotels and that Guilin was now China's top tourist trap. Nevertheless, I covered a lot of ground during my stay and I feel that I could not have crammed much more into my itinerary without becoming completely exhausted.

'In China, no change name, all equal,' commented the clerk at the Foreign Affairs Department in Shanghai when I applied for a travel permit to visit Shaoxing. She noted with amusement that I had taken my husband's name on marriage and reverted to my maiden name on divorce. The Chinese like to convey to foreigners the impression that men and women are regarded as equals and to some extent this is true. Women hold positions at all levels in the state hierarchy and perform jobs in all spheres of employment, including those which were previously regarded as male preserves, like heavy manual labour, building and engineering. However, it appears that traditional attitudes die hard and chauvinism still flourishes, particularly in remote, rural areas. As a reminder of the old days, it is still possible to see little old ladies hobbling along on tiny bound feet, although this barbaric practice is no longer carried out.

I was fortunate to be able to stay with a couple who were English lecturers (officially designated 'foreign experts') at one of the universities in Shanghai, and I was therefore permitted to attend cultural functions arranged for them by the university liaison officer. I participated in a discussion about the role of women in society with two members of the Shanghai Women's Federation, which was set up after the 1949 Revolution to 'protect and assist women and to promote the education of children'. Both women were remarkably frank and open about their activities, which took me by surprise. The Federation acts as a marriage guidance counselling service and birth control advice centre; it aims to help women whose husbands or mothers-in-law have treated them badly and to educate women to recognise the importance of restricting the size of their families to one child only (the alternative being that China would be unable to feed her expanding population). The women admitted that, although the aim of the state was complete sexual equality, it was impossible to educate the entire population to this way of thinking; many couples, particularly those who had grown up since the revolution, were equal partners in marriage and shared the chores and cooking but traditional values frequently prevailed in the rural areas and many women received a raw deal. In the family order, wives often take second place to their mothers-in-law, which causes obvious problems. Nevertheless, the overall tone was one of optimistic determination.

Apart from students and teachers, the only other Chinese I met who openly associated with foreigners were intellectual dissidents, writers and artists who had already blotted their copybooks and had little else to lose. Several of them had spent long periods in jail for openly criticising the state and failing to comply with the government's idea of creative art, and one had since compounded these crimes by marrying a German woman teacher. The state granted him permission to marry an alien but delayed issuing him with a passport and thus he was unable to leave China with his wife when her contract expired – apparently not an uncommon form of harassment and one which led to the breakdown of the marriage. Though an extreme (and unusual) case this illustrates the extent to which the state pervades all aspects of life in China, from where you live and what work you are allocated, to when you may marry and when you may have a child. The regime has, however, become more lenient in recent years towards intellectual dissidents and religious minorities. A new programme of religious tolerance was recently introduced which permits groups of religious minorities to visit sacred shrines in other provinces. I saw several hundred Buddhist pilgrims from Yunnan Province visiting, for the first time, a beautiful temple in Ling Yin, near Hangzhou, over a thousand miles from their home.

Travelling in China is manageable on the whole and sometimes quite pleasant. Difficulties inevitably arise as a result of the language barrier but few problems are insoluble. I travelled long distances by plane to save time but took the train for shorter journeys, which was a good way to meet ordinary people and see some open countryside. Going by bus is very cheap and fine if you don't mind being squashed. The best way to get around Beijing is on a bicycle; pedestrians and cyclists appear to have the right of way over motorists which leads to some lively confrontations, but slow progress if you are in a taxi.

Hotels, although they appear somewhat dilapidated, are generally clean and comfortable and warm, apart from the often cavernous dining rooms which are usually freezing, and the antique plumbing works more often than not. You will probably encounter officious travel agents, surly ticket clerks, sullen waiters and uncooperative shop assistants; you may have to queue for several hours to purchase an air ticket or confirm a reservation and you will become infuriated by the word 'meio' (there aren't any). But for the most part, I found the Chinese people friendly, kind and helpful. On several occasions, I was plucked from the tail of a long queue at the railway station and pushed firmly to the front, and at Shaoxing the woman in charge of the station invited me to wait for the train in the relative luxury of her office and to sip green tea by the pot-belly stove. I was often given the impression of being an honoured guest, and this, among other factors, made journeys that were often hard (and dull) generally enjoyable and certainly worthwhile.

▨ **Ruth Crosskey was one of the first independent travellers to go into Tibet in September 1984. She spent three weeks in Lhasa and a further week travelling in Tibet.**

While I was travelling in China with an Australian friend, Alba, Lhasa was officially opened to individual travellers. We were very excited, obtained the necessary permits and paid the expensive airfare via Chengdu to Lhasa. The flight over great mountain ridges was spectacular and in the distance, we caught a glimpse of Everest.

We spent some time in Lhasa, visiting the great monasteries of Sera, Drepung and Ganden, now decaying and with only a token number of monks. We ate *mamos* – yak-filled samosas – and *chang* – the local beer – and drank butter tea in the little teahouses. We wandered through the mudstreets of old Lhasa, where the houses are decorated with floral designs, attempted to learn Tibetan words from Nepali and Tibetan traders who had come up from Kathmandu and could speak some English, and had a barbecue by the river with some of the other Western travellers who had also rushed to Lhasa as soon as they heard it was open.

Alba and I did not wish to leave Lhasa by the official route – flying back to Chengdu – but to try travelling overland. There are only three real routes. The road back to Chengdu, probably the most spectacular and at least ten days' hard driving over many passes, was graphically described as 'broken'. The road to Kathmandu, about three days' drive and a walk across the border, was not then open to foreigners and a heavy Chinese police presence made truck drivers reluctant to take us as passengers. The only viable option was the north road, two or three days travel across the Tibetan plateau to the city of Golmud, officially 'closed' but a railhead for Chinese supply convoys. Unofficially, we negotiated and paid for tickets on a truck returning to Golmud and bought provisions –

dried noodle soup, green tea, biscuits – and warm clothes. We hoped we wouldn't be caught in the outskirts of Lhasa, the Public Security can make life difficult for foreigners if they wish.

We travelled in a convoy of three trucks, Alba and I in separate cabs. Our drivers were Chinese, only one was literate, and although verbal communication was difficult, we got on well with them, and their attitude towards us was protective. The driving was very hard. Although the road had few steep gradients, it was the roughest I have ever been on, and for long distances I just clung on to the iron bars in front of me and hoped I wouldn't go through the windscreen. The drivers chain-smoked and looked exhausted after ten hours of driving with only a short pause for lunch. The old Russian-built trucks had a tendency to break down. One night my driver had to change a back wheel on the side of the road by the light of a blowtorch. Over particularly rough patches, the bonnet would shake loose and occasionally the engine came near to boiling over. The inadequacies of their lorries, the nonchalance with which the drivers set out to drive one of the most arduous roads in the world made their macho American equivalent look rather silly.

During the day we crawled across sparsely grassed plateaux towards the distant snow-covered ridges. Occasionally we came across herds of yaks and mud-hut settlements with an eating house and diesel pumps. At night we shared the drivers' food and slept in a row on the mattresses in the back of the truck, warmed by each other's bodies. In the morning the drivers would unfreeze the engines with blowtorches and crank-start them and we would be off again.

We arrived in Golmud late at night and our drivers took us to the hotel used by Chinese officials. The next day Public Security registered us and put us on a train to Xining, the capital of the state of Qinghai, which was once part of Tibet, and which we did have permits for. The steam engine pulled us through desert landscape, then grasslands and then dry river valleys, the banks lined with insubstantial trees.

At Xining, quite by coincidence we arrived on the 35th Anniversary of the Founding of the People's Republic of China. Having passed illegally through the state, we were surprised to find ourselves swept into a round of banquets, films, command performances and processions. We became quite accustomed to meeting the governor and having our photographs taken with him. Such is China.

What problems did we experience? The most basic difficulties were those experienced as much by men as women – physical exhaustion from the journey, problems of communication and worry about the attitude of Public Security to our then illegal venture. Although we were not exposed to danger, drivers can fall asleep at the wheel, trucks do come off the road, and there can be problems too with exposure and altitude sickness. Women travelling, of any nationality, are very, very rare, especially in northern Tibet, which seemed to us to have an almost Wild West-pioneer atmosphere as it is being opened up by the Chinese. Large numbers of the men in this region are unmarried or have not been close to a woman for years. Sleeping together at night in the back of the truck the third driver tried to cuddle me. It was an opportunistic gesture, not intimidating in any way, but it made me realise how entirely dependent we were on these men – regardless of what happens, you can't just flounce off into the Tibetan plateau.

TRAVEL NOTES

Language Standard Chinese (*putong hua* – 'common speech' or Mandarin) is based on Beijing Chinese and understood everywhere to a degree. In addition there are major dialects such as Cantonese and Fujianese, plus distinct minority languages. English and Japanese are the main second languages taught in schools, but English is still spoken mainly in the bigger cities and by younger people. It is essential to learn some basic Chinese words and phrases and recognise the basic place names in characters. The best practical language guide is *China Travellers Phrase Book* (Eurasia Press, New York, 1980).

Transport Visas are easily obtained from travel agents in Hong Kong, and once you've got one you can visit around 240 'open' cities without a permit – which should cover more or less anywhere you might want to go. Lhasa is now open, as is the overland route from Kathmandu. For other places you need an alien's travel permit, which you can pick up at nominal cost from any Public Security Bureau. The situation is, however, constantly changing; contact CITS or the Embassy for the most up-to-date information.

Prices vary, but tourists tend to pay 70 per cent more on trains (sometimes 100 per cent more on planes) than Chinese. *CITS* (Chinese International Travel Service) offices are a good place to buy train tickets. Students get local prices on trains. Hitching is possible for short distances, but not really advisable if you're on your own.

Accommodation Tourists are designated specific hotels, generally the more expensive; in practice most hotels will put you up in their dormitories or cheaper rooms if you are persistent.

Special problems The Chinese authorities are very interested in foreign currency and may overcharge you: ask politely for cheaper price, room, meal etc. The black market for FECs (Foreign Exchange Certificates), especially in the south, is now flourishing. You can exchange your money for 'people's money' (*renminbi*) at lucrative rates – but be aware that the authorities are clamping down on this – Chinese can get jailed or shot if caught, tourists deported first class at their own expense. The use of false student cards is also now being cracked down upon by the Chinese.

Health problems include colds, nose and throat infections, caused by the dry atmosphere and industrial pollution. Chemist shops, however, are well stocked and local pills potent.

Special problems for Tibet Altitude sickness can afflict people quite badly – Lhasa is at 12,000 feet. Don't do anything too energetic for several days after flying in. Outside Lhasa medical facilities are rare and unsophisticated. Travelling around Tibet, trucks will give you free lifts for short journeys, but long journeys in the cab you will usually have to pay for. Hiring jeeps is very expensive. Public Security will try to stop you going anywhere you shouldn't, but at the same time seemed to take a resigned approach when directing one back to the straight and narrow.

Guides Rhonda Evans, Catharine Sanders and Chris Stewart, *The Rough Guide to China* (RKP, 1986). Most up-to-date of the independent guides. Alan Samagalski and Michael Buckley, *China, A Travel Survival Kit* (Lonely Planet, 1984). A thorough, almost encyclopaedic, 800-page guide, now carried by just about every Australian in China.

CONTACTS

There are branches of the **All China Women's Federation** in most cities, but you will probably need a special introduction by someone at the university or other body of authority in order to meet any representatives of these organisations.

Society for Anglo-Chinese Understanding (SACU), 152 Camden High Street, London NW1 (Tel. 01-267 9840). First operators of tours to China. A good source of information and also short language courses.

BOOKS

Elizabeth Croll, *Chinese Women Since Mao* (Zed Books, 1984). Informed analysis of the effect of new policies – in the economy, marriage and employment. Useful for the earlier Maoist decades is the same author's *Feminism and Socialism in China* (RKP, 1978).

Beverley Hooper, *Youth in China* (Penguin, 1985). Compiled from living in China before and after the Cultural Revolution; includes a chapter on 'From feminism to femininity'.

Dympna Cuzack, *Chinese Women Speak* (Century, 1985). Classic, in-depth study of Chinese women, researched from the 1950s on.

Agnes Smedley, *China Correspondent* (1943, Pandora Press, 1985). Compelling account – from a feminist perspective – of women's role in the Revolutionary period.

Hsieh Ping-Ying, *Autobiography of a Chinese girl* (Pandora Press, 1985). Pre-revolutionary childhood narrative of one of China's lending women writers.

David Bonavia, *The Chinese* (Pelican, 1982). Well-informed and very readable account of contemporary Chinese life and all its contradictions.

Minority Rights Group, *The Tibetans* (report no 49, 1983) includes two cultural perspectives, of a British journalist and a Tibetan.

Travel notes compiled by Gladys Morton.

Thanks to Kaye Stearman and Chris Hough for background information and help in putting together this chapter.

HONG KONG

Hong Kong with its rampant consumerism and affluence can be a bewildering and overpowering place; whether you travel from Europe or through South-East Asia the city will come as a shock, despite all its superficial aspects of current British colonialism.

The British, whose 99-year lease expires in 1997, have turned this tiny colony into a multinational business venture using the various incentives of low taxes, free trade and few currency restrictions. The cost of living is high but then so are the wages and many women with British qualifications (secretarial, teaching, journalism) come here for 2–3 years to boost savings. Luxury hotels, apartment blocks, an amazing range of restaurants and clubs and the much-touted shopping areas of Kowloon and Hong Kong Island reflect the lavish lifestyle of the business community, as well as catering for nearly 3 million visitors a year.

Within the Chinese community itself there are enormous disparities of wealth. Smuggling, especially high-tech goods, weapons, pornography and drugs, have underpinned a few dynastic families. The majority of the

5 million Hong Kong Chinese have to cope with severe social problems: intense overcrowding, unemployment and a very high crime rate. The situation is aggravated by the somewhat laissez-faire indifference of the British colonial authorities. Lack of government intervention may benefit the financial community and wealthy tourists, but the other side of the picture is a dearth of state welfare and schools and no free health service.

▨ **Louise Byrne has been to Hong Kong twice. Once for a week, a year later for six months, during which time she worked as a journalist.**

The first time I visited Hong Kong I hated it. I returned a year later and loved it so much that I stayed for six months. The secret, I discovered on that second trip, was to fight my way out of the tourist ghetto and into the narrow back streets and alleyways that litter Hong Kong. There I found the gabbling, steaming, chopstick-clicking Hong Kong sounds and smells issuing surprisingly from what looked like cluttered pigeon holes stacked sky high. Only then did I realise how fascinating this seemingly tiny pinpoint of a place is.

I was continually surprised by the resilience of the Chinese. It takes more than stoicism to cope with the urban deprivation and the frenetic pace of Hong Kong city life. The seamier side of free enterprise – long and hard working conditions, pervasive indifference to welfare rights by the British colonial authorities and the notoriously high incidence of organised violent crime – are facts of life for many of these people. But the dreams and aspirations of making fast money are not easy to surrender.

There's a common saying amongst Hong Kong Chinese that there is only one country they would like to be governed by less than Britain and that is mainland China. It's difficult to know whether such statements are fact or fiction because, true to popular myth, the Chinese can be inscrutable. As a tourist, one simply doesn't strike up a conversation with the local shopkeeper or taxi driver and the only way in which I was able to mix at all was by teaching English to a group of young students at one of Hong Kong's many language schools.

Eighteen out of a class of twenty were women and nearly all of them worked as clerical staff with Western or Chinese companies. Amongst them I found a great sense of being Chinese, which suggests that whatever the political implications of 1997, the new government will never be as fundamentally foreign to the local people as Whitehall always has been. Learning English is a serious business, and in a community obsessed with upward mobility, a reasonable command of the language is one of the best ways of securing a good job. The emphasis is usually on educating male members of the family first, although the ratio in my class suggested that the bias is changing.

The women students were obviously curious to know how I managed to avoid some of the less enviable commitments they faced. For women to travel abroad alone is not so much shocking to them as daring and, like many women in South-East Asia, they assumed my travels were financed by my parents. When the curriculum allowed, we discussed the general lack of equality between the sexes. With only a few of them did I ever feel that this meant anything more than equal pay, itself a long way off in Hong Kong. These intelligent hardworking women are still, it seems, inextricably bound to the famous Chinese family unit with all its advantages and disadvantages.

If you've got five days in Hong Kong, don't spend four of them shopping. You may not find the time or the opportunity to study the local community in detail, but it would be unforgiveable not to make an effort to escape the lure of the shops. There were three things I never tired of doing: going up on to the Peak at sunset and watching the whole of Hong Kong slowly light up below, crossing the harbour on the famous Star Ferry, probably the cheapest and most memorable harbour ride anywhere in the world, and visiting Lantau and Cheung Chau, just two of Hong Kong's 235 outlying islands.

Travelling alone in Hong Kong you won't have many problems because, on the whole, the men are indifferent to foreign women. Harassment and violent crime certainly prevail but are almost entirely contained within the community, for whom the traveller, except as a consumer, is largely irrelevant.

TRAVEL NOTES

Language Cantonese and English both widely spoken in commercial/tourist situations.

Transport Easy and cheap by bus, ferry, tram and train.

Accommodation There's plenty of it but it tends to be expensive. Cheapest are probably the YMCAs (Salisbury Road, Kowloon, Tel. 3–692–211, and overspill, 23 Waterloo Road (Yaumatei), Kowloon Tel. 3–319–111), which admit both women and men.

Guides *The Rough Guide to China* (RKP, 1986) includes a chapter on Hong Kong; the local tourist board also supply reams of information at points of arrival.

CONTACTS

Association for the Advancement of Feminism in Hong Kong, Room 1202, Yam Tze Commercial Building, 17–23 Thomson Road, Wanchai Hong Kong.

Hong Kong Council of Women, GPO Box 819, Hong Kong, Tel. 3–715–505. Originally set up by Chinese women to fight (successfully) for the abolition of concubines. Now a fully-fledged feminist group fighting for a wide range of women's rights in Hong Kong.

Asian Students Association (ASA) 511 Nathan Road, 1/F, Kowloon, Hong Kong. The ASA takes a strong anti-imperialist, anti-colonialist and anti-racist stand. Its

Women's Commission, set up in 1975, is currently chaired by the League of Filipino Students (LFS) and promotes the emancipation of women and encourages the formation of national women's groups. ASA publishes a bi-monthly Asian Students News which includes regular information about women's struggles in Asia.

BOOKS
J.W. Salaff, *Working Daughters of Hong Kong: Filial Piety or Power in the Family?* (Cambridge University Press, 1981). In depth study of working women in Hong Kong and the effects of industrialisation upon family life there.

Thanks to Lindsey Darking.

JAPAN

For many Japanese there's a certain amount of kudos attached to having a *gaijin* or foreigner as a friend. Not only are you an honoured visitor to whom traditional hospitality and courtesy is due, but you also have great curiosity value, as a direct link to the rock, sport, fashion and film scene of the West. Going there as a tourist, the crowds and hectic pace of life can be hard to adjust to. Sexual harassment is prevalent, though it is not usually directed towards Western tourists in any sort of coercive or threatening way. If you are going there to live and work, it may be hard to get used to what is essentially a conservative, male-dominated society.

Leading the world in high technology and fashion, Japan epitomises an enviably modern, successful nation. Yet it's a society in which women are still very much expected to play a secondary role. Soft porn is evident and available everywhere — in newspapers, advertisements, even early evening television. In the country that virtually created sex tourism in Asia, even a business deal is incomplete without the visit to the nightclub for 'hostess' entertainment.

The Japanese work ethic, the incredible devotion to a group, a company, a job, is made viable by the invisible labour of women — who nurture, service and maintain the workforce. Home is about the only place where Japanese women have power. They dominate household affairs and the upbringing of children, often acting as home tutors within the highly competitive educational system. It is not uncommon for a husband to give his wife his pay cheque and then be allocated an allowance.

Women are heavily discriminated against in the workplace. Usually they are only taken on by companies as temporary, supplementary labour — indeed it is one of the factors often cited in Japan's current economic success. As part-time workers, these women, quite apart from their very low wages, are denied the security and benefits available for full-time workers, even pension and sickness benefits. It is also quite common for pressure to be exerted on female employees to retire 'voluntarily' when they reach 30.

The main focus for the **Japanese feminist movement** at present is the Equal Employment Law, which is intended to comply with the UN Convention on the Elimination of Discrimination at work. The argument is that the present bill fails to legislate against discrimination in *hiring*, and that it endangers existing legislation which protects women against the excessive hours of the typical male Japanese worker. More worryingly, in a recent survey 70 per cent of working women in Japan were unfamiliar with the content of this important bill.

▰ **Alison Williams lived and worked in Japan for three years and travelled throughout the country. In a postscript she describes a visit to Hiroshima.**

Whatever claims you want to make for Japan, even as you do so, you realise that the opposite is also true. It is a very wealthy country (look at the GNP and the amount spent on consumer goods), but it is also impoverished in many ways, with a dearth of welfare and public facilities. The beauty of the landscape is outstanding, but is matched only by the ugliness of rabid industrial development which sprawls down the coast from Tokyo for hundreds of miles. A newly arrived visitor is struck by the pristine cleanliness of her surroundings: streets, stations, shops, people, all look equally fresh and well-scrubbed, but the seas and rivers are made sluggish with chemical effluence and, in this supposed bastion of high tech, less than half the houses are on a main drainage system. The Japanese are renowned for being polite, and so they are, but only if the situation calls for it and it is appropriate to extend courtesy. Fortunately, foreign visitors fall into this category.

If you are visiting Japan as part of an East-West overland route, you are likely to encounter far fewer travellers than in other Asian countries. Away from the Tokyo-Kyoto circuit, it may even be lonely, especially as their natural shyness makes many Japanese reluctant to approach a foreigner. Also, even in their own country, the Japanese tend to travel in groups who do everything together and are difficult to break into, and you may also be regarded as weird if you are alone. Even so, it is well worth going off the beaten track, especially if you can muster a few words of Japanese. Rural people have more time for you, and even though they may never have met a foreigner before, they are less inhibited than Tokyoites. It is also in the countryside that you will find the traditions of Japan preserved and, if you can communicate, you are bound to be invited for meals, visits, local festivals or tours of the locality.

This is where hitching helps: it gives you the rare opportunity to make a Japanese friend. Although you almost never see a Japanese hitching, they are extraordinarily kind to thumbing foreigners, and once accepted aboard you are then subject to the rules of Japanese hospitality. I do not think I ever had a lift where the driver did not go out of his or her way to take me closer to my destination. I was also bought meals, drinks, souvenirs and photographed frequently. The only drawback is feeling overwhelmed at being given so much, especially if you are unable to converse with your driver, so it is a good idea to have a supply of 'presents' – foreign cigarettes, snacks, even postcards of home.

That said, if you are travelling alone and are picked up by a single man, it is as well not to appear too friendly, however grateful you are to get a lift. Some women have had bad experiences. Most of the problems that a foreign woman has in Japan are because she has been unaware of how her behaviour, perfectly normal in her own society, is likely to be misread by a Japanese man. Remember that there is little socialising between Japanese men and women and platonic friendship is rare. Inter-action between the sexes is largely for the purpose of having sex, so that accepting an invitation, say to supper, unaccompanied, could be seen as tantamount to agreeing to sex. Few men, however, would force them-selves on you, it would rather be a case of misinterpreting your attitude. I should add that, personally, I have never had any serious problems even hitching alone (in fact some of my happiest times in Japan were as a direct result of hitching).

If you are going to be in Japan for some time and would like to meet other women, you might like to join a tea-ceremony group or flower arranging class. Here you will meet mainly young women getting a basic grounding in the arts considered desirable in a good bride. If you can overcome your repugnance at such an institution, you might be pleasantly surprised. These kinds of classes give you the opportunity to learn some-thing not only of ancient Japanese philosophy and their approach to aesthetics, but also about the lives and aspirations of young women contrasted with the wisdom (disillusion?) of the teacher who is likely to be elderly. If this sounds too prissy for you, why not join a women's aikido class? You can also meet people at youth hostels; although these tend to be too institutionalised for Western taste (organised games anyone?) they can, however, sometimes provide useful lifts and contacts, and are good on local information. Finally, there is always the local *sento* or public bath.

The Japanese bath ritual is one of the most pleasurable experiences available to a traveller in Japan, especially during the icier months. Until recently, the majority of homes were not fitted with bathrooms, which meant that families used the local sento. Even now, many Japanese still prefer to bath at their 'local', as it is often the centre of the community and for women especially, a chance to meet friends and have some time to themselves without constant demands being made on them by men. Women come here to relax, meet friends, get clean and occasionally have a go on the massage machine. The atmosphere is warm and congenial and for once you will not feel that you are being stared at. The sento is one of the better Japanese institutions, cheap and easily accessible to foreigners. It also provides a way of meeting women that is refreshingly informal in this otherwise rigid society.

HIROSHIMA

Forty years since the bomb dropped, nearly 400,000 people are still suffering the effects of radiation. Many of the *hibakusha* (A-bomb victims) are women, often ostracised by their husbands and families, and they and their children still suffer and die early from radiation-related diseases, especially cancers.

I visited the Peace Museum in Hiroshima on a cold, grey winter's day. Freezing rain fell on this modern industrial city, and the bleakness of the climate was an appropriate match for the exhibition inside. Nothing can prepare you for what you will see there, so go with a friend if you can, but in any case go.

The events surrounding the bombing are well-documented and meticulously detailed. You learn what certain individuals were doing at the time, how a quirk of fate saved Mr Ito, why the bathhouse attendant was particularly unfortunate, and how the bomb was especially 'effective', most people being out on a hot summer's day, enjoying the 'all clear' after a recent air-raid. Facts are substantiated by a variety of exhibits and relics – melted roof tiles, pieces of exploded plumbing, photographs of half-destroyed bodies, tumours and hospital work still being carried out today, life-size wax models of victims struggling to the River Ota with skin and clothes torn off. One particularly memorable exhibit was the shreds of a woman's blouse. It was made of a checked material, and the white part of the design remained, while the rest had been burned away, giving a lattice effect. An accompanying photograph showed the similar effect this had had on her body.

The evidence is baldly laid before you, with no embellishment or attempt to sensationalise, and this adds to its force. When you have seen as much as you can take, you can add your protest to those in the visitors' book and visit the bookshop, a boon for anyone interested in the Peace Movement. The area surrounding the museum has been made into a Peace Park (Heiwa Koen), with memorials, greenery and water, and statues adorned with thousands of coloured origami lucky cranes made by school children from all over Japan. The park's most outstanding feature is the dome 'dōmu'. This is the skeleton of the Industrial Promotions Hall (and, incidentally, the only ruin allowed to remain), over which the bomb exploded. It stands in direct line with the eternally burning Flame of Peace, the canal and the museum, at once a reminder and a warning.

To offset the heavy emotional experience of the museum, I recommend a visit to the nearby sacred island of Miyajima, which is traditionally one of the three scenic spots of Japan. The shrine's huge orange gate (Japan's largest) stands in the sea and is as much a symbol of Japan as Mount Fuji. The shrine itself is lovely, especially at high tide, and you should also climb Mount Misen for fantastic views of the Inland Sea.

If you are interested in anti-nuke activities, use the Tourist Information Centre (TIC) to put you in touch with a local group; many *hibakusha* are members, and there is always a mass rally held in the Peace Park on the anniversary of the bombing, August 6th.

◤ **Kate Ferguson has been living and working in Tokyo for the last two years.**

As a foreigner in Japan, you are always a slight oddity and might hear yourself referred to as a 'henna gaijin' – strange foreigner. Since a certain degree of strange behaviour is expected, foreigners can act in a freer way than a Japanese can. For instance, as a foreign woman I have been able to visit a variety of different bars, including a few of the infamous hostess bars, and have entered bars on my own. A Japanese woman would not be able to feel comfortable in such situations, and indeed, it is sometimes frowned upon for a Japanese woman even to be seen drinking at all.

A foreigner in Japan often has the feeling of being permanently on show, like being some kind of rare animal. Women with fair hair particularly can expect to be approached by people eager to touch their hair. In spite of this, all the women travellers to whom I have spoken agree that the annoyance of receiving too much attention is far outweighed by the delights of travelling in Japan for a woman. The most important of these is the almost complete safety of travel and the freedom to walk alone at night. The situation is of course slightly different for a foreign woman working and living in Japan for a longer period of time. It would be hard for most foreign women to live outside the main centres of Tokyo, or the Kansai area of Osaka, Kobe or Kyoto, because of the feeling of being constantly watched and also because of the isolation – the lack of people with a good knowledge of English and similar ideas with whom to establish a friendship.

I am fortunate to be working in an all women's department of a British company in Tokyo. The women are expected to take on certain responsibilities usually reserved for male workers, and make important decisions about their work. However, as my comprehension of Japanese has improved, I have been surprised by the way in which some of the senior men address the women in the office. They will call them 'kimi' or 'omae' which are both derogatory ways of saying 'you' to a woman. I have also noticed that, in addition to the male superiority ethos, Japanese men are under a lot of pressure to conform and not stand out as different from their associates. A relationship with a foreign woman is considered to be nonconformist and, as a lot of Japanese men are also frightened by the image of an independent, aggressive Western woman, there are few such relationships.

Among my acquaintances, there are some women with Japanese boyfriends or husbands. The men tend to be out-of-the-ordinary Japanese, such as designers, architects or musicians who live fairly unconventional lifestyles. It would probably be difficult to have a relationship with a businessman. I met one American woman who was involved with a Japanese man whom she had met in the States. When they came to Japan, their relationship suffered under the strain of his late working hours: he would often return home in fairly typical Japanese style at three or four in the morning, and sometimes even sleep at the office – again not uncommon. Such loyalty to the company and expectation that work should be given priority over wife or girlfriend is difficult for a lot of Western women to comprehend and adjust to.

Learning the language has enabled me to make a lot of Japanese women friends in Tokyo. This is a chance often denied to people who speak no Japanese, who are limited to getting to know the few Japanese women who have spent a fair amount of time overseas.

My friends include Yoko Kumaki (aged 29) who attended a missionary school as a child, as her mother believed she would benefit from a more practical English training than is usually available in Japanese high schools. She also studied English at the YMCA in Tokyo and then continued her studies at a university in Australia. She returned to Tokyo at the age of 26, to an arranged marriage. (The majority of marriages in Japan are arranged and sometimes a private detective is used to check up on the partner's suitability.) Yoko has continued to work in an increasingly responsible position for a British company in Tokyo.

Sumie Iwatsuki, on the other hand, is more like the politically orientated feminists of the West. Her hobby is, she says, designing and building houses for communes. Sumie has lived in communes that she has helped build for fifteen years and her latest house, opened in January 1985, is a women-only house in Chiba prefecture, just outside Tokyo. The commune is purpose-built with sleeping, eating and meeting quarters as well as a music rehearsal room. There is also a plan to have a room set aside as a video studio. The brains and energy behind this project seem to be Sumie's, who spends her time writing, illustrating and making music in the feminist cause. She stands as an example of quite a different kind of Japanese workaholic.

This may all paint a rather too rosy picture of the situation of women in Japan. In fact it is no coincidence that both these women live in Tokyo. Any woman outside the capital who wished to follow a lifestyle which differed from the traditional housebound role would find life difficult. It may seem strange to a Western woman that Japanese women rarely complain about their situation. In fact, only a minority (for example Sumie) complain about anything in the political context. Perhaps this is due to the adherence to the 'shikata ga nai' philosophy in Japan. 'Shikata ga nai' means 'it can't be helped' and there is undoubtedly a tendency to accept things as they are, rather than disturbing the social harmony by protesting about grievances. Moreover, many Japanese men and women would argue that their society works better than most others, and see little justification in making fundamental changes.

TRAVEL NOTES

Language Japanese. Little English is spoken outside the cities, though many Japanese write English better than they speak it. Be prepared to speak slowly and clearly – and smile! Japanese are often nervous of approaches from a *gaijin*.

Transport Extensive, efficient and expensive – make use of the Japanese two-week rail pass. Hitching is very unusual but possible. Taxi drivers in Tokyo often have to be 'bribed' after midnight.

Accommodation Japanese style hotels (*ryokan*) are difficult to cope with unless you've knowledge of the language. Go to the tourist office for advice. Look for 'business hotels' which can be up to 50 per cent cheaper than normal ones, and avoid 'love hotels' unless you have a particular purpose in mind.

Guides Ian McQueen, *Japan – A Travel Survival Kit* (Lonely Planet, 1985). Essential guide, recently updated and revised. *Tokyo Journal* is a monthly publication in English with what's on information and articles for foreigners living in Tokyo; *Kansai Time Out* does the same for Kansai.

CONTACTS

TWIN (Tokyo Women's Information Network) c/o Agora, Shinjuku 1–9–6, Shinjuku-ku, Tokyo 160. The best general source of information on feminist groups in Japan and abroad. Also makes referrals for legal services, medical consultation, housing, child care and research facilities. Operates by telephone, 03–354 8565, Mon to Fri in English and Japanese.

International Feminists of Japan (Tel. 03–793 6241). Aims to forge better links between Japanese feminist groups and their counterparts abroad. A group of feminists from the foreign community living in Japan meets on the first Sunday of each month at the Fujujoko centre near Tokyo's Alledonobashi station.

Gayon House Bookshop, next to Tokyo Union Church, (nearest station Omoe Sando), Tokyo. Feminist and anti-nuclear books.

Tokyo Rape Relief Centre open Monday, Wed and Friday from 7pm to 10pm. Tel. 03–207 3692. Provides women lawyers and gynaecologists sensitive to the needs of rape victims and has plans to sponsor assertiveness-training and self-defence courses.

Kyoto Feminist Group, Kyoto YWCA, Muromachi, Demizu-agaru. Meets every second and fourth Sunday. The group welcomes foreign women. Tel. Sue 075–722 0686.

Asian Women's Association c/o Masako Goto, 112 Sakura Gauka, Hodogaya-ku, Yokohama 240, Tel. 03–508 7070. Campaigning group opposed to the use of cheap female labour in Japan and South-East Asia, and also against Japanese sex tourism in Seoul, Taipei and Bangkok.

Lesbian Feminists Centre, c/o PO Box, 84 Nakano Post Office, Nakano-ku, Tokyo 164. Activities range from dances to karate lessons for women.

Women's International Network. Meets monthly in Umeda, Osaka; check listings of *Kansai Time Out*.

National Women's Education Centre, 728 Sugaya, Ranzan-machi, Hiki-gun, Saitama-ken. Centre for study, research, exchange in and out of Japan.

BOOKS

Sachiko Ariyoshi, *Letters from Sachiko* (transl. Abacus, 1984). These letters were written to her sister in the West highlighting the differences in women's aspirations between East and West – offers important insights into contemporary Japanese life.

Yuko Tsushima, *Child of Fortune* (Kodansha, Tokyo, 1985). The heroine is a Japanese woman living in Tokyo, battling against dependence and the expectations of deference. Recommended.

Michiko Yamamoto, *Betty San: Four Stories* (1973; Kodansha transl. 1985). Again addresses the subservient domestic roles of Japanese women – and also East-West incompatibilities.

Shizuko Go, *Requiem* (1973, The Women's Press, 1986). Diary narrative of the last months of the last war, as experienced by the 'daughters of military Japan'.

Junichiro Tanizaki, *The Makioka Sisters* (Picador, 1983). Very well-known in Japan, with a quintessential Japanese heroine struggling between passivity and self-will.

Susan Pharr, *Political Women in Japan: The Search for a Place in Political Life* (California UP, 1981). Exploration of women's images of self and society and of expectations, from first-hand interviews.

Liza Crihfield Dalby, *Geisha* (California UP, 1983). Contemporary study – of a living phenomenon. The author, an anthropologist, became a geisha during her stay in Kyoto.

Leonie Caldecott, 'At the Foot of the Mountain: The Shibokusa Women of Kita Fuji', in Lynne Jones (ed.), *Keeping the Peace* (The Women's Press, 1983). Moving and extraordinary account of a rural and local peace group at the foot of Mount Fuji and their defence of their community through disrupting military exercises in the region.

Thanks to Liz Gorst.

SOUTH KOREA

Since the 1950s war, which devastated both North and **South Korea**, there has been rapid industrialisation in the South, propelled by massive injections of US aid. The government is very keen to increase South Korea's international standing – Seoul is the site of the 1988 Olympics – and to attract big business to its luxury hotels and conference centres. So far, however, few places outside the capital have become commercialised, and most of your fellow tourists are likely to be Korean daytrippers. As a foreigner you may attract curious stares, and find it hard to communicate, but there is very little danger of harassment.

Though you won't be directly affected, it's hard to ignore the undercurrent of violence and repression in South Korean society – seen most recently in the student riots in Kwangju. The government is rigidly authoritarian and has only recently lifted a curfew imposed after the Korean War. And for all its business, the country remains isolated – from Soviet-aligned North Korea by cold war and from Japan by bitter memories of colonial rule.

Korean culture owes much to Chinese influences but has its own distinctive features, like its unique female *shammans* (religious leaders). In general, the position of women is still dictated by Confucianism, and the disparity in the way daughters are valued in comparison to sons is so glaring that there has been an educational campaign to try and redress the balance.

Conditions of work make South Korean women some of the most exploited in all Asia. For many, the growth of agribusiness and industry has left little option apart from assembly-line work in one of the many multinational factories. These have moved their operations to Korea to take advantage of the very low wages, and often cut costs even further with unsafe, unhygienic, improperly lighted workplaces. Women's organisations have begun to militate to improve conditions and to educate workers about their rights, but many women are too afraid of losing their jobs to resist the intimidation and sexual harassment common to such factories. Often these workers are young daughters sent to the factories to provide the main source of family income.

Kisaengs, hostesses or, in fact, prostitutes, also tend to be dispossessed women from the rural areas, who flood to the cities to find work. They are a very lucrative part of the tourist industry and the price of a kisaeng is often included as part of the package deal. The Japanese, who used thousands of Korean women as their prostitutes during the last World War, remain the chief customers, and come to Korea often in group tours for sex. Some Asian women's groups, especially in Japan, are now campaigning against this form of tourism.

◤ **Ann Ward worked as a teacher of English at the University of Seoul for two years, and travelled throughout the country.**

Although it is considered a little unusual to travel alone in Korea for fun, I always felt quite safe on my own. My greatest problem was the language. Many Koreans have studied English at school, but few have the ability or confidence to speak it. But the language barrier apart, it is fairly easy to mix in – as a foreigner you tend to attract attention and a great deal of friendly interest. Quite often I received gifts and offers of food; Koreans are enthusiastic picnickers, preparing elaborate meals for the open air, and may invite you to join the party.

Whilst I was never harassed or hassled for money, I was, like most visitors, amazed and infuriated by the amount of pushing and jostling that goes on in the streets. There seems to be nothing personal in this; whoever you are, you will get shoved aside. On the other hand, a complete stranger at a bus stop will remove hairs from your collar in a totally abstracted way, just as a seated passenger on a crowded bus will grab your bag and hold it for you on his or her lap.

Seoul is a good place to start a tour of Korea, not least because there you can find out more about getting around. It is also worth a visit in its own right. In the centre of Seoul, impressively set among mountains, are several former palaces, with museums in their grounds. I particularly liked the Secret Garden, also in the centre of the city, but amazingly quiet with lakes and pavilions set in extensive grounds. On the outskirts of the city there are royal tomb sites, tumuli surrounded by giant stone statues of warriors, officials and animals. Seoul has far outstripped its former boundaries, reminders of which are the East and South Gates. Both gates have giant markets nearby, selling everything from pigs' heads to computers.

Outside Seoul, there are several sites which are popular with tourists and Korean day and weekend trippers alike, such as Mount Sorak National Park, Pusan and Cheju Island. Most Buddhist temples seem to be on mountainsides, many only accessible by foot. The Mount Sorak area is rugged, with trails leading to remote temples and hidden water-falls, especially beautiful in autumn. Pusan is a seaport and Korea's second largest city. It has a beach, (unbelievably crowded in high summer), casino, and the kind of facilities intended to attract male Japanese tourists in search of cheap sex. But it also has a fascinating quayside market which is a good place to sample raw fish (much cheaper in Korea than in Japan).

Over the last decade, Cheju's popularity as a tourist destination has grown. Increased affluence has brought many Korean visitors, notably honeymooners, to the island. It is large, far to the south of the mainland, with a warmer climate, lush vegetation and a rich volcanic soil, in which tropical flowers and fruit, including pineapples can be grown. The majority of holidaymakers go there in August. I went in July and was surprised by how few people were there, even in the most popular beauty spots.

Driving in the centre of the island, we came across a group of excited Korean tourists photographing a field of black and white cows. Much that is exotic about the place to visitors from the mainland seems commonplace to visitors from the British Isles. White farmhouses with thatched roofs, dry stone walls, green fields: it's easy to imagine yourself in the west of Ireland, especially since they knit and sell very beautiful Arran sweaters.

Cheju is famous for its women divers. Look out to sea at almost any point around the coast, and you will see a float and the wet-suited figure of a diver. The souvenir shops sell postcards of swimsuited glamour girls, poised daintily on a rock, but this is hardly representative of the highly skilled, businesslike women divers I saw. These were wives and mothers rather than teenage mermaids and, amazingly fit, they seem to continue diving well into middle age. More than that, they have a kind of poise and confidence that I have not seen anywhere else. They spend long hours in the water, collecting shellfish and other delicacies and sometimes spearing large fish. Their economic independence has long been estab-lished and it shows in their demeanour.

TRAVEL NOTES

Language Korean, which has its own alphabet, *Hangul*. English is little spoken, in spite of the strong American presence.

Transport Mostly by bus or coach. There are few private cars.

Accommodation Beware some of the hotels with real Western beds instead of mattresses on the floor – Carmel Pavageau stayed in two in Suwon, unknowingly (at first) in the red-light area.

Guide Geoff Crowther, *Korea and Taiwan – a Travel Survival Kit* (Lonely Planet, 1984).

CONTACTS

National Council of Women, 40–427,428 The Third Street of the Han River, Youngsan-Ku, Seoul.

BOOKS

From the Womb of Han: Stories of Korean Women Workers (CCA, Hong Kong, 1982). Collection of stories, many direct transcriptions. Available from CCA-URM, 57 Peking Rd, Kowloon, Hong Kong.

AUSTRALIA AND THE PACIFIC

Chapter Fifteen

AUSTRALIA

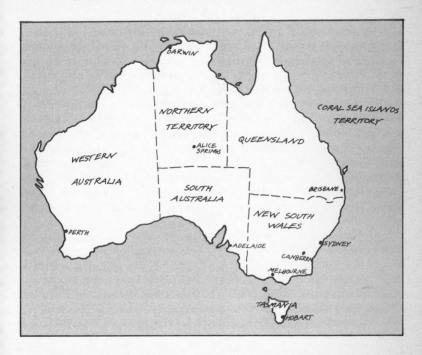

Australia is a vast country, almost the size of North America, yet with 15 million people it has the same population as Holland. The country is divided into six states: Western Australia, Queensland, South Australia, New South Wales, Victoria and the island of Tasmania; and the Northern and Australian Capital territories. The latter contains the modern capital, Canberra, home of central government, currently under the Labour Party leadership of prime minister Robert Hawke. Whereas central government directly controls the two territories, each state is to some extent self-governing and very much has its own characteristics.

Contrary to popular belief, Australia was not 'discovered' by Captain Cook. Aboriginal people had already been there for some 40,000 years when white colonisers arrived to disrupt and destroy their harmony with the land. Thousands were wiped out, either brutally murdered or killed off by imported diseases. Their descendants now form a small minority, increasingly prepared to fight for self-determination. The rest of the population, about 40 per cent of whom are first-generation Australian, originate from a variety of countries including Britain (probably still the dominant group), Ireland, Greece (Melbourne has the third largest Greek population of all cities), Germany, Italy, Poland and, most recently, Indochina. Nearly all, however, consider themselves first and foremost Australians.

The vast scale and emptiness of Australia make it in some ways a difficult country to explore. Long distances and the high cost of living mean that public transport is expensive, whilst hitching is not generally recommended. If you have time one of the best ways to see the magnificent outback is to team up with a group and buy a camper van. Temporary work, well paid by British standards, is relatively easy to find, especially if you have a working holiday visa, which must be issued in your home country before leaving. Over half the population live in less than ten towns. Largest and generally most popular with travellers is Sydney, capital of New South Wales. It's not only striking for its position, dominated by a beautiful harbour, but a lively, cosmopolitan city, competing only with Melbourne as the country's leading centre of the arts and alternative culture. Sydney houses many radical groups, including women's film, theatre and music collectives.

The Australian **Women's Movement** achieved significant gains in the 1970s when the then Labour government introduced a number of measures that benefited women. Equal opportunity and anti-discrimination laws were passed, in some states at least, and an impressive network of health centres, battered women's refuges and rape crisis centres was set up across the country. However, a period of Conservative rule followed by continuing cuts in government funding have meant that women have had to fight hard to maintain these services. Feminism today is also very much linked to the environmental and anti-nuclear movement; some 900 women went to the first women's peace camp at Pine Gap in 1983.

■ **Rosemary Frances went to Australia on a one-year contract to write a course for an adult migrant education programme.**

I find it hard to share my experience of Australia: it is difficult to focus on particulars. I didn't have a bad time there but I can't say I had a good time either, perhaps because my stay was dominated by the frustration of trying to set up a project against a quite impenetrable wall of bureaucracy. Small things like trying to obtain information or get documents processed were always a major operation. Many professional people seem to have little commitment to their work; endless coffee and chat seemed to be the norm, with a lot of emphasis on recreation. For once, though, money wasn't the problem.

I did most of my travelling alone, using buses, once a train and once hiring a camper van with friends. The personal columns of city newspapers usually have offers of long-distance rides, sharing petrol, but I was put off by the risk of a long journey with a stranger who might drive (or do other things) like a maniac. Hitching is reputed to be hazardous.

I made it to most of the main cities plus smaller places in a total of about eight months. The outback myth is still widely upheld, but in reality most people are highly urbanised with cars, TVs and videos – Australia is said to have the highest rate of video ownership in the world. Although I crossed the desert several times whilst traversing the continent vertically and horizontally, I never really experienced the outback because of the hassles in doing so alone and, not least, the high cost of travel. In sheer frustration I eventually joined the first tour I've ever been on – four days on the edge of a sheep station in Western Australia – which turned out to be surprisingly enjoyable.

I was shocked by the attitudes of many Australians, including the otherwise liberal, to the indigenous people. Apart from the maintenance of the nonsense that Australia was discovered by Captain Cook, many seemingly rational people claim that 'Abos' are dirty, lazy, alcoholic, irreligious and without any rights to the land. My attempts to argue were invariably met with: 'You're a pommie visitor and don't understand what it's like.' I did in the end make sufficient contacts to get a permit to visit an Aboriginal outback area, but decided such sightseeing was intrusive. A festival for Aboriginal women has started annually in Adelaide and I enjoyed watching some of the women-only dances and learning more about the people, although yet again I felt this was a voyeuristic and white-managed affair.

In contrast, the position of migrants is generally positive. There has been much criticism of Australia seeming to have an all-white migration policy, to which the current government has responded by taking in refugees from Eritrea and Ethiopia and business people from India. But all migrants do have the legislated right to hostel accommodation and fulltime paid English classes for three months on arrival, plus less intensive classes after that. To outsiders the impact of so many cultures manifests itself mainly as ethnic exotica — restaurants and dance groups – although governments are beginning to support more comprehensive cultural and language programmes. Perhaps because so many migrants have willingly abandoned their roots in search of an economic dream, their attitude as individuals is often to assimilate. Consequently the culture and power structures seem dominated by 'Anglo' concerns, including celebration of the Queen's birthday.

There are many myths about Australia that are current not only in the rest of the world but also amongst urban Australians. The weather is one. Whilst it is, of course, hot in the tropical north, Melbourne and

Adelaide in particular can have six-month winters little different from above-zero southern England – at least they feel similar because of the strong winds and lack of adequate heating. People are friendly, but only at surface level and I found it much more difficult to build relationships than I'd expected. 'Barbies' (barbecues), do not prevail, nor do hats with corks hanging off, and the growth of Australian designs mean that many people dress extremely well. I never met a truly 'Ocker' male. Legislation in favour of women's rights is strong in most states – at least it is on paper. Australia is reputedly the land of the free and classless; certainly the class concept isn't the complex one of Britain, but differentiation and discrimination clearly exist.

For the visitor or traveller though, Australia certainly has wide and immediate potential. If it's a stop-off point on your way round the world and you wish to work then it's easy to earn a lot of money. If you want to opt out into a society where it's easy to become wrapped in bourgeois comfort and close your eyes to anything else, then migrate. If you have definite issues to explore on your travels, like the women's movement, peace issues, alternative comedy, contemporary political art forms, etc., then it's dynamic and exciting. And if you're a desert freak who's highly organised with a lot of money and companions and can get permission to go to certain areas, then it's reputed to be wonderful. But if you're there because it's there (in my case I was invited to work by the Australian Immigration Department) then I guess, like me, your feelings, positive, negative or neutral, will entirely depend on your personal experiences and contacts.

◪ **Vicki Cheater worked in Australia to finance a two-and-a-half year stay. Her most memorable experience was a long trip by motorbike across the outback.**

The Australian outback can be dangerous country for travellers. Incidents of mechanical breakdown throw you on your own resources at a moment's notice. You can imagine, then, the trepidation with which I set out from Perth, pillion on a Honda 750cc, destined for Sydney via the Northern Territory and Queensland.

Travelling by bike was tough, journeys averaging 500 kilometres per day, and at times the falls, punctures, inevitable breakdowns and sheer torture of riding on dirt roads made the whole trip an endurance test. A feeling of utter helplessness and smallness would take over everytime I looked at a map, and despite a mechanically minded male companion I would sometimes become over-preoccupied with arriving. However, I found compensation of such exposure to the elements in unleashed surges of pure freedom, in an atmosphere pulsating with heat where the air itself becomes an entity. I would unhesitatingly recommend a similar trip to any sensible, resourceful adventurer.

The outback abounds with curious sights and rare wildlife: 10-foot termite mounds that rise like gravestones out of the ground, baobob trees, whose bottle-necked hollow trunks were once used to imprison Aborigines, and shoals of seawater fish, fed by hand off the pier in Darwin. It is difficult to convey the thrill of all this, and to see it you don't have to take off on your own, or by bike. There are organised adventure trips and safaris from Darwin – to the Katherine Gorge, for example, where a park ranger will help you to penetrate the silent centre.

I travelled from West to East and would recommend a trip in that direction, as I found the movement from the dry flat desert scrub of Western Australia to the sub-tropical rainforest of Queensland a heartening experience and refreshing therapy for a bleached soul. It's a good idea to use official camping sites en route, whether at a roadhouse or in a remote National Park, for there is a real fear of being trampled on by wild cattle if you opt for a roadside spot.

Australia has an impressive system of National Parks, most provide basic camping, and as areas of designated natural beauty with a protected wildlife they provide good vantage points for seeing the weird and wonderful flora and fauna. If you want a combination of bushwalking and swimming, then I would recommend going to the National Park gorges. Off the beaten track in the Kimberleys, Western Australia, is Windjana Gorge where, if you're lucky, your only company will be the wildlife. All water has to be boiled here as you share the watering hole with cattle and freshwater crocodiles. There are other similar, equally beautiful gorges, however, which offer further chances to birdspot and bushwalk on more sophisticated levels of camping – Geikie Gorge in WA and Carnarvon Gorge in Queensland, for instance.

In a parched landscape I tended to seek out watering holes, and these vary from cool, clear undiscovered pools and cascading waterfalls to hot thermal springs, dams, billabongs, and beaches. The hot springs at Mataranka, south of Darwin are good for massaging aching, well-travelled limbs, days prior to the long haul east. Equally self-indulgent days can be spent at Broome, north of the Great Sandy Desert, WA. Here there is a camping ground adjacent to the beach and some days you can spot porpoises on the horizon. Broome supports a pearling industry, originally introduced by the descendants of the town's Chinese population and you can pick up pure and cultured pearls at rock bottom prices.

To finance my travels I worked in the north, having arrived in Australia on a working-holiday visa. Waitressing and barmaid jobs were relatively easy to come by, though you need to make certain exactly what the job is about – there's a fine line between waitressing and 'hostess' work which amounts to prostitution. Short stints of casual work, however, are quite the norm; my shortest was three days, my longest three months – each one just right for supplementing the coffers. As an aid to seasonal work the CES (the DHSS equivalent) provides a useful chart showing when and where fruit picking is available.

▨ **Karen Hooper's work for an alternative Queensland radio station brought a lot of contact with Australian, and travelling, women. She wrote this piece in Brisbane, her base for nearly eighteen months.**

In a country that has been settled by so many different races I'm disillusioned by the extent to which there is racism in Australia, not only towards Aboriginal people but other minority communities such as the Asians. Though it must be said my view has undoubtedly been tainted by spending most of my time living in the country's most oppressed state, Queensland – ironically the Sunshine State – dominated by the right-wing politics of Premier Sir Joh Bjelke Petersen and his big happy family of the National Party.

Joh and wife Flo were introduced at a recent National Party convention as 'Papa and Mama Bear!' Joh believes he and his Christian 'nats' are guardians of the morals of Queenslanders and it looks as if only an act of God will usurp him. In the Sunshine State there is a burning contempt for anything that strays from the 'norm'. And that includes feminists and gays – even more so as the attitude to the recent Aids scare reaches hysterical proportions. A woman's place is in the home, so we don't need a state sex discrimination act here, says Joh – consequently the Federal Bill does not cover women working in state departments. In 1979, women campaigned successfully to block abortion legislation that would have turned the clocks back, but there are still only two abortion clinics and, in theory, it is still illegal to have an abortion in Queensland.

I've been living and working in the state capital Brisbane, courtesy of a journalism award from the International Rotary Foundation. I have studied film and politics, media and postwar feminism, worked as a sub-editor on a Sunday newspaper and helped to set up the women's radio collective *MEGAHERS* at the alternative radio station here, 4ZZZ. Thankfully, there is a strong and positive movement against the state policies here from women's and community groups. And, despite all odds, a place like Women's House has just been able to celebrate its 10th anniversary – this year moving into larger West End accommodation to continue providing a rape crisis centre and many other services for women in the community. 4ZZZ itself is also an important resource, reaching 60,000 people on the Queensland airwaves (see Travel Notes). It is run, collectively, without any government grant and recently decided that 30 per cent of its music output must be devoted to women artists.

With the archaic views currently circulating in Queensland it is, however, a relief to see a Federal Labour government in power. While legislation won't necessarily change people's consciousness, government policy on women's unemployment and discrimination have gone some way to underline the problems. There is now a women's bureau within the Employment Department which decides on policy. And there are women in positions of real power. Like Senator Susan Ryan, appointed Minister for Education and Youth Affairs last year, the first Labour woman in cabinet and architect of the Sex Discrimination Bill. And Dr Anne Summers, author of the acclaimed *Damned Whores and God's Police, the Colonisation of Women in Australia*, now occupying the title of First Assistant Secretary, Office of the Status of Women, in the Prime Minister and Cabinet Department.

Australian men have been slow to accept equality with women and discrimination remains rife. In many isolated country areas gang rape is still a regular occurrence. If you do decide to take off to more remote parts of the country I'd think twice about hitching alone. And I can't imagine men taking kindly to displays of affection between women. Avoid country towns was the main advice I received from fellow travellers. One woman I spoke to was accused of being a 'cunt-sucker' simply because, sitting in a pub, she put her arm around her friend. Last year she was with a group of Women for Survival on their way to the Pine Gap Women's Peace Camp. In a pub in Tennant's Creek a guy shouted 'We love nuclear bombs', and threw a glass at a woman who spoke up for the cause.

But it's not all like that. Just when you think you can't take another harsh comment from a beer-bellied bigot, you'll find an Aussie male who just wants to be your feminist groupie and can understand perfectly 'where you're coming from'. Just as the leers are getting too much, you'll find a wonderful gay male who wants to know more about female sexuality than you know yourself and who will offer a sensitive alternative in the macho madhouse.

◢ Maria Maw visited Pine Gap Women's Peace Camp towards the end of a long trip around Australia.

Pine Gap is about twenty miles south of Alice Springs, an area sacred to the Aboriginals. It is also the site of a joint US/Australian Defence Space Research base. Towards the end of 1982 Women for Survival groups nationwide, and particularly in Alice, decided to start a camp in order to draw the public's attention to the base.

I heard about Pine Gap almost as soon as I arrived in Australia. It was shortly before the day in December 1982 when thousands of women encircled the base at Greenham Common. Hearing about the events in England made me quite homesick and, although I try to travel without definite plans, I immediately made a mental note of when the Australian women's camp was due to begin, the following November.

By that time I had spent almost a year hitching and travelling around the country, mostly with Australian men. I was tired of explaining my aversion to being called a 'chick', which inevitably led to discussions on feminism, and looked forward to spending some time in feminist company. The morning I decided to head north from Adelaide there was no mistaking the group of women chattering excitedly in the bus terminal café: flamboyant haircuts, seemingly haphazard outfits of brightly coloured, well-worn and handmade clothes, with a liberal sprinkling of feminist badges, earrings and motifs. I plucked up courage and asked them if they were going to Pine Gap. I can't describe the wave of warmth that washed over me as I answered yes, I was going too. After months of playing verbal games with people here was a group who spiritually embraced me immediately, in common sisterhood. They came from Adelaide and I became an Adelaide woman.

Travelling from Adelaide to Alice is a unique experience. About two thousand miles of dead straight road, most of which is unsealed – just corrugated red dust. The land is flat, topped by a layer of spindly silver-green scrub, and the air like the exhaust from a vacuum cleaner, hot, dry and dusty. The only sign of humans was a littering of abandoned cars along the verge, all to our delight sprayed with women's and peace slogans. That day the air was still and clear, the largest expanse of sky I had ever seen, deep blue, sprinkled with a frosting of cotton-wool clouds. I felt elated.

The 11th was still a few days off. We were one of many groups that arrived that evening at the temporary camp set up at Roe Creek, a few miles out of Alice. In daylight it turned out to be an idyllic spot; a dry river bed lined with tall, shady eucalyptus trees. There was so much colour with the huddles of tents, tarps and banners, pale golden sand, a brilliant blue sky and the silvery green of those unforgettable trees. The spectacle grew as more women arrived, hundreds of them, having bussed, driven and hitched from all over Australia.

Finally, at dawn on the 11th we packed up and congregated on the road to the base. There were about a thousand women walking the one kilometre to the gates, and most of us helped to carry the longest banner ever, each section made by women who couldn't be present in person. The press and security guards were the only spectators and I think even they were impressed by the flood of colour.

Our new camp stretched along a narrow, treeless strip on one side of the road, the other side being Aboriginal land which was only to be used for recreation. Affinity groups, averaging twelve women, formed individual communal camps, each with its own kitchen area. Every day there was some form of action, usually spontaneous and symbolic – singing, dancing, drama and, one day, a CIA Olympic Games. But twice in the first week these led to more direct action, with women climbing over the fence and the gates being forced down. And there were endless meetings.

The most hotly debated issue was the presence of men in the camp, which became further confused with support of Aboriginal Land Rights. Some of the women representatives of Aboriginal communities were accompanied by men. Unfortunately this resulted in a separate Aboriginal camp, although many women did join the main camp for meetings and camp-fire gatherings. In the end, after many hours of discussion in small groups, it was agreed that the camp had little choice but to incorporate the male help already present.

There was further criticism from Aboriginal women about the methods used in the action, and the lack of information and misinformation the Aboriginal communities had been given. One spokeswoman claimed that they had been led to believe that the camp would be effective in closing the base. She was also upset at the risk of arrest. Prison is not unfamiliar to some Aboriginal women and there was a danger that other women's actions might have adverse effects on the Aboriginal community with respect to Land Rights' claims and their treatment during detention. She went on to explain the Aboriginal way of action which involved prayer, trust in God, men and women working together, and hours of discussion over many years if necessary. Her conclusion was a warning: no more direct action which would involve arrest, and no extension of the planned two-week camp. It was clear that incorporating land rights into the women's peace campaigning had not been sufficiently considered.

TRAVEL NOTES

Languages English is the official language, but you'll also find Italian, Greek, Serbo-Croat, Turkish, Arabic, Chinese, and numerous Aboriginal languages.

Transport A good system of trains, buses and planes connects all major cities. All public transport is expensive, but prices are competitive so it's a good idea to look around. Petrol is cheap by British standards so it's worth buying your own vehicle if you have the time and money. Hitching is not advisable for single women, especially in outback areas and along the Queensland coast.

Accommodation Suburban motels tend to be much cheaper than centrally situated hotels. Sydney, especially, has lots of hostels geared to travellers. Australians are generally very hospitable so don't be afraid to use any contacts you may have. University notice boards can also be good sources (and for lifts too).

Special problems Working visas are becoming increasingly hard to get. Applications should be made well before you leave home and you will need evidence of sufficient funds to cover your trip.

Guide Tony Wheeler, *Australia: A Travel Survival Kit* (Lonely Planet, rev. 1986). A thorough guide, though one written from an Australian perspective and sometimes assuming a bit too much knowledge.

CONTACTS

It would be impossible to include here all Australian **feminist groups**. The following list covers some of the major cities – for more details take it from there. SYDNEY: **Women's Liberation House**, 62 Regent Street, Chippendale 2008 (Tel. 699–5281); **Leichhart Women's Health Centre**, 164 Flood Street, Leichhart 2040 (Tel. 560–3011); **Rape Crisis Centre** – Tel. 819–6565.

Out in the wilds of New South Wales there's a **women's commune** which has been running since 1974. If you want to visit, write first to **Amazon Acres**, The Mountain, c/o PO Birdwood, Via Wauchope, NS Wales 2446, Australia.

MELBOURNE: **Women's Centre**, 259 Victoria Street, West Melbourne 3000 (Tel. 329–8515). Groups at this address include: Women Against Rape; Lesbian Line; Women and Children in Transition; Women's Liberation Newsletter; Women's Radio Collective; and Women's Legal Resources Group.

NORTHERN TERRITORY: **Women's Information Service**, PO Box 2043, Darwin 5794 (Tel. 81–2668); **Women's House/Crisis Centre**, PO Box 3219, Alice Springs 5750 (Tel. 52–6075).

CANBERRA: **Women's Centre**, 3 Lobelia Street, O'Connor 2601 (Tel. 47–8070); **Women's Shopfront Information Service**, Ground Floor, CML Building, Darwin Place, Canberra 2600 (Tel. 46–7266); **Rape Crisis Centre**, Tel. 47–2525.

BRISBANE: **Women's House**, 30 Victoria Street, West End 4101 (Tel. 44–4008); **Brisbane Women's Health Centre**, PO Box 205, Woolloongabba 4102 (Tel. 393–1175); **Rape Crisis Centre** c/o Women's House (as above). For women's radio in the city and immediate area tune into **Megahers** on 102FM (5pm, Tuesdays).

PERTH: **Women's Information and Resource Centre**, 103 Fitzgerald Road, North Perth 6006 (Tel. 328–5717); **Women's Health Care House**, 95 Thomas Street, West Perth 6005 (Tel. 321–1751). No Rape Crisis Centre.

ADELAIDE: **Women's Liberation House**, 1st Floor, 234A Rundle Street, Adelaide 5000 (Tel. 223–1809); **Working Women's Centre**, 31 Gilbert Place, Adelaide 5000 (Tel. 212–3722); **Adelaide Women's Community Health Centre**, 64 Pennington Terrace, North Adelaide 5006 (Tel. 321–1751); **Hindmarsh Women's Health Centre**, 6 Mary Street, Hindmarsh 5077 (Tel. 46–6521); **Rape Crisis Centre**, Tel. 268–8882.

TASMANIA: **Women's Information Service**, 4 Milles Street, South Hobart 7000 (Tel. 23–6547); **Lesbian Line**, 6–10 pm, Tuesdays, Tel. 34–5839.

Women's bookshops include:
SYDNEY: **The Feminist Bookshop**, 315 Balmain Road, Lilyfield 2040 (Tel. 810–2666).

VICTORIA: **Shrew**, 37 Gertrude Street, Fitzroy 3065, (Tel. 419–5595).

BRISBANE: **Women's Book, Gift & Music Centre**, Cnr Gladstone Road and Dorchester Street, Highgate Hill 4101 (Tel. 44–6650).

ADELAIDE: **Murphy Sisters Bookshop**, 240 The Parade, Noward 5067 (Tel. 332–7508).

There are numerous **feminist magazines** in Australia, including *Girl's Own*, *Hecate*, *Womanspeak*, *Scarlet Woman* and *Liberation*.

BOOKS

Dorothy Hewett, *Bobbin Up* (Virago, 1985) Entertaining portrait of working-class life in Australia in the 1950s. Only novel by one of the country's leading women playwrights, first published in 1959.

Susan Mitchell, *Tall Poppies* (Penguin, 1983). Profile of ten successful Australian women – an inspiring, well-balanced read (the women come from all backgrounds and nationalities) and a phenomenal best seller in the country.

Anne Summers, *Damned Whores and God's Police: The Colonisation of Women in Australia* (Penguin, 1975).

Isobel White et al., ed., *Fighters and Singers: The Lives of Some Australian Women* (Allen & Unwin, 1984). Collection of stories focusing on the lives and strong characters of a number of Aboriginal women.

Robyn Davidson, *Tracks* (Paladin Books, 1982). Compelling, very personal story of how she learned to train wild camels and eventually sets off with four of them and a dog to explore the Australian desert.

Jill Julius Mathews, *Good and Mad Women* (Allen & Unwin, 1984). Traces a history of the Australian traditions which have created the meaning of the ideal of the 'good woman'.

David Adams, ed., *The Letters of Rachel Henning* (Penguin, 1985). Written between 1853 and 1882, the letters give a vivid account of life in colonial Australia as seen through the eyes of a previously sheltered young Englishwoman.

Also **novels** by Henry Handel Richardson, Miles Franklin and Christina Stead – classics by and about women.

Thanks to Karen Hooper, Tessa Matykiewicz and Christine Bond for their individual contributions to these Travel Notes.

Chapter Sixteen

NEW ZEALAND AND THE SOUTH PACIFIC

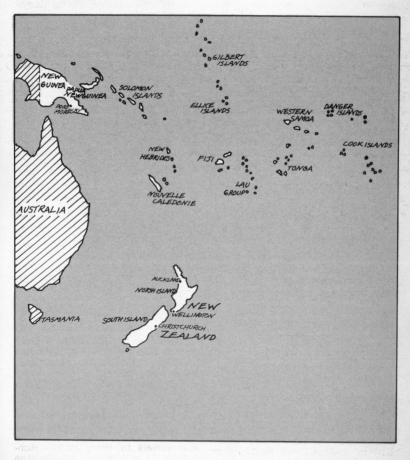

The **South Pacific** is an immense area dotted with thousands of mostly tiny islands. The main exceptions are the vast island of New Guinea, situated in the south-west, north of Australia, and the two principal islands of New Zealand in the south-east. The many clusters which lie in between make up the countries of Fiji, the Samoas, French Polynesia, Tonga, Vanuatu and New Caledonia, to name just a few.

New Zealand, with its predominantly white-settler population, is unique in sharing more affinities with Australia than with its Pacific neighbours. As inhabitants of a former British colony, with the Queen of England as formal Head of State, most New Zealanders are proud upholders of British tradition. However, the indigenous Maori (some 10 per cent of the population), having managed to survive the early ravages of colonisation, are beginning more and more to assert their own separate cultural identity and fight for appropriate political representation. In spite of these grievances, Maori people are generally open and friendly towards Western tourists, and the country as a whole has a reputation as a relaxed and easy place to travel.

Until recently, inaccessibility and limited facilities kept much of the rest of the Pacific relatively unknown, both to package tourists and independent travellers. Nowadays, though, a growing number of islands threaten to follow the fate of **Tahiti**, which commercial interests have virtually succeeded in transforming from Pacific paradise into tourist nightmare. If you're really seeking adventure, choose very carefully or else head straight for **Papua New Guinea**.

Depending on where you go, your choice of accommodation will vary from luxury hotel to village hut; the cost of food and transport will differ enormously too. In terms of safety, it's again hard to generalise, but provided you're careful and respect local customs there shouldn't be much problem of sexual harassment, at least from local people.

A few Pacific nations, among them American Samoa and French Polynesia, have quite large foreign communities, for they've been maintained as overseas territories by the countries which colonised them. Others, controlled at various times by Britain, France, Germany, the United States, New Zealand and, in the case of New Guinea, Indonesia and Australia, still remain under the thumb of foreign powers, even after official independence. Colonialism is a key political issue in the Pacific, along with escalating concern about French and American nuclear tests and the dumping of foreign nuclear waste into the ocean. In recent years, a vast network of nuclear bases, ports and airfields has been set up throughout the region with little, if any, consultation with the indigenous people. The result is an impressively united and growing movement for a nuclear-free and independent Pacific in which women play a leading role.

From 1975, when the First Pacific Women's Regional Conference took place in Fiji, the **Pacific Women's Movement** has spread to more and more countries. Much of its work is co-ordinated by the Pacific Women's Resource Centre which links up groups and spreads information with the help of a satellite communications system. As well as the vital nuclear issue, the concerns of the movement include violence against women, racist and sexist use of experimental contraception, tourist exploitation, and the need for a feminist approach to development projects.

We received very little response to our request for articles on the Pacific and the following cover only **New Zealand** and **Papua New Guinea**. Further contributions on other countries in the region would be very welcome for the next edition of this book.

NEW ZEALAND

New Zealand comprises two main islands, North and South, situated some 2,000 km south-east of Australia. Despite the huge distance separating it from the 'old mother country', very strong links are retained with Britain. Most travellers are struck by New Zealand hospitality, but the British tend to be quite overwhelmed.

The original Maori population now live mainly on the North Island. Maori society is tribal, traditionally associated in complete harmony with land and sea, and tied closely to the bonds of family life and the village community. Although far more integrated into white European immigrant (*pakeha*) society than, say, the Australian Aboriginals, they have been badly disrupted by rapid urbanisation. Together with age-old land grievances, high unemployment, unequal pay, educational failure and low standards of health and housing have all contributed to the rapid acceleration of Maori protest in recent years.

New Zealand is a great place if you like the outdoor life. The countryside is wild and beautiful, far more varied than the common image of acres of grazing sheep (they outnumber people 20 to 1) would suggest. It also feels unusually safe to travel around alone. Hitching is widely accepted and there is plenty of accommodation to suit all tastes, youth hostels being the best bet for a cheap, clean place to stay.

There is quite a strong **Women's Movement** in New Zealand, illustrated by a range of organisations from Maori women's groups to town-based women's resource centres and groups campaigning for peace. The anti-nuclear issue, supported by Prime Minister David Lange, is very much in the forefront of debate, especially in relation to nuclear testing and the dumping of nuclear waste in the Pacific.

▧ **Kathryn Ann Ephgrave spent six months in New Zealand, most of the time 'tramping'.**

From the beginning I planned to spend as much time as possible in the national parks and forestry reserves. Working out my route, various government departments and park rangers were extremely helpful and constructive in providing information, maps and advice. Regardless of my sex, their main concern was, as with all trampers, my safety. But provided I had adequate equipment, plenty of food and had registered my intentions in the registration book, my ability to hike deep into some of the remotest regions of wilderness was never questioned. It is well accepted that New Zealand women are as keen on outdoor pursuits as men, in fact a well-respected bond is established between men and women while on the tracks. The ability to tell a good story around a campfire at the end of a day with a burly bunch of males is all that is required. It is however very unwise to trek alone, as some of the tracks are rarely used.

For the keen walker I would recommend trips around Arthur's Pass, Mount Cook, Mount Aspiring and Fiordland in the South Island; Tongariro and Lake Waikaremoana national parks in the North Island. Many alternatives are available though, and if you are short of time the Millford Sound and Routebourn tracks are outstandingly beautiful, relatively easy and very popular with overseas visitors. All the national parks have a network of huts with basic amenities, even mattresses, enabling you to plan a trip of several days.

Travelling around New Zealand as a whole can be a problem, especially in some of the remote regions where public transport is scarce. Generally I preferred to hitchhike, partly because I was short of cash, but also as the best way to meet the local people. It wasn't always straightforward but I never felt unsafe, and was constantly being offered accommodation. New Zealanders (certainly the ones I met) seem by nature to be hospitable, friendly and concerned to see that you're all right. While hitchhiking, incidentally, don't be surprised if a light aircraft should circle overhead, land in a nearby field and offer you a lift somewhere – it happened to me. Pilots are quite often willing to offer a ride in their aircraft and if you turn up at an aerodrome in a small town and ask around, people are only too keen to assist.

From Bluff, on the south coast of the South Island, it is possible to pick up a ride on a boat to the Campbell Islands. This involves several days' sailing on a supply ship, doing a rare relief of the meteorological station. It's an excellent opportunity to photograph wildlife and to get as far south as you can go towards Antarctica. You could also get a boat to Stewart Island from Bluff, only about three hours' ride depending on weather conditions. The island has been designated as a national park and has no road network, apart from at the tiny port of Oban. In the rugged dense interior there's a variety of wildlife, including penguins, seals, kiwis and the very rare kakapo.

New Zealand is very much geared towards the hitchhiker, cyclist and off-beat explorer. Apart from the extensive network of the Youth Hostel Associations, there are motor camps which offer a variety of very cheap basic cabins and tent sites. There are also cheap independent hostels and lodges, particularly in the North Island. Alternatively, you can often find somewhere to sleep in the communes or in some of the 'back-to-nature' villages scattered around the Coromandel Peninsula and the East Cape, and similarly Maori communities offer shelter to travellers in their *marae* (traditional Maori meeting house).

If you want to work in New Zealand in order to stay longer, the most obvious possibilities are seasonal fruit picking, roughly between December to March, in Alexandra, Nelson, Tauranga and Keri-Keri. Keri-Keri also offers the unusual opportunity to pick oysters – a kind of manual work equally open to women. Likewise, seasonal work is available in Queenstown during the skiing season, mainly in hotels, restaurants and bars.

Because of the kindness of the people I met and the general cheap cost throughout, I was able to live well on a very low budget. A great percentage of my stay was in unpaid accommodation, greatly reducing the overall costs. I'd definitely recommend a visit to anybody, and I look forward to my own return.

TRAVEL NOTES

Languages English and Maori.

Transport The two islands are connected by regular ferry services between Picton and Wellington. If you can afford the hire, a camper van is much the best way of seeing the country. Trains are limited, but buses operate to most outlying areas and many women hitch.

Accommodation Hotels, lodges and hostels (with dormitories or private rooms) are reasonably priced by Western, or Australian standards. As well as providing camping facilities, motor camps have cabins and caravans for hire and are widely spread throughout New Zealand.

Guides Tony Wheeler, *New Zealand – a Travel Survival Kit* (Lonely Planet, rev. 1985). The most comprehensive guide for independent travellers. Jim DuFresne, *Tramping in New Zealand*

(Lonely Planet, 1982) offers additional information for really keen hikers.

CONTACTS
The following information is taken from **Broadsheet** (June 1985), New Zealand's main national feminist magazine. You can usually buy it from *Sisterwrite* or *Silver Moon* bookshops in London or else write directly to **Broadsheet**, Box 68–026, Newton, Auckland. The groups, etc. below are listed alphabetically by town.

AUCKLAND: **Broadsheet Bookshop**, 485 Karangahape Road (Tel. 398–895); **HELP Counselling for Victims of Sexual Assault**, PO Box 68–165, Newton (Tel. 399–185); **Lesbian Social Group**, PO Box 44–167, Pt Chevalier; **Rape Crisis Centre**, 63 Ponsonby Road (Tel. 764–404); **Snapdragon Women's Bookshop**, 256 Jervois Road, Herne

Bay (Tel. 768–978); **West Auckland Women's Centre**, 111 McLeod Road, Henderson (Tel. 836–2470); **Womanline**, Telephone Information and Referral Service, open Mon-Fri, 11am–8.30pm (Tel. 765–173).

CHRISTCHURCH: **Kate Sheppard Women's Bookshop**, 202A High Street; **Lesbian Line**, (Tel. 794–796), Thurs 7.30–10.30pm; **Rape Crisis Collective** (Tel. 794–793); **THAW The Health Alternative for Women**, Cnr Peterborough and Montreal Streets (Tel. 796–970).

DUNEDIN: **Lesbian Line** (Tel. 778–765), Mon 7.30–10pm; **Rape Crisis Centre**, Rm 6 Regent Chambers, Octagon (Tel. 741–592); **Women's Resource Centre**, Rm 10 Regent Chambers, Octagon, 2–5pm Weds (books, space, coffee).

GISBORNE: **Women's Centre** (Tel. 76–247).

HAMILTON: **Women's Centre**, PO Box 7025, Subway Shops, Claudelands Bridge.

NAPIER/HASTINGS: **Napier Women's Emergency Centre,** (Tel. 436–515).

NELSON: **Women's Centre and Rape Crisis**, 320 Hardy Street, Nelson (Tel. 82–407).

NEW PLYMOUTH: **Women's Centre**, 66 Brougham Street, (Tel. 84–957).

PALMERSTON NORTH/MANAWATU: **Rape Crisis Centre**, 165B Broadway Avenue (Tel. 76–805); **Women's Health Collective**, Old Firestation, Cuba Street, (Tel. 70–314); **Womyn's Resource Centre**, 165B Broadway Avenue, open Mon-Fri, 10am–3pm (Tel. 774–26).

TAURANGA: **Women's Centre**, PO Box 368, 42 Grey Street (Govt Life Bldg) (Tel. 83–530).

TE AWAMUTU: **Te Awamutu Feminists**, c/o Carol Lamb, 111 Hazelmere Crescent (Tel. 4485) or June Bright, 20 Thorncombe Road (Tel. 5901).

WELLINGTON: **Access Radio** 783 khz, **Woman Zone**, 10am Sundays, **Lesbian programme**, 11am, contact the collective via Radio NZ (Tel. 721–777); **Lesbian Line**, (Tel. 898–082), Tue-Thur, 7–10pm; **Rape Crisis Centre** (Tel. 898–288); **The Woman's Place**, feminist bookshop, 289 Cuba Street (Tel. 851–802); **Women for Peace**, PO Box 9314 Wellington, contact Celia Lampe (Tel. 758–063, evenings).

BOOKS

Keri Hulme, *The Bone People* (Hodder & Stoughton, 1985). Extraordinary semi-autobiographical novel weaving in Maori myth, custom, magic and language. Originally published by a New Zealand feminist co-operative it won the English Booker award – and unexpected wide and international distribution.

Phillida Bunkle and Beryl Hughes, eds. *Women in New Zealand Society* (Allen & Unwin, Sydney, 1980).

Amiria Manutahi Stirling, *Amiria* (Reed, Wellington, 1976). Life of a Maori woman told by Anne Salmond.

Janet Frame, *The Envoy from Mirror City*, *To the Is-land*, *Living in the Maniototo* and others The Women's Press, 1984. Inner, psychological novels by possibly New Zealand's most established writer.

Lady Barker, *Station Life in New Zealand* (Virago, 1984). First published in 1870, this is a classic story of early colonial life told with warmth and a real feeling of adventure.

Robert Macdonald, *The Maori of New Zealand* (Minority Rights Group Report, No 70, 1986). Excellent background to Maori history and grievances up to the present day. Obtainable from good bookshops or MRG, 36 Craven Street, London WC2N 5NG.

Thanks to Kaye Stearman of MRG for access to the above report before publication and Kathryn Ann Ephgrave for general background and Travel Notes.

PAPUA NEW GUINEA

Papua New Guinea, the eastern half of New Guinea, is the second largest island in the world. Only a narrow stretch of sea separates it from Australia, but its Melanesian people have quite different physical features and social structures from the Australian Aborigines. Parts of the island have been claimed at various times by the Spanish, Portuguese, Dutch, Germans, British and Australians. Independence and self-government were finally achieved in 1975, but Papua New Guinea is still dependent on massive inputs of Australian aid and has modelled much of its bureaucracy on the Australian system.

Travel is necessarily adventurous. Ninety per cent of the population live in villages, often remote and producing most of their own food. Transport is erratic and accommodation expensive and limited; tourist facilities are mainly restricted to the capital, Port Moresby, the east coast, the Sepik river and a few islands accessible by plane. However, people are friendly and hospitable and, with the help of local guides, one of the best ways of getting to know the island is on foot – bush-walking.

As food producers, cooks and mothers, the **women** of Papua New Guinea have always had certain status and power in the community. Any myths of male superiority stem largely from the implantation of white ways and values through development programmes initiated by the colonial administration. Although there is no feminist movement as we may know it, women are organising more and more to reverse such prejudices and defend their rights. The core of this work is done through a network of district women's associations. Affiliated to the National Council of Women in Papua New Guinea, they are concerned with promoting self-reliance, improving health and childcare facilities and providing training in different skills, including leadership and management. The Maprik District Women's Association, comprising about 90 women's groups, hopes to have opened its own women's centre by the end of 1985. They welcome resources and news of the activities of other women around the world.

◢ **Ann Fairnington spent two years working in a rural area.**

Perhaps my most general and lasting impression of Papua New Guinea is of a country being stretched in time: at one end the cities, with their blocks of flats, airports, bars and computers; and at the other, self-sufficient villages where money has no practical use except to be strung round the neck as a decoration, or else paid to a woman's family as part of the traditional bride price. So far, the stretching force between these two worlds doesn't seem to have damaged the people as much as in other developing countries. This is partly due to the positive reinforcement of traditional ways which is promoted in schools and on the radio. Virtually everyone, including monied bureaucrats, has a strong sense of belonging to their own village or clan.

Women are generally respected but, as usual, have been oppressed by a series of cultural devices which are still very much part of traditional life. In the remoter parts of Oro Province where I lived and, I suspect, in other areas, girls at puberty are shut in a small hut for several weeks. During this time they are fed rich foods and allowed out only briefly after dark. When they emerge from their confinement their skins are pale from lack of sun and they are fatter – both characteristics associated with beauty. They are dressed up and their skins oiled in order to show them off in their best light to prospective husbands. Women marry young and a bride price is arranged between the families involved. This price is paid off in instalments over the next few years and if the woman proves to be less than perfect, if she does not have children or obey her husband, then the contract can be cancelled and the money refunded.

Menstrual blood is considered poisonous and so women should never step over food or people's legs. However a group of women told me that although, in theory, if a woman steps over food it should be discarded, in practice that is only done if a man *sees* the woman step over food.

Older women seem to have considerable status in traditional society. They appear to be free to insult and issue instructions to younger men and women, and are often involved in the decision-making processes of the village.

The clear distinction between men and women's work in the country-side makes it easy to spend time with groups of women, washing clothes in the river or selling their produce in the large colourful markets. Usually they are very friendly. As far as men go, I learned to expect more unwanted attention from British and Australian residents than from Papua New Guineans. The country has a high proportion of single white men sent out by their companies to cut their business teeth in the commercial backwaters. They can be extremely hospitable to (white) women travellers, providing information or a spare bed, but some definitely seem to expect a return.

Despite my good experiences with Papua New Guinean men, you will almost certainly hear a host of horror stories as soon as you encounter the wealthy expatriates of Port Moresby. No doubt they contain some truth, but one can avoid many problems by taking simple precautions. I never walked around the towns alone after dark and I was careful not to offend local customs by my dress. In PNG a woman's thighs are considered more erotic than her breasts and are not meant to be exposed in public. Thus I wore shorts only on the rare occasions when I was with a predominantly expatriate group. Much of the time I wore a lap-lap, a large oblong piece of brightly coloured cloth, cheaply and readily available everywhere. They are worn as skirts by most women and some men, and are invaluable to the traveller as they can be used as a sheet, towel, dress or shawl.

In the highlands I often wore loose cotton trousers, especially when climbing in and out of PMVs (public motor vehicles) the main form of transport on the few roads in each province. Virtually anyone with a truck and a driving licence can get a PMV licence and wear the blue number plate on his truck to indicate he will carry passengers for a fare. Fares are regulated by the government and are very reasonable: you pay towards the end of the journey, but if you want to go a long way it's wise to discuss the fare before starting. Vehicles range from open-back utility trucks to mini buses and often carry piglets and women with huge piles of garden produce going to the market. They can be dusty and uncomfortable but are always friendly and full of interest.

Travel between provinces is usually by small planes of the Talair or Air Nuigini airlines and is truly spectacular as one flies between mountains and low over tropical rain forest. On the less popular routes the planes may have as few as 6 seats. The pilots are often Australian men who work for a year or so with Talair to get enough flying hours to join an Australian airline. White women are often invited to travel in the co-pilot's seat to keep the pilot company.

A very pleasant way to travel up the east coast, often overlooked by tourists, is on the boats of the Lutheran Shipping company. For a very reasonable fare one gets a bunk in a sort of dormitory with open sides where one can laze and see the coastal villages slip by and watch schools of dolphins and tuna fish swim alongside.

To enjoy PNG's transport systems to the full, expect them to be late starting and delayed on route. Throwing away the tense expectations and timetables of Western travel can be a liberating experience take a good book and something refreshing to drink, and relax.

TRAVEL NOTES

Languages There are more than 700 distinct languages, but in most areas you will find someone who has some schooling and speaks English, the official language. If you plan to stay any length of time, it's fun to learn some Pidgin – roughly derived from English, spelt phonetically with simple grammatical rules. For example, as there's no word for prince, Prince Charles is known as 'Nambawan pikinini bilong Misus Kwin'. Pidgin phrase books are available to help you on your way.

Transport Rugged territory has prevented the development of a cross-country road network and most tourists travel by plane. Buses operate in major towns; otherwise the most common form of transport is the PMV, or public motor vehicle (see text).

Accommodation Hotels and motels tend to be expensive.

Special problems Be careful not to offend local customs by your dress (again see text); don't wear shorts.

Guides Mark Lightbody and Tony Wheeler, *Papua New Guinea – a Travel Survival Kit* (Lonely Planet, rev. 1985). Invaluable for its concise detailed information on every aspect of travelling in PNG. Riall W. Nolan, *Bush-Walking in Papua New Guinea* (Lonely Planet, 1983). Describes 11 walks and climbs of various lengths and difficulty, backed up by good practical information. The best general guide to the South Pacific region as a whole is David Stanley's *South Pacific Handbook* (Moon Publications, US, 1984).

CONTACTS

Maprik District Women's Association, Maprik Administration Community School, PO Box 30, Maprik ESP (see introduction).

National Council of Women, Port Moresby.

Women's Resource Centre, PO Box 520, Port Moresby.

For more general information on the Pacific Women's Movement, write to the **South Pacific Women's Bureau**, South Pacific Commission, PO Box D5, Noumea Cedex, New Caledonia.

BOOKS

Christina Dodwell, *In Papua New Guinea* (Picador, 1985). One of a new generation of intrepid women travellers, she tells the story of her lone two-year expedition in some of the remotest parts of the country.

Marilyn Strathern, *Women in Between: Female Roles in a Male World – Mount Hagan, New Guinea* (ANU Seminar Press, London, 1972). Deals with women's status and relations between the sexes in the New Guinea highlands: what women do, how they see themselves and the rights they demand in a world where most affairs of 'significance' are dominated by males.

An excellent article by Vanessa Griffin on the Pacific women's movement is included in *Sisterhood is Global* (see General Bibliography).

Thanks to Helen Massil for additional background on Papua New Guinea.

LATIN AMERICA

Chapter Seventeen

MEXICO AND CENTRAL AMERICA

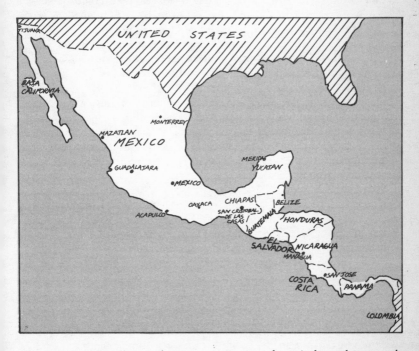

Mexico attracts millions of visitors every year, from independent travellers to holidaymakers in search of sun and sea. If you can tolerate the *machismo*, its culture and physical beauty alone make it one of the most rewarding countries to visit in Latin America.

Few people, however, would think of travelling through **Central America**. Guatemala and El Salvador are each caught up in a bloody civil war which has left thousands dead and forced over 1½ million people from their homes in the past ten years. Most of them are poor peasants, victimised by a succession of corrupt and repressive regimes determined, with the help of massive US aid, to hang on to their power. Tension has also spilt over into the border areas of Mexico and Honduras where refugee camps are frequently raided by government troops in search of 'subversives'.

Apart from Panama in the far south, only **Belize** and Costa Rica remain relatively untouched by the conflict. The first, tucked away in an almost forgotten corner between Mexico, Guatemala and the Caribbean sea, has a history of British rule followed by democratic government, leaving it somewhat removed from the roots of revolt elsewhere. **Costa Rica** also has a reputation for democracy. The army was abolished in 1949 and certain progressive policies have led to comparative comfort for the largely white population. Poverty exists of course – and women, as usual, are the worst hit – but not on the scale likely to provoke a revolution. It's debatable how long Costa Rica can remain unscathed by the war in neighbouring Nicaragua, but for the meantime tourists still go there, attracted by its famous natural beauty and apparently easy-going political atmosphere.

For a country under siege **Nicaragua** continues to receive a remarkable number of foreign visitors, many of them feminists eager to see for themselves and learn from the much publicised involvement of women in the Nicaraguan revolution. From all accounts travellers are welcome, especially Spanish-speakers who have skills to offer or can at least report home on what is happening.

MEXICO

Mexico is a chaotic and exciting country with a tremendous amount to offer the traveller. Between the highly developed resorts lie miles of untouched beaches, but most of the interest lies inland. Large areas of central and southern Mexico are rich in colonial history, Indian traditions and the relics of ancient civilisations – not to mention magnificent scenery. An extensive bus network makes it easy to get around and, depending on the exchange rate (Mexico is in a permanent state of economic crisis), there's plenty of cheap accommodation.

After a very stormy past, Mexico is nowadays regarded as one of the most stable countries in Latin America. This stability is based more on its strength as an advanced industrial power, than on just or democratic government. Despite efforts to present a radical face to the outside world, the Institutional Revolutionary Party, in power for over 40 years, is deeply conservative. Little has been done to implement the kind of social changes symbolised by the famous 1911 Revolution.

Many people are very poor and resent the affluence of their northern neighbours in the United States. Some of this anger is inevitably focussed on tourists, which can be hard to cope with, especially tied up with machismo. *Gringas*, (foreign women) representing both wealth and a type of sexuality denied to Mexican men, are the easiest targets for resentment. Approaches from men tend to be aggressive, so you need to feel strong. It's also worth making a great effort to learn at least some Spanish – a relatively easy language – before you go.

Not only foreigners need to arm themselves against machismo. **Mexican feminists** have long recognised it as a deep-rooted obstacle in their struggle for equality and freedom. However, as in the rest of Latin America, more urgent concern is given to the denial of basic economic and social rights suffered by most of the female population. Since it began in 1970, a large section of the Women's Movement has been closely linked to various political parties of the Left. At the same time there is an autonomous movement, for which abortion is a central issue, and there are several organised lesbian groups. Although certain reforms, such as the elimination of discriminatory laws, have been passed on paper, Mexican women see themselves as having a lot more to fight for.

◥ **Margo Sheridan spent a summer travelling alone in Mexico.**

Unusually, I found Mexico a fairly relaxed place to travel, both with other women and by myself. The people I met tended to be a self-selected and therefore limited group, i.e. middle-class men and very few women. You need to make a deliberate effort to meet women as, traditionally, they're unlikely to approach you. The men paid lip service to feminism but when challenged became proud and edgy. One thing that helped to build my self-confidence was always having a notebook or sketchbook with me. It changed people's perceptions of me into a 'doer' rather than a passive object and I think improved their attitude to me as a lone female tourist.

One of the great Mexican clichés is the melting pot synthesis of Pre-Colombian and Spanish culture. Great official pride is taken in the prehispanic heritage, in ironic contrast to the unofficial casual racism shown towards the Indian population. Two towns, San Cristobal de las Casas and Oaxaca, illustrate this sometimes uneasy blend of cultures.

San Cristobal, near the Guatemalan border, is the southernmost outpost of Mexico's well-established gringo trail. The area is stunningly beautiful, with a large Indian population, making it a popular focus for anthropologists as well as other travellers. The journey there, through Tuxtla Gutierrez and Chiapa de Corzo, is spectacular and very slow, the bus crawling up through the hills of Chiapas, winding through pine forests, patches of eroded red earth and strangely Alpine valleys of bright green maize.

The town stands at about 6,000 feet with a view of mountains at the end of every cobbled street. The colonial-style houses are built low against earthquakes and painted a variety of pastel shades under red-tiled roofs. From the tourist's point of view, San Cristobal is at its best right now. Twenty years ago you would have been intruding on a totally Indian way of life, as the town was only accessible by dirt roads. In a few years' time the package coaches will arrive. Meanwhile, it's one of the most atmospheric places in Mexico.

The town is the headquarters of *CARGUA*, a group providing much-needed help to Guatemalan refugees on the border. It also seems to be a magnet for 'right-on' North Americans learning Indian dialects, conserving the jungle, saving the Quetzal bird, etc. This lends a certain radical-chic air which I found rather appealing.

Becoming increasingly hostile to these invaders, however, are the unassuming Indians who flock to the town on market day. Four main tribes descend from the surrounding hills, each with their distinctive dress. The men's costume is often more colourful than the women's, their straw hats decorated with cascades of brightly coloured ribbons floating freely to indicate bachelorhood or tied to denote marriage. (The entire population of Zinacantecan Indians seemed to flaunt single status!) Women almost always go barefoot, half-walking, half-running along the streets, whilst the men wear the heavy woven leather sandals which go back to Mayan times.

Oaxaca again combines Indian culture and colonial style, but on a much larger scale. Its elegant buildings of jade-green stone, wrought-iron grilles and carved porches are more reminiscent of Spain and it's fast becoming an important industrial centre; yet the huge Saturday market, attracting Indians from villages all around, still gives you a glimpse of ancient times. The city has a pleasant cosmopolitan air and there's always something going on in the tree-lined main square: a band playing, a demonstration against local government corruption, food vendors, children touting flowers, and all sorts of people passing through. Apart from visiting the market, it's worth entering the famous church of Santo Domingo, a riot of Mexican Rococo with brightly painted, rouged cherubs stepping off the walls and roof in all directions and an astonishing wealth of gold leaf. Also take a bus to the archaelogical site of Monte Alban, a Zapotec temple complex in a magnificent mountaintop position not far from the town.

◤ **Debbie Garlick, who lived for a year in Mexico, adds a few warnings.**

I arrived at the Nuevo Laredo border exhausted after two days' bus-ride from Chicago. It was New Year's Eve and the immigration building seemed flooded with happy jostling families, mostly North Americans taking advantage of the holiday. There was no sign of the friend I had arranged to meet and I felt very alone.

As I sat trying to avoid the attentions of Mexican men and wondering about the complications of obtaining a visa, an immigration official suddenly leant across his desk and inquired if I spoke English and Spanish. I nodded and, before I had time to think, a desk appeared in front of me and I was explaining the immigration procedure to American tourists. The men who had been hassling me only minutes before were suddenly bringing me cups of tea, directing people towards me for briefing and generally acting with great respect.

I was kept busy all night and when morning dawned I mentioned my own visa to the official who had co-opted me into the immigration department. 'No problem,' he smiled through tobacco-stained teeth, giving me the maximum time limit.

All Mexican border crossings are unpredictable, depending on the mood of officials. You are entering the world of *mordidas* (bribes), so be on your guard and don't be conned into paying unnecessarily for visas or tourist cards.

Machismo also rules in Mexico. As a woman you have to tolerate a constant stream of *propios* (indecent suggestions), this being a national sport. The best way to cope is to grit your teeth and ignore it, for although it is a constant irritation, it's quite possible to travel alone. I often travelled by bus, truck and train on my own and several women friends have done the same. The main thing is to know some Spanish, however basic. It gives you more independence, more idea of what's going on around you and makes you less reliant on finding an English speaker to impart essential information. I recommend travelling with another woman largely for moral support.

I only cracked up once under the strain of machismo, when I was once pursued for three hours around the streets of Guadalajara by a Mexican on a bicycle who wanted me to model in his bedroom furniture show-room. I tried desperately to shake him off, determined not to let him know where I lived. In the end, out of sheer frustration and anger, I knocked him off his bicycle and started hitting him with my bag to loud applause from everyone in the street café nearby. Usually 'va al infierno' (go to hell) or 'dejarme en paz, desgraciademente hombre' (leave me in peace you unfortunate man), said with vehemence, is enough to get rid of an unwanted pursuer.

TRAVEL NOTES

Languages Spanish and various Indian dialects.
Transport Buses are by far the best means of getting around. First-class buses cost more but are generally quicker and more reliable and comfort-able. Many towns have a modern central bus station where you can shop around.

Make sure you're not sold a ticket for a bus that's already gone – it can be awkward to change it. Trains are cheaper, but much more limited and very slow. Hitching is more hassle than it's worth with the additional threat of police harassment.

Accommodation Cheap hotels are usually easy to find and it's worth haggling if you feel you're being over-charged. In cities you'll find most of them concentrated around the central square or *zocalo*.

Special problems Many women have enjoyed travelling alone through Mexico, in spite of sexual harassment. Self-confidence and some knowledge of Spanish seems to help.

Don't get involved with or ever trust the police. Police bribery is a common racket (especially if you're driving). If approached it's best to act as if you don't know a word of Spanish. Talk a lot in English about the British Embassy and Tourista (a government agency in charge of looking after tourists), offer them less than half of what they ask and only pay once a reasonable price has been reached.

Don't touch drugs. It's usual for a dealer to sell them to someone, sell the information to the police and then get half the drugs once his victim has been arrested.

Tampons are scarce outside the capital.

Guide John Fisher *The Rough Guide to Mexico (RKP, 1985)*. Probably the best of the Rough Guide series, practical, informed and often amusing – invaluable for any Mexican travel.

CONTACTS

Movimiento Nacional Para Mujeres, San Juan de Letran 11–411, Mexico DF (Tel. 512–58 41). National women's organisation, useful for contacts throughout the country.

Grupo Lambada, Apartado Postal 73–130, Mexico DF. Lesbian group.

Asociacion Por Salud Maternal, San Luis Potosi 101, Apartado 7–150, Mexico DF 7 (Tel. 564–68 11) Provides sex education and contraceptive advice.

Centro de Apoyo a las Mujeres Violadas, Calle 17 No 122, Col San Pedro de los Pinos, Div Personal Astronomos 40–8, Mexico 8 DF (Tel. 277–0901). Support centre for raped women. Open Mon to Fri 4–8pm.

FEM, Martha Lamas, Begonia 13, San Angel INN, Mexico 20 DF. Recommended feminist magazine.

Colectivo Cine Mujer, Angelas Negoechea, Penunuri 19, Sede Casa Oyoacan, Mexico DF. Women's film collective, established in 1974 and still going strong.

CIDHAL, Apartado 579, Cuernavaca, Morelos. Women's documentation centre. (Cuernavaca is about 50 miles from the capital).

Organizacion Nacional Para Mujeres, Apartado Postal 6–29, Guadalajara, (Tel. 15–92 88).

BOOKS

Sybille Bedford, *A Visit to Don Otavio* (1953, Eland Books, 1984). An extremely enjoyable, often hilarious, occasionally lyrical and surprisingly relevant account of travels in 1950s Mexico.

Oscar Lewis, *The Children of Sanchez* (Penguin, 1966). Chronicles the lives of a working-class family in Mexico City in the 1940s. Oral history at its best.

Octavio Paz, *The Labyrinth of Solitude* (Grove Press, 1961). Collection of essays exploring the social and political state of modern Mexico, by one of the country's leading philosophers.

BELIZE

Belize is a tiny, eccentric country quite different from the rest of Central America. Formerly British Honduras, it was colonised by the British and most people speak English. Roughly half the population of 150,000 are Creoles. Others include Mayan Indians, mestizos, Garifunas (of mixed African and Amerindian descent) and a handful of Europeans. Whilst the majority are peasant farmers, one-third live in Belize City, the country's impoverished commercial capital and the only urban area of any size. The countryside, largely covered by forest, feels remarkably empty.

Belize's chief tourist attractions are some fine Mayan ruins and a chain of coral islands called the Cays which are surrounded by the second largest barrier reef in the world. It is also something of a democratic oasis in Central America. Frustration and tension, stemming from decades of colonial repression and non-development, exist beneath the surface but the only external threat comes from Guatemala with which Belize has a long-running dispute over land rights. Outside the City, where women travellers are especially seen as easy prey for local gangs, and Orange Walk, dangerous due to increased drug-trafficking, it feels a very peaceful place.

There is said to be a growing **feminist movement** in Belize as more women seek employment and independence, particularly in the capital. The recently elected United Democratic Party advocates equal rights and claims to want to integrate women more fully into the nation's social and political structure. The Women's Bureau, funded by the government, initiates self-help groups to improve health care and encourage income-generating projects around the country; and there are a few independent women's groups in existence. All the same, Belize is very much a Third World country with many families living in remote areas where there are no roads and people have little contact with the rest of the country. Women in these communities are mostly unaffected by the changes taking place elsewhere.

■ **Jessica Barry first went to Belize specifically to research community development in a newly independent commonwealth country. She liked it so much that she returned two years later.**

I first visited Belize in 1982, only a year after independence. My immediate feeling was one of dismay at the state of neglect that the British had left behind. Belize City seemed a sorrowful place: ragged children played amongst heaps of rubbish; there was an overpowering smell from the open drains that ran along each side of the unpaved streets and emptied raw sewage into a network of fetid canals; decrepit wooden houses, some no more than shacks, leant crazily together in muddy yards. It took me some time to come to terms with my initial response to the city, and to see that beneath its shabby surface lay a richly diverse street life which years of colonial repression had done little to destroy. By the end of four months, during which I travelled around extensively, I was quite bewitched by Belize and knew that I'd eventually return.

The opportunity finally arose in 1984. As I rattled along into the old capital (the new capital, Belmopan, was established as the administrative centre in 1970 but Belize City remains the chief town) in an ancient taxi – there are no buses from the airport – I wondered if I'd notice many changes. 'What's happened?' I asked the fat cheerful taxi driver in amazement as we turned into the main street. No sign of rotting garbage and the surface had been paved. He looked over his shoulder, his pork-pie hat wobbling precariously, 'De opposition won de local election', he grinned.

It was early evening and barefooted boys were loitering in front of the supermarket selling the weekly newspapers. 'Beacon-Reporter-Amandala', they shouted, running three names into one. The pavements were crowded with families enjoying a stroll after the heat of the day.

Night descends quickly in the tropics and before dark I, too, wandered through the city reviving memories. I explored the narrow back streets, and in these poor alleyways nothing had changed: overburdened clothes lines in each back yard; the pungent smell of cooking rice; sounds of reggae music and laughter. I went down Pinks Alley and into Water Lane, crossing over onto Bliss Promenade where the old courthouse is an evocative reminder of a gracious and, for some, more privileged age.

Only a few old colonials remain in Belize. Their place has been taken by international aid-workers and Peace Corps volunteers. Many non-Belizeans love the country, but some find the seediness of the city hard to accept. Crime is rampant and Westerners a prime target. It's hard to be inconspicuous in such a small community. During my first visit I was constantly aware that everything I did was being observed. But apart from one occasion, when a guy I didn't know accused me of being 'uptight' for not talking to him, I was never hassled. Now, as I wandered around on that first warm evening of my return, I felt suddenly at home.

I went to the covered market near the swing bridge hoping to find Mavis, an old Creole woman who sold vegetables. Even before I reached her dimly lit stall I could see the tip of her cigarette glowing in the gloom. She was sitting in her usual place, perched up on the edge of her counter among the cabbages and sweet potatoes. She was even wearing the same faded red cardigan and battered panama. We talked about the trouble she was having trying to stop the chickens from eating the spinach in her yard as around us people started to pack up for the night. Lean sombreroed farmers went past carrying sacks of water melons and yellow grapefruit. Old weatherbeaten Indian women gossiped at the entrance and everywhere there was bustle and noise.

Later I thought again about the extraordinary contrasts in Belize – not only amongst the people but in the land itself. Up in the Maya mountains, beyond the tangled green jungle, there are miles of scented pine forests and hidden trails. Here the silence and solitude is only interrupted by animals and birds. Scarlet parrots, like swift red arrows, streak across your path. Wild orchids, Belize's national flower, grow in abundance. There are waterfalls and views of misted hills which make you catch your breath.

Aldous Huxley once wrote, 'If the world had any ends, Belize would certainly be one of them.'

A more recent saying emblazoned on children's T-shirts gives another perspective. 'If you are good and say your prayers, when you die you'll go to Belize.'

TRAVEL NOTES

Languages English is the official language. Spanish is widely spoken in the north and west. Other languages include Maya and Garifuna.

Transport Buses run from Belize City to the six district towns. Only the northern and western highways are paved. The Hummingbird highway going south is often impassable beyond Dangriga because of heavy rains. There is no railway system.

To reach some of the islands take a speed boat from near the swing bridge in Belize City. They leave every morning.

Accommodation There are many small guest houses and hotels in the City. Outside there are small, cheap and very basic hotels in each major town.

Special problems Belize City isn't safe after dark. Drug smuggling in the north, in and around Orange Walk, is leading to violence and all travellers should take care. Everywhere else is generally safe. Punta Gorda is a particularly friendly and hospitable town.

Guides The *South American Handbook*, (Trade & Travel Publications, Bath) updated yearly, contains less than 20 pages on Belize, but they are packed with useful information.

CONTACTS

The Women's Bureau 44 Gabourel Lane, Belize City. Contact with the Women's Bureau should be made through Norris Hall, Chief Information Officer, Government Information Office, Belmopan. He will also provide information about other women's groups.

Legal Aid Centre (just off Regent Street), 6 Adam Lane, Belize City. Women lawyers at the centre are active in campaigning for women's rights and equal opportunities for girls entering employment. There are also plans for a women's resource centre for research and information.

BOOKS

Zee Edgell, *Beka Lamb* (Heinemann Caribbean Writers Series, 1982). Poignant novel about growing up in Belize City by the former director of the Women's Bureau.

William David Setzekorn, *Formerly British Honduras: The New Nation of Belize* (Ohio University Press, USA). Informative and recently updated account of Belize's history.

NICARAGUA

Nicaragua is at war. Ever since the triumph of the revolution (*el triunfo*) in July 1979, when the age-old dynasty of Anastasio Somoza was finally overthrown, most of the country's people have been fighting to defend themselves against destabilisation and the threat of a full-scale invasion from the United States. A former ally of Somoza, the US government is determined to defeat the ruling Sandinistas, its most dangerous expression of hostility being support of the *contras*, a paramilitary terrorist organisation made up of Somoza's old National Guard, former supporters of the FSLN (Frente Sandinista Liberacion National) and other disenchanted groups.

The combination of this crisis, together with Nicaragua's ongoing efforts to develop the social revolutionary process at every level, make it impossible to visit the country as a 'detached' tourist. However, there are still plenty of foreigners around, from curious travellers to people eager to contribute much-needed skills, and most Nicaraguans will be only too pleased to meet you.

Since it's assumed that you have a purpose, you won't be an oddity travelling alone. Outside war zones, mainly on the borders with Honduras and Costa Rica, you'll find few restrictions on your movements, provided you carry a passport at all times. Transport and accommodation are cheap, if not the most comfortable. Machismo has by no means been eradicated, despite the impressive participation of women in the Nicaraguan revolution, but there's little threat of physical harassment.

The huge involvement of **women in the Nicaraguan Revolution** – at one stage they made up 30 per cent of the army including some in high command – has made it a case-study for feminists and women in national liberation movements everywhere. Today women no longer play a leading military role in defence of their country, but through their central association, AMNLAE, many continue to risk their lives as couriers as well as participating in a wide range of projects.

◤ **Carole Fabian went on a tour organised by the London-based Nicaragua Solidarity Campaign.**

Travel to Nicaragua from London is easy to arrange. Our tour company (Progressive Tours) handled all the ticket and insurance details (no entry visas necessary) and the Nicaragua Solidarity Campaign presented us with a full and organised programme arranged with Turnica, the Nicaraguan tourist agency.

Once in Nicaragua, there appear no restrictions on the movements of visitors. Anywhere we could reach by boat, bus or plane was open (including war zones) and guides and speakers were cooperative. Yet the war and the economic blockade exert a visible reality. Should your tour include a visit that happens to be currently in the line of contras fire, your programme might have to be hastily re-arranged. Transport was laid on for us, but is now a scarce commodity and needed for purposes other than ferrying tourists around. Spare parts cannot be obtained and petrol is short. We had only two days' supply left for our bus towards the end of our tour and I was struck by the pure delight of our coach driver when I offered him two small batteries from my camera to use for his headlights.

The ability to dispense with Western luxuries is essential. Our special Turnica bus was soft and new, but sometimes we had to travel in an ancient and very bumpy coach from the University of Managua. And accommodation can be spartan – all our hotels were pre-booked and at one, near Masaya, we slept three to a room with one sheet per bed (a water shortage prevented much washing), and there was no soap or toilet paper. Also, don't expect great efficiency. On top of all the practical problems, Nicaragua maintains a 'mañana' view of the world which creates a warm relaxed atmosphere but can be very frustrating. One-or two-hour waits for lunch in restaurants we'd booked into, and the sudden cancellation of visits because nobody had checked opening times or the availability of speakers, were a familiar occurrence. However, they were only the one real irritant in a short, crowded and exciting programme.

Stepping off the plane at Managua airport, you are immediately involved in the plight of Nicaragua. Everyone, from government and trade-union officials to nursery nurses, teachers, peasants and mothers whose children have been kidnapped by the contras, wants to explain to you what's happening in their country. A strong sense that the outside world is only fed inadequate and distorted information is accompanied by a painfully moving belief that, seeing the reality, visitors can return home to increase understanding and support for what Nicaragua's trying to achieve. It was impossible not to be impressed by the gains of the Revolution and the clarity, patience, friendliness and humour with which so many aspects of society were explained and shown to us.

The most fundamental and lasting change has probably been in agricultural reform. Most Nicaraguans are peasants and one of the first acts of the Sandinista government was to give them the land so long denied to them. For women, too, there has been some remarkable progress in the last six years. In Esteli we met Clorinda, the regional secretary of *AMNLAE* (Nicaraguan Women's Association Luisa Amanda Espinosa, named after an FSLN commander who died in the fighting). A calm woman with short dark hair and a strong voice, she explained how AMNLAE (formerly AMPRONAC) had begun as women's response to the repression of the Somoza dictatorship. Through the 1970s they organised mass demonstrations, looked after the wounded, acted as couriers and provided safe houses, as well as being active combatants in the fighting. Since the success of the Revolution, she said, priorities had changed. Women's concerns now include education, improving health-care and increasing their role in production. Voluntary brigades of women build their own houses whilst others are learning mechanical skills.

In a visit later to the government newspaper *Barricada*, we learned of women office cleaners who, after gaining some education, were now fully fledged journalists. Everywhere, in fact, I was struck by the confidence of the women we met, yet their progress is still hampered by deeply entrenched male attitudes – women on television are still shown inspiring their men to action rather than fighting beside them. But with energies so absorbed by the war against the contras, it's hardly surprising that machismo has been able to maintain its grip.

For a country at war, I found Nicaragua an amazingly open society and police and soldiers were unfailingly friendly and polite. We experienced no harassment from men and, language permitting, were free to approach anyone we wished. In fact the government is only too anxious to promote tourism.

Ann Ogidi spent five weeks in Nicaragua, mainly to research a dissertation on liberation theology.

Foreigners in Managua tend to concentrate in one small area: nearly all information is exchanged at the Inter-Continental Hotel, the only other building besides the Bank of America which stands over seven storeys high. Given the general chaos of communication and street planning, everyone takes their bearings from these two beacons.

There are no tourists in Nicaragua, only travellers, *brigadistas*, *internacionalistas* and crazy *gringos*. This international community, centred in Managua, ignores the subtle distinction between journalists, diplomats and artists; they're all here with a theory, a story, an angle that someone will be interested in. In my efforts to arrange interviews, gain access to libraries and organise travel, I found no substitute for the international circuit. Most of my really useful contacts and meetings stemmed from casual conversation in the Inter-Continental, the Yerba Buena or Comedor Sara. (The last two are evening eating places frequented by the foreign population of Managua). But Nicaragua has very little in common with this exciting but insular world, so when you're feeling relaxed and confident about your Spanish go north.

Travelling north through Esteli, Matagalpa, Jinotega and Ocotal takes you through some of the most beautiful parts of the country. High up in the mountains of the Selva Negra the nights are freezing cold, even in summer, but it's worth going for the rich variety of vegetation and wildlife. Almost everywhere you'll find the contra war a part of everyday life. Soldiers seem to be permanently mobilised, moving from area to area in buses, on foot and in trucks. Compulsory military service makes it an accepted social fact, yet it doesn't seem to have brutalised the people. Culture is an important part of education and poetry workshops are encouraged in both the army and the police force. With this emphasis on the humanity of the security forces, it's not uncommon for a villager to approach a policeman for advice on a domestic problem.

It is impossible not to draw attention to yourself because you'll be the one stepping in potholes, getting caught in the downpours and the one waiting at the wrong bus-stop. Ask twenty different people a direction and you will get twenty different answers. Nicaraguans, courteous and friendly, would rather give you a wrong answer than none at all. The thing to remember is just take everything as it comes, as one taxi-driver said to me: 'This is Nicaragua, don't give yourself any more problems than you've already got.'

As a black woman, I attracted special curiosity. I got quite used to explaining that, firstly, I wasn't from Bluefields and secondly, I wasn't Cuban and I spoke very little Spanish. People just couldn't resolve the apparent contradiction between black skin and England. Sometimes I'd be introduced as a British journalist living in Nigeria, which was even more confusing, or a Nigerian working for the British government. On the street level I was a definite oddity; often in the north, women would come out of their shops and openly stare. Once at a bus stop a mother thrust a crying child into my arms and asked me to talk to it while she went to do her shopping. People I was interviewing, to illustrate a point, would often draw analogies from Africa in order to indicate a level of common understanding or experience of exploitation and I was usually invited back to meet the wife/husband and children. After Britain, it made a great change to be able to use colour politics positively.

My encounters with sexism ranged from light banter to irritating drunk hassle, but it was mostly verbal. Obvious tourist attractions, such as beaches, crater lakes and the hot springs at Tipitapa, are the dodgiest areas, where I wouldn't recommend that you travel alone. Amongst Nicaraguans leisure tends to be a family activity, and you'll quite often find yourself being more hassled by Western men.

TRAVEL NOTES

Languages Spanish, with one of the harder accents to understand in Latin America. English is spoken on the Atlantic Coast, where you also might find the Spanish easier to understand. Also Miskitu and other Amerindian languages.

Transport Taxis are cheap and operate

as a public transport system with fixed rates. Chartered taxis from the stand outside the Hotel Inter-Continental are necessary for awkward journeys, and the driver will rip you off at foreigners' rates – haggle but expect to pay a premium. Buses in Managua are very cheap but overcrowded and uncomfortable; the 118/119, which you get outside the Hotel IC, is notorious for pickpockets.

Accommodation There seems to be no medium in Managua between the $60 a night + *Hotel IC* and the rock bottom *hospedajes*. Just opened this year, is a small government-built pension, *El Colibri*, exceptional value and reasonably priced but highly sought after by the travellers. If you don't book into here first try again until there is a vacancy. All the tourist *hospedajes* (boarding houses), equally unrecommendable, are clustered in one area near the cine Dorado, Avenida España.

Special problems Don't change money on the black market. It's illegal and there's little difference from the official rate. Bring dollars and make sure you change them into local currency in Managua as you'll only be charged the exorbitant 'airport official rate' outside. Take a torch with you. Power cuts are frequent and you'll really appreciate having your own light.

Other information: If you get the chance, don't miss a trip to the Atlantic Coast. Bluefields, home of the Miskitu Indians, is a war zone but the Nicara-guan tourist agency, Turnica, organise tours including an unforgettable boat trip back across Lake Nicaragua.

Contact the *Nicaragua Solidarity Campaign*, 20–21 Compton Terrace, London N1 2UN (Tel. 01–359 8982) for details of study tours and up-to-date information. Also, Progressive Tours Ltd, 12 Porchester Place, London W2 2BS (Tel. 01–262 1676) who have links with the NSC.

Guide The *South American Handbook* (see Belize) has limited coverage. If you can read Italian, there's a good – and radical – guide published to Nicaragua by Clup, Milano.

CONTACTS
Any contact with women's groups is best made through the central office of **AMNLAE**, Apt. Postal A238, Managua.

BOOKS
Cain et al., *Sweet Ramparts* (NSC/War on Want, 1983). Traces the history of the Nicaraguan revolution and assesses achievements and their limitations for women since 1979. Recommended.

Margaret Randall, *Sandino's Daughters* (Zed Books, 1981). Tells the story of women's participation in the revolution through a number of interviews made shortly after 1979.

For a general historical summary of Nicaraguan history up to that period, read George Black, *Triumph of the People* (Zed Books, 1981).

COSTA RICA

Costa Rica is known in the United States as the tourist's paradise. The country is rich in wildlife and tropical vegetation, much of it preserved in well-kept nature reserves and national parks, and there are some beautiful beaches. A further attraction is its reputation as a peaceful haven of democracy amidst the political turmoil of Central America.

With no army, a relatively high standard of living and its own national health service, Costa Rica is certainly the most socially and economically advanced country in the region. But it is heavily dependent on the United States whose influence is everywhere. In contrast to its northern neighbours, especially Mexico, the preponderance of burger joints and baseball caps in the capital, San José, can be quite a shock. There is also little evidence of an indigenous population. Apart from a tiny minority of Indians and a few black and *mestizo* communities, most people are of Spanish descent.

Costa Rica is not a particularly difficult place for women travellers, but for Costa Rican women life is often very hard. 52 per cent of families are headed by single women, burdened with all the responsibility of earning a wage and looking after children, old people and itinerant men. As a result, in poor neighbourhoods, they tend to be the first to get involved in any kind of community action.

Although the **Women's Movement** in Costa Rica is largely middle class, one group, *CEFEMINA* (Feminist Centre for Information and Action), is able to work with poor women through its links with *COPAN*, a popular community organisation with 80 per cent women members. Their work includes co-ordinating self-help groups on issues such as nutrition, breast-feeding, contraception and sexuality, and bringing out a monthly newsletter. Other feminist organisations in San José are *Ventana*, who concentrate on theoretical discussion, and *Colmena*, mainly involved in health and social assistance.

◪ **Jane Horton lived in Costa Rica for almost two years, teaching English.**

Tourism in Costa Rica has suffered considerably in recent years as a result of tensions on the northern border – Nicaragua is only six hours by bus from San José. Nevertheless, large numbers of Americans continue to visit the country, recommended as a long stop-off for anyone travelling up or down through Latin America. If you're passionately interested in flora and fauna, it's even worth an (expensive) one-off holiday.

San José lies in the middle of Costa Rica, cradled between steep hills and fertile land where everything imaginable seems to grow. We once planted a two-foot banana tree in our garden and ten months later it was at least ten-foot high and bearing 400 bananas! Along with coffee, the major export, bananas are one of the country's main sources of revenue.

Rolling hills, little wooden farmsteads, and coffee and banana plantations lead down from the central valley to the tropical coasts of the Pacific and the Caribbean. Both are accessible by bus or train, but the train journey, though slower, is by far the more memorable in both directions. Puerto Limón, on the Caribbean side, is a fascinating place: a ramshackle port with a palm-fringed promenade and a largely black community, speaking a mixture of Spanish and English. From here you can take a bus to one of the loveliest national parks at Cahuita. It's possible to camp in the park, by the beach, but mind out for theft, the wild ocean, falling coconuts and buying hash when there's a policeman behind the next tree. There's another park north of Puerto Limón, called Tortuguero, which is only accessible by boat. Almost an island, linked to the mainland by only a tiny strip of land with water and jungle on all sides, it's a real adventure. Canoes can be rented to explore the tropical rain forest and there are cheap cabins to stay in; you will, though, tire of beans and rice by the time you leave.

The two best spots to visit on the Pacific are the parks of Manuel Antonio and Santa Rosa. Manuel Antonio, six hours' uncomfortable bus-ride from San José, is great for a few lazy days on the beach. It is well geared up to campers, with showers, wooden tables and well-marked footpaths, and the beaches are idyllic – the sort you never expect to see outside a travel brochure. Santa Rosa is much more demanding. Unless you have a vehicle, expect a steep 12-kilometre walk from the park entrance to the beach. This is where turtles come up in their thousands every so often to lay eggs – all I found was a giant shell. There is nowhere to stay except a camping ground, so take a tent if you can and all your food supplies.

Finally, a park with a difference is Monteverde. A huge nature reserve, Monteverde is a cloud forest way up in the mountains above the busy resort of Puntarenas (to be avoided). On the edge lies a small village, Santa Elena, where you can stay and talk to the American Quaker community who settled there after the war and were largely responsible for the protection of the forest. This park, unlike the others, has an entrance fee but it is worth it for the spectacular scenery and remarkable animal life.

I usually travelled with a man or with a group of people, but I don't think travelling alone is a problem in Costa Rica. Men stare but they're not aggressive, at least outside the capital. Propositioning gringas is something of a sport in San José.

It was when I had a baby that I really noticed the attitudes of men and women around me. When my belly swelled I wasn't bothered at all; instead men would stop me in the street and say: 'How lovely! When is the little one due? Children are gifts of God you know. . . .'. When Ana was born I breastfed her in the most public places, bus stations, cafés, parks. Again men would turn and look, only to smile and complement me on my beautiful baby and affirm that 'mother's milk is best'. The first time I went out without her and with my newly flattened belly I was hassled again.

Women showered me with advice. Time and time again I was told to stop Ana's protruding navel with a cork and a cent coin and tie a belt around her middle. On top of advice to shave her head and even cut her eyelashes (to make her hair grow faster), the most common refrain was: 'Oh, she must be cold. Why hasn't she got a hat on?'. No matter how hot the weather – and the same seems to apply to most Latin and Third World countries – babies are knitted up from top to toe.

I chose to pay for a room to have Ana, although private treatment increases the risk of having to suffer a 'high-tech' birth. (The process is much more 'natural' in public hospitals where there simply isn't enough money for modern equipment.) But I did have a lot of choice: only one night in hospital with my baby beside me, a bed for my partner, and a friend allowed into the delivery room. The loveliest thing about having Ana in Costa Rica was the view which greeted her into the world, of the green green hills around San José silhouetted against the early morning sky.

TRAVEL NOTES

Languages Spanish is the main language, but quite a few people speak English in tourist areas and, especially, along the Atlantic coast.

Transport Buses go virtually everywhere and are cheap and regular. It's best to book a day or two in advance for long trips and to be sure of a seat you must arrive an hour before departure time. Avoid special tours arranged by travel agents – they're designed for rich gringos. Taxis are worth taking to the suburbs of San José or late at night.

Trains to both coasts are cheap, bumpy and fascinating.

Accommodation San José tends to be expensive, but outside the city there are quite a few cheap, basic hotels. Camping is commonplace in the national parks, but obviously carries an element of risk.

Special problems Women are advised not to wear shorts or strapless sundresses in San José. Also keep your passport and papers in order and on you at all times. Spot checks by the police are frequent due to drug traffic and the continuing rise in illegal immigration. Pickpocketing is on the increase in large towns, especially San José.

Guide The *South American Handbook* (see Belize) contains some 30 pages on Costa Rica including listings for hotels of every kind.

CONTACTS
CEFEMINA, Apartado 949, San José. See introduction.
Revista Ventana, Apartado 925, Centro Colón, San José. Magazine with an emphasis on feminist theory.

BOOKS
Paula Palmer, *What Happen* (obtainable from: The Bookshop, Av. 1, Calle 1 and 3, San José). Fascinating oral history of the black people of the Atlantic Coast written by a North American woman who lived in an Atlantic village for several years.

We also strongly recommend two **other books on Central America**:
Elisabeth Burgos-Debray, ed., *I. . . . Rigoberta Menchu* (Verso, 1984). An Indian woman from Guatemala chronicles the repression and history of resistance in her country, including insights into religion, feminism and family life.
Manlio Argueta, *One Day of a Life* (Chatto, 1984). Using the perspective of a Salvadorean peasant woman, this novel movingly conveys the everyday horrors of the war in El Salvador.

Chapter Eighteen

SOUTH AMERICA

Along with Mexico and the central strip, almost all the countries of **South America** share a history of Spanish colonisation. The one exception is Brazil, covering roughly half the continent, which was colonised by the Portuguese.

More than 400 years later these countries still have a lot in common, from their Latin/Indian ethnic mix to their ongoing political instability. Although this unity is quite superficial – the difference between countries is one of the most striking things about travelling in South America – certain characteristics do apply collectively to travellers.

Whether in Bolivia, Colombia, Ecuador or Peru, for instance, as a foreigner you will always be a *gringa*. Although it may sometimes come across as an insult, usually from people hostile to the wealth and power of North America with which you will inevitably be associated, the expression is not in itself offensive.

In terms of attitudes to women, the area is renowned for its **machismo** — the untrammelled sexism of its male Latin population, often characterised by a kind of tough, swaggering bravado. This has been repeatedly challenged by Latin American feminists who form one of the most militant women's movements in the Third World. Machismo may prove a burden for women travellers, especially in resort areas, isolated beaches and the larger towns, but don't be put off. As a foreigner and a curiosity you're likely to elicit more help and hospitality than harassment.

Tourism is not well developed in South America. Apart from areas of famous archaeological sites, some stretches of coast, notably in Brazil and Venezuela, and the odd ski resort, the predominance of high mountains, huge flat plains and dense rain forest has left it relatively untouched by commercialised travel. It is still a place to go for adventure.

The following articles cover seven of the thirteen South American countries. We would like to have included **Argentina** but at present British travellers are not granted visas for non-commercial visits and we were unable to find an up-to-date, post Falklands/Malvinas account. We would also like to have included **Uruguay** – now returned to civilian rule – and hope to do so in the next edition of this book.

VENEZUELA

Of all the countries in South America, **Venezuela** is one of the least touched by tourism. This is partly due to the government's lack of interest in trying to attract foreign visitors; but also because, until devaluation in 1982, the country was impossibly expensive.

Almost a million Europeans have settled in Venezuela since the Second World War, to join a mixed population of Indian, Spanish and African descent. The entire coast borders on the Caribbean and people everywhere tend to share the relaxed, casual attitude to life associated with that part of the world. In general they are friendly and helpful, especially if you speak Spanish.

Thanks to oil, Venezuela is a rich country by Latin American standards. However, the government, whose democracy stands out in the region, has not been able to prevent rising unemployment. Already half the population live in the country's eight major cities where there are few jobs and no security, the crime rate is high and more and more families are classed as 'marginal'. Over 52 per cent of the population (including the President) are illegitimate, and large numbers of families have no paternal support of any kind.

Venezuela's reputation for democratic rule in fact only very partially extends to **women**. True, it had a female governor as long ago as 1524 and women took part in the fight for independence from Spanish rule, but today, even basic rights still need to be fought for. Less than three years ago groups of women organised marches through the capital of Caracas to try and improve their legal position. Backed by the Venezuelan Federation of women lawyers, these demonstrations had some success: reforms to the Civil Code gave financial responsibility to the fathers of illegitimate children, made divorce easier and improved women's property rights. The new legislation, plus the existence of a government family planning service, makes Venezuela appear fairly liberal, particularly in the South American context. But the laws and the contraceptives aren't much use without an education programme; most women aren't aware of their personal or political rights and so the exploitation carries on.

Feminists have a hard time in the face of a small but powerful opposition from groups backed by the church. Giovanna Espino wrote a book about the need for legal abortion in Venezuela. At the launch she and some of her feminist colleagues were attacked – verbally and physically – by a pro-life group.

Among the few **feminist groups**. *Miercoles*, made a film about Isma-elina, a Venezuelan peasant woman who died, aged 42, in her 24th pregnancy. She had earned the family living making flower pots, looked after the house and brought up the children single-handed. Although the film highlights the need for sexual education and a change in attitudes, its distribution tends to be limited to middle-class intellectuals who are already sympathetic to the problems. One organisation which has had success in breaking out of these limits is *8 de Marzo*, who work in the industrial city of Valencia. They write simple plays about women's issues and perform them in the *barrio* slums.

◤ **Mary Farquharson lived in Venezuela for seventeen months, working on the *Daily Journal*, an English-language newspaper with a circulation of 15,000 largely aimed at expatriates.**

Venezuela is a physically imposing country. Rivers are impassable, mountains are high and the plains stretch out for days without a hint of civilisation. Its isolation from tourism makes travelling hard but exciting. Outside the ugly northern cities and the few equally ugly resorts, there is the choice between staying in a very basic hotel or just slinging a hammock between two trees. The climate favours the second option, though not without a mosquito net.

I had expected that two females would be constantly bothered by local men who are unused to visitors let alone women with backpacks. As it turned out we were treated with great respect; people from all walks of life went out of their way to help us.

In the Venezuelan Amazon a navy captain helped us to reach an Amerindian community living on the banks of the Orinoco; in the middle of the *llanos* (plains) a family gave us a lift to the nearest town – four hours away – and insisted that we go to their home for a meal and a shower. Travelling with a man, I found the people friendly but they weren't quite so helpful.

The only problems I encountered in nearly two years in Venezuela were at the coast. Almost every trip I made with another woman to the more isolated Caribbean beaches were ruined by men exposing themselves, hassling us and, on one occasion, stealing from us and physically threatening us. But stick to the busier beaches – and there are plenty to choose from – and this is less likely to happen.

I chose not to travel on my own in Venezuela because most of the interesting places are very isolated and visitors are still uncommon. It is not like Brazil or Peru where the main problem can be avoiding other foreigners. Although the easiest way to travel is with a car, it is possible to visit interesting places by public transport. Internal flights are cheap and a good way to start a journey into the wilder reaches of the country. Puerto Ayacucho, the capital of the Venezuelan Amazon, has a small airport. It is a sleepy jungle town where the military are supposed to check permits before allowing travellers to visit Amerindian communities.

With time and patience, a lift to the banks of the Orinoco can be negotiated and from there it is a question of waiting for the local doctor or
a tribesman to offer a lift in his motorised canoe.

Alternatively, a flight to Ciudad Bolivar can be the start of the long
journey towards Brazil. When the local owner of an old American car
can find five passengers he leaves the city for El Dorado, the rough mining
town with a top security prison where Papillon was once housed. Between
the main street and the prison is a river infested with electric eels. Very
few prisoners escape. El Dorado is civilised in comparison with Kilometer
88, a hostile village that provides temporary accommodation for thousands of gold miners. There are only a few women in Kilometer 88 and
most of them are prostitutes. Unless travellers are interested in tasting
the extremity of he-man culture, the main reason for visiting this
aggressive spot is to catch a jeep across the savannah to Brazil. There is
only one road across the huge plain; it is unpaved and sometimes unpass-
able. The scenery is superb: grassy plains stretching for as far as the eye
can see, interrupted only by flat-topped mountains and an occasional
Amerindian settlement.

Perhaps the most civilised adventure in Venezuela is to explore the
Andes, to the west of the country. The capital, Merida, is a university
town with several decent hotels, a good market and plenty of sunny
squares. The world's highest cable-car takes tourists to a café at the top
of the mountain which overlooks the town, but more enlightened travellers get off at the station before the last. From here, there is a path to
the village of Los Nevados – apparently a three-hour hike for locals
although it took us nearly seven. A cluster of red roofs sit in a valley
surrounded by green hills. As the dying sun catches the village and the
mules are put to bed, it is hard to imagine anywhere more tranquil.

Not far from Merida the mountains give way to mile upon mile of flat
marshy plain. The contrast is striking not only in the scenery but in the
people and the way of life. The llanos are cowboy country. Men herd
cattle by day and, at nightfall, they play the *cuatro* – small guitar – and
sing plaintive songs about the land. Women are kept in the kitchen; they
appear more subdued than in other parts of the country. Although female
travellers aren't made to feel particularly welcome in the llanos, the
rewards for anyone interested in wildlife are immense. One swamp will
reveal flocks of heron, scarlet ibis, the odd eagle, plenty of snakes, lizards
and iguana.

One of the most exciting trips I made was to a mountain five hours
by bus from Caracas. Known as Sorte, it is the centre of the Maria Lionza
black magic cult which plays an important part in the lives of most poor
Venezuelans. Every weekend busloads of believers come from the cities
and build small shrines in the mountain clearings. Smoking fat cigars and
beating African drums between their thighs they call the spirits; each

group has a medium who, once the spirit has been contacted, will walk on glass and perform other rituals to help and protect the group. Women dominate these ceremonies. Men go too but they tend to hide, like guilty children, in the shadows.

TRAVEL NOTES

Languages Spanish and some native Indian languages and dialects.

Transport Apart from good bus services between major cities, *colectivo* taxis known as *por puestos* monopolise transport to and from smaller towns and villages. In general, few tourists means few facilities for making travelling easy. Visit one of Corpotourismo's offices in Caracas to discuss plans, but don't let them put you off the more exciting destinations.

Accommodation Hotels tend to be expensive although good, cheap places can be found if you look around. Camping is popular, especially in the resort areas, but there are no special camp sites for travellers and women are definitely not advised to sleep out in isolated areas.

Special problems Bureaucracy can be maddening. Carry your passport at all times as the police are fond of doing spot checks. Thieving is common, mainly in Caracas where it's unsafe for women to travel alone at night. Hold on to valuables and don't wear jewellery at any time.

Guide The *South American Handbook* (Trade and Travel Publications, Bath). Updated yearly, carries about 50 pages on Venezuela and is still the best guidebook around.

CONTACTS

Circulos Femeninos Populares, Apartado 4240, Caracas 1010–A, Venezuela. Umbrella organisation co-ordinating and training local women's groups in rural areas and poor neighbourhoods. Publishes a bulletin, *Mujeres en la Lucha* (Women in Struggle) which includes articles about their activities and issues such as housing, water, food, health.

Grupo Femenista Miercoles, Apartado 668, San Cristobal 50001–A, Tachira, Venezuela (see introduction).

La Mala Vida is a lively feminist publication, available from Apartado Postal 47659, Caracas 1041, Venezuela.

COLOMBIA

Colombia is a violent country. Robberies and muggings are common and it's the centre of illicit drug traffic in Latin America. Smugglers see tourists as an easy target to use as innocent carriers, making them a prime suspect for the police who themselves may not think twice about planting drugs on the unwary traveller.

Political conflict adds to Colombia's dangerous reputation. As recently as 1950, thousands of people were being killed in a long and bloody war between Liberals and Conservatives. Today the main battle is between the military and widespread guerrilla and other popular opposition movements. Recent peace initiatives by the relatively democratic Conservative government of President Betancur seem to have had little effect.

Not surprisingly, Colombia is one of the least popular Latin American destinations for travellers and Europeans are a rare sighting. Being a woman in a strong *machista* culture makes problems worse and without a male companion be prepared for continual sexual harassment.

Feminism in Colombia has made a lot of progress since the first groups started up in 1975. Besides being the venue of the successful First Feminist Meeting of Latin America and the Caribbean, the country has witnessed several women's demonstrations; the publication of feminist literature; the development of research; and the formation of new autonomous groups as well as others, such as *Mujer en la Lucha*, which are directly linked to political parties.

Reaching women of all backgrounds is a major problem for the Women's Movement in a country where social and economic divisions are so rigid. One of the most progressive groups in Colombia is *Cine Mujer*, a women's film-making collective which has made some headway in gaining access to the all-important mass media of cinema and television. Even the poorest families in Colombia tend to have TV, and cinema is a popular form of entertainment. Cine Mujer have made several short films about the position of women in Colombian society, which have been shown up until recently in cinemas throughout the country. As long as they don't openly attack the church or the hallowed concept of the family, the group can use this access to a mass audience to challenge many popular myths. As they take advantage of the increasing use of video, there are hopes of achieving an even wider distribution.

◢ **Karen Stowe and Emma Lilly spent six months travelling together in Colombia and Ecuador. They specifically visited Colombia to find out about the Women's Movement.**

In Colombia we wanted to make contact with as many women's groups, organisations and campaigns as possible, to find out the kind of services they offer and what problems they have encountered. However, our experiences brought home the immense difficulties in communicating across cultures; and the gulf between Western feminist assumptions and the reality of women's lives in the Third World.

We spent two months in the capital, Bogotá, a dirty, inhospitable city, sprawling across an Andean plateau at a height of 10,000 feet with a dramatic climate, fluctuating between oppressive brooding storms and bursts of clear sunlight. This uneasy atmosphere, together with the prevalence of street crime and political tension makes for a city which has little attraction for the outsider.

One of the first places we visited was the *Casa de la Mujer* (Women's House), which was set up in 1982 as a centre for rape-crisis counselling, providing psychological and legal support for women. We were initially apprehensive, with no idea of what reception to expect as European outsiders. In fact we were quickly put at ease. The centre – which is run by six paid women and twenty volunteers – was a place we returned to regularly, both as a source of information and advice and as a haven from the hassles of life in Bogotá.

The Casa de la Mujer (see Travel Notes for address), though primarily a counselling service, is very much involved in all Colombian women's issues. It runs courses on health and sexuality, prenatal instruction and creative classes for children. It is publicised on local radio, has a large and comfortable meeting space, and has been used by over 2,000 women in the three years since it opened.

Through the Casa we were also introduced to a private, non-profit-making organisation which runs a health service for women. A much-needed supplement to the ill-equipped and underfinanced government health centres, these women's clinics offer cervical smears, pregnancy tests, family planning, and, though officially illegal in Catholic Colombia, abortions. These, carried out within ten weeks of conception for a fee of about $50, are performed under the guise of 'completing' unsuccessful backstreet or self-induced abortions. The government, probably for strictly economic reasons, turns a blind eye.

We were surprised by this level of women's activity and organisation in Bogotá and impressed by the services on both practical and emotional levels. Inevitably, though, we found the organisers predominantly middle-class. And the poorest women in Bogotá – those living in the *barrios* (shanty towns) at the edge of the city – were both socially and geographically marginalised, even from the free services. They could barely afford the bus fare in to one of the clinics, let alone the time.

This is something the Casa de la Mujer is well aware of, and they have begun setting up women's projects in the barrios themselves. We were interested in visiting one of these – they seem to have met with over-whelming success – but were discouraged on the grounds that this might lead to a breakdown in the delicate relations of trust. We accepted the argument. However, we still felt that, despite the gulf between the barrio women and ourselves, we could learn a lot by meeting some of them and talking.

A chance to do this eventually arose when we met a Jesuit priest, Francisco, who had chosen to live in one of the poorest barrios. He invited us to meet a woman called Graciela, a mother of eight children, who had impressed him with her efforts to organise and improve conditions in the community. The barrio in which they lived was a straggle of two towns – Sucre and San Martin – just a small part of the vast network of shanties that have sprung up in the last thirty years on Bogotá's outskirts. Francisco drove us out along dirt tracks clinging to the steep hillsides, the buildings, overlooking the skyscrapers of central

Bogotá, a ramshackle collection of wood, corrugated iron and breeze block.

Graciela received us at Sucre, gave us lunch, and talked passionately about developments over the last ten years. She described how she came to realise the futility of relying on men to effect change, and how she set up a *consultorio* (committee), made up predominantly of women, to answer some of the community's health needs. There were considerable problems and struggles. The local men strongly resisted any kind of women's solidarity outside the home and, though they were happy enough to let women work long hours in the worst service sector jobs, would often prevent their attending meetings. But, as Graciela made clear, there was and is determination. 'We have to bear the blows and persevere – if women don't try to change things here nobody else will.'

At Sucre, in fact, women take responsibility for more or less everything in the community – for food, clothing, health and education. Men seem to have little commitment to family life. Those that do have jobs, usually on construction sites, spend their free time and money on beer – 'which,' as Graciela says, 'only goes to the government.' For the money to keep things going, women are forced into work as maids, waitresses, cooks and cleaners in the wealthier Bogotá households, jobs in which they are periodically sacked, since otherwise their employers would have to pay *prestaciones*, a form of social security.

Our encounter with Graciela – and the several occasions when we returned to Sucre and San Martin – are among the most powerful memories of our time in Colombia, and we felt strongly inspired by the way we saw her and other barrio women organising in the face of all odds. Since leaving in 1984, though, we have had no news of the community. For all we know it may even have disappeared. A decision by the government to build a new road, means that the shanties, and the social problem they pose, are, for a while, 'solved'.

TRAVEL NOTES

Languages Spanish.

Transport Buses are cheap and frequent. All long-distance routes are covered by coaches – comfortable but a bit more expensive. There are few passenger trains. Never travel in a taxi without a meter as you'll be overcharged.

Accommodation The poor exchange rate on the peso makes Colombia one of the most expensive South American countries. However, hotels outside the main cities can be very cheap. Camping isn't advised.

Special problems Thieves and pickpockets are rife – hang on to your luggage at all times, watch your pockets and don't wear a watch or jewellery. Expect harassment from all kinds of men, including the police and the military. With a largely mestizo population, Colombia is perhaps the worst country in South America for *machismo*. Bus stations can be particularly frightening places for harassment of all kinds. The drug scene is very heavy. Buses are periodically searched by the police and it's common for drug pushers to set people up. Never carry packages for other people without checking the contents. Sentences for possession can be very long.

Guide The *South American Handbook* (see Venezuela) includes over 100 pages on Colombia.

CONTACTS

Casa de la Mujer, CRA 19 56–29 Bogotá. (Tel. 2496317). Women's centre.

Centro de Informacion y Recursos para la Mujer. C1 36 17–44, Bogotá (Tel. 2454266). Advice centre for rape crisis counselling, family planning etc.

Cine Mujer, Av. 25c 49–24, Apartado 202, Bogotá (Tel. 2426184). Women's film-making collective.

Unidad de Orientacion Materna y Assistencia, CRA 17–33–50, Bogotá (Tel. 2850910). Women's health clinic.

BRAZIL

Brazil is huge, with land ranging from the tropical rain forest of the Amazon Basin, to partially arid Highlands, down to the heavily industrialised coastal strip. And its population too is diverse. After the centuries of decimation which began with colonisation only a fraction of the indigenous Indian population remains. The rest are mainly descended from the Portuguese colonists, the African slaves they brought with them, and the millions of European families who more recently flocked to the country for work.

A lot of Brazil's wealth and most of its European population are concentrated in the south around the two largest cities, Rio de Janeiro and São Paulo. In contrast, the north-east, containing one-third of all Brazilian people, is strikingly poor; the birthrate is very high, wages are low and there's widespread malnutrition. Parts of these areas, especially Rio and the larger cities of the north-east, are becoming increasingly unsafe and women are advised never to travel alone at night.

Brazil is presently emerging in great confusion from a long period of military rule. In January 1985 Tancredo Neves, known popularly as 'Dr Tancredo', was elected President by an overwhelming majority, marking the start of a much-heralded transition to democracy. Two months later he died, leaving his successor to build a government based on the uneasy alliance of communists and conservatives, big business and the trade unions.

Many students, trade unionists and other political activists went into exile during the 1960s when the army was particularly repressive. Among them were feminists who later returned with ideas from Europe and the United States. They are just one of the influences behind Brazil's growing **Women's Movement**. Today groups range from autonomous feminist organisations campaigning on issues such as health, sexist education,

male violence and women's legal rights, to more hierarchical organisations directly linked to political parties.

▨ **Ines Rieder has been living in Brazil since 1984. She is active in the
Women's Movement and contributes to the feminist national newspaper,
Mulherio.**

Every time I set off to a new place I mean to avoid comparisons, but I
end up bringing out my collection of memories, trying to fit the new into
the familiar patterns of the past.

This happened when I first came to Brazil. Everything seemed strange
and yet I felt I'd seen it before. Finally I found the answer: all the
ingredients I recognised from other places were suddenly mixed together
here in one country. There are the Brazilian cities which are slightly
poorer imitations of North American ones; and there is the countryside
with all its reminiscence of Africa – red soil, lush green vegetation,
simplicity – but already much more under the influence of mechanisation
and agribusiness. Then there are the Brazilian people, a mingling of so
many races but still defined by their own class rules.

The descendants of Portuguese colonial families are still major landowners in Brazil and, together with a few other European and Arab
families who have made it as merchants and factory-owners, control most
of the political power. Beneath them lies a sizeable, mainly white, middle
class. The majority of poor are black and *mulatto*, landless peasants who
continue to migrate to the cities to survive. Their cultural and religious
life is still influenced by African traditions, but the ever-present TV is
teaching them how to adapt to the values of a consumer society. Whatever
there exists of 'true' Brazilian culture is being eroded by car pollution
and replaced with plastic.

I did not arrive in Brazil expecting to find a tropical paradise or to
have *the* sensual experience of my life. I just wish the promoters of such
fantasies would show me where they encountered them. Entering Brazil
from Peru – we had decided to take boats from Iquitos down to Belem
– I was prepared for the worst. But compared to Peru, the Brazil I saw
as a tourist was calm. We walked the streets without fearing robberies
or violent clashes between the police and unemployed or striking workers.

Travelling down the Amazon was a three-week introduction to life in
what remains of the jungle. It was also a good opportunity to observe
the mechanisms of Brazilian society, of which boats are a microcosm.
There were women huddled in their hammocks, surrounded by and caring
for their children; the men playing cards and getting drunk on beer; the
teenagers who played their seductive games; the ageing artist, making up
stories of his never-realised glorious career; the North American
missionary, preaching the Bible to the Indians to prepare them for the

arrival of business; and the handful of tourists – European and Latin American – staring at the endless forests, the almost untouchable horizon and the waters of the river. The thoughts and conversations of the foreigners focussed on one question: how much longer will all this exist? Large chunks of the forest have already been destroyed, and with the help of chemicals, among them the infamous 'agent orange', the process is accelerating fast.

Life in the towns along the way was less entertaining. Heat and humidity keep everyone in their houses, watching television; soap operas around the clock, only interrupted by commercials. Without an ample supply of good books I would have suffered.

Along the Amazon and along the 6,000 kilometres of Atlantic coast, people are used to invasions, whether from missionaries, colonisers or 'just' tourists. However, inland, especially in the drought-plagued northeast, I felt much more conspicuous. Marlene, my travel companion from São Paulo, and I, native of Central Europe, were stopped as we walked down the streets by women, curious to know what we were doing in their town. One woman suspected we were either Germans or gypsies; others, who saw me reading a book, thought I must be a preacher. Why else would anyone bother to read? Our 'whole-earth' type sandals caused further speculations, ranging from nun to hippie. Nobody could imagine that we were just two ordinary women, curious and privileged enough to be travelling for the sake of it.

▮ **At the time of writing Pat Treasure is living in Rio de Janeiro, where she has found work teaching English.**

Brazilians seem very relaxed and open in their attitudes to sex and sexuality. A man will interpret a look as an expression of interest far more readily than his European counterpart, but I can't say I've felt sexually threatened so far. The major danger in Rio is undoubtedly robbery.

With no Welfare State, high inflation and insecure employment, there's a lot of crippling poverty in Brazil. Over half of Rio's population live in conditions impossible for most Europeans to imagine, in *favelas* (slum ghettoes), sometimes within metres of expensive apartment blocks. To wander down to the water's edge at dusk to admire the sunset, as I did, clearly marks you out as a tourist target. My advice in such a situation is to forget about self-defence and hand over your money with as much good grace as you can muster. When I asked, my robbers at least gave me back enough money for the bus fare home! I still haven't been involved in any of the mass bus robberies which seem to happen periodically but I've learnt not to carry much money around.

I'm partly living off savings and with dollar travellers' cheques to convert to *cruzeiros* the cost of living is very reasonable. As long as you're careful, it's worth changing money on the black market, when you'll get about one-third above the official rate. It's also an experience in itself – reminiscent of a Humphrey Bogart movie!

Working is a much better way of meeting people than being a permanent tourist. With only a tourist visa the possibilities are obviously limited, but part-time English teaching is a good bet and you'll be particularly in demand if you have teaching experience or qualifications. There are plenty of private Language Schools and the back-up and facilities in the one where I am working seem excellent. They also provide contacts for teaching private lessons – far better paid if less secure. Remember, though, that Brazilians tend to avoid making decisions until the last moment – and then frequently change their minds.

If you're planning to spend a long time in Brazil it's important to try to have some contacts before you set out. The culture shock is considerable no matter how prepared you think you are. There are a lot of Brazilians living and studying in the UK who really enjoy talking about their country and who may well suggest people to ring up or visit. Try asking around or putting an advert at your nearest university, or go along to Brazilian Contemporary Arts in London. English isn't as common as one might expect and even if Brazilians have learnt it in school, the association of English language with American imperialism in South America engenders a lot of hostility. The struggle to learn Portuguese is definitely worth it.

TRAVEL NOTES

Language Portuguese. Don't assume everyone speaks Spanish. It won't be appreciated.

Transport Modern buses criss-cross the country almost any time of day or night. They are cheap, comfortable and fast. Internal air travel is well developed. If time is more of a problem than money, it may be worth purchasing a 21-day airpass which allows you unlimited travel as long as you don't repeat your route. Airpasses must be bought outside the country. Hitching is difficult and not recommended.

Accommodation There are plenty of cheap hotels throughout Brazil.

Special problems Avoid going alone to isolated beaches or walking around alone at night in any city. Robberies and assaults on residents and travellers alike are becoming increasingly frequent.

Other information Homosexuality and lesbianism have their own barely recorded history in Brazil. Rumours have it that in Recife 40 per cent of the population have been or are involved in homosexual activities, but this hasn't led to an expressive gay lifestyle. Both Salvador and São Paulo have their own lesbian organisations (see below). Much of gay life and gay encounters take place at night in bars and nightclubs or on beaches during the day. None of these places are for women or men only, though some, like *Ferro's Bar* in São Paulo, are preferred lesbian hang-outs. And most of them aren't exclusively gay.

Guide Again the *South American Handbook* (see Venezuela) has a lengthy (200 page) chapter on Brazil.

CONTACTS

There are so many women's organisations it would be impossible to list them all here. Also, groups are forever moving and changing. Probably the best central organisation to contact is **Centro Informacao Mulher** (CIM), Rua Leoncio Gurgel, 11–Luz 01103, São Paulo/SP (Tel. 229 4818). Postal address: Caixa Postal 11.399, 05499 São Paulo/SP, Brazil. CIM publishes regular lists of different women's organisations throughout the country.

The following three groups are also recommended by Ines Rieder.

Casa da Mulher, Comba Marques Porto, Rua Debret 23–Sala 1316, 20.030 Rio de Janeiro.

SOS Corpo (women's health group), Rua do Hospicio 859, apto. 14, 50.000 Recife.

Brasil Mulher Terezinha Goncalves, Av. Princesa Leopoldina 38b, apto. 1301, 40.000 Salvador, Bahia.

BOOKS
June Hahner, *Women in Latin American History – Their Lives and Views* (UCLA Latin America Center Publications, Los Angeles, 1976). Includes Brazil.

ECUADOR

Ecuador is one of the smallest, richest and most beautiful countries in South America. It also has a reputation as one of the most peaceful, in spite of a noticeable military presence.

The current civilian government is supposedly committed to a long-term programme of social and economic reform. Oil resources have helped to bolster up the economy – as the saying goes: 'We may be poor, but down there [Peru] they're dying of hunger.' Nevertheless, political unrest continues to be fuelled by unemployment, rising prices and uneven economic growth.

The country is divided into two main areas: coast and *sierra*, the latter dominated by the Andes mountains. The majority of Ecuador's Indian population (roughly 40 per cent in all) eke out a living from working on the land of the sierra. Despite certain progressive agricultural policies, both here and along the more-developed coast, a growing number of people flock to the towns for work. More than half of them are women.

Ecuador has a gradually awakening **Women's Movement**, the core of which is dedicated to developing and working with grass-roots women's organisations. An important group is *CEPAM* (Centre for the Promotion and Action of Ecuadorean Women) whose work led to the opening of the country's first women's centre in the capital, Quito, in 1983. CEPAM runs various training programmes for rural and urban women; publishes resources on issues such as health and women's legal rights; and helps to co-ordinate most of the 20 or so other women's groups active in and around Quito. The Centre is keen to make contact with feminist groups from other countries in order to exchange ideas and promote understanding about the situation and activities of Ecuadorean women.

▧ **Elizabeth Gowans lived in Ecuador from 1966 to 1968. Recently she returned for a month to find very little had changed.**

Second smallest country with the second highest capital, Ecuador packs more scenery and history per inch than any other in South America. Outside the towns there is a wealth of Indian presence.

The Indians remain scrupulously detached from both travellers, their own civilian *mestizo* cousins and from the (black) *mulatto* coastal population of shipwrecked/escaped slaves. The Indians present no threat to the female traveller. In fact it is difficult for even their mestizo counterparts to reach through to them, living as they do in a sort of Andean time-warp. The mestizo overlay presents no threats to solitary women travellers either – being steeped in the more compassionate elements of Catholicism and exuding an enriching sense of the worth of each individual person. They want to know *you*, your *family*, your *pensamientos* (thoughts). Take the time to look in their treasure troves (usually a biscuit tin) at the five post cards and six photographs of foreign visitors they have had . . . the bundle of letters in a rubber band.

Geography has been kind in inhibiting communications/contact internally and externally. And it still is, to the extent that travelling schedules can be arbitrary and the people remain 'safe to be amongst', prepared to put themselves out to help you and basically family oriented. This means that they will see you, the female, as either a sister, mother, aunt, grandmother, daughter, which makes it very safe, but calls for reciprocal respect. For those of us coming from fragmented non-nuclear family situations it can mean taking on a new identity.

Basically, personal relationships lie at the heart of Ecuadorean society. It is not the *solving* of a problem but the *discussing* of it that they value. All situations are seen as a means of interacting and people's urge to help you is sometimes so great they will let it override the fact they don't know where a place is and go ahead and direct you anyway, half hoping someone will correct you later. (The exception is, of course, the military. Asking a soldier outside the Casa de Cultura, after much thought, he stated honestly that he didn't know where the Casa de Cultura was.) If you find a person (bank or hotel) who understands the nature and importance of *información*, ask every question you can think of. But if you can't find the information, start the journey without it. There is an Ecuadorean saying: 'El que esperar, desesperar', he who waits, despairs. This applies to transport. The times at which buses and planes should leave has no significance. They go when they are full.

The two most infuriating words for Westerners are: 'No hay' and 'Ya mismo'. 'Ya mismo', meaning 'Right now', has topped the list for twenty years and shows no sign of budging. 'When is the bus coming?' 'Ya mismo . . .'. Probably in three days' time so start walking and flag it down when it passes. 'No hay' means 'There isn't any' and is most often applied to water when you want a shower. Checking into a residencia, leave no hole unplugged. 'Is there water?' 'Yes.' 'Is there water always?' 'Yes.' 'Is there water now?' 'Yes.' Go to the room. Try that tap. 'There is no water.' Often places do have a water pump (*bomba*) but are loathe to use it because of the electricity. So negotiate before checking in: 'Do you have a water pump? (Yes) Will you put it on once a day for me?' There is an element of game here because people find it intensely amusing that you, being so well informed, would not know their place has no water pressure or even that you would expect them to put on the pump so you can wash your jeans when the laundry costs only 20p.

Ecuador is very much at its own place in time and history. You can today visit the Stone Age, the 16th century – in places the 21st century – but there is no homogeneity. Coffee shop intellectuals still roll 1960s political ideology round in their mouths (one feels more for style than applied conviction), say they dream of going to Cuba, exporting the revolution . . . The students and country as a whole are quite cut off from the modernity of thinking of say Chile, Peru, Argentina and beyond. But this does not make it backward. Ecuador was the first South American country to thumb its nose at United States interference in the 1966 Punte del Este conference and does not look about for nations to follow.

You can't vote unless you can read and write. There are 14 political parties. Oil-financed development has benefited local rather than foreign interests and although there is well-founded dissatisfaction with the way things are run, it could be much worse. Social security is for those who pay in only. The rest get by on the family system.

It would be dangerous to apply imported interpretations of all this. Even Ecuador's rich are poor in terms of being unable to leave their lives and spend it elsewhere. They are often tied in obligations to those who wear their handdowns and a clear sense of 'accountability' comes through. Even the existence of poverty is not what it seems.

Ecuadorean juxtaposing of officialdom and 'getting there in the end' is illustrated by the following. Recently a tourist, virtually asking to have his wallet removed in the crowded San Roque market, Quito, was accordingly separated from it. The thief, having sequestrated the money and traveller's cheques (but left the passport, air tickets and credit card) followed the man to a café, where he had unwittingly ordered food, and skidded the wallet across the floor to him. The police response was first to return to his hotel room and buy up as many of his and his wife's clothes as they could be persuaded to part with, thus providing the money to tide them over until the banks opened on Monday. They also clubbed together to spend some three weeks' salary on securing his bottle of duty free Scotch (which, of course, travellers are not allowed to sell). Finally, they begged him earnestly to sell his camera to their CID department as theirs had been stolen and they couldn't photograph criminals. Unfortunately they couldn't raise the price of even one lens.

If this happens to you, get a copy of the police report for your insurance, but don't wait around. It just means more haggling over what the police cannot afford to buy off you, listening to their tales of misfortune and getting bogged down. The same with traveller's cheques. Fill out the claim form with a forwarding address, then go. He who waits, despairs.

As you may have guessed, there is a market in second-hand clothes. A nice gesture is to take a spare suitcase or bag of good, clean, warm jumble-sale gear and deliver it to the downtown offices of one of the two charities, *CAFOD* or *CARITAS*, or direct to the Bishop's Conference itself (address: *Conferencia Episcopal Ecuatoriana*, Av. America 1866 y la Gasca, Quito – tel. 52–45–68). The women have their own distribution system for used clothing. Nights in the Andes can be very cold and it makes a change for visitors to go with something to give instead of just cameras to 'take' with. NB Don't tell the Customs you're bringing in clothes you will part with or they may be tempted to ask for Import Duty.

TRAVEL NOTES

Languages Spanish, Quechua, Jivaroa.
Transport Buses are very cheap and frequent, but don't expect the same spacious coaches as Peru. For long journeys try to buy tickets in advance from the office. When buying tickets on a bus, make sure the driver doesn't overcharge you. Trains are also very cheap, but erratic. Make sure you buy your ticket the day before. The train from Quito to Guyaquil is famous for its series of switch-backs and wonderful scenery. Flying is cheap and irregular. Probably most useful for trips into the more remote regions of the Amazon.
Accommodation Hotels are cheap, especially outside the main cities, but always ask to see the room. It is also possible to bargain in the cheaper *pensiones* or *residencials*.
Guides The *South American Handbook* (see Venezuela) has at least 70 pages on Ecuador. Rob Rachowiecki, *Climbing and Hiking in Ecuador* (Bradt Enterprises, 1984). Useful for the adventurous. Available from Bradt Enterprises, 41 Nortoft Road, Chalfont St Peter, Bucks SLA OLA, England.

CONTACTS
CEPAM, Los Rios y Gandara, Quito (see introduction); and **Centro Accion de las Mujeres**, Casilla 10201, Guayaquil. Activities include organising literacy campaigns, healthcare, producing audio-visual resources and running a women's bookshop.

BOOKS
Audrey Bronstein, ed., *The Triple Struggle: Latin American Peasant Women* (War on Want Campaigns, London, 1982). Includes interviews with women from Ecuador.
A good bookshop in Quito is *Libri Mundi*, Juan Leon Mera 851 y Veintemilia. The proprietor is European (married to an Ecuadorean Indian) and has information in almost any language. He also keeps a noticeboard for 'What's on in Quito?'

PERU

Peru is one of the most travelled countries in South America, largely due to its magnificent Inca sites. It also, however, has one of the poorest and most isolated Indian populations in the entire continent. Erratic changes in government, combined with the development of the coast and the Amazon (rich in oil) at the expense of the *sierra*, have restricted any positive moves to improve their position in recent years.

At the time of writing Peru is in a state of some upheaval due to the terrorist activities of *Sendero Luminoso* ('Shining Path'), a group which first made itself known on election day 1980 when ballot boxes were blown up by a bomb in a remote mountain village south of the capital Lima. Maoist in belief, the organisation is allegedly dedicated to achieving self-sufficiency for Peru's largely Indian peasant population. Whatever its motives, Sendero Luminoso's continuing campaign of bomb attacks, coupled with the government's violent response, have led to a wave of terror previously unknown in Peru. For the traveller this means that at least one section of the country, the mountainous area around Ayacucho, is completely out of bounds.

Peru has a relatively active **Women's Movement**. As in all Latin American countries, most of its groups are socialist-feminist in outlook, meaning that they are based on the belief that the majority of Peruvian women (70 per cent of the illiterate population) are doubly oppressed, as women and as members of the poorest socio-economic class. At the same time, they are concerned with issues such as the legalisation of free abortion on demand, the right to contraception, and the campaign against male violence, all of which have been consistently neglected by the traditional Left.

Most of Peru's women's organisations are centred in Lima, venue of the 1983 Second Latin American and Caribbean Feminist Meeting.

◤ **Frances Brown travelled throughout Peru during the winter season (May-June).**

Peru is two countries. In the big cities along the flat coastal strip it is a land of 'white' Peruvians of Spanish descent. But the high, desolate Andean regions to the east are predominantly peopled by Indians, Quechua-speaking survivors of the ancient Inca Empire.

I spent five weeks travelling the length of the country on public transport and sampled both worlds. There is no doubt about which one is in charge. Peru is governed and run almost entirely by and for whites, while the Indians remain peasant farmers scratching a living from the thin

Andean soil, or crowded together in shanty towns outside the cities which promised — but failed — to give them work.

In the mountains the Indian women are the mainstay of all the local markets, and often work as vendors boarding trains and buses to sell produce and cooked food. Life is tough — washing laundry in an icy stream takes all day — and children help out from an early age, perhaps tending a few animals, or running errands. The men work just as hard too; as human pack animals, they are often almost entirely obscured by the loads they transport from one place to another. Both sexes work on whatever tiny plot of land they may own.

But despite their high profile, Indian women seem suspicious, even afraid of strangers. The Latin women are more open and friendly, but even they are rarely to be seen in bars or cafés, where the men are often quite chatty and interested to exchange views of their country and yours.

For this purpose it is essential to know some Spanish. Hardly anyone in Peru speaks English, and without the language you will be cut off from the whole population. What's more, regulations concerning the buying of rail and bus tickets are sometimes absurdly complex; conflicting times of departure may be given by two people in the same office and delays are fairly frequent. It helps if you have at least some idea of what is going on. And if you ask for directions be prepared to be sent on a wild goose chase. Peruvians have a very strong notion of courtesy and honour, which I at first did not understand. It would be a terrible loss of face for them to admit that they don't know the way somewhere, so when that happens they simply make it up. This can be immensely frustrating, especially when you are tired, and constitutes my worst memory of Peru, along with one other — water.

All over the country, even on the shores of Lake Titicaca, there are problems of supply. In cheaper hotels, especially in the mountains, only cold water is normally available, whatever the hotel signs may say. Supplies are frequently cut, but rarely when the management is expecting it. We were driven out of one hotel in Huaraz, which had no water for two days, despite repeated assurances that it would be switched on at any minute.

These frustrations made me glad I had a travelling companion for mutual moaning and support. It was also nice to be able to share the undoubted good times such as listening to real Peruvian folk music in local cafés; or collapsing over a simple meal after a hard day's travelling and listening to other people's conversations; not to mention just enjoying the scenery. Although I was travelling with a man I made plenty of sorties on my own, sometimes at night, and at no time did I feel threatened or was I sexually harassed. Whilst *machismo* is justifiably notorious in Latin America as a whole, I did not find Peruvians particularly afflicted by it. I was stared at because I was a *gringa*, not because I was a woman.

■ Kirstie Shedden travelled alone around Peru for three months; she writes on Cuzco and Lake Titicaca.

Once centre of the Inca Empire, Cuzco stands at a height of 3,500 metres in the Andes. It is where the Spanish went in search of gold and ended up wiping out a whole civilisation. I arrived there at night, my nerves frayed from the twenty-hour train ride from Arequipa, on the notorious robber line. Eighty per cent of tourists have things stolen. I was told that Cuzco, too, was full of thieves so my pack was wrapped in a sack, I kept my money and passport hidden around my waist. People who don't take these kinds of precautions are almost certain to suffer.

I explored Cuzco slowly over the next few weeks. It is a strange place, full of history, but geared to tourism. Because of this you are more sharply aware of the poverty. Everyone is trying to sell something and at the bottom of the pile are the small children who follow you into restaurants or chase after you in the street, wanting you to buy a cigarette or a postcard. They have swollen bellies, grubby tattered clothes and sleep in doorways at night.

Again because of tourism, there is an element of danger. Apart from the thieves, there are stories of women who have been raped and of men who have been beaten up. I suspect that the fact that it happens at all is why people talk about it so much, because violence is not usual in Peru. However, I was dragged across the street by drunken men a couple of times and I tried to avoid walking alone at night.

Most days I went to the market to eat, passing pockets of Inca stone-work and the vast churches. I wrote letters, read books, talked to people and took Spanish lessons. At night I went to a *peña* and listened and danced to Peruvian music. I learned to dance very quickly after once being hurled on to an empty dance floor by an enthusiastic Peruvian.

One morning I crammed myself into a small bus going to Pisac, a village some 32 kilometres north of Cuzco in the Urubamba valley. Just as you think they couldn't possibly get any more people on the bus they stop and squeeze on another enormous *campesina* woman with her baby and her bundle of coca leaves.

Pisac has a regular Sunday market, basically for tourists so it's expensive. The village is especially famous for its beads – you can watch children in the little shops hand-painting intricate designs on them all day. There is also some impressive archaeology up on the mountains nearby. A three-hour walk takes you up through stunning scenery to three Inca hill fortifications, the highest of which is a huge fortress, very well preserved. Inca architecture blends so much into the landscape that you practically fall over a settlement before it's visible.

To get back from Pisac I had to hitch a ride since all the buses were full. After waiting politely for an hour I hurled myself into the back of a truck with everyone else.

My favourite place was Chincheros. About 20 kilometres from Cuzco, this small pueblo is still unspoiled by tourism. There are no bars or restaurants, simply the mud-brick houses of the *campesinos*. The market here is authentic, where people from neighbouring villages bring their wares and spread them out on the ground. I walked from Chincheros away down into the next valley and saw no one.

For a woman travelling alone in South America, the islands of Lake Titicaca are places where you can regain your sanity. There is peace, beauty and no machismo. You feel completely safe. Lake Titicaca lies between Peru and Bolivia and I travelled there from Cuzco, arriving at night in Puno, the major Peruvian town on the lake. The sooner you get out of Puno the better. Dirty and ugly, it is renowned for thieves.

Boats out to the islands leave early in the morning and I found the harbour a little late, after getting lost in the mud and concrete slums on the edge of the town. I took a motor launch to Taquile with three people I had met in Cuzco. Once you leave the dull reedy water around the harbour, the lake becomes the magical, legendary place you read about. It is impossible to describe the blueness of the water – so vast it's more like an ocean – and the extraordinary silver quality of the light.

We landed at Taquile at midday and climbed a steep, rocky Inca path to the island's only village. The centre of the pueblo is Spanish with a large square surrounded by mud-brick buildings, a few of which serve as restaurants purely for the benefit of visitors. I saw one woman crouched in the dusty plaza selling bread and oranges to the islanders, but there are no shops. Families farm and are self-sufficient.

The islanders are all Indian campesinos, most of whom speak only Quechua. They preserve their Inca heritage in other ways too. Everything is shared and decisions are reached by consensus. A man is especially appointed to allocate rooms to visitors with different families. That way no one family profits by visitors more than another.

We were taken to our room by a young woman with a tiny cross-eyed baby peeking out of the black shawl tied across her back. She walked incredibly fast, barefoot, spinning wool in her hands as she went. I was always being amazed by the toughness of the campesinos in Peru. This woman lived with her husband, two daughters and parents-in-law in a complex of thatched-roof, mud-brick buildings built around an open courtyard. There was a storeroom, a room for cooking and sleeping in, and a guest room which I shared with my three travelling companions. The walls were laced with straw for added warmth.

That afternoon we walked to one end of the island and back. We saw Inca ruins scattered on the highest ground and looked at the most wonderful views. You can even see snow-capped mountains across the lake. The whole island is covered in Inca terraces although they are no longer all cultivated. Many traditions disappeared with the arrival of the

Spanish and, although the Indian people look bright-eyed and healthy, in reality the range and quality of the crops they produce are not sufficient to maintain a balanced diet. Life is short.

At night I tried to talk to the family. The husband spoke some Spanish and told us a little about his wife and children, but he was mainly concerned with showing us the clothes he made, in the hope that we would buy something. His wife spoke only Quechua and wouldn't return a smile. I suppose she just saw us as intruders.

The following morning I walked to the other end of the island alone, glad to have a few hours to myself. Families were taking their animals up to plough the terraces. Ploughing itself is done by the men, whilst the women and children walk along behind and break up the soil – more tiring but less prestigious than the men's work.

▰ **Alison Cork spent most of her time in Peru walking through the Amazonas.**

Most tourists tend to stay in the south of Peru, attracted by Cuzco and its surrounding sites. I gave these places a miss, partly because of the growing guerrilla activity in the south, but mainly because I'd gone to Peru for what I hoped would be the spectacular scenery of the north, and the accompanying quiet.

Travel within Peru can be a problem. Most roads, except the coastal highway, are in very bad condition and deteriorate in the rainy season, often leaving the traveller stranded. Aeroplanes are more reliable, but likely to be booked up far in advance and subject to long delays. We were lucky and managed to take a plane from Lima to the northern coastal town of Chiclayo. From there we took a bus inland and up into the Amazonas.

The journey lasted twenty-one hours which seemed a very long time, especially as I suffered badly from *soroche* (altitude sickness). By the time we reached Chachapoyas, the capital of Amazonas, we were at a height of about 3,500 metres. From there we travelled on by truck.

There is only one road in Amazonas – an unsurfaced and unprotected dirt track, dynamited out of the mountain sides. Small wooden crosses stand at intervals along the roadside, marking the point where vehicles have crashed and hurtled over the edge. The trucks we rode in were very old, continually breaking down and packed to bursting point with people, animals and goods. Not surprisingly, it's a ritual for both passengers and driver to cross themselves before each journey and I joined in, just in case.

We stayed for seven weeks in the Amazonas, walking over the mountains from one remote village settlement to another. Most of them were situated on mountain tops, some 3,000 metres up. They were small and poor, inhabited entirely by Indian campesinos. These villages can be spotted from far away, their corrugated iron roofs glittering in the sun amongst the patchwork of fields, where farmers have managed to clear vast areas of the Amazon jungle.

Since we were quite near the Equator, the vegetation on the mountains was lush and almost tropical with creepers sometimes twenty feet high, giant ferns and brilliantly coloured flowers, including orchids. Swarms of multicoloured butterflies were our constant companions. The sunsets and sunrises were the most arresting I have ever seen – and that includes those in the Himalayas.

I was continually astonished and delighted at the unquestioning hospitality offered by the people we met. We usually came to a village in the afternoon or evening, where we would stay the night. The children always came out to greet us first. They would run up, touch me quickly and then run away, calling 'gringita', meaning 'the little foreign woman'. Then the parents ventured out and we would begin to communicate in what was, for my part, pidgin Spanish. We had little to offer, other than postcards, biros and stories about England. To offer money would have been an insult. And although they obviously had little conception as to where England was, or why we had come so far just to look at mountains, the friendship and kindness never wavered.

We carried a tent, but the villagers nearly always insisted we stay in one of their houses. Accommodation was primitive. A family of seventeen, including the grandparents, would eat, sleep and work in a one-roomed hut. The only light came through several ventilation holes in the walls. There was no electricity, running water or heat – animals were kept inside to generate warmth. I spent one night with two hens, a cockerel, twelve guinea-pigs, the dog and, I suspect, a rat.

To begin with, people were often amazed to find that I was a woman. With my hair up and wearing typical walking clothes I must, in retrospect, have passed for a man. Once this was cleared up, they invariably wanted to know if my companion and I were married. The fact that we weren't didn't seem to matter – it was my 'barrenness' that they found hardest to accept. Most Peruvian girls marry at around 15, and have children continuously until they are past child-bearing age.

I was pleasantly surprised by the respect shown to me by the men. I was often taken into their confidence and felt treated very much as an equal. I never once felt unsafe, and if all travel in Peru could be under the same conditions, I wouldn't hesitate to recommend it to women travelling on their own.

TRAVEL NOTES

Languages Spanish, Quechua and Aymara.

Transport There is a pretty comprehensive network of long-distance buses, which covers all but the most remote Andean towns and the Amazon region. There is no railway in the mountains except between Lima and Huancayo and across the flat *altiplano* between Cuzco and Lake Titicaca. It is sometimes impossible to buy train tickets more than one day in advance of the time you want to travel. Hitching is fairly common. You are expected to pay, but it's not usually much cheaper than public transport.

Accommodation There are far more cheap than expensive hotels in Peru. Indeed outside the big cities and towns basic accommodation is often all that is available. Check the price and ask to see the room first – it could be a shock if you haven't been in a Third World country before. Many larger towns have a Hotel Turistas which should be up to a certain standard and still be reasonably priced, but even here don't expect constant water.

Special problems Peru is the home of very skilled pickpockets and grab-and-run thieves so take care everywhere, especially when arriving in towns at night by public transport. Remember that thieves very often work in groups – sometimes families – where *gringos* are caught off-guard by the distracting appealing glances of a small wide-eyed child. It is a livelihood.

Coca leaves, the raw material of cocaine, are freely and legally available for chewing and brewing. However the government, with American assistance, has mounted a big campaign against smuggling and production of the drug itself. Police have a habit of arresting gringos, especially in Lima, and demanding a ransom for their release – otherwise drug-handling charges are threatened. Five years in a Peruvian jail is no joke, so make sure there is absolutely no reason for you to be under suspicion.

Guide Dilwyn Jenkins *The Rough Guide to Peru* (RKP) is probably the best guidebook to any individual South American Country. Practical and culturally sensitive.

CONTACTS

Flora Tristán, Centro de la Mujer Peruana Av. Arenales 601, Lima. Women's centre dedicated to the growth, development and strengthening of the feminist movement in Peru. Allied to the United Left (Apron) party, with the basic tenet 'first socialism, then the feminist revolution.'

Movimiento Manuela Ramos Camana 280–Oficina 305, Apartado Postal 11176, Lima 14. Mainly concerned with co-ordinating projects with working-class women. Write first.

If you speak Spanish there are quite a few **feminist publications** in Peru. Watch out for *Mujer y Sociedad*, *La Tortuga* and *La Manzana*. For help, literature or advice try *Flora Tristán*, the *Libreria de la Mujer* **bookshop** (near the start of Av. Arenales, Lima) or the women's centre which is run by nuns near the centre of Lima (in Quilca, just half a block from Av. Wilson)

BOOKS

Dervla Murphy *Eight Feet in the Andes* (John Murray, 1983). Describes the author's journey with her 9-year-old daughter and a mule 1,300 miles through the Andes.

Audrey Bronstein, ed, *The Triple Struggle: Latin American Peasant Women* (War on Want Campaigns, London 1982). See General Bibliography.

Michael Reid, *Peru-Paths to Poverty* (Latin America Bureau, London, 1985). Good account of the political situation from the 1950s to the present day.

Mario Vargas Llosa, *Aunt Julia* and the *Scriptwriter* (Picador, 1984) *Conversations in the Cathedral* (Faber, 1986) and others. Llosa is Peru's best known novelist – highly readable with incidental, sometimes crazy insights into life in Lima.

BOLIVIA

In **Bolivia** things are seldom straightforward. Schedules can be disrupted by anything from floods through strikes and road blocks to plain bureaucracy – all hazards you have to take philosophically. The country itself, though, is one of the most exciting for South American travellers. The scenery, ranging from a height of zero to 16,000 feet, is often spectacularly beautiful and the people (two-thirds Indian) still seem steeped in tradition. Bolivia is also the cheapest country in Latin America for travellers with dollars.

The situation is, however, pretty desperate for the average Bolivian, for whom prices are the main topic of conversation. At the time of writing (November 1985) Bolivia's experiment at a vaguely left-wing government has been tried and seen to fail. Since the elections in July the new style is a kind of extreme Thatcherism, incorporating privatisation and decentralisation of all important state enterprises, abolition of the minimum wage, and an end to restrictions on the hiring and firing of labour. Unemployment is rocketing along with the ever-increasing rate of inflation which recently reached 40 to 50,000 per cent. Bolivia is no longer the cheapest Latin American country for tourists, as the price of eating out, accommodation and transport also rise in line with the new government's policies.

In Bolivia there is no women's liberation movement in the western feminist sense, but more and more **women** are demonstrating for economic and political change. They were a key factor in the defeat of the Banzer dictatorship in 1978 when women from the mines staged a hunger strike in the capital, La Paz, in demand for an amnesty for political exiles. In the last congress of the COB (Bolivian Workers Federation) women delegates insistently demanded more representation on its committees and participation in general, which they obtained.

There are **women's groups** and organisations of all types, from conservative upper-middle-class associations through all shades of the political spectrum to the far left. Two of the most notable are the widespread Women's Peasant Federation and the Amas de Casa de la Ciudad, a group of poor women who run a health clinic and various education programmes in the slums of La Paz. Both are remarkable in being grassroots women's organisations who believe in the value of excluding men from specific discussions and decisions in order for women to gain the confidence to stand up for their rights.

◣ **Alison Sadler has been working in Bolivia since August 1982, as a documentalist/librarian, initially in Cochabamba, then La Paz. She is currently working in the documentation department of an educational research and action centre committed to educational alternatives in Bolivia and involved in various projects in the slum areas of the city.**

My personal experience of women in Bolivia is based mainly on contact with middle-class women – most of whom I've met through work – and the fleeting but constant relations with the *cholitas* or market sellers I buy from. Having had a lot of working contact with fairly progressive organisations in Bolivia (popular education, women's organisations, *campesino* development, etc.), it's nice to know that there are a lot of very committed, politically aware women around. Their reactions towards me have varied immensely. Some regard me with a mixture of admiration and awe at being a *gringa* who has had the privilege of living in that wonderful consumer society 'out there', with videos, washing machines and beautiful clothes; others as a complete curiosity with my long red hair and strange clothes, rather like an exhibit in a zoo; and others simply regard me as a *compañera* in our work together.

Male attitudes vary in a different way. In general campesinos are very shy of foreign women and, especially in the high altiplano where so many live, you're unlikely to be bothered, even verbally, in the street. The people of the lowlands tend to be more extrovert, but peasant women, like the market traders of Cochabamba who are famous for their traditional leading role in running the family, have a reputation for independence. As a gringa, you'll probably receive comments and stares from men, but as an independent woman you're less of an oddity down here. Middle-class men, who are almost bound to be *mestizo* (mixed race) in origin, display the usual Latin characteristics of *machismo*. Husbands often frown on or totally forbid their wives to work outside the home, so you may be seen as a threat, but I've not found harassment a problem on any great scale.

In terms of places to visit in Bolivia, I recommend the Yungas as not to be missed. My first trip there and the many times I've returned since have convinced me that, if you have limited time, this is the one place to go. The Yungas valleys are a semi-tropical paradise about 100 km and three to four hours' bus-ride east of La Paz. It is possible to travel to one part of the area and back in one day, but I would suggest that you need two or three days, or even more, to fully appreciate its beauty.

My first trip there, on the back of a motorbike and consequently open to all the elements and subtle changes in climate and atmosphere, was a revelation. We climbed out of La Paz through Villa Fatima towards La

Cumbre Pass, at over 16,000 feet which leads to Yungas. You are out of the city within 15 minutes and pass through scenery I thought very reminiscent of Scotland – stark, imposing mountains, some snow-capped depending on the season, and barren moorland. If you are lucky the sun will be out, but climbing over the pass can be quite an ordeal, as freezing mist and fog more often than not cover the whole area.

Winding down through gaps in the mountains more grass and trees slowly appear. A natural break in the journey is the tiny collection of corrugated iron shacks lining the road which is known as Unduavi. To my mind it is a miserable, damp, blot on the landscape, but you can get a coffee and semblance of a hot snack or meal if you feel so inclined.

From here changes in vegetation, climate and scenery really make themselves felt. The air becomes warmer and more humid, charged with a delicious spicy scent; the way down, now a one-track dirt road, is lined with papaya trees, ferns and hanging plants of all types. Following the steep side of the valley, it gradually descends to a village called Yolosa which, like Unduavi, is more or less an extended transport café but, unlike Unduavi, is pleasantly hot and has the rapid, cascading river nearby as an added attraction. I remember the unusual sight of several black cholitas with their children, wearing the same traditional bowler hats and full skirts of the La Paz women.

Leaving Yolosa there is a short climb of about half-an-hour up to Coroico, one of the principal towns of the Yungas area. It is perched around the top of one of the many ridges and folds in the valley and the distinctive buildings of the Hotel Prefectural, virtually the only hotel worth staying in in Coroico, can be made out from some distance. If you like walking this is a lovely area to explore. You can walk down to the river in about an hour, passing through orange groves and past isolated houses. I found it quite a thrill to actually pick a grapefruit from the tree instead of a supermarket shelf. The river is lovely to bathe in if you find the right spot and, if you don't have the energy to climb back up to the town, you can hitch a ride to Yolosa and thence back to Coroico.

The other main town of the Yungas region is Chulumani, a little further from La Paz than Coroico, and not quite as picturesque, but you can spend a very pleasant weekend in one of its motels. The San Antonio, on a bend in the road about 20 minutes before Chulumani, is beautifully situated overlooking the valleys, has a decent swimming pool and very nice rooms, all in a setting of banana, poinsettia and frangipani trees. Like all average hotels in Bolivia, it is very cheap. Further on, actually in Chulumani, is the San Bartolomé, a week-end watering hole of the upper-middle-class Bolivian but if you can stomach the company, the surroundings are absolutely spectacular: the cleanest swimming pool in Bolivia, gourmet food at giveaway prices, and pretty chalet-type accommodation for the guests, not to mention the magnificent views.

TRAVEL NOTES

Languages Spanish, Quechua, Aymara and other minor Indian languages.

Transport Taxis are easily identifiable by their red number plates and will take as many people as can be squashed in, so it's worth stopping one that looks full. *Micros* (small buses) cover most points of the city, each route being allocated a letter. There are set stops but they will usually stop on every corner. Pay the driver on entering. *Flotas*, or long-distance buses, run from the city's main bus terminal to most other towns in the country, except those towns within the Department of La Paz, which are served by buses leaving from various points within the city. Ask at your hotel, travel agent or tourist information kiosk. Air transport within Bolivia is very cheap.

Accommodation Although prices are rising fast, there are still plenty of cheap, basic hotels by European standards. Only La Paz tends to get booked up, so try to arrive early in the day.

Special problems Avoid going to a doctor, dentist, clinic or hospital unless absolutely necessary. The Bolivian medical profession has an unhealthy reliance on the prescription of (unnecessary) drugs. Take with you all the sanitary protection you will need as tampons are incredibly expensive. Most varieties of contraceptive pills can be bought over the counter at chemists.

Don't bring British currency to Bolivia. If you manage to change sterling it will be at a very low rate. Everything revolves around the dollar here.

Guide The *South American Handbook* (see Venezuela) has 50 pages on Bolivia.

CONTACTS

Centro de Promoción de la Mujer Gregoria Apaza, Edificio Muritto, 3rd Floor Office no 2, Calle Murillo, La Paz Tel 327932 – Postal address: Casilla 21170, La Paz, Bolivia.

Centro de Información y Desarrollo de la Mujer (CIDEM), Avenida Villazon no 1958, 3rd Floor, Office no 3A, La Paz (opposite University), No telephone – Postal address: Casilla 3961, La Paz, Bolivia.

BOOKS

Audrey Bronstein ed. *The Triple Struggle: Latin American Peasant Women* (see Peru). Includes interviews with Bolivian women.

Domitila Barrios de Chungara. *Let Me Speak* (Stage 1, London, 1978). First-hand account of the life of one of the founder members of the Housewives Committees of Siglo XX, one of Bolivia's largest mining complexes. A more recent pamphlet by Domitila is included in Miranda Davies (ed.), *Third World – Second Sex* (Zed Books, 1983). See General Bibliography.

James Dunkerley, *Bolivia: Coup d'Etat* (Latin America Bureau, London, 1980). *Rebellion in the Veins: Political Struggle in Bolivia, 1952–82* (Verso, 1984).

CHILE

Chile is the home of one of the most brutally repressive governments in Latin America. Chileans are friendly and hospitable; but the presence of the Pinochet dictatorship is bound to temper the tourist's enjoyment.

General Pinochet has been in power since the coup of September 1973 which toppled the elected government of President Salvador Allende. Thousands of Chileans were imprisoned, murdered, tortured or went into exile, and the present government's economic policies have led to poverty, unemployment, malnutrition and massive division between rich and poor. There are few foreign tourists despite the government's attempts to revamp its image abroad.

Women are very active in the struggle for democracy in Chile. *CODEM* (Defence Committee for Women's Rights) co-ordinates a large network of working-class **women's organisations**. Local groups in different parts of the country develop training schemes for women in areas like health and technical skills; they campaign for women's legal rights, for adequate housing, and for the release of political prisoners; and organise soup kitchens, alternative schools, cultural events and protest activities, especially in the shanty towns. All this work, like the struggles of women in trade unions, is intrinsically linked with the Chilean opposition movement against the government.

At the time of writing, there are two or three women's centres in Santiago. One of them, *DOMOS*, in the heart of the capital, is a meeting place and centre for contact with different groups. The women there also produce educational materials, offer a free advice service and run workshops on various themes. However, as with all such groups, their future is always uncertain, both for lack of money and the constant threat of political censorship.

▨ **Paula Brown is involved in *CAMUR*, a group of British and Chilean women in London, which campaigns to provide materials and funds for the various projects being undertaken by *CODEM* in Chile. She describes her first visit to Chile.**

I flew into Chile from Rio, across the snow-capped Andes. Elated at having arrived, with Santiago bathed in spring sunshine, I passed through immigration. There the atmosphere was tense and the guards heavily armed. The contrast between the country's beauty, caught between the Andes and the Pacific Ocean, and the often brutal realities of its political regime stayed in my mind throughout my visit.

Chile is long and thin, ranging in climate from the northern deserts, through the Mediterranean warmth of Santiago, to the damp, cold south. I spent most of my stay in a small southern town, set among rivers, lakes and volcanic mountains.

The Chileans are an intensely patriotic people, uncomfortably aware of their country's bad press overseas. They are very curious and stare unashamedly, wanting to know why you come and what you think of Chile; and they automatically assume you must be rich and privileged — which in comparative terms at least, you are.

In the shanty towns people are suspicious and hostile, in a permanent state of siege from the police and the army; and in a remote village small boys threw stones at me. A stranger is a threat, and a woman alone stands out especially in a country where men are dominant. In Chile, if you are accompanied by a man it is automatically assumed you are married to him; and it is often least troublesome to go along with this. It is also assumed you have or will have children; otherwise you become an object of pity. Gay men are derided, though more or less tolerated; but lesbians meet actual hostility and run the risk of being incarcerated as mentally unstable.

During my stay I lived in a series of pensions. High unemployment, which particularly affects women, leads many families to let rooms as a source of income. My first pension was a small wooden house run by a middle-aged widow. With her lived two daughters and a son. The elder daughter was a cashier in a supermarket; the younger was unemployed but made a little money organising Tupperware parties – something new in Chile. The son too was unemployed, but while the two women worked all day, he did no housework at all. It is thought dishonourable for men to do domestic work. Two naive but fervent teenage American Mormons were also staying in the pension. Although the town was small, the Mormons had their own mission and a hot-line to Utah: part of the widespread invasion of American-backed evangelists since the coup.

The atmosphere between myself and these boys became strained; besides which the house was bitterly divided politically. The mother and younger daughter supported the government, while the son and elder daughter opposed it. It was a tense time, leading up to the tenth anniversary of the coup. The 8th September was a day of protest, on which there were several deaths and many people were arrested or injured. The government mounted a massive propaganda campaign in the media, to draw attention to 'ten years of national liberation'. Señora Pinochet featured prominently in these promotions, appearing on television to talk about law and order and condemn the 'criminality and vandalism' of the protesters.

In the pension the television became the focus of the political battle in the family. It is inescapable in Chile, in houses, shops, bars and restaurants. And it's an unreservedly reactionary force towards women, universally presented as stereotypes, usually white-skinned, fair-haired, over made-up and dressed in clothes so tight they would be impossible to move in. A great deal of pornographic material, too, is sold in the streets.

One of the most rewarding parts of my trip was the visits I made, bringing news and greetings to the families of friends exiled in Europe. In spite of their poverty they showed me enormous warmth and kindness, and we exchanged presents. They live in hope that the ban on exile will one day be lifted, and as the years pass find it hard to grasp what has happened.

Unlike its neighbours, Peru and Bolivia, Chile's Indians have been largely exterminated or assimilated, except in the south where the largest remaining group, the Mapuche, have lost their land and are reduced to beggars or virtual slaves on the big estates. Their plight dates from the nineteenth century when the government gave away vast tracts of Indian land to white settlers, many of whom were Germans. The German community today is prosperous and self-contained, maintaining links with Germany where they send their children to university. They felt threatened under the Allende government and are keen supporters of the dictatorship. I spent an afternoon with such a family and was amazed that it seemed like going back fifty years to a pre-war way of life. To the women of the family the rest of Latin America seemed to mean nothing: their holidays were spent in Europe or the United States – or just possibly on the beaches of Rio.

During my last days in Chile I visited the shanty towns around Santiago to make contact with members of *CODEM*. A major focus of the centre there is on health and sexuality – crucial in a country where there is no National Health Service, no family planning help and, as a result, a high rate of dangerous illegal abortion. Private health care is beyond the reach of most women.

The women's centre has a theatre group which performs in the shanty towns plays on themes of housing, health, sexuality and unemployment, followed by discussion. All these activities provide a great source of strength for women, as they counteract the false images put out by the media in a male-dominated society. Chilean women are strong, and growing stronger: they know that no lasting freedom will be won until they themselves are free.

TRAVEL NOTES

Languages Spanish and some remaining indigenous languages.
Transport Buses are many and frequent. Travelling directly from north to south, or vice-versa, internal flights are quick and comfortable, but you obviously miss out on much.
Accommodation A wide range of hotels and pensions at all prices can be found throughout the country. Most towns have a tourist information office for guidance or it's easy just to ask in the street.
Special problems Remember to buy Chilean-made products whenever possible. You are usually offered brand-name imported goods at highly inflated prices. Beware of taking part in any overt anti-government activity. A foreign passport doesn't necessarily make you immune to police brutality.
Guide The *South American Handbook* once again has a chapter on Chile (see Venezuela).

CONTACTS

Any radical organisation in Chile is liable to police raids at any time. This includes most premises used by women's groups, so it is impossible to list any reliable addresses. For up-to-date information it is best to contact any of the following organisations based in London:
CAMUR South Camden Women's Centre, 90 Cromer Street, London WC1.
Chile Democratico, 95/97 Old Street, London EC1. Tel. 01–608 1920.
Chile Solidarity Campaign Women's Group 129 Seven Sisters Road, London N7 7QG. Or write to *Isis International* (Women's Information and Communication Service), Casilla 2067, Correo Central, Santiago, Chile. (Tel. 490 271).

BOOKS

Latin American and Caribbean Women's Collective *Slaves of Slaves the Challenge of Latin American Women* (Zed Books, 1980). Portrays women's struggles in 11 different countries, including Chile.

Joan Jara, *Victor, An Unfinished Song* (Jonathan Cape, 1983). Moving account of her life with Victor Jara. legendary Chilean folksinger, who was murdered by the military in 1973.

Pablo Neruda *Memoirs* (Penguin, 1975). Autobiography of Chile's best loved poet.

Chapter Nineteen

THE CARIBBEAN

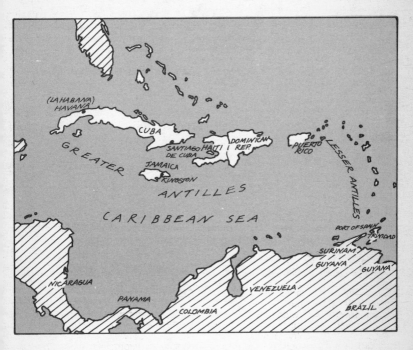

The islands of the **Caribbean** form a vast chain, starting with Cuba, less than 100 miles from the tip of Florida, and curving south to end in Trinidad. Most tourists go to a few selected islands, seduced by a hedonistic vision of sun, sea and fine white sand. Parts of Jamaica, especially, have been developed for this purpose. Independent travellers are not well catered for; cheap accommodation is scarce and the cost of living expensive. Wherever you are, it takes an effort to explore the country and it's a lot easier if you know someone – but it can be well worth it.

It's all too easy to generalise about the Caribbean, renowned for the music, the slow pace of life and the excellent rum. The islands may share these appealing characteristics, along with a history of slavery and exploitation (first by the Spanish, followed by years at the mercy of competing foreign powers), but each nation is strongly determined to establish its cultural identity.

Only Cuba saw independence before this century and then it took a revolution to throw off domination by the United States. The rest of the Caribbean retains close economic links with the States whose government is always ready to intervene in the region. It is also largely responsible for the recent growth of organised tourism. This background of foreign exploitation has led to a certain amount of hostility towards white people, especially in the West Indies. If you're white, you can expect to be teased and shouted at but, away from the 'ghettoes', few women report being seriously threatened. It you really can't handle it don't go.

Only three islands are included here: **Cuba, Jamaica** and **Trinidad**. We would welcome pieces on others, or on Caribbean island-hopping in general, for the next edition.

CUBA

Since the decisive revolution of 1959, **Cuba** has become something of a showpiece of Latin American socialism. Foreign visitors still go to witness the impressive social reforms, but the days of being confined to an organised study tour appear to be over. Cuba is becoming increasingly open to tourists (except for North Americans who continue to have difficulties obtaining a visa) and its blend of social equality, physical beauty and warm, outgoing people makes it one of the most appealing countries in the world.

Cuba is an enormous island, by far the largest in the Caribbean. Bus and rail services are a bit erratic and accommodation can be a problem – the relatively few cheap hotels are much in demand – but with time, patience and the help of the official tourist agency, *Cubatur*, it's possible to travel extensively around the country. There is none of the extreme poverty which characterises most Latin American countries and people are generally friendly and relaxed. Personal safety seems to be only a minor hazard, although the official intimidation of gay people has been reported in the past.

The **status of women** has changed markedly since the Revolution: successful efforts have been made to ensure they have equal access to education and job opportunities; and they have played a leading role in health and literacy campaigns. Most of this work is carried out through the *Federation of Cuban Women* which was set up by the government in 1960. With well over 2 million members, the Federation has the ability to organise and change women's lives on a massive scale. Its achievements are impressive, but the fact remains that few, if any, Cuban women hold any high position of power in the government and the Family Code, for all its radical stipulations, has done little to persuade men to share the housework.

▰ **Christina Jacqueline Johns spent a month in Cuba. Her visit from Mexico was entirely organised by *Cubatur*.**

Since the Revolution, when Havana ceased to be the 'sin city' of wealthy North Americans, the island hasn't figured prominently on the tourist map. The Cuban government, however, is working hard to change this situation. There are now a number of package tours to Cuba with enticing names like 'Cuba Waits for You' and 'Scuba in Cuba'. I took one of these package tours to Havana and it was one of the most interesting and enjoyable holidays I've ever had.

Many people say that Cuba is characterised more by 'Fidelismo' than 'socialismo'. What they mean is that socialism in Cuba is strongly influenced by the relaxed nature of Latin culture and temperament, and the remarkable mixture of conviction and tolerance symbolised by Fidel Castro. There is nothing rigid about Cuban socialist society. And there is nothing rigid about the package tours organised by Cubatur, the government tourist agency. The excursions – to beaches, museums, day-care centres and state farms – are partly determined by those in the tour group and all excursions are optional. If you like, you can spend your entire visit to Cuba exploring on your own. There are no restrictions whatever on where you can go and public transport is available.

The organised excursions, however, give you a good sense of just how Cuba's particular brand of socialism works. At Las Naranjas State Farm you can see the housing provided free to workers who choose to work on the farm. There are also farm stores where some goods are sold on an unrestricted basis and others (more scarce) within set limits. A blackboard in the store tells the shopper how much of these limited goods can be bought at one time. Day-care centres, where you can see small groups of children cheerfully playing and reading while their parents work, are also free.

But Cuba is not all state farms and day-care centres. Most tours include at least one day at Varadero Beach, the country's chief resort and a really beautiful Caribbean beach. And there are a number of very active night spots, including the famous outdoor *Tropicana*. A night there is like walking straight back into the 1950s.

Food is not one of Cuba's strong points. There is an odd left-over American influence which results in lots of rather dry hamburgers and sandwiches. But there are two excellent restaurants in Havana – the *Floridita*, one of Hemingway's old haunts, which specialises in seafood, and *El Bodigita* which features traditional Cuban dishes. And Cuban ice cream is not to be missed. For many years after the Revolution, ice cream wasn't available and now that it is, it has become something of a national obsession. There is a park near the centre of Havana which has seven or eight different outdoor ice cream pavilions which are usually packed late into the night.

Visiting the various museums and the monuments in Havana is interesting too, but probably the most rewarding pastime is talking to people. Cubans are extremely friendly, open and generous with their time. And they are amazingly patient about answering questions, showing almost none of the resentment of tourists you find in many other countries. Cuba needs the foreign currency brought in by tourists and Cubans are proud to show off what they've achieved in the twenty-five years since the Revolution. Your interest and your questions are viewed as a compliment – a statement of just how important Cuba is. I found myself using our English-speaking tour guide as something of a walking encyclopedia. Every morning I had a dozen questions about the mechanics of life in Cuba.

I had a very interesting conversation one afternoon in a coffee shop with a Cuban psychiatrist who was also an Anglican minister. 'Before the Revolution,' he said to me 'the people in government were very religious, and they stole the country blind. These people are Marxists, and they have no religion, now everybody in the country eats. I vote for the Communists.' Not all Cubans are so positive. There are the *discustados* as well, those who don't like the new Revolutionary Cuba, but they are just as interesting to talk with and just as open in expressing their views. Language schools are free to everyone and I found that many Cubans speak at least some English, making it relatively easy to start up a conversation.

It was obvious from my first midnight walk through the streets of Havana that life for women in Cuba was very different from that of most other women in Latin America. After about two hours, I started to realise that the sense of watchful wariness a woman develops in, say, Mexico was unnecessary here. I didn't have to be cautious when passing a group of men talking on a street corner. They might look, but they didn't leer. They might be interested, but never in that way that makes a woman feel she is being sized up as a potential victim. I experienced none of the vaguely obscene and aggressive comments a woman learns studiously to ignore in Mexico.

I mentioned this difference to the Cuban psychiatrist. 'Yes,' he said. 'It's true. In Cuba we take the women very seriously.' What I learned about Cuba while I was there seemed to confirm his opinion. Our tour guide told me that there used to be messages on television – between programmes – which, in his words, 'encouraged the mens to be gentle with the womens'. The Family Code of Cuba states explicitly that men and women have the right to practise their profession or skill and that they share equal responsibility for household tasks and childcare.

Needless to say, all is not perfect despite these advances. One of the most revealing discussions I had was with a Cuban man and his Puerto Rican wife in a bar one afternoon. The woman had travelled in Central America, Mexico and the United States and had for the past four years lived in Cuba with her husband. I asked if she thought the status of women in Cuba was better than their status in Puerto Rico or Mexico. 'Oh yes,' she replied. 'But Cuban men, in the home, are still very macho – even worse than the Mexicans.' After my own experience I was very surprised. Her husband started shaking his head. 'No, no. That's not true.' Ignoring him, the woman continued. 'In the home they think it must be their way because they are the man.' 'You don't understand', he said, 'You're not Cuban.' The more questions I asked, the more they disagreed until I became more or less irrelevant to the argument they were having with each other. After a while they reached something of an impasse. 'I am a woman and I see these things', she said as a parting shot. 'It is only your colonial mentality that makes you think this way,' he replied grumpily. She looked over at me and winked.

TRAVEL NOTES

Language Spanish. It seems that relatively few Cubans speak any English (though reports vary) so it's advisable to learn at least some Spanish before you go.

Transport Bus and train services are quite extensive, but tend to be slow and generally inefficient. Theoretically, hitching is illegal, but in practice it works quite well if you're prepared for the inevitable risks involved.

Accommodation Unless you're on an organised tour you may well have problems finding somewhere reasonably cheap to stay. Travelling independently, you're still obliged to book five days' accommodation in advance and from then it's still advisable to book through the official *Cubatur* office, Calle 23, No 156, Velado, Havana (Tel. 32–4521), as the cheaper hotels tend to fill up quickly, especially in the provinces.

Guide Paula DiPerna, *The Complete Travel Guide to Cuba* (St Martin's Press, New York, 1979). Very out of date, but still the most comprehensive guide; available from: Carila Latin American Resource Centre, 29 Islington Park St, London N1. The *South American Handbook* also carries a chapter on Cuba.

CONTACTS
Federation of Cuban Women, Calle 11 214, La Habana, Cuba. Central organisation for making contact with women's groups throughout the country.

BOOKS
Margaret Randall, *Cuban Women Now: Interviews with Cuban Women* (The Women's Press, Toronto, 1974). Women from diverse backgrounds talk about their lives and aspirations in the wake of the revolution.
Elizabeth Stone, ed., *Women and the Cuban Revolution* (Pathfinder Press, New York, 1981). Collection of speeches and documents, including the thoughts of Fidel Castro.
Inger Holt-Seeland, *Women of Cuba* (Lawrence Hill, New York, 1981). Yet more interviews, with six women ranging from a farmworker to a university teacher.

For a more recent feminist view of women in contemporary Cuba read Germaine Greer's chapter in *Women – a World Report* (see General Bibliography).

Thanks to Tricia Barnett for travel information.

TRINIDAD

Trinidad is the largest island in the Eastern Caribbean, with a population of about a million people, and the closest to the mainland. Only seven miles away, Venezuela can be clearly seen from the hills.

Like Venezuela, Trinidad is an oil state, but the collapse of oil prices since the great boom period of the 1970s has left the island in bad financial trouble. Even so, the middle-classes continue to live a comfortable life, driving around in large gas-guzzling American cars (petrol, despite a couple of recent price increases, is still cheap), eating in overpriced restaurants boasting international cuisine, and building large sprawling houses along the coastal strips beside the capital, Port of Spain, and San Fernando in the south. The poor have been hard hit. Bullock-drawn carts and ploughs co-exist with expensive imported cars and tractors, and many smallholders live in tumbledown shacks in the hills.

Outside carnival there is little tourism in Trinidad. Trinidadians themselves take their holidays on the much smaller sister island of Tobago which, as a classic 'tropical paradise,' has far more tourist facilities. Wherever you go, even staying in small guest houses or with local families, the cost of living is high. But people are generally friendly and hospitable and, if you love music and dancing (this is the home of the calypso and the steel band), there's lots of cheap entertainment. At the same time without a male companion you can expect endless propositions from local men.

Although there are some vociferous feminists within the trade unions, the **Women's Movement** has been slow to develop. Trinidad is ethnically very mixed – broadly a combination of people of African, Indian and, to a much lesser extent, European, Chinese and Syrian descent. While relations are harmonious, people are always aware of the possibilities of friction between the different groups, especially with rising unemployment. The political parties tend to be split along racial lines, but an attempt is always made to keep some balance of races within the government. People are far more conscious of this issue than they are of sexism.

◢ **Sue Ward visited Trinidad for a week as a guest of the University of the West Indies.**

Port of Spain is a sprawling harbour town with some beautiful old colonial buildings, now largely housing government offices. Some of the town was redeveloped during the oil boom when the price of land shot up to ridiculous levels. There are roads of near-motorway standard around the edges and several shopping malls, mostly half unlet, while the other part of the town is a grid system of narrow streets permanently choked with traffic.

One consequence of an economy based on cheap petrol is that no Trinidadian who can afford it ever walks anywhere if he or she can drive. Several times before I got wise to it I was offered lifts to places only a short distance away on foot, only to be taken on a huge detour to avoid the traffic jams.

The Trinidadians I met were friendly and hospitable – embarrassingly so in fact, so that I wasn't allowed to pay for a single meal. Any British guest would have been treated well, but people were especially unwilling to see a woman pay for anything, even though I was on an expenses-paid trip.

Long queues and very slow service in the banks and government offices were, I was told, standard for their laid-back lifestyle, something the country certainly has – very attractive until you actually want something done in a hurry.

Apart from the heat I found no problems walking around or taking buses on my own, but the middle-class Trinidadians at the university were quite paranoid about security and personal safety. They claimed that unemployed youths, many of them Rastafarians, were responsible for a spate of muggings and burglaries; the Professor who was my host had a high wire fence with padlocked gates around his house, and a fierce dog who roamed loose in the garden at night.

Since Trinidad is so close to the Equator, days and nights are roughly the same length, darkness falling at about 6pm all year round. The first couple of evenings I went out alone after dark, but I was warned so many times that it was dangerous that I became jumpy, which greatly restricted my movements.

When I left everyone said 'You must return for Carnival.' Trinidad celebrates the beginning of Lent with the biggest and most spectacular carnival in the Caribbean, nearly a whole week of 'jumping up,' steel bands and drinking. By November many workshops creating the costumes and floats were in evidence and there were money-raising parties advertised for every weekend in all the towns I visited. It's impossible to find a hotel during Carnival, but everyone expects to find friends and acquaintances, and even vague friends of friends, turning up and sleeping on the floor. In any case, the amount of sleep you get is limited – you're too busy drinking and dancing.

◤ **Ursula Ryland spent a large part of her childhood in Trinidad up to 1949. Accompanied by her husband, she finally returned for a week in 1985.**

I first knew the island at child level, pedalling energetically up and down around an oilfield community where the roads smelt of pitch at midday and became sticky under the pulling tread of tyres and burnt the soles of bare feet. The immediate landscape was made up of widespreading houses surrounded by gardens of cut kutch grass and often edged with hedges of hibiscus or bougainvillea, the flowers red, magenta or purple, all hot-looking. There were massive trees whose branches reached out away from the road edge over the silken sea below. The long grass fields were forbidden because of poisonous snakes and at nightfall the pedals were pushed with immense fury to escape the time of the wheeling bats, some of which were said to spread disease and suck the blood of sleeping cattle.

More than three decades later I found myself, a tourist, being driven out of Port of Spain along the scenic route towards Maracas Bay. Our driver was adamant: 'This country's a confusion, man! God I'm telling you it's a helluva confusion. It's time they in charge put on some cultural tours. You don't know what in the hell you're looking at.'

The route wound through mountains covered by deep forest, birds nests hanging like string bags from the trees. High up a wisp of wet-looking cloud drifted from a jagged point. A few dead cars lay crumpled by the roadside. Way below, between craggy tentacles of land, the green sea shimmered in the distance. It was Easter Monday and everyone was enjoying the holiday; Muslims, Hindus, Jews, Christians, regardless of faith. When we reached the beaches there were cars and people everywhere. Not liking crowds, we decided to move on. Driving south we passed ramshackle buildings on stilts, some with rusty corrugated iron roofs. We also saw rows of identical modern houses, arranged like desks in a general office and intended for occupants in that wage bracket. There were lean-to's near the highway with people selling great green melons and advertising 'loud' tomatoes (loud means good). At one point in our journey the road curled around a group of houses whose occupants had refused to move to allow the originally planned lie of the highway.

Just outside San Fernando, the island's second largest town, we came to a roundabout with more illegal stalls selling beautiful looking fruit and vegetables. Entrepreneurs are hard to quash in Trinidad. The Savannah in Port of Spain, a focal point for cricket, horse-racing and Carnival, is said to be the largest roundabout in the world due to the temporary one-way system introduced some years ago. It's also a great free market-place.

Finally, we turned towards La Brea and the famous pitch lake not far from San Fernando. The lake, a vast expanse of hot black tar, provides a significant, if decreasing, source of revenue for Trinidad's flailing economy. Two guides ran alongside the car as we approached. One of them spoke enthusiastically of the lake, describing it as the 'mother rock of oil'. He spoke of the lake's skin creeping up the incline towards its old rim, as rebirth, where it would fold in and return to the mother of the lake.

A man with dreadlocks was standing in the middle of the lake, his face and clenched fists raised to the hot sky, and I heard the words 'Oh God, these mother-fucking white men'. No one took any notice, but I turned away.

TRAVEL NOTES

Languages English is the main language although, laced with Creole expressions, it can be hard to understand. In some areas Spanish and a French patois are spoken.

Transport Buses are cheap, but tend to be very overcrowded. Out-of-town services are limited, so, as long as you can decipher the complicated system, it's often best to get a taxi. Make sure you pay after local people in order to determine the fare, or else agree a price in advance. It's not worth hitching. As well as being risky, you'll probably be picked up by a pirate taxi anyway. The *South American Handbook* (see below) includes a good run-down on how the taxi system works.

Accommodation Like everything, hotels are expensive and prices more than double at Carnival times. The Trinidad and Tobago Tourist Board, 56 Frederick Street, Port of Spain, said to be very helpful, provides information on a range of places to stay, including guest houses which are more reasonably priced.

Guide The *South American Handbook* (Trade and Travel Publications, Bath), updated yearly, includes a short chapter on Trinidad and Tobago.

CONTACTS

There are at least two women's organisations in Trinidad: **Concerned Women for Progress**, socialist in orientation and closely linked to trade unions; and **The Group**, made up largely of professional, middle-class women lobbying against various forms of sex discrimination.

We've been unable to trace any addresses, but try writing to the **Women and Development Unit**, University of West Indies, Extra-Mural Department, Pinelands, St Michael, Barbados, which co-ordinates information on women in the Caribbean.

BOOKS

Merle Hodge, *Crick Crack Monkey* (Heinemann, 1981). Revealing novel about growing up and coping with the caste system in Trinidad.

JAMAICA

Jamaica has mountains, beautiful beaches and a tropical climate with high temperatures all the year round. Tourism is integral to the island's economy and strings of discotheques, expensive restaurants, and organised water-sports centres line the coast roads. At the same time beaches are never crowded and, outside major resorts like Montego Bay, there's plenty of scope for more adventurous travel – although it won't be cheap.

Communication can prove an unexpected problem. Although British colonisation has left English as the official language, most people speak a local patois which is very difficult for outsiders to understand. It's much easier and probably safer to travel with someone who knows 'Jamaica talk'.

Safety is mainly a hazard in and around the capital, Kingston. The people of Jamaica are mostly very poor; unemployment is high and violence, much of it politically motivated, has become a regular feature of life in the city. No traveller is advised to walk there alone, especially at night, but tension fades visibly as you move away from the area. You can expect comments from men wherever you go, but no general threat of sexual attack.

The importance of reggae music amongst young people; the practice of Rastafarianism, a cult based on the divinity of the late Emperor Haile Selassie of Ethiopia; and moves to achieve official recognition of Jamaican dialect as a language in its own right, are all signs of a nation struggling to define its cultural identity. **Women** are integral to this process, for they have always been greatly responsible for preserving African tradition through the passing down of customs through the family. Recognition of the hitherto submerged role of women in Caribbean history lies at the core of Jamaica's most radical women's group, *Sistren* (meaning sisters), a theatre collective for working-class women. According to Honor Ford-Smith, one of Sistren's members, the group use drama as a consciousness-raising tool, 'a means of breaking silence, of stimulating discussion, of posing problems and experimenting with their solutions'. This approach is far removed from other women's organisations which tend to focus on domestic and handicraft schemes which do little to challenge the actual position of women in society.

▰ **Jenny Morrison spent a year teaching at an all-girls' school 70 miles from Kingston.**

Saturday morning and the markets mushroom throughout rural Jamaica. Women sit cross-legged before their heaps of breadfruit, yams and sweet potatoes. Others perch on their haunches, sucking eagerly at the old clay pipes jammed between their toothless gums. The picture, quite rightly, implies the tough, resilient and independent nature of these women.

The Jamaican woman is special. She moves with a serene sense of dignity and has a natural and balanced awareness of herself, her grace and beauty. But she is still a long way from achieving any form of sexual equality. At least one-third of women in Jamaica are heads of household with the responsibility of earning money to support their families, and the numbers are rising.

I was teaching in Mandeville, a mountain town west of Kingston. Working in an all girls' school taught me, more than anything, the difficulties of growing up in such a troubled society. Half of one class was probably fatherless in the sense that Daddy, attracted by migrant labour, had smuggled himself into nearby Miami to seek his fortune, not bothering to return; or else gone off to live with another of his women. Outside this family situation, teenage prostitution is ridiculously high. Rumour had it that many of the fifth-form girls were selling themselves simply to pay for their bus fares, exam fees and books!

The raw deal experienced by Jamaican women, however strong they may be, is nowhere more obvious than in the budding Rastafarian cult, which, with its red, black, green and yellow paraphernalia, has captivated many of the island's young people. The cult itself has many good points – its bouncy energy, pulsating music and ethnic pride – but attitudes to female members hit the depth of chauvinism. The role of any woman in the group is that of an individual queen or partner. Fidelity is expected of her and any sexual misdemeanours are condemned by the Old Testament, also used to sanction the infidelity of the male. Birth control is rejected as a 'white ploy to kill black people' and during menstruation women are considered unclean, thus unwanted and abandoned temporarily by their men.

I slowly discovered Jamaica throughout my stay. I say 'slowly' because travelling is seriously handicapped by transport problems. Little fifteen-seater minibuses have been shipped to the island to speed its inhabitants from A to B. Apart from the fact that they can be as hard to catch as mosquitoes, you need a strong nerve to survive being spun along the coast roads. And don't expect to have a seat to yourself. Often thirty people are squashed into a vehicle equipped to carry half that number, many actually outside, clinging desperately on to windows and doors. There are compensations. If you do get an inside place, you're bound to find a friendly soul willing to entrust her life secrets to you, hoping you'll do likewise.

Arriving almost anywhere makes the long crush seem worth it. Most tourists think of Ocho Rios or Montego Bay, but there are many deserted coves, tropical gardens, waterfalls and bamboo-lined walks to enjoy. Whatever the landscape, physically, Jamaica is Paradise.

Tempting fate one night I shunned the glamorous hotels and, with three friends, set up a small tent on a still sweltering sandy beach. Peeny-wally fireflies sparked around our heads, escorting us on our midnight swim, and the cries of local crab-catchers haunted our dreams. We were, however, woken by local police who commended us on our bravery for camping on a beach notorious for all manner of crimes.

Jamaica's reputation as a peace-loving country was badly maimed by political riots, triggered by the 1980 elections, and continues to sink. Crime is on the increase and random shootings have become a common occurrence in Kingston. In the face of mounting poverty and social problems far too much emphasis is placed on tourism (the largest source of foreign exchange). The perceived needs of the wealthy American holiday-maker are all too often catered for at the expense of local people.

◪ **Mara Benetti spent ten weeks in Jamaica.**

My first three weeks were a gentle breaking-in period during which I got used to being shouted at in the street 'Ehi! Whitie! Whitie!' from passing cars and lorries and learned how to cope with the constant hassling which tourists can expect to suffer. With time I felt stronger within myself and decided to travel around the island.

With its eruptive vitality and alien ways Jamaica is an intimidating country for a woman to travel alone. However, in the end I much preferred it to travelling with white friends. Alone it was easier to divorce myself from the wealthy tourist hordes and, although I certainly felt insecure and threatened at times, I always ended up having some interesting encounter. I learned to get used to the men who swarm around almost any white woman with caressing looks and sweet words. They are different from, say, the Italian 'pappagallo' or the North African male champion; in Jamaica attitudes to sex are more free and easy, sexual taboos appear to be less strong, and I came to the conclusion that the dominant reason beind these seductive approaches was the 'subtle charm of the bourgeoisie' which white skin exerts on people who are very poor. If you go out with a Jamaican man don't be surprised to find yourself paying for two.

Contacts with women in Jamaica aren't easy. Unlike the men, they aren't particularly inclined to strike up a conversation, partly because they're too busy making ends meet, and partly because they see Western women, with the allure exerted on Jamaican men by their wealth, as dangerous competition. From a distance I was struck by the preponderance of strong 'mother' figures, mainly a result of the high number of 'baby mothers', that is women who are single parents. Relatively little importance is placed on the institution of marriage, but womanhood in Jamaica seems to revolve around children.

With its total rejection of birth control, this emphasis on children is especially strong within the Rastafarian community. The rasta queen is meant to be entirely subordinate to her king. Yet the rastawomen I met struck me with their strength of character, confidence and self-possession. They stood firm and independent. Many lived with their children without men in their lives. The community was generally supportive and the baby father gave some erratic contribution to the upbringing of his offspring, but it was the women who provided for most of their needs and ran the household. This was the life of one of the few rastawomen I had the chance to meet.

My encounter dated back to the very beginning of my stay when I made a trip north with Tekula, an American black dreadlock woman I had met through a friend. Tekula was incredibly beautiful and, with her unusual light blue eyes, aroused great interest in everyone she met. She was also very stylish, always dressed in clothes dyed and designed by herself with great inventiveness and skill. Something must have attracted the rastawoman who approached us as we sat on the beach at Orange Bay. With a sense of purpose she walked straight up to Tekula and after exchanging a few words invited her to her hut in the bush. I was taken along as a sort of special concession for the woman took one look at me and announced: 'The Bible says woman shall not wear men's clothing', staring at my baggy trousers which, up to that moment, I'd thought very respectable.

Our guide, who was tall, well-built and in about her mid-thirties, led the way up a hill along a path which soon disappeared to leave us scrambling through tropical vegetation. After the first hill we descended into a valley covered with small coconut trees, then up again, past another valley in which grazed half a dozen goats, then up yet another hill. I can hardly remember how many hills and valleys we walked, but we finally made our way along the edge of a mound at the end of which a couple of bamboo sheds stood on a flattened open space. The first, largish and built on a raised platform, had a couple of beds in it and most of her belongings – a plastic bag full of rags, clothes and several blankets – as well as a wooden table cluttered with tobacco leaves and small parcels of *ganja* characteristically wrapped in brown paper. The other hut was her kitchen, open on two sides, with an open fire and a few makeshift seats made of old beer barrels.

The woman lived alone, although that day several of her men friends were present, all young rastas looking proud and dignified despite their unkempt appearance. They were poorly dressed and no one wore shoes. We were ushered into the first hut and told to make ourselves comfortable and take a seat on her bed. She rolled up a massive joint for herself and offered me some tobacco when I said that ganja was too strong. It began to rain and everyone came to take shelter and the hut became really crowded. As the only white woman and a 'bald head' (the rasta expression for all non-Rastafarians) I felt so out of place I could only sit in silence and soak up the scene. The conversation was in patois, double-dutch to me, and I could only understand the usual 'Praise Jah, Rastafari', repeated by everyone so often and regularly that it gave a musical rhythmic quality to what was being said.

Our hostess seemed to rule like a queen. She pointed to the banana and the coconut trees that grew around the hut; at the yam, the green beans and the chickens clucking underneath the wooden floor; at the breadfruit she had just collected from the lower branches of a tree and launched into a thanksgiving litany to Jah. At some point – I didn't understand why or what in the conversation had prompted it – she started to undo her flowery headscarf. It was an automatic movement, one gesture after another, as she kept on talking to her attentive public. Finally her dreadlocks tumbled down from the top of her head, heavy, long, twenty years of them perhaps? She looked suddenly younger and more graceful, even slightly bashful. For a brief moment she stood there and gave us all a proud satisfied smile before wrapping her hair up again and folding everything into place.

TRAVEL NOTES

Languages Most people speak patois or 'Jamaica talk' amongst themselves, but can easily switch into English. Language problems usually depend on the situation you find youself in.

Transport Buses are cheap, but slow and the driving can be pretty wild. Minibuses also operate on all the main routes, always jam-packed since they only set off when full. Some taxis have meters, but it's wise to sort out the fare before you set off. Hitching is not recommended.

Accommodation Hotels tend to be expensive and it's usually better to try to find a room for rent. There are lots of houses on the beach at Negril which offer inexpensive rooms. Recommended in Kingston are the *Four Seasons* and the *Sandhurst Lodge.*

Special problems There are varying reports about the safety of Kingston — the shanty town areas in the south-west of the capital are definitely to be avoided — but provided you feel confident and carry very little money it's worth a visit.

Market prices shoot up 100 per cent at the sight of a white face, so bargaining is a must.

Standard medical care is very dubious and medicines expensive, so make sure you are insured and, as far as possible, take your own supplies.

Ganja or marijuana is widely grown and smoked, but it's illegal. It's also very very strong.

Guide The *South American Handbook* (see Trinidad) only has 8 pages on Jamaica but, unlike other guides, at least it doesn't just cater for the luxury tourist.

CONTACTS
Sistren Theatre Collective 100 Hope Road, Kingston 6 Tel. 927–8800. The group works mainly in the shanty towns and in rural areas, but it's worth getting in touch to try and see them in action.

BOOKS
Michelle Cliff, *Abeng* (The Crossing Press, New York, 1984). Explores the life of a young girl growing up among the contradictions of class, and colour, blood and Jamaica's history of colonisation and slavery.

Erna Brodber, *Jane and Louisa Will Soon Come Home* (New Beacon Books, 1980). The author's first novel, written in the form of a long prose poem about life in Jamaica.

Ziggi Alexander and Audrey Dewjee eds., *The Wonderful Adventures of Mrs Seacole in Many Lands* (1957, Falling Wall Press 1984). Mary Seacole, who was born into Jamaican slave society, writes about her life and travels.

Pamela Mordecai and Mervyn Morris, eds, *Jamaica Woman* (Heinemann, 1982). Exciting anthology of poems by 15 Jamaican women.

Also look out for the work of Jamaica's best-known woman poet, Miss Louise Bennett.

Thanks to Carolyn Wood for help with these Travel Notes. Also to Catherine Black for background information used in the regional introduction.

NORTH AMERICA

Chapter Twenty

THE USA AND CANADA

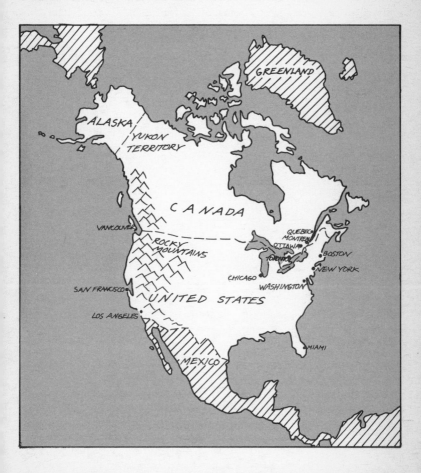

Most travellers have a set image of **North America**, especially its cities, from its worldwide domination of TV and film screens. But what may take you by surprise is the sheer size of the area – the sense of space which is exciting and exhilarating. You should also be prepared for much greater regional diversity and ethnic mix than is portrayed in the media.

There are the indigenous North Americans, Inuits and Indians, and large immigrant communities in most big towns – Hispanics, Chinese, Italians, Irish and Polish.

It can sometimes seem to a foreigner that North Americans, especially the youth, are permanently on the move. It's partly the ease of travel and partly the greater distances between communities – people think nothing of driving 100 miles to a party and back in the same evening. Although regional loyalties are strong, outside Middle America you'll meet few people who live in the town they were born in – society is much more fluid than in Britain. A lot of North Americans are tourists in their own country too: the dream of driving from coast to coast in a big car, tuned into the radio, is very much an American one.

In the North American **Women's Movements**, the euphoria at the hardwon battles of the 1960s and 1970s has given way to a re-appraisal of aims in the austere 1980s. Feminists retain an influential, organised presence at a local level, but at a national one they are marking time in a climate epitomised by the defeat of Equal Rights Amendment in the US and the advent of neo-feminist groups.

USA

Despite any sense of familiarity you may feel you have with US culture you're bound to experience some degree of culture shock on arrival in the States. New York especially can leave you feeling too small, too vulnerable and too pedestrian alongside the pace and hustle of its city life. But it doesn't take long to gain confidence – even to feel quite relaxed about travelling. So many American women travel from state to state that for the most part you won't be given a second glance; it is only in situations where you're readily identifiable as a tourist that you may find yourself attracting hustlers. Big cities, however, do have definite no-go areas – which you'll be warned about – and travelling anywhere in urban America it is always wise to avoid carrying extra cash.

The exchange rate is not as bad as it was, but money can still be a major concern. There are numerous networks of cheap hotels, but some can be very sparse places catering for the bottom of the heap of migrant Americans. The reputation that Americans have for hospitality is, however, well deserved and even the briefest encounter can lead to offers of floorspace or a bed for the night. Hitching is considered fairly risky (more so than in the UK) but you can usually get to whichever town you want on a Greyhound or Trailway bus.

It's very easy to be a tourist in America and 'do the sites' – the Grand Canyon, Las Vegas Golden Mile, Yosemite National Park, Disneyland. On this sort of circuit you may find fragments of Amerindian culture cynically packaged and presented to the tourists. It's all part of the recent rehabilitation of native American culture, particularly offensive in the light of the continued erosion of native Indian territories and lifestyles and discrimination at all levels against these peoples. Considering the size and number of America's ethnic minorities, integration has in fact been a reality for a comparative few. Colour discrimination, notorious in the South, remains an enduring fact of life – Black and Hispanic urban ghettoes tend to be the poorest, most deprived in the country.

Regional chauvinism is strong, each state having its own legislation and political affiliations. Between them attitudes towards women (and towards Reagan and God) vary widely. The Moral Majority and associated groups like the Pro-Lifers have recently strengthened and extended their base. They are proving effective as an anti-abortion lobby and in the current climate of hysteria surrounding the spread of Aids, are receiving growing support for their tough line on 'sexual deviance'. In many states women are being forced to campaign to protect gains made in the 1970s from an onslaught of retrogressive legislation – the defeat of the Equal Rights Amendment being just one symptom of this trend.

The spectrum of activities and discourse described as **feminist** is much wider than in Europe, and in many areas, notably among Black American feminists the process, aims and objectives of the movement seem more clearly defined and developed. In making contact with women's groups it can be hard to adjust to a subtly different *modus operandi* and style of communication, but, as for everything in America, it is always possible to find a niche.

See Mary Hockaday's piece below for more details on the Women's Movement.

◪ Mary Hockaday spent a year living and studying in New York and travelled all over the States.

After a year in the USA, I still find it a place of paradox, not least when it comes to the status of women. An enduring image for me is that of Geraldine Ferraro, the country's first woman vice-presidential candidate and important role model for women aspiring to political office, in a Diet Pepsi television ad with her two daughters saying, 'We can be whatever we want to be, and being a mother is one of the choices I'm most proud of.' New achievements and old habits live side by side.

As a visitor take the precautions you would anywhere, especially with money and personal property. You should be particularly careful in the big cities. In one way they are more relaxing for a woman on her own than some European cities since there is less low-level sexual harassment on the streets. But then again the chance of high-level harassment, of rape, is greater. I always tried to look as if I knew where I was going, even if I didn't. Hustlers and hasslers are drawn like moths to a flame to hesitancy and unease.

A British accent is a mixed blessing. Usually it draws oohs and aahs and the rightly famed American hospitality. Brush up on your royal family trivia – I felt ungracious several times because I couldn't pay back kindness with even the name of Princess Di's hairdresser. Your accent does mark you as a foreigner, if not a tourist, so watch out for suddenly raised prices in bars and taxis.

New York is rich enough in experience to keep any visitor busy for some time. But it is not America. Nor is the East Coast, or hardly even the West and East Coasts. The middle is vast, varied and offers staggering landscapes – even the patches of flatness and emptiness can be breathtaking. There is no substitute for driving through. I never had any trouble travelling, either alone or with another woman. But I would not hitch in either situation.

Every state is different, from North Carolina with churches and advertisements for God, to California with its lesbian bars and advertisements for gay politicians. The one area I am sorry to have missed is the deep South, but I would probably not travel there as a white woman alone. In many places in the States a single woman traveller would not be given a second glance. Off the beaten track people may be surprised, but you are no more an oddity as a foreigner or a woman than someone from New York. America is an inward-looking nation and lack of interest in or coverage of European and world affairs amazes many visitors. The one region that gets more attention than in Britain is South and especially Central America, although attention is no guarantee of accuracy.

The history of the North American Women's Movement is in some ways parallel to the British. The US had its own pioneer women and 19th-century free thinkers and suffragettes, and women there have organised similar campaigns for the vote, equal pay, contraception and abortion, fairer tax credit and divorce law and toleration of lesbianism. But the shape of the recent movement is different. It drew strength and lessons from the Black Civil Rights movement of the 1960s, and the voice of Black feminists is stronger than in Britain.

In one way it seems that the themes and dreams of the Women's Movement are more fully assimilated, among men as well as women, than in Britain. It is relaxing; I find myself less defensive than at home. But this is a rhetorical country, and the rhetoric hides much difference and actual resistance. Feminism is taken for granted and institutionalised, but in embryo form. There are state and city offices for women but incredibly, in a country which prides itself on its Constitution and Declaration of Rights, there is still no Equal Rights Amendment.

Feminism has become more than an indulgent umbrella word in America. It is a whole canopy. I, like many other Europeans I met, was surprised by how readily it covers 'right-wing feminism', and Republican women. I think of them as individualist feminists, the ones who believe the ads screaming 'You can have it all', or indeed already have it. They are the women who wear high heels with their navy suits at the law office, and sneakers on the subway home. They have done well. The Women's Movement of the 1970s got more women into the professions, and they are notably more visible in business and politics than in Britain. There are women's banks, and corporate childcare is better. But the story at the other end of the scale is very different. It is the story of the 'feminisation of poverty', as more and more families are headed by single women on inadequate salaries or social security that under Reagan is dwindling. Minority women have it even harder than white.

There are many who bewail the stagnation if not the death of the US Women's Movement, and it certainly has none of the vitality and feel of a movement bringing about radical change as women say it did in the 1960s and 1970s. But it is not defeated. A major concern now, and one that reflects an extension from middle-class issues, is equal pay – not just for equal work but for women's work that is comparable to men's, in an effort to raise the wages for undervalued traditionally female jobs like nursing and clerical work.

This is a new fight, but some of the old ones are breaking out again. Frustratingly, the movement faces the wearisome prospect of having to defend legal abortion all over again. Fanatical 'Pro-Lifers', as they call themselves, bombed and set fire to abortion clinics last year (1984). The Catholic Church, the administration, fundamentalists, and even some on the left who are beginning to place 'foetal rights' over women's rights, are co-ordinating a sophisticated anti-abortion campaign, that is turning the issue away from choice for living women.

I was not prepared for the pervasiveness and power of religion in the US. For many it is a source of community and cultural vitality, and there are some churches in the vanguard of civil rights campaigns. But others certainly do not help women's interests.

As far as the administration is concerned, Reagan has asked the Supreme Court (the highest judicial body with one judge out of nine a woman) to overrule earlier pro-choice legislation, and make the availability of abortion a matter for each state to decide. Affirmative action (a kind of positive discrimination) is also under attack. But the federal government is not America. Because of the country's size, and because of the distance of Washington from so many places, local politics at a state and city level are more lively and important than local politics often are in Britain. Ethnic, grassroots and feminist organisations can exercise more sway at this level than the administration might like.

One major impression I have of America is the eagerness and ability of women to organise, to fund-raise, to lobby. Anywhere you go you can find a woman doing something, and in many cities there are extensive networks for every political, sexual, religious and racial shade imaginable: groups for women artists, Jewish lesbians, women business owners, women jazz drummers, women against pornography, women against women against pornography, etc., etc. There's a joke that you may be one in a million, but go to New York and you'll find seven others just like you, and they will have started a group.

■ **Margaret Cowley and her partner W.L.G. made use of the 'drive-away' system, taking a car across the States.**

Wonderful, I thought, driving along with the city behind us and those wide American roads in front. San Francisco is, as cities go, beautiful and often captivating. But our visit this time had been so traumatised by the strong surge of sado-masochism among the lesbian feminists we'd met that my lover and I felt a strong sense of relief when the country opened up in front and we left it all behind.

The drive-away system that operates in the USA is very convenient for women who wish to travel independently and yet have little money to do so. It's a basic delivery service, whereby Americans who are moving from one area to another hire a company to transport their car. We were to deliver a VW Scirocco from Oakland, California, to Espanola, New Mexico. We left the $100 deposit, to be returned on completion of the task, and drove off with a free tank-full of petrol. One is meant to travel on the most direct route and within a certain number of days, but the time allowed for delivery is generous and obviously varies according to the distance.

I sat behind the wheel with all the excitement that surges through me every time I start an adventure. For me there is no other feeling in the world like this: a sense of freedom, of the mystery of a different country and culture – and no electricity or telephone bills to worry about. It was March, barely out of winter, but it was sunny and I wanted to feel the heat of the sun on my body. The radio played old 1960s songs, and we sang along, feeling like a couple of old hippies. Heading south, we crossed the San Joaquin Valley with its agricultural landscape of vineyards, orchards and fields displaying the first growth of annual crops. We then took the route to Barstow. The countryside was now mountainous in parts and increasingly arid. We had our first glimpse of 'tumble-weeds', conjuring up memories of a particular type of early Hollywood western, and causing us great glee.

We were aiming to arrive at the Grand Canyon in Arizona at sunset, and although we did get there in time, the full magnificence of this event was spoiled by an overcast sky. We had hoped to stay the night there but the motels were all outrageously expensive. Not surprised or too disheartened, we drove the 59 miles back to the main highway and found a cheap downtown motel in the town of Williams – $6 a night each for the room, with colour TV and vibrating bed attachment thrown in. The bed wasn't the sensual experience of a lifetime – it made me feel seasick and I had to get off.

Our route took us further west and we were able for a time to motor along a minor and surprisingly deserted road, following the Canyon's edge. The mist lifted, the rain became patchier and we had the opportunity to realise its sheer vastness, the amazing geographical structures, the colours and its unique beauty. We drove across the Painted Desert, land of the Hopi, Apache and Navajo Indians. Several times that day we stopped for coffee at roadside places and it appeared that strangers were an unaccustomed sight. Nobody was rude to us, but there was an air that we were intruding. On the radio at this point we could only receive that particular brand of American country and western music which seems to romanticise women being abused in a variety of ways. All the liberal attitudes of the Californian life were far behind.

We crossed the State line into New Mexico and stopped the night in the town of Gallup at another motel. This one was run by a sari-clad Indian woman, and we found that several of the cheapest motels in the south-west were run by women from India; we were always treated well, and our rooms always clean and comfortable. Our next stop was Albequerque, where we found the women's bookshop *Full Circle*. The feminists there spoke of the strong lesbian/feminist movement in Albequerque and events that were very definitely women only. This was heartening news after our experience in San Francisco where we found no women-only clubs, regular events or space (even the Women Building, with the exception of one very small room, was mixed). We were hoping that the women at Full Circle could help with directions to the ARF women's land: we had heard vague descriptions of it, and wanted to find out more, but the best they could do was provide us with another address, *Mama Lola's Restaurant* in Santa Fe, where 'someone would be arriving that evening and knew the address.' This was true and with hand-drawn map and a few extra handy landmarks verbally installed in our heads, we set off. It was roughly 25 miles to ARF, driving up into the hills which were covered in small trees and other hardy growth.

Without too much trouble we found the ARF land, but rain was now falling heavily and it was just on dusk. We spoke with two women in the first house we came to, explaining that we had been offered a women's teepee for the night. It was revealed that the teepee was on a hill which we could only just see through binoculars and the journey to it would take some 1½ hours by foot. Normally the opportunity to make such a trek and sleep under canvas would have been a very enticing proposition. But the rain, the knee-deep mud and the undeniable darkness seemed to hint at all manner of disasters, and with unpleasant thoughts of poisonous snakes and large brown bears we looked glum. Seeing our hesitation, the women invited us to stay with them, which we gladly accepted. Their house wasn't part of the women's land so, as we left the following morning, we never actually got to ARF. We delivered the car to its owner the next day. She signed our delivery slip, necessary to recover our deposit, and drove us into Santa Fe to the Greyhound Bus Station.

■ **Diane Speakman describes her experience of New York, a city she is getting to know.**

Try to stay at least ten full days in New York. I wish someone had given me this advice, because the combined effects of jet-lag and culture shock reduced me, as they might well you, to a zomboid state. People often expect things to be approximately as they are at home. They're not! We've flown from the Old World to the New: historical perspectives, culture, people's attitudes, are very different and New York's are the most different of all. People there are more sophisticated, there's a more varied ethnic mix, life runs at a faster pace and much more ruthlessly.

It is also a startlingly expensive city – I sometimes felt like one of those swollen creatures in a George Grosz caricature *eating* dollar bills. Anything other than a budget-class hotel will seriously set you back, and in those you tend to pay in paranoia what you save in money. Nor can you afford to eat every meal out like middle-class Manhattanites do. A glass of beer or a cocktail in any of the singles bars in the city, even a coffee, are crippling by British standards; so too are entry charges to museums and even off-Broadway theatres ($25+ a seat). At least roller-skating to your Sony Walkman or, more popular, jogging in Central Park are free.

Obviously you can cut costs by choosing your hotel location carefully and using the buses or subway rather than cabs, assuming, that is, you can tolerate the subway's visual (and sometimes physical) assaults, and come to grips with the complexity of its three lines. A friend of mine got on the IND A express train expecting to be able to get out at 72nd Street, and ended up at 125th Street – in Harlem. Although there is a three-hour bus tour into the area run by Blacks (Penny Sightseeing Co., 303 West 42nd Street, 247 2860), it seems unhealthily voyeuristic to me, and

I prefer to abide by the 'rule' that Harlem is a no-go area, especially for white women.

This hinges into the whole question of where and why one feels safe in New York, which is partly a subjective thing. I heard that any street above 100 was suspect if not dangerous; ten years ago it might have been one above 90 – gentrificiation proceeds apace. I had been told so often about bag-snatching and hold-ups and knew people on business trips who'd been mugged because they were sauntering and looking prosperous, that I was far from relaxed. The first morning I was in New York, which happened to be the unseasonably hot and humid day of the Marathon (October 28), I left my bag behind in the door-keepered apartment I was lucky enough to be staying in, off Columbus Avenue, and walked a mile or two from west-to east-side Manhattan with just a $5-dollar bill in my trouser pocket: by the time I had cheered myself hoarse encouraging friends running in the Marathon and needed a drink/ice-cream, it had gone.

If you're planning to visit Manhattan alone, I'd suggest taking a short self-defence course first, not so much to use as to boost your confidence. Be aware all the time of the lie of the street, odd groups of men, and be very careful if you go into Central Park (even men are likely to be gang-raped if they stray into a rather attractive area known as The Ramble) Everywhere walk confidently and briskly, head up, don't carry a map or a lot of money; wear your bag slung across your body and if you are accosted as opposed to attacked or menaced with a knife, be prepared to do something lateral. Learn too, if you want to make contact with people in Manhattan, about 'apartmenting' – which address means what in terms of money, acceptable status, social mobility, ethnic surroundings. The swapping of addresses and ritual discussion of space, if my experience is anything to go by, will form at least the first cultural exchange you may have with Manhattanites lucky enough to have some kind of job and any degree of financial security.

My last trip was part business. I wanted to make contact with some feminists working in publishing and the arts. Half my sessions with these women were sticky and inert since we seemed to have such different ways of operating and communicating. We were, I suppose, stressed, intent on conveying or gaining information about our separate set-ups, functions, views, in a short time; and Manhattanites are demanding in a work context – everything must be sharper, faster, more efficient. But there were exceptions, occasional meetings where we could slow the pace, relax and share our different work experiences.

My most pleasurable memories of New York are made up of particular moments: looking at the two Rembrandt self-portraits in the Frick Museum; eating a Mexican meal on Columbus Avenue watching the world go by; witnessing a happening – a tap-dancer suddenly starting up in the street below the apartment; experiencing the diversity and gusto of the South St Seaport area and the atmosphere of the Annual Village Halloween Parade; and, above all, visiting the foyer of Grand Central Station (East 42nd St) and being a participant in that reel of film which was America to so many of my peer group in England during the 1940s and 1950s.

■ **Maureen Duff won a trip to Hawaii through a short-story competition in _Woman's Own_. The groups of islands, which includes Oahu, Maui and Kauai, became the 50th American state in 1959.**

In Oahu (capital Honolulu) one paradise has been replaced by another. The first, unchanged for thousands of years, was free, and still is – coco-palms, beaches and beautiful mountains. The second, a hotel resort built in the 1960s on top of the Hawaiian royal family's favourite beach, Waikiki, reminded me of a vast modern hospital complex where people suffering from twentieth-century exhaustion might come to convalesce. The seventeen-hour flight certainly put us in that category for a few days but for the privilege of recovery we had to cough up.

High prices mean that apart from Japanese honeymooners you'll meet only a certain type of American tourist on Oahu. One restaurant had named an omelette after two of them – 'Harold and Gladys from Okla-homa'. The original Hawaiian culture has been practically squashed out of all existence by a couple of centuries of invasion – by missionaries, immigrants, Americanisation and tourism. Hackneyed and poignant examples of old Hawaiian life can be found tucked away in such places as restaurants (photographs on the walls) and in cabarets, clubs and hotels (Polynesian dancing shows). The Kodak Hula Show for instance is free, entertaining and incorporates a little Hula philosophy – nobody is allowed to leave until the musicians (in traditional mu-mu costume) and Hula dancers (in green ti-leaf grass skirts) have posed for tourist photographs. There were several wives of the military in the audience the day we went. They were given a special mention by the aged MC who bore an uncanny resemblance to Ronald Reagan, complete with cowboy hat.

One place to avoid is the Polynesian Cultural Centre on the windward side of Oahu. Run by the Mormons, this establishment is the nadir against which every other experience of Hawaii must be measured. Its brochure claims to show 'the islands as you hoped they'd always be'. For an extortionate $14 it's like a trip to the zoo, to see students perform dances in artificially created Polynesian villages, separated by waterways down which the happy islanders paddle and sing on their way to entertain the next batch of tourists. We found it offensive and, avoiding the Kentucky-style cafeteria, hotfooted our way out.

Indigenous Hawaiians have benefited little from the influx of US multi-corporate investors, who tend to cream off the profits of tourism. During a 'Circle Island' bus tour we saw the camping sites of 'beach people', the casualties of American property developers' refusal, among other wrongs, to pay back-rent on developed areas many of them still own. Those with real grievances are denied access to the courts to redress the wrongs, and a land rights movement is not yet organised enough for effective action. In the meantime the beach people are shunted around the island, and often dragged from their tents, in an embarrassed attempt to keep them out of sight of the tourists.

I have to admit our experience of Hawaii was not the most wonderful. Of course we would have had a vastly different kind of time if we'd had more money. For instance it costs at least $40 one way to visit another island by plane, and, although there were one or two special offers on when we were there, we just couldn't justify the expense against the possibility that the experience of another island would not be greatly different to the one we were already on. On Maui, for instance, there is in progress the erection of another 'Waikiki-type' nightmare resort, only bigger. Kauai is more tropical than the other islands and remains as yet undeveloped, due partly to its lack of beaches.

As far as women travelling alone is concerned, Hawaii poses the same problems as you are likely to come across in any Westernised culture. You can meet men in bars or discos if that's what you want. We were warned, however, not to wait around for a bus out of town in the dark. The politeness of Hawaiians was both wonderful and bizarre. Nobody was rude, ever, but at the same time it was impossible to penetrate the smiling faces and good moods. In the end, our suspicious European minds had to concede that it was not just 'good business sense' but genuine friendliness. In fact smiling was like a national policy. Towards the end of our stay one woman shopkeeper wanted to know 'Now have you been treated well?' A serious question demanding a serious answer. 'Yes,' we said, 'definitely.' She smiled with satisfaction. People in Hawaii take their caring very seriously and that blanket friendliness was simple, non-European and genuine. We missed it when we came home. And it was really only then that I began to realise how much the American veneer of Hawaii is merely a disguise thrown over a group of islands whose roots lie in an ancient, alien culture. Hawaii has something you can't pin down, an exotic but lost quality as if the islanders themselves have consciously forgotten their origins but still move instinctively to the old rhythms.

TRAVEL NOTES

Language English – but there's a significant first-generation immigrant population who don't necessarily speak it. This is particularly true of the Spanish-speaking Americans in California, New Mexico and New York.

Accommodation Generally expensive, with budget-price hotels often in fairly seedy or 'unsafe' parts of town. On the road, *Motel 6* are worth looking for as they are cheap, plentiful and will book ahead for you; so too are youth hostels; safe, cheap and not usually requiring membership – many are more like small hotels.

Transport For internal travel there are *Greyhound* and *Trailway Bus* networks (stations often unsalubrious though) and cheap internal flights. Petrol is also inexpensive, as is carhire in most states. To drive-away you just need a passport and valid driving licence. Hitching is dodgy for either sex and not recommended.

Special problems Entrance visas are compulsory, and work visas hard to come by. Immigration procedures can be harrowing, with very close questioning – it helps to have names and addresses of contacts, a credit card and a return flight ticket. Cost and bureaucracy of US health care is horrific. You must take out medical insurance. If you think there is any chance you will need gynaecological care double-check your policy. Some don't cover it, and it is very expensive. So is contraception, so bring your own. Planned Parenthood is the US family planning organisation; they often have clinics giving swift, good help. University hospitals are usually good places for medical care.

Guides *Moneywise* (published by Travelaid) and *Let's Go* (Colombia Press) both publish practical low-budget guides to the US as a whole and to California. For New York there's a new *Rough Guide* (RKP, 1986).

CONTACTS

Two important resources:

The Index/Directory of Women's Media (published by Women's Institute for Freedom of the Press, 3306 Ross Place, NW Washington DC 20008, (Tel. 202–966 7783)). Lists women's periodicals, presses and publishers, bookstores, theatre groups, film and music groups, women's news services, writers' groups, media organisations, women's radio, special library collections, etc. Invaluable and updated yearly.

The National Organisation for Women (15 West 18th Street, 9th Floor, New York, 10011 and 425 13th Street, NW Washington DC 20004). Has groups all across the country: a good place to get referrals to more specific concerns.: rape crisis centres and counselling services, feminist bookshops and lesbian bars.

Most towns of size have women's groups, rape crisis centres and counselling services; big cities have feminist bookshops and lesbian bars, whilst universities and colleges are all good resources, many with women's centres of their own.

Below is a **select list of contacts** for the major cities and some states:

NEW YORK: **Women's Center**, Barnard College, 117th Street Broadway, (Tel. 212–280 2067). (Collection of books articles, periodicals, and clearing house for information on women's organisations studies, conferences, events); **Women's International Resource Exchange** (WIRE), 2700 Broadway, Room 7, (Tel. 212–666 4622); **Ceres** (women's gallery), 91 Franklin Street; **First Women's Bank**, 111 East 57th Street; **Djuna Books**, 154 West 10th Street and **Womanbooks**, 201 West 92nd Street; **Qui Travel** (Women's travel agent), 165 West 74th Street; **Women's Peace Camp,** Seneca Army Depot, New York State (sister camp to Greenham).

WASHINGTON: **Women's Information Network and Emergency Services,** 3918 W Street, NW Washington 20007 (Tel. 201–337 2217 (answering service), 333 9696 (guest house)); **International Center for Research on Women** (ICRW), 1010 16th Street, NW 20036 (collection and dissemination of current research on women especially related to development; library, and organises workshops, conferences); **National Women's Health Network**, 224th 7th Street, SE, 20003 (national organisation devoted to women and health, the 'umbrella' of women's health movement; also publishes guides to specific women related health problems); **Lammas** (women's bookshop), 321 7th Street, SE (Tel. 202–546 7299); **Rape Crisis**

Center PO Box 21005, Washington DC 20009.

BOSTON,CAMBRIDGE: **Information on women's groups, activities** Tel. 417–555 1212; **Cambridge Women's Center,** 46 Pleasant (Centre of information for Mass); **Boston Women's Health Book Collective**, Box 192 West Somerville, Mass 02144 (best known for **Our Bodies Our Selves**, book on women's sexuality and health; also projects, activists' network, collective monitors issues and policies affecting women's health in US and abroad).

In Lexington: **Women's International Network**, 187 Grant Street, 02173 (organisation with wide range of topics of concern, i.e. development; publishes reports from round world in quarterly *WIN News*): **New Words** (women's bookshop) Inman Square, Cambridge; *Marquis* (bar), Massachusetts Avenue (Central Square), Cambridge.

CHICAGO: **National Organisation for Women** 1957 E 73rd Street, 60649 (centre for information for Illinois); **Northwestern University Women's Center**, 619 Emerson, Evanston 60201, (Tel. 312–492 3146). (good for information about women's groups and offers counselling on rape and abortion); **Jane Addam's Bookstore**, 5 South Wabbash, Room 1508, Chicago (Tel. 312–782 9798).

SAN FRANCISCO/NORTHERN CALIFORNIA: **Women's Building**, off Valencia Street, Mission District (Tel. 415–863 5255) (information, art gallery, housing boards, classes); **Berkeley Women's Center**, 2112 Channing Way, Cal. 94704 (Tel. 415–552 2709); **A Women's Place Bookstore**, corner of Broadway and College Av., in Oakland: **Old Wives Tales Women's Bookshop** (also has readings), 1009 Valencia Street, S.F. **Clementina's**, Bay Brick Inn, 1190 Folsom Street and *Amelia's*, 647 Valencia Street/17th Street, women's bars/discos in San Francisco.

·LOS ANGELES/SOUTHERN CALIFORNIA: **Women's House/Building,** 1727 North Spring Street, LA 90012 (Tel. 213–221 6161) (public centre, art projects and gallery, studio and video centre); **Center for Women's Studies and Services**, 908 E Street, San Diego, Cal 92101 (centre for studies, women's health and therapy services, advice and information; organises educational and cultural activities like free feminist university); **Lesbian Political Action Center**,

1428 Fuller Avenue, Hollywood 90046 (Tel 213–874 8312); **A Different Light Bookstore**, 4014 Santa Monica Blvd., Hollywood, 90029 (Tel. 213 – 668 0629) (lesbian and gay books); **Sisterhood Books**, Westwood Blvd., Wilshir/Santa Monica, (bookroom and newsletters); **Page One Bookstore**, 45E Colorado Blvd, Pasadena (Tel. 213 – 792 9011); **Feminist Poetry and Graphic Center,** 40 4175 Kansas Street, San Diego 92104.

DETROIT: **Women's Liberation News and Letters** (branches throughout US), 2832 East Grand Blvd., Room 316, MI 43211; **Herself Bookstore** – recently moved, for address call information Detroit (women's books, record, periodicals).

MINNEAPOLIS: **Amazon Bookstore Inc.,** 2607 Hennepin Avenue South (Tel. 612–374 5507) (list of rooms, apts, housing and other interests available); **A Women's Coffee House**, 1 Groveland, nr Franklin.

PENNSYLVANIA: **Women's Center**, 616 North Highland Avenue, Pittsburgh 15206 (Tel. 412–661 6066).

TEXAS: **Women's Center**, Houston 792 4403.

WISCONSIN: **Wisconsin's Women's Building**, PO Box 17647, Milwaukee, WI 53217.

MONTANA: **Women's Resource Center**, University of Montana, Missouka, Montana 59812 (research and publications on women and technology and development).

ARIZONA: **Women's Place Bookstore**, Dept U. 2401, N 32nd Street, Phoenix, Arizona 85008.

COLORADO: **Women to Women Bookstore**, Denver, Colorado (Tel. 303–320 5972).

FLORIDA: **Pagoda's Women's Space** Coastal Highway, St Augustine, Florida 32084 (Tel. 904–829 2970) (holiday centre for women); **Ellies Nest**. (women's guest house) 1414 Newton Street, Key West, Florida 33040 (Tel. 305–296 5757).

FREELAND: **Heathcote**, 21300 Heathcote Road, Freeland, MD 21053. (women's community and retreat centre).

Feminist magazines include:
New York: *Womanews, New Directions, Quest.*
Washington: *Off Our Backs.*
Boston: *Sojourner.*

San Francisco: *Plexus*.
Nationwide (and almost mainstream): *Ms*.

BOOKS

More an idiosyncratic dip into the pile than any sort of a 'representative sample'.

Cherie Moraga and Gloria Anzaldua (eds), *This Bridge Called My Back, Writings by Radical Women of Color* (Kitchen Table: Women of Color Press, 1983). Includes prose, poetry, personal narrative and analysis by Afro American, Asian, American, Latina and Native American Women.

Hester Eisenstein, *Contemporary Feminist Thought* (Allen & Unwin, 1984). Readable background on American Feminist theory.

Gloria Steinem, *Outrageous Acts and Everyday Rebellions* (1983, Flamingo 1985). Illuminating collection of journalist/feminist writings of 1960s and 1970s.

Adrienne Rich, *On Lies, Secrets and Silence – Selected Prose 1966–78* (Virago, 1980). Feminist and lesbian essays, speeches and reviews.

Kate Millet, *Sexual politics* (1969, Virago 1979). Seminal work of feminist literary and cultural analysis.

Betty Friedan, '*It Changed My Life*' (Norton, 1986). Collection of influential writings, and now historic speeches, that provides a first-hand account of the development and continuing impact of the American Women's Movement.

FICTION

Marge Piercy, *Braided Lives* (Penguin, 1984). Semi-autobiographical, novel covering the youth, adolescence and 'college days' of a girl seeking to escape working class Detroit and the repressions of the McCarthy era. Also by Marge Piercy are *Vida* (The Women's Press, 1980) the tale of a political activist forced underground in the sixties – a powerful evocation of the political and cultural shifts over those ten years; and *Woman on the Edge of Time* (The Women's Press, 1977) her feminist utopia.

Maxine Hong Kingston, *The Woman Warrior* (Picador, 1981). A beautifully crafted book unravelling the Chinese cultural traditions and myths that helped her form her identity as a first generation Chinese/American.

Tillie Olsen, *Tell Me a Riddle* (1960, Virago, 1983); *Yonnondio* (1974, Virago, 1980). 'Riddle' is a collection of four short stories exploring some of the 'pain and promise of fundamental American experience'; Yonnondio her only novel, set in the mid-West, about a working-class family struggling to better their lives during the Depression.

Toni Cade Bambara, *The Salt Eaters* (1960, Virago, 1982). Brilliant novel by one of America's leading Black women writers, recently followed by the collection of short stories *Gorilla, My Love* (Virago, 1984). She writes in a wonderful racy style, described as 'reading like jazz'.

Toni Morrison, *Song of Solomon* (1970, Triad/Granada 1982). Complex, beautifully told fable set in the deep south of America. Also recommended is her first novel, *The Bluest Eye* (Triad/Granada, 1981), which chronicles the tragic lives of a poor black family in Ohio through the eyes of a young girl.

Ntozake Shange, *Sassafrass, Cypress and Indigo* (Methuen, 1984). Story of three sisters by the author of the great play *For Colored Girls who Considered Suicide when the Rainbow is Enuf*. Her most recent book, *Betsey Brown* (Methuen, 1985), tells the story of a girl growing up in St Louis around the time of the Black Civil Rights movement.

Barbara Smith, ed., *Home Girls – a Black Feminist Anthology* (Kitchen Table: Women of Color Press, USA, 1983). Includes the writing of 34 black women.

Audre Lorde, *Zami* (Sheba, 1984). Powerful evocation of what it's like to be black and lesbian in a white hetero-sexual society.

Paule Marshall *Brown Girl, Brownstones* (Virago, 1982). Powerful novel of daughter of Barbadian immigrants coming of age in New York during the Depression.

Marilyn French *The Women's Room* (Sphere, 1979). Ground-breaking novel of the 1970s of woman's growth to feminism.

Joyce Johnson, *Minor Characters* (Picador, 1983). Gripping memoir of her life as part of the wild 1950s Beat generation growing up in the world of jazz, poetry and black-stockinged Bohemia in New York.

Claudia Tate, ed., *Black Women Writers at Work* (Oldcastle Books, 1985). Interviews with many of the greats, from Maya Angelou and Alice Walker to Audre Lorde.

Thanks to Susan Traill.

CANADA

If you travel to **Canada** from the US, you'll probably find it less sophisticated and (if only relatively) poorer. It has a far less dense population and for many it's the mountains, forests, rivers, and vast, empty plains that are the principal attraction. You should have little problem travelling, alone or with another woman, though as in the States it's best to find out which areas of the bigger towns to avoid. Getting around is straightforward, on buses, trains and internal flights.

In such a huge country, you would expect to find regional differences between people, but there are also national ones, stemming back to the colonisation by British and French. There has always been some degree of tension between English and French Canadians, particularly in **Quebec Province**. The 1970s was an explosive time when the Quebecois separatist movement was at its height, but since the passing of the language laws by which French is Quebec's official language, relations have been easier. The government is explicitly committed to developing a bilingual national identity and attempts to do this by emphasising a common cultural heritage, and by regulating foreign, mainly US, influence. Dependence on American investment and technology and the degree to which Canadian culture and lifestyle has been Americanised are a source of continued resentment.

Struggles within national minorities for identity, rights and property have all influenced the **Women's Movement** and determined its diverse, regional and very active nature. In almost every town you will find a women's bookshop, café, feminist theatre, art gallery and local health centre. There are Indian and Inuit (Eskimo) groups, women's causes in national political parties and active trade union women's groups. The largest national organisation, the *National Action Committee on the Status of Women (NAC)* is a coalition of over 220 groups and represents two million women. The main controversy within the Women's Movement at present is over the censorship of pornographic material. The NAC favours censorship laws, but more radical women's groups claim that this is merely lending feminist legitimacy to repressive and masculinist regulations. A recent and alarming development is a new group called *Real Women* (Realistic Equal Active For Life). Formed in 1984, they have adopted a number of feminist issues while attacking abortion, positive discrimination and 'no-fault' divorce; Canadian feminists have yet to come up with a way of combating them or including them within the bounds of the movement.

◪ **Kate Pullinger hitchhiked through the Yukon Territory, a massive area north of British Columbia in western Canada.**

The Yukon is basically the Great Outdoors, and not much else. Exceptionally underpopulated, with less than 25,000 people in an area almost as large as France, it is a mountain-lake-forest-river-lover's dream come true. I think the best way to see it, at least in summer, is to hitchhike. I have always found hitching in the Yukon relatively fast, easy and safe, mainly because towns are far apart and nobody is going to leave anyone standing on the side of the road in the middle of nowhere at −20°C, or, in summer, in all that dust.

Last summer I stood on the side of the road outside the Yukon's capital, Whitehorse. My thumb stuck out, I was heading for Dawson City 333 miles away. The first vehicle to stop was an old Ford truck, flat bed on back with two extremely large sled dogs hanging out over its sides. They barked at me ferociously. A woman jumped out and asked how far I was going. I told her, and she said she was only going fifty miles, but that was a good start. So I jumped in.

She was young, had long plaited hair, and was wearing men's shorts and a felt hat. Next to her sat a small dark baby, who looked at me curiously. The woman didn't say anything so neither did I. After a few miles she reached above the windscreen and pulled a cigar from behind the sunshade. She smoked it as she drove, clenching it between her teeth when she changed gear. I looked out of the window over the hills and vast, peopleless landscape.

After fifty miles she pulled off the road onto the dirt track that led to her house and I thanked her and jumped out. I slammed the truck door so it shut properly and she and the baby sped off. The sled dogs barked at me until I was far out of their sight. I stood again at the side of the road. A small Toyota two-door stopped. I put my pack in the backseat and climbed in front. This driver was also a woman. She wore a skirt and her hair was wet. We began to chat and I learned that she was just driving home from a swimming lesson in Whitehorse − a trip of two hundred miles, every Friday. There aren't very many swimming pools in the Yukon. The conversation led to a familiar story: she came up to the Yukon ten years ago to visit a friend and stayed. She said she wouldn't leave for anything, and now her brother lives up here too. I began to think there must be something special about this place.

Where she dropped me it was very quiet. There were trees everywhere I looked. In fact, all I could see was trees. I had to wait here around twenty minutes before I heard what sounded like a truck. I saw the dust before I could see it, great clouds of dirt billowing up into the sky. Then I saw the truck and stood on my tiptoes and tried to make my thumb bigger. The driver saw me and started to slow down. It took him a long time to do so and he went past me. I could no longer see, there was so much dust, and I held my scarf over my mouth. When it settled I walked to the truck – a long way up – and negotiated the lift, another fifty miles.

After hoisting my pack up I climbed in. The driver started the engine and headed down the road. I smiled to myself, thinking I was in front of the dust now. The truck driver seemed to change gears a hundred times before we were up to the right speed. Steaming along, past the endless lakes and hills, he told me about his children going to school, having babies and working in Edmonton. I listened and then asked how long he'd been here. He said he came for a year thirty years ago. There is something about this place.

Dropped at another turnoff I ran into the bushes for protection from all that dust. When he and his cloud were out of sight, I climbed back to the road. A few more cars went by and then a van stopped. It was a newish van, brown with a sunset painted on the exterior. I knew about this kind of van: lush interior, shag carpets on the walls, a stereo. They call them sin-bins, glam-vans, or more straightforwardly, fuck-trucks. Thinking of my vulnerability, I took a look at the driver. He was male, of course, and looked about forty-five. He was wearing a nylon shirt with bucking broncos on it. He had a skinny black moustache and shiny hair. He asked where I was going and said he was too, he didn't know these parts and would like some company. The voice inside me said he was okay. I got into the van.

The driver was called Dan and came from Fort St John. He talked away about his family and I began to relax. He said he was a professional gambler which made me sit up: gambling is illegal in most of Canada. Dan told me all about the gambling circuit in British Columbia, the late-night games in Trail, Kelowna, Hope, the nights when he'd walked away with $4,000 in his pocket. He told me about the cards, the passwords and the bribes to the Mounties. I was astounded, this was a whole new side to Beautiful But Boring British Columbia. I asked him what he was doing up here. Then I remembered: Dawson City is the only place in Canada where gambling is legal. And Dawson City was where I was headed.

It was evening by the time we arrived and Dan dropped me off at the crossing to the campsite. Satiated with gambling stories, I sat down beside the river and waited for the little ferry to take me across. It was full of other hitchhikers: Germans, Americans, Quebecois. It was 8 pm and the sky was as bright as mid-morning. I ate and then took the ferry back across to the town, strolling along the wild west wooden sidewalks, past the false-front saloons, hotels and shops and ending up in front of Diamond Tooth Gerties, the casino. I went in, thinking I wouldn't play, just have a look around. The place was full and everyone was drinking, smoking and gambling. There were dancing girls, and a vaudeville show and card-dealers with waistcoats and bow ties and armbands. I had a drink and wondered if this was what it had looked like in 1905. Standing beside the blackjack table I figured out how to play, and watched as people won and lost. I wasn't going to play, just watch.

Many bottles of Molson Canadian and five hours later, I came out, $10.00 up. It was 2am, broad daylight; if the sun ever went down, I missed it. Running to catch the ferry back to the campsite, I talked and laughed with all the other gamblers I had met. Feeling rather rich and drunk, I crawled into my tent. Someone had built a campfire and people were milling about doing campfire sorts of things but it didn't seem right, campfire and campsongs in broad daylight. I closed my eyes and thought that perhaps after a few nights of lucrative gambling I would hitch that brief 150 miles up into the Arctic Circle. There is definitely something about this place.

▨ **Marcia Kahan is a Canadian playwright based in London. She visits Montreal regularly, an unusual city in North American terms in that it is predominantly French-speaking.**

Montreal, at its best, is both relaxed and cosmopolitan, the most European of North American cities and entirely accessible to the woman traveller. Unlike Manhattan – whose breathless pace makes you wonder why you aren't indoors, accomplishing something – or Toronto – which feels like a flat southern Ontario town multiplied by a thousand – Montreal is neither overwhelming nor boring.

The city is predominantly French-speaking, and all the signs are in French. But if you've learned your French from Parisian sources, you may have difficulty following the rapid, slurred Quebecois accent. *Demain* – 'tomorrow' – sounds like 'ts-meh' in Quebecois; *oui* – 'yes' – is pronounced 'way'. This shouldn't discourage an attempt to make your way in French, and although many residents still live entirely unilingual lives, the opportunity to speak two languages and experience two cultures, simultaneously, should not be missed. As Montreal poet F. R. Scott noted, you may find a menu offering 'deep apple pie/tarte aux pommes profondes' or a sign warning 'This elevator will not run on Ascension Day'.

The issue of language informs every aspect of Quebec society, since the survival of French ensures the survival of French Canada in North America. The motto on car licence plates was recently changed from the innocuous 'La belle province' to the more ominous 'Je me souviens' – I remember. What is remembered, presumably, is the victory of the British over the French in 1759, an event which established English economic and political power in the province. From the eighteenth century until 'the quiet revolution' of the 1960s, French Canada remained a rural

Catholic society. The majority of Quebecois citizens served in menial ways and made all the compromises, while the English or Anglophones ran things.

During the last 25 years all that has changed. The province is now industrialised, with managerial posts filled by French Canadians; half the population now lives in the metropolis; the Church no longer dominates education and social habits. Quebecois women, who finally obtained the vote in 1940, no longer accept the role of Catholic matriarch. By 1984, the birthrate had fallen to 1.45 per cent per women, amongst the lowest in the world. Yet many have argued that industrialisation is not enough, that the survival of Quebec culture is dependent upon the province's separation from the rest of Canada. Although the 1980 provincial referendum on that issue was defeated, there has been recent legislation which uncompromisingly establishes French as the primary language of business, justice, education and public service – and for the first time in history more than 50 per cent of Quebec's Anglophones are bilingual.

Politically this is an interesting time to visit Montreal. Some French Canadians are happy with the reforms, others, notably academics and social scientists, will never feel secure until Quebec becomes an independent state. Many English Quebeckers resent the severity of the new language laws and some immigrants similarly are angry that they can no longer have their children educated in English. I have met bilingual Anglophones who have left the province feeling rejected by their Francophone counterparts. I also know many who have remained, relishing the complexity and richness of a bilingual society.

The best starting point to explore central Montreal is the network of streets running west-east from Mackay to Mountain (de la Montagne) where you will find a variety of shops, restaurants, cafés and galleries. My own idea of a good afternoon in downtown Montreal would include a visit to the Musée des Beaux Arts on Sherbrooke or to a gallery or two on Bishop and Crescent, a cappucino at the *Coffee Mill* (*Le Moulin à Cafe*) on Mountain, a browse round the *Cheap Thrills* secondhand bookshop on Bishop, a Fellini or Truffault film at Concordia University's de Maisonneuve campus, and finally a smoked meat special at Ben's all-night delicatessen at Mansfield and de Maisonneuve.

As far as safety goes, take similar precautions as for any other large city, particularly after dark. I've walked freely in all quarters of the city without hassle, though I once waited for the 150 bus at Dorchester and St Laurent, and discovered that every woman on that corner after 10 pm is assumed to be a prostitute.

Montreal's climate tends to extremes. Winters are very cold, with temperatures as low as minus 40. The city may be hit by spectacular blizzards any time from December to April, which brings things to a hushed standstill before the snow-ploughs do their work. The 'underground' city links large parts of downtown – shops, cinemas and the cultural centre, Place des Arts – by metro. Spring tends to be delightful, though its appearance is unpredictable. By June, the humidity of summer has set in, with temperatures as high as 90°F. A good way to become involved in the city during a summer visit is to enrol in a French course offered by one of the universities. Concordia University also has an institute specifically for women's studies. Fall is a particularly good time of year to be in Montreal; the tourist crowds have thinned, the trees burst into flame and the annual film festival is on.

TRAVEL NOTES

Language English and French; in Quebec, French is the main language.

Transport *Greyhound* coaches to most towns – a good value three-month pass is usually available, valid for travel across Canada. Inexpensive flights to most centres within provinces, although cross-country flights are rather more expensive. Canadian Pacific Railway and Canadian National Railway across southern Canada. Hitching is possible but not always advisable alone on the open, lonely roads.

Accommodation YWCAs are usually a good bet: full details from the national office in Toronto (571 Jarvis Street, M4Y JJ1; Tel 416–921 2117).

Guides Mark Lightbody, *Canada – A Travel Survival Kit* (Lonely Planet, 1984). *Moneywise Guide to North America* (Travelaid, 1984) includes a Canada section.

Recommended for the Yukon is *The Alaska–Yukon Handbook* (Moon Publications, US, 1985).

CONTACTS

A very good source for addresses and information about the women's movement in Canada is *Everywoman's Almanac* (The Women's Press, Canada, also distributed in UK and available in women's bookshops here).

Also useful the **Canadian Women's Mailing List** for up-to-date information of events, publications, services is published by WEB Women's Information Exchange, 9280 Arvida Avenue, Richmond BC 604–274 5335.

Established centres include:

MONTREAL: **The Montreal Women's Yellow Pages** (available in most bookshops) list resources for women; **Institute for Women's Studies, Institute Simone de Beauvoir,** Concordia University, 1455 de Maisonneuve Blvd. W., Montreal H3G 1MB; **Androgny** (gay/feminist bookshop), 1217 Crescent. **Women's Information Centre**, 3595 St Urbain; (tel 514–842 4781); *YWCA* 1355 Dorchester Blvd, West (Tel 514–866 9941).

QUEBEC: **Centre-Femmes**, 855 Holland (Tel. 418–683 2548).

OTTAWA: **Ottawa Women's Network**, PO Box 2053, Station D, Ottawa K1P 5W3 (Tel 613–224 7210).

TORONTO: **Feminist Party of Canada**, 100 Bain Street, 32 The Lindens, Toronto M5A 2R3; **Resources for Feminist Research**, Dept of Sociology, Ontario Institute for studies in Education, 252 Bloor Street, West Toronto M5S 1V6 (research and studies on women's action and issues in West and Third World, publishes quarterly journal); **Rape Crisis Centre** (Tel 416–964 7477; **Voice of Women** (World Peace Organisation), 175 Carlton Street, Toronto M5A 2K3; **Women's Bookstore**, 73 Harboard St.

LONDON, ONTARIO: **Womanspirit** (art research & resource centre), 359 Dundee Street, Main Floor, N6B 1V5.

SCARBOROUGH, ONTARIO: **Canadian Women's Studies/Les Cahiers de la Femme**, Centennial College Women's Studies, 651 Warden Avenue (bilingual journal with lots of information on women and work).

EDMONTON, ALBERTA: **The Everywoman's Place**, 9926–112 Street (Tel. 403–488 2748; **Commonwoman Books**, 8210–104 Street.

NEW BRUNSWICK: **Fredericton**

Women's Centre, 629 King's Street (Tel. 506–455 3309).
ST JOHN'S, NEWFOUNDLAND: **Women's Centre**, 88 Military Road (Tel. 709–753 0220) (also has bookstore).
WINNIPEG, MANITOBA: **The Women's Building**, 730 Alexander Avenue (Tel. 204–783 7889).
REGINA, SASKETCHEWAN: **Regina Women's Community Centre**, 219–1808 Smith Street (Tel. 306–522 2777).
VANCOUVER: **Downtown Eastside Women's Centre**, 412 East Hastings Street (Tel. 604–255 1614); **North Shore Women's Centre**, 8–117 E 15 Street, North Vancouver V7L 2P7; **Vancouver Women's Bookstore**, Cambic Street (Tel. 604–684 052); **Ariel Books**, W 4th Av, at McDonalds: **Vancouver Women in Focus**, 456 West Broadway (Tel. 604–872 2250) (Feminist arts and media centre).
CALGARY, ALBERTA: **Women's Resource Centre-YWCA**, 320–5th Avenue, S.E., Calgary T2G 0E5 (Tel. 403–263 1550).
WHITEHORSE, YUKON TERRITORY: **Victoria Faulkner Women's Centre**, 302 Steele Street (Tel. 403–667 2693).

BOOKS

M. Fitzgerald, C. Guberman & M. Wolfe, eds., *Still Ain't Satisfied* (Woman's Press, Canada) Canadian Feminism today.
Varta Burstyn, *Women Against Censorship* (Douglas & MacIntyre, Canada 1985). Account of the current censorship debate in the Canadian Feminist movement.
Michele Landsberg, *Women and Children First* (Penguin, Canada). Clear insight into Canadian life, politics and feminism by columnist with the Toronto *Star*.
Susan Crean, *Newsworthy: The Lives of Media Women* (Stoddart, Canada 1985). Examination of how women have overcome the 'twin barriers of self-doubt and discrimination' and established themselves in print and electronic media.
Penney Kome, *Women of Influence: Canadian Women and Politics* (Doubleday, New York, 1985).
Susanna Moodie, *Roughing it in the Bush: or Forest life in Canada* (Virago, 1985). Sharp, enduring account by an early British settler; new introduction by novelist Margaret Atwood.

FICTION

Joan Barfoot, *Gaining Ground* (first published 1978, The Women's Press, 1980). Novel about a woman who leaves her husband, children and suburban security to live as a hermit deep in the Canadian countryside.
Jane Rule, *The Desert of the Heart* (Talonbooks, Toronto, 1964) and *Outlander*, short stories (Naiad, Toronto, 1981) are just two of the books we recommend by one of the country's leading lesbian feminist writers.
Margaret Atwood, *The Edible Woman* (1969, Virago 1986), *Surfacing* (1962, Virago, 1979), and others By Canada's leading novelist and woman poet – they're more about psychological conflicts than about Canada.
Ann Cameron, *Daughters of Copper Woman* (Women's Press, Canada, 1985). Novel of matriarchal secret legends of Nootka women, off Vancouver island.
Willa Cather, *Shadows on the Rock* (1937, Virago 1984). Classic novel about French settlers in Canada.
Margaret Lawrence, *A Jest of God, Bird in the House* (New Canadian Library). Two novels set in rural Ontario.
Alice Munro, *Beggar Maid* (Penguin, 1981). Best-known book of this Canadian author, again set in rural Ontario and in Toronto.

Thanks to Anne O'Byrne and Catherine Pepinster for introductory information and Travel Notes.

GENERAL BIBLIOGRAPHY

Some of the books detailed below have been included, for their specific concerns, in individual country bibliographies – and in the case of the excellent *Sisterhood is Global* and *Women: A World Report*, more than once. We would like to acknowledge our debt to these, and to the whole range of books listed (and often suggested by contributors), in the compilation of *Half The Earth*.

WORLDWIDE CONCERNS/ANTHOLOGIES

Robin Morgan, ed., *Sisterhood is Global* (Penguin, 1985). Anthology made up of original articles from feminists all over the world, preceded by statistics and other little-known information on the history and status of women. Especially useful for an overview of the Women's Movement in each country, 70 in all.

New Internationalist, *Women: A World Report* (Methuen, 1985). Aimed to coincide with the end of the United Nations Decade for Women, this book provides a review of UN information on the status of women, followed by accounts by ten writers, each of whom visited a different country to report on women's experience; for example, Angela Davis on Egypt, Germaine Greer on Cuba and Manny Shirazi on the Soviet Union.

Miranda Davies, ed., *Third World – Second Sex: Women's Struggles and National Liberation* (Zed Books, 1983). Compilation of the experiences and perspectives of women's organisations from over 20 Third World countries. Topics include women, politics and organisation, the role of women in national liberation movements, autonomous women's movements, campaigns around health, work and against violence.

Women and Development: a Resource Guide for Organisation and Action (Isis, 1983). Provides a much-needed feminist perspective to the whole issue of development focusing on certain key areas like women's role in food production, health, communication and education, and the effects of migration, tourism and the recruitment of labour by multinational companies. Shows how women are organising and fighting to control their own lives, each chapter being followed by a comprehensive selection of books, pamphlets, research centres, women's groups and other resources.

Kumari Jayawardena, *Feminism and Nationalism in the Third World* (Zed Books, 1986). Authoritative – and pioneering – study of women's participation in the democratic and revolutionary struggles of Asia and the Middle East from the late nineteenth century onwards.

Mineke Schippef, ed., *Unheard Words: Women and Literature in Africa, the Arab World, Asia, the Caribbean and Latin America* (Allison & Busby, 1986). Informative introduction to women's literary achievement in the Third World – including proverbs, essays and interviews.

World View (Pluto Press, 1984). Political yearbook providing a survey of facts, news and statistics from a socialist perspective. Covers all the major regions of the world. Unfortunately its future is uncertain and there's been no update since 1984. Also the *The New State of the World Atlas* (Pluto, 1985)

AFRICAN WOMEN

Margaret Jean Hay and Sharon Stitcher, eds., *African Women South of the Sahara* (Longman, 1984). Specifically for students, this is a comprehensive study of the economic, social and political roles of women in Africa, past and present.

Asma El Dareer *Woman, Why Do You Weep? Circumcision and Its Consequences* (Zed Books, 1982). Scholarly survey based on large-scale statistical research of circumcision and infibulation in her native Sudan. She deals with attitudes to it of both women and men, related health problems, the history of circumcision, and suggestions for concrete steps – all relevant to many other areas of Africa as well as Sudan.

Christine Obbo *African Women Their Struggle for Economic Independence* (Zed Books, 1980).

Nici Nelson *Why Has Development Neglected Rural Women?* (Pergamon, 1979). First volume of the Women in Development series, it reviews the current literature, confronts the question of why development so often by-passes women and makes a set of recommendations for researchers, planners and administrators on how that can be changed.

Anne Cloudsley *Women of Omburman Victims of Circumcision* (Ethnographica, 1983, reprinted 1984). The author lived and worked with Sudanese women, learned about their rituals, celebrations, marriages, births. Important book about women in traditional societies, on the social context in which female circumcision is performed.

Charlotte H. Bruner, ed., *Unwinding Threads: A Collection of African Women Writers* (Heinemann, 1983)

Raqiya H. Dualeh Abdalla, *Sisters in Affliction: Circumcision and Infibulation of Women in Africa* (Zed Books, 1982). A good account which provides historical background and a political context to customs and practices within a Muslim framework. Also discusses the economics of marriage and provides community field studies.

MUSLIM WOMEN

Lois Beck and Nikki Keddie, eds., *Women in the Muslim World* (Harvard University Press, 1978). Authoritative collection of essays, predominantly by anthropologists, on women in different Muslim countries.

Ann Dearden, ed. *Arab Women* (Minority Rights Group Report no. 27, revised 1983). Useful survey on the position of women in different Arab countries.

Elizabeth Warnock Fernea and Basima Qattan Bezirgan, eds, *Middle Eastern Muslim Women Speak* (1977, University of Texas Press 1984). A collection of autobiographical and biographical writings by and about Middle Eastern women.

Fatima Mernissi, *Beyond the Veil* (1975,

Al Saqi Books 1985). Exploration of male-female relations in the Muslim world, focussing on such themes as conflict between husbands and wives, the pervasive and often destructive role of the mother-in-law and the constricting physical boundaries of women's lives.

Fatna A. Sabbah, *Women in the Muslim Unconscious* (Pergamon Press, 1984). Detailed exposé of the elements in Islamic culture that combine to ingrain attitudes towards women in Muslim societies.

Juliette Minces, *The House of Obedience – Women in Arab Society* (Zed Books, 1982). A general account about women in the Arab world with one specific chapter on women in Algeria and Egypt.

Nawal El Saadawi, *The Hidden Face of Eve* (Zed Books, 1980). A personal, often disturbing account of what it is like to grow up as a woman in the Islamic world of the Middle East.

Germaine Tillion, *The Republic of Cousins* (1966, Al Saqi Books, 1985). Account by distinguished French anthropologist of the effects of cultural prehistory of Mediterranean region on lives of the women.

ASIAN WOMEN

Women in Asia Minority Rights Group Report no 45, revised 1982 edition. Survey on status, role, employment, work, political participation and issues and considerations of women of Pakistan, India, Sri Lanka, Bangladesh, Philippines, Indonesia, South Korea, Japan, China.

LATIN AMERICAN WOMEN

Audrey Bronstein *The Triple Struggle: Latin American Peasant Women* (War on Want Campaigns, 1982). Women in Bolivia, Ecuador, El Salvador, Guatemala and Peru express in their own words the struggle against the oppression of underdevelopment, poverty and the position of women in male-dominated societies.

Latin American and Caribbean Women's Collective, *Slaves of Slaves: the Challenge of Latin American Women* (Zed Books, 1982). Summary of women's struggles in a number of countries, including accounts of their historical roles in the different wars of independence.

Latin American Women (Minority Rights

Group Report no. 57, 1983). Excellent survey of women's exploitation at home and in the workplace, including information on how women are organising, both on specific issues such as health and for wider revolutionary change.

Women Organising in Latin America (Isis International Journal no. 5, 1986). Collection of articles by feminist activists from Chile, Peru, Mexico, Uruguay, the Dominican Republic and Argentina, focusing on developments in the Latin American Women's Movement over the last decade. Available form Isis International (See Italy Travel Notes for Rome address).

A Note on Bookshops:
In Britain, the best general source for most books detailed here is *Sisterwrite* (190 Upper St., London N1 *O.S.C.* (Tel. 01–226 9782); *The Travel Bookshop* (13 Blenheim Crescent, London W11; (Tel 01–229 5260) is useful for the more esoteric guidebooks; *Collet's International Bookshop* (129/131 Charing Cross Road, London WC2 (Tel. 01–734 0782) for East European/Soviet literature; *Carila Latin American Resource Centre* (29 Islington Park St, London N1 (Tel. 01–359 2270) has a good selection of books, but mostly in Spanish.

HALF THE EARTH: THE SECOND EDITION

This first edition of **Half The Earth** has been almost two years in the making, in the course of which we've tried to commission articles (and gather information) on as wide as possible a range of experiences and countries. At all stages, though, it has been clear how much the book is really a developing and shifting project, as events have overtaken us, or travellers directed our attention at destinations we'd previously imagined closed or impossible. . .

We plan to produce a **second edition** of the book in around two years' time. For this, we'll be printing largely fresh contributions and experiences, as well as updating all the travel notes and bibliographies. If you feel you could contribute, whether by writing an article (between 500 and 2,500 works), or updating advice or contacts, or simply recommending a book, we'd very much like to hear from you.

Please write to:

Half the Earth **(The Rough Guide Series)**
Pandora Press
11 New Fetter Lane
London EC4P 4EE.